# FOLLOWING THE LAND

**A Genealogical History of Some of the PARKERs of Nansemond County, Virginia, And Chowan/Hertford/Gates Counties, North Carolina 1604-2004**

**Raymond Parker Fouts**

1506 Cambridge Drive
Cocoa, FL 32922-6416

USA

# Contents

Chapter 1    William[1] PARKER                                                                                    1

Chapter 2    Richard[2] PARKER (William[1])                                                                    9

Chapter 3    Some Richard[4] PARKER (Richard[3],Richard[2],William[1]) Descendants    19

Chapter 4    More Richard[4] PARKER (Richard[3],Richard[2],William[1]) Descendants    31

Chapter 5    William[4] PARKER (Thomas[3],Richard[2],William[1])                                47

Chapter 6    Thomas[6] PARKER (Thomas[5],William[4],Thomas[3],Richard[2],William[1])    55

Chapter 7    Thomas[2] PARKER (William[1])                                                                  69

Chapter 8    Other descendants of William[3] PARKER (Thomas[2],William[1])            83

Chapter 9    Descendants and siblings of Kindred[6] PARKER                              99

Chapter 10   Peter[3] PARKER (Thomas[2],William[1])                                          123

Chapter 11   Other descendants of Peter[3] PARKER (Thomas[2],William[1])              145

Chapter 12   Jobe[5] PARKER and some of his descendants                                    157

Chapter 13   Thomas[3] PARKER (Thomas[2],William[1])                                        169

Chapter 14   Children of Joseph[5] PARKER (Joseph[4],Thomas[3],Thomas[2],William[1])    187

Chapter 15   John[6] PARKER (Joseph[5],Joseph[4],Thomas[3],Thomas[2],William[1])        203

Chapter 16   Descendants of Nathan G.[7] PARKER                                            215

Appendix     Family Photos                                                                    229

Female Name Index                                                                              233

Name Index                                                                                      245

Location Index                                                                                  275

## *MAPS & PHOTOS*

Map depicting part of Upper Parish of Nansemond County, VA     8

Map depicting PARKER lands in Nansemond County     18

Map depicting Virginia Land Patents of Richard[4] PARKER     30

Map depicting 1740/41 North Carolina Land Grant to Peter[5] PARKER     46

Photograph of PARKERs Methodist Church in Gates County, North Carolina     67

Map depicting 1825 division of land of Thomas[6] PARKER     68

Map depicting Virginia Land Patents to Thomas[2], Thomas[3] and John[4] PARKER     81

Map depicting William[3] PARKER's 1706 Virginia Land Patent     82

Map depicting 1810 division of land of John[5] PARKER     98

Map depicting 1838 division of land of Reuben[6] PARKER     122

Map depicting 1714 NC Land Grants to Thomas[3], Peter[3] and John PARKER in Chowan County     144

Survey map on Chowan River by Jonathan PRICE, 1799     168

Map depicting 1716 North Carolina Land Grant to Aaron BLANSHARD     186

Photograph of gravestones in Nathan G. PARKER Cemetery, Gates County, North Carolina     214

# *PREFACE*

This book is the culmination of 32 years of research and collection of a wide variety of source materials concerning the Parker families mentioned in the title. The use of land records, and estate records concerning land, has been central to that research in establishing relationships among family members.

There are numerous references to these families on the Internet, as well as in printed material, but most seem to lack reliable documentation. An attempt has been made here to provide the reader with as much diverse primary-source data on these families as possible, with the hope that it will provide a basis for further research by future generations.

The Internet resources used here are digital images of the original documents, lodged in such repositories as the Virginia State Library and Archives, and the North Carolina State Archives. Deeds, wills and other documents, referred to in the text as "transcribed here in full," are *verbatim* transcriptions, either from xerographic copies, or microform images of original documents. The plats included here were created with Steve Broyles' DeedMapper™ computer program and maps. Secondary sources have been restricted to those most trusted by the author.

Certain families have been selected to be traced in each line, as representative of what may be accomplished by use of the available data. Most of them have been followed to the 10th generation. Birth and marriage records have been omitted for those born after 1930, in the interest of privacy and security for the living. Chowan and Gates Counties records are quite complete and provide the researcher ample documentation to continue tracing these Parker families and allied lines.

All names appear in the Name Index. Female names, both maiden and married, also appear in a separate index. Clerks of Court, Constables, County Surveyors, Judges, Justices of the Peace, Public Administrators, Public Registers and Sheriffs appear in the main index, under their own names and also separately under those headings. Blacks have been indexed under the heading of "Negroes," the term in use at the creation of these records. All surnames have been entered in bold capital letters. Any one name may appear more than once on a given page. All spellings of every name are indexed.

"~~Thomas~~" denotes a crossed-out word. "Stump*ty*" emphasizes verbatim spelling. "Chap__" denotes missing or illegible letters. /In the/ denotes interlined words. All transcriptions within quotation marks are verbatim.

The writer has most gratefully received the kindness and generosity of family and friends for the duration of this endeavor. My husband Robert's infinite patience, assistance and encouragement have been my most valuable assets, as always. I would also like to express my deep gratitude to Weynette Parks Haun for her friendship, guidance and all the superb transcriptions of county records that made this book possible.

Others who have made such valuable contributions are George P. Bauguess, Rebecca L. Dozier, Marianne N. Ordway, Judith Cox Whipple, Jim and Julie Sizemore and the numerous others who have been credited in the footnotes. Thank you.

# FOLLOWING THE LAND

## A Genealogical History of Some of the PARKERs of Nansemond County, Virginia, And Chowan/Hertford/Gates Counties, North Carolina 1604-2004

### William[1] PARKER

The system of land distribution in the Colony of Virginia made the acquisition of land a relatively easy task. In order to settle the colony sufficiently to make a profit for the investors in England, 50 acres of land were granted to individuals for the payment of their own transportation from England and 50 more for every other person whose transportation they also paid. Many of the persons so transported were young, indentured servants, who were able and willing to work to acquire the means to pay the transportation of others, after fulfilling the terms of their own indentures. William[1] PARKER fits this description. Patentees were often living in the Colony several years prior to the date of their first land patent. The tragic loss of the other Nansemond County records elevates the patents and grants to a position of prime importance. They are used here to show the location of the lands he and his descendants acquired, and their continued and close association with the neighboring landowners.

The first record of William[1] PARKER appears to be the Muster of the inhabitants of Virginia on 7 February 1624/25. He was 20 years of age and came to Virginia in 1616, in the ship *Charles*.[1] This would place his year of birth circa 1604. His next appearance in the records is in a Virginia Patent to John **BUSH**, dated 1 December 1624, wherein he is mentioned as being one of two servants who came in the *Charles* in 1621. John **BUSH** received part of the 300 acres due him for his own personal right for coming over in the ship *Neptune*, in 1618, and part for the transportation of his wife, Elizabeth, and daughters Elizabeth and Mary, in the *Guift*, in 1619.[2] His patent was in the parish of "Kiccoughton in the Corporation of Elizabeth City," slightly northwest of Ragged Island, now in Isle of Wight County. He may well have been here a few years earlier than 1618, with William[1] **PARKER** as a servant, or purchased his indenture from some unknown party. The *Charles* made several voyages to Virginia from the port of London, England.[3]

As William[1] **PARKER** arrived here at the tender age of approximately 12 years, it is most likely that he was orphaned, and unlikely that his ancestry can be readily determined. Assuming that he was indentured at age 12, for the usual period of seven years, he would have earned his freedom by 1623 and been 19 years of age. His circumstances in the interim are unknown, but he had acquired sufficient means to pay the transportation of seven persons into the Colony of Virginia by the last day of May 1636. On that date, he obtained a patent for 350 acres of land, "in the Countie of Warrisquoake beginning at a little Creeke on the South side of Nanzemund river abutting Northwest Upon the said river against Dumplinge Island and South east into the woods."[4] This land lies near Dumpling Island Creek, now known as Oyster House Creek, and east of Wilroy Swamp, in Suffolk City, formerly Nansemond County.[5]

[1] American Plantations and Colonies, Virginia People, 1624/5, Thomas Langford, c. 1997-2001 http://englishamerica.home.att.net/index.html

[2] Virginia State Library and Archives, Land Patents, 1:31, http://ajax.lva.lib.va.us/F/?func=file&file_name=find-b-clas30&local_base=CLAS30, hereafter VSLA

[3] American Plantations and Colonies, Virginia People, 1624/5, http://www.primenet.com /langford/ships/shp-c01.htm#Charles

[4] VSLA, 1:362

[5] USGS Topo Map, Microsoft TerraServer, (Cont.)

## Chapter 1: William[1] PARKER

William[1] **PARKER** patented another 350 acres of land in the "Countie of Upper New Norfolke," on 18 June 1638. It is described as "runing South East into the woods Northwest Upon Nansmund river beginning at a Creek called **POWELL**s Creeke and butting Upon the lands of the said William **PARKER** the said three hundred and fiftie acres of land being due unto him...for the transportation of Seaven prsons..."[6] The names of the headrights are different from the ones in the 1636 patent. It will be noted that Nansemond County was known as Warrisquoake in 1636 and Upper New Norfolke by 1637.

Thomas **POWELL** obtained two patents in "the Upper Countie of New Norfolke" in 1637. The first patent, 10 June, was "on the South side of Nansimond river bounded East south East into the woods butting Northerly into the marsh," and contained 100 acres.[7] The second was granted 20 June 1637, and was also in the Upper County of New Norfolk, "lying one mile from the plantation of the said Thomas **POWELL**, the [sic] runs Westerly winding about a point of Marsh Southerly running into the woods South East," and contained 200 acres.[8] This land lies just south of the two patents to William[1] **PARKER**.

Samuel **STEPHENS**, gentleman, son of Capt. Richard **STEPHENS**, late of Virginia, Esqr., received a patent for 2,000 acres 20 July 1639. It is described as "being in the Upper countie of New Norfolke in Nansamund river on both sides of the head of a Creeke called dumpling Island Creeke bounding Easterly into the woods Unto a greate Arrow reed swampe northerly to the side of the Land of Percivall **CHAMPION** and Westerly Upon the head of **CHAMPION**s Land Alsoe westerly Upon the head of William **SANDERS** land and runing Southerly by the head of William **PARKER**s land and extending to the head of Thomas **POWELL**s Land..."[9] This patent further delineates the lands of William[1] **PARKER** and will be of significance at a later time.

William[1] **PARKER** served as a Burgess for Upper Norfolk in the General Assembly of Virginia as of 12 January 1642/43, along with John **CARTER**, Daniell **COOGAN** and Thomas **DEWE**.[10] At that time, he owned a minimum of 700 acres of land and apparently purchased other lands by deeds that are no longer of record.

A patent to one Toby **SMYTH**, Gent. 25 September 1644, was bounded "eastward with a Creek Called Dumpling Island Creek wch Creek parteth from the Land of William **PARKER**," which confirms his ownership, and probable residence there, to that date.[11] Between 25 September 1644, and 3 February 1647/48, William[1] **PARKER** apparently moved almost directly across the Southern Branch of the Nansemond River, to the Western Branch, as evidenced in a patent to Edward **COOK** for 100 acres of land, 17 March 1654/55, on the Western Branch. This patent states that his land joins on that of William **PARKER** and shows that his residence had changed from the Southern Branch to the Western Branch of the Nansemond River. One of the headrights on this patent was one George **GOURDON**, who will be mentioned later.[12] Leonard **GUINNS** obtained a patent 9 June 1648, for the 150 acres he had purchased of Toby **SMITH** on 3 February 1647/48. This land was the same patented by **SMITH** 25 September 1644, with one important difference: Dumpling Island Creek then "parteth from the Land of Thomas **PARKER**."[13] It is apparent that this Thomas **PARKER** was William[1] **PARKER**'s son. This same period may have been the time that William[1] sold his 1636 and 1638 patents, and Thomas **POWELL** sold his 100-acre, 1637 patent to the father of John **WRIGHT**, as evidenced in his patent of 10 November 1678.[14] This is the last mention of William[1] **PARKER** of the Western Branch.

---

http://terraserver.microsoft.com/printimage.asp?S=12&T=451&y=5093&Z=18&W=1

[6] VSLA, 1:543

[7] Ibid., 1:501

[8] Ibid., 1:501

[9] Ibid., 1:667

[10] *The General Assembly of Virginia July 30, 1619-January 11, 1978, Bicentennial Register of Members*, Compiled by Cynthia Miller Leonard, Published for the General Assembly of Virginia by the Virginia State Library, Richmond, 1978, p. 20

[11] VSLA, 2:13

[12] Ibid., 3:316

[13] Ibid., 2:137

[14] Ibid., 6:669

# Chapter 1: William[1] **PARKER**

Thomas **DEW** first appears in Nansemond County records with a patent for 150 acres, dated 1 August 1638. It lay "in the Upper Countie of New Norfolke in Nansemond river beginning at the first point next to the land now seated by Thomas **POWELL** runing into the woods South East..."[15] The next patent for him was also dated 1 August 1638, and included 400 acres of land "scituate lying and being in Nansamond river wth in the Countie of the Upper Norfolke lying one mile or thereabouts from the plantaçon of Thomas **POWELL** the river Westerly winding about a point of marsh Southerly runing into the woods South East..." Two hundred acres were by assignment from Thomas **POWELL**, and two hundred for the transportation of four persons.[16] His next patent was dated 10 October 1638, for 300 acres "scituate lying and being in the County of Upper Norfolke in Nansemond river beginning at a small Creeke at the old Indian towne...runing South East into the woods a small Island being opposite against the said land..." for the transportation of six persons.[17]

Thomas **DEW** obtained an assignment of 250 acres from John **WRIGHT** 7 November 1640. It was also in the Upper County of New Norfolk, "upon the miles end of a pattent of Mr. Thomas **DEW**es... runing East and by South through a great reedy Poquoson..." This transaction was witnessed by one Thomas **BUSH**.[18] Thomas **DEW** is mentioned in a patent to Randall **CREW** for 450 acres, 13 November 1640, "in the Countie of the Upper New Norfolke Upon the head of a Creeke which issueth from the Southerne branch of Namsamund river beginning at a point of Land opposite to a feild called **GEORGE**s feild runing behind the land of Mr Thomas **DEW** and on the other Side bounded by the maine Poquoson..."[19] This patent will be mentioned again.

The location of some of the lands of Thomas **DEW** becomes more evident with the description of the lands he received in a patent of 750 acres 8 January 1643/44. It is described as "being in Upper Norfolke and lying on the Eastward side of the Southward branch of Nansamund river and beginning at a marked pine standing on the Southward Side of the Mouth of a Creeke called Craney Creeke and opposite to two small Islands Called Craney and New haven and runing for length from the said pine South East three hundred and twentie poles Unto a marked post standing in the Mouth of a branch and soe North West eighty pole Unto a marked white oake and soe South west Unto the Lands of Mr. Randall **CREW**..." Three hundred acres of this patent is a renewal of the patent of 10 October 1638, and the remaining 450 acres were his right for the transportation of nine persons.[20] This land lies south west of the City of Suffolk, between Suffolk Municipal Airport and Lake Kilby.[21]

There were two Craney Creeks in the same county and this one retained its name until at least 28 September 1732, when Joseph **STALLINGS** obtained a patent for 26 acres in Nansemond County. It is described as "Beginning At a white Oak on the North West side of the beaverdam als Craney Creek in William **HILL**s Line and runs thence due West One hundred thirty Six pole to a black Oak thence South Sixty seven Degrees East One hundred thirty twoe pole Crossing the said Beaverdam Swamp to John **CAMPBELL**s Miles End..."[22] Beaverdam Swamp is noted as Beaverdam R. on the Confederate Engineers' Map of Isle of Wight and part of Nansemond, by J. F. **GILMER**, Chief Engineer.[23] The other Craney Creek, and Island, has retained its name and lies at the mouth of the Elizabeth River, just above Portsmouth, VA. It is readily located on a current road map.

William **HATFEILD** obtained three patents in the Upper County of New Norfolk. The clerk who recorded them dated the first one as "22th" of August 1638. The other two are clearly the 24th, with all three recorded over two pages. The first was for 300 acres "scituate lying and being in Nansamond river within the Upper Countie of New Norfolke next adjoyning to the Lands of Percivall **CHAMPION** and runing Up a Creeke called Dumpling Island Creeke being on the East side of the

---

[15] VSLA, 1:587

[16] Ibid., 1:587

[17] Ibid., 1:632

[18] Ibid., 1:692

[19] Ibid., 1:721

[20] Ibid., 1:942

[21] USGS Topo Map, Microsoft Terraserver, http://terraserver.homeadvisor.m.../printimage.asp?S=14&T=2&X=111&Y=1269&Z=18&W=

[22] VSLA, 14:511

[23] Confederate Engineers Maps, Jeremy Francis Gilmer Collection, Virginia Historical Society, Isle of Wight and part of Nansemond, sheets 47-49,81, 912.755

Said Creeke South and by West upon the said Creeke and North & by East into the woods…"[24] This land is very near that of William[1] **PARKER**. The other two patents are for 100 and 200 acres, respectively, but contain no useful description of the land.[25] These patents will be mentioned at a later time. It appears that he had at least one other patent, or perhaps a purchase from some individual, as of 25 July 1646. On that date, John **GARRET** had a patent for 400 acres "being in the County of The Upper Norfolke Upon the head of a Creek or branch Called Indian Creek which Issueth from the Western branch of Nansimum river beginning at a marked Pocikery and adjoyning on and belowe a percell of Land of William **HATFEILD**s runing for Length North North East over A reedy Swamp…"[26]

George **GOURDEN** obtained a patent for 100 acres 18 March 1662/63. It is described as "being in the Western branch of Nancemond River Beginning at a marked white oak on a point by a marsh side and so runing for Length north by East three hundred and twenty poles joining to Wm. **PARKER**s Land so again from the first mentioned Oak East by South for breadth Fifty poles, butting on his Own Land to a marked tree and so again for length North by East Three hundred and twenty poles Joining to his own Land including the said Quantity. The said Land being formerly granted unto Edward **COAKE** by patent dated the Seventeenth of march One thousand six hundred and fifty four and by the said **COAKE** Assigned and set over unto the said **GOURDEN**…"[27] When land was granted multiple times, it retained the wording of the original patent, including the names of adjoining landowners at that time. It does not necessarily mean that those same landowners were still there at the date of the latest patent. William[1] **PARKER** was alive as of 17 March 1654/55, but may have been deceased by 18 March 1662/63.

Randall **CREW** came to Virginia in the *Charles* in 1621, with William[1] **PARKER**. He was living at West & Sherley Hundred, in the Corporation of Charles City, as of 22 January 1624/25. He was 20 years old and a servant of one Mr. **BENETT**.[28] His first patent appears to be one for 750 acres of land 24 July 1638, in "the Upper Countie of New Norfolke Easterly up a Creek in Nansemond river Northerly Upon the river running Westerly along the river Southerly into the woods… The said Seaven hundred and fifty acres of Land being due Unto him… (Vizt) one hundred acres according to an order of Court bearing date the 5th of October Anno domi 1631 in right of his wife Dorothy **BEHETHLAND** and six hundred and fiftie acres in right of transportation of Thirteen prsons…"[29] This description is not helpful in locating the land, but a slightly earlier patent to Abraham **PELTREE**, 25 February 1638/39, gives a clearer perception of the approximate location. **PELTREE**'s patent is "fiftie acres of Land scituate lying and being in the upper County of New Norfolke wth in Nansamond river als Matrevers river lying Southerly upon Mr Randall **CREW** /his/ Creek Easterly towards the Swamp Westerly towards the maine river and Northerly towards the land of Thomas **POWELL**…for his own prsonall Adventure…"[30] This description places this patent of Randall **CREW** near the first large bend in Nansemond River between Brock Point and Thompson Landing.[31]

His next patent was for 450 acres, 13 November 1640. It was "in the Countie of the Upper New Norfolke Upon the head of a Creeke which issueth from the Southerne branch of Namsamund river beginning at a point of Land opposite to a feild called **GEORGE**s feild runing behind the land of Mr Thomas **DEW** and on the other Side bounded by the maine Poquoson runing South west for length…"[32] This land was at the head of Crany Creek and will be mentioned again, at a later time. His next patent was for 460 acres, dated 9 September 1648. It was "Scituate or being in the County of Nancemond being on the Eastward side of the Southern branch of Nancemond River and beginning at

---

[24] VSLA, 1:592

[25] Ibid., 1:593

[26] Ibid., 2:71

[27] Ibid., 5:175

[28] American Plantations and Colonies, Virginia People, 1624/5, Thomas Langford, c. 1997-2001 http://englishamerica.home.att.net/index.html

[29] VSLA, 1:584

[30] Ibid., 1:620

[31] USGS Topo Map, Microsoft Terraserver, http://terraserver.microsoft.com/printimage.asp?S=12&T=2&X=451&Y=5089&Z=18&W=1

[32] VSLA, 1:721

a Marked oake standing on a point on the Northward side of the Mouth of a Creek Called Craneyed [sic] Creek and runing North North East two hundred and four poles by the Maine Branch Side Unto a Marked red oake and Soe South East three hundred and twenty poles on the Land of William **HATFEILD** Unto a marked red oake and Soe South South East be [sic] South three hundred and twenty poles Unto a Marked white oake Standing by the Side of the Said Craney Creeke and Soe runing down by or Nigh on the Side of the Said Creeke unto the first Mentioned Marked tree…"[33]

William[1] **PARKER** was born circa 1604, in England, and came to Virginia as early as 1616, in the ship *Charles*. He was an indentured servant to John **BUSH**, who paid the transportation for his second voyage from England, in the *Charles*, in 1621. By 18 June 1638, he had acquired at least 700 acres of land in what became known as the Upper Parish of Nansemond County, now the City of Suffolk. This land was located on the southern branch of Nansemond River. As a respectable planter, he served as a Burgess for Upper Norfolke [Nansemond,] in the General Assembly of Virginia in 1642/43, and was acquainted with Thomas **DEW**, another Burgess in the same period. By 1654, or earlier, he had moved across the Nansemond River to the western branch. He sold those original patents to the father of one John **WRIGHT**. No record remains of other lands he may have purchased, sold or bequeathed to descendants. The population of this area was very small and greatly dependent upon each other for protection from the native peoples, and assistance in many other ways. William[1] **PARKER** knew his neighbors, including William **HATFEILD**, Randall **CREW**, his shipmate, and Thomas **DEW**. These families moved in the same social circle and were associated for many years, as will be shown. William[1] **PARKER** probably died some time after 1655, and possibly as late as 1663.

There were two distinctly different men named Thomas **PARKER**, both of whom lived in Isle of Wight County, VA. The elder Thomas is probably the one whose transportation was paid by John **SWEETE**, mentioned as a headright in his 26 September 1643, patent of 1,540 acres lying in Isle of Wight County.[34] The first record of landownership for this man is a patent for 300 acres, 15 November 1647. It is described as being located in Isle of Wight County, "upon a branch of a Creeke Called **EDWARDS** Creeke the Sayd branch known by the Name of ashen Swamp," adjoining the land of Richard **JACKSON**, and "by Virtue of a former Patent granted Unto Thomas **MORREY** Dated ye. 7th of Aprill 1641 and by the Said **MURREY** [sic] assigned to the Said **PARKER**."[35]

This patent is a good example of some of the problems encountered in transcription. Lookalike and faint letters, ink blots, and poor penmanship also plagued the clerks who had to transcribe these patents from the originals into the patent books. Another opportunity for error to creep into the records arose on the occasion of the normal wear and tear of everyday use that necessitated the transcription to yet another book. The abovementioned patent to Thomas **MORREY** clarifies at least one of these problems. It reads "Upon a branch of a Creeke called **SEAWARD**s Creeke…[36]" That one small detail enables quite accurate placement of this patent. Chuckatuck Creek has had several names, including Chuckatuck River, Warresquicke River, and New Town Haven River. It has also been known as being in both Nansemond and Isle of Wight Counties. **EDWARDS** Creek only appears in the patents in that one instance and **SEAWARD**s Creeke appears in numerous other patents on that creek, thus the latter is the correct name.

One of John **SEAWARD**s several patents, dated 18 June 1638, for 400 acres, was in Isle of Wight County, "Upon Warresquicke river now called new Towne haven," near a former patent of 600 acres.[37] A patent to Richard **JACKSON** for 450 acres, 13 March 1641/42, was "in the Countie of the Isle of Wight lying upon the head of a branch of the South bay Creeke called **SEWARD**s Creeke."[38] "South Bay" refers to the second bay on the west side of Chuckatuck Creek. **SEWARD**s Creek parallels U. S. Highway 17, between Bartlett and Crittenden, VA.

Thomas **PARKER**'s next patent was granted 18 March 1650/51, and contained 380 acres. It lay a short distance north and west of the 1647 patent, in Isle of Wight County. It is described as "Begining at a Point of Land Called the Island Neare **TAPSCER**s Creeke and thence runing west South

---

[33] VSLA, 2:148
[34] Ibid., 1:911
[35] Ibid., 2:85
[36] Ibid., 1:747
[37] Ibid., 1:634
[38] Ibid., 1:772

west westerly Eighty Eight perches to a Marked pine tree thence west South west Seventy Eight poles to the Corner tree of Mr. **NORSWORTHY**es Miles End...”[39] This land was due him for the transportation of eight persons into the Colony of Virginia. Those names appear in this record as Thomas **PARKER**, Joane, Francis, Elizabeth and Thomas, Children, John **MASON**, Sarah his wife and Mary **DAULDING**. The patent is rather ambiguous concerning the children's names, but they do appear later with Thomas **PARKER**, with the exception of the name “Joane.” It was most probably meant to read “John.”

The “Mr. **NORSWORTHY**” referred to in this patent was Tristram **NORSWORTHY**. He had several patents of earlier date, but the one for 670 acres, 6 December 1641, is the most helpful in locating the 1650/51 patent of Thomas **PARKER**. It is described as “Six hundred and Seventy Acres of Land and Marsh...in the Maine River and in the County of the Upper Norfolke...behind ye. Rugged Island Creeke...and Soe East by South on the New Town haven river Bay...the Said quantity of Land being Commonly known by the name of the Ragged Islands...”[40] This part of what was to become Nansemond County, then known as “Upper Norfolke,” was cut off to Isle of Wight County by 1650. Ragged Island still retains its name and is crossed at the southern end of the James River Bridge. Another of **NORSWORTHY**s patents, for 150 acres 3 May 1643, is described as “being in the County of the Isle of Wight and lying on the Westward side of a great marshe behinde an Island called by the name of the long ponds...”[41]

Thomas **PARKER** and James **BAGNOLL** were granted a patent for 470 acres, 29 May 1683. It is described as “four hundred and seventy Acres of High land and Marsh scittuate on the West side of **TAPSTER**s (alias ye long Ponds) Creek in ye Lower prish of Isle of Wight County fifty Acres part thereof being granted to Peter **MOUNTAGUE** by Pattent dated ye. 25th. of ffebruary 1638 [/39] and after severall Assignments Conveyed to Thomas **PARKER** (whose Widdow ye abovesd. Thomas Intermarryed.) and three hundred and Eighty Acres joyning to ye. former, being Granted to the aforesaid Thomas **PARKER** deced by Pattent Dated ye 18th. of March 1650 ye. Remaining forty Acres being within ye. former Bounds wch. ꝑsells descended to Dortthy & Sarah Daughters to ye. aforesaid Thomas **PARKER**, ye. Eldest whereof being Marryed, and of full Age, Did together with her husband Sell and Convey their Rights to their Father in Law Thomas **PARKER** abovesaid, the younger being lately Marryed to James **BAGNOLL** abovesaid, ye. whole being thus Bounded, Begining att ye. Mouth of **TAPTSTER**s [sic] Creeke aforesaid, and thence up the said Creeke to a Small Gutt, a little above **GARRETT**s poynt, then up the said Gutt North thirty degrees West seventy four poles, then West south West a hundred twenty four poles to a Sweet Gum, then South West by South a hundred and fifty poles to a greate white Oake then North West by North a hundred & Eighty poles to a Small Spanish Oake, then North East by North thirty two poles to a Branch of ye. Ballasting Marsh Creeke, then down ye. said Branch, North North West ninety four poles to Wm **SMITH**'s Line, and so by his Line East North East three hundred thirty four poles to ye. Back Creeke, then down ye. Said back Creeke to ye. ballasting Marsh Creeke, and Down yt. Creeke to ye first Station. The said Forty Acres being Due by and for ye. Transportation of one prson...”[42] Part of the land in this patent has been eroded away by the James River. Ballasting Marsh Creek is now known as **BALLARD** Creek, just to the northwest of Ragged Island.

The 50 acre patent to Peter **MONTAGUE** was granted 25 February 1638/39, and was “Land Scituate lying and being in the Upper Countie of new Norfolke North East Upon a Creeke called by the name of the Long pond Creeke South East buting Upon the Land of William **EYRES** South west into the woods called by the name of Oyster banck...”[43] Peter **MONTAGUE** assigned this land to Thomas **PARKER**, who eventually married **MONTAGUE**'s widow. Her name was Frances, as evidenced by her request for administration of Thomas **PARKER**'s estate 29 February 1663/64. His will specified that she should have the third part of his Estate, with the other two thirds to his children who

---

[39] VSLA, 2:289
[40] Ibid., 2:19
[41] Ibid., 1:928
[42] Ibid., 7:293
[43] Ibid., 1:616

are not named.[44]   The securities on this administration bond were Nicholas **SMITH** and Thomas **PARKER**.

The patents are quite consistent in mentioning relationships between father and son in regrants of lands originally patented to the father.   No such relationship appears between Thomas **PARKER** of the 1650 patent and Thomas **PARKER** of the 1683 patent.   The latter Thomas made his will 16 November 1685.   It was proved in court by his executrix, Frances **PARKER**, 9 February 1685/86.   Her bond was granted 1 May 1686.[45]   Children named in this will were eldest son, John, sons Thomas, Francis and George.   Daughters were Elizabeth, Mary and Ann.   All were under age.   Thomas stated that he was "aged 56 years or thereabout."   That would place his date of birth circa 1629.   The fact that both these men named some of their children the same, and lived on the same land, makes a good case for them to have been father and son.   This family may be further traced in the records of Isle of Wight County.

The elder Thomas would have been too old to be Thomas[2] **PARKER** *(William[1])*.   The younger man would have been the proper age to be Thomas[2], and the names of his children are repeated in later generations in the William[1] **PARKER** family, but further proof would be required to make that claim.   There is the possibility that Thomas **PARKER** who was dead by 29 February 1663/64, was a brother of William[1] **PARKER**, though no proof has become available to date.   More information has been found on Thomas[2] **PARKER** *(William[1])* of Nansemond County, and will be included later.

---

[44]   Chapman, Blanche Adams, *Wills and Administrations of Isle of Wight County, Virginia, 1647-1800*, (Baltimore: Genealogical Publishing Co., c. 1975.) p. 62

[45]   VSLA, Isle of Wight Co., Record of Wills, Deeds, Etc., Vol. 2, 1661-1719, pp. 58;247-248

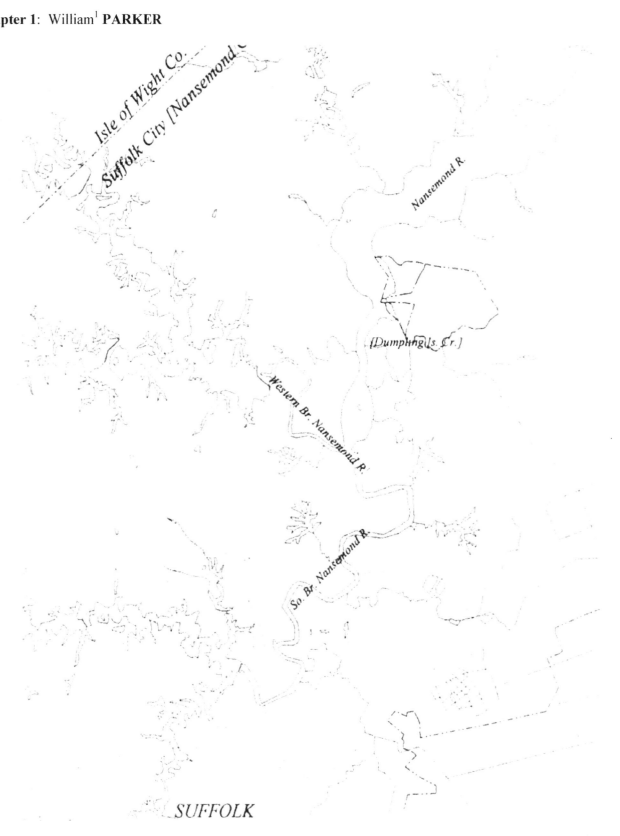

Scale: 1.52 mi/in

Map of part of Upper Parish of Nansemond County, VA, illustrating location of Dumpling Island Creek relative to the Southern and Western Branches of Nansemond River. USGS computer map used in DeedMapper™.

## Richard[2] PARKER (*William[1]*)

Richard[2] **PARKER** (*William[1]*) of Nansemond County, VA, is estimated here to have been born circa 1624, in that county. This man has long been claimed as being the Richard **PARKER**, "Chirurgeon," of Charles City and Henrico Counties, born in Cornwall, England in 1630. He is not the same man, though they were contemporaries. This has been ably proven by Waunita **POWELL** in her book, *Three Richard Parkers*. Dr. **PARKER** was in Charles City County, VA, by 1654, and married Mary **PERKINS**, widow of Nicholas **PERKINS**.[1] By September, 1664, he had moved to Henrico County and died some time after February 1679/80.[2] There appears to be no evidence whatsoever that this man ever set foot in Nansemond County, VA.

The commonly accepted statement that "Richard **PARKER** of Nansemond married Elizabeth **BAILEY**, daughter of Capt. Richard **BAILEY**," is a myth easily laid to rest by use of a single primary source. His wife's name is unknown, but it definitely was not "Elizabeth **BAILEY**," as evidenced by a suit brought in Accomack County Court, 28 September 1695. This action was brought by the Reverend Thomas **TEAKLE**, plaintiff, versus Mr. Phillip **PARKER** and Elizabeth his wife. She was accused of taking a number of goods from Mr. **TEAKLE**, while visiting his daughter, Margaret, in his absence. The verdict was that Phillip **PARKER** must pay £29 Sterling in damages. The foreman of the jury on this case was one William **PARKER**. In the deposition of John **ADDISON**, "aged 40 years or thereabouts," he relates the events of 2 February last, stating that Margaret **TEAKLE** sent her servant woman to invite Elizabeth **PARKER**, wife of Phillip, to her home. About an hour later, Elizabeth, Samuel **DOE**, his wife and daughter, came to her house "and a Negro fidler with them belonging to Capt Richard **BAYLEY** whose fiddle was Sent for or brought after him and one James **FAIREFAX** came for the fiddler and the Sd Elizabeth **PARKER** replyed she had borrowed the Fidler of her Sister Ursula **BAYLY** wife of the Sd Capt Richard **BAYLY**."[3] Further research on the people mentioned in this suit may divulge Elizabeth and Ursula's maiden name, for those seeking that information. In addition to the above evidence, Richard[2] **PARKER** had been dead 15 to 20 years earlier than the creation of this court record.

The first instance of the name Richard **PARKER** found in Nell Marion **NUGENT**'s excellent work, *Cavaliers and Pioneers, Abstracts of Virginia Land Patents and Grants, 1623-1666*, p. 150, is as a headright in a patent of 300 acres to John **CARTER**, 22 December 1643. This land was "in the County of Upper Norfolk and lying on the Westward side of the Southward branch of Nansamund river over against a prsell of lands of Mr Thomas **DEW** and beginning at a marked white oake standing on the Southward side of the Mouth of a small gutt and runing west twoe hundred and one pole on the land of William **TUCKER** unto a marked Gum tree standing by a Swamp side and soe South one hundred fortie six pole by or nigh unto a small Creeke side unto a marked pine standing on a point on the Eastward side of the Mouth of the said Creek...for the transportacon of six prsons..."[4] William **TUCKER** was granted a patent 6 January 1642, "adjoyning on a pattent of Land of Mr Thomas **HAMPTON** Clerke."[5] Thomas **HAMPTON** was granted a patent 21 September 1637, "in the Upper Countie of New Norfolke bounded North Easterly wth the prting [parting] of the Southerne and westerne branches of Nansamond river Easterly...on an old Indian field."[6] This locates the **CARTER** patent as being on the Western Branch of the Nansemond River, probably in the same area in which William[1] **PARKER** lived by then. The "lands of Thomas **DEW**" were the former patents of Thomas **POWELL**. This area is easily located on a current road-map of Virginia.

---

[1] Powell, Waunita, *Three Richard Parkers*, c. 1991, pp. 9;13
[2] Ibid., p. 11
[3] VA State Library Microfilm Reel 79, Accomack County Orders 1690-1697, pp. 160a-165, courtesy of George P. Bauguess
[4] VSLA,1:93
[5] Ibid., 1:864
[6] Ibid., 1:482

It should be noted that John **CARTER**, as well as Thomas **DEW**, was also a Burgess at the same time William[1] **PARKER** served in that office, so all were well acquainted. By 1643, Richard[2] **PARKER** would have been about 19 years of age, and old enough to have been returning from England, after possibly visiting family and receiving his education there. His name appears again as a headright, in a patent to Lawrence **PETERS** for 300 acres, 17 June 1647. It lay in Nansemond County, "on the westward side on ye. Head of a branch of the North west branch of Nansimum river Called the Indian Creeke" and adjoined William **STORY** and John **GARWOOD**.[7] His father was living on the Western Branch and probably also knew Lawrence **PETERS**, whose surname is connected with later generations of his family. In all probability, the headrights in this patent had been purchased, as they are essentially the same as the ones in the **CARTER** patent, thus do not necessarily represent a second trip for this Richard.

Richard[2] **PARKER** appears to have inherited, or purchased, some land before receiving his first Nansemond County patent, 5 October 1654. That patent gives "unto Mr. Richard **PARKER** four hundred Acres of Land Scituate or being in the southern branch of Nansemond River begining at a marked white Oake and Soe running for breadth East North East two hundred poles to a marked Gum buting on the Land of Mr. William **WRIGHT** and Soe againe for length South South East three hundred and twenty poles to a marked tree and Soe againe for breadth West South West two hundred poles to a marked Gum and Soe againe for length North North West three hundred and twenty poles Joyning to his Owne Land to the first mentioned marked tree...for the Transportacon of Eight Persons..."[8] The date of acquisition, by whatever means, of "his own land," is unknown. In this patent, he was addressed as "Mr.," a term of respect with more meaning than it bears today. Checking preceding and following pages of Patent Book 3, reveals that this is not a routinely-used term by the transcribing clerk. Being a landowner, with perhaps more education than the average man at that period, would earn him that address. Richard[2] renewed this patent 18 March 1662/63.[9] Some of the reasons for a person to renew a patent were acquisition of adjoining land, failure to seat the land within the allotted time, an inaccurate survey and boundary disputes with neighbors.

William **WRIGHT** was granted a patent in Nansemond County, for 2,250 acres, 15 February 1655/56, just a brief time after Richard's first patent.[10] One of the lines of **WRIGHT**'s patent crossed a small creek called Marracoones Creek. It will be mentioned here again. One of the 45 persons whose transportation justified this patent was one Ann **PARKER**. Her relationship, if any, to Richard[2] **PARKER** is unknown. He was granted another patent for 200 acres, on that same date, at the head of **PARKER**'s Creek.[11] Patentees usually occupied the land for several years prior to issuance of the patent, thus it would not be unusual for a creek on Richard[2]'s land to have been called **PARKER**'s Creek.

Edmund **VAHANE** was granted a patent of 250 acres, 9 April 1662. It lay "in the Southern branch of Nancemond River 200 Acres thereof at the Easter [sic] Side of the branch Beginning at a Maple a Corner tree of Thomas **HARWOOD**s Land runing the head of his Land for Length & by William **WRIGHT**s Land South South West..."[12] He received another 100 acres, 29 March 1666, under the name of Edward **VAUGHN**. Spelling variations are common in these records and this patent contains two. The second is Thomas **HARWOOD**, who shows up in other patents as Thomas **HARROW** and Thomas **HARRELL**, the current spelling. This property lay "in the upper Parish of the County of Nancemond Beginning at a burnt stump being the Corner tree of Sylvester **BAKER**s Land, and runing South West three hundred and twenty poles on the miles end of Randolphe [sic] **CREW**es Land to a marked oak and buting on the Land of Richard **PARKER** and So south East fifty poles to a marked pine & so North East three hundred and twenty poles Joining to **PARKER**s Land Mr. **WRIGHT**s & Thomas **HARROW**s Land to **HARROW**s Corner tree by the Creek side..."[13]

---

[7] VSLA, 2:85

[8] Ibid., 3:371

[9] Ibid., 5:323

[10] Ibid., 4:13

[11] Ibid., 4:27

[12] Ibid., 4:387

[13] Ibid., 5:668

**Chapter 2:** Richard[2] **PARKER** *(William[1])*

These patents place Richard[2] **PARKER** as a neighbor of Randall/Randolphe **CREW** and William **WRIGHT**. The 1648 patent of Randall **CREW** has already established that both he and William **HATFEILD** owned land on Craney Creek.

Richard[2] **PARKER** purchased both of William **HATFEILD**'s 1638 patents, and Randall **CREW**'s 1648 patent. He was dead before 23 April 1681. That is the date of a patent to Thomas, Richard and Francis **PARKER**, "the three Sons of Richard **PARKER** deced One thowsand fower hundred and twenty acres of Land with Marsh adjoyning lying and being in the Southerne branch of Nanzemund begining at a red oake standing on a point to the Northward of Craney Creeks Mouth and opposite to a small Island called Crany Island at **CRAIN**s Ehan_ing [sic] thence runing downe by the Maine branch side according to the severall turnings and windings of the said branch till it comes to a great decayed white oake standing a little above the Creeke or Mouth which is called **PARKER**s Creeke thence South East Crossing over the said Creeke ___ and Extending three hundred and twenty pole to John **SMALL** his owne white oake thence South West one hundred Eighty fower pole to a markt white oake beeing the begining tree of the Crosse Swampe Pattent and runs the due Courses of the said Pattent Vizt East North East two hundred pole to a markt Gum thence [line crossed out] South South East three hundred & twenty pole to a markt Ash by a Gum in a great woody pocoson or maine [?] Runing thence West South West twoe hundred pole to a markt Gum thence North North West one hundred sixty fower pole to a markt Gum Standing by a branch being in the head line of **HOOD** neck Pattent thence South West by West one hundred forty six pole to a white oake standing by and towards the head of Crany Creeke thence downe or nigh the said Creek to the Mouth thereof and thence as the Southern Northerne branch runs downe to the first mentioned red oake including the first quantity three hundred acres whereof being formerly granted to William **HATFEILD** by two Patents the one for twoe hundred the other for one hundred acres dated the 24th August 1638 and fower hundred and sixty acres more of the Same Said Land formerly grannted Unto Randall **CREWE** by Pattent dated the 9th September 1648 all which by deeds and Surrender become the prper right of Richard **PARKER** Senir decest fower hundred acres more of the said Land was formerly grannted to the said Richard **PARKER** Senir by Pattent the 18th March 1662[/63] and one hundred acres more being greatest ___ be Marsh was alsoe formerly granted to Richard **PARKER** one of the now Pattentees by patent dated the 24th ffebruary 1675/76 all which by the said Pattents and their ffathers Will being now the right and in possession of the Said Thomas Richard and ffrancis **PARKER** the one hundred & sixty acres ___ being a ___ ___ & Marsh found to be conteyned wthin the said bounds and due by and for the transportacon of fower prsons &c... 23d Day of Aprill Anno Domi 1681..."[14]

Another important patent for a Richard **PARKER** was for 100 acres, granted 24 February 1675/76, mentioned above. It is described as "one hundred acres of Land With marsh the Greater part Adjoyning lying & being in the County of nanzimond at a Island Called **HOOD**s neck in the Southern branch & Joyning to other Land of the said **PARKER** beginning at the mouth of a Small Creeke or Gutt a little below a Small Island of Woodland and Runing Up by the maine branch side near N. W. 136 po. till it turnes the ___ poynt of marsh and then runs S. W. or near thereabouts by the branches Side passing by a Long point of Woodland 120 po. Then S. E. to a marked white ___ oke Standing by the wood Side & So Extending over Severall points 136 po. By an old line of markt trees of Said **PARKER**s to a white Gum Standing on a point by or near the marsh & butting on the Lands of Tho: **PARKER** now liveth on, thence N: E: or near there abouts to the forementioned small Creek or Gutt & runing according to the Several turnings & windings thereof till it Comes to the mouth where itt first Begins meandring...for the Transportation of two prsons..."[15] This is obviously the patent referred to in the one to Thomas[3], Richard[3], and Francis[3] **PARKER**, and this man is Richard[3] **PARKER**, "one of the *now* Pattentees." It is quite probable that Richard[2] **PARKER** was already dead by this date, as he is not mentioned as an adjoining landowner.

Thomas **DEW** was granted a patent of 450 acres, 20 April 1681. It is described as being "in the Upper prish of Nanzemond at the head of a Creeke called Crany Creeke which issues out of the Southard branch begining att a small saplin hiccory standing by or neare twoe markt Saplin pines in the line of **HOOD**s neck Pattent & which now belongs to ffrancis **PARKER** & runs thence to a

---

[14] VSLA, 7:93
[15] Ibid., 6:595

white oake by Crany Creeke side by markt trees of the said **PARKER**s...& Joynes at a markt stake wth the line of Georg [sic] **SPIVEY**es gent [?] Thence South East Crossing the Beverdam...the said land being formerly granted to Randall **CREWE** by Pattent bearing date the thirteenth of November 1640 the which after severall Surrenders & discent [sic] is now of right in possession & in fee belonging to the said Coll Thomas **DEWE**..."[16]

Francis[3] **PARKER** was granted a patent for 20 acres, 16 April 1683. It is described as "being in the upper Parish of Nansemund County Begining at a marked Hickory wch stands by or nigh two small markt Saplin Pines in the line of **HOOD**s neck now in the Possession of the said **PARKER** and runs by the Said **PARKER**s line North East and by East fifty two pole to a line of Marked trees of the Cross Swamp Pattent, which was Granted to Richard **PARKER** Senr. Father to the said frrancis and goes by that Pattents Line South South East one hundred twenty four pole, and intersects and Joynes to the land & Line of Jerrico now belonging to Coll Thomas **DEW**, and so by the Said **DEW**s marked trees North West to the first Station...for the transportation of one prson..."[17] This appears to be the last reference to Francis[3] **PARKER** *(Richard[2],William[1])* in the patents. He does appear in the Quit Rent Rolls of 1704, for Nansemond County, with 170 acres of land. He is estimated here to have been born circa 1652. Francis[4] **PARKER**, Jr., appears in that same listing, under "Persons living out of the County and others that will not pay or give account," with no land mentioned.[18]

Thomas[3] **PARKER** *(Richard[2],William[1])* appears to have received at least part of the Cross Swamp patent of Richard[2] **PARKER**, as evidenced by a patent for 430 acres to Thomas **DUKE**, 23 April 1681. It is described as "Land lying and being in the upper parish of Nansemund begining at a markt oake about five pole from Thomas **HARRELL**s Corner dogwood and runs South South West one hundred pole to a Live oake thence North West by West sixteene pole to the Corner Gum of Thomas **PARKER** thence by the said **PARKER**s South South East line of the Cross Swamp three hundred and twenty pole to a markt Ash by a great old Gum at his Miles end thence North East twoe hundred sixty twoe poles to a markt Gum at the Miles end of the Pattent of twoe hundred acres formerly belonging to William **WRIGHT** and thence North North East One hundred pole to a markt holy [sic] neare Thomas **HARRELL**s corner Saplin Gum at his Miles end and _?_ thence by markt trees West North West three hundred and twenty pole to the first station two hundred acres of the said Land being formerly graunted to William **WRIGHT** by patent bearing date the 18th March 1662 and by him conveyed to the said Thomas **DUKE** the twoe hundred and thirty acres residue being due by and for the transportation of five prsons &c..."[19] This is the patent granted to **WRIGHT** 15 February 1655/56, and renewed 18 March 1662.

Thomas[3] **PARKER** was granted a patent for 150 acres, 16 April 1683. It is described as "land and marsh lying and in [sic] ye upper prish of Nanzimund, Begining att a marked Pine a corner tree which begins the land of Col Thomas **DEW** att the mouth of a Creek Called Crainy Creek isueing out of ye Southern Branch and runing South East by ye. Said **DEW**es land three hundred & twenty poles to a marked white Gum, thence north East thirty Eight pole, to a marked Hickory standing by or nigh ye. Creek Side, and so down the said Creeke, according to the Severall Turnings and Windings thereof (includeing a small Island called Rackoone Island) to the first mentioned marked Pine..."[20] Rackoone Island may well be the source of the name "Marracoones Creek." Thomas[3] **PARKER** was still living on this land in 1698, as evidenced by a patent of 48 acres to Richard **PARKER**, 15 October 1698. It was on the "eastermost Side of Southern branch of nansamond River in ye County of nansamond beginning at a white oake a Corner tree of Thomas **PARKER** Running thence northeastwardly forty five degrees one hundred and twenty poles to a pine thence South eastwardly fortyty [sic] five degrees fifty poles to a white oake thence northeastwardly forty five degrees one hundred fifty Seven pole to a Dogwood a Corner tree of Thomas **HARRELL**s thence South Eastwardly Seventy nine degrees Seven poles to a white oake a Corner tree of Thos **DUKE**s...to a maple a Corner tree of Richd **PARKER**s

---

[16] VSLA, 7:90

[17] Ibid., 7:261

[18] Wertenbaker, Thomas J., *The Planters of Colonial Virginia*, Russell & Russell, c. 1959, Appendix, pp. 197-201

[19] VSLA, 7:88

[20] Ibid., 7:259

Cross Swamp patent Line two hundred and ten pole to ye first Station..."[21] This establishes his residence in the area near Suffolk, and distinguishes him from another Thomas **PARKER** who lived nearer the border of Isle of Wight and Nansemond Counties, at the same time. He is estimated here to have been born circa 1648.

In 1698, Richard[3] **PARKER** was still living on the land he inherited from his father. His son, Richard[4], was granted two patents dated 26 April 1698. The first was for 100 acres..."with __ marsh the greater part...at a place Called **HOOD**s neck in the Southern branch and Joyning to other lands of the said **PARKER**s fathers...butting on the land Thomas **PARKER** now dwells on...the said one hundred Acres of land was formerly granted unto Mr. Richd **PARKER** Senr, by patent dated ye 24th ffeb 1675/76 and was by him deserted and is since granted unto his son Richd **PARKER** by order Of the Genll. Court bearing date ye 15th of Apll 1697 and is further due unto him by and for the transportation of two persons into this Colony..."[22] The second patent was for 400 acres and was "formerly granted unto Mr. Richd **PARKER** by patent dated ye 15th October 1654 and renued in his Maj name by order ye Quarter Court and also granted by patent dated ye 18th march 1662 to the said Richd. **PARKER** and by him deserted and since granted to the patentee by order of ye. Genll. Court dated ye 15th apll. 1697...for the transportation of eight persons into this colony..."[23] The 100-acre patent was very specific as to the relationship of father and son. The 400-acre patent does not make that distinction. This is obviously the same land patented by Richard[2], grandfather to this Richard[4]. Richard[4] **PARKER** *(Richard[3],Richard[2],William[1])* is estimated here to have been born circa 1676. He appears on the Quit Rent Roll of 1704, as owning 514 acres in Nansemond County.[24] Richard[3] **PARKER** may have died between 1698 and 1704.

On 28 April 1711, a patent of 49 acres was granted to Thomas **DUKE**, Jr., and his brother, John. It is described as "being in the upper parish of Nansemond County on the Westward Side of the Southerne Branch of Nansemond River and...Begining at a Maple Standing in their father Thomas **DUKE**s Line and Near unto a Corner tree of the Land of Frances **MACE** and Runns thence bounding on the Said **DUKE**...to the Line of the aforesaid **MACE**..."[25] This, and the 1681 patent to Thomas **DUKE**, establishes the location of the land of Francis **MACE**, and where Richard[4] **PARKER** received his next patent. It was of 44 acres, granted 28 April 1711, and lay on the "Eastward Side of the Southern Branch of Nansemond River near the head of a Runn Called **OLIVER**s Runn," and began at a Black Gum corner tree of Francis **MACE**.[26] This is the last patent recorded for this Richard **PARKER**, in this area.

Some time in the ensuing three years, he moved south to the present Gates County, NC/Suffolk City, VA, border area. One of his first patents there was for 302 acres, for the importation of six persons, dated 16 June 1714. It was "near the head of **BENNETT**'s Creek in the upper parish of Nansemond County...near **HOOD**s Mare branch."[27] On that same date, he had another patent for 304 acres, near the head of **BENNETT**'s Creek, also on **HOOD**'s Mare Branch.[28] This land adjoins the western lines of that first parcel of 302 acres. He allowed this patent to lapse for want of seating and planting and it was re-granted to Daniel and Jonathan **PARKER**, 12 July 1718.[29]

A patent of 200 acres was granted to one Samuel **PARKER** 16 June 1714. It is described as "being in the upper parish of Nansemond County near the head of **BENNITT**s Creek & bounded as followeth to wit, beginning at a maple Richard **PARKER**'s Corner tree Standing in **HOOD**'s mare branch & runs thence down by the same south Easterly fifteen degrees eighty pole to a pine thence south westerly seventy three degrees two hundred fifty two pole to a pine standing near the side of **DAVY**es mare branch thence by or nigh the Same north westerly eighty three degrees sixty two pole

[21] VSLA, 9:175

[22] Ibid., 9:142

[23] Ibid., 9:144

[24] Wertenbaker, Thomas J., *The Planters of Colonial Virginia*, Russell & Russell, c. 1959, Appendix, pp. 197-201

[25] VSLA, 10:32

[26] Ibid., 10:10

[27] Ibid., 10:133

[28] Ibid., 10:185

[29] Ibid., 10:388

to a pine thence north westerly twenty Degrees ninety three pole to a pine thence north Easterly thirty eight degrees twenty pole to a Pine thence north Easterly eighty two degrees three hundred & two pole bounding on the land of the Said Richard **PARKER** to the first station...”[30] That last call of “N82E. 302 pole,” matches the southern boundary of the 304-acre parcel. This patent was re-granted to Richard[4] **PARKER**, in Nansemond County, 12 July 1718, for the sum of 20 shillings.[31] The identity of this Samuel **PARKER** is unknown.

On 1 March 1719/20, William **SPITES** was granted 400 acres by North Carolina, “in Chowan precinct.” It began “at a dead pine Saml **PARKER**s line tree So along his line various Courses to a pine ye. Said **PARKER**s corner tree on mare branch...”[32] The border disputes between North Carolina and Virginia led to land being granted by both governments in the same area. The lack of communication between the two is apparent in that Richard[4] **PARKER** had owned Samuel’s patent for nearly two years when William **SPITES** received his 400 acres. The larger portion of the above lands lie within the current boundaries of Gates County, NC.

Richard[4] **PARKER** continued to acquire land in his lifetime, both by patent and purchase. After the dividing line was run in 1728, Richard[4] patented at least three other parcels that remained in Nansemond County. The first was for 399 acres, 28 September 1730, and was granted to “Richard **PARKER** of North Carolina...Beginning at a Pine a Corner tree of his own Land...” This parcel bounded on the “Country [State] line,” Thomas **ODUM**, on the head of the Beech Swamp, John **WILLIAMS**, Thomas **GOFF** and Edward **ROBERTS**.[33] Beech Swamp is now known as Mill Swamp and flows out of Somerton Swamp. It parallels the border until it nears U. S. 13, where it dips down into Gates County. Beech Swamp re-enters Virginia just above Piney Wood Chapel. The head of the swamp lies in Nansemond County.

The next Virginia patent for this man was for 388 acres, 25 August 1731, also to “Richard **PARKER** of North Carolina.”[34] This land began at a pine corner of his own land, of the 1730 patent, and adjoined Joseph **HORTON**. There is yet another Virginia patent for Richard[4] **PARKER**, but it is listed in the index to the Virginia Land Office Patents and Grants under the name “John **PARKER**.” This parcel was of 371 acres, 20 June 1733. It also began at his corner pine and adjoined both the 1730 and 1731 patents, as well as the “Country line,” and one John **KNIGHT**.[35] Each of these three properties cost the sum of 40 shillings.

When the dividing line was drawn in 1728, about half of Richard[4]’s Nansemond County lands were then in Chowan County, NC. The missing minutes of Chowan County Court of Pleas and Quarter Sessions prevent earlier documentation, but by 16 July 1730, it appears that Richard[4] **PARKER** had been appointed a Justice of the peace for that county.[36] His last known appointment to that office was made at a court held 17 October 1734.[37]

He continued to fulfill his civic responsibilities in the community through his membership in the Episcopal Church of St. Paul’s Parish. He was first named as a vestryman for St. Paul’s by Easter Monday 1731.[38] He was chosen a Church Warden at the July 1731 meeting of the Vestry, in Edenton, and was re-elected vestryman Easter Monday, 3 April 1738, and 7 April 1740.[39] At a Vestry held at the Indian Town Chapel, 18 April 1741, it was ordered that Richard **PARKER**, Isaac **HUNTOR**, Thomas **WALTON** and John **SUMNER** hire workmen to build a chapel at or near James **COSTEN**’s, and another at or near James **BRADDEY**’s. They were each to be built to the specifications of “Thirty five foot Long and Twenty two foot and a halfe wide Eleven foot in the pitch betwee [sic] Sill

---

[30] VSLA, 10:186

[31] Ibid., 10:388

[32] Secretary of State, North Carolina Land Grants, 8:218, File No. 887, hereafter NCLG

[33] VSLA, 14:137

[34] Ibid., 14:296

[35] Ibid., 15:67

[36] Haun, Weynette Parks, *Chowan County North Carolina County Court Minutes Pleas & Quarter sessions 1730-1745*, c. 1983, 1:#3

[37] Ibid., 19:#56

[38] Fouts, Raymond Parker, *Vestry Minutes of St. Paul’s Parish, Chowan County, North Carolina 1701-1776*, Second Edition, c. 1998, 25:#56, hereafter, Fouts, *Vestry Minutes*

[39] Ibid., 17:#60;35:#84;38:#90

and plate and a Roof workmanlike near a Squear and to be a Good fraim Gott out of Good Timber and coverd with Good Siprus Shingles and weather boarded with feather Edged plank nine inches broad with Good Lapp of two Inches at the least and Good Sleapers and flowers [floors] of Good plank of Inch and a qtr thick and Sealed [ceiled] with Good plank with three windows Suitable for Such a hows or howses and two Doars Suitable with a pulpitt...”[40]   The chapel at James **BRADDEY**'s was built near the Knotty Pine Swamp, now known as Buckland Mill Branch.  The chapel at James **COSTEN**'s was built near Sunbury.

The Vestry met at Thomas **WALTON**'s home, 8 August 1741.  The contract for the chapels had been drawn up and it was then ordered that Richard **BOND** and Jonathan **PARKER** “Be allowed and payd by this prish the Sums of Money by them a greed [sic] for by this Vestrey for the building of Two Chappells when their work is Done according to their a greemt.”[41]  The next meeting was held 10 April 1742, at “The Chappell at Meherin,” another name for the one at James **COSTEN**'s, near Meherrin Swamp.  It was then ordered that “the Ch wds. pay to Jonathan **PARKER** forty Two Pounds and Ten Shillings proclamation Monney for his Trouble and Charge in building a Chappell at the Knotty Pine.”[42]  This Jonathan **PARKER** was one of Richard[4] **PARKER**'s sons.

Processioning of lands was to be done every three years, by an act of the Lords Proprietors, titled “An Act for settling the Titles and Bounds of Lands,” dated 23 November 1723.  The Justices of each precinct court were to order the vestry of each parish to divide them into convenient districts for processioning every person's land between 1 October and the last day of April, following the order of the Court.  In 1729, this law was altered to allow the vestries to appoint the required two freeholders for each district as processioners, without the court order.  They were required to make a return of their proceedings to the next Court, including any lands which had not been processioned, and the reasons for failing to comply with the order.  Persons who had their lands processioned twice were deemed the sole owner.[43]  Processioning was done, quite literally, by the processioners, the landowners, and some neighbors walking along the boundaries of each parcel, noting and renewing boundary marks.  Between October and April, harvesting of crops was complete and there was time and opportunity for the processioners to make their appointed rounds, and make return to the Court.  Illness and inclement weather were the main hindrances to making timely returns.

At a Vestry meeting held at Edenton, 12 March 1742, Demsey **SUMNER** and Jonathan **PARKER** were appointed processioners for the district from the Knotty Pine to the Perquimans Road at Loosing Swamp, and all contained between that and **BENNETT**s Creek Swamp to the bridge, then from **BENNETT**s Creek Bridge to the Knotty Pine.  It was also ordered that John and Richard **PARKER**, Sr., be appointed processioners from the Knotty Pine up the road that leads to the Virginia line, to the said line and Perquimans line and all contained between that and the Loosing Swamp.[44]  Loosing Swamp is now known as Folly Swamp, in the eastern edge of present-day Gates County.

Richard[4] **PARKER**'s final Virginia patent was granted 20 May 1749, for 82 acres in Nansemond County, on Thomas **BOYT**'s land on the west side of Somerton Swamp, and adjoining Robert **PARKER** and William **ROGERS**.[45]  The wording of this patent omits the fact that Richard was living in Chowan County, NC, then, but it was transcribed from an earlier book and was probably omitted at that time.

Several deeds concerning Richard[4] **PARKER** are found in the records of Chowan County.  The first of these is a deed for 50 acres from Jonathan **KITTERELL**, of Chowan Prect., to Richard **PARKER** of the Upper Parish of Nansemond Co., VA, dated 23 March 1723/24.  It was “part of a greater tract Granted by Patent to sd. John **KITTERELL** as by his Patent dated 4th July 1723...& is bounded Vizt:  Begining at a Red Oak a line tree of the Pattent neer the line of Jno. **STALLINGS**, thence by a Row of Mark'd trees to a Mark'd Pine Neer the Side of White Pott Pocoson, thence Run-

---

[40]  Fouts, *Vestry Minutes*, 40:#94

[41]  Ibid., 25:#56

[42]  Ibid., 40:#96

[43]  Clark, Walter, ed. *The State Records of North Carolina, Vol. XXIII, Laws 1715-1776*, Goldsboro, NC; State of North Carolina, 1904, pp. 103-106;114;115, courtesy of Weynette Parks Haun, Durham, NC.

[44]  Fouts, *Vestry Minutes*, 45:#104

[45]  VSLA, 27:181

ing to a Mark'd White Oak a Corner tree of sd **KITTERELL**s neer the line of Thos. **BEAGLIN**s [**BENGLINS** ?] land, thence Runing along the Patent Line to a mark'd Pine a corner tree of the Patent, thence runing the course of the Patent to a mark'd Red Oak another corner tree of the Patent neer the line of sd. Jno. **STALLINGS** Land, thence runing the course of the Patent to the first station...50 Acres...sd. **KITTERELL** hath right in fee simple to sell...land is clear of all sales, bargains, Entails etc... Signd: Johnan (K) **KITTERELL**..." Witnesses were Geo. (G) **SPIVEY** and Jas. (|) **SPIVEY**. It was acknowledged in court, "26 March 1723." This date should read "26 March 1724," as it is the second day of the new year, at that time.[46] No record of this patent has been found in either VA or NC.

On 19 October 1742, John **SMALL** sold Richard[4] **PARKER** 203 acres, part of a patent to his father, John **SMALL**, dated 31 October 1726. This land began at "a gum in the maple Pocoson and running thence NoE 18 po. to Thos. **SPIGHT**s Corner Pine thence Bounding on the Sd. Thos **SPIGHT**s Line to Daniel **PUGH**s Corner Pine thence the Several courses of the sd. Patten and Regard being had thereto more full and at Large Doth and may appear...to the 1st station..." Witnesses to this deed were Jonathan[5] and Daniel[5] **PARKER**, and it was proved in court 9 March 1742/43.[47] The elder **SMALL**'s patent is of record in the Virginia Land Office.

On 10 December 1742, Richard[4] **PARKER** also purchased 100 acres from Robert **ABRAMS**. It was part of a patent to William **SUMNER**, 3 April 1723, beginning "at a markt red oak Standing in a Small Branch which issueth out of the Bound Pocoson & Runs into a Pocoson Commonly Called **FRIOR**s Pocoson so along that Br. SE to a Markt white oak Standing in The Forked Branch it being in the Pattent Line that line to a Pine standing by the Elm Swamp up Elm Sw. to a Pine in the Bear Branch thence Binding on Thos. **HOUSE**s Line to a Pine Corner Tree of Christopher **GOWIN**s, his line to the first station..." Jonathan[5] and Daniel[5] (D) **PARKER** also witnessed this deed.[48] Jonathan[5] and Daniel[5] were two of his sons, as evidenced by his will.

Richard[4] sold 150 acres of his land to his son, Peter[5] **PARKER**, 10 January 1748/49, for 45 barrels of tar. The land is described as being in Chowan, "it being the land whereon the sd. Peter **PARKER** now dwelleth and bounded as followeth... Beginning at the Country line on a branch called the mill dam branch so runing down the sd. Branch to a marked gum standing by or nigh the sd. Branch thence by a line of markt trees to a white oak markt & standing nigh to afors'd Branch so down the said branch to the mouth thereof then crossing the sd. Peter **PARKER**s mill pond to a marked white oak standing on the South west side of the sd. pond thence by a line of marked trees to Wm. **DOUGHTRIE**s Line thence along Wm. **DOUGHTRIE**s to a branch commonly Called the Little mare branch so down the said branch to the mouth of a branch commonly called the bay tree branch so up the sd. bay tree branch to a chesnut oak Moses **BOYCE**s to the bay tree branch thence up the sd. branch to the country line thence west along the said country line to the first station, containing by Estimation 150 acres..." Witnesses to this deed were Jonathan **PARKER**, John **BENTON**, Jr., and John **BENTON**. It was proved in April Court 1749.[49] This 150 acres is part of Richard[4]'s 16 June 1714 patent of 302 acres.

On 28 May 1736, Richard and Ann **HINES** of the upper Parish of Nansemond Co., VA, sold 200 acres of land in Chowan Co., NC, to Moses **BOYCE**, also of Nansemond. It is described as being "near the head of **BENNETT**s Creek beginning at a White Oak standing on the North West side of a branch called the Bay Tree Branch running thence No. Westerly forty six degrees one hundred thirteen & a half pole to a Red Oak a corner tree of Rd. **PARKER**s land thence bounded on his patent line No. East twenty two degrees, Two Hundred Twenty two poles to a pine..." The latter is one of the calls on the southeast side of the above mentioned patent. Richard **HINES** purchased this land from the original Virginia patentee, Bryant **OQUIN**.[50]

---

[46]  Chowan Co., NC, Deed Bk. C#1:342-343. Verbatim transcription of this deed courtesy of Weynette Parks Haun, 13 July 2002, from Chowan County Deeds, Microfilm Reel C.024.48002
[47]  Chowan County Deed Book A#1:167
[48]  Ibid., A#1:166
[49]  Ibid., C#:152-153
[50]  Haun, Weynette Parks, *Chowan County, North Carolina Deed Books: W-1 1729-1738;C-2 1738-1740;D 1748-1806 and various earlier & later dates Vol. I.*, c. 1998, Deed Bk. W#1:312-313, 22:#119

Richard[4] **PARKER** sold other parcels of land, to John **MOORE** and Thomas **FRAZIER**, some time in the year 1750, though the deeds appear not to have survived. The Chowan Cross Index to Deeds-Grantor 1695-1878, shows these names for Book F#1, but having been deemed "non-reproducible," there are no page numbers.[51] That same Cross Index to Deeds also shows a deed of gift from Jonathan **PARKER** to Richard **PARKER**, in Book F#1. The deed to John **MOORE** was proved by the oath of Demsey **SUMNER** in Chowan County October Court 1750, and the one to Thomas **FRAZIER** was proved in January Court 1750/51.[52] A partial record remains in the Chowan County deed of John **MOORE** to Demsey **SUMNER**, dated 6 April 1757. It is described as "two parcels of land being the land & plantation whereon sd John **MOORE** now liveth bounded according to the most ancient known & reputed bounds thereof & is joining the lands of Wm. **DAUGHTIE**, Peter **PARKER**, Daniel **PARKER** and others & is on the No:ern & So:ern side of a swamp known as the Great Maer [sic] Branch in Chowan Co. part of which land was sold to sd John **MOORE** by Richd. **PARKER** & the other part thereof by Jonathan **PARKER** as by their deed registered in Chowan Co. containing in the whole 590 A. Wit: Demsey **SUMNER**, Richd. **PARKER**, Geo **GOLSON** [sic] jurat. Pvd Jan Ct. 1758 by Geo. **POLSON**..."[53]

These records establish Richard[4] **PARKER** as living near the present community known as Drum Hill, in Gates County. Some of these land descriptions will be repeated in following chapters.

---

[51] NCSA, C.024.49501, Chowan Cross Index to Deeds Grantor 1695-1878, Vol. A
[52] Haun, Weynette Parks, *Chowan County North Carolina Court Minutes 1749-1754*, c. 1992, 33:#57;40#72
[53] Chowan County, NC, Deed Book, H#1:246, 119:#714 courtesy of Weynette Parks Haun, Durham, NC

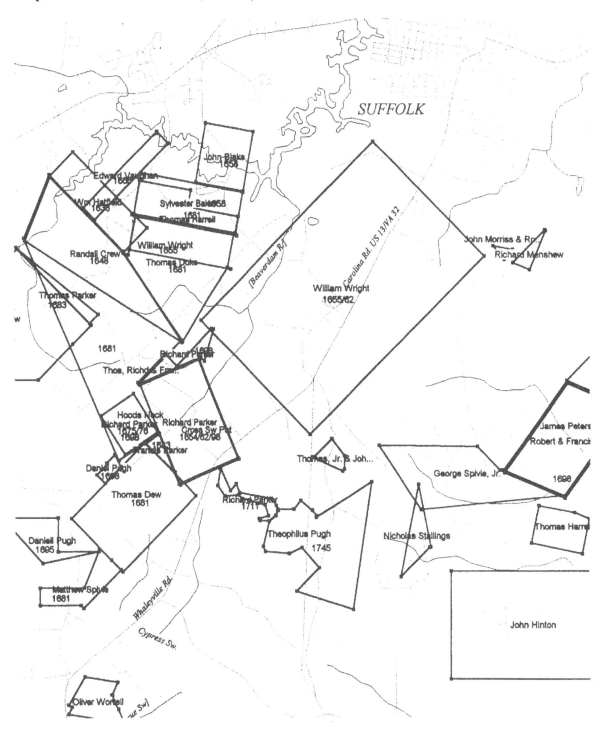

Scale: 0.76 mi/in

Map depicting location and plats of **PARKER** lands in Nansemond County, VA, 1654-1683, including the **HOOD**'s Neck and Cross Swamp Patents.

**Some Richard[4] PARKER *(Richard[3],Richard[2],William[1])* Descendants**

The following is a verbatim transcription of the last will and testament of Richard[4] **PARKER**:
[p. 1] "North Carolina ss  In the Name of God Amen

I Richard **PARKER** of Chowan County in the Province afore Said Do Make and ordain this my Last will and Testament I/n/ manner and form following that is to Say furst I Give My Sole into the hands of God who Gave it and my Body to Be Bured at the Discrecsion of my Executors heare after Named And what worldly Goods I have I do Dispose there of as foll [sic] foloweth

Imprimis  I give and Bequeth unto My Son Richard **PARKER** My Land and Plantaton whare I now Live Bounded By a Branch from the mouth thare of up the Said Branch to a markt white Oak thence a Long the Said Branch Side by a line of markt Trees to a Gum thence up the Said Branch to a markt tree Standing in the fork of the Said Branch thence by a line of markt Trees into a Pocoson a Corner tree Thence a long a line to Joseph **HORTON**s Line thence a Long the Said Line to Joseph **HORTON**s Corner Tree thence Running a Long Willam **EVERET**s [?] line to his Corner Tree thence Runing a Long a Line of Trees in the gaulberry Pocoson thence Runing a long a line of _____ [crossed out] markt Trees in the fork of the Litelle Mare Branch from thence Runing Down the Said Branch to a white oak Standing By the Side of the Mill Pond from thence Crossing the Mill Pond to the firt Stat/i/on Containing a bout five Hundred acres I Say to him and his hairs [sic] forever

Item  I give and Bqueath /To my/ son Daniel **PARKER** the Plantation and Land wher_ he now Liveth Containing about three Hundred & fifty Acres and Bounded as followeth Vizt [?] Begining at the Mill Swamp So Bindig [sic] on the Last Line of the Land alredy made a Long a line of markt Trees a Corner tree thence Runing a Long John **MORE**s Line thence Runing a Long a Line to John **MORE**s Corner tree thence Runing a long a Line of markt /Trees/ **PUGH**s thence Runing a Long a Line of trees In or neare the Contry Line thence Runing a Long a Line of trees to a Coner tree Standing in the gaulber/r/y Pocoson thence to Amarkt tree [?] Standing in the fork of the Mare Branch To turn over  [Stamped #3030]
[p. 2]  So Down the Said Branch to the first Station I say to him and his Hairs for ever

Item  I give and Bequeath to my Son Francis **PARKER** a parsel of Land Containing ab/o/ut Three hundred & fifty Acr/e/s and Bounded as fol [sic] followeth Begining At a Markt pine Standing By a pond and near the Contry Line thence a Long the Contry Line to a markt tree in Charls **RUSSEL**s Line So a Long **RUSSEL**s Line to a markt pine a Corner tree Standing in the head of a Branch So Down the Said Branch as far as the Parcell Extendeth thence Joining on the Land formerly be Longing to John **WILLIAMS** and Thomas **GOFF** So Binding on John **HASLIT**s [?] Land to a Corner Tree in his Line thence by a Line of markt Trees to a Corner Tree Standing in the Pocoson thence By Several Corses to the first Station I Say to him and his heirs for Ever...Ever [sic]

Item  I give and Bequeath to My Son Stephen **PARKER** the Plantation and Land that I Bought of Moses **HALL** and of Mikel **JONES** Containing abou/t/ Two hundred and Twenty Acers I Say to him the Said Stephen **PARK/ER/** And his heirs for Ever...

Item  I Give and Bequeath to my Son Francis **PARKER** the Tract of Land I Took up & Surveyed Lying on Somerton Swamp and Containing Eighty Two acres I Say To him and his heirs for Ever

Item   Give and Bequeath to my Said Sons Richard **PARKER** Peter **PARKER** Daniel **PARKER** Stephen **PARKER** Robart **PARKER** Francis **PARKER** and to Each of them fifty acres of Land Lying on Mehearon Pocoson Below **PUGH**s ferrey I Say to them and thair heirs for Ever

Item   I Give and Bequeath to my Sons Richard **PARKER** Stephen **PARKER** Francis **PARKER** the Land I purchased of John **SMALL** Lying on the Timber Porqonson [sic] Containing aboute two hundred Acres I Say to them and thair heirs for Ever

Item  I Give and Bequeath to my Son Richard **PARKER** fifty Acres of Land I purchased of H [?] **KITTRLIN** [**KITTRELL**] Lying neare the Loosing Sw [sic] Swamp I Say to him and his heirs for Ever

Item   I Give and Bequeath /my/ frind Jonhn [sic] **BENTON** a Parsel of Land Joyning on **BENET**s Crek and **BENTON**s land and So along the Bay Branch upon the Prov/iser/iser that he Pays forty three Barrels of Tarr If he Justly Pays the tarr to me or my /fore young [?] Sons/ Sons [sic] I Say then /the [?]/ Land to him and his h<u>ar</u>s for Ever    Turn over [Stamped #3031]

[p. 3]  Item  I Give and Bequeath to my Granson Richard **PARKER** five Shilling Currant money of Virginia I Say to him In full for his Part of all my Estate movicable and onmovisable [?]

Item  I Give and Bequeath to my Granson Will/i/am **PARKER** five Shilling Currant money of Virginia I Say to him in full for his Part of all my Estate maulable and onmovisable [?] I Say to him and his hairs forever  [No stamped number. Appears to be on back of previous page.]

[p. 4]  Item  I Give and Bequath to my Said Son Robart **PARKER**, the Plantation and Land I Bought of James **ELLIS** Containing a bout Sixty ac<u>rs</u> I Say to him and his hairs for Ever...

Item  I Give and Bequeath to my fore Said Son Robart **PARKER** five Shillings Cash to him in full for his Part of my Parsonable Estate I Say to him and his heirs for Ever...

Item  I Give and Bequeath to my Said Son Peter **PARKER** my water Mill Stones and five Shillings Cash to him in full for his Part of my Personable Estate I Say to him and his heirs for Ever

Item  I Give and Bequeath to my Son Daniel **PARKER** five Cows and wan [one] Mire [Mare] Named Boney Branded with H formerly Belonging to Joseph **HORTON** to him in full for his Part of my Parsonable Estate I Say to him and his heirs for Ever

Item  I Give and Bequeath to my son Jonathan **PARKER** Three Peices of Seven Eights Linnen to him In full for his /part/ of Personable Estate I Say to him and his heirs for Ever...

Item  I Give and Bequeath to my Son Jonas **PARKER** my Negro Girl named **DOLL** to him In full for his Part of my P/e/arsonable Esta<u>t</u> I Say to him and his heirs for Ever

Item  I Give and Bequeath to my three Daughters Elizabeth **HUNTER** and Ann **SP/I/VEY** and Alse **DAUGHTREY** Ten Shillings apice [sic] I Say to Each of them In full for thare Sheares of my Parsonable Estate

Item  All the Remainar of my Estate of what Natur or Kind So ever I leave to be Equally Divided amongst my five Cheldren Namley Jacob Stephen Francis Richard Patience  I Nominiate [sic] and appoint My Loving Wife and my son Peter **PARKER** to be Executrix /Er/ Executer to this my Last will and Testament And I do hereby Revoke Diss A Null and make Void all former Wills by me heare to fore made in Witness Where of I have heare Unto Set my hand and fixt my Seal the twenteth Second Day of September in the year of Christ one thousand Seven hundred and forty Forty [sic] Nine

Richard **PARK[ER]**

Signed Sealed and By the Testeter }
Published and Declared to Be his Last }
Will and Testament in Presents of }
John **WILLIAMSON** Jurat
Wm. **DOUGHTIE** Jurat
      his
John    X      **MOORE** Jurat
      Mark
[Stamped #3032]
[p. 5] Chowan county}ss April Court 1752  Present His Majestys Justices
Then was the within will Proved in open Court by the oaths of John **WILLIAMSON** William **DOUGHTIE** and John **MOORE** Three of the subscribing Evidences thereto in Due form of Law Jaˢ: **CRAVEN** Cl __ [No stamped number.]
[Reverse of document:] Richard **PARKER**'s Will
Letters issd the 17th July 1752 as appears on the Bond  [Handwritten #3033]"[1]

The page of this will that appears between pages three and four, in xerographic copies, is rather unusual in that it contains only those two small bequests to his grandsons, Richard⁶ and William⁶ **PARKER**.  That is only one of the peculiar circumstances concerning this will.  His death occurred prior to the middle of December, 1751, and his will was not proved in court until the following April.  He was deceased prior to 14 December 1751, as evidenced by a Gates County deed of Richard⁵ **PARKER** "of Hartford Co., NC, to Jacob **SUMNER** of Nancemond Co., VA," for 250 acres, dated 12 March 1778. "Hartford Co." was actually Hertford County at that time, just before the formation of

---

[1] NCSA, NC Wills, Vol. XXII, pp. 57-58, Chowan County Wills

Gates in 1779. The land lies just west of the part of **BENNETT**s Creek now known as **GOODMAN** Swamp. It is described as land "whereon said Richard **PARKER** lately dwelt...beginning at the mouth of a branch out of Elisha **PARKER**'s Millpond, to a oak, marked trees binding on Elisha **PARKER's** land to Virginia line, west along the line to line of trees that runs into fork of Little Mare Branch, down sd. Branch to an oak near aforsd. Millpond, crossing pond to the first station...part of pattent to Richard **PARKER** the Elder 16 June 1714, descended to his grandson, Richard **PARKER** of Nancemond Co., VA, was sold by him to Richard **PARKER**, party to these presents by deed dated 14 December 1751, registered in Hartford Co..." It was signed by Richard **PARKER** and witnessed by Isreal **BEEMAN**, Jacob (X) **RABEY**, Henry **KING**, and James (X) **JONES**.[2]

A second, though earlier, deed explains how Richard[6] **PARKER** of Nansemond County was able to dispose of his rights in two different pieces of property that had belonged to his grandfather. It is from "Richard **PARKER** of the upper parish of Nancemond County to Daniel **PARKER** of Chowan Co. in NC, 21 December 1751, 350 acres for 'love and good will...towards sd. Daniel **PARKER** his uncle,' but more especially for the sum of 10 shillings...land in Chowan County whereon sd. Daniel **PARKER** now liveth, beginning at Peter **PARKER**'s Mill swamp thence binding on the lands of Richd **PARKER** and John **MOORE** or on land which said Daniel bought of Fra. **PUGH**, then by a line of marked trees on or near the county line, then to corner in Galberry pocoson, then to tree in the fork of Mare Branch, down the said Mare Branch to the first station...which sd. Tract was granted to Richd **PARKER** grandfather to the partie to these presents who never had disposed of the same in his life time and dying without will that is known of the said land descend to sd. Richd **PARKER** as heir at law to his Grandfather..." It was signed by Richard[6] **PARKER** and witnessed by John (J) **MORE**, John **BENTON**, and Demsey **SUMNER**, Jurat.[3]

Richard[4] **PARKER** was supposed to have "died without will that is known of," and the only way his grandson could inherit all his real estate would be if he were the eldest son of Richard[4]'s eldest son, under the rule of primogeniture. That son's name appears to have been William[5]. He was granted 145 acres by North Carolina on 14 August 1723. It is described as "lying in Chowan precinct on the Beech Swamp beginning at a Gum in the Swamp at the mouth of a Branch Aaron **ODAM**'s corner running with his line N.17W.158 pole to a pine John **DAVIS**'s corner then along Aaron **ODAM**'s line N.40E.170 pole to two pines and a White Oak his corner then N.60W.22 pole to a red Oak in Tho. **ODAM**'s line then with his line N.76W.31 pole to a pine Thomas **ODAM**'s corner then with another of **ODAM**'s lines N.25W.64 pole to a Spanish Oak **ODAM**'s corner on the Beech Swamp thence the courses of the Said Swamp to the first Station..."[4] This parcel shares a boundary line with Thomas **ODAM**, [**ODOM**] as does the 28 September 1730, VA patent to Richard[4] **PARKER**, and places this land to the west of, and very near Richard[4]'s 1714 patents. William[5] **PARKER** does not appear on John **ALSTON**'s list of tithables taken in 1743, and may have removed to Nansemond County, where his son lived and died.[5] It would appear that William[5] **PARKER** *(Richard[4],Richard[3],Richard[2],William[1])* died prior to 1749.

Richard[6] **PARKER** *(William[5],Richard[4],Richard[3],Richard[2],William[1])* grandson of Richard[4] **PARKER**, lived in Nansemond County, VA, as evidenced by deeds and his will. He wrote his will 28 October 1760, and stated that he was "of the upper Parrish of Nansemond County being sick & weak but of a Well Disposing Mind and Memory..." He left to his uncle, Peter[5] **PARKER**, all his land in Hertford County, NC, in trust, to "sell the said land and the Money Arising therefrom to be Applied to my son David **PARKER** and to his heirs and Assigns forever. I also give to my said son my Negro Woman Named **HAGAR** provided he shall pay to my Daughter Ede **PARKER** the sum of Twenty pounds...or shall Deliver to my said Daughter the first Child the said Negro shall bear that shall be living when my said son arrives to the age of Twenty one years." He left the rest of his estate to be equally divided among his wife, son and daughter, and named "Friends" Demsey **SUMNER** and Abraham **PARKER** executors. He signed his will as "Richd. **PARKER**." The witnesses were Dempsey **SUMNER**, John **BIRD**, Abraham **PARKER**, and Jesse **BIRD**. It was proved by Abraham

---

[2] Gates County, NC Deed Book A, first section, p. 10

[3] Chowan County, NC Deed Book H#1:249

[4] NCLG 3:168, File No. 579

[5] NCSA, Stack File CCR 190, Taxes & Accounts 1679-1754, Tax Lists, Chowan

**PARKER,** 13 February 1764, at Nansemond County Court. Abraham refused the executorship of the will and made oath that he saw John and Jesse **BIRD** sign it as witnesses, and that they had since moved to North Carolina. Dempsey **SUMNER** gave bond, with John **COLES**, Jr., and Abram **PARKER** as his securities.[6] His land in Hertford County was 170 acres purchased of his uncle, Peter[5] **PARKER**, 1 December 1755.[7] This will is a copy, not the original, and the specific reason for it being in Isle of Wight County, VA, is unknown to this writer. No further information on Ede[7] or David[7] **PARKER**.

Whether Richard[4]'s will was simply misplaced, or deliberately concealed, is unknown. All of his children appear to have been of majority age as there is no indication that any of them were minors at the time of his decease. In April Court of 1752, a summons was ordered to be issued to the executrix and executor of the will of Richard **PARKER**, deceased, to appear and show cause why they didn't qualify thereto. It was noted that the executrix was not named in the will, so the summons could not issue. The will was proved in April Court, 1752, by John **WILLIAMSON**, William **DOUGHTIE**, and John **MOORE**.[8] On 26 June 1752, a summons issued from the court for Demsey **SUMNER**, John **NORFLEET** and John **BENTON**, "all of the County aforesaid Planters Personally to be and appear before our Justices at our next Court to be held for our Said County at the Court house in Edenton on the third Thursday in July next then and there to Testify all and Singular those things which you and Each of you Shall Know in a Certain Cause Pending undetermined wherein Francis **PARKER** is Plft [sic] and Peter **PARKER** Deft on the Part and behalf of the Deft: and to be tried on the first Day of the said Court..."[9] This suit does not appear in the county court minutes, but it may have gone to a higher court, or have been withdrawn. The point of contention between Francis[5] and Peter[5] probably concerned their father's estate.

The next record reveals the name of Richard[4]'s wife. At July Court, 1752, Peter[5] **PARKER** and Hannah **PARKER**, executor and executrix to Richard[4] **PARKER**s will, came into court and relinquished their right of executorship and refused to qualify. Stephen[5] **PARKER** prayed the administration on the estate, with the will annexed. It was granted upon his giving bond and security in the amount of £1,000, with Demsey **SUMNER** Esqr., and Jacob[5] **PARKER** as sureties.[10] At October Court, 1752, Stephen[5] petitioned the court and it was ordered that Demsey **SUMNER** Esq., John **BENTON**, John **MOORE** and William **HUGHS**, Jr., or any three of them, divide the estate. That division was returned and filed in January Court, 1753.[11]

Demsey **SUMNER**, John **BENTON** and John **MOORE** made the final division of the personal estate of Richard[4] **PARKER**, among his five children. These were probably the children of his union with Hannah, thus were his youngest. Earlier wives' names are unknown to the writer, though others have attributed several different ones to him. Each heir received one slave, from 12 to 15 pounds of old pewter, and well over 200 pounds of pork, among other items, for a total of £46..1..3, each. Francis[5] and Stephen[5] each received a Bible and Richard[5] was given a Testament. Jacob[5] and Patience[5] received other items. This document was sworn to by the "dividers" 17 January 1753.[12]

Among the Chowan County Miscellaneous Papers, there are two lists of tithables that appear to be dated 1755. They both contain a number of the same names. The shorter of the two appears to have been written by John **ALSTON**, though unsigned, and seems to be incomplete. The longer list was taken by Demsey **SUMNER** and shows a total of 470 tithables.[13] The more likely date of the

---

[6] Found among loose papers in the Clerk's office, Isle of Wight County Court House, by Mr. Alvin P. Reynolds, Jr., genealogist, and submitted to Virginia Tidewater Society and published Vol. 12, #4, Dec. 1982, p. 142. courtesy of the late Martha J. Hawkins, genealogist, of Monticello, AR

[7] Chowan County Deed Book H#1:126

[8] Haun, *Chowan County North Carolina Court Minutes 1749-1754, Book III*, c. 1992, 66:#130;#132

[9] NCSA, C.024.99004, Chowan County Miscellaneous Papers 1748-1753 Vol. VI:56

[10] Haun, *Chowan County North Carolina Court Minutes 1749-1754, Book III*, c. 1992, 71:#141;82:#165

[11] Ibid., 78:#157

[12] NCSA, C.024.99004, Chowan County Miscellaneous Papers 1748-1753, Vol. VI:124

[13] Ibid., C.024.99005, Vol. VII:100;104

Chapter 3: Some Richard[4] **PARKER** (Richard[3],Richard[2],William[1]) Descendants

**ALSTON** list is between 1752 and 1754.[14] It shows Hannah **PARKER** between Peter[5] and Daniel[5] **PARKER**. Peter[5] and Daniel[5] **PARKER** also appear on the 1755 **SUMNER** list, but Hannah does not. There is no further record of her, thus she was probably deceased by 1755.

Richard[5] **PARKER** (Richard[4],Richard[3],Richard[2],William[1]) sold all of the 500 acres of land willed to him by his father, on 12 March 1778, to Jacob **SUMNER**, of Nansemond County, VA, as mentioned earlier, though that deed shows only 250 acres of it. The other 250 acres would have been of record in Nansemond County. On that date, Jacob **SUMNER** entered into a bond in the amount of £1,000, the condition of which was that Richard[5] **PARKER** had executed deeds for 500 acres in Hertford County, NC, and Nansemond County, VA, for the purpose of procuring a sum of ready money and that Jacob should pay Richard[5]'s debt to Luke **SUMNER**. If Richard[5] should repay all sums advanced by Jacob, within one year and eight months of the date of the bond, he would return the lands, deeds and titles. Should Richard[5] fail to repay him all sums, including interest, Jacob would advertise the said land, and after deducting the debt, interest, and costs, "shall equally divide and pay the Residue of the Money to Patience **FRYER** Sister of the said Richard **PARKER** and to all her children then Living..." It was further agreed that if Richard[5] should fail to appear according to the time within mentioned, then Jacob would take into his possession all and every part of his personal estate and sell the same and divide the proceeds as within ordered. The witnesses to this document were Jacob (J) **RABEY**, Israel **BEEMAN**, and Henry **KING**.[15]

On 16 August 1783, Jacob **SUMNER** and wife Sarah sold that 250 acres that lay in Gates County, NC, to one Willis **PARKER**, of Nansemond County, VA.[16] It appears that Richard[5] **PARKER** died intestate, and without issue, just prior to that sale. In Gates County August Court, 1783, Thomas **FRYER** moved for administration on the estate of Richard[5] **PARKER**, deceased, by his attorney, John **BRICKELL**, Esqr. Administration was granted and he gave bond of £200 specie, with James **BRADDY** and Israel **BEEMAN** as securities. He exhibited an inventory of the goods and chattels, rights and credits of Richard[5]'s estate in November Court of that year.[17] Thomas **FRYER** lodged a complaint with the Gates County Court in an undated document. It details the bond given by Jacob **SUMNER** 12 March 1778, in the sum of £1,000, which was then of the value of £352..11.1 and one farthing, current money of the State, that was to have been paid to Richard[5] **PARKER**. Jacob was often required to pay the same to Richard[5] in his lifetime and then to Thomas **FRYER**, as his administrator, but refused to do so in both instances.[18]

In the Gates County August Court 1784, in a suit between Thomas **FRYER**, Administrator of Richard[5] **PARKER** deceased and Jacob **SUMNER**, the jury said that the conditions were not performed and assessed for the Plaintiff's damages of £355..11.0 and costs. Jacob prayed an appeal to the Superior Court and gave bond and security 21 August 1784, in the sum of £711..2, in specie, to pay Thomas **FRYER**, if his appeal should fail. The bondsmen were William **HARRISS** and Isaac **MILLER**.[19] The foregoing records prove that Richard[5] **PARKER** (Richard[4],Richard[3], Richard[2], William[1]) died intestate by August 1783, was not married, and had no descendants. His sister, Patience[5] **(PARKER) FRYER**, and her children, were his sole beneficiaries. No further information.

Daniel[5] **PARKER** (Richard[4],Richard[3],Richard[2],William[1]) first appears in the records 13 July 1718, as co-patentee with Jonathan[5] **PARKER**, on that 304-acre patent that Richard[4] allowed to lapse. He purchased 400 acres of land from Francis **PUGH** 18 October 1734, adjoining William **SPIKES** and John **KING**.[20] This is the parcel mentioned by Richard[6] in his 1751 deed to his uncle, Daniel[5] **PARKER**. His next purchase was made 15 April 1742, from his brother, Peter[5]. That parcel was 120

---

[14] Haun, *Chowan County North Carolina Court Minutes 1749-1754, Book III*, c. 1992, 78:#155. John Alston returned a list of tithables for the year 1752. His handwriting, on other signed lists, was compared to the one in question.
[15] NCSA, D.C.R. 2.023.12, Edenton District Estates Records, , Richard Parker File
[16] Gates County, NC Deed Book A:48, second section
[17] Fouts, *Minutes of County Court of Pleas and Quarter Sessions, Gates County, North Carolina 1779-1786*, c. 1994, 61:#120; 66:#131
[18] NCSA, D.C.R. 2.023.12, Edenton District Estates Records, Richard Parker File
[19] Ibid.
[20] Chowan County, NC Deed Book C#2:1

acres on Richard **FELTON** and Richard **PARKER**, on Merry hill Pocosin, part of a patent of 640 acres to Peter[5] **PARKER**, 11 March 1740. Jonathan[5] **PARKER** witnessed that deed.[21] All of Richard[4]'s children lived to the west of **BENNETT**s Creek, when that part of Chowan County was cut off to Hertford County in 1759. The only record found for Daniel[5] during the 20 years between 1759 and 1779, when Gates County was created, is a Hertford County Tax record. He was listed as having three taxables for the year 1768.[22] They were probably his sons, Demsey[6], Isaac[6] and Robert[6] **PARKER**.

Daniel[5] **PARKER** made his will in Gates County, 30 November 1780, and it was probated in May Court, 1781. He named his wife, Mary, grandson Daniel[7], son of Luke[6] **PARKER**, to whom he gave his plantation and all his lands, plus Negro girl **RHODA**. If Daniel[7] should die without heir, the land was to be equally divided amongst his sons Demsey[6], Isaac[6] and Robert[6] **PARKER**. Under that same circumstance, the Negro girl was to be divided amongst all his children. He bequeathed his daughter, Sarah[6] **HORTON**, one Negro girl named **HAGOR**, then in her possession. All the remainder of his Negroes, and all the beds and furniture, were to be equally divided amongst sons Demsey[6], Isaac[6], and Robert[6] **PARKER**, and daughter Ruth[6] **RIDDICK** and his son, Luke[6] **PARKER**'s children, after the decease of his loving wife, Mary **PARKER**. He also gave one cow and calf to grandson William[7] **GRIFFIN**, son of his daughter Judah[6] **GRIFFIN**. He nominated sons Demsey[6], Isaac[6] and Robert[6] **PARKER** as Executors. Witnesses were Elisha[6] **PARKER**, Thomas **FRYER**, Peter[5] **PARKER**, and Jacob **SUMNER**. Daniel[5] signed his will with his mark, "DP," formed as a combined letter. The following is written beneath the witnesses and his signature: "Item I Give to my Gran Son Willis **CHITREL** Son of my Daughter Mary **CHITREL** one Cow and Calf to he and his heirs for Ever. Item I Give to my Gran Son Benjaman **CHITREL** Son of my Daughter Abigal one Cow and Calf to he and his heirs for Ever." It was exhibited into May Court by the executors and proved by oath of Jacob **SUMNER**, and ordered to be recorded. It was "Recorded in Book A Folio 17 & 18."[23] His son, Luke[6] **PARKER**, was still in Hertford County in 1770.[24]

Some researchers have mistakenly believed that this Daniel[5] **PARKER** married Mary **FARLEE**, daughter of James **FARLEE**, of Chowan County. This is not the case, as evidenced by the will of James **FARLEE**, and a conveyance of land from Mary and her husband, Amos **PARKER**. James **FARLEE** made his will 12 January 1750/51. He named his wife, Rachel, daughters Mary **PARKER**, Sarah and Christian **FARLEE**, sons Samuel and James **FARLEE**. It was witnessed by William **BOYD**, Amos **PARKER**, and John [His mark is in the shape of a new moon.] **BACKCUS**, with John **CAMPBELL**, merchant of Bertie County, as, executor. It was probated 17 January 1750/51, just five days later.[25]

On 31 August 1761, Amos **PARKER** and Mary **PARKER** his wife, of Chowan Province, sold 100 acres of land to William **HARPER**, of same. This land began at the head of the Spring Branch and adjoined David **WELSH**, Poplar run, and James **PARKER**. It was taken out of a larger tract belonging to James **PARKER**.[26] These two documents should dispel any doubt as to the real name of Mary **FARLEE**'s husband. From the **PARKER**s' long and close association with the **SUMNER**s, it is likely that Daniel's wife was of that family. They were close neighbors, near the head of **BENNETT**'s Creek, and the **FARLEE**s lived near **BALLARD**s Bridge, well down into present-day Chowan County. Daniel[5] and Mary's eldest son was named "Luke," a **SUMNER** name.

Demsey[6] **PARKER** *(Daniel[5],Richard[4],Richard[3],Richard[2],William[1])* made his will 6 May 1807. He directed his executors to sell 50 acres of his land, adjoining Edwin **SUMNER** and William **GATLING**, Sr., to pay his debts. He bequeathed the remainder of his lands to his son Miles[7]. The remainder of his estate was to be equally divided between his daughter, Edith **VANN**, and the heirs of his deceased son, Robert[7] **PARKER**. His brother Isaac[6] was one of the witnesses and his will was

---

[21] Chowan County, NC Deed Book A#1:69

[22] Fouts, *William Murfree Tax Receipt Book, Hertford County, North Carolina, 1768-1770*, c. 1993, 13:#16

[24] NCSA, C.R.041.801.8, Gates County Wills 1762-1904, Daniel Parker, courtesy of Rebecca L. Dozier, Augusta, GA

[24] Fouts, *William Murfree Tax Receipt Book Hertford County, North Carolina 1768-1770*, c. 1993, 45:#90

[25] NCSA, NC Wills, SS-James Farlee

[26] Chowan County, NC, Deed Book L#1:17

probated in February Court, 1808.[27] He was actually dead by 11 December 1807, when Hillory **WIL-LEY**, one of his executors, took the inventory of his estate. The sales of his personal property were made 9 January 1808.[28] No further information included here.

Francis[5] **PARKER** *(Richard[4],Richard[3],Richard[2],William[1])* first appears in the Chowan County records in a deed dated 1 November 1753, from him and Stephen[5] **PARKER** to Richard **BOND** for 203 acres in Chowan County, as by patent dated 31 October 1726, to John **SMALL**.[29] It adjoined Thomas **SPIGHT** and Daniel **PUGH** on the Maple Pocoson and it was the same land bequeathed to them and their brother, Richard[5], by their father. Richard[5] may have given them a quit-claim deed for his share, though it was never recorded.

Francis[5] **PARKER** purchased 330 acres of land in Gates County, 15 November 1786, from Isaac, Mary, Richard, and Ann **CROOM**, of Dobbs County, NC. It began at a corner of Henry **KING**'s land on Cypress Swamp and lay on the Deep Cypress Swamp, to the Flat Cypress Swamp near a spring and opposite William **HOOKS**, Jr. It also adjoined Francis **SAUNDERS** and a former line of Joseph **BALLARD**'s. This deed was witnessed by Sherrard **BARROW**, Abraham **SAUN-DERS**, and Spiner **CALDWELL**. Just five months later, 7 April 1787, he purchased another 350 acres of land. This parcel was from Silas, John, James, and Jesse **COPELAND**, all of Nansemond County, VA. It lay on the south side of the Cypress Swamp, being the "residue of a patent granted to Charles **SANDERS**, deceased, by a patent 25 June 1762, and by a deed before the date of these presents sold to William **ODOM** 300 acres of the aforesaid patent." This deed was witnessed by Abraham **SANDERS** and Mary **COPELAND**.[30] These were not his first purchases, as evidenced by a Chowan County deed of gift from Thomas **HARE**, of Bertie County, to Demsey **SUMNER**, 14 August 1779. He gave him 150 acres adjoining Francis **SAUNDERS**, Joseph **SPEIGHT**, Henry **KING**, Catherine **KING**, and Francis **PARKER**, on the Deep Cypress.[31] Francis[5] sold an unspecified number of acres to Benjamin **SAUNDERS** 10 February 1789, on Reedy Branch, "the patent line," and Henry **KING**. It was part of the patent to Charles **SAUNDERS**, 25 June 1762.[32]

Francis[5] **PARKER** made his will in Gates County 6 April 1791, probated in August Court of that year. He left the use of his plantation to his wife, "Febury" **PARKER**, during her natural life or widowhood, with some stock and household utensils, then to his son, Miles[6]. He bequeathed all his land and plantation in Pitt County, on "little Contentency Creek," to his son, Wilday[6] **PARKER**. One researcher has suggested that this name may actually be "Dilday," from a surname in the same area, but the handwriting in this original will is very clear and is relied upon here. The remainder of his estate was to be sold and equally divided "amongst all my children and loving Wife." His wife and William **GOODMAN** were appointed executrix and executor. The witnesses were William **ODAM**, Solomon **KING**, and John (X) **SUMNER**.[33]

An inventory of Francis[5] **PARKER**'s estate was taken by Pheriby **PARKER**, 22 July 1791. Jesse **SAUNDERS**, Benjamin **BARNES**, and Francis **SPEIGHT** signed a guardian bond 21 August 1793, for Jesse **SAUNDERS** to be guardian to Miles[6] **PARKER**, orphan of Francis[5] **PARKER**. The names of the other children of Francis[5] and Pheriby are revealed by the division of the estate, made 12 August 1795, by Isaac **PIPKIN**, Jr., Henry **SPEIGHT**, Philip **LEWIS** and Francis **SPEIGHT**. The widow and each of the children named received £39.8.9[3/4]. They were Bethany[6], Polly[6], Edith[6], Salley[6], Abigail[6] and Miles[6].[34] There is no mention of Wilday[6] in these records. Under yet another spelling of her name, Fereby **PARKER** was charged a tax on 67 acres of land in Pitt County for 1791 and on 330 acres in Gates County. She continued to list that Gates County land through 1806.[35]

---

[27] Almasy, Sandra L., *Gates County, North Carolina Wills 1807-1838, Vol. II*, c. 1985, 2:3 Hereafter, "Almasy."
[28] NCSA, G.041.2194760, Gates County Estates, Record of 1765-1920, Vol. Odom-Parker, Folder: Parker, Demsey 1808, Doc. #1021;2030
[29] Chowan County, NC, Deed Book G#1:185
[30] Gates County, NC Deed Book 1:245:1:276
[31] Chowan County, NC Deed Book A#1:19
[32] NCSA, C.041.40002, Gates County Real Estate Conveyances 1786-1795, Vol: 2, 3, 2:38
[33] NCSA, C.R.041.801.8, Gates County Wills 1762-1904, Francis Parker, courtesy of Rebecca L. Dozier
[34] NCSA, C.R.041.508.85- Gates County Estate Records, Folder: Francis Parker
[35] NCSA, C.041.70001 Gates County Tax Lists 1784-1831, [1784-1806] p. 110, 1791, William Goodman's Captaincy

Fereby **PARKER** made her will 4 November 1807, probated in November Court, with William **GOODMAN** as executor. She directed that the rest of her estate, over and above the minor bequests to her children, be sold.[36] The names Polly[6] and Wilday[6] are not mentioned in her will. She was dead by 13 November 1807, when William **GOODMAN** took the inventory of her estate.[37]

Miles[6] **PARKER** *(Francis[5],Richard[4],Richard[3],Richard[2],William[1])* appears to have married Martha **SAUNDERS**, widow of Lawrence **SAUNDERS**. Lawrence made his will 7 April 1815, probated in August Court 1815. He made bequests to his wife, Martha and nephews, children of his three brothers, Bray, Brian and Robert **SAUNDERS**. He also made bequests to Thomas and Mary **SAUNDERS**, as well as John Anthony **MARCH**, Eli **ELEY**, Henry **JONES** and $300 to Miles **PARKER**. Lewis **EURE** and Henry **HARE** witnessed this will[38].

On 17 February 1826, Thomas **SAUNDERS**, of Hertford County, sold Miles **PARKER** 200 acres of land for $600.00. It was described as "begining at the reedy Branch a Corner of the said **PARKER**s line thence along a line of marked trees to Miles **HOWELL**s line thence along said **HOWELL**s line to a popular on the Cypress Swamp thence down said Swamp to the mouth of a branch the Land of David **BOYET**s decd. thence up Said Branch to Jesse **WIGGINS** line thence a long Said line a Corner tree on the Sand banks a Corner tree on Jesse **SAUNDERS** decd. thence along Said line to the Galbush below the High Hill adjoining the Land of the Said **PARKER** thence along said line to the first Station which Said Tract belong[d]. to a certain Lawrance **SAUNDERS**..."[39] Another deed from Thomas **SAUNDERS** provides more information on the family. It was made to Jason **SAUNDERS** of Gates County, and John A. **MARCH** of Nansemond County, VA, for 400 acres, dated 23 January 1830. It was described as "all my right & title to all the land that was given to me by Lawrence **SAUNDERS**, after the death of his wife, (except the land I Sold Miles **PARKER**, per deed)...400 acres...Beginning at a corner on Miles **PARKER** line at the head of the gaul bush, thence along said [sic] to Jesse **WIGGINS** line (formerly **SUMNER**s) to a corner on the great marsh, thence down said marsh, to Chowan river near the stoney landing thence down said River to near **COPELAND** Seine place, thence E. a direct course on **SUMNER**s line to a corner in **PARKER**s line near **BALLARD**s Pocoson, thence along said Pocoson to the beginning also another tract formerly belonged to John **SUMNER** marked & bounded as follows. Beginning at a corner on the Cypress swamp running E. on Henry **JONES** line to **PARKER**s line, thence along **PARKER**s line to **LANG**s corner snag, thence along said line to the Cypress swamp, thence up said swamp to the first station..." He also did "warrant & ever defend all rights, titles, claims or demands whatsoever to the said tracts or parcel of Land after the death of Martha **PARKER**." Myles **PARKER** and James **SAUNDERS** witnessed this deed.[40]

Miles[6] was listed on the Tax List with 333 acres of land in 1807.[41] This was the land he received on his mother's death, in accordance with his father's will. He acquired several other parcels of land in his lifetime and owned 643 acres in 1842, as listed by his administrators.[42] In Gates County Court of Pleas and Quarter Sessions, begun 15 November 1841, it was "Ordered that Riddick **GATLING** & Lemuel **PARKER** be appointed Admrs on the Estate of Miles **PARKER** decd. & give bond in the sum of $40,000. Also on the Estate of Martha Ann **PARKER** & Mary Jane **PARKER** and give bond in the sum of $10,000 each with Mills **ROBERTS** & Jno B. **LANGSTON** for security."[43] Those bonds were taken out the next day on all three estates.[44] An inventory of Miles[6'] estate was

---

[36] Almasy, *Gates County, North Carolina Wills 1807-1838, Vol. II*, c. 1985, 2:2

[37] NCSA, G.041.2194761, Gates County Estates, Record of 1765-1920, Vol. Parker, E.-Parker, M., Folder: Parker, Fereba 1807, Doc. #495

[38] Almasy, *Gates County, North Carolina Wills 1807-1838, Vol. II*, c. 1985, 2:44

[39] NCSA, C.041.40006, Gates County Real Estate Conveyances 1819-1829, Vol: 11-13, 12:114-115

[40] NCSA, C.041.40007, Gates County Real Estate Conveyances 1829-1836, Vol: 14,15, 14:168-169

[41] NCSA, C.041.70001, Gates County Tax Lists 1784-1831,[1807-1831] p. 6, 1807, Jonathan Rogers Captaincy

[42] NCSA, C.041.70002, Gates County Tax Lists 1832-1851, [1842-1851] p. 14, 1842, William H. Goodman Captaincy

[43] NCSA, C041.30003, Gates County Court Minutes 1827-1850, November Court 1841 [Pages are not numbered.]

[44] NCSA, C.041.50011, Gates County Administrators' Bonds 1822-1847, 3 Vols., [1836-1847] #111-113

taken 19 February 1842, by Riddick **GATLING** and Lemuel E.[7] **PARKER**, his administrators.[45] That is an unusual date for an inventory, as the date of sales of the personal property was 7 December 1841, the same day Mary Ann's year's provision was laid off to her by order of November Court, 1841. Mary Ann **PARKER** was listed as the widow, who purchased the large majority of the items.[46] Mary Ann appears to be his second wife.

In a petition to November Term of Court 1842, Lemuel E.[7] and Mary Ann **PARKER** requested a division of Negroes that had belonged to Mary Jane[7] **PARKER** and Martha Ann[7] **PARKER**, and that they were "infants & heirs at Law of Myles **PARKER** decd. died some time in the year 1841, leaving sundry Negroes, that They are the only heirs at Law of the said Mary & Martha..."[47] Another undated petition for the same purpose states that "Your petitioners Mary **PARKER** widow of the late Myles **PARKER**, Leml. **PARKER** only son of said Myles and the administrators of Martha Ann & Mary Jane **PARKER** represents to your worships that the said Myles died intestate and we pray your worships to appoint commissioners to divide the Negroes belonging to estate of said decd. between your petitioners, the said Mary **PARKER** & Lemuel **PARKER** and the administrators of said Martha Ann & Mary Jane **PARKER** and your petitioners as in duty bound will ever pray &c."[48] This petition apparently preceded the one in November Court, as it requested a division of Miles[6'] Negroes and the one in November requested the division of the Negroes who were set apart to the estates of the two girls. Miles[6] **PARKER** died between August and November, 1841, and left as heirs his wife, Mary Ann, only son Lemuel E.[7], and Mary Jane[7] and Martha Ann[7] **PARKER**, also deceased.

On 8 December 1841, jurors laid off and set apart Mary **PARKER**'s dower in her husband's lands, described as "Begining at a Gum Standing on Cypress Swamp thence a Cross the Swamp to the deep Cypress Swamp thence down Said Swamp to the fork thence up the Flat Cypress Swamp thence runing a line of mark [sic] trees to Said Swamp thence up Said Swamp to a mark pine thence nearly a north Corse a line of mark trees to Francis **SAUNDERS** line runing Said line to Henry **KING**s line thence runing Said [sic] to the Cypress Branch near its head thence down Said Branch to a former line of Joseph **BALLARD**s line thence a long Said line to the first Station it being the land & Plantation whereon Miles **PARKER** decd. lived and died also Fifteen acres of land which Said Miles **PARKER** decd. purchased of William **BEASLEY**..."[49]

Lemuel[7] E. **PARKER** *(Miles[6],Francis[5],Richard[4],Richard[3],Richard[2],William[1])* purchased 200 acres of land from his father 30 November 1839, for $1,500.00. This land adjoined "the lands of the late Miles **HOWELL** & James **SUMNER** decd. & John **JONES** & others, being the same tract piece or parcel of land that formerly belonged to Lawrence **SAUNDERS** decsd..."[50] Lemuel[7] E. **PARKER** owned 1,553 acres of land at his death in 1851.[51]

In 1850, his family consisted of himself, age 32, Emily, age 35, Texana T.[8], age 7, Martha E.[8], age 5, Miles[8] H., age 2, and one Mildred **HARRELL**, age 32.[52] This would place his birth circa 1818 and an approximation of his marriage date to circa 1842, though no record has been found. A writ of dower was issued from the Gates County Court in November 1851, for Emily **PARKER**, widow of Lemuel E. **PARKER**, who "departed this life some time in the year of 1851 intestate, seized and possessed at the time of his death of large tracts of land situated in said Conty [sic.]" It was ordered to be returned to February Term of 1852.[53]

On 18 December 1851, Emily's dower rights in Lemuel[7]'s lands were laid off to her and described as "adjoining the lands of Mills H **EURE** Riddick **GATLING** and others containing five hun-

---

[45]  NCSA, G.041.2194762, Gates County Estates, Record of 1765-1920, Vol. Parker-Pierce, Folder:  Parker, Miles 1842, Doc. #8
[46]  Ibid., Doc. #12-24; Doc. #26-27
[47]  Ibid., Doc. #40
[48]  Ibid., Doc .# 35
[49]  Ibid., Doc. #31
[50]  NCSA, C.041.40008, Gates County Real Estate Conveyances 1836-1842, Vol: 16,17, 17:204-205
[51]  NCSA, C.041.70002, Gates County Tax Lists 1832-1851, [1842-1851] 1850, p. 323, Brick House District
[52]  Almasy, *Gates County, North Carolina Census 1850 & 1860*, c. 1987, p. 34
[53]  NCSA, G.041.2194761, Gates County Estates, Record of 1765-1920, Vol. Parker, E.-Parker, M., Folder: Parker, Lemuel 1852, Doc. #1846

dred acres more or less" and allotting her one-third of that amount "included and comprised in the following limits and bounds to wit ~~Beginning at~~ the whole of the plantation whareon [sic] Lemuel E **PARKER** died with that portion of the Lawrance **SAUNDERS** plantation on the South side of the main road leading from Somerton to **MANNEY**s Ferrey including the dwelling house or mansion of the Said Lemuel E. **PARKER** in which he most Generally dwelt next before and at the time of his death and all the out houses offices and improvements thereunto belonging..."[54]

Riddick **GATLING** Administrator, made the sales of the perishable estate of Lemuel E.[7] **PARKER** on 18 December 1851. A large portion of the items were sold to the widow and the total sale amounted to $1,920.70½.[55] He submitted an account to the Court, beginning August Term, 1851, ending 20 November 1853. The balance due the estate was $2,971.85½ and was divided among Emily **PARKER**, Widow, and Timothy E. **LANGSTON**, guardian for Texana,[8] Martha E.[8], Mills [sic] H.[8] and Margaret[8] **PARKER**, each receiving $345.86½. Margaret Ann[8] **PARKER** was born after 21 August 1850, the date of the enumeration of the 1850 Census.

Elisha **CROSS** appeared on a marriage bond with Mrs. Emily **PARKER** 31 August 1858, with J. M. H. **LEE** as his bondsman.[56] In November Term, 1858, "Elisha and wife Emily, Texanna, Martha, Margaret Ann infants by their Guardian Timothy E **LANGSTON** showeth unto your Worships that they are tenants in common of these slaves viz **ISAAC, JACK, JIM, DAVE, DAVID, MILLS, SILAS, NED, ASHLY, HENRY LEWIS, KIDDY, ANN, JANE LUCY** and **LAURA** [?] they desire to hold their shares in severalty and to that end pray your Worships to appoint three free holders unconnected by affinity or consanguinity to divide the slaves into four equal shares..." That division was made 29 December 1858. Emily received **MILLS, HENRY, JACK** and **KIDDY**.[57] Emily **CROSS** is noted as the "late widow" of Lemuel E.[7] **PARKER**.

By 1860, Riddick **GATLING**, Sr., had become guardian to Texas T.[8] **PARKER**, Margaret A.[8] and Martha E.[8] **PARKER**, as shown in his return dated 18 February 1861.[58]

On 19 April 1866, Riddick **GATLING**, Sr. was given notice to appear in Court on the third Monday in May, 1866, to renew his guardian bond for "the orphans of Lem. **PARKER** decd."[59] He made a guardian return to February Court, 1867, with Martha E.[8] **GOODMAN** & husband Wm Mac **GOODMAN**. Martha[8] E. was noted as "**GOODMAN** Alias **PARKER**, Orphan of L. E. **PARKER**" in an April 1865, account, so had married by that time. The balance due her was $51.80, "in Confederate & Bank Money." The balance due Margaret E.[8] **PARKER** was $65.13, in the same currency.[60]

Emily **CROSS** made her will 25 June 1859, probated May Court 1863. It was witnessed by J. M. H. **LEE** and Wm. H. **LEE**. As she did not name an executor, it was permitted by the Court for Elisha **CROSS** to administer on her estate under bond of $10,000.00. She bequeathed "all the Negroes which descended to me from my former husband S. [L.] E. **PARKER** and from my son Harrison **PARKER** viz. **KITTY, JACK, MILLS** and **HENRY** ..." to her husband, E. **CROSS**.[61] The "Miles H." **PARKER** in the 1850 Census appears to have died at a very early age and his full name was Miles Harrison[8] **PARKER**.

Edwin **CROSS** appeared on a marriage bond with Miss Texanna[8] **PARKER**, dated 12 September 1865, with William Henry **LEE** as his bondsman.[62] Texanna[8] **CROSS** appears in the 1900 Federal Census, as "Tex E.," widowed head of household, born December 1842, age 57. Lemuel[9] E. **CROSS** is listed as her son, born November 1865, age 34. Ages are listed in the Census as of the last birthday, thus this date may be in error. Rosa[9] E. was her daughter, born June 1878, age 21, and

---

[54]  NCSA, G.041.2194761, Gates County Estates, Record of 1765-1920, Vol. Parker, E.-Parker, M., Folder: Parker, Lemuel 1852, Doc. #1895-1896

[55]  Ibid., Doc. #1869-1876

[56]  Almasy, *Gates County, North Carolina Marriage Bonds 1778-1868*, c. 1987, p. 20

[57]  NCSA, G.041.2194761, Gates County Estates, Record of 1765-1920, Vol. Parker, E.-Parker, M., Folder: Parker, Lemuel 1852, Doc. #1764-1765;1767

[58]  Ibid., Doc. 1837-1842

[59]  Ibid., Doc. #1850-1851

[60]  Ibid., Doc. #1854-1857

[61]  Almasy, *Gates County, North Carolina Wills 1838-1867, Vol. III*, c. 1987, p. 122

[62]  Almasy, *Gates County, North Carolina Marriage Bonds 1778-1868*, c. 1987, p. 20

Henry P.[9] **CROSS**, a son, born August 1882.[63] William M. P. **GOODMAN** appears in that same Census, born December 1847, age 52, with wife Martha E.[8], age 55, born March 1845, son James I.[9], age 30, born December 1879, Sue M.[9], age 26, born May 1876, and sons William T.[9], age 17, born February 1883 and Harry H.[9], age 13, born September 1886.[64] No further information included here.

Jonathan[5] **PARKER** *(Richard[4],Richard[3],Richard[2],William[1])* first appears in the records of Nansemond County, on the lapsed patent to Richard[4] **PARKER**, 12 July 1718.[65] He was co-patentee with his brother, Daniel[5]. On 18 October 1734, he purchased 400 acres of land from Francis **PUGH**, of Bertie County. It was part of a NC patent to **PUGH** of 29 October 1726. This parcel began at a dead pine on Saml. **PARKER**, and adjoined the Mare Branch, Thomas **GOFF**, Edward **DOUGHTY**, and John **KING**.

He has been referenced previously as being the builder of the Knotty Pine Chapel, between 8 August 1741 and 10 April 1742, as well as being a processioner in 1742, and witnessing several family deeds. On 20 October 1743, Jonathan[5] **PARKER** proved in court that his family consisted of seven white persons, including himself, Charity his wife, William, Rachel, Jess, Elizabeth, and Persilia.[66] Charity **PARKER** was one of the daughters of John **BENTON**, who made his will 25 February 1748/49. Secondary sources have mistaken the name "Jes" in that will to be "Jas." John named his sons, Epaphro__tus, Elijah, Jethro, and John **BENTON**. He bequeathed one Mulatto woman named **HANNAH** to his daughter, Judith **RABEY**, and one shilling Sterling each to grandsons William[6] **PARKER**, son of his daughter Mary **PARKER**, and to Jes[6] **PARKER**, son of his daughter Charity **PARKER**. Witnesses to this will were Henry (X) **MORGIN**, John **WEAVER**, and William (X) **PARKER**, and it was probated in Chowan County Court, October 1750.[67] Jesse[6]'s full name appears in the Gates County records in only one instance. In August Court, 1797, he is on a list of jurors to be summoned for the next term, as Jesse Benton[6] **PARKER**, although his name is crossed out.[68]

Jonathan[5] **PARKER** apparently died after Hertford County was formed in 1759, and before Gates was formed in 1779. That may also be true of Stephen[5], Jacob[5] and Jonas[5] **PARKER**. Jacob[5] is known to have still been living in 1770, as evidenced by his name on a tax list for that year.[69] There is an indication that at least some of Richard[4] **PARKER**s descendants moved to Tennessee. A power of attorney was made in Gates County 14 February 1831, by a Jonathan **PARKER** of Rutherford County, TN, to Hillory **WILLEY**, to sell "land as called out in old grant, Wm. **BAKER**s line, and Notty Pine Swamp."[70]

[63] Powell, David, *1900 Gates County Census*, c. 1994, p. 206-207

[64] Ibid., p. 206

[65] VSLA, 10:388

[66] Haun, *Chowan County North Carolina County Court Minutes Pleas & Quarter Sessions 1730-1745*, c. 1983, 73:#161

[67] NCSA, Chowan County, NC SS Wills-John Benton

[68] Fouts, *Minutes of County Court of Pleas and Quarter Sessions Gates County, North Carolina 1794-1799, Vol. I*, c. 1984, 85:170

[69] Fouts, *William Murfree Tax Receipt Book Hertford County, North Carolina 1768-1770*, c. 1993, 44:#89

[70] Gates County, NC, Deed Book 14:257

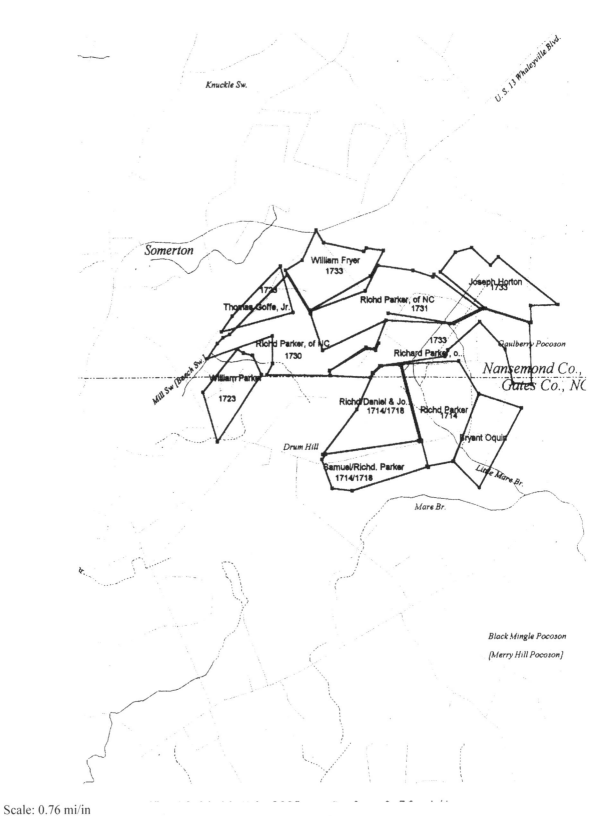

Scale: 0.76 mi/in

Map depicting Virginia Land Patents of Richard[4] **PARKER** on border between Nansemond County, VA, and Chowan/Hertford/Gates Counties, NC.

## More Richard[4] PARKER *(Richard[3],Richard[2],William[1])* Descendants

Peter[5] **PARKER** *(Richard[4],Richard[3],Richard[2],William[1])* first appears in the records 10 November 1739, with a purchase of 100 acres from Samuel **HARRELL**, son of John **HARRELL**, Jr., of Virginia. This land lay in Chowan County at a place called Gum Branch, or the Bulls Skull, and was patented 19 January 1716, by Richard **BERRYMAN**. **HARRELL** had purchased it from one **LASSITER**, and it began at a pine in or near a small branch, then N55W 108 poles to a pine in the Merry Hill Pocoson. Richard **TAYLOR**, Daniel (DP) **PARKER** and Robert (RP) **PARKER** were witnesses.[1]

On 11 March 1740/41, Peter[5] received a NC land grant of 640 acres, "Beginning at a pine in Merry Hill pocoson, running No 49Et.54 po. to a pine, then So.20Et.100 pole to a Live Oak then N.81Et.20 pole to a pine, then So.46Et.101 po. along Peter **PARKER**s line to a Black Gum, then No.80.Et.20 po. to a Gum in Gum Branch, then No.13.Et.61 po. along **PARKER**s line to a pine then S.11.Et.21 po to a white Oak in Adam **RABEY**s line, so So.44Et.7 po. to a White Oak, so S.38Wt.220 po. along **RABY**'s line to a White Oak then No. 71.Wt.43 po. to a gum, then So.88Wt.20 pole to a Gum then No.72Wt.44 po to a Chinquapin Oak, then So.37Wt.40 pole to a pine, then No.60Wt.80 po. to a red Oak, then No.73Wt.108 po to a pine along **BAKER**s line, then No.35.Wt.75 po. to a Gum, then No.160 po. to a Red Oak, then No.40Et.100 po. to a pine by **WATERS** corner tree, then So.70.Et.174 po. to a pine then So.20Wt.50 pole to the first Station. To hold &c. Dated the 11th Day of March 1740/41..."[2]

He sold 120 acres of this land to Daniel[5] **PARKER** 15 April 1742, adjoining his own land, Richard **FELTON**, and Richard **PARKER**. It was bounded on one side by the patent line and joined Merry Hill Pocoson. Jonathan **PARKER**, Jesse **RIDDICK** and Demsey **SUMNER** were witnesses.[3]

On 10 January 1748/49, Richard[4] **PARKER** conveyed 150 acres of land to Peter[5] **PARKER**, in Chowan County. It is described as "being the land whereon the sd. Peter **PARKER** now dwelleth and bounded as followeth...Beginning at the Country line on a branch called the mill dam branch so runing down the sd. Branch to a marked gum standing by or nigh the sd. Branch thence by a line of markt trees to a white oak markt & standing nigh to afors'd Branch so down the said branch to the mouth thereof then crossing the sd. Peter **PARKER**'s mill pond to a marked white oak standing on the South west side of the sd. Pond thence by a line of marked trees to Wm. **DOUGHTRIE**s Line thence along Wm. **DOUGHTRIE**s to a branch commonly Called the Little mare branch so down the said branch to the mouth of a branch commonly called the bay tree branch so up the sd. Bay tree branch to a chesnut oak Moses **BOYCE**s corner to [sic] thence various courses binding on the land of the said Moses **BOYCE** to the bay tree branch thence up the sd. branch to the country line thence west along said country line to the first station..." It was witnessed by Jonathan **PARKER**, John **BENTON** and John **BENTON**, Jr.[4]

On 17 April 1749, Peter[5] made a deed to his son, Jonathan[6] **PARKER**, for 250 acres for the sum of 30 shillings. It began at "a white oak from thence runing along **RABIE**s to a corner Pine on Peter **PARKER**s line runing along sd line to a corner Pine in the edge of Merryhill Percoson runing the various courses of the sd percoson to a corner pine of ye. sd. Peter **PARKER**s..." Moses, Demsey and Daniel[5] (DP) **PARKER** were witnesses.[5]

Peter[5] sold another 150 acres of his 1740 patent to Epaphroditus **BOYCE** 24 November 1753. It lay in Merry Hill Pocosin, beginning at a swamp or branch called the "Norwest," and on Richard **BAKER**, by the patent line and near William **WALTERS** corner.[6] Peter was also in the part of

---

[1] Chowan County, NC Deed Book C#2:64

[2] NCLG, 5:70, File No. 645

[3] Chowan County, NC, Deed Bk. A#1:69

[4] Ibid., C#2:152-153

[5] Ibid., C#2:150

[6] Haun, *Chowan Co., North Carolina Deed Books: A-1,E-1,F-1,F-2, G-1 (Deeds dated 1701-1755), Vol. II.,* c. 1999, 119:549, G#1:129

Chowan County that was cut off to Hertford County in 1759. It appears that he was dead by 12 March 1778, the date of the deed from Richard[5] **PARKER**, of Hertford County, to Jacob **SUMNER**. In that deed, one of the references is to "Elisha **PARKER**'s Millpond." It is obvious that Elisha[6] **PARKER** is another son of Peter[5] **PARKER**.

Peter[5] sold 150 acres to Richard[6] **PARKER** *(William[5],Richard[4],Richard[3],Richard[2],William[1])* of Nansemond County, VA, 1 December 1755. The land was in Chowan County, on and in Merry Hill Pocoson, "beginning at a maple on the gum swamp binding on Richard **BAKER** land to North West swamp, to the head thereof to a pine near Willm **WALTERS** corner binding by the patent line to corner in Daniel **PARKER**s land on **COLE**s Island, then by a line called **COLE**s line to the first station...part of a pattent of 640 acres to sd. Peter **PARKER**..." Moses **PARKER**, Elisha **PARKER** and Demsey **SUMNER** witnessed that deed.[7] This was the land directed to be sold in the 1760 will of Richard[6] **PARKER**. Moses[6] **PARKER** appears to have been another son of Peter[5] **PARKER**.

Elisha[6] **PARKER** *(Peter[5],Richard[4],Richard[3],Richard[2],William1)* is listed in the Gates County Tax Lists as owning 950 acres in 1785.[8] He had sold James **PRUDEN** 100 acres of land 26 October 1784. It was described as "Lying and being in Gates County aforsaid and Lying at a place Colled [sic] and Known by the name of the Gum Branch...begining at a markt pine Standing in a Small Branch thence by Various Courses according to the Known and antient Bounds of the Said Land to William **TREVATHAN** line thence Binding on the Land of the Said William **TREVATHAN** till it Comes to the antient and Known bounds of the Said land again then by Various Courses to the first Station..." This deed was witnessed by Isaac **MILLER**, John **PARKER** and Mary **PARKER**.[9] This parcel will be recognized as the one his father, Peter[5] **PARKER**, had purchased from Samuel **HARRELL** in 1739.

On 3 March 1786, Elisha[6] **PARKER** gave his son Peter[7] **PARKER** 125 acres of land for the sum of five Shillings. It is described as "being the Land & Plantation whereon the said Peter **PARKER** now Liveth and Bound as Followeth that is to say Beginning at the Contry Line on a branch Colld [sic] the Mill Dam branch so runing down the said branch to a Marked Gum by or nigh the Said Branch thence by a Line of Marked Trees to a white Oake Markt standing nigh the afore said Branch so Down the Said Branch to a markt Gum Thence by a Line of Markt Trees to a Branch Commonly Colled the Little Mare Branch so Down the Said Branch to the mouth of a Branch Commonly Colled the Bay Branch so up the said bay Branch to Chesnut oak Moses **HINES**'es Corner tree thence various Courses Binding on the Lands of the Said Moses **HINES** to the Said bay Branch Thence up the Said Branch to the Contry Line thence west along the said Contry Line to the first Station..." It was witnessed by Demsey **WILLIAMS**, Abraham **SUMNER** and Josiah **BENTON**, and proved in May Court 1786.[10]

Elisha[6] **PARKER** received a North Carolina Land Grant of 300 acres 28 September 1791. It is described as "Begining at a water Oak James **PRUDEN**s and Isaa [sic] **WALTERS** Corner tree standing on the Side of Merry hill pocoson thence along said **PRUDEN**s line and binding thereon North Sixty five East one Hundred and thirty four poles to a dead pine Jethro **BENTON**s Corner tree thence binding on Said **BENTON**s Line North thirty three East fourteen poles to a pine North Forty four poles then North fifty five West fourty Eight poles to a Read Oak thence North Ten west Twenty two poles then North thirty six west thirty four poles thence north Eleven East Sixty one poles to the Centre of pine Gum and read Oak thence North forty five Eighty two poles to a pine Stump William **WALTERS**'s Corner thence North twenty Eight West twenty Six poles to a pine on the Pocoson Side thence along the Several turnings & windings of Said Pocoson three Hundred & Twenty five poles to a Marked pine Thence into the Pocon [sic] South fifty six East one hundred and Sixty poles to a pine then South fifteen East thirty poles to a Red Oak in Isaac **WALTERS**'s line thence with his Line North Fifty five East twenty two poles to a pine On the Pocoson Side thence along the pocoson Binding on Said **WALTERS**'s line to the first Station..."[11]

---

[7] Chowan County, NC, Deed Bk. H#1:126

[8] NCSA, C.041.70001, Gates County Tax Lists 1784-1831, [1784-1806,] 1785, p. 16, James Arline's Captaincy

[9] NCSA, C.041.40001, Gates County Real Estate Conveyances 1776-1788, Vol: A,1, 1:53-54

[10] Ibid., 1:213-214

[11] NCSA, C.041.40002, Gates County Real Estate Conveyances 1786-1795, Vol: 2,3, 3:37-38

Elisha[6] **PARKER** made his will 26 August 1793, probated in February Court 1794. He bequeathed to his son Peter[7], and daughters Elizabeth[7] **EASON** and Mary[7] **GRIFFIN**, ten pounds each. He gave son John[7] **PARKER** one Negro fellow named **JILES**, provided that he "brings in a bond for which I came security to **SPARLING & LAWRENCE** Merchts..." His son Jesse[7] received 370 acres of land "comonly called **PUGH**s Land Begining at Danl. **PARKER**s corner thence with sd. **PARKER**s line to Elisha **CROSS**es line thence binding on sd. **CROSS**es line & the land of John **KITTRELL** to Isaac **WALTERS** land to a maple standing in the first station..." He also gave Jesse[7] a feather bed and furniture and another to his daughter Peggy[7] **PARKER**. Son Elisha[7] **PARKER** received the "manner plantation whereon I now live with all lands not before given, except three hundred acres in Merryhil pocoson to him and his heirs forever." He directed that 300 acres to be sold. Daughters Christian[7] and Nancy[7] **PARKER** each received ten pounds, one feather bed and furniture, two cows and calves, two ewes and lambs. Christian[7] also received a desk and Nancy[7] a chest.

Elisha[6] bequeathed thirty pounds to his grandson, John[8] **GRIFFIN**. He stated that "The true intent and meaning of this my last will and Testament is that my well beloved Wife Esther **PARKER** should occupy hold and enjoy the whole of my Lands except 300 acres in the pocoson ---- undisturbed during the term of her natural life or widowhood with the remaining part of my perishable property not before given for the better maintenance & preferment of my young children, then at the experation of her life or widowhood the remaining part to be equally divided between my five children namely Jesse, Peggy, Elisha, Christian and Nancy **PARKER** to them & their heirs forever. I nominate my well beloved Wife Esther **PARKER** Jesse **PARKER**, and Elisha **PARKER** my sole executors to this my last will and Testament..." John **PARKER**, Daniel **PARKER** and Pa. **HERGERTY** witnessed this will.[12]

On 20 July 1796, Esther **PARKER** sold that 300-acre patent to R. **HUNTER** of Nansemond County, VA, as directed by Elisha[6]'s will. The deed was witnessed by Peter[7] **PARKER** and Elisha[7] **PARKER**.[13] In August Court, begun 15 August 1796, that deed was proved by the oath of Elisha[7] **PARKER** and was from Esther **PARKER** to Riddick **HUNTER**.[14] An inventory of Elisha[6]'s estate was exhibited into February Court 1794, by Esther **PARKER**.[15] That inventory is in the Estate Record for Elisha[6] **PARKER** and it is signed by his executrix, "Easter **PARKER**." The first item in that record is 890 acres of land.[16]

Esther was deceased by 21 March 1804, when Elisha[7] **PARKER** took an inventory of "that part of Elisha **PARKER**'s estate left to his wife Esther **PARKER** now deceased, which was in her possession at her Death..."[17] One of the items is "1 Ewe and Lamb at Cherry **PARKER**s." Cherry **PARKER** was her daughter-in-law, as will be shown. A sale of her estate was made 30 May 1804.[18]

On 16 February 1807, Humphrey **PARKER**, John **POWELL** of Jacob, & Patrick **HEGARTY**, all of Gates County, entered into a bond in the sum of £500, for Humphrey to become guardian to "Peggy **PARKER** a Dumb Woman Daughter of Elisha **PARKER** decd."[19] In a February 1807 Court order, her condition is more fully explained by the fact that Humphrey is appointed guardian to "Peggy **PARKER** who is about Thirty years of age perfectly dumb from her Infancy..."[20] Humphrey was guardian to Peggy[7] as early as May 1805, as evidenced by a guardian return of 1806. He paid Moses H. **SMALL** for four and one-half months' board, and also charged her account for nine

---

[12] Gates County, NC, Will Book 1:119

[13] NCSA, C.041.40003, Gates County Real Estate Conveyances 1794-1803, Vol: 4,5, 4:81-82

[14] Fouts, *Minutes of County Court of Pleas and Quarter Sessions Gates County, North Carolina 1794-1799, Vol. I*, c. 1984, 59:#120

[15] Ibid., 3:#4

[16] NCSA, G.041.2194761, Gates County Estates, Record of 1765-1920, Vol. Parker, E.-Parker, M., Folder: Parker, Elisha, Sr. 1795, Doc. #245

[17] Ibid., Doc. #254

[18] Ibid., Doc. # 261

[19] Ibid., Doc. #247

[20] Fouts, *Minutes of County Court of Pleas and Quarter Sessions Gates County, North Carolina 1806-1811, Vol. III*, c. 1985, 24:#523

months' board. He paid cash to the Executor of Elisha[7] **PARKER** Junr., deceased.[21] She was deceased by February Court 1812, when Humphrey **PARKER** came into court and moved for administration on the estate of Peggy[7] **PARKER**.[22]

Elisha[7] **PARKER**, Jr., *(Elisha[6],Peter[5],Richard[4],Richard[3],Richard[2],William[1])* made his will 30 September 1806, wherein he gave a life estate to his "well beloved wife Peggy," and after her death or marriage, one half of his lands to each of his two daughters, Elizabeth Pipkin[8] **PARKER** and Polly Lee[8] **PARKER**. Both girls were minors at that time. Jonathan **ROGERS** and Hillery **WILLEY** were appointed his executors and Daniel **PARKER** and Pa. **HAGERTY** were the witnesses.[23] "Peggy" and "Polly" are diminutives of "Margaret" and "Mary."

Jonathan **ROGERS**, Executor, took an inventory of Elisha[7] **PARKER**'s estate 15 November 1806. The only tools mentioned in that inventory were "a parcel of Cuppers [Cooper's] tools."[24] In November Term 1806, the petition of Margaret **PARKER**, widow of Elisha[7] **PARKER**, deceased, stated that "after having duly made his last Will and testament that your Petitioner not being satisfyed with the same so far as regards the Lands of her said husband came into Court and openly dissented from the same." His lands were described as "adjoining the Lands of Jesse **SAVAGE** Isaac **WALTERS** Danl. **PARKER** and others..." A Writ of Dower, dated 17 November 1806, issued 16 December 1806, was to be returned to February Term 1807. It directed that 12 freeholders were to "lay off Divide and set apart on oath the Dower of Margaret **PARKER** relict of Elisha **PARKER** deceased..."[25] In February Court, 1812, Jonathan **WILLIAMS** exhibited his guardian accounts with Elizabeth P.[8] and Polly L.[8] **PARKER**. He remained their guardian through 1816, but only for Polly L.[8] **PARKER** for 1817.[26] The last guardian return for Polly L.[8] **PARKER** was exhibited in February Court 1820.[27]

Jesse[7] **PARKER** *(Elisha[6],Peter[5],Richard[4],Richard[3],Richard[2],William[1])* was initially listed for taxes on one poll in the year 1795, until his death in 1800.[28] His birth is estimated as circa 1773. His father had bequeathed 370 acres to him, after the death of his mother. He predeceased her, thus never took possession. He appeared on a marriage bond with Cherry **CROSS**, dated 10 February 1794. Elisha **CROSS** was his bondsman.[29] He made his will 12 September 1800, and stated that he was "sick." It was probated in November Court 1800, the next court following the date of his death. His wife was to have a life estate in his property, then to be equally divided between his two children. He named Elisha **PARKER** and John **CROSS**, Jr., to be his executors, but did not name his wife, nor his children. R. **HUNTER** and Hardy **CROSS** were witnesses.[30] Jesse[7] **PARKER** was dead by 26 September 1800, when the inventory of his estate was taken by Elisha **PARKER** and John **CROSS**. The account of the sales of his estate is dated 13 November 1800.[31]

Cherry **PARKER** came into May Court 1804, and moved for the "Guardianship of her two Sons Hardy D **PARKER** & Hardy [sic] **PARKER** orphans of Jesse **PARKER** decd Ordered that she give Bond & Security in the sum of two hundred pounds for each at same time John **CROSS** & Hardy

---

[21] NCSA, G.041.2194761, Gates County Estates, Record of 1765-1920, Vol. Parker, E.-Parker, M., Folder: Parker, Elisha, Sr. 1795, Doc. #249

[22] Fouts, *Minutes of County Court of Pleas and Quarter Sessions Gates County, North Carolina 1812-1817, Vol. IV*, c. 1986, 7:#745

[23] Almasy, *Gates County, North Carolina Wills 1779-1807, Vol. I*, c. 1984, p. 194-195, Will Book 1:119-121

[24] NCSA, G.041.2194761, Gates County Estates, Record of 1765-1920, Vol. Parker, E.-Parker, M., Folder: Parker, Elisha 1806, Doc.#282

[25] Ibid., Doc. #291-292

[26] Fouts, *Minutes of County Court of Pleas and Quarter Sessions Gates County, North Carolina 1812-1817, Vol. IV*, c. 1986, 5:#742; 29:#786; 50:#825; 76:#872; 109:#923; 138:#976

[27] Ibid., *1818-1823, Vol. V*, c. 1987, 60:#1118

[28] NCSA, C.041.70001, Gates County Tax Lists 1784-1831, [1784-1806] pp.179,195,209,228,236,262, Jesse Benton's Captaincy

[29] Almasy, *Gates County, North Carolina Marriage Bonds 1778-1868*, c. 1987, p. 67

[30] Almasy, *Gates County, North Carolina Wills 1779-1807, Vol. I*, c. 1984, pp. 153-154, Will Book 1:177

[31] NCSA, G.041.2194761, Gates County Estates, Record of 1765-1920, Vol. Parker, E.-Parker, M., Folder: Parker, Jesse 1800, Doc. #977-979;982-983

**CROSS** came into Court and offered themselves as Security &c."[32] This is an obvious error by the Clerk. That bond was signed 21 May 1804, in the sum of £500, for Cherry **PARKER** to be guardian to Hardy D. **PARKER**.[33] The second son's name does not appear in any of the Court or Estate Records, including Guardian Returns.

Charity **PARKER** appears in the Gates County Tax Lists for 1807 and 1808, as guardian to Hardy[8] **PARKER**, with no polls and 370 acres of land.[34] That is the acreage left to Jesse[7], after the death of his mother, which had then descended to Hardy[8]. There was no "equal division" of Jesse[7]'s lands. Charity **PARKER** was dead by 21 November 1808, when John **CROSS** entered into an administrator's bond on her estate with Henry **COPELAND** and Hillory **WILLEY**. Her administrator took an inventory of her estate 17 December 1808. In an Account Current with her estate, dated 12 January 1811, John **CROSS** listed "To Do. pd. for Schooling Orphans of said decd Entered? in the lifetime of the decsd} 4:88"[35] There is no mention of either child's name.

Though no other record of the second child has been found, his name is finally revealed in the will of Hardy **CROSS**, made 13 July 1813 and exhibited into court by September 1815. In that will, Hardy gave "unto my GrandSons Hardy **PARKER** & Joseph **PARKER** sons of Charity **PARKER**, one negro man **LEWIS** that I bought of Dempsey **ODOM** to them and their heirs forever, also one feather bed and furniture to Joseph **PARKER** to him his heirs and assigns forever." He also mentioned his son, John **CROSS**.[36] Joseph[8] **PARKER** seems to have died young. No further information for him.

John **CROSS** entered into bond of £500 and was appointed guardian to Hardy D.[8] **PARKER**, 21 November 1808.[37] At a court held 15 February 1813, it was ordered that William **LEE** be appointed guardian to Hardy[8] **PARKER**, orphan of Jesse[7] **PARKER**, deceased, in the sum of £1,000.[38] He continued as guardian through 1815.

Hardy D.[8] **PARKER** *(Jesse[7],Elisha[6],Peter[5],Richard[4],Richard[3],Richard[2],William[1])* became liable for a poll tax after his twenty-first birthday in 1816, thus he was born in 1795. He is listed with one poll, 370 acres and two Black polls for that year.[39]

On 25 January 1818, Hardy D.[8] **PARKER** sold William **BABB** 13 acres of land for $100.00. It was described as "Begining at a Gum Stump in the branch at the Corner of a piece of Land that Elisha **WILLIAMS** purchased of Isaac **WALTERS** thence runing S.37 E.46 poles to a Pine **WILLIAMS**'s Corner thence runing N.70° E2½ pole to a Pine in Isaac **WALTERS** decsd. line thence N7½° W44 Pole to a Gum in the swamp thence runing up the swamp N87° W34 pole up the swamp thence S62° W23 pole to the first Station..." It was witnessed by Isaac H. **JINKINS** [sic] and Wiley W. **JINKINS**, proved in February Court 1818.[40]

Another of his land transactions was a purchase of 180 acres, for $600.00, on 14 September 1824. It was from Enos **ROGERS** and his wife Elizabeth, Elisha **ROGERS** and his wife Mary of the County of Nancemond and state of Virginia and Jonathan **WILLIAMS** and his wife Margaret, of the County of Gates. It was described as "adjoining the Lands of Jesse **SAVAGE** Daniel **PARKER** and the said Hardy D. **PARKER** the heirs of Isaac **WALTERS** Decd. and Robert **WILSON** it being all and singular that tract or parcel of Land whereon /Elisha/ ==== **PARKER** Decd. formally [sic]

---

[32] Fouts, *Minutes of County Court of Pleas and Quarter Sessions Gates County, North Carolina 1800-1805, Vol. II*, c. 1985, 98:#428

[33] NCSA, G.041.2194761, Gates County Estates, Record of 1765-1920, Vol. Parker, E.-Parker, M., Folder: Parker, Jesse 1800, Doc. #980-981

[34] NCSA, C.041.70001, Gates County Tax Lists 1784-1831, [1807-1831] p. 6;22, Jonathan Rogers Captaincy

[35] NCSA, G.041.2194760, Gates County Estates, Record of 1765-1920, Vol. Odom-Parker, Folder: Parker, Charity 1808, Doc. #1279;1281;1286

[36] Almasy, *Gates County, North Carolina Wills 1807-1838, Vol. II*, c. 1985, pp.50-51, Will Book 2:118-121

[37] NCSA, G.041.2194761, Gates County Estates, Record of 1765-1920, Vol. Parker, E.-Parker, M., Folder: Parker, Jesse 1800, Doc. #990

[38] Fouts, *Minutes of County Court of Pleas and Quarter Sessions Gates County, North Carolina 1812-1817, Vol. IV*, c. 1986, 27:#783

[39] NCSA, C.041.70001, Gates County Tax Lists 1784-1831, [1807-1831] p.154, Seth Morgan's Captaincy

[40] NCSA, C.041.40005, Gates County Real Estate Conveyances, Vol: 9,10, 1811-1812,1815-1819, 10:341

lived..." The private examination of all three women was taken and they agreed to the sale.[41] This is the land of Hardy[8]'s uncle, Elisha[7] **PARKER**.

The land records prove their usefulness in genealogical research, and this one is an excellent example for identifying female names found in other records. Enos **ROGERS** appeared on a marriage bond with one Betsy **PARKER**, 7 April 1818, with William **BYRD** as his bondsman. Elisha **ROGERS** appeared on another bond with Mary **PARKER**, 1 January 1821, with George **WILLIAMS** as his bondsman.[42] Considering the dates of the guardian returns for Elizabeth Pipkin[8] **PARKER**, and Polly Lee[8] **PARKER**, and the dates of the marriage bonds, their identities become clear. They owned the land whereon their father "formerly lived," so would have authority, along with their husbands, to sell it. Jonathan **WILLIAMS** was executor on Elisha[7]'s will and he obviously married the widow Margaret, who also had an interest in the land.

Hardy D.[8] **PARKER** appears in the 1850 U. S. Census records as being 55 years of age, with Elizabeth, age 50, George E.[9], age 24, Jethro W.[9], age 21, Mildred Ann[9], age 20 and Mary E.[9], age 13. His son, Edmond J.[9] **PARKER**, lived next door and is shown as age 27, Jane R., age 22, Lazarus J.[10], age 5, Jesse E.[10], age 3, and Mary L.[10], age 2. Hardy D.[8] and Elizabeth were living in Haslett District in 1860, with M. E.[9] and Jethro[9] **PARKER** still living with them.[43]

Hardy D.[8] **PARKER** made his will 5 March 1869, probated 30 August 1869. He bequeathed a life estate to his beloved wife, Elizabeth, in the land whereon he lived, "except a certain part thereof lying on the North side of the Public road herein after given away which said land thus loaned is separated from the tract of land on which my son, Edmon J., now lives by a line hereinafter more particularly specified, also the piece of land which I gave my Grandson, Junius Hardy..." She was also to receive all his crop, bonds and money left after all debts and funeral expenses were paid. He lent unto his "son Edmon J. the tract of land lying North of the public road by a line beginning at the white oak near the public road thence with a ditch crossing said road to a cedar post at the head of said ditch thence a straight to a large pine on the old **PRATT** path in the line formerly Jesse **WIGGINS** up said **WIGGINS** line to **COLLINS** line up said **COLLINS** line to **BAKER**s line down **BAKER**'s line to the road thence down the road east to the white oak, to him his life after his death to his widow, Mildred A. during her life as? his widow; after her death or widowhood to my Grand Children Joseph A. and Alice E. **PARKER** to them and their heirs. I also lend unto my said son Edmon J. all the land lying on the south side of the public road beginning at the white oak near the public road thence down the branch to **WILLEROT**s [sic] line thence up said **WALTERS** line to the land formerly belonging to George **SMITH** along **SMITH**s line to the public road to the white oak to him his life after his death to my Grand Children George Thomas and William Lafayette **PARKER**." The tract of 200 acres that he purchased from Thomas **PARKER** went to his son, George E.[9] **PARKER**, who was living on it at the time. It adjoined Barnes **GOODMAN** and others. All the lands and chattel property that he had loaned to his wife were directed to go to his son, Jethro̲w W.[9] **PARKER**, along with "all the lands thus loaned lying on the south side of the public road and the small field lying directly opposite the dwelling house, beginning at the gate a little west of the house lot thence along the lane to the back of the said field thence running with the back fence around to the road..."

His daughter, Mildred A.[9], was given all the land he owned in Virginia, beginning at the State line to Frank **ROGERS** line, **SMITH** and others, back to the State line. Daughter Mary Elizabeth[9] was given "one certain tract or parcel of land lying on the North side of the public road beginning at a hollow bridge in the said public road near the head of Jimmies branch thence with the ditch across the cleared land to the head of said ditch from the head of said ditch Straight to the State line on **SAVAGE**'s line, thence down **SAVAGE**'s line to the road, thence up the road to the corner of the field to Jethrow W.'s line around the front to the road thence up the road to the hollow bridge with the exemption of the small field and suburbs given to my son Jethrow W..."

He gave his grandson, Junius Hardy[10] **PARKER**, "all the land lying on both sides of the road, beginning at the branch where my son Edmon J.'s line makes into the Jimmies branch thence running up the branch to the road to my daughter Mary Elizabeth's line thence up her line to the State line

---

[41] NCSA, C.041.40006, Gates County Real Estate Conveyances, Vol: 11-13, 13:6
[42] Almasy, *Gates County, North Carolina Marriage Bonds 1778-1868*, c. 1987, p. 79
[43] Almasy, *Gates County North Carolina Census 1850 & 1860*, c. 1987, p. 40;128

thence up the State line to the pine at the corner on Edmon J. line thence down Edmon J's line to the starting point on the south side of the road in Jimmies branch..."

He appointed his son, Edmon J.[9] **PARKER**, as his sole Executor, who submitted the following to R. B. G. **COWPER**, Judge of probate, 30 August 1869: "In the matter of the Will of Hardy D. **PARKER** dec'd. Edm<u>un</u>d J. **PARKER** being sworn, doth say that Hardy D. **PARKER**, late of said County is dead & having first made and published his last Will and testament and that he the said Edmund J. **PARKER** is the Executor therein named. Further that the property of the said Hardy D. **PARKER** consisting of realty and personal __ is worth about Three Thousand dollars so far as can be ascertained as of the date of this application and that the said Edmond J. **PARKER** and wife Mildred Ann and their children George T.[10], William L.[10] Alice E.[10], Joseph A.[10] and Junius H.[10] **PARKER**, George E.[9] **PARKER**, Jethro W.[9] **PARKER**, Mildred A.[9] **WIGGINS**, wife of Wilie **WIGGINS** and Mary E.[9] **COBB**, wife of F. W. **COBB** are the parties entitled to the property under said will and live in Gates Co., N. C. E. J. **PARKER**"[44]

Edmond J.[9] **PARKER** *(Hardy D.[8],Jesse[7],Elisha[6],Peter[5],Richard[4],Richard[3],Richard[2],William[1])* married Jane R. **ARLINE** 9 November 1843, according to a Bible record originally owned by him. Three of their children were Lazarus J.[10] **PARKER**, born 7 October 1844, Jesse A.[10] **PARKER**, born 31 August 1846, and Mary Jane R.[10] **PARKER**, born 31 May 1848. Edmond J.[9] married secondly Mildred A. **SPEIRS** 31 December 1857.[45] The 1860 Census lists another child, Geo.[10] **PARKER**, age 10, omitted in the Bible record. The other children listed are Wm.[10] **PARKER**, age 8, James[10] **PARKER**, age 4, and Alice[10] **PARKER**, age 2. The next household consisted of one Fred **COBB**, age 30.[46] He married Mary E.[9] **PARKER** 14 September 1865.[47] Jane R. **ARLINE** was Jane Rebecca **ARLINE**, daughter of Jesse and Mary **ARLINE**.[48]

◫◫◫◫◫◫◫◫◫◫◫◫◫◫◫◫◫◫◫◫◫◫◫◫◫◫◫◫◫◫◫◫◫◫◫◫◫◫◫◫◫◫◫◫◫◫◫◫◫◫

Robert[5] **PARKER** *(Richard[4],Richard[3],Richard[2],William[1])* first appeared in the records of Chowan County as a witness to a deed from Samuel **HARRELL** to his elder brother, Peter[5] **PARKER**, 10 November 1739.[49]

Robert[5] **PARKER**, of Hertford County, NC, purchased 750 acres of land from John **ALSTON**, of Orange County, NC, 9 February 1778. The land was situated in Hertford County and was described as "Beginning at A pine Standing on the North Side **BENNET**s Creek on the Creek Side Jesse **BROWN**s Corner tree thence Along the Sd **BROWN**s line to the haw tree Branch thence running up the Sd Branch to James **HAYSE**s line thence Along his line to Lawrence **BAKER**s Line and along the Sd. **BAKER**s line to George **PILAND**s line thence Down the Sd **PILAND**s line to Seasbrook **WILSON**s Line thence Down the Sd **WILSON**s line to **BENNET**s Creek thence up the Sd Creek to the first Beginning it being the land and plantation whareon [sic] Colo John **ALSTON** formerly Lived..." The witnesses were Wm. **ALSTON**, Charles **HORTON** and James (X) **BROWN**.[50] This deed is dated the year before Gates County was formed from Chowan, Hertford and Perquimans Counties. Robert[5] **PARKER**, Sr., sold Jonathan **TRADER** 75 acres of land 11 May 1781. Both men were termed "of the County of Gates." It was paid for by £40 "North Carolina Currency (Viz) one Hundred Silver Spanish Milled Dollars," to be "taken out of Sd. **PARKER**s Lands belonging to the Deeded Lands on Which he dwells begining at A Red oake on the back Swamp thence Runing Along a line of marked treese [sic] near a N W Course to a White oake a Corner Tree thence along another Marked [sic] Treese to **BENNET**s road to A red Oak Standing On the Sd Road thence runing down sd. road to a branch named the half way Run then Down sd. half way run to a white oake on the back Swamp then Down the back Swamp to the first Station." Though she is never mentioned in the deed,

---

[44] Gates County, NC Will Book 4:4-7

[45] Gates County Historical Society, *Bible Records of Gates County, N. C.*, c. unknown, p. 144

[46] Almasy, *Gates County North Carolina Census 1850 & 1860*, c. 1987, p. 141

[47] Almasy, *Gates County North Carolina Marriage Bonds 1778-1868*, c. 1987, p. 17

[48] Almasy, *Gates County, North Carolina Wills 1838-1867, Vol. III*, c. 1987, p. 22, Will Bk. 3:37-39, Will of Jesse Arline

[49] Chowan County, NC Deed Book C#2:64

[50] NCSA, C.041.40001, Gates County Real Estate Conveyances 1776-1788, Vol.: A, 1, Book A, Section 1:10. This book contains two sections, with separate page-numbering. Section 1 contains 116 deeds.

Abigal **PARKER** also signed it. The clerk transcribed his signature as "Robart **PARKER**," and hers as "Abtgall **PARKER**." Thos. **GARRETT**, Jr., and Seasbrook **WILSON** witnessed this deed.[51]

He sold John **POLSON** 100 acres of this land 20 February 1782. It began at a gum on the side of the Halfway Run, then along that branch a northwest course to **BENNETT**'s Creek Road, to a corner, then nearly a South course to George **PILAND**'s line, then to his own line to the first station. Evans **MURPHERY** and Wm. **BROOKS** witnessed this deed.[52]

His next land conveyance was for 100 acres to Willis[6] **PARKER**, for the sum of five Shillings, made 18 November 1783. Both are named as being "of Hertford," even though they lived in Gates County, and the land was situated there. It was described as "Begining on the North Side of **BENET**s Creek at the Run thence Runing along **GARRETT**s line to A Warter Oak Standing On the east Side of the Main Road a Corner tree thence Along A Row of Marked Trees near a South E course to A pine a corner Tree Standing in A branch thence down the Branch to the Creek then Down the Creek to the first Station..." George **WILLIAMS** and Jacob **BAGLEY** witnessed this deed.[53]

On 20 November 1783, Robert[5] **PARKER**, Sr., made a deed to Robert[6] **PARKER**, Jr., for 100 acres, for the same sum of five Shillings. This land was also in Gates County, though it was referred to as being "situate in Hertford County." It was described as "Begining at a pine Standing in A Branch Willis **PARKER**s Corner tree thence Runing Along a Row of Marked Trees near a SE course to the back Swamp thence down /sd/ swamp to **BENET**s Creek then down sd. Creek to Willis **PARKER**s Line then along said **PARKER**s line to the first Station..." The same witnesses appear on this deed as the previous deed to Willis[6] **PARKER**.[54]

Robert[5] **PARKER** purchased a parcel of 90 acres of land from Jesse **BROWN**, and his wife Mary, 20 January 1789. It was described as "Begining at a pine on **BENNET** Creek thence Runing a Line of Marked Trees to the haw tree Branch down the Said Branch to the pine from thence from thence [sic] to **BENNET**s Run down the Various Courses Creek [sic] to the first Station." Abm. **RIDDICK**, Seasbrook **WILSON** and Moor **CARTER** witnessed this deed.[55]

Willis[6] and Robert[6] **PARKER** were two of the sons of Robert[5] **PARKER**, Sr., and his first wife, name unknown. Willis[6] **PARKER** *(Robert[5], Richard[4], Richard[3], Richard[2], William[1])* retained and paid taxes on the 100 acres deeded to him by his father until 1793. Willis[6] **PARKER** died between May and August, 1793. Mary **PARKER** and Robert[6] **PARKER** were granted administration on his estate in August Court of that year, and entered into bond of £1,000, with John **VANN** and John **LEWIS** as bondsmen. An inventory of his estate was exhibited into Court and an order given for them to sell so much of his estate as would pay his debts. In that same court session, Robert[6] **PARKER**, Jr., was appointed overseer of the road "in the Room of Willis **PARKER** dec."[56] Willis[6] left minor children, as evidenced by the Tax List for 1794, when Robert[5] **PARKER**, Sr., was listed with the tax, "for Willis **PARKER**'s orphans," on that 100 acres.[57] Willis[6] and wife Mary had two known children, named Nancy[7] and Mary[7] **PARKER**.

In May Court 1811, a division of land of Willis[6] **PARKER**, deceased, was ordered to be made by Daniel **SOUTHALL**, William W. **RIDDICK**, Esqrs., Willis **BROWN**, William **HINTON** and James **BOOTH**, or any three of them, plus the County Surveyor, if needed. It was done as follows: "Set apart and allotted to Nancy **BOND** Survey No. 1 Containing Thirty and one acres, Begining at the fork of the Road near Mr. **SOUTHALLS** thence along the Honey Pot road 60 poles thence leaving the road & running N 73E52 poles to a Small Gum Corner Standing in a branch Dividing Said Willis & Robert **PARKER**s Land thence down said Branch 44 poles to a Gum & pine a Corner in the Dividing line thence with said line S47 west ninety eight poles to a Small Dogwood on the path side in

---

[51] NCSA, C.041.40001, Gates County Real Estate Conveyances 1776-1788, Vol.: A, 1, Book A, Section 1:82

[52] Ibid., A, Section 1:111

[53] Ibid., A, Section 2:75

[54] Ibid., A, Section 2:75;76

[55] NCSA, C.041.40002, Gates County Real Estate Conveyances 1786-1795, Vol: 2,3, Book 2:97

[56] Fouts, *Minutes of County Court of Pleas and Quarter Sessions Gates County, North Carolina 1787-1793*, c. 1995, 138:#258;139:#260;140:#262

[57] NCSA, C.041.70001, Gates County Tax Lists 1784-1831, 1794, p. 166, William Harriss' Captaincy

**WALTON**s line thence with said line N.55.west 18.po. to a Gum and poplar in a branch thence up said Branch to the Begining, to be her part.

Set apart to Polly **PARKER** Survey No. 2 Containing Forty and five Acres Including the Dwelling Begining at a Dogwood by the old path in **WALTON**s line running across the Land N.47E.98 poles to a Gum & pine in Robert **PARKER**s Branch thence down said Branch to **WAL-TON**s line thence with said line N55.W.102 poles to the first Station for her share. Given under our hands & Seals this 30th July 1811. Willis **BROWN** (Seal) Wm. W. **RIDDICK** (Seal) James **BOOTH** (Seal) Pa **HEGERTY** (Seal)"[58] Mary is referred to here by the nickname "Polly." Patrick **HEGERTY** was the County Surveyor at that time.

Nancy[7] **PARKER** appeared on a Gates County marriage bond with Thomas **BOND**, 12 December 1809, with John **WALTON** as bondsman. Mary[7] **PARKER** appeared on another bond with Warren **CRAPER**, 10 June 1817, with Thomas **BOND** as bondsman.[59]

Robert[5] **PARKER** married his second wife, Abigail, prior to 1781, as evidenced by the deed to Jonathan **TRADER**. She also appeared on a deed from Robert[5] **PARKER**, Sr., to William **BOYCE**, for 112 acres, dated 17 November 1789. It is described as "Begining at a pine Standing on **BENNET**s Creek thence Runing along the Patten Line to a Gum A Corner tree Standing in the Great haw Tree ~~Branch~~ Swamp thence down the Swamp to **BENNET**s thence Down the Creek to the first Station." Isaac **MILLER**, Henry **FORREST** and William **CLEAVES** witnessed this deed.[60] This parcel appears to be the "90 acres" purchased from Jesse and Mary **BROWN** in January of that year.

Robert[5] **PARKER**, Sr., was dead by 21 August 1797, when Robert[6] **PARKER** took an inventory of his estate. The first entry on that inventory is "480 Acres of Land."[61] Robert[6] **PARKER** entered into a bond for the sum of £1,500 for administration on the estate of Robert[5] **PARKER**, deceased, on 23 August 1797. James **FREEMAN** and Henry Ebron **SEARS** were his bondsmen.[62] The account of sales of the estate was made 28 September 1797, naming many of his family members, among others.[63] In August Court 1798, it was ordered that William W. **RIDDICK**, William **BROOKS**, Miles **GATLING**, Michael **LAWRENCE** and Thomas **MARSHALL** meet with the County Surveyor and make a division of the real estate of Robert[5] **PARKER**, deceased.[64] The first four of these men returned the division in November Court 1798.[65] It was never recorded, but is partially preserved in later deeds.

A Writ of Dower was issued 20 November 1797, for Abigail **PARKER**, relict of Robert[5] **PARKER**, deceased. Her dower was laid off 28 December of that year, and was described as "Begining at the fork of the New Road at the Carner [sic] of **SOUTHALL**s plantation Thence along the New Road to the Swamp the back Swamp [sic] thence up sd. swamp to a white Oak at the Corner of the apple Orchard thence Southern Course along a Row of young peach Trees thence to the Corner of the Said Orchard Thence to a Stake about A North Course to a Red Oak on the side of the Aforesaid Back Swamp thence up said Swamp to a Sliped pine in the Mouth of a Branch thence up Sd. branch to a Slipd. pine & holdes? at the Cart path thence along the Cart Path that leads towards **POLSON**s to the Edenton Road Thence along the Sd Road towards the Court house To the first Station."[66] The quantity of land is not mentioned in this document, but is partially revealed in a deed dated 30 November 1801, from Lewis (X) and Abigail (X) **MORGAN**. Lewis **MORGAN** and Abigail **PARKER** appeared on a Gates County marriage bond dated 21 January 1801. Halan **WILLIAMS** was his bondsman.[67]

[58] NCSA, C.041.40005, Gates County Real Estate Conveyances 1811-1812, 1815-1819, Vol: 9,10, 9:48-49

[59] Almasy, *Gates County, North Carolina Marriage Bonds 1778-1868*, c. 1987, pp. 9, 19

[60] NCSA, C.041.40002, Gates County Real Estate Conveyances 1786-1795, Vol: 2,3, 2:111

[61] NCSA, G.041.2194762, Gates County Estates, Record of 1765-1920, Vol. Parker-Pierce, Folder: Parker, Robert 1797, Doc. #357

[62] Ibid., Doc. #352

[63] Ibid., Doc. #345-349

[64] Fouts, *Minutes of County Court of Pleas and Quarter Sessions Gates County, North Carolina 1794-1799, Vol. I*, c. 1984, 106:#208

[65] Ibid., 111:#219

[66] NCSA, G.041.2194762, Gates County Estates, Record of 1765-1920, Vol. Parker-Pierce, , Folder: Parker, Robert 1797, Doc. #339-341

[67] Almasy, *Gates County, North Carolina Marriage Bonds 1778-1868*, c. 1987, p. 63

They sold Daniel **SOUTHALL** 50 acres for $10.00. It is described as "Beginning at a Gum Tree Standing on the New Road a little this side of the plantation of Robert **PARKER** Decd. being a Corner tree Between Abraham **PARKER** & Willis **PARKER**s Orphans thence along said Abraham **PARKER**s line to a Corner Red Oak Standing on the Main Road Opposite to the Dwelling House of Willis **BROWN** thence binding on the Main Road the Various Courses thereoff [sic] to the fork Just above Gates Court House from thence runing the Various Courses of the New Road & binding thereon to the first Station Containing Fifty Acres be the same more or Less the said Tract of Land being a part of the Dower of said Abigail **MORGAN** during life..." Jesse **SOUTHALL** and Willis **BROWN**, Jr., witnessed this deed and it was proved by them in November Court 1802.[68]

Robert[5] and Abigail **PARKER** had two minor children at the time of his death. They were William[6] and Sarah[6] **PARKER**. William[6] was at least 14 years of age 19 May 1801. He came into Court and chose Willis **BROWN** as his guardian, who entered into a bond of £500, with Demsey **ODOM** and Thomas **FREEMAN** as bondsmen.[69] Benjamin **HAYSE** entered a bond of £500 to become guardian of Sarah[6] **PARKER**, orphan of Robert **PARKER**, deceased, on 18 August 1806. Kinchen **NORFLEET** and Mills R. **FIELD** were his bondsmen.[70]

William[6], John[6], Willis[6], Christian[6], Robert[6] and Nancy[6] were the children of Robert[5] **PARKER** and his first wife. Priscilla[6], Elizabeth[6], Jesse[6], Abraham[6], Richard[6], William[6] and Sally[6] **PARKER** appear to be children of Abigail, as will be shown.

Willis[6] **PARKER** first appears in Gates County records as a witness to a deed from James and Jean **GREGORY** to John **WALTON**, dated 6 December 1782.[71] Willis[6], Willis[7] **BROWNE** and Jonathan **SMITH** were appointed as "Patterolls" [Patrols] in August Court of 1783, in Captain Christopher **RIDDICK**'s district.[72] There were at least two contemporaneous Willis **PARKER**s in Gates County. They are differentiated by the districts in which they lived. The Willis[6] treated here is found in the tax district, or captaincy, of Christopher **RIDDICK**, along with his father, Robert[5] **PARKER**.

Christian[6] **PARKER** married James **BROWN**, as evidenced by her application for administration on his estate, with Robert[6] **PARKER**, Jr., in February Term of Gates County Court 1797.[73] She made her will 5 October 1799, probated in November Court of that year. She bequeathed to her "beloved son," James[7] **BROWN**, 100 acres of land lying on Honey Pot Road, "that fell to me in the division of my fathers land provided my son James pays my son Robert **BROWN** twenty dollars when he arrives to the age of Twenty one years..." She left $5 to her son, Willis[7] **BROWN**, as his full share of her estate, and named Polley[7], Nancy[7], Elizabeth[7], Luiza[7] and Robert[7] **BROWN**, all of whom would share equally in the division of her perishable estate. She named Willis[7] **BROWN** executor and had Jethro **WILLIAMS** and George **WILLIAMS** as witnesses to her will.[74] In February Court 1807, Robert[6] **PARKER**, guardian to Robert[7] **BROWN**, orphan of James **BROWN**, exhibited his accounts. The balance due the orphan amounted to £14.10.7.[75] This is the only guardian account found for Robert[7] **BROWN**, thus it may have been the final one, having achieved the age of 21 in late 1806, or the first month in 1807.

Robert[6] **PARKER** made his will in Gates County on 5 November 1822. It is transcribed here in full:

"State of No. Carolina
Gates County

---

[68] NCSA, C.041.40003, Gates County Real Estate Conveyances 1794-1803, Vol: 4,5, 5:357

[69] NCSA, G.041.2194762, Gates County Estates, Record of 1765-1920, Vol. Parker-Pierce, Folder: Parker, Robert 1797, Doc. #354; Fouts, *Minutes of County Court of Pleas and Quarter Sessions Gates County, North Carolina 1800-1805, Vol. II*, c. 1985, 33:#318

[70] NCSA, G.041.2194762, Gates County Estates, Record of 1765-1920, Vol. Parker-Pierce, Folder: Parker, Robert 1804, Doc. #366

[71] NCSA, C.041.40001, Gates County Real Estate Conveyances 1776-1788, Vol.: A, 1, A, Section 2:37

[72] Fouts, *Minutes of County Court of Pleas and Quarter Sessions Gates County, North Carolina 1779-1786*, c. 1994, 64:#127

[73] Ibid., *1794-1799, Vol. I*, c. 1984, 69:#140

[74] Almasy, *Gates County, North Carolina Wills 1779-1807, Vol. 1*, c. 1984, 147-148; Will Bk. 1:168-169

[75] Fouts, *Minutes of County Court of Pleas and Quarter Sessions Gates County, North Carolina 1806-1811, Vol. III*, c. 1985, 28:#530

Know all men by these presents that I Robert **PARKER** of the County & State aforesaid being of sound & perfect mind & memory do make & ordain this instrument to be my last will & testament in manner & form (viz) First it is my will that all my Just debts be paid in as short time after my decd. by the sale of my parishable Estate as the Law will permit.

2nd. I give unto James **BROWN** my Nephew, all my land & plantation whereon I now live also my two negro woman [sic] **AGGY** & **MILLEY** with a desire they may remain on the plantation & that said James **BROWN** shall pay unto Abraham **PARKER** one hundred dollars unto Ezikiel [sic] **LASSITER** one hundred dollars & unto Mary **CROSS** one Hundred Dollars, to them & their heirs forever.

3rd. I give unto my Neice Elizabeth **PARKER** my negro man **GILES** to her & her Heirs Lawfully begotten & if she should die without an heir aforesaid, said negro to be divided between James **BROWN**, Abram **PARKER** & Mary **CROSS** Equally.

4th It is my will that my parishable estate be sold & out the Money arising therefore I give unto Louisa **PARKER**, Eliza **PARKER** wife of Peter, James **BROWN**, Willis **BROWN** my Nephew, Prissila **HAYS** & Nancy **BOND** Each Five Shillings to be paid by my executors hereafter named.

5th. Lastly I appoint Abraham **PARKER** & James **BROWN** my executors to Carry into Execution this my last will & Testament revoking all other or former wills, as witness I have hereunto set my hand 5th Novr. 1822

Signd. in presence of                                        Robert **PARKER**

H. **GILLIAM**

Codicil

I give unto the Heirs of Abraham **PARKER** decd. each Five shillings & the remainder of my Estate of whatever nature I leave to be Equally Divided between A **PARKER** & Jas. **BROWN**, also I give unto Richard **PARKER** my half brother five shillings also unto Eliz. **BULLOCK** five Shillings, the heirs of William **PARKER** decd. Each five Shillings, Mary **EVANS** five Shillings as witness my hand & Seal 10th January 1823.

Witness                                        Robert **PARKER**

H. **GILLIAM**

State of North Carolina

   Gates County    August County Court of Pleas &c 1823

The last will of Robert **PARKER** decd. was exhibited into court by James **BROWN** & Abraham **PARKER** the Executors therein appointed and was proved by the oath of Henry **GILLIAM** the subscribing witness thereto & ordered to be recorded at the same time the said Executors was duly qualified for that Office and prayed an order for letters testamentary thereon which was granted &c.

         Teste  J. **SUMNER**, Clk."[76]

An inventory of his estate was taken and a sale of his personal property was made 12 August 1823, by his Executors. This was usually done within a very short time of the death of the person. It contained all the usual implements and stock needed on a farm, as well as kitchen utensils and shoemaker's tools. The shoemaker's tools were sold to Ezekiel **LASSITER**. Some of the purchasers were Abram, Henry, James, Eliza. and Peter **PARKER**. James, Jesse, and James **BROWN**, "of Willis," also purchased items.[77]

A petition for partition of the lands of Robert[6] **PARKER**, deceased, was submitted to Gates County Court in February Term, 1824. It is an exceptional document in the extent of the detailed account of complex family relationships, and is transcribed here in full:

"To the Worshipful, the justices of the county Court of Gates Febr. Term 1824.

The petition of Nancey **BOND**, Mary **CRAPER**, John **EVANS** & wife Mary, Ezekiel **LASSITER** & wife Nancy, James **PARKER**, /& wife Luisa/ Peter **PARKER** /& wife Eliza/ Sophia /**PARKER**/ & Penny **PARKER** Thos **COLLINS** & Nancy his wife Robert **PARKER**, Henry **PARKER** & Cherry/arity/ [Charity] **PARKER**, Benja. **HAYS** & wife Priscilla Sidny [sic] **PARKER**, Thirsa **PARKER**, Magt. **PARKER** & Jane **BROWN** by their Guardian Jethro **SUMNER**, Abram

[76] Gates County, NC, Will Book 2:201-202

[77]  NCSA, G.041.2194762, Gates County Estates, Record of 1765-1920, Vol. Parker-Pierce, Folder: Parker, Robert 1823, Doc. #385;#398-404

**PARKER** & his wife Sally humbly sheweth that Robt **PARKER** died on or about __ [blank] day 1803 intestate (without issue[78] [sic]—leaving brothers & sisters of the whole blood Willis **PARKER**, Christiana **PARKER** and Nancey **PARKER** – Willis **PARKER** /died &/ had issue Nancey **BOND** & Mary **CRAPER** -- Christiana **PARKER** died & had issue Mary **EVANS**, Nancy **LASSITER**, Willis **BROWN**, Betsey **PARKER** – Louisa **PARKER** – Nancy **PARKER** died & left issue Jane **BROWN** – Robt. **PARKER** likewise left bothers [sic] & sisters of the half blood to wit Priscilla **HAYS**, Eliza **BULLOCK**, Jessee [sic] **PARKER**,[79] Abram **PARKER**, Richard **PARKER**, Wm. **PARKER**, Sally **PARKER** – Jesse since died leaving Sophia, Penny Sidey, Thirsa, & Magaret [sic] **PARKER**, Abm. **PARKER** is likewise dead leaving Nancy Robt. Henry & Charity.

Yr. petitioners further shew that the [sic] Robt. **PARKER** died seized & possessed of a certain tract of land lying & being in the county aforesaid containing by estimation ___ [blank] Acres adjoing [sic] the lands of Nancy **BOND** & Mary **CRAPER** & Danl **SOUTHALL** – Yr. petitioners therefore pray that Commissioners be appointed to divide Sd. into ten parts to wit to ~~Mary~~ /Nancy/ **BOND** ~~one tenth,~~ & ~~to~~ Mary **CRAPER** one tenth to Mary **EVANS**, Nancy **LASSITER**, Willis **BROWN**, Eliza. **PARKER**, Ja **BROWN** & Betsey **PARKER** & Louisa **PARKER** one tenth being the children of Christiana **PARKER** – to Jane **BROWN** one tenth – To Priscilla **HAYS** one tenth – to Eliza **BUL-LOCK** one tenth, to Sophia Penny, Sidney Thirsa & Magt **PARKER** daughters of Jesse **PARKER** one tenth – to Nancy, Henry, Robt. & Charity daughter [sic] of Abm. **PARKER** one tenth – to Richd **PARKER** one tenth – ~~to Wm. PARKER one tenth~~ Will **PARKER** one tenth – to Sally **PARKER** one tenth. Yr. petitioners further pray that /Subpinas/ [sic] & Copies of this petition issue to Ja **BROWN**, /Abr **PARKER**/ David **BULLOCK** & wife Eliz[a]., Rich[d] **PARKER** & wife, & Will **PARKER** & wife, & Willis **BROWN** to shew cause if any they have why a partition should not be had agreeably to the prayer of the petitioioners [sic] & agreeably to the Act of Assembly in such Case made & provided, & do whatsoever all? yr worships may deem meet & proper &c Jno L. **BAILY** Atto for the petition__ "[80] The Peter **PARKER** in this petition will appear again, at a later time.

James[7] **BROWN** filed his answer to this petition wherein he set forth that Robert[6] **PARKER** made his will 5 November 1822, bequeathing the whole of the "premises set forth in the above petition" as cause for not granting the prayer of the petition. A further answer was to the effect that the land could not be divided without "a disparagement of the value." This document is undated.[81]

A division of the land of Robert[6] **PARKER**, deceased, was ordered to be made 21 February 1825, by Thomas **RIDDICK**, William W. **RIDDICK**, Pryor **SAVAGE**, Kinchen **NORFLEET** & James **WILLIAMS** with the County Surveyor. The actual division was made by Wm. W. **RIDDICK**, James **WILLIAMS** and Pryer **SAVAGE**, with Benbury **WALTON**, County Surveyor, 8 November 1825. Number 1 was described as "beginning at a bridge in the road leading from Gates Court House to Suffolk," joining on a line of John D. **PIPKIN** and contained 24 acres. It was drawn by Nancy[7], Henry[7], Robert[7] and Charity[7] **PARKER**, children of Abram[6] **PARKER**. Number 2 began at a pine corner of No. 1 at the road, then to a corner of Nancy[7] **BOND**, and other courses, containing 24 acres drawn by Richard[6] **PARKER**. Number 3 began at a corner in **PIPKIN**'s branch, with other courses, containing 24 acres, and was drawn by William[6] **PARKER**. Number 4 began at "a stake a corner of No. 1 at the dividing line," to a corner of No. 2 in a branch, containing 24 acres, drawn by Sophia[7], Penny[7], Lidia[7], [sic] Thursa[7] and Mary[7] **PARKER**, Children of Jesse[6] **PARKER**. Number 5 began at a black gum in a branch **PIPKIN**'s line, to corners on numbers three and four, containing 24 acres, drawn by Sally[6] **PARKER**. Number 6 mentions "the Creek Swamp," which would refer to **BEN-NETTS** Creek, contained 24 acres and was drawn by Nancy[7] **BOND** & Mary[7] **CRAPER**, children of Willis[6] **PARKER**. Number 7 began at "at a large Cypress a corner of No. 9 in the Creek Swamp,

---

[78] The above will of Robert Parker corrects the erroneous date of his death in this document. In this instance, the attorney has used "intestate" to mean "without issue," instead of the correct definition of "without making a will."

[79] Part of this document is obscured on film by an apparent fold. A copy of it is found on Doc. #368, in Folder: Parker, Robert 1804, and has been used to supply the illegible words.

[80] NCSA, G.041.2194762, Gates County Estates, Record of 1765-1920, Vol. Parker-Pierce, Folder: Parker, Robert 1804, Doc. #368; Folder: Parker, Robert 1823, Doc. #411

[81] Ibid., Doc. #387

thence S 61.W73. poles to a pine a corner of No. 6. No 8 & No 9. thence N31½.W 57. poles to a small pine a corner of No. 4. No. 5. & No. 6. thence N.53.E. by a line of marked trees, to the run of a branch, **PIPKIN**'s line, thence down said branch its various courses to the first Station, Containing 24 acres, drawn by James **BROWN**, & others (Children of Christian **BROWN** and receives from No. 1. Nancy **PARKER**, Henry **PARKER**, Robert **PARKER** & Charity **PARKER**, (Children of Abram **PARKER**, $9." Number 8 began at a pine corner of No. 6 at the edge of the Creek Swamp, near a branch, to a corner of No. 6, No. 7 & No. 9, thence to a corner of No. 10, "crossing an Island and along the Creek Swamp to the run of a branch which emties [sic] in **BENNETS** Creek, thence up said branch to the first Station," containing 24 acres. It was drawn by Jane[7] **BROWN**. Number 9 began at a black gum, near the Creek at the old landing, and contained 34 acres, drawn by Elizabeth[6] **BUL-LOCK**. Number 10 was described as "Beginning at a small Cypress, a corner of No. 8, in the dividing line thence S40 W. across an Island and along the Creek swamp, to the run of a branch, which emties in the Creek, thence down Said branch to the Creek, thence up the Creek, on the edge thereof to a black gum at the old landing, thence N31½ W.57 poles to the first Station Containing 34 acres, drawn by Prissilla **HAYS**..."[82] Each parcel's value was assessed by the commissioners chosen to make this division, and they determined the cash amount owed to equalize the value among the petitioners, as shown in Number 7.

It will be noted that in the codicil to Robert[6] **PARKER**'s will, of 10 January 1823, "the heirs of William **PARKER** decd." are mentioned. On 7 March 1812, John[6] **PARKER** conveyed 80 acres of his land to Abraham[6] **PARKER**, for £90. It was described as "Situate lying and being in the County of Gates and State aforesaid Bounded on Robert **PARKER**s Benjn. **HAYS**es & Moses **DAV-IS**es lands which said Tract of land the said John **PARKER** become Heir to from his Fathers Estate... The Condition of the Above Conveyence [sic] is Such that whereas the said Abraham **PARKER** have [sic] become Security for the said John **PARKER** in A Refunding Bond for the Sum of Eighty Pounds given to Robert **PARKER** Administrator to the Estate of Robert **PARKER** decd. and he the said Abraham **PARKER** not feeling Willing to make himself liable to pay any Debt or damages that may be recovered against the said John as heir of his Father and the said John being Willing to Secure the said Abraham **PARKER** from any debt which may be Recovered against the Estate of Robert **PARKER** decd. hath Conveyed and Sold to the said Abraham as Security to the above mentioned Bond given to Robert **PARKER** Admr. & the above Conveyence will be Void otherwise to Remain in full force & Virtue. John his (X) mark **PARKER** (Seal.)" Witnesses to this deed were Mills **RID-DICK** and Robert[6] **PARKER**. It was acknowledged in May Court 1812.[83]

On 29 July 1813, John[6] **PARKER** conveyed that same land to Daniel **SOUTHALL** for £80. It was described as "lying on the road Leading from Gates Ct House to the honey Potts, Bounded by the Lands of Benjamin **HAYS**, the land formerly William **PARKER**s, Moses **DAVIS** & Robert **PARKER**, it being the same tract of Land allotted to me in the Division of my Fathers real Estate No. 11th. in s[d] Division containing by Estimation one hundred acres be the same more or less by the known And reputed Boundaries of the sd tract of Land... John his X mark **PARKER** (Seal.)" Witnesses to this deed were Wm C **BROOKS** (Jurat) and John W **SOUTHALL**. It was proved in August Court 1815, by the oath of Wm. C. **BROOKS** and registered 27 June 1816.[84]

The above John[6] **PARKER** received the "11th" portion of the real estate of his father. There is no record of that division of land in Gates County deeds, as previously mentioned. This man was John[6] **PARKER**, son of Robert[5] **PARKER**, which is also stated in a deed from Daniel **SOUTHALL** to Arthur and George **WILLIAMS**, all of Gates County, on 30 May 1816, "it being the lot of Land give [sic] to John **PARKER**, Son of Robert **PARKER** Decsd. in the division of Said Land...the bounds of which are fully expressed, in the said division..."[85] He was deceased prior to the date of the will of Robert[6] **PARKER**, without heirs. The William **PARKER** mentioned in the codicil, and the 1813 deed of John[6] **PARKER**, may have been another deceased son, and brother to that Robert **PARKER**. It was not uncommon for a family to give a second child the same name as a previously

[82] NCSA, C.041.40007, Gates County Real Estate Conveyances 1829-1836, Vol: 14,15, 14:106-108

[83] NCSA, C.041.40005, Gates County Real Estate Conveyances 1811-1812, 1815-1819, Vol: 9,10, 9:131

[84] Ibid., 10:142-143

[85] NCSA, C.041.40006, Gates County Real Estate Conveyances 1819-1829, Vols: 11-13, 11:84

deceased child. The second William[6] **PARKER** received a full share in the division of his half-brother Robert[6]'s land, 8 November 1825.

The lands of both Robert **PARKER**s were sold by the heirs to just a few individuals. The first sale recorded, after Abigail **MORGAN**'s dower, was 80 acres from Abraham[6] **PARKER** to Daniel **SOUTHALL**, 14 May 1802, for 240 Spanish Milled Dollars. It was described as "Beginning at a White Oak Standing on **BENNITT**s [sic] Creek Old Road that leads to the Court House thence So. 70 East 169 pole to a Stake on the New Road thence down the said New Road to a branch thence up the Branch to a pine thence a line of Marked trees 104 on [sic] the aforesaid Old Road thence up the said Road to the first Station...it being a propotion [sic] of land allotted to said Abraham **PARKER** out of his Father Robert **PARKER** Decd. lands and plantation..." Jesse **SOUTHALL**, Wm. **BROOKS** and Robert[6] **PARKER** were witnesses. It was proved in November Court of that year.[86]

Nancy[7] and Elizabeth[7] **PARKER** sold Daniel **SOUTHALL** 50 acres for 140 Silver Dollars, 7 February 1804. It was one half of an undivided tract "Beginning at a Red Oak Standing on the Main Road that leads from Gates Court House Nearly Opposite to Willis **BROWN**s Dwilling [sic] House thence Runing No. 85 East 104 pole to a Pine in a branch A Corner Tree thence along a line of Marked Trees to the Honey Pot Road thence along the said Road the Various Courses thereof and Binding thereon to the old Road that leads from the Court House thence along the said Old Road...to the first station...which Tract of Land fell to the said Nancy **PARKER** and Elizabeth **PARKER** in the lands and plantation belonging to our Grandfather Robert **PARKER** Decd..." Nancy[7] signed her name and Elizabeth[7] used "X" as her mark. Jethro **MELTEAR**, Jr., and M. **RIDDICK** were witnesses. This deed was proved in May Court 1806.[87]

Benjamin **HAYS** and his wife, Priscilla[6], sold Daniel **SOUTHALL** 110 acres for 220 Silver Dollars, 30 December 1806. It began "at a White Oak A Corner Tree in George **WILLIAMS**'s line thence North Fifty Six pole to a Pine thence South Seventy one Degrees East Two hundred and Thirty Six pole to a Red Oak A corner Tree on the New Road Thence Binding along the said Road toward the Court House To a Pine a Corner Tree thence North Twenty Nine Degrees West Two Hundred and Fifty Eight Pole to A Pine thence along A line of Marked Trees To the Beginning...it being A Certain Tract of Land Aloted [sic] as in the division of the lands of Robert **PARKER** Deceased..." Both Benjamin and Priscilla[6] used the "X" as their marks. The witnesses were Jesse **SOUTHALL** and Abraham **BEEMAN**.[88]

A further description of the lands of Robert[5] **PARKER** is provided by a deed from Richard[6] **PARKER** to Daniel **SOUTHALL**. It was made 4 December 1806, by "Richard **PARKER** of the County of Henderson and State of Tenessee, in consideration of the sum of $300.00," and was described as being in Gates County and "Beginning at a Stake on the New Road a Corner between Richard **PARKER** and Daniel **SOUTHALL** thence Runing and binding on the line of said Daniel **SOUTHALL** Eighty pole to a Stake thence runing North Thirty degrees East One Hundred Pole to a Pine thence South Seventy five Degrees East One hundred and three pole to the New Road thence along said Road and binding on the Various Courses thereof to the Beginning Fifty five Acres it being a Certain Tract of land Allotted me in the division of my Father Robert **PARKER** Deceased..." Witnesses were Jacob **HUNTER** and Timothy **WALTON**, Jr. It was registered in May Court 1807.[89]

The land of John[6] **PARKER** mentioned earlier, as sold by Daniel **SOUTHALL** to Arthur and George **WILLIAMS**, was sold by the latter, then of Hertford County, on 28 December 1822, to Charles **NEWSOM**, also of Hertford. This deed is more specific in the description of this parcel and facilitates determination of the exact location of these lands. This 100 acres is described as "lying on the north side of **BENNET**s Creek Runing as follows begining at the road where the run of the Swamp Crosses thence runing down the main run of said swamp to the Creek thence runing up the /sd./ Creek to Moses **DAVIS** line thence along Moses **DAVIS** line to the deep branch & corners thence along Benjamin **HAYES** line to the road at a pine standing at the Clay hill where the path strikes out to go through said land thence runing down the road to the run of sd. Swamp at the first station." It was

---

[86] NCSA, C.041.40003, Gates County Real Estate Conveyances 1794-1803, Vol: 4,5, 5:344

[87] NCSA, C.041.40004, 1803-1810, Vol: 6,7,8, 6:301-303

[88] Ibid., 7:211-212. This deed is repeated on 7:229 and proved in August Court, 1808.

[89] Ibid., 7:39-40

witnessed by E. H. **NEWSOM** and M. E. **NEWSOM**.[90] This particular parcel is now covered by the waters of the northwest end of Merchant's Millpond. Some of Robert[5] **PARKER**'s lands are now bisected by U. S. Highway 158, between Central Junior High School and County High School. This highway crosses Honey Pot Swamp, between the two schools.

Willis[7] **BROWN** sold all his right and title in land formerly the property of Robert[6] **PARKER**, deceased, to John **MATTHEWS** for the sum of $18.00, on 16 May 1826.[91] On 11 March 1826, Penninah[7] and Sophia[7] **PARKER** sold him their right in the right of their father, Jesse[6] **PARKER**, "the tract of land whereon the late Robert decd formerly lived situate in said County near the Court House and bounded by the lands of Davis **SOUTHALL** & Mary **BROTHERS** and others..." for $36.00. Isaiah **MATTHEWS** and Lassiter **RIDDICK** witnessed this deed.[92] Jesse[6] **PARKER**, who had "Sophia, Penny Si<u>dey</u>, Thirsa, & Magaret," appeared on a marriage bond with Nancy **BRADY** 19 December 1799. Willis **BROWN** was his bondsman.[93]

On 10 June 1826, Abraham[6] and Sarah **PARKER** sold John **MATTHEWS** 24 acres of land, "by actual survey," for $150.00. It was part of the estate of Robert[6] **PARKER**, deceased, and was their part of the division of that estate, adjoining John D. **PIPKIN**, John **MATTHEWS**, William[6] **PARKER**'s heirs and the those of Christian[6] **BROWN**. Abraham[6] signed his name and Sarah used "+" as her mark.[94] It was proved in August Court 1828.

On 6 July 1826, Henry[7] and Cherry[7] **PARKER** sold one sixth of one legal share of Robert's land for $36.00. It adjoined John D. **PIPKIN**, William[6] **PARKER**'s heirs, Richard[6] **PARKER**'s heirs and Daniel **SOUTHALL**. On 4 July 1826, Elizabeth[7] and Louisa[7] **PARKER**, had sold their eight acres to John **MATTHEWS** for the same price.[95]

On 16 January 1827, Bryant **BROTHERS** and wife Mary[7], sold John **MATTHEWS** 12 acres "all our right title and interest in & to the lands of the late Robert **PARKER** decd... adjoining the lands of Mrs. Nancy **BOND**, the said Bryant **BROTHERS** & others..." The witnesses were the same as to the previous deed. Mary[7] **BROTHERS** signed with "+" as her mark. Mary[7] could not conveniently attend the court to be privately examined on her assent to this deed, but was examined by two Justices, who made a return of that examination on 22 May 1827.[96] Mary[7] was formerly Mary[7] **CRAPER**, but had appeared on a marriage bond with Bryant **BROTHERS** 21 November 1825. Clement **HILL** was Bryant's bondsman.[97] On 1 December 1827, James[7] **BROWN** also sold to John **MATTHEWS** "Formally [sic] the lands of Robert **PARKER** Decd. and one six part of one Legal sh<u>ear</u>," bounded by John D. **PIPKIN**, Elizabeth[6] **BULLOCK** and Nancy[6] **BOND**. H. **GILLIAM** was the sole witness to this deed.[98] John **MATTHEWS** made several other purchases of these **PARKER** lands from various heirs.

---

[90] NCSA, C.041.40006, Gates County Real Estate Conveyances 1819-1829, Vols: 11-13, 11:230

[91] Ibid., 12:128

[92] Ibid., 12:128-129

[93] Almasy, *Gates County, North Carolina Marriage Bonds 1778-1868*, c. 1987, p. 67

[94] NCSA, C.041.40006, Gates County Real Estate Conveyances 1819-1829, Vols: 11-13, 13:183-184

[95] Ibid., 13:185;186

[96] Ibid., 13:9-11

[97] Almasy, *Gates County, North Carolina Marriage Bonds 1778-1868*, c. 1987, p.13

[98] NCSA, C.041.40006, Gates County Real Estate Conveyances 1819-1829, Vols: 11-13, 13:90-91

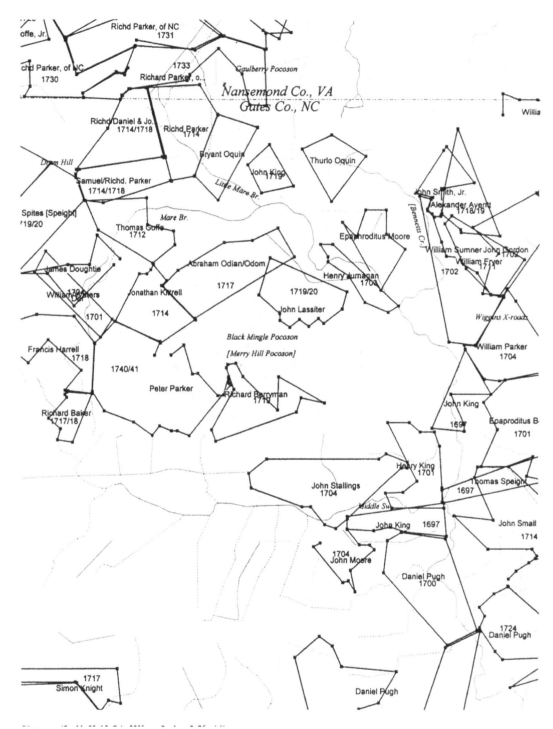

Scale: 0.76 mi/in

Map depicting the 1740/41 North Carolina Land Grant to Peter[5] **PARKER**, relative to some of the holdings of his father, Richard[4] **PARKER**.

## William[4] PARKER *(Thomas[3],Richard[2],William[1])*

For many years, William[4] **PARKER** has been claimed as the son of the Thomas **PARKER** who made his will in Chowan County on 23 January 1717. All the children mentioned in that will were less than 18 years of age on that date. William[4] **PARKER** obtained a Virginia patent for 282 acres in Nansemond County, 20 October 1704. His birth date is estimated here to have been ca. 1683. He would most likely have been at least 21 years of age in 1704, therefore could not possibly be the William **PARKER** who was son of the Thomas who made that will in 1717.

Naming patterns in the families descending from William[1] **PARKER** are quite consistent down through the generations. Each generation traced thus far from Richard[2] named a son Richard. Richard[4] named his eldest son William. The name "Thomas" never appears in this family. William[4] **PARKER** named one of his sons William, and another Thomas. Thomas is repeated in this family in the same manner as that of Richard[2]. The name "Richard" is never used in the early generations of this family. The loss of the Nansemond County records prevents a positive identification of the parentage of William[4] **PARKER,** but a logical premise is that he is the son of Thomas[3] **PARKER** (Richard[2],William[1]) who was still living on the Cross Swamp patent in Nansemond in 1698. That premise is used here. Any documented proof to the contrary will be gratefully accepted.

William[4] **PARKER** was granted 282 acres in the Upper Parish of Nansemond 20 October 1704, as previously noted. It is described as "near the head of **BENNETTS** Creek a branch of Chowan river begining at a stake standing in John **KING**s line & a Corner stake of **BENTON**s land & runing thence North Westerly thirty degrees one hundd. & Sixteen pole to a poplar a Corner tree of John **KING**s Land thence North Westerly twelve degrees sixteen poles crossing a branch to a white oake a Line tree of **SUMNER**s land thence South easterly Eighty three degrs. Fourty two pole to a pine thence North Easterly thirty one degrees two hundred & Sixteen poles bounding in part on the said **SUMNER** to a pine thence North Easterly thirty three degrees fifty one pole to a pine thence South Easterly thirty two degrees two hundd. & thirty pole to a White Oake thence South Westerly twelve degrees fourty two pole to a pine a Corner tree of **BENTON**s land thence South Westerly Eighty two degrees one hundd. Eighty four pole to a pine bounding on the said **BENTON** to another pine his Corner tree thence bounding on him the said **BENTON** his Land to the first Stacon...for the transportacon of six persons..."[1] This land lies at **WIGGINS** Crossroads, now in Gates County. The "**SUMNER**" referred to above was William **SUMNER**, and "**BENTON**" was Epaphroditus **BENTON**.

William[4] **PARKER** is reputed to have married Ann **KING**, daughter of Henry **KING**, who made his will in 1714. Early researchers stated that there was a "**KING** Bible" that showed this William **PARKER** as married to his daughter, Ann, and that Richard **PARKER** married her sister, Mary **KING**. No evidence of such a record has ever been found for William[4] and Ann, and Richard **PARKER** has been proven to have been married to a Hannah, of unknown surname.

William[4] **PARKER**, Planter, sold 75 acres to James **HUBBARD**, Wheelwright, "this day of October 1736." This parcel is described as "part of a tract of 170 acres granted to John **SMALL**, Jr. by patent 10 July 1719, by sd. John **SMALL** made over to W. **PARKER** by deed dated 25 Nov 1724 as by records of Nansemd. Beginning at a Gum standing in a branch called the Flatt Branch thence No. Easterly to a certain Pine thence East to a Gum standing in the Loosing Swamp thence down sd swamp to **POWELL**s corner tree a Gum thence along **POWELL**s line to a Gum standing in the sd Flatt Branch so along sd branch the several courses thereof & bounded thereon to the first mentioned [sic]..." Witnesses to this deed were James ( | ) **BENTON**, Thos. **PARKER**, and John **BENTON**.[2]

William[4] **PARKER** purchased 50 acres of land from John **GRIFFIN** on 17 March 1736. This land lay on the west side of **BENNETT**'s Creek, beginning at a red oak by the side of the creek, John **KING**'s corner, on his line, then northwest to a pine "in dividing line of sd. **GRIFFIN**s and

---

[1] VSLA, 9:635

[2] Haun, *Chowan County, North Carolina Deed Books: W-1 1729-1738; C-2 1738-1740; D 1748-1806 and various earlier & later dates, Vol. I,* c. 1998, W#1:304, #111:21

**PARKER**, down sd. Line NE to a red oak by side of Mare Branch, down Mare Branch to **BENNETT**'s Creek to the first station." It was part of a tract granted to Henry **JOURNIGAN** in 1703.[3] He sold that 50 acres of land to John **WILLIAMSON**, 11 June 1742.[4] It was located on the south side of Mare Branch and mentions "the patent line." This deed was proved 8 March 1742/43.

William[4] **PARKER** appears to have purchased other lands adjoining the John **SMALL**, Jr., patent, as well as the 75 acres he sold to James **HUBBARD**. As this land was in Nansemond County, no record remains of any other purchases he made prior to 1729. James and Elisabeth **JONES**, sold Thomas **WIGGINS** 89 acres on 30 September 1741, part of a "tract lying on the head of a swamp known by the name of the Lo<u>ss</u>ing [sic] Swamp...part of a tract Granted to John **SMALL** Sener. [sic] by patent dated in VA 11 Jul 1719 & sold by sd John **SMALL** by Deed of Sale dated 20 Oct 1724 to John **JONES**..." It began at a pine on the south side of the Loosing Swamp, to the Flat Branch and to a corner on William **PARKER** and back to the Loosing Swamp.[5] Loosing Swamp is now known as "Folly Swamp," in Gates County, and flows west from the Dismal Swamp.

William[4] **PARKER** made his will in Chowan County 27 December 1750. It began, "In the Name of God amen I William **PARKER** of Chowan County in the province of North Carolina being Sick and weak do make and Ordain this my Last will and Testament in manner and forme following that is to Say first I Bequeath my soul to almighty God hopeing that my lord and God will pardon all my Sins And Recieve me into his mantions of Etarnal Bliss and as for what worldly Goods it hath Pleased almighty God to bestow upon me I Do Give and Dispose thereof as followeth Viz

Imprimis first I will that all my Just Debts be honestly payd and Discharged

Item    I Leave to my Loving wife Ann **PARKER** the use of my plantation whereon I now Live Dureing her Natural Life and after her Decead I Do give and Bequeath my Said Plantation together with all the Land I Now Own to my Son James **PARKER** and to his heirs and assigns for ever

Item    I Leave the use of all my other Estate of what Nature or Kindsoever to my Said Wife Ann **PARKER** Dureing her widdowhood and at the Change of her Condition Either By Marriage or Death then I Give to my Son Benjamine **PARKER** One Likely Cow and Calf and then I also give to my Daughter Judeth **DUKE** the wife of Thomas **DUKE** one Cow and Calf and one Shilling Sterling I Give to the heirs of My Daughter Ann **FRENCH** And [sic] all the Rest and Residue of my Said Estate at the Decease or marriage of my Said Wife I Do give to be Equally Divided amongst All my children (<u>to</u>witt) James **PARKER** William **PARKER** Thomas **PARKER** Benjamine **PARKER** John **PARKER** Mary **FRYER** and Judeth **DUKE** in Equal Divisions ___ [torn] to Shear and Shear aLike to Each of them

___ [Illegible word] I Nominate and appoint my Said Wife Ann **PARKER** and My Son James **PARKER** to be Executrix and Executor to this my Last will and Testament to See it honestly fulfilled in Each perticuler in witness whereof I have hereunto Set my hand and fixt my Seal the twenty Seventh Day of December anno Dominia 1750

William **PARKER** {Seal}

Signed and Sealed and by the Testator    }
Published and Declaired to be his           }         Exerx Qualified
Last will and Testament in the presents of}         Mr. **SUMNER** to pay    pd
       his
William  W  **WATERS**
       mark
       his
Henry  H  **GRIFFEN** Jurat
       marke
Demsey **SUMNER** Jurat

---

[3]  Chowan County, NC Deed Book W#1:303
[4]  Haun, *Chowan County, North Carolina Deed Books: A-1, E-1, F-1, F-2, G-1 (Deeds dated 1701-1755) Vol. II,* c. 1999, A#1:162, 29:#126
[5]  Ibid., A#1:28, 5:#22

## Chapter 5:  William[4] **PARKER** *(Thomas[3],Richard[2],William[1])*

North Carolina  }                                          July county Court 1751
Chowan County}ss        Present his Majestys Justices
These may Certifies [sic] that Henry **GRIFFEN** and Demsey **SUMNER** two of the Subscribing Eve-
dences to the within will appeared in open Court and made oath on the Holy Evangelists of almighty
God that they were Present and Saw William **PARKER** sign seal Publish and declare the within to be
and Contain his Last will and Testament and that the said William **PARKER** was then and at that time
of Sound and Disposing Memory and they also Saw William **WALTORS** the other Subscribing Eve-
dance Sign his Name thereto at the same time: then also appeared Ann **PARKER** Executrix of the
within will and Testament named in open Court and took the Executors oath in due form of Law.  Ordered that the Honol. Nathaniel **RICE** Esqr Secratary of said Province or his Deputy have Notice
thereof that letters Testamentory Issue thereon as the Law Directs  Test J. H **CRAVEN** C. C."[6]

James[5] **PARKER** *(William[4],Thomas[3],Richard[2],William[1])* first appears in Chowan County
Court records as one of the witnesses proving the will of John **HUBBARD** on 17 April 1735/36.  At
that same court, he was also a witness proving a deed from Moses **HALL** to John **HUBBARD**, dated
28 January 1734/35[7].  William[4] **PARKER** was one of the other witnesses to both those documents.[8]
James[5] also witnessed a deed from John **HUBBARD** to Thomas **PARKER** on 15 June 1736, and one
from John **BENTON** to James **BENTON**, 22 September 1736.[9]  His year of birth is estimated here to
have been circa 1713.  The **BENTON**s, **SUMNER**s and **PARKER**s had remained friends and neighbors for at least 31 years.  The William[4] **PARKER** family lived to the east of **BENNETT**'s Creek, thus
remained in Chowan County in 1759, when Hertford County was formed.

James[5] **PARKER** made oath in Chowan County Court 19 January 1743/44, that his family
consisted of four white persons, including himself, his wife, William[6] and James[6].  During the course of
that same court, he was appointed overseer of the road, "from the parting of the Road at John **BEN-
TON**s to the County line."[10]  In references to October Court 1752, a deed of sale of land from William
and Ann **JONES** to James **PARKER** was acknowledged and ordered to be registered.[11]  It does not
appear in the Chowan County Deed Books, but it should have been in the infamous Book F#1.  A description of this land appears later in Gates County records.

James[5] shared property lines with his brother, Benjamin[5] **PARKER**, John **WILLIAMSON**,
Demsey **SUMNER,** and Elijah and Jethro **BENTON**, in 1756.[12]  These are obviously some of the lands
left to him by his father.  In an order for processioning for all the land between Flat Branch and the
Country line, and along **BENNETT**'s Creek to the main road, issued 23 October 1764, James[5] shared
lines with Edward **ARNELL**, John **DARDEN**, Epaphroditus **BENTON**, and Demsey **SUMNER**.
Jacob **NORFLEET** and David **JONES** were the processioners.[13]

On 11 May 1780, James[5] **PARKER**, Sr., sold 84½ acres of land in Gates County to William[5]
**PARKER**, Sr., for £20.  It is described as the "tract, plantation & parcel of land that the said James
**PARKER** bought of Wm. **JONES**...situated in the fork between the rich thicket and Oarepeak Swamp.
Beginning at Joseph **JONES** corner on the south side of Oarepeake Swamp and running down the said
swamp binding thereon the rich thicket swamp thence up the said swamp till it intersects the land of
Joseph **JONES** aforesaid, thence along his line to the first station, 84½ acres and being a part of a tract
containing 159 acres granted to Wm. **JONES** baring [sic] date by patent 17 Nov. 1700 and by the said
Wm. **JONES** Senior in his last will and Testament given to his son John **JONES** during his natural life

---

[6]  NCSA, Chowan County, NC Wills, SS/AR

[7]  Haun, *Chowan County, North Carolina Deed Books: W-1 1729-1738; C-2 1738-1740; D 1748-1806 and various earlier & later dates, Vol. I*, c. 1998, W#1:264, 13:#72,

[8]   Haun, *Chowan County North Carolina County Court Minutes (Court of Pleas & Quarter Sessions) 1735-
1738:1746-1748, Book II*, c. 1983, 4:#7

[9]  Haun, *Chowan County, North Carolina Deed Books: W-1 1729-1738; C-2 1738-1740; D 1748-1806 and various earlier & later dates, Vol. I*, c. 1998, W#1:305-306;305, 21:#113,#112

[10]  Haun, *Chowan County North Carolina County Court Minutes Pleas & Quarter Sessions 1730-1745*, c. 1983,
79:#170;#171

[11]  Haun, *Chowan County North Carolina County Court Minutes 1749-1754 Book III*, c. 1992, 77:#154

[12]  Fouts, *Processioners' Records Chowan County, North Carolina 1755/1756; 1764/1765; 1795-1797; 1800
and 1808*, c. 1993, 2:#2;7:#11-12;13:#22

[13]  Ibid., 21-22:#39

**Chapter 5:** William[4] **PARKER** *(Thomas[3],Richard[2],William[1])*

and after his decease to his grandson Wm. **JONES** by a deed of sale the said **JONES** conveyed the same to James **PARKER** above, said party to these presents..." Witnesses to this deed were Demcy (X) **JONES**, William and Edward **ARNOLD**.[14] This is the land he purchased in 1752, from William and Ann **JONES**.

In February, 1783, James[5] **PARKER** made a deed of gift to his son, Amos[6] **PARKER**. It was made "this day of February" and was for the "love and good will that I have for my son Amos **PARKER** of said County, give and grant all and singly goods and chattels-all my lands and plantation, all my stoc both Horces and Cattle and Negro in Dores and out of Dores-To have and to hold..." It was signed by James[5] and witnessed by William **ARNOLD** and Josiah **BRINCKLEY**.[15] No record of his death has been found. The purpose in tracing this James **PARKER** is to separate him from another James, who also had a son named Amos. They are easily blended into one without careful use of the land records.

Amos[6] **PARKER** was probably the youngest son of James[5] **PARKER,** as he had stated in 1744 that his children were named William[6] and James[6]. Further proof of this is found in the will of William[6] **PARKER**, Sr., *(James[5],William[4],Thomas[3],Richard[2],William[1])* made 28 October 1788, in Gates County. He initially left all his lands and plantation, Negroes, stock of all kinds, and all his goods, to his "well beloved wife Elisabeth **PARKER**," during her natural life and widowhood. He gave his son John[7] one Negro boy and £7..10 in Virginia Currency. He gave to son William[7] "my an-nuel Plantation, a Boffat belonging to my House, but if he should die without Heirs, to fall to my son Kedar." The rest of his worldly estate was to be equally divided among the rest of his children, "namely viz my Son William **PARKER**, Willis **PARKER**, Kedar **PARKER**, Treacy **PARKER**, Polly **PARKER**, Umphry **PARKER**, James **PARKER**, Hugh Griffin **PARKER**." He named his wife, Elizabeth, son William[7], and "my Brother Amos **PARKER**" as executors to his will. It was witnessed by Kedar[7] (X) **PARKER**, Willis[7] (X) **PARKER**, and Abraham **VINCENT**.[16] This will, along with an inventory of the estate, was exhibited in May Court 1789, by William[7] and Amos[6] **PARKER**, and proved by the oaths of Kedar[7] and Willis[7] **PARKER**, who relinquished their rights as legatees.[17]

William[6] **PARKER** was dead by 22 January 1789, as evidenced by the inventory of his estate taken that day by William[7] (X) and Amos[6] (X) **PARKER**.[18] It is unclear as to the reason for the delay in exhibiting the will and inventory, completely bypassing the February Court. Elizabeth **PARKER**'s maiden name was most probably **GRIFFIN**, as the names Humphrey and Hugh both appear in that family. Naming a child "Hugh Griffin **PARKER**" would certainly lend weight to that conclusion. She was dead before 2 April 1804, when an inventory of her estate was taken. Humphrey[7] **PARKER**, John **DUKE** and Moses H. (X) **SMALL** appeared on an administration bond 21 May 1804, in the amount of £200, for Humphrey[7] to administer on the estate of Elizabeth **PARKER**, deceased.[19]

Not all of William[6] **PARKER**'s children were adults at the time of his death. In May Court 1796, it was ordered "that Humphry **PARKER**, orphan of William **PARKER**, decd about Eighteen years of age be bound as an Apprentice to Charles **JONES** to learn the Buisiness [sic] of a Taylor &c." In November Court 1796, it was ordered "that James **PARKER**, orphan of William **PARKER**, about Sixteen years of age be bound an Apprentice to Thomas **PARKER** to learn the Buisiness of Cooper &c."[20]

William[6] **PARKER** purchased 100 acres of land in Chowan County 2 July 1753, from Mat-thew **HUBBARD**, of Bertie County. It is described as "Lying on a Swamp commonly Called the Rich Thicket Swamp and beginning at a pine on the south side of said Swamp near the mouth of a small branch and runs thence according to the Course of the Patent of the said land SW 80 deg 200 po. to a

---

[14] Gates County Deed Book A:59

[15] Ibid., A:53, Second Section

[16] Almasy, *Gates County, North Carolina Wills 1779-1807*, c. 1984, p. 74, Will Book 1:80

[17] Fouts, *Minutes of County Court of Pleas and Quarter Sessions Gates County, North Carolina 1787-1793*, c. 1995, 40:#71

[18] NCSA, C.R.041.508.88, Gates County Estates Records Folder: William Parker, Sr. 1789

[19] NCSA, G.041.2194761, Gates County Estates, Record of 1765-1920, Vol. Parker, E.-Parker, M., Folder: Parker, Elizabeth 1804, Doc. #577;579

[20] Fouts, *Minutes of County Court of Pleas and Quarter Sessions Gates County, North Carolina 1794-1799, Volume I*, c. 1984, 55:#112; 67:#135

pine thence NW 5d 74 po. to a poplar, thence NE 82d 96 po to a Live oak thence NE 35d so far as to include the quantity of 100 acres and thence on an Easterly course down the Poquotion to the Extint of the afsd. Patent-part of a patent of 500 acres granted to Thomas **MILNER** 7 November 1700—sold by **MILNER** to John **HUBARD** Father to sd. Mathew **HUBARD** partie to these presents who by last will and testament 15 October 1734 gave to said Mathew..." William[6] **PARKER** sold 21 acres of this land to Edward **ARNELL** 11 June 1774, and he and his wife, Elizabeth, sold 79 more acres to John **DUKE** 3 February 1775.[21]

William[7] **PARKER**, Jr., *(William[6],James[5],William[4],Thomas[3],Richard[2],William[1])* died in August 1793. An inventory of his estate was taken on 17 August 1793, and on 20 August an administrator's bond was issued for Sarah (X) **PARKER** and Amos[6] (X) **PARKER** to administer on the estate of William[7] **PARKER**, deceased. Jethro **BENTON** and James **JONES** were bondsmen. He was termed "William **PARKER**, Jr." in the account of sales of part of his estate dated 13 September 1793, by James **GATLING**, Sheriff.[22] In May Court 1796, it was "Ordered Kedar **BALLARD**, Esq., Miles **BENTON**, James **KNIGHT**, and Jethro **BENTON** audit the accounts of Amos **PARKER**, Administrator of William **PARKER**, junr., dec'd and that they make a division of the Estate of William **PARKER**, Sen. and William **PARKER**, junr. dec'd."[23] Those two accounts were settled 18 November 1797. The one for William[7] **PARKER**, Jr., was an account with Amos[6] **PARKER**, Admr., and Sarah **PARKER**, Admrx. In that account, the widow was paid £12.10 "for Keeping the Orphan Child 18 months." The child is not named in this record. Sarah received £21.3.11½ as her right of dower. The balance was divided among his brothers and sisters, with each allotted £6.1.1.¾. They were named as John[7], Willis[7], Kedar[7], Humphrey[7], James[7], and Mary[7] **PARKER**, and Theresa[7] **WIGGINS**. It appears that Hugh Griffin[7] **PARKER** did not survive.

In May term 1804, a petition submitted to Gates County Court sheds a great deal of light on the family of William[7] **PARKER, Jr.** It is fully transcribed here and is self-explanatory.

"May Term 1804 Gates County

To the Worshipful Court Now Sitting – The petition of Humphry **PARKER**, in behalf of himself and John **PARKER**, Willis **PARKER**, Kedah **PARKER**, and James **PARKER**, brothers of William **PARKER** des'd, Son of Wm. **PARKER** Senr decsd'. Humbly Sheweth that on or about the year 1789 Wm. **PARKER** Senr departed this Life, Leaving a Written Will &c by which Will he devised to his Son William Certain Lands, and in Case the Sd. Wm. Junr. should die without Issue, then the Said Land was to be to Kadah **PARKER** Son of the decsd But So it Was, the Said Wm. Junr departed this Life on or about the Year 1794 [sic] Leaving a daughter by the name of Esther, and the Said Esther departed this life on or about the Year 1795, your petitioner on his own part, and on the part of his other brothers above Named, Considering themselves the legal representatives Heirs of the Said William **PARKER** Junr dec'd., Prays your Worships to take the Case Under Your Consideration and pass an Order for the division of Said Land, that Was the property of Sd. William Junr. & his daughter Esther between your petitioner and his brothers above Namd and your petitioner as in duty bound Will Ever pray &c Humphry **PARKER**

NB  William **PARKER** Junr intermarried with Sarah **BROTHERS**, having one daughter Esther, She died as aforesd, Sarah, relict of the Said William Intermarried with William **BRINKLEY** by whom she hath two Children Still living &c. H. **P.**

Kedar **BALLARD** & Miles **BENTON** Esqs. Ordered that Thomas **PARKER**, Thomas **BALLARD** and Elisha **HARE**, make a division of the Real Estate, a Greable to the prayer of the Petitioners with the Surveyor."[24] William[7] **PARKER** appears on a marriage bond with Sarah **BROTHERS** dated 24 December 1791, with Amos **PARKER** as his bondsman.[25]

Humphrey[7] **PARKER** *(William[6],James[5],William[4],Thomas[3],Richard[2],William[1])* raised a family

---

[21]  Chowan County, NC, Deed Book G#1:9; Q#1:50; Q#1:211

[22]  NCSA, C.R.041.508.88, Gates County Estates Records, , Folder: William Parker 1793

[23]  NCSA, G.041.2194762, Gates County Estates, Record of 1765-1920, Vol. Parker-Pierce, Folder: Parker, William, Jr. 1793, Doc. #712

[24]  NCSA, G.041.2194762, Gates County Estates, Record of 1765-1920, Vol. Parker-Pierce, Folder: Parker, William, Jr. 1793, Doc. #717-718

[25]  Almasy, *Gates County, North Carolina Marriage Bonds 1778-1868*, c. 1987, p. 69

of his own, in Gates County, and was dead by November 1854. E. R. **HARRELL** was his administrator.[26] The well-preserved records of Gates County provide ample resources for the researcher to further trace the members of these families.

Benjamin[5] **PARKER** *(William[4],Thomas[3],Richard[2],William[1])* first appears in the Chowan County records when he was excused from Grand Jury duty in April Court 1743.[27] In order to be a juror, he would be required to be 21 years of age, and a freeholder in the county. He witnessed a deed from Joseph **JONES** to Moses **HAIR**, 29 August 1747.[28] Benjamin[5] purchased 195 acres of land on the south side of Elmn [sic] Swamp, from James **ELLIOTT** 12 April 1749, "beginning at a gum in **WOODS** line as by Patent granted Demsey **SUMNER**, 10 June 1728, several courses of said patent to the first station...sold by Demsey **SUMNER** to James **ELLIOTT**..."[29] This deed was witnessed by Thomas **FRAZER**, William **PARKER**, and Hardy (H) **MORGIN**.

Benjamin[5] **PARKER** appears to have been married to Sarah **JONES**, daughter of Henry **JONES**, who made his will in Chowan County 11 February 1754. In that will, he bequeathed one cow and calf to his daughter, May **LOVEL**, one Shilling Sterling to daughter Jane **CHAMPION**, one Shilling Sterling to son William **JONES**, and one cow and calf to daughter Sarah **PARKER**. The rest of his estate was left to his wife, Elizabeth **JONES**. She, and Benjamin **PARKER,** were appointed executrix and executor. Henry signed his will with "H" as his mark, and his witnesses were Henry **BONNER**, John **LUTEN**, and Samuel **LUTEN**. The will was exhibited into April Court 1754, and proved by the witnesses. Elizabeth **JONES** came into court and qualified as executrix, but there is no mention of Benjamin **PARKER**. He may have simply refused to serve.[30] He was still living as of 2 April 1756, when his land was processioned in the Corapeake area.[31] No further information.

Thomas[5] **PARKER** *(William[4],Thomas[3],Richard[2],William[1])* first appears in Chowan County records in a deed for 40 acres of land from Littleton **SPIVEY**, son of John **SPIVEY**, to John **BENTON**, dated 30 October 1733. John **SPIVEY** left his patent to his sons, Littleton and John, and it began at a corner tree of John **BENTON**'s patent and was bounded on his line to a "marked pine standing in or near a dividing line between John **BENTON** & one Thomas **PARKER**..."[32] Thomas' date of birth is estimated here to have been circa. 1712. On 15 June 1736, John (+) **HUBBARD** sold Thomas **PARKER** two tracts of an estimated 145 acres of land. The beginning of this deed reads as though it were between John **HUBBARD** and William **PARKER,** but the other references to the grantee as Thomas **PARKER** correct that. This land is described as "part whereof was by LW&T of John **HUBBARD** deceased given & bequeathed to sd John **HUBBARD** party to these presents Vizt: I give unto my son John **HUBBARD** part of land that I took up which binds upon Moses **HALLS** land & Richd. **FELTON**s & John **NORFLET**s land unto a pine an old corner tree & from thence near about a West Course with a line of markd. Trees unto a Gum a markd tree of same survey...with privilege of getting Timber & Trees upon my land given unto my son Mathew...as by the sd Will dated 15 Oct 1734... The other tract lately purchased by sd John **HUBBARD** party to these presents, beginning at a White Oak a line tree of **LASSITOR**s land..." Witnesses to this deed were W. **PARKER**, Thos. **PARKER**, and James **PARKER**.[33] Thomas[5] has already been mentioned as a witness to the deed from William **PARKER** to James **HUBBARD**, dated October 1736.

Richard **FELTON** sold 75 acres of land to Thomas[5] **PARKER** 21 January 1737/38. It is described as "part of a patent granted to Jno. **SMALL** for 150 acres, 13 November 1721, and sold to **FELTON** by **SMALL** 23 October 1722, beginning at a marked pine, to a gum and by line of marked

---

[26] NCSA, C.R.041.508.85, Gates County Estates Records, Humphrey Parker 1854 File

[27] Haun, *Chowan County, North Carolina Miscellaneous Papers 1685-1744, Book I*, 110:#433-64

[28] Haun, *Chowan County, North Carolina Deed Books: W-1 1729-1738, C-2 1738-1740, D 1748-1806 and various earlier & later dates, Vol. I*, c. 1998, C#2:182-183, 115:#583

[29] Chowan County, North Carolina, Deed Book F#1:221

[30] NCSA, Chowan County, NC Wills, SS

[31] Fouts, *Processioners' Records Chowan County, North Carolina 1755/1756; 1764/1765; 1795-1797; 1800 and 1808*, c. 1993, 7:12

[32] Haun, *Chowan County, North Carolina Deed Books: W-1 1729-1738, C-2 1738-1740, D 1748-1806 and various earlier & later dates, Vol. I*, c. 1998, W#1:226-227, 6:#32

[33] Haun, *Chowan County, North Carolina Deed Books: W-1 1729-1738, C-2 1738-1740, D 1748-1806 and various earlier & later dates, Vol. I*, c. 1998, W#1:305-306, 21:#113

trees to a pine in the dividing line between sd. Thos. **PARKER** and Rd. **BOND** who hath bought the other part or quantity of 75 acres..." Witnesses to this deed were James **GRIFFIN**, Junr., John (S) **FULKS**, and Jno. **SUMNER**.[34] Thomas[5] sold this parcel to Joseph **JONES** 10 October 1738. Witnesses to this deed were Jno. **SUMNER**, Jno. **JOHNSTON**, and Edward (E) **ARNALL**.[35]

John **LASSITER** was granted a patent for 82 acres 23 October 1703. It is described as "Land Scituate & being in the upper parish of Nansemond County near a place called the Rich thicket begining at a pine a Corner tree of Thomas **MILNER**s Land & runing thence South Westerly Sixty Six degrees ninety Six pole to a white Oake thence North Westerly forty eight degrees Eighty pole to a Maple thence North Easterly twenty two degrees Sixty pole to a white Oake thence North Easterly Sixty three degs. Thirty Six pole to a poplar standing in the sd **MILNER**s line thence along his line South Easterly Eighty two degs: Eighty Eight pole to a poplar **MILNER**s corner tree thence South Easterly five degs. Seventy four pole bounding on **MILNER** to the first Stacon..."[36] John **LASSITER** sold this parcel of land to Thomas[5] **PARKER** in a Chowan County deed that begins "The beginning of this Deed is tore out of the Book." The index lists this deed as being created in 1739.[37] This parcel of land stayed in the family.

Thomas[5] **PARKER** made his will in Chowan County 23 August 1762, as transcribed here in full: "In the name of God amen I Thomas **PARKER** of Chowan County being sick and weak of Body but thanks be to god of perfect mind and memory and calling to mind the uncertain State of this life do make constitute and ordain this my last will and testament in manner and form following

First I recommend my soul to god who gave it and my Body to the Earth hoping to obtain throw this merit of my saviour a happy Resurrection and as touching my temporal Estate which almighty God has bestowed upon me after my Just debts are paid I give and bequeath as follows.

I give to my son Thomas my manor plantation unto it belonging containing two hundred and seventy three acres to be the same more or less to him and his heirs forever.

It is my desire that all the remainder part of my Estate both real and personal be equally devided among my nine children Viz Pricilla, Sarah, Abm, Absolam, Judith, Ruth, Telpah, Thomas & Margaret

Lastly I nominate and appoint my daughter Pricilla and my friend Jethro **BENTON** to be executrix and Executor of this my last will Revoking all former Wills by me made heretofore and acknowledge this only to be my last Will In Witness I have hereunto set my hand and seal the 23rd day of August 1762.

<table>
<tr><td>Sealed, and delivered in presence</td><td>Thomas **PARKER**</td></tr>
<tr><td>of William **PARKER**</td><td></td></tr>
<tr><td>James **PARKER**</td><td></td></tr>
<tr><td>Jacob **NORFLEET**</td><td></td></tr>
<tr><td>James **HARRIS**"[38]</td><td></td></tr>
</table>

This will was produced in open court 18 December 1771, proved by the oath of William **PARKER**, and Jethro **BENTON** qualified as one of the executors.[39] He made the sale of the estate on 9 January 1772.[40] Thomas[6] **PARKER**, to whom his father had left all his lands, bought several items at that sale, including "One Walnutt desk, One Looking Glass, One pine Chest, and One Trunk." The only other children who made any purchases were Ruth[6] and Judith[6] **PARKER**, though other relatives also appear. Among them were James, William, Judith, Josiah, John, Luke and Moses **PARKER**. Jethro **BENTON**'s account with the estate of Thomas **PARKER** is dated 11 June 1772, and the amount of the sale was £562:12:11. After all outstanding accounts were paid, "Their being nine Childring [sic] to Shear the Estate it amounts of £46..0..5½ to each is £432:4:1½. Their is a balance

---

[34] Chowan County, NC Deed Book W#1:373

[35] Ibid., C#2:63

[36] VSLA, 9:567-8

[37] Chowan County, NC Deed Book C#2:222

[38] Chowan County, NC Will Book A:220

[39] NCSA, C.024.30007, Chowan County Court Minutes & Ref. Docket, Pleas & Quarter Sessions 1762-1772, Court session from 18 December to 20 December 1771. Pages are not numbered.

[40] NCSA, C.024.50001, Chowan County Record of Estates 1701-1790, 1 Vol., pages not numbered, courtesy of Weynette Parks Haun, Durham, NC

£1.9.1¾ deducted from Each Shear which brings the Above Portion to £46..11.3¾."[41]

The petition of Enos **ROGERS** and his wife, Telpha, [sic] states that "Thomas **PARKER** late of Chowan County father of your Petitioner Telpha being possessed of a considerable Estate amounting to the Sum two thousand pounds specie and upwards on or about the Twenty Third day of August in the year of our Lord one thousand seven hundred and sixty two made & published his last Will & Testament in Writing by which after giving his Plantation to one of his Sons, directed that all the Remainder part of his Estate == both Real & personal should be equally divided between his Nine Children and appointed a certain Jethro **BENTON** and his Daughter Priscilla his Executors and soon after died leaving your Petitioner and eight other Children Your Petitioners further Shew that soon after the death of the said Thomas **PARKER** the said Jethro **BENTON** proved the said Will and took upon ~~His~~ himself the Execution of the ~~said~~ same and possessed himself of the whole Estate of the said Testator of the Value aforesaid sold the same at publick vendue and applied the money to his own use never having rendered any answer to your Petitioners tho they have often requested him to come to a Settlement and to Account with them for the principal & Interest, which the said Jethro hath...refused..."[42] The petition requested of the court that they compel Jethro **BENTON** to settle the account with them. This petition also states that Telpha had married Enos **ROGERS** after the death of her father. A penciled date of 1762, on the bottom of this document, is obviously in error. The document itself is undated, but must have been submitted to the court well after 9 January 1772, the date of the sale of the estate. There is quite a discrepancy between the amounts of money in these two records. No record of a resolution of this issue has been found.

---

[41]  NCSA  G.041.2194762, Gates County Estates, Record of 1765-1920, Vol. Parker-Pierce, Folder:  Parker, Thomas 1772, Doc. #531-533
[42]  Ibid., Folder: Parker, Thomas 1762, Doc. #527-528

## Thomas[6] PARKER *(Thomas[5],William[4],Thomas[3],Richard[2],William[1])*

Thomas[6] **PARKER** *(Thomas[5],William[4],Thomas[3],Richard[2],William[1])* married Mary **ARNOLD** 20 March 1773.[1] His date of birth is estimated here to be circa 1752. Mary is reputed to have been a daughter of William **ARNOLD**, but that appears to be in error. She was the daughter of Edward **ARNOLD** who died circa 1777. The division of his estate was made 13 June 1777, to heirs named William, Edward, John, and Richard **ARNOLD**, as well as Elizabeth **NORFLEET**, Pleasant **KNIGHT**, Mary **PARKER**, Bathsheba **ARNOLD**, and Esther **ARNOLD**.[2] Thomas[6] and Mary were married about four years before the death of her father. They named their first child Edward.

The first identifiable land record for Thomas[6] **PARKER** is a deed from James **KNIGHT**, of Nansemond County, VA, 15 October 1775, to "Thomas **PARKER**, son of Thomas of Chowan County" for 50 acres of land. It lay at a place called the Ridge Thicket, beginning on the south west of the Ridge Thicket Road, binding on the lands of Edward **ARNELL** until it joined the lands of Thomas **PARKER**, "party to these presents." It was one-half of a parcel purchased from Thomas **MILNER** 21 March 1737. It is further described as running along Thomas's line until it joined other lands of Edward **ARNELL**, then along his line to Ridge Thicket Road, then along the road southeasterly to the first station.[3] Part of the "lands of Edward **ARNELL**" mentioned in this deed is the parcel that William[6] **PARKER** sold to **ARNELL** 11 June 1774. When James **KNIGHT** bought it from Thomas **MILNER**, it was adjoining John **HUBBARD**.[4]

Thomas[6] **PARKER**'s main occupation was cooper, a maker of barrels, kegs, casks and tubs. On 1 May 1780, Thomas **CASPEY**, orphan of William **CASPEY**, about the age of 12 years, was bound as an apprentice to Thomas[6] **PARKER** to "Learn the Buisiness [sic] of a Cooper."[5] He has been previously mentioned as having taken James[7] **PARKER**, son of William[6], as an apprentice cooper. His third apprentice to that trade was Nathl. **HALL**, a mulatto boy about 20 years of age, in February 1806.[6] His fourth apprentice was William **MINOR**, bound to him 18 August 1817.[7] It should be kept in mind that the Census enumerators would count these young men as part of the family.

Thomas[6] was a well-respected member of his community as evidenced by the Gates County Court having appointed him, Edward **ARNELL**, and Isaac **WALTERS** as Assessors to assess the taxable property in the District or Muster Bounds of Captains Jethro **SUMNER** and James **ARLINE** in August of 1781.[8] In November court of that year, it was ordered that the Assessors be allowed $300 for each and every day they were employed in assessing the taxable property in their districts.[9] This record is rather ambiguous as to whether the amount paid was to each Assessor, or to each group of three who were so appointed. The latter is the more likely of the two possibilities.

Thomas[6] next purchased 70 acres from Edward **ARNOLD** 15 December 1786. It lay on the west side of the Thicket Road, on the south side of a new line of marked trees and ran up a certain branch near a place called the "Turnup Patch," to the said **PARKER**'s line and was part of a patent for 200 acres to Thomas **MILNER**. **MILNER** sold it to John **HUBBARD**, "who by his last will and testament dated 15 October 1734, did devise the said land to his son Mathew, who sold it to Wm. **PARKER**, who sold it to John **DUKE**, who sold it to Edward **ARNOLD** whose heir was Wm. **AR-**

---

[1] Gates County Historical Society, *Bible Records of Gates County, NC*, c. unknown, p. 152

[2] NCSA, C.024.99009, Chowan Co. Misc. Papers, 1772-1782, Vols. 15, 16, 15:123-125

[3] Chowan County, NC, Deed Bk. Q#1:269

[4] Haun, *Chowan County, North Carolina Deed Books: W-1 1729-1738; C-2 1738-1740; D 1748-1806 and various earlier & later dates Vol. I*, c. 1998, W#1:374-375, 34:#184

[5] Fouts, *Minutes of County Court of Pleas and Quarter Sessions Gates County, North Carolina 1779-1786*, c. 1994, 16:#28

[6] Ibid., *1806-1811 Vol. III*, c. 1985, 9:#499

[7] Ibid., *1812-1817, Vol. IV*, c. 1986, 149:#995

[8] Ibid., *1779-1786*, c. 1994, 35:#68

[9] Ibid., 40:#78

**NOLD** who gave it to Edward **ARNOLD**, partie to these presents..." It also joined to other lands of both **ARNOLD** and **PARKER**, as well as Moses **HARE** and Elizabeth **NORFLEET**.[10]

On 6 November 1788, Edward **ARNOLD,** and wife Elizabeth, sold Thomas[6] **PARKER** 58½ acres of land. It lay on the west side of Thicket Road, "Beginning where William **JONES** and said Thomas **PARKER**s line Joins, thence along the Said Road North fifty seven Degrees Sixty Six pole to William **ARNOLD**s line, then South thirty one Degrees west Seventy Eight Pole to a Holly thence south Eighteen Degrees West one Hundred & Seventy Six pole to a Sweet Gum a Corner Tree on Moses **BENTON**s line thence South fifty three Degrees East forty pole to a Gum thence North twenty three Degrees West thirty three pole to a white Oak Thence North fifty eight Degrees East thirty four pole to a Gum thence North thirty five Degrees East one Hundred & forty Nine pole to the first station...and is part of the land which William **ARNOLD** conveyed to Said Edward **ARNOLD** & is Known by the Name of the Thicket Perquoson..."[11]

They sold Thomas[6] another 27 acres 16 April 1789. This parcel lies on the west side of Thicket Road near the mouth of a small branch issuing out of Thicket Swamp. It then ran along the road to his line, then leaving the road, south 65° west, 48 poles, then north and east. It has the same chain of title as the 1786 deed for 70 acres.[12]

On Wednesday, 16 November 1790, Thomas[6] **PARKER** attended court and moved for administration on the estate of Elizabeth **NORFLEET**, his sister-in-law. He gave bond and security for his performance in the amount of £2,000, with William **HARRISS** and William **ELLIS** as his securities.[13]

In May Court of 1791, Thomas[6] **PARKER** was appointed guardian to Kinchen **NORFLEET**, orphan of Jacob **NORFLEET**, with bond and security for £1,000 with Jethro **BALLARD** and Abraham **MORGAN** as securities. In that same court session, Kinchen **NORFLEET**, about 16 years of age, was bound as an apprentice to William **LEWIS** to learn the business of house carpenter and joiner.[14] Jacob **NORFLEET** made his will 12 December 1778 and it was proved in August court 1780. He named his wife, Elizabeth, as executrix, along with son Kinchen and brother Abraham **NORFLEET** as his executors.[15] By November court of 1791, Thomas[6] **PARKER** had become administrator of both Jacob and Elizabeth and returned an account of sales of the perishable part of the said estates. Abraham **NORFLEET** was probably dead, as well as Elizabeth, and Kinchen was not of age, so could not administer on the estates.[16] Thomas[6] **PARKER** was also one of the executors to the will of Moses **BENTON** who died in August of 1793.[17] He was frequently a juror on both grand and petit juries and was appointed overseer of the road in May 1794.[18]

Thomas[6] made at least two more purchases of land. One was 32 acres from William **JONES**, 28 August 1801. It was a tract of "Woodland Ground...Beginning at Mills **ELLIS** line at the publick Road thence North 57° E 30 po. to a Gum Saplin thence North 20 East 21 po to a Red Oak thence North 44° wt. 34 pole to a pine the [sic] North 53° wt 75 pole to a Corner pine thence South 28° w 41 pole to the Aforesaid Road thence Binding on said Road to the first Station..." The second was another 14½ acres of "Woodland Ground" from Mills **ELLIS**, on 29 August 1801. It was described as being "on the North side of the Rich thicket Road Beginning at the Eastward Corner of a piece I purchased yesterday of William **JONES** thence North 57° East 30 pole to a Gum Saplin thence South 62° E 82 pole to a Holly in **NORFLEET**s line thence S 25° Wt 18 pole to a Water Oak thence binding on a line of Marked Trees and Various Courses Eastward until it Intersects with the aforesaid Road

---

[10] Gates County, NC Deed Book 1:259

[11] NCSA, C.041.40002, Gates County Real Estate Conveyances 1786-1795, Vol: 2,3, 2:46-47

[12] Gates County, NC Deeds, 2:16

[13] Fouts, *Minutes of County Court of Pleas and Quarter Sessions Gates County, North Carolina 1787-1793*, c. 1995, 72:#132

[14] Ibid., 83:#153-154

[15] Almasy, *Gates Co., NC Wills 1779-1807, Vol. I*, p. 7, Will Book 1:7

[16] Fouts, *Minutes of County Court of Pleas and Quarter Sessions Gates County, North Carolina 1787-1793*, c. 1995, 96:#178

[17] Ibid., 133:#248

[18] Fouts, *Minutes of County Court of Pleas and Quarter Sessions Gates County, North Carolina, 1794-1799, Vol. I*, c. 1984, 14:25

thence along said Road and binding on the same Westward to the First Station..." His son, Edward[7], was a witness to that deed.[19] Thomas[6] **PARKER**'s lands encompassed a large area in Northeastern Gates County, including the surrounding area of the community now known as "**PARKER**'s Fork."

His last land transaction appears to have been 1 June 1813, when he deeded one acre of land to Isaac **HUNTER**, Sr., Humphrey **PARKER**, Thomas **PARKER**, David **PARKER**, John **GWIN**, John **POWELL** and Jonathan **WILLIAMS**, trustees, in trust "that they Shall Erect and Build or Cause to be Erected and Built thereon A House or Place of Worship for the Use of the members of the Methodist Episcopal Church in the United States of America." It was described as "A Certain Lott or Piece of Ground...Beginning at a large Post Oak on Esther **HARE**s line runing to a Post Oak Humphrey **PARKER**s Corner thence to a Red Oak a New made Corner thence about a West Course 53 Steps to a Red Oak Oak [sic] a New made Corner thence along a line of Marked Trees 93 Steps to the Beginning..."[20] **PARKER**'s Methodist Church now stands on that acre of land.

Thomas[6] **PARKER** came into court on 16 February 1814, and moved for administration on the estate of his eldest son, Edward[7] **PARKER**, deceased. He gave bond of £1,000 and Moses **SPEIGHT** and John **DUKE** offered themselves as securities, who were approved by the court.[21] Thomas[6] took an inventory of Edward[7]'s estate, but the record is not dated. The sale of the estate was made 1 April 1814. Items were sold to Humphrey and Thomas **PARKER**, Richard H. and Kedar **BALLARD**, James **BENTON**, Mary **MINOR**, Jesse L. **HARE** and Joshua **SMALL**, among others.[22] Thomas[6] **PARKER** exhibited both inventory and account of sales into court 16 May 1814.[23]

Thomas[6] **PARKER** made his will 16 April 1825, as transcribed here in full:

"In the name of God amen I Thomas **PARKER** of Gates County and State of North Carolina being of sound & perfect mind and memory blessed be God I do this sixteenth day of April in the year of our lord One Thousand eight Hundred & twenty five make and publish this my last will and Testament in manner following that is to say.

Item I give and bequeath to my Daughter Margaret **PARKER** one <u>n</u>egro girl named **DINAH** one Bed & Furniture & one pine Chist

Item I give unto my Grand son Jordan **PARKER** one negro Man named **SAM** and all my Coopers Tools of every discription.

Item I give & bequeath to my Grand son Alfred **PARKER** one feather Bead & Furniture one Cow & Calf one sow & Pigs and four hundred Dollars in money.

Item I lend unto my Daughter Ruth **BRINKLEY** the houses & land whereon she now lives or as much land together with the plantation on which she lives as will make one Hundred Acres during her natural life. I also give her one Hundred Dollars in money.

Item I give unto my Daughter Elizabeth **MINOR** the I/n/terest of Six Hundred dollars during her natural life my <u>d</u>isire is that my friend John C **GORDON** who I shall appoint one of my Executors shall keep the above named Sum of Six Hundred dollars in his possession and pay the Interest on the same to my Daughter Elizabeth in that way and manner that he may think best for her and after her death to divide the principal equally between all her Children.

Item I give and bequeath the land above loaned to my daughter Ruth **BRINKLEY** there being one Hundred acres to be equally divided between all her Children after her death to them and their heirs forever.

Item I give and bequeath to my grand Daughter Margaret Ann **BALLARD** one Bed & furniture.

Item I give & bequeath all my lands not before given away to be equally divided between my daughters Ann **BALLARD** Mary **ODOM**, Margaret **PARKER** & Sarah **BRINKLEY** & to my grand

---

[19]  NCSA, C.041.40003, Gates County Real Estate Conveyances 1794-1803, Vol:4,5, 5:278-279

[20]  NCSA, C.041.40005, Gates County Real Estate Conveyances 1811-1812, 1815-1819, Vol: 9,10, 10:57-59

[21]  Fouts, *Minutes of County Court of Pleas and Quarter Sessions Gates County, North Carolina, 1812-1817, Vol. IV*, c. 1986, 49:#824

[22]   NCSA, G.041.2194761, Gates County Estates, Record of 1765-1920, Vol. Parker, E.-Parker, M. Folder: Parker, Edward 1814, Doc. #65; #61-64

[23]  Fouts, *Minutes of County Court of Pleas and Quarter Sessions Gates County, North Carolina, 1812-1817, Vol. IV*, c. 1986, 57:#837

Children Margaret Ann **BALLARD**, Jordan **PARKER** & Alfred **PARKER**, my will and disire is that the lines to make the division of my land between my above named Children & Grand children should run North and South and that my Daughter Margaret **PARKER** should have the lot whereon my dwelling House stands and my grand son Jordan **PARKER** to have his lot on the East side of and Joining Margaret **PARKER** and alfred [sic] **PARKER** to have his lot on the West side of & Joining Margaret **PARKER**s. To them & their heirs forever

Lastly The Residue of my property of every discription not given away I wish to be sold and the ballance after paying my Just debts and the legacies before given to be equally divided between all my Children.

I nominate and appoint my worthy friends Dempsey **KNIGHT** James **MORGAN** & John C **GORDAN** Executors of this my last will and Testament

Thomas **PARKER** (Seal)

Signed Sealed published and
Declared by Thos. **PARKER** the
Testator in the presence of us
    Witness
Teste James B. **ARNOLD**
Thomas **DRAKE** Jurat
State of North Carolina}
    Gates County    }        ~~November~~ /August/ County Court of Pleas &c 1825
The last will and Testament of Thomas **PARKER** decd. ------ [Crossed out & illegible word] ~~appointed~~ was exhibited into Court by John C **GORDAN** one of the Executors therein appointed and was duly proved by the Oath of Thomas **DRAKE** one of the subscribing witnesses thereto and on motion was ordered to be recorded at the same time the Said Executor was qualified for that office and prayed an Order for letters Testamentary thereon which was accordingly granted Teste J **SUMNER** Clk" [24]

The inventory of his estate was taken by John C. **GORDON** 5 June 1825, just five days after Thomas[6] died on 31 May.[25] The sale of his estate was made 21 June 1825, as transcribed here in full:[26]

"1

Account of Sales of the property belonging to the Estate of Thomas **PARKER** dec[d]. sold 21st June 1825 on a credit of six months                  $ Cts

| | | | |
|---|---|---|---|
| 1 Dagon plow | To Alfred **BALLARD** | 2.50 | |
| 1 ditto " | " Jethro **BRINKLEY** | 1..00 | |
| 1 ditto " | " Alfred **BALLARD** | 1..00 | |
| 2 ditto " | " Theop[s]. **HARRELL** | 1..75 | |
| 2 weeding do | " John C. **GORDON** | ..49 | |
| 1 pair traces &c | " Ditto | 1..35 | |
| 1 pair ditto | " Alfred **BALLARD** | 1..40 | |
| 1 D. Plow &c | " James M. **RIDDICK** | ..50 | |
| 1 Box & old Iron | " Humphrey **PARKER** | 3..00 | |
| 2 Sheep Skins | " Abraham **PARKER** | ..37½ | 13..36½ |
| 1 Set Black Smith's Tools | " David **BENTON** | 32..00 | |
| 1 Ox Cart & Wheels | " Jethro **SUMNER** | 10..57 | |
| 1 pr. Cart Wheels | " William **MINER** | 4..00 | |
| 1 Horse Cart & wheels | " John **HOFFLER** | 14..50 | |
| 2 Rakes | " T. W. **CARR** | ..37½ | |
| 1 Plow, Bridle &c | " Jesse L. **HARE** | ..32 | |

---

[24] Gates County Will Book 2:240-242
[25] Gates County Historical Society, *Bible Records of Gates County, NC*, c. unknown, p. 152
[26] NCSA, G.041.2194762 Gates County Estates, Record of 1765-1920, Vol. Parker-Pierce, Folder: Parker, Thomas 1825, Doc. #552-560

| | | | |
|---|---|---|---|
| 3 Grubing hoes | " T. W. **CARR** | 1..15 | |
| 3 Weeding hoes | " Dempsey **KNIGHT** | 1..13 | |
| 1 Hoe & axe | " Alfred **BALLARD** | 1.50 | |
| 1 Hoe | " Mary **ODOM** | ..40 | 65  94½ |
| 2 Axes | " T. W. **CARR** | 1..00 | |
| 2 ditto & adze | " Jethro **BRI/N/KLEY** | 1..00 | |
| 1 pr. Wedges | " T. W. **CARR** | 1..00 | |
| 1 ditto | " Ditto | 0..62½ | |
| 1 Spade | " Jesse L. **HARE** | ..25 | |
| 3 Baskets | " Dempsey **KNIGHT** | ..46 | |
| 4 ditto | " R. H. **BALLARD** | ..25 | |
| 1 Augur, plain &c | " Jesse L. **HARE** | ..76 | |
| 2 Plains | " William **MINER** | ..26 | |
| 2 Augurs | " Humphey [sic] **PARKER** | ..67 | 6.27½ |
| | Amt. Carrᵈ forward | | $  85..58½ |

**2**

| | | | |
|---|---|---|---|
| | Amot. Brot. Forward | dolls. | 85..58½ |
| 3 Augurs | " To William **MINER** | ..12.½ | |
| 2 Chissels & gouge | " Humphey **PARKER** | ..35 | |
| Hammer, mallet &c | " Abram **PARKER** | ..18¾ | |
| 1 Chissel & Saw Set | " James **MORGAN** | ..12½ | |
| 1 Copper Kittle | " Kedar **BALLARD** | 3..30 | |
| 1 Tumbler & Log Cart | " R. H. **BALLARD** | ..26 | |
| 1 Bbl. Cart | " Kedar **BALLARD** | 1..13 | |
| 1 pr. Old wheels | " Wm **MINER** | ..75 | |
| 1 Waggon Frame | " Samuel **MORGAN** | ..25 | |
| 5 Barrels 1 Choice | " John O. **HUNTER** | 2..60 | |
| 8 ditto | " ditto | 1..79 | |
| 10 Empty Barrels | " Jesse **MATHIAS** | 1..87 | 12..73¾ |
| Balance of do | " Ditto | 2..00 | |
| 1 Grind Stone | " Benj: **BALLARD** | 1..50 | |
| 1 Brandy Still | " Humphrey **PARKER** | 70.12½ | |
| 1 Barrel Brandy Nᵒ 1 | " Alfred **BALLARD** | 19.60 | |
| 1 ditto  "        2 | " Benj. **BALLARD** | 19.05 | |
| 1 ditto  "        3 | " Jethro **BRINKLEY** | 19.06¼ | |
| 1 ditto  "        4 | " Ditto | 19.06¼ | |
| 13½ galls." @74¾ Cts | " Etheldred **MATTHEWS** | 10.02¼ | |
| 75ʷ Lard | " Kedar **BALLARD** | 6.75 | |
| 36ʷ do | " Alfred **BALLARD** | 3.24 | |
| 1 Fat Keg | " Jno. **TAYLOR** | ..20= | 170..62¼ |
| 1 Bbl. Pork | " Jethro **BRINKLEY** | 12.62½ | |
| 143ʷ Pork @ 7ᶜᵗˢ | " Kedar **BALLARD** | 10.01 | |
| 106ʷ do | " Alfred **BALLARD** | 8.21½ | |
| 2 Bbls fish | " Kedar **BALLARD** | 8.15 | |
| ½ Bbl. Do | " Alfred **BALLARD** | 2.07 | |
| 1 Keg & oil | " John **HOFFLER** | ..51 | |
| 1 Bbl. Vinegar  Nᵒ 2 | " Samuel **MORGAN** | 1..00 | |
| 1 large Jug | " Seth R. **MORGAN** | ..77 | |
| 2 Oil ditto | " Jethro **BRINKLEY** | ..12½ | |
| ½ Bush. 2 Bbls. &c | " Ditto | ..40 | |
| 1 Brandy Bbl | " John O. **HUNTER** | ..25 | |
| 1 Black Horse | " Henry **WALTON** | 49..00 | 93..12½ |
| | Amot. Carrd. Forward | dolls. | 362..07 |

| | **3** | $ Ct | |
|---|---|---|---|
| | Amot. Brot forward | 362..07 | |
| 1 Bay Horse | To Alfred **BALLARD** | 50..00 | |
| 1 Gig & Harness | " William **TABER** | 20..00 | |
| 1 Yoke Oxen | " John **BENTON** | 34..00 | |
| 1 Bull Stag | " Dempsey **VANN** | 6.09 | |
| 1 Small pied Steer | " Rich[d] H. **BALLARD** | 3..55 | |
| 1 Brindle Cow | " Henry **PUGH** | 8.65 | |
| 1 Red Cow & yearling | " John O. **HUNTER** | 10..00 | |
| 1 Brindle do  do | " Jethro **BRINKLEY** | 9..55 | |
| 1  do   & calf | " Mary **ODOM** | 10.62½ | |
| 1  do   do | " Alfred **BALLARD** | 10..06¼ | |
| 9 head Sheep | " John **HOFFLER** | 11.25 | 173..77¾ |
| 177[w] fodder | " Thos. **DRAKE** | 1..81¼ | |
| 5 barrels Corn | " Mary **ODOM** | 14..30 | |
| 10 Barrels do | " Kedar **BALLARD** | 30..00 | |
| 5 ditto | " Saml. **MORGAN** | 15..00 | |
| 5 ditto | " Alfred **BALLARD** | 15..05 | |
| 10 ditto | "  ditto | 30..00 | |
| 5 ditto | "  ditto | 14..95 | |
| 5 ditto | " Jethro **BRINKLEY** | 14..55 | |
| 5 ditto | " Jethro **SUMNER** | 14..60 | |
| 3 bushels Corn | " Alfred **BALLARD** | 1..74 | |
| 3 barrels shatter do @ 185 | " Humphrey **PARKER** | 5..55 | |
| 2 Bbls. Ditto | " James **MORGAN** | 3..70 | = 161..25¼ |
| 1 measuring tul [tool] | " David **BENTON** | ..76 | |
| 1 Negro man **BRITTIAN** | " Jethro **BRINKLEY** | 220..00 | |
| 1 ditto    **JACK** | " John **BENTON** | ..12½ | |
| 1 ditto    **TOM** | " William **MINER** | 10..10 | |
| 1 Old woman **DINAH** | " Edward **ARNOLD** | 11..00 | |
| Orchard, field Corn &c | " Alfred **BALLARD** | 39..99 | |
| Pond field | "  ditto | 50..25 | |
| 2 Pocosin do | " Jesse L. **HARE** | 12..25 | |
| Long field | " James **MORGAN** | 15..00 | |
| Oat Patch | " **BALLARD & CARR** | 12..61 | |
| 5 Shoates | " Alfred **BALLARD** | 4..01 | |
| 17 ditto | "  ditto | 15..45 | |
| 1 Boar | " Humphrey **PARKER** | 3..00 | |
| 1 Sow & pigs | " Alfred **BALLARD** | 4..67 = | 399..21½ |
| | Amot carr[d] forward | dolls | 1096..31½ |

| | **4** | | |
|---|---|---|---|
| | | $ Cts. | |
| | Amot Brot forward | | 1096..31½ |
| 1 Sow & pigs | To William **MINER** | 4..08 | |
| 1 ditto | " Alfred **BALLARD** | 3..05 | |
| 1 ditto | " John **DAVIS** | 2..14 | |
| 1 ditto | " Isaac **BARR** | 2..20 | |
| 1 ditto | " Alfred **BALLARD** | 2.12½ | |
| 1 Sow | " Joseph **HANIFORD** | 1.60 | |
| 300[w] Bacon @ 6¢ | " Alfred **BALLARD** | 18.00 | |
| 100[w] ditto | " Humphrey **PARKER** | 8..00 | |

| | | | |
|---|---|---|---|
| 100 ditto | " Kedar **BALLARD** | 7..75 | |
| 274[w] ditto | " John **HARE** | 21.92 | |
| 1 Bbl. Soap | " Alfred **BALLARD** | ..65 | |
| 1 X cut saw | " Abr[m]. **MORGAN** Sen[r]. | 8..26 | 79..77½ |
| 1 ox yoke & rope | " John **BENTON** | ..75 | |
| 1 Small Steelyards | " Alfred **BALLARD** | ..90 | |
| 1 pr. Ditto | " David **BENTON** | 2..49 | |
| 2 woolen wheels | " Alfred **BALLARD** | 1..00 | |
| 1 Linen ditto | " Jethro **BRINKLEY** | 1..87½ | |
| 1 ditto | " William **MINER** | 1..76 | |
| 1 Keg | " Thos. **DRAKE** | ..19 | |
| 1 Broad axe | " Jesse **MATHIAS** | ..30 | |
| 1 large pot | " Alfred **BALLARD** | 1..00 | |
| 1 ditto & hooks | " Jethro **BRINKLEY** | ..75 | |
| 1 Dutch oven | " Thos. **DRAKE** | ..51 | |
| 1 Pot & Hooks | " Alfred **BALLARD** | ..56 | |
| 1 ditto | " ditto | ..25 | |
| 1 Pan | " ditto | ..12½ | 12..46 |
| 1 Dutch Oven | " ditto | ..50 | |
| 1 Griddle | " ditto | ..38 | |
| 1 Grid Iron | " Mary **ODOM** | ..40 | |
| 1 Tea Kittle | " Alfred **BALLARD** | ..25 | |
| 1 Spit | " Ditto | ..20 | |
| 1 Hand Mill | " Abrm. C. **MORGAN** | 5..15 | |
| 1 Mortar | " Alfred **BALLARD** | ..05 | |
| 1 Loom & Gear | " ditto | ..50 | |
| 2 pewter basins | " Mary **ODOM** | ..56 | |
| 2 do dishes | " ditto | ..94 | |
| 2 Trays | " Alfred **BALLARD** | ..10 | |
| 2 pails | " Mary **ODOM** | ..50 | 9..53 |
| | Amot carr[d] forwd | dolls | 1198..08 |

**5**

| | | | |
|---|---|---|---|
| | Amot Brot forward | | 1198..08 |
| 2 Pails | To Kedar **BALLARD** | 92 | |
| 2 tubs | " ditto | 16½ | |
| 1 Sifter | " Alfred **BALLARD** | 16 | |
| 1 Keg | " Edward **ARNOLD** | 06¼ | |
| 207 ft. Scantling | " Jesse **MATHIAS** | 1..74 | |
| 171 do. Plank | " T. W. **CARR** | 1..47 | |
| Plat form & basket | " Alfred **BALLARD** | ..68 | |
| 1 Apple Mill | " Dempsey **KNIGHT** | 4..05 | |
| 12[w] Wool @ 37½ | " John C. **GORDON** | 4..50 | |
| Empty barrels &c | " Jethro **BRINKLEY** | ..52 | |
| 1 Trough | " John C. **GORDON** | ..60 | |
| 1 ditto | " T. W. **CARR** | ..62½ | 15..49¼ |
| 2 do | " Thos. **DRAKE** | ..73 | |
| 2 ditto | " Kedar **BALLARD** | ..46 | |
| 1 Tub & meal | " Alfred **BALLARD** | 2..00 | |
| 1 do do | " Kedar **BALLARD** | 1..38 | |
| 2 Tubs | " Wm. **MINER** | ..74 | |
| 1 Bird roaster | " Alfred **BALLARD** | ..13 | |
| 3 Tin measures | " John C. **GORDON** | 1..00 | |
| 1 Spice mortar | " Kedar **BALLARD** | 2..99 | |

| | | | |
|---|---|---|---|
| 1 lot Tin | " Wm. **MINER** | ..26 | |
| 2 butter pots &c | " Alfred **BALLARD** | ..51 | |
| 1 pr Waffle Irons | " R. H. **BALLARD** | 1..52 | |
| 2 reap hooks & tub | " Edward **ARNOLD** | ..56 | |
| Cart Wheel Hubs | " Alfred **BALLARD** | 1..00 | |
| 1 Tub | "   ditto | 14 | 13..43 |
| 1 Scythe | "   ditto | 1..03 | |
| 1 ditto | " Wm. **MINER** | ..07 | |
| 1 ditto | " Kedar **BALLARD** | ..12½ | |
| 1 Stock Bees | " Matthias **MORGAN** | 1..00 | |
| 1   ditto | " Jesse L. **HARE** | ..52 | |
| 1 Gun | " Alfred **BALLARD** | ..05 | |
| Empty Barrels | "   ditto | ..52 | |
| 19 Geese | "   ditto | 5..51 | |
| 2 pr pot Trammels | "   ditto | 2..43 | |
| 5 Tann[d] Sheep skins | " Jesse L **HARE** | 1..12½ | |
| 1 Conch Shell | " John **BENTON** | ..15 | |
| 1 Gun | " Kedar **TAYLOR** | 4..31 | |
| 1 ditto | " T. W. **CARR** | 2..45 | |
| 1 ditto | " Wm. **TABER** | 1..00 = | 20..29 |
| | Amot carr[d] forward | dolls. | 1247..29¼ |

**6**

| | | | |
|---|---|---|---|
| | Amot brot. Forward | | 1247..29¼ |
| 2 Bridle bits &c | To Alfred **BALLARD** | 51 | |
| 1 Currying knife | " Benj. **BALLARD** | .85 | |
| 1 Augur & gouge | " David **BENTON** | 63 | |
| 1 Tea board | " Thos. **DRAKE** | 1..90 | |
| 1 ditto & wash stand | "   ditto | 1..31 | |
| 1 pr Candle Sticks | " Alfred **BALLARD** | 1..12½ | |
| 1 Hackle | "   do | ..26 | |
| 1 Candle Stand | "   do | 1..00 | |
| 1 dressing table | " Ben. **BALLARD** | 1..15 | |
| 1 Case &c | " Alfred **BALLARD** | ..31 | |
| ½ doz Chairs | "   ditto | 2..15 | |
| 2 Chairs | "   ditto | ..30 | |
| 10 ditto | " Wm. **MINER** | 1..99 | 13..48½ |
| ½ doz Silver Spoons | " Alfred **BALLARD** | 15..80 | |
| 5 small ditto | "   ditto | 2..76 | |
| 1 pr brass hand Irons | " Ben. **BALLARD** | 3..00 | |
| 1 pr Iron do &c | " Afred [sic] **BALLARD** | 1..02 | |
| 1 pr Sad Irons | "   ditto | 31 | |
| 1 Beaufat | "   ditto | 21..01 | |
| 1 Case & Bottles | " Albridgeton **BROWN** | 2..26 | |
| 1 Walnut Table | " Mary **ODOM** | 5..01 | |
| 1   ditto | " Alfred **BALLARD** | 4..00 | |
| 1 Clock | " Jethro **BRINKLEY** | 8..50 | |
| 1 Desk | " Benj. **JONES** | 5..00 | 68..67 |
| 1 Razor & Strap | " Alfred **BALLARD** | ..87½ | |
| 1 Hone &c | " Kedar **BALLARD** | ..65 | |
| Steel &c | " Alfred **BALLARD** | ..49 | |
| 1 Slate &c | "   ditto | ..22 | |
| 1 Ink Stand | "   ditto | ..06 | |
| 1 Bible | " Kedar **BALLARD** | 2..00 | |

| | | | |
|---|---|---|---|
| 4 Vol. Magazines | " Benj. **BALLARD** | 3..05 | |
| American Magazine | " ditto | ..41 | |
| life of Dr.**COOK** | " John C. **GORDON** | ..65 | |
| American Biography | " Alfred **BALLARD** | 2..00 | |
| 3 Vol. Sermons | " Dempsey **KNIGHT** | ..55 | |
| Appeals &c | " John C. **GORDON** | ..20 | |
| Parcel of Old books | " Jesse **PARKER** | ..06¼ | |
| A tea table | " A. **BROWN** | 2..00 | 13..21¾ |
| | Amot carr[d] forward | Dolls. 1342..66½ | |

7

| | | | |
|---|---|---|---|
| | Amot. Brot forward | $  1342..66½ | |
| 1 Looking glass | To Alfred **BALLARD** | ..25 | |
| 2 yds. Brd. Cloth | " Benj. **BALLARD** | 8..25 | |
| 2 large tumblers | " Alfred **BALLARD** | ..44 | |
| ½ doz tumblers & 2 decants. | " ditto | ..62½ | |
| 4 Bowls | " ditto | ..31¼ | |
| 1 Castor | " ditto | 1..00 | |
| 1 Waiter &c | " ditto | 1..25 | |
| Crockery in Cupboard | " Jethro **BRINKLEY** | ..31¼ | |
| 5 dishes | " Alfred **BALLARD** | 1..05 | |
| 1½ doz plates | " ditto | ..75 | |
| Knives forks &c | " ditto | ..75 | |
| 1 Pine table | " ditto | ..41 | |
| 1 Chest | " Martha **SOUTHALL** | ..31 | |
| 1 Gig box | " Alfred **BALLARD** | ..08 | 15..79 |
| 1 bed & furniture | " Ben. **BALLARD** | 17..00 | |
| 1 ditto | " Jesse **PARKER** | 15..25 | |
| 1 bedstead | " Solomon **ELLIS** | 9..02 | |
| 120 R. O. Staves | " Jethro **BRINKLEY** | ..66 | |
| 390 ditto | " ditto | 2..37½ | |
| 118 W. O. ditto | " William **MINER** | 1..70 | |
| 1 hand saw | " Alfred **BALLARD** | ..75 | |
| Oyster Shells | " Dempsey **KNIGHT** | ..50 | |
| 1 work bench | " Alfred **BALLARD** | 1..55 | |
| 1 funnel | " ditto | ..06 | |
| 2 Hoes | " Matthias **MORGAN** | ..46 | |
| 1 Grind Stone | " Jethro **BRINKLEY** | ..05 | |
| Cart Wheel timber &c | " Wm. **MINER** | 1..00 | 50..37½ |
| 1 Bbl Vinegar | " A. **BALLARD** | 1..15 | |
| Corn field | " ditto | 29..50 | |
| 10 Shoates | " Humphey [sic] **PARKER** | 8..00 | |
| 10 ditto | " Jethro **BRINKLEY** | 7..00 | |
| 1 Sow & pigs | " Alfred **BALLARD** | 3..25 | |
| 1 ditto | " ditto | 2..00 | |
| 1 Basket of leather | " Jethro **BRINKLEY** | 1..00 | |
| 1 large tub | " Alfred **BALLARD** | ..80 | |
| 1 Side leather | " Will. **MINER** | ..50 | |
| Leather Stands &c | " Humphrey **PARKER** | 5..88 | |
| 1 Ox yoke | " Jethro **BRINKLEY** | ..12 | |
| 1 Saddle | " John C. **GORDON** | ..25 | 59..45 |
| | Amot carr[d] forward | Dolls.  1468..28 | |

Amot Brot forward    $    1468..28½ [sic]

| Warping bars | To Alfred **BALLARD** | ..25 | |
|---|---|---|---|
| 1 Bbl fish | " ditto | 3..76 | |
| 1 Bed &c | " John C. **GORDON** | 13..00 | |
| 1 Cow & Calf | " Alfred **BALLARD** | 6..15 | |
| 1 ditto | " Thos. **DRAKE** | 8..30 | |
| 1 yoke Oxen | " John C. **GORDON** | 20..95 | |
| 5 barrels Corn | " Washington **JONES** | 15..00 | |
| a parcel Corn | " T. W. **CARR** | 4..62½ | 71..21½ |
| | | | 1539..50 |

Subtract for Alfred **PARKER**s property Sold at Sale

| 1 Bed | $15..00 | |
|---|---|---|
| 1 Sow & Pigs | 4..00 | |
| 1 Cow & Calf | 10..00 | |
| | $29..00 | 29..00 |
| | | $1510..50" |

The purpose of including the above record here is to illustrate some of the personal possessions owned by a prosperous farmer, and the items utilized in everyday life in that era. Two items that may have been previously owned by Thomas[5] **PARKER** were the "Looking glass" purchased by Alfred **BALLARD**, and a desk purchased by Benjamin **JONES**.

During November term of 1825, a petition was submitted to the court by Benjamin **SUMNER**, attorney, for the division of the real estate of Thomas[6] **PARKER**, deceased. The petitioners were Kedar **BALLARD** and Ann[7] his wife, Mary[7] **ODOM**, Alfred **BALLARD** & Margaret[7] his wife, Jethro **BRINKLEY** and Sarah[7] his wife, Margaret Ann[8] **BALLARD** by her next friend and father, Benjamin **BALLARD**, Jordan[8] **PARKER** by his guardian Joseph **GORDON**, and Alfred[8] **PARKER** by his guardian, Alfred **BALLARD**, and William **BRINKLEY** and his wife, Ruth[7]. This petition provides specific confirmation concerning the heirs, in that it states that "Ann **BALLARD** mentioned in the Will aforesaid is the wife of your petitioner Kedar **BALLARD**, that Margaret **PARKER** also mentioned in the said Will has since the publication thereof intermarried with your petitioner Alfred **BALLARD**, and that Sarah **BRINKLEY**...is the wife of Jethro **BRINKLEY**."[27] In that same term, it was ordered "that Humphry **PARKER**, Demsey **KNIGHT**, James **MORGAN**, David **BENTON** and Jacob P. **JONES** be appointed Commissioners with a Surveyor to make a division of the real estate of Thomas **PARKER** dec[d]. among his legatees...and make due return of your proceedings...with actual surveys of the same, to this Court at next siting [sic] hereunto annexed." That survey was made 20 December 1825. It was stated that the whole tract "by actual survey contains six hundred and nineteen acres."[28] When the metes and bounds in this division are plotted, they only encompass an area of 532.7 acres.

The following document was submitted to the Court in November 1829. "We the undersigned having been appointed by the County Court of Gates to Divide the plantation of Thomas **PARKER** late of Gates County, Decd, amongst the heirs, did, agreeably to the order of said Court, meet and divide said land, and make due return of our proceedings, never the less we have since been informed that said report is not to be found on the Registers books of this County, neither can the original be found in the Office of the Register, therefore, by request of those concerned, We proceed to make a duplicate of said report which we hope will be admitted to record, it being a correct transcript of the Original. We divided the plantation as followeth: Set off and allotted unto Jethro **BRINKLEY**, in right of his Wife, lot No. 1. Containing 74 acres, and to receive from lot No. 4 one hundred and Eighty five dollars. Set off and allotted unto Margaret A. **BALLARD** lot No 2. 74 acres, and to receive from No. 5 one hundred and sixty six dollars and fifty Cents. Set off and allotted unto Jordan **PARKER** lot No. 3. 74 acres, and to receive from No. 6. Seventy four dollars, and from No. 5. Eighteen dollars and fifty Cents Set off and allotted unto Alfred **BALLARD** lot No. 4. 74 acres, and to pay to No. 1. One hundred and Eighty five dollars. Set off and allotted unto Alfred **PARKER** lot No 5, 74 acres, and to

---

[27] NCSA, G.041.2194762 Gates County Estates, Record of 1765-1920, Vol. Parker-Pierce, Folder: Parker, Thomas 1825,Doc. #536-538
[28] Ibid., Doc. #571

pay to No 2. One hundred and sixty six dollars and fifty Cents, and to No. 3 Eighteen dollars and fifty cents. Set off and allotted unto Kedar **BALLARD** lot No 6 74 acres and to pay No. 3 Seventy four dollars, lot No. 7. 74 acres, set off and allotted unto Mary **ODOM**, valued 370 dollars, being an average proportion of Said property agreeably to Valuation by us made. Given under our hands and Seals the 17th day of Oct 1829. James **MORGAN**, Humphrey **PARKER**, Jacob P. his P. mark **JONES**"[29]

A division of Thomas[6] **PARKER**'s personal estate, agreeable to his will, was ordered in August Court 1827, and was made 27 October 1827, by Joseph **GORDON**, James **MORGAN**, and Isaac R. **HUNTER**. It states that "Agreable to the Auditors report there is in the Hands of his Executor the Sum of Eight Hundred and Sixty [?] Nine dollars & 88 Cents, this Sum Scaled down in equal propotion agreable [sic] to the different legacies, leaves the Sum of four Hundred & Sixty three dollars & 64 Cents to the Heirs of Elizabeth **MINOR**, three Hundred and Nine dollars & Ten Cents to Alfred **PARKER** & Seventy Seven dollars & 28 Cents to William **BRINKLEY** in right of his wife Ruth **BRINKLEY** given under Our hand the day & date as Above."[30] The children named in Thomas[6] **PARKER**'s will were Ruth[7] **BRINKLEY**, Elizabeth[7] **MINOR**, Ann[7] **BALLARD**, Mary[7] **ODOM**, Margaret[7] **PARKER** and Sarah[7] **BRINKLEY**. The grandchildren were Jordan and Alfred **PARKER**, and Margaret Ann **BALLARD**. The family Bible, owned by the George **KITTRELL** family of Corapeake, NC, gives the following listing of Thomas[6] and Mary's children:

"Edward **PARKER** born 25 December 1775
Nancy **PARKER** born 1 March 1778
Mary **PARKER** born 20 May 1780
Elizabeth **PARKER** born 16 February 1782
Sarah **PARKER** born 7 December 1783
Peggy **PARKER** born 21 Jan 1786
Alesey **PARKER** born 11 May 1788
Ruth **PARKER** born 10 September 1790
Thomas **PARKER** born 19 November 1792"[31]

Edward[7], Alesey[7], and Thomas[7] all died before their father. Edward[7] **PARKER**, born 25 December 1775, is reputed to have married Elizabeth **WILLIAMS** in 1801. They named their first child Alba[8] **PARKER**, born 15 September 1803. The second child, Jordan Williams[8] **PARKER**, was born 26 October 1807. Alfred[8] **PARKER**, the third child, was born 26 March 1810, and died 28 April 1829.[32] The fourth, and last, child was born 10 April 1814, and Elizabeth named him Edward[8] **PARKER**. His father had died just before his birth, very near 1 April 1814, when Thomas[6] made the sale of Edward[7]'s estate.[33]

Jordan Williams[8] **PARKER** entered into a marriage bond with Penelope **WALTON** 27 January 1830, with Humphrey **PARKER** as bondsman.[34] Penelope (**WALTON**) **PARKER** submitted a petition for dower in November Court, 1867, and stated therein that Jordan[8] **PARKER** died in July 1867, and his heirs were George T.[9], David W.[9], James R.[9], Richard H.[9], Edward J.[9], Margarett A.[9] **PARKER**, and Issabella[9], wife of Exum **WHITE**.[35] A receipt from Edward **PARKER** to J. A. **KNIGHT**, administrator of Reverend Jordan[8] **PARKER**, in the amount of $2.40, for 240 bricks for his grave, was paid in full 17 December 1867.[36]

His administrator, John A. **KNIGHT**, sold Richard H.[9] **PARKER** 128 acres of his land for $290.00, known as the "Home Tract." It was bounded on the northeast by the road leading from **PARKER**'s Meeting House to the Suffolk Road, and south by the road leading to John T. **MOR-**

[29] NCSA, G.041.2194762 Gates County Estates, Record of 1765-1920, Vol. Parker-Pierce., Folder: Parker, Thomas 1825 Doc. #578 The original division, with plat, appears on Doc. #570, 572 and 573.
[30] Ibid., Doc. #577
[31] Gates County Historical Society, *Bible Records of Gates County, NC*, c. unknown, p. 152-153
[32] Ibid., p. 152
[33] NCSA, G.041.2194761 Gates Co. Estates, Record of 1765-1920 Vol. Parker, E.-Parker, M. . Folder: Parker, Edward 1814, Doc #61-64
[34] Almasy, *Gates County, North Carolina Marriage Bonds 1778-1868*, c. 1987, p. 68
[35] NCSA, G.041.2194761 Gates Co. Estates, Record of 1765-1920 Vol. Parker, E.-Parker, M. . Folder: Parker, Jordan 1868 Doc. #1497
[36] Ibid., Doc. 1444

GAN's. This tract was also known as the "Ruthy **BRINKLEY** tract." The reason for this sale, on 10 November 1869, was to pay the debts of the decedent.[37]

Nancy[7] **PARKER**, born 1 March 1778, was also called "Ann" in her father's will. Her first marriage was to Miles **BENTON** who entered into a marriage bond with her on 28 February 1803, with Kinchen **NORFLEET** as bondsman.[38] Miles **BENTON** made his will 27 June 1805. He left the use of one third of his land and plantation whereon he lived, among other things, to his "loving wife Nansey **BENTON**." He decreed that the lands he purchased of Luke **SUMNER** were to be sold by his executors on a credit of 12 months. That money was to be lent at interest and the interest was to be applied to building a school house and hiring a teacher for the purpose of a free school and "that said school have to be built within two miles of the place where I now reside and all children with [sic] four miles of my place of residence be permitted to be taught in said school." The land he purchased of Luke **SUMNER** was a 600-acre tract that lies on the "Southwest Side of the Great Dismal Swamp, and well Known by the name of the White Oak Spring marsh," on 17 April 1798.[39] He appointed his friends, Kedar **BALLARD** and Thomas **PARKER**, his executors. The witnesses to this will were Joseph John **SUMNER**, James **KNIGHT**, and Jacob **BENTON**. It was exhibited into court at November term, 1805.[40] At the session begun 18 November 1805, the will was dissented to by Nancy **BENTON** on 19 November 1805.[41]

Her second marriage was to Kedar **BALLARD** who entered into a marriage bond 7 November 1808, to marry Nansey **BENTON**. Jethro **SUMNER** was his bondsman and one Martha B. **SUMNER** was a witness.[42] Kedar **BALLARD** was one of the Justices for Gates County for many years.

Mary[7] **PARKER** was born 20 May 1780, and appears on a marriage bond with Benjamin **ODOM** on 18 June 1818, with George **KITTRELL** as bondsman.[43] Benjamin **ODOM** was the son of Demsey **ODOM** and he made his will 11 September 1821. It was exhibited into court at February term 1822, by his executor, George **KITTRELL**.[44]

Elizabeth[7] **PARKER** was born 16 February 1782, and was dead before 27 October 1827. The division of her father's personal estate on that date refers to the "heirs of Elizabeth **MINOR**."[45] She appears on a marriage bond with James **SOUTHALL**, of Amelia County, VA, 6 November 1806, with Jesse **SOUTHALL** as bondsman, and Jacob **HUNTER** as witness.[46] Their children were Martha Ann[8] **SOUTHALL**, born 29 August 1807, Thomas James[8] **SOUTHALL**, born 9 August 1809, and Mary Elizabeth[8] **SOUTHALL**, born 18 October 1811.[47] In November term, 1822, Daniel **SOUTHALL** was appointed guardian to all three children.[48] Their mother, Elizabeth[7], had returned to Gates County and was remarried by that date. She appears on a marriage bond 30 September 1822, as "Betsey **SOUTHALL**," to marry William **MINER**. William **ARNOLD** was the bondsman.[49] William **MINER** will be remembered as an apprentice to Thomas[5] **PARKER** in 1817.

Sarah[7] **PARKER** was born 7 December 1783, and was married to Jethro **BRINKLEY** some time before 16 April 1825, when her father made his will.

---

[37] NCSA, G.041.2194761 Gates Co. Estates, Record of 1765-1920 Vol. Parker, E.-Parker, M. . Folder: Parker, Jordan 1868, Doc. #1504

[38] Almasy, *Gates County, North Carolina Marriage Bonds 1778-1868*, c. 1987, p. 6

[39] NCSA, C.041.40003, Gates County Real Estate Conveyances 1794-1803, Vol:4,5, 4:236-237

[40] Almasy, *Gates Co., NC Wills 1779-1807, Vol. I*, c. 1984, p. 7, Will Book 1:224-227

[41] Fouts, *Minutes of County Court of Pleas and Quarter Sessions Gates County, North Carolina 1800-1805, Vol. II*, c. 1985, 131:#478;132:481

[42] Almasy, *Gates County, North Carolina Marriage Bonds 1778-1868*, c. 1987, p. 4

[43] Ibid., p. 65

[44] Almasy, *Gates Co., NC Wills 1807-1838, Vol. II*, c. 1985, p. 80, Will Book 2:179-181

[45] NCSA, G.041.2194762, Gates County Estates, Record of 1765-1920, Vol. Parker-Pierce. Folder: Parker, Thomas 1825, Doc. #577

[46] Almasy, *Gates County, North Carolina Marriage Bonds 1778-1868*, c. 1987, p. 87

[47] Gates County Historical Society, *Bible Records of Gates County, NC*, , c. unknown, p. 152-153

[48] Fouts, *Minutes of County Court of Pleas and Quarter Sessions Gates County, North Carolina 1818-1823, Vol. V*, c. 1987, 139:#1251

[49] Almasy, *Gates County, North Carolina Marriage Bonds 1778-1868*, c. 1987, p. 63

**Chapter 6:** Thomas[6] **PARKER** *(Thomas[5],William[4],Thomas[3],Richard[2],William[1])*

Peggy[7] **PARKER** was born 21 January 1786, and was named as "Margaret **PARKER**" on a marriage bond taken out by Alfred **BALLARD** 27 June 1825. James **MORGAN** was his bondsman.[50]

Alesey[7] **PARKER** was born 11 May 1788 and was named in a marriage bond entered into by Benjamin **BALLARD** 26 November 1812. Richard A. **BALLARD** was bondsman.[51] She was dead prior to 16 April 1825, when her father made his will. Margaret Ann[8] **BALLARD** was their only known child, born 16 October 1813[52].

Ruth[7] **PARKER** was born 10 September 1790, and was named in a marriage bond entered into by William **BRINKLEY** 5 February 1812. Jethro **BRINKLEY** and John **BARNES** were his bondsmen.[53]

Thomas[7] **PARKER** was born 19 November 1792, and did not survive his father.[54]

Later generations of this family are easily traced in the Gates County records. No further information included here.

Parker's Methodist Church, Parker's Fork, Gates County, NC. Photo taken by the author in July 1983.

---

[50] Almasy, *Gates County, North Carolina Marriage Bonds 1778-1868*, c. 1987, p. 3

[51] Ibid., p. 3

[52] Gates County Historical Society, *Bible Records of Gates County, NC*, c. unknown, p. 152-153

[53] Almasy, *Gates County, North Carolina Marriage Bonds 1778-1868*, c. 1987, p. 12

[54] Gates County Historical Society, *Bible Records of Gates County, NC*, c. unknown, p. 152-153

**Chapter 6:** Thomas[6] **PARKER** *(Thomas[5],William[4],Thomas[3],Richard[2],William[1])*

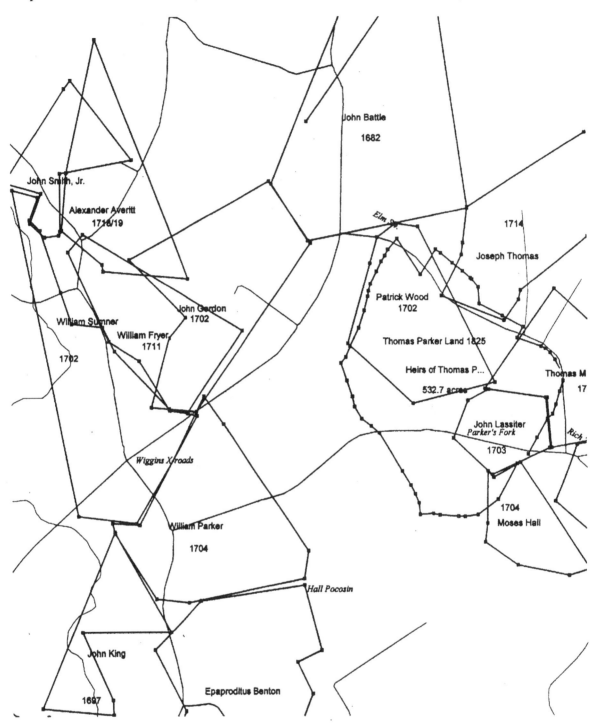

Scale: 2000 ft/in
Map depicting the 1825 division of land of Thomas[6] **PARKER**, relative to the 1704 VA Land
Patent to William[6] **PARKER**, in Gates County, NC.

## Thomas[2] PARKER *(William[1])*

Thomas **PARKER**, of the northern part of Isle of Wight County, VA, was still living there in May of 1683.[1] Thomas[3] **PARKER** *(Richard[2],William[1])* was living near the Cross Swamp patent in Nansemond County, in 1698.[2] These facts place them in widely separated areas, and some distance from the following Thomas **PARKER**.

Thomas[2] **PARKER**, *(William[1])* brother to Richard[2] **PARKER**, was mentioned in a patent to Leonard **GUINNS**, as owning land on Dumpling Island Creek, in 1648. There is no remaining record of the disposition of his land in that area. This Thomas could possibly be a generation later, but until proof to the contrary becomes available, he will be considered here as the second generation. His birth is estimated here to have been ca. 1626.

He patented 600 acres on 25 April 1679. It is described as being "near ye. Head of ye. Southerne branch of Nansemond River begining at a mrked White oak standing by ye. branch side & soe runing for length north 320 po: to a mrked White oak & soe for breadth W: 300 po: to a mrked pine & soe again for length Soly: 320 po: to a mrked oak standing by ye. branch side & Soe East by ye. branch side 300 po: to ye. first mentoned tree. The said land being for<u>mly</u> granted to ffrancis **WELLS** by pattent dated ye. 20<sup>th</sup> October 1665 And Purchased by ye sd. Thomas **PARKER** of Symon **IRONS** who married Dorothy ye. Daughter & Sole heir of ffran: **WELLS** aforsd..."[3] That purchase may have been as early as 1672.

The "head of the Southern Branch of Nansemond River" was located between the community of Holland, VA, near U.S. 58 Business and the present border with Isle of Wight County, of what was then the Upper Parish of Nansemond County. Commercial and agricultural activities have altered the drainage in the area to the extent that it is no longer discernible as such.

James **COLLINS**, Jr., was granted 450 acres 10 July 1680. This land is described as "being in the upper prsh of Nanzemond at the head of the land formerly grannted by Pattent to David **LOYD** and now possessed by Samuell **WATSON**." It adjoined Thomas **PARKER**'s line.[4] The patent to David **LOYD** was granted to David "**FLOYD**," 20 October 1665.[5]

Just two years after the 1679 patent, Thomas[2] **PARKER** was granted 700 acres on 20 April 1681. This patent contained 500 acres of the **WELLS** patent, plus 200 acres more for the transportation of four persons, thereby confirming his title to the entire 700 acres. This parcel was located "neare the County line," and adjoined William **BUSH**'s land[6]. He most probably had sold, or given away, the other 100 acres at some time within the span of those two years. There were numerous conveyances of land between individuals that were never mentioned in subsequent patents.

Thomas **MANDUE** patented 320 acres of land 20 April 1682. It lay "on ye blackwater branches in ye Isle of Wight county," and adjoined George **PERCE**s land, then in possession of Phillip **WRAYFORD**, Matthew **STRICKLAND**, and "ye Coblers line..." One of the headrights claimed in this patent was one Thomas **PARKER**.[7] Thomas **MANDUE** patented another 390 acres 28 October 1702. It lay in Isle of Wight County, on the south side of the Blackwater River and Nottaway Swamp. This patent will be mentioned again, at a later time.

On 23 October 1690, Thomas[3] **PARKER**, Jr., *(Thomas[2],William[1])* was granted 240 acres of land in the Upper Parish of Nansemond County, near Kingsale. It adjoined Thomas **PARKER**, Sr., James **COLLINS**, Edward **THELWELL**, **OSBORNE**, and Nicholas **PERROT**.[8] The terms "Sr." and "Jr." were used to denote two *living* men of the same name, though of different ages. They were

---

[1] See Chapter 1, pp. 5-7, for discussion of this Thomas Parker.
[2] See Chapter 2, pp. 12-13, for discussion of this Thomas Parker.
[3] VSLA, 6:681
[4] Ibid., 7:36
[5] Ibid., 5:563
[6] Ibid., 7:92
[7] Ibid., 9:473
[8] Ibid., 8:92

not always father and son, though that appears to be the case in this instance. This Thomas[3] **PARKER**, Jr.'s birth is estimated here to have been circa 1649. This patent adjoined the western side of Thomas[2] **PARKER**'s 1681 patent. Kingsale Swamp rises northeast of Holland, VA, and flows west into the Blackwater River.

Henry **SANDERS** was granted a tract of 118 acres on 26 April 1698. It is described as being "in the lower parrish of Isle of white [sic] County near King sale beginning at a pine a Corner tree of Thomas **PARKER**s," and adjoined Edward **FELWELL** [THELWELL,] John **BRYANT**, and John **ROBERTS**.[9] This patent lies on the northwest bounds of the 1690 patent to Thomas[3] **PARKER**, Jr., though he is called only "Thomas **PARKER**," without that distinction. It appears that Thomas[2] **PARKER**, Sr., was dead by that time. No further mention of him is found in the Virginia patents.

Henry **GAY** was granted a tract of 400 acres in the Upper Parish of Nansemond County on 22 April 1669. It began at the mile's end of James **COLLINS**' land.[10] James **COLLINS** had patented 400 acres on 11 March 1664, near Thomas **MASON**, and still owned that parcel.[11]

John **PARKER**, Cooper, was granted a patent of 87 acres on 29 October 1696. It is described as "Scituate Lying and being in the Western [sic] Branch of nansemd. Rivr: in ye Uper parish beginning at a marked Red oake a Line Tree of Henry **GRAY**s [sic] Land and run thence a Long **GRAY**s Line trees North North East foure hundred Sixty eight poles to a Saplin Red oake, thence bounding on Saml **WATSON**s Land Northwesterly Seventy Degrees one hundred Eighteen poles to a Corner white oake of Peter **PARKER**s, thence Bounding Peter **PARKER**s Line trees South Easterly five Degrees two hundred twenty two poles thence Southeasterly Eighty five Degrees twenty two pole to ye first Station..."[12] These patents place Thomas[3], Peter[3] and John[4] **PARKER** on lands adjoining the lands of Thomas[2] **PARKER**. When this patent is plotted, it becomes obvious that it is inaccurate. There may have been some controversy between John[4] and one of his neighbors, necessitating another survey, and a new patent to confirm his title. That corrected survey was patented 28 October 1697, for 83 acres, but the name was misread and recorded under "John **BARKER**."[13] When the calls are plotted, the acreage is actually 84.6 acres. There were two headrights for each patent, but they were not the same names. Another inaccuracy in these patents is the name Henry "**GRAY**." Extensive reading of other patents makes it clear that this was Henry **GAY**. Errors of this type are quite common.

There is no record of a patent for the Peter **PARKER** whose land adjoined John[4]'s patent. It is likely that Peter[3] **PARKER** was given, or sold, that missing 100-acre parcel that belonged to Thomas[2] **PARKER** between 1679 and 1681. John[4] and Peter[3] **PARKER** had removed to Chowan County, NC, by 1700. Thomas[3] **PARKER** followed circa 1707, as will be shown.

Of the three William **PARKER**s who patented land within the present bounds of Gates County, the third appears to be the youngest son of Thomas[2] **PARKER** (*William[1].*) William[3] **PARKER**'s birth is estimated here to have been circa 1678. He patented 250 acres of land 2 May 1706, which is described as "being on the Eastward Side of a branch or swamp wch. Comes out of Saram main swamp in the upper Parish of Nansemond County begining at a marked gum a Corner tree of Richd **BAREFIELD**s Standing on the Eastward side the aforesd branch or swamp and runing along the aforesd **BAREFIELD**s Line trees North Easterly forty degrs. Easterly one hundd. & thirteen Poles to a markt white Oake thence North Westerly thirteen degrees three hundred ninety Poles to a markt red Oake thence North Westerly Eighty four degrees one hundred poles to a markt pine in the main swamp thence down the Swamp and bounding thereon according to the Sevll. Courses thereof to the first Stacon the Sd. Land was formerly granted unto Peter **PHEBUS** by Patent dated the 20th of Aprill 1694 & by him deserted & Since granted to the sd. Wm. **PARKER** by order of the Genll Court dated the 16th day of October 1705...for the transportacon of five persons..."[14]

Richard **BAREFIELD** patented the land mentioned above on 20 April 1694, and one of his

---

[9] VSLA, 9:148

[10] Ibid., 6:242

[11] Ibid., 5:89

[12] Ibid., 9:47

[13] Ibid., 9:99

[14] Ibid., 9:730

headrights was named William **PARKER**.[15] This may be another instance of a young man returning from receiving his education in England. He may also have had a family connection with Richard **BAREFIELD**.

The location of the above lands becomes more evident with the description of a North Carolina patent to one Samuel **MERRIOTT** on 27 August 1714, for 366 acres. It is described as being "in Chowan Precinct on the Et. Side of **MILLS**'s Swamp, beginning at a pine on ye. Swamp side Wm. **PARKER**s Corner tree, then Et. 130 pole to a pine, then No. 144 pole to an Oak, then No. 40 Et. 382 pole to a Lightwood Stump, then Wt. 160 pole to a pine on ye Wt. Side of ye Beaver dam branch, then along ye said branch to ye head of **MILLS**'s Swamp, then up ye. Said Swamp to ye. First Station..."[16] This description places William[3] **PARKER**'s land near the community of Sarem, in Gates County. "**MILLS**'s Swamp" and "Mill Swamp" are in the same general area, but are entirely different streams. **MILLS**' Swamp is now known as Flat Swamp, near Sarem. It derived its name from Henry **MILLS**, who had a patent of 500 acres on "Sarum Swamp," 20 April 1685.[17] Mill Swamp was formerly known as "Beech Swamp."

William[3] **PARKER** (*Thomas[2], William[1]*) is mentioned as an adjoining landowner to Samuel **MERRITT** in several Chowan County deeds as late as 1740. The repetition of land descriptions from earlier conveyances makes it difficult to determine if the names mentioned are of current neighbors, at that date. One of those deeds was from Jno. **PIPKIN**, Jr., to Moses **HARE**, for 180 acres, "begining at **PETTERS** Swamp & runing up sd Swamp to the mouth of the Long Branch & runing up sd Branch to Samuel **MERRELL**s [sic] line & along his line to Wm. **PARKER**s line & along his line to 1st. Sta. sd. land purchased of Jos. [?] **BRADLEY** 2 Aug 1736..."[18] There is no date in this deed, but it was proved in court 16 October 1740. When John **PIPKIN**, Jr., purchased that 180 acres, the grantor's name was spelled "**BRADDY**."[19]

It would appear that William[3] **PARKER** had died some time before 4 June 1746, the date of the deed from John **COLLINS**, of Bertie County, for 125 acres of land to Isaac **WILLIAMS** of Chowan County. It is described as "beginning on a branch or Flatt that issueth out of **MILES** [sic] Swamp that makes the Horse [?] Pocoson bounding on sd Pocoson to the West end then a direct North corse to the patent line thence along the of [sic] sd patent to **MILES** Swamp thence up sd swamp to the first station, sd land being part of a pattent granted to William **PARKER** for 250 acres 2 May 1706..."[20] All of William[3] **PARKER**'s lands lie in the part of Chowan County that was cut off to form Hertford County in 1759. There is no extant record of any of his possible purchases, or sales, of land that might have been mentioned in deeds between 1759 and 1779, when Gates County was formed. He does not appear in the extant Chowan County Court Minutes, nor in any other of the deeds for that county.

On 14 September 1736, Thomas **PILAND** sold 200 acres of land in Chowan Precinct to Stephen **SHEPARD**. It was "part of a patent granted to sd **PILAND** 400 A dated 20 Nov 1728, beginning on the South side of **MILLS**'s Swamp on the line of Charles **SCOTT** & so runs by a line of markd trees to a White Oak on the No. side of Roap? (Roass?) Pecoson then East to **MILLS**'s line thence along **MILLS**'s line to the afsd. swamp thence up the swamp to the first station..." This deed was acknowledged 7 July 1737.[21]

Another of Stephen **SHEPARD**'s acquisitions was from Robert **REDDICK** 25 March 1739, for 50 acres. It was "part of Richd. **BAREFIELD**s pattent being on the south side of **MILLS**es Swamp begining on the Wt. side of **PATTERES** [sic] Swamp beginning at a White Oak a corner tree a runing line in boregarden [sic] to a markd White Oak a corner tree thence a runing line to a markd

---

[15] VSLA, 8:338

[16] NCLG, 1:229 File No. 149

[17] VSLA, 7:478

[18] Haun, *Chowan County, North Carolina Deed Books:W-1 1729-1738; C-2 1738-1740; D 1748-1806, Vol. I*, c. 1998, C#2:78, 101:#512

[19] Ibid., W#1:295, 18:#102

[20] Haun, , *Chowan County, North Carolina Deed Books: A-1, E-1, F-1, F-2, G-1 (Deeds dated 1701-1755) Vol. II*, c. 1999, E#1:144-145, 73:#337

[21] Haun, *Chowan County, North Carolina Deed Books:W-1 1729-1738; C-2 1738-1740; D 1748-1806, Vol. I*, c. 1998, W#1:349-350, 29:#160

Gum a corner tree thence runing down **MILLS**es Swamp to the mouth of **PETTERS** Swamp thence up the Swamp to 1st Sta. ..."[22] "Boregarden" is now known as "Beargarden," next to Sarem.

These deeds establish William[3] **PARKER**'s land as being on **MILLS'** Swamp, the Beargarden and land owned by Stephen **SHEPARD** and Thomas **PILAND**.

Robert **PARKER** purchased 50 acres of land from Jacob **RODGERS** 24 June 1755, by an unrecorded Chowan County deed. It is exceptional in its detailed history, and is included here in its entirety.

"This Indenture made the twenty fourth Day of June in the year of Our Lord Christ one Thousand Seven hundred fifty & Five Between Jacob **RODGERS** of Chowan County in the province of North Carolina of the One part and Robert **PARKER** of the Same County of the other part Witnesseth that the Said Jacob **RODGERS** for and in Consideration of the Sum of Eighteen pounds Current money of Virginia to him in hand paid the receipt whereof he Doth hereby Acknowledge and himself there with fully paid and Satisfied he the Said Jacob **RODGERS** have given granted Bargained and Sold and Do by these presents fully Clearly & absolutely, Give, Grant Bargain, Sell Alien Enfieoff Convey and forever make Over and Confirm unto him the Said Robert **PARKER** & to his heirs & assigns forever, all that Messuage plantation Tract And parcel of Land Scituate Lying & Being in Chowan County aforesaid and Lying On the Western Side of a Swamp formerly Called **MILLS**es Swamp & Bounded as follows That is to Say Begining at a White Oak Standing in the mouth of a Branch that Issueth out of a Swamp /Called/ **PETER**'s Swamp on the westward Side thereof and Runs A Long Stephen **SHIPPARD**s Line to the Head Line of the patent, thence to the head of a branch so Down the Said Branch to the aforesaid Swamp then Down the Swamp to the first Station all which Said Land so Bounded as aforesaid Contains By Estimation fifty Acres Be the Same more or Less & is part of a patent for Ninety Acres Granted to Richard **BARFIELD** Dated the 20th. of April 1~7~694 and by Right of Inheritance Did fall to John **BARFIELD**, and was by him Sold & Conveyed to James **MATHEWS** by a Deed of Bargain and Sale Dated the 29th Day of July 1729 and was by the Said **MATHEWS** Sold and Conveyed to Abraham **ODOM** by an Indorsement Both On the Back of the Deed and also On the Back of the patent and was in the Same manner Sold & Conveyed By the Said Abraham **ODOM** to richard **WILLIAMS** and was by him in the Same forme Conveyed & Sold to John **ODOM** and was by the Said John **ODOM** in the manner & forme aforesaid Conveyed & Sold to Thomas **ROOKS**, and did fall by Right of Inheritance to Joseph **ROOKS**, and was by the Said Joseph **ROOKS** In the forme aforesaid Sold & Conveyed to the said Jacob **RODGERS** the partie to these presents, With the revertion & Revertions & Remainder & Remainders of all & Singular the premises and Every part & parcel thereof to him the Said Robert **PARKER** and to his heirs and assigns forever To Have and to Hold the Said Lands & premises with All and Singular the appurtenances freely & Clearly acqu~ited~ and Discharged from Him the Said Jacob **RODGERS** and his heirs forever and the Said Jacob **RODGERS** do by these presents promise and Warrent that he will against himself and against all & Every other person or persons whatsoever Defend the Said Lands & premises free from any manner of Incumbrance to him the Said Robert **PARKER** and to his Heirs and assigns forever in Witness where of the Said Jacob **RODGERS** hath Hereunto Sett his hand and fix't his Seal the Day & Year above Written                    Jacob **RODGERS**

Signed Sealed & Delivered}
in the presents of              }
Demsey **SUMNER** sr Jurat
Thomas **FRYER**
Demsey **SUMNER**" [23]

This land adjoined Stephen **SHEPHARD** and is part of the patent to Richard **BARFIELD**. **BARFIELD**'s Nansemond County patent adjoined that of Peter **PHEBUS** in 1694, then William **PARKER** when it was patented to him in 1706. This Robert **PARKER** appears to be Robert[4], (*William[3], Thomas[2], William[1]*) a son of William[3] **PARKER**. He owned land adjoining the land of William[3] **PARKER** and is most likely Josiah[5] **PARKER**'s father. Robert[4] is mentioned in the processioning of

---

[22]  Haun, *Chowan County, North Carolina Deed Books: W-1 1729-1738; C-2 1738-1740; D 1748-1806, Vol. I*, c. 1998, C#2:77, 101:#511

[23]  NCSA, C.024.99005, Chowan County Miscellaneous Papers 1753-1756, Vols. VII, VIII—Vol. VII:62

his and Stephen **SHEPARD**'s adjoining land 25 February 1756.[24] His birth is estimated here to be ca. 1710. Both Robert[4] and Josiah[5] **PARKER** paid one poll tax each in Hertford County from 1768 through 1770.[25] Robert[4] **PARKER** was most likely dead before 1784, as he does not appear in the Gates County tax list for that year.[26] The name Robert also appeared in the family of Josiah[5] through several generations. The birth of Josiah[5] **PARKER** is estimated here to be ca. 1735.

On 10 February 1786, Josiah[5] **PARKER**, Sr., made a deed of gift to his son, James[6] **PARKER**, "for and in Consideration of the Natural Love and affection wh[ich] he hath and Bareth unto the Said James **PARKER** his son as also for the Better Maintainance and Perfirmant [sic] of the Said James **PARKER**..." It is described as "100 acres of land on the south side of **MILLS** Swamp, it being one Moiety of a Tract of Land the Said Josiah **PARKER** bought of Stephen **SHEPHARD** by a Deed baring date the Twentieth Day of August in the year of Our Lord one Thousand Seven Hundred & Fifty Six...Be___ning at a pine a Corner Tree in **ROGERS**'s Line on the South Side of **MIL__** Swamp thence Runing a long **ROGERS**'s Line to a White Oake a Corner ___ on the other side of Toe [?] [the?] Pecoson thence Eastwardly binding on Thoma_ **PILAND**s Line to a Red Oak thence near Northwestwardly along a L___ marked Trees to a Chenkapen Oak Standing in the Edge of **MIL__** Swamp thence up the Said Swamp to the first Station..."[27] He signed this deed by his mark, a stylized letter "J," consisting of a vertical line crossed at the top, center and bottom. There is no extant record of his wife's name.

On 14 August 1786, Josiah[5] **PARKER** sold 25 acres of land to Stephen **SHEPHERD**, part of a previously mentioned patent to Thomas **PILAND** for 400 acres, dated 20 November 1728. It is described as "begining at a white Oake where Thomas **PILAND** Corners at **MILLES** patent line thence along **MILLES** Line to a Red Oake and Corners thence running Near a west Course Joining the Sd. Josiah **PARKER** by a line of Marked trees to a post Oke and Red oke Corner Trees from thence Running Near a South Course to Thomas **PILAND**s line to the first Station..."[28] He used the same mark on this document.

On 1 February 1787, Josiah[5] **PARKER** leased to James[6] **PARKER** for £1:10 rents, "land whereon Josiah **PARKER** Liveth during next six years..."[29] He used that same mark on this document as well, and Josiah[6] **PARKER**, Jr. was one of the witnesses. He signed with his own mark, a letter "X."

In 1784 and 1785, Josiah[5] is shown in the Gates County Tax Lists as owning 175 acres in Captain William **GOODMAN**'s Captaincy. He gave son James[6] 100 acres, and sold another 25 to Stephen **SHEPHERD** in 1786, which should have left him with 50 acres. In 1787, James[6] is shown with the 100 acres and Josiah[5], Sr., is shown with 75 acres. In 1788, he listed 100 acres, though there appears to be no recorded conveyance of any sale or acquisition. Josiah[5] no longer appears in the Tax Lists as of 1789, and James[6] **PARKER** then listed 175 acres.[30] It is clear that Josiah[5] (*Robert[4],William[3],Thomas[2],William[1]*) died in 1788-1789, and his land consisted of 75 acres at that time. He died intestate and left no estate records.

Josiah[6] **PARKER** appeared in the Court of Pleas and Quarter Sessions 19 February 1782, and "came into Court and Confesed his begeting a Basturd Child on the Body of Naomi **WILLIAMS** Ordered that he give Security in the sum of One Hundred pounds Gold and Silver money at the same time Moor **CARTER** and Thomas **VANN** came into Court and offered themselves as Securitys for keeping the said child from becoming Chargeable to the said County."[31] Naomi was the daughter of Samuel and Mary **WILLIAMS** of Gates County, and was mentioned in Samuel's will of 11 April

---

[24] Fouts, *Processioners' Records Chowan County, North Carolina 1755/1756; 1764/1765; 1795-1797; 1800 and 1808,* c. 1993, 16-17:.#25

[25] Fouts, *William Murfree Tax Receipt Book Hertford County, North Carolina 1768-1770,* c. 1993, 27:#47; 50:#104

[26] NCSA, C.041.70001, Gates Tax Lists 1784-1831, 2 Vols., Vol. 1:3, Capt. Wm. Goodman's Captaincy

[27] Gates Co., NC, Deed Book 1:172 Copy, courtesy of Jim and Julie Sizemore, Gates County, NC.

[28] Ibid., 1:223, courtesy of Jim and Julie Sizemore.

[29] Ibid., 2:57, courtesy of Jim and Julie Sizemore.

[30] NCSA, C.041.70001, Gates Tax Lists 1784-1831, 2 Vols., Vol. 1:4;25;32;62;79.

[31] Fouts, *Minutes of County Court of Pleas and Quarter Sessions Gates County, North Carolina 1779-1786,* c. 1994, 44:#86

1789, as "Naomi **PARKER**."[32] This will was proved in February Court 1791. There is no extant marriage record for Josiah[6] and Naomi.

On 16 August 1791, Timothy **WALTON** sold Josiah **PARKER** 150 acres described as "beginning at the mouth of a small branch that issueth out of **BENNET**s Creek Pircoson by name of Crooked Branch, meanders of said branch to a pine at the head, straight course to a pine in Horsepen Swamp, down the Swamp to a pine now the line of George **OUTLAW**, his line to a pine near the head of a small branch out of the Percoson, down the branch to the Percoson, to a juniper 50 yards below Cow Bridge, to a juniper in the Reads to a Juniper within 10 yards of Sd. Timothy **WALTON**'s bridge, to the high lands 10 yards below sd. bridge, along the high land to the first station...part of a pattent granted to Chowan Indiens on **BENNETT**'s Creak..."[33] This land is located in Indian Neck, south of Gatesville. Indian Neck is formed by **BENNETT**'s Creek and Catherine Creek.

On 15 February 1794, Josiah[6] **PARKER**, and Oma his wife, sold 37½ acres to James[6] **PARKER** and it was described as "on the South Side of **MILLS**'s Swamp Begining at a Live Oak being a Corner tree on James **RIDDICK's** Line and so Runing along the Sd **RIDDICK's** Line untill it comes on **SHEPHARD**s Line & so runing along the Said **SHEPHERD**s line untill it Comes to a Corner tree being a Red Oak a new line made by the Sd. Josiah & James **PARKER**..."[34] This sale was Josiah[6]'s remaining interest in his father's land.

On 19 January 1799, Timothy **FREEMAN** sold 200 acres to Josiah[6] **PARKER**, being all the high land, beginning on the side of the "purcoson in Robert **TAYLOR**'s line, to the horsepen Swamp, along the swamp to Charles **SMITH**'s line, his line to Timothy **WALTON**'s line, to the purcoson to the first station..."[35]

Josiah[6] **PARKER** sold 140 acres of the 150 he had purchased in 1791, to James **BAKER** on 15 February 1799, and another three acres to Timothy **FREEMAN** on 25 July 1800.[36] He sold the 200 acres to Riddick **TROTMAN** on 25 August 1800.[37]

The 1786 State Census for Gates County shows Josiah[5] **PARKER**, Sr., with one white male between 21 and 60 years of age, and one either under 21, or above 60. His son, James[6], was still under 21 in 1786. He began paying a poll tax in 1787.[38] His birth is estimated here as ca. 1765. Josiah[6] **PARKER**, Jr., was obviously an elder son, as he was paying a poll tax in 1784, and perhaps before.[39] He is listed in the 1786 Census with the identical enumeration of white males in his household.[40] A study of later records makes it apparent that his eldest son was also named Josiah[7]. Josiah[6] **PARKER** (*Josiah[5],Robert[4],William[3],Thomas[2],William[1]*) was dead by February 1827, as shown by an order of Court "that Robert **PARKER** orphan of Josiah **PARKER** decd. be bound to Francis **ELLINOR** to learn the trade of a taylor."[41] Timothy **HAYSE** was appointed Guardian to Robert[7] **PARKER**, orphan of Josiah[6] in May Court 1828, in the amount of $500, with William **HAYSE** and Zacheriah **HAYSE** as his securities.[42]

James[6] **PARKER** (*Josiah[5],Robert[4],William[3],Thomas[2],William[1]*) lived his entire life on the land his father gave him, at Sarem. He was dead before 9 February 1805, when the inventory of his estate was taken by his administrator.[43] It included 250 acres of land. On 18 February 1805, Henry

[32] Almasy, *Gates County, North Carolina Wills 1779-1807, Volume I*, c. 1984, Gates Co., p. 85-86, Will Book 1:90-91

[33] Gates County, NC Deed Book 2:263

[34] Ibid., 3:119

[35] Ibid., 4:334

[36] Ibid., 5:28; 5:237

[37] Ibid., 5:161

[38] NCSA, C.041.70001, Gates Co. Tax Lists 1784-1831 [1784-1806] p. 32, William Goodman's Captaincy

[39] Ibid., p. 4

[40] Register, Alvaretta Kenan, *State Census of North Carolina 1784-1787*, Second Edition, c. 1973, Genealogical Publishing Co., Baltimore, MD, Gates County, p. 38

[41] Fouts, *Minutes of County Court of Pleas and Quarter Sessions Gates County, North Carolina 1824-1827, Vol. VI*, c. 1988, 127:#1466

[42] Ibid., *1828-1831 "Rough Minutes" May 1827-May 1833, Vol. VII*, c. 1990, 17:#23

[43] NCSA, G.041.2194761, Gates County Estates, Record of 1765-1920, Vol. Parker, E.- Parker, M., Folder: Parker, James 1805, Doc.#838-842, hereafter Gates County Estates. The document number is above the record,

**COPELAND** went into Court and moved for the administration on the estate of James[6] **PARKER**, deceased, which was granted on his giving bond and security in the sum of £800. William **GOODMAN**, Esqr. and William **GOODMAN**, of Joel, came into Court and offered themselves as his securities. Henry **COPELAND** exhibited the inventory of James[6]' estate in that same court.[44]

The sale of the perishable estate of James[6] **PARKER** was made 28 February 1805. Items were sold to James, Judah, Nancy, Peter, John & Miles **PARKER**, Henry **COPELAND**, James **BRADDY** and Isaac **PIPKIN**, among others.[45] Judith **PARKER** petitioned the Court for provisions for her and her family for one year, as the widow of James[6] **PARKER**, deceased, in November 1805.[46] The Court ordered that Isaac **PIPKIN**, Esquire, Thomas **BARNES**, Henry **GOODMAN** and James **GATLING** lay off to Judith "so much of the Stock, Crop & provisions as shall be sufficient for hers & her familys support for one year."[47] A division of the estate of James[6] **PARKER** was made 17 August 1808, to Judith, Peter[7], James[7], John[7], Jesse[7], Polley[7], Milley[7], Robert[7] and Asa[7] **PARKER**.[48] This division consisted of the funds left in the accounts of Henry **COPELAND**, Administrator, after all the debts were paid, out of the cash in the house and the amount of sales of the perishable property. Each heir received £9.12.8½.

James[6] and Judith had another child, but she was dead by September, 1805. James D. **MOSELEY** presented a bill for a visit and medications in September 1805, to the "Estate of Miss Ann E.[7] **PARKER** daughter of James **PARKER** decd."[49] It was proved 5 July 1806. A receipt from Whitmel **EURE** to "Henry **COPELAND** Administrator of the Estate of Jas. **PARKER** Decd. 10 Shillings for Making a Coffin for Nancey **PARKER**," was dated 20 May 1806, and witnessed by John **LEWIS**.[50]

A writ of partition for lands of James[6] **PARKER** was dated 20 August 1810, and the division of his real estate was made 15 January 1811, to James[7], Peter[7], John[7], Robert[7], Milly[7], Jesse[7], Polly[7] and Asy[7] **PARKER**.[51]

In August Court, 1810, it was ordered that James **GATLING**, Thomas **BARNES**, John **WARREN** and Mills **LEWIS**, with the County Surveyor, make a division of the real estate of James **PARKER**, deceased. This order was in response to a petition of Peter and James **PARKER** for that purpose.[52] The division of the real estate of James[6] **PARKER** is presented here, in full: "Pursuant to an Order of Court hereunto annexd [sic] We the Subscribers being Qualified for the purpose of making a Division of the Real Estate of James **PARKER** decd /between the Heirs/ Report in manner and form following Viz

Set a Part to James **PARKER** Survey No 1-containing Nineteen acres On which stands the Dwelling House Beginning at Isaac **PIPKIN**s Corner in **MILLS**'s Swamp then On his line S22 E 64 po to a markd [sic] Gum by the path thence along said Path S 64 W 18 po to a Post Oak thence S 5 E 100 po to a Sweet Gum in John **SHEPHERD**s line thence On his line West 15 po to his Corner pine thence N 5 W 165 po to a Corner Water Oak in the Swamp thence Down the run to the First Station.

Set a Part to Peter **PARKER** Survey No 2 Contng [sic] Nineteen Acres Beginning at a markd Gum standing On the North side of a Path thence as the Path goes S64 W 18 po to a post Oak thence S 5 E 100 po to a Sweet Gum in John **SHEPHERD** line thence On his line E 42 po to a pine in Isaac **PIPKIN**s line thence On his line N 8 W 18 pole thence N 22 W 88 po to the first Station.

---

on the film.

[44] Fouts, *Minutes of County Court of Pleas and Quarter Sessions Gates County, North Carolina 1800-1805, Vol. II*, c. 1985, 114:#453

[45] NCSA, G.041.2194761, Gates County Estates, Folder: Parker, James 1805. Doc. #776-1781

[46] Ibid., Doc. #798-799

[47] Fouts, *Minutes of County Court of Pleas and Quarter Sessions Gates County, North Carolina 1800-1805, Vol. II*, c. 1985,132:#480

[48] NCSA, G.041.2194761, Gates County Estates, Folder: Parker, James 1805. Doc. #785-788

[49] Ibid., Doc. #827

[50] Ibid., Doc. #833

[51] Ibid., Folder: Parker, James 1798 Doc. #770-771;765-769. These documents are misfiled, and belong in the 1805 folder.

[52] Fouts, *Minutes of County Court of Pleas and Quarter Sessions Gates County, North Carolina 1806-1811, Vol. III*, c. 1985,117:#665

Set a Part to John **PARKER** Survey No 3- Begining at a Corner Water Oak Standing in **MILLS** Swamp his Brother James Corner tree thence On his line S 5 E 166 po to a pine John **SHEPHERD**s Corner thence West 20 po to a Pine thence N 5 W 166 po to a Corner Gum in the Swamp thence Down the run to the first Station.

Set a Part to Robert **PARKER** Survey No. 4 Containing Twenty & Four Acres Beginning at a Marked Gum Brother Johns Corner in **MILLS**s Swamp thence On his line S5E166 po to a Corner pine thence W36 po to post O [sic] thence N3E 150 po to a Gum in the Swamp thence down the run to the first Station.

Set a Part to Milly **PARKER** Survey No. 5-Beginning at her Brother Roberts Corner Gum in **MILLS**'s Swamp thence On his line S 3 W 150 po to a Corner Post Oak thence West 34 po thence from a Corner Maple thence N 10 E 60 po to Gum in a Branch thence Down the Meanders of said Branch to **MILLS**'s Swamp thence down the Swamp binding the run to the Beginning.
Containing Twenty three Acres. [sic]

Set a part to Jesse **PARKER** Survey No. 6 Containing Twenty & One Acres Begining at Gum Jams [sic] **JONES** Corner in **MILLS** Swamp thence On his line S 17 W 150 po to a Pine thence East 36 po to a Corner Maple thence N 10 E 60 po to a markd Gum in a Branch thence down Said Branch to the run of the Swamp thence up the Run to the Beginning.

Set a Part to Polly **PARKER** Survey No. 7-beginning at a Pine John **SHEPHERD**s Corner thence with his line S 64 po to a pine thence W 70 po to a Corner Sweet Gum in Col **BAKER**s line thence N 64 po to a pine thence East 70 po to the Beginning Containing Twenty eight /Acres/

Set a Part to Asy **PARKER** Survey No. 8 containing Twenty eight acres Begining at a Col [sic] **BAKER**s corner White Oak thence On his line N 69 E 6 po to White Oak thence East 80 po to a Sweet Gum a Corner thence N 64 po to a Pine thence West 57 po to a pine in James **JONES** line thence with his line S 26 W 57 po thence S 20 W 15 po to the Beginning.

Given under Our hands & Seals this 15th January 1811 John **WARREN** {Seal} Mills **LEWIS** {Seal} James **GATLING** {Seal} Pa.. **HEGERTY** Sur {Seal} NB: Surveying & making out the Report 4 days}"[53]

Jesse[7] **PARKER**, son of James[6] **PARKER**, was born circa 1792. He was "about fifteen years of age" when he was bound as an apprentice to Richard **RAWLS** to learn to be a house carpenter in August Court, 1807. Robert[7] **PARKER**, another son of James[6], was born ca. 1799. In that same Court, he was bound an apprentice to Reuben **HARRELL**, "to learn the business of a Cooper," having been "about eight years of age."[54]

Asa[7] was the youngest child in this family. Peter[7] **PARKER** was appointed guardian to Asa[7], "orphan of James **PARKER**, decd." in November Court, 1819. An order was made in August Court, 1823, "that a Sci Fa to issue against Peter **PARKER** Guardian to Asa **PARKER** Orphan of James **PARKER** decd. to appear at next Court and renew his Guardian Bond or give other or Counter Security for the said Guardianship as the Court may direct &c."[55] No record of earlier guardian bonds has been found. Asa[7] **PARKER** was born ca. 1804, not long before his father died.

Judith, widow of James[6] **PARKER**, made her will as Judith **EURE**, 23 February 1821. It was probated in August Court, 1823. She gave all her lands to her grandsons, Asa H.[8] **PARKER** and Theophilus[8] **PARKER**, "to be Equally divided between them after the death of my sun [sic] Peter **PARKER** and Elizabeth **PARKER**." Most of her stock went to grandsons Wiley[8] **PARKER** and James[8] **PARKER**, also after their parents' death. She mentioned her daughters, Mildred[7] **PILAND** and Mary[7] **HENDRIN**, and granddaughter Sally E.[8] **PARKER**. Peter **PILAND** was one of the witnesses to this will. Judith made a codicil to that will 30 April 1823, wherein she bequeathed to her "son Peter **PARKER**, all my right title and interest in and to that part of my former Husbands Estate James **PARKER** which was lately resolved in our last Soperour [sic] Court...whatever amount may

---

[53] NCSA, C.041.2194761, Gates County Estates, Folder: Parker, James 1798 Doc. #765-767 These documents are misfiled, and belong in the 1805 folder.

[54] Fouts, *Minutes of County Court of Pleas and Quarter Sessions Gates County, North Carolina 1806-1811, Vol. III,* c. 1985, 40:#547

[55] Ibid., *1818-1823, Vol. V,* c. 1987, 53:#1106;165#1287

fall to my part...,"⁵⁶

Peter⁷ **PARKER** (*James⁶,Josiah⁵,Robert⁴,William³,Thomas²,William¹*) first appeared in the Gates County Tax List for 1806, paying one poll-tax, with no land.⁵⁷ He continued with that status until 1815, when he appeared with the 175 acres his mother, Judith **PARKER**, had listed in 1807 and 1808.⁵⁸ The only other person who listed 175 acres for taxes in the same captaincy was one John **PARKER**, in 1809.⁵⁹ He was most probably John⁷ **PARKER**, brother of Peter⁷ **PARKER**. Peter⁷ does not appear in the list of taxables for the county after 1826. That listing shows he owned 52 acres.⁶⁰ It would appear that Peter⁷ **PARKER** had died circa 1826. His son, Theophilus⁸ **PARKER** appeared on the Tax Lists with that 52 acres beginning in the year 1827.⁶¹

Peter⁷ **PARKER** appeared on a marriage bond with Betsey **BROWN**, dated 19 June 1805.⁶² She will be remembered as the daughter of James and Christian (**PARKER**) **BROWN**, discussed in Chapter 3.

A petition to the Spring Term of the Court of Equity for 1846 is transcribed here:
"State of North Carolina}
            Gates County}        In Equity Spring Term 1846
To the Honorable the Judge of the Court of Equity of said County.

The petition of James **PARKER**, Wiley **PARKER**, Edwin **PARKER**, Peter **PARKER**, Westley **PARKER**, Richard [sic] **CROSS** and Wife Eliza Jesse **DUNFORD** and Wife Siddy of Sophie Robert and Dossey **PARKER**, infants, by their next friend John **WILLY** humbly complaining Sheweth

That Peter **PARKER** late of said County died some few years since, intestate, seized and possessed of a certain tract or parcel of land lying in said County adjoining the lands of Jno. D. **PIPKIN**, Blake **BRADY**, John **RIDDICK** and others, and containing fifty acres more or less.

That said Intestate left him surviving his children and heirs at law James **PARKER** Wiley **PARKER**, Edwin **PARKER**, Peter **PARKER**, Westly **PARKER**, Eliza **CROSS** intermarried with Richard **CROSS** and Theophilus **PARKER** who has since died intestate leaving his widow Siddy since intermarried with Jesse **DUNFORD**, and his three infant children Sophie, Robert, and Dossey who are without guardian to whom the said lands have been transmitted, and who yet hold the same as tenants in Common- as follows.

The petioners James **PARKER** Wiley **PARKER**, Edwin **PARKER**, Peter **PARKER**, and Westly **PARKER** being Each Entitled to one Seventh part thereof; The said Richard **CROSS** and Wife Eliza to one Seventh part; the petitioners Jesse **DUNFORD** & Wife Siddy to a life Estate in one third of the remaining Seventh part, and the petitioners Sophie, Robert, and Dossey being Entitled to the residue of the last mentioned Seventh, in Equal shares.

Your Petitioners further shew that they are desirous to have partition of the said descended lands among the co-tenants according to their respective shares, in order that Each may possess his and her part in severalty-and that an actual division, from the number of tenants and the small Extent of the land, could not be made without serious injury to their several interests in the premises.

Your Petitioners therefore pray your Honor to order and decree that a sale be made of the lands aforesaid, for the purpose of division, and that the clerk and Master be directed to conduct such sale, making due advertisement thereof and selling at the Court House door on such reasonable credit and taking such security for the purchase money, as shall on the one hand tend to Enhance the value of the property and secure the money at which the premises may be bidden [sic] off-and make due return at the next term of this Honorable Court

And that your Honor would from time to time make all other and further needful orders as

---

⁵⁶ Almasy, *Gates County, North Carolina Wills 1807-1838, Vol. II*, c. 1985, p. 89, Will Book 2:198-199
⁵⁷ NCSA, C.041.70001, Gates Tax Lists, 1784-1831, two volumes [1784-1806] Mills Lewis' Captaincy, 1806, p. 357
⁵⁸ Ibid., [1807-1831] Richard Barnes' Captaincy, 1807, p. 8; 1808, p. 24; Richard Smiths' Captaincy, 1815, p. 133
⁵⁹ Ibid., Richard Barnes; Captaincy, 1809, p. 39[1807-1831]
⁶⁰ Ibid., John Speight's Captaincy, 1826, p. 338
⁶¹ Ibid., p. 364, Richard Odom's Captaincy
⁶² Almasy, *Gates County, North Carolina Marriage Bonds 1778-1868*, c. 1987, p. 68

shall be just and proper and tend to the more Effectual relief of your petitioners in the premises. And as in duty bound &c                    Wm: J **BAKER** Sol for Petitioners"

An affidavit of John **RIDDICK**, attesting that a division could not be made of the land "without serious injury," appears at the bottom of this document.[63]  On the basis of this petition, a decree was handed down that the Clerk and Master in Equity should offer the land for sale, on a credit of 12 months with interest from the day of sale.[64]  The Clerk and Master made his report to the Fall Term of Court, 1846.  He offered the land for sale "before the Court House door in the Town of Gatesville on the 18th day of May 1846, when one Jesse **DUNFORD** appeared and bid the sum of One Hundred dollars, which being the highest and last bid said land was Knocked off to said **DUNFORD**..."[65]

It will be noted that in the above petition, the name "Richard **CROSS**" is used.  On 6 October 1847, Riddick **CROSS** and Eliza **CROSS**, his wife, sold to Rufus K. **SPEED** "for the Consideration of Twelve dollars & thirty two Cents all the money now in the hands of the Clerk & Master in Equity of the County aforesaid arising from the sales of the land belonging to the heirs at law of Peter **PARKER** deceased under a decree of the Court of Equity..."  Riddick **CROSS** signed his name and Eliza used her mark of "X", with the name Sarah Eliza **CROSS**.  They appeared on a marriage bond dated 11 November 1845, as Riddick **CROSS** and Sarah E. **PARKER**, with Richard **CROSS** as bondsman.

Theophilus[8] **PARKER** (*Peter[7],James[6],Josiah[5],Robert[4],William[3],Thomas[2],William[1]*) and Sidney **PARKER** appeared on a marriage bond dated 5 January 1830, with John **WILLEY** as bondsman. Sidney **PARKER** will be remembered as the daughter of Jesse and Ann (**BRADY**) **PARKER**, discussed in Chapter 4.[66]  Theophilus died circa 1840.  His last appearance in the Tax Lists was for 1839, when he was listed with that 52 acres.[67]  His was an uncommon name and it underwent unexpected changes to appear quite differently in the records.  The petition for dower of Siddy [sic] **DUNFORD** is transcribed here in full:

"North Carolina}          Court of Pleas & Quarter Sessions Nov? Term 1844

Gates County  } To the worshipful the Justices of the Court of Pleas & Quarter Sessions of said, [sic] the petition of Siddy **DUNFORD**, the widow of Orpha **PARKER** deceased, late of Said County Sheweth your worships that her Said husband Orpha **PARKER** departed this life about four years ago intestate, seized in fee of a tract of land in Said County devised to him by one Judith **EURE**, adjoining the lands of Wm W **COWPER** Jesse **PARKER**, and John D **PIPKIN** Containing by estimation fifty Acres, on which your petitioner is entitled to dower.

Your petitioner sheweth your worships that no administration has been taken out upon her deceased husband's estate and that no guardian has been appointed for the Children of her said husband, namely Sophia Ann, James Robert, & Dawson **PARKER**.  She there fore prays your worships, to appoint some discreet person guardian ad litem /to accept service of this petition/ and to order the sheriff of Said County, to summon a jury to go upon the premises and lay off Dower to her according to law: and that they make their report to the next term of this Court.

Wm: J **BAKER** Sol for Petitioner

The reverse of this document shows "Jesse **DUNFORD** Siddy **DUNFORD** his wife widow of Orpha **PARKER** decd. Petition for Dower To The Court  Filed at Nov Term 1844  Service accepted W G **DAUGHTRY**."[68]  The Writ of Dower to the Sheriff of the county shows his name as "Offa" **PARKER**.[69]

James B.[8] **PARKER**, (*Peter[7],James[6],Josiah[5],Robert[4],William[3],Thomas[2],William[1]*) was born 14 October 1814, and died 12 January 1895.[70]  He appeared on a marriage bond dated 27 December 1847,

---

[63]  NCSA, C.041.2194762, Gates County Estates, Vol. Parker-Pierce, Folder:  Parker, Peter 1846, Doc. #176-178

[64]  Ibid., Doc. #184

[65]  Ibid., Doc. #180

[66]  Almasy, *Gates County, North Carolina Marriage Bonds 1778-1868*, c. 1987, p. 67, Jesse Parker and Nancy Brady marriage bond, dated 19 Dec. 1799, Willis Brown bondsman.

[67]  NCSA, C.041.70002, Gates County Tax Lists 1832-1851, [1832-1841] p. 228, Wm. H. Goodman's Captaincy

[68]  NCSA, G.041.2194762, Gates County Estates, Vol. Parker-Pierce, Folder:  Parker, Orpha 1844, Doc. #149

[69]  Ibid., Folder:  Parker, Offa 1845, Doc. #144

[70]  Fouts, Raymond Parker, personal transcription of gravestone in Parker Cemetery at Sarem, Gates Co., NC 18 September 1977.  Hereafter, Parker Cemetery at Sarem.

with Priscilla **HAYES**. Asa **HILL** was his bondsman.[71] He was obviously a widower, as he had a daughter named Roxanna[9] **PARKER** who was born 13 February 1842. Roxanna[9] died 29 June 1931.[72] She married Thomas **HOLLAND**, son of J. J. and Carrie **HOLLAND**, 31 January 1878.[73] Thomas **HOLLAND** preceded her in death 11 September 1927.[74]

James B.[8] **PARKER** and his first wife had Roxanna[9] and he and Priscilla had Edward[9], John W.[9], Elizabeth A.[9] Sarah A.[9] Timothy[9], Lucy[9], William[9], Emily[9] and Susan[9] **PARKER**.[75]

John W.[9] **PARKER** was born 20 September 1854, and died 26 July 1935.[76] He married Emily O. **BROWN** 22 January 1884, by Thomas T. **SPEIGHT**, Minister.[77] Emily was born 29 April 1864, and died 2 September 1936.[78] No further information.

Elizabeth A.[9] **PARKER**, age 39, married Isaac W. **CRAWFORD**, age 62, son of Abram and Elizabeth **CRAWFORD**, on 15 October 1895.[79] No further information.

Timothy[9] **PARKER** was born Timothy Edward[9] **PARKER**, on 12 September 1859. He died 2 February 1927, of pneumonia.[80] He married Emily Hortense **ROUNTREE** 21 March 1894, at J. A. **ROUNTREE**'s residence. She was the daughter of John A. and Emily **ROUNTREE**.[81] Emily was born 27 August 1870, and died 1 June 1952.[82] No further information.

William[9] **PARKER** was 25 years old when he married Annie E. **HOFLER**, age 23, on 20 January 1892. She was the daughter of Hance and Caroline **HOFLER**.[83] No further information.

Wiley[8] **PARKER** (*Peter[7],James[6],Josiah[5],Robert[4],William[3],Thomas[2],William[1]*) lived just three doors away from James B.[8] **PARKER** in 1860. He was 49 years of age, thus would have been born circa 1811. The other members of his family were his wife, Susan, age 33, and children Emmy[9], age 16, Sarah[9], age 13, "B. F.[9]", a male child age eight and James, age five.[84] Wiley[8] died between August and November, 1860, after the census enumeration for that year. Susan **PARKER**, as his widow, petitioned the Court in November Term, 1860, for her year's provisions. She stated that "her said husband died intestate in the County aforesaid since the last session of this Court..."[85]

In November Term, 1861, the following petition was submitted to the Court of Pleas and Quarter Sessions: "To the worshipful the Justices of the said Court. The petition of Henry C. **WILLEY** & Riddick **GATLING**, Jr Administrators of Wiley **PARKER** Complaining respectfully sheweth unto your worships that their intestate Wiley **PARKER** departed this life sometime in the year 1860 domicilled [sic] in the County of Gates and intestate, That administration upon the Estate of said intestate was Granted by this Court to your petitioners at ~~May Ter~~ Febry Term 1861 Your petitioners show unto your worships that said intestate owned a small personal Estate which has been sold by your petitioners and amounts to about the sum of Twenty five dollars. That said intestate was at his death seized and processed [sic] of a tract of land lying in said County and bounded by the lands of John **WILLEY** Sr John H [?] **PARKER** & ~~Elisha~~ James **ROOKS**, containing thirty acres or about that quantity. Upon which there are several small log houses of but little value. One third of said tract is cleared and in an ordinary state of cultivation That the land is poore? & is worth about the sum of One hundred and fifty dollars, subject as it is to the dower right of Susan **PARKER** the widow of the said intestate. Your petitioner shows unto your worships that the land herein described descended at

---

[71] Almasy, *Gates County, North Carolina Marriage Bonds 1778-1868*, c. 1987, p. 67

[72] Parker Cemetery at Sarem.

[73] Register of Deeds Office, Gatesville, NC, Gates County Marriage Register 1867-1882

[74] Parker Cemetery at Sarem

[75] US Census, Gates Co., NC, 1860, Roll #898, p. 16, Reynoldson Twp., Fam #595; 1870, Roll M593-1139, p. 4, Reynoldson Twp., Fam #30; 1880, Roll T9#964, p. 1, Reynoldson Twp.,Fam #3,

[76] Parker cemetery at Sarem

[77] Register of Deeds Office, Gates County Marriage Register 1883-1923, 1884

[78] Parker Cemetery at Sarem

[79] Powell, David, *Late Nineteenth Century Gates County Marriages from 1883 to 1900*, c. 1997, p. 32

[80] Register of Deeds Office, Gates County Death Records, 3:185

[81] Powell, David, *Late Nineteenth Century Gates County Marriages from 1883 to 1900*, c. 1997, p. 113

[82] Parker Cemetery at Sarem

[83] Powell, David, *Late Nineteenth Century Gates County Marriages from 1883 to 1900*, c. 1997, p. 112

[84] US Census, Gates Co., NC, 1860, Roll #898, 1860, Roll #898, p. 16, Reynoldson Twp., Fam #596

[85] NCSA, C.041.2194762, Gates County Estates, Vol. Parker-Pierce, Folder: Parker, Wiley 1861, Doc. #690

the death of said intestate to Mary **EURE** now the wife of ~~Nolley~~ /Jas. O./ **EURE**, of full age, and Emma Jane ~~Mary Susan~~, /Sarah Eliza/, Cornelius and ~~Mills~~ /Francis/ **PARKER** infants subject to the dower right of the widow aforesaid. The said infants have no Guardian to protect their rights." They requested of the Court that they appoint a guardian ad litem for the children and give them license to sell the land for the purpose of enabling them to settle the estate. The Court ordered that Henry L. **EURE** be appointed guardian ad litem "to Emma ~~EURE~~ /PARKER/ Sarah ~~EURE~~ /PARKER/ Eliza ~~EURE~~ /PARKER/ Cornelius ~~EURE~~ / PARKER/ and Francis ~~EURE~~ /PARKER/ heirs at law and orphans of Wiley **PARKER** decd..."[86]

In that same November Court, Susan **PARKER** submitted her petition for dower in the lands of her deceased husband, Wiley. In that petition, she names his heirs as "Mary **EURE**, wife of 'Nolley' **EURE**, Emma Jane, Cornelius and Frank **PARKER**."[87]

James O. **EURE** appeared on a marriage bond 21 February 1854, but the bride's name was left blank. His bondsman was Quinton **BRADY**.[88] The above documents prove that his bride was Mary[9] **PARKER**, daughter of Wiley[8] **PARKER** and his first wife, whose name is unknown. Susan would most likely have been too young to be Mary's mother. Mary[9] E. **PARKER** was born 15 April 1841, and died 22 September 1910. Her husband, James O. **EURE**, was born 1 July 1834, and died 25 August 1908.[89] They appear in the 1900 Gates County Census as having three sons at home. Their names were Charly[10], born August 1873, Nollie E.[10], born July 1878, and Lenward[10], born June 1881. The last name may have been "Leonard." Mary[9] is listed as mother of 10, with five living.[90] The only other known child of this couple was named Ella **EURE**, born 1859.[91] No further information.

Edwin[8] **PARKER** (*Peter[7],James[6],Josiah[5],Robert[4],William[3],Thomas[2],William[1]*) first appeared in the Gates County Tax Lists in 1842, listed as paying for one poll, with no land. That held true for 1843, as well. In 1844, he was listed as being liable for one poll tax and 52 acres of land.[92] He made no other appearances on these lists after 1844.

Peter[8] **PARKER** (*Peter[7],James[6],Josiah[5],Robert[4],William[3],Thomas[2],William[1]*) was born 4 October 1818, and died 15 April 1883. His wife was Elizabeth Ann **HOFLER**, born 1 April 1837, and died 23 May 1890.[93] They appeared on a marriage bond dated 21 January 1858.[94] On 5 October 1883, an order was made in the Gates County Court for allotting a year's provision to Elizabeth A. **PARKER**, widow of Peter **PARKER** deceased, and her family of four children under 15 years of age. Among the items allowed her were cattle, hogs, a horse, household and kitchen furniture, a clock, two tables, a common desk, two looking glasses and a sewing machine, all the potato and cotton crops, and all the carpenter's tools, which amounted to a value of $620.00.[95]

In the 1885 Spring Term of Superior Court for Gates County, Elizabeth A. **PARKER** initiated an action against J[as]. R. **PARKER** and L. L. **SMITH**, Trustee. The complaint was "That on the 3d. Sept. 1877 J. R. **PARKER** was indebted to Peter **PARKER** decd by note upon which was due that day $552.60, with interest thereafter at six per cent given for the purchase of a tract of land in Gates County...which note was in the hands of L. L. **SMITH** for collection."[96] In Spring Term of Superior Court, 1885, in the case of "Elizabeth **PARKER** against Jas. R. **PARKER** & Lewis [?] L. **SMITH**

---

[86] NCSA, G.041.2194762, Gates County Estates, Vol. Parker-Pierce, Folder: Parker, Wiley 1861, Doc. #678-680

[87] NCSA, G.041.2194762, Gates County Estates, Vol. Parker-Pierce, Folder: Parker, Wiley 1861 Doc. #671

[88] Almasy, *Gates County, North Carolina Marriage Bonds 1778-1868*, c. 1987, p. 28. Ms. Almasy noted that the "1860 census shows a female named Mary age 22."

[89] Gates County Cemetery Survey, http://www.throughwire.net/gates/family/jamesoeure.htm, by Julianne Sizemore. There are excellent pictures of this cemetery, including close-ups of the stones on this site.

[90] Powell, David, *1900 Gates County Census*, c. 1994, p. 208

[91] Almasy, *Gates County, North Carolina Census 1850 & 1860*, c. 1987, 1860, p. 144

[92] NCSA, C.041.70002, Gates County Tax Lists 1832-1851, [1842-1851] 1842, p. 14, William H. Goodman's Captaincy; 1843, p. 48; 1844, p. 80

[93] Gates County, NC, Historical Society, *Bible Records of Gates County N. C.*, c. unknown, p. 150

[94] Almasy, *Gates County, North Carolina Marriage Bonds 1778-1868*, c. 1987, p. 48

[95] NCSA, G.041.2194762, Gates County Estates, Vol. Parker-Pierce, Folder: Parker, Peter 1883, Doc. #188-190

[96] Ibid., Doc. #192-195

Trustee &c Present Hon Wm. M. **SHIFF** Judge presiding: This cause coming now to be heard by the Court and a jury & the jury having found all the issues in favor of the plaintiff and assign her damages at Twenty nine dollars and it further appearing that the said amount is secured by a conveyance of the following real estate to the defendant L. L. **SMITH** Trustee: Beginning at a maple, corner of Henry G **WILLIAMS** heirs [?] and L. W. **PARKER**-thence south 11° E 37 ½ poles to a gum near the gate, thence nearly the same course a line of marked trees 156 poles to a large white oak corner on Mr **UN-FLEET**s [sic] heirs-thence N 75 W 22 poles to a gum-thence nearly the same course a line marked trees 67 poles to a Small pine, corner on J **SEARS** line & the balance of the said tract above mentioned, thence due North 168 poles to the run of Knotty pine Swamp thence up the run of said Swamp & down the line of H G **WILLIAMS** land to the first station containing 72 acres-In Book #28 page 185 On motion of ____ [illegible words] of counsel for the plaintiff, it is adjudged that the plaintiff recover of the defendant J. R. **PARKER** the sum of Twenty Nine Dollars, with interest thereon till paid together with the sum of $ ___[blank] costs here of And it is further adjudged that unless the said defendant pay to the plaintiff or into Court for her use the amount herein before adjudged against him in sixty days after the adjournment of this court, then the defendant **SMITH** is required to sell the above described land, after thirty days public notice, at the Court house door in Gatesville and three other public places in said County, at the said Court house door and out of the proceeds of Sale pay the judgment ___ and principal, interest and cost, together with the cost of sale and the balance pay the said **PARKER**."[97]

Peter[8] and Elizabeth **PARKER** had the following children: Harriett Ann[9], born 9 October 1859, died 21 December 1879; Charles Thomas[9], born 8 August 1861, died in November 1880; Indiana Riddick[9], born 4 September 1862, died 3 September 1924 and was married to Harrison L. **BROWN**; William Ambrose[9], born 7 September 1864, died 21 May 1890; James Edward[9], born 1 October 1866, died 30 September 1939; Stephen Arnold Douglas[9], born 4 July 1869, died 1 September 1948; Julia Etta[9], born 20 January 1873, died 29 May 1890; Sally Mary[9], born 15 August 1876, died 22 January 1947, and Louis Claiborne[9] **PARKER**, born 10 April 1881, died 7 October 1948.[98] No further information included here.

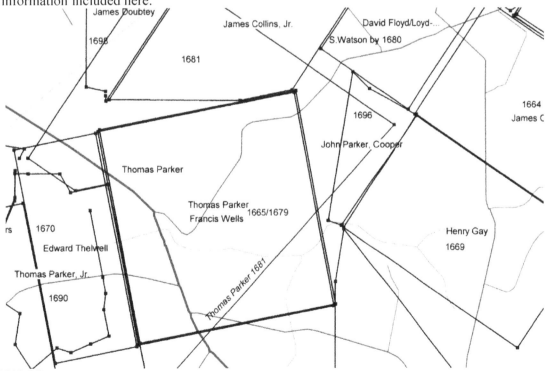

Scale: 2000 ft/in

Map depicting VA Land Patents to Thomas[2], Thomas[3] and John[4] **PARKER**, near the Nansemond and Isle of Wight County border, north of Holland, VA.

---

[97] NCSA, G.041.2194762, Gates County Estates, Vol. Parker-Pierce, Folder: Parker, Peter 1883, Doc. 198-200
[98] Gates County, NC, Historical Society, *Bible Records of Gates County N. C.*, c. unknown, p. 150

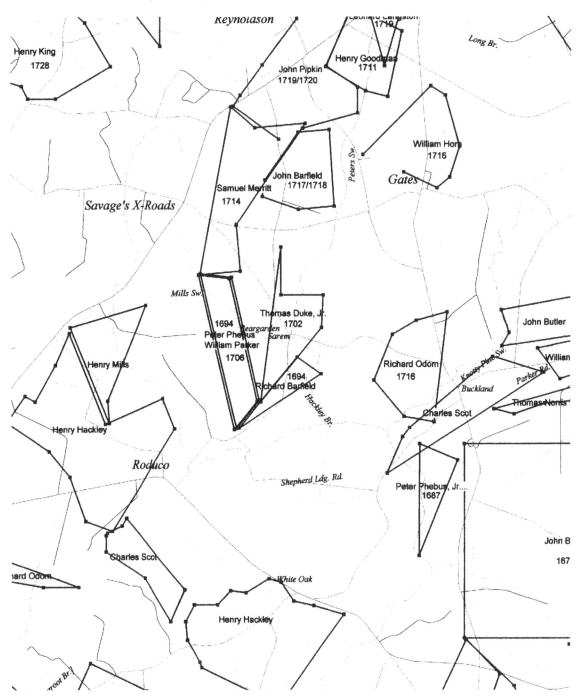

Map depicting William[3] **PARKER**'s 1706 VA Land Patent between **MILLS** and **PETERS** Swamps in Gates County, NC.

## Other descendants of William³ PARKER *(Thomas²,William¹)*

John⁴ **PARKER** *(William³,Thomas²,William¹)* first appears in Chowan County records at a Vestry held in Edenton on 12 March 1742/43.  It was then "Ordered that Mr: John & Mr: Richard **PARKER** Senr: be & they are hereby Appointed P[r]ocessioners from the Knotty Pine up the Road that Leads to the Virginia Line to the Said Line & perquim͟ons Line & all Contained between that & the Loosing Swamp &c."[1]  According to law, two freeholders in each canton, or district, were appointed to go around and mark the boundaries of each person's land once in every three years, as explained in Chapter 2.  Given that John⁴ **PARKER** would be required to be owner of a minimum of 50 acres, and at least 21 years of age to be considered a "freeholder," his birth would have occurred no later than 1722.  He may well have been born several years earlier.

His land is mentioned in a deed from Charles **RUSSELL**, of the Upper Parish of Nansemond County, VA, to William **FRIER**, of Chowan County, NC, dated 19 April 1744.  It is described as being "held by a Patent granted to John **LANGSTON** to these presents [sic] as by his sd Patent dated 30 Jul 1726, begining at a Corner Pine of John **PARKER**s standing on the side of Robert **ROGERS** Branch being a corner of Richard **ODOM**s & so runing from thence by a line of marked trees to Thomas **LANGSTON**s line near a Northerly Course runing along this line to a corner White Oak being a dividing corner between Charles **RUSSELL** & William **FRIER** & then runing along Thomas **LANGSTON**s line to the [sic] Thos. **PILINT**s [**PILAND**'s] line & so runing along Thomas **PILINT**s line to corner Gum of William **UMFLET**'s & so runing along Wm. **UMFLET**s line to the corner tree of sd **UMFLET**s standing on John **PARKER**s line being formerly a line of Richard **ODOM**s & so runing along John **PARKER**s line to the first station a corner Pine..."[2]

On 1 March 1718/19, Richard **ODOM** received a patent of 300 acres "lying in Chowan precinct Beginning at a Gum on the Marsh Cyprus run, then W. 112 pole to a pine, then W. 10 N 128 pole to a pine, then N. 95 W 140 pole to a pine, then by various courses down the Marsh Cyprus to the first Station..."[3]  This patent will be mentioned again.

In Chowan County October Court 1744, was read the petition of "sundry of the Inhabitants of Sarum Scratch Hall and Places adjacent which follows in these Words, Vizt, &ca.  Granted so far as relates to the Road and Ordered that the following Persons be and is [sic] hereby appointed a Jury to lay out the Same according to the prayer of the said Petition and to Make return thereof the next Court, Vizt:  Edwd. **VANN** Junr, John **LEWIS**, Willm. **SKINNER**, John **SKINNER**, John **TAYLOE**, William **TAYLOE**, James **HENTON**, Edwd. **WARREN**, Calum **ROSS**, John **ODOM**, William **LANGSTON**, William **LANGSTON**, Junr."[4]

In October Court 1745, the return for this order was made and the following persons laid off the road:  "John **LEWIS**, John **SKINNER**, Wm. **TALOE** [?] (**TALOR** [?]) Edwd. **WARREN**, Callum **ROSS**, Wm. **LANGSTON** Sen., Wm. **LANGSTON**, Edward **HARE**, Henry **KING**, Isaac **WILLIAMS**, Francis **SPEIGHT** & Moses **HARE**, and at the prayer of the said Persons, Isaac **WILLIAMS** and Wm. **JONES** are appointed overseers of the said Road and ordered that the following Persons & their hands work thereon Vizt:  Wm. **TAYLOR**, Jno. **MOOR**, Robt. **SMITH**, Callum **ROSS**, Jno. **THOMAS**, Wm. **WALLACE**, Jno. **HYNDS**, Joseph **CRAWFORD**, John **ODAM**, Robert **MANOR**, James **ELLIS**, James **ELLIS** Jur., Wm. **LANGSTON**, Wm. **LANGSTON**, Jur., Lenord. **LANGSTON**, Charles **RUSSELL**, Saml. **EUER**, Epaphrods: **JONES**, John **PARKER**, Jos: **VAN**, Thos: **LANGSTON**, Alex: **CARTER**, Edwd: **HARE**, _____ **KING**, Moses **ODAM**, Wm: **GOODMAN**, Martha **PIPKIN**s hands, Henry **GOODMAN**, Moses **HAIR** & Alexander **OLIVER**

---

[1]  Fouts, Vestry Minutes of St. Paul's Parish Chowan County, North Carolina 1701-1776, Second Edition, c. 1998, 45:104

[2]  Haun, *Chowan County, North Carolina Deed Books: A-1, E-1, F-1, F-2, G-1 (Deeds dated 1701-1755) Vol. II*, c. 1999, A#1:239-241, 41-42:#192,

[3]  NCLG, 1:270, File No. 186

[4]  Haun, *Chowan County North Carolina County Court Minutes Pleas & Quarter Sessions 1730-1745*, c. 1983, 99:#207

and that they are exempted from working on any other Roads."[5]  These records establish the location of this John **PARKER**'s residence in what became Gates County, and give the names of his neighbors.

On 12 December 1748, Jacob **ODOM** and Aaron **ODOM** sold John[4] **PARKER** 234 acres.  It is described as "part of a pattent to Richard **ODOM** 1 Mar 1718 and by the Sd. Richard **ODOM** given & bequeathed to sd. Jacob **ODOM** & Aaron **ODOM** Parties to these presents...lying on a branch known by the Name of **ROGGERS**es branch, beginning at a pine Standing on the East side of the said branch down said branch to a branch that divides James **ELLIS**es land from ye hereby granted & released land to a corner white oak in the mouth of a bottom Thence up the said branch to a branch called the Licking root branch to a water oak standing in the senter of the said branch, so up the said branch till it intersects with the pattent Line to a black gum thence West along ye sd line to the first station..."[6]

A deed of gift, [which amounts to a last will and testament,] was made from James **ELLIS** to his sons, James, Jacob, Joseph, William and Daniel **ELLIS**, 2 May 1752.  It gives to James, his eldest son, 66 acres, "as I purchased of Andrew **ROSS** & John **ODOM** patented by Richard **ODOM** and John **ODOM** the first patent dated 1 Mar 1718 & the other dated 25 Mar 1734 [?] & is bounded as followeth:  beginning at a Hickory standing near the Cyprus Swamp a corner tree that is Frances **LANGSTON**s thence along her line to John **PARKER**s line thence with his line to the Lickingroot Branch thence down sd branch to a marked Pine thence along a line of marked trees to the Cyprus Swamp thence up sd swamp to the mouth of the Likingroot [sic] Branch from thence up sd swamp to the first station;  To my Son Jacob **ELLIS** I give 50 A on the South side of a certain branch begining at a Pine standing in the head of the sd branch in John **PARKER**s line thence down the branch to a marked Gum standing in the side of the Cyprus Swamp from thence by a line of marked trees to the run of sd Cyprus Swamp..."[7]  Lickingroot Branch is now known as "Licking Branch," and lies just to the east of the community of Eure.

On 22 June 1754, Jacob **ODOM** sold John[4] **PARKER** 100 acres for £7 current money of Virginia.  It is described as "begining at a marked pine tree of James **ELLIS** Junr standing on the South side of the sand bank Swamp and Runing from the said pine by a Row of marked trees to a Corner Red oak Standing in the patent line and so Runing the Several Courses of the patent to a Corner Gum tree of John **ODOM**s and so Runing from the Sd. Corner along John **ODOM**s line to the sand bank Swamp and thence Runing down the said Swamp and binding on the Run to the first Station a Corner pine tree of James **ELLIS** Junr...being part of a patent granted unto Richard **ODOM** which bears date the first day of March 1718..."[8]

John[4] **PARKER**'s next purchase was 100 acres from Henry **BAKER** on 17 July 1754.  It is described as "being part of a patent granted to Henry **BAKER** Deceased for 640 acres bearing date the 28th Day of July 1730...as may more fully appear...begining at James **ELLIS**es Corner pine and runs thence on **ELLIS**s 200 pole to a pine on the River pocoson then along the River pocoson 108 pole to a pine thence No. 220 po. to a pine thence South 65E 120 pole to the first station..."  Nath **WILLIAMS**, Tho. **FRYER** and Joseph **WARREN** witnessed that deed.[9]

This is the last reference to John[4] **PARKER** prior to the formation of Hertford County in 1759.  The records of the intervening 20 years, between 1759 and 1779, when Gates County was formed, are forever lost, with two exceptions.  First, in the Processioners' return of Jacob **ODOM** and Jeames [James] **BRADEY**, on 11 February 1756, his land, and "his other land" was done.  John[4] was present, as were John **ODOM** and James **ELLIS**.[10]

Secondly, in the William **MURFREE** Tax Lists for Hertford County, he is termed "John

[5]  Haun, *Chowan County North Carolina County Court Minutes (Court of Pleas & Quarter Sessions) 1735-1738:1746-1748, Book II*, c. 1983, 93:155-156

[6]  Chowan County, NC Deed Book C#2:155

[7]  Haun, *Chowan County, North Carolina Deed Books: A-1,E-1,F-1,F-2,G-1 (Deeds dated 1701-1755) Vol. II*, c. 1999, G#1:71-74

[8]  Chowan County, NC Deed Book G#1:228

[9]  Ibid., G#1:225

[10]  Fouts, *Processioners' Records Chowan County, North Carolina 1755/1756; 1764/1765; 1795-1797; 1800 and 1808*, c. 1993, 3:4

**PARKER**, Senr." with two taxes paid in 1768. In 1769, and 1770, he is listed with three taxes.[11] During the Colonial period, a man was taxable at age 16, thus it would appear that John[4] **PARKER** may have had two sons who had attained that age by 1769. One of those sons would be John[5]. In 1754, he owned at least 484 acres of land and was a respected member of his community. He served as a processioner and was on the Grand Jury for the county.

John[4] **PARKER** was dead by 15 February 1783, as evidenced by the inventory of his estate taken by John[5] **PARKER**. That inventory is transcribed here to illustrate the variety of items in use at that time in an above-average home. It appears that John[4] was a minister.

"A True Inventory of the Estate of John **PARKER** Deceasd febary [sic] the 15 Day 1783

1 Horse

3 feather Beeds & Furnitude [Beds & Furniture]

1 Dush [Dish]

1 Case of Bottels

14 Puter Dishes

10 Puter Basons

14 puter plaits

14 Spoons

1 puter Tankard

3 Chist [Chest]

16 Table knifs

2 Table forks

4 axes

7 Hoes

2 Tabels

2 Plows & 1 Colter

1 Cross Cut Saw

1 han Saw

3 fryen pans

1 Box iorn an heatrs

1 trunk

6 [?] Stone mugs

1 [?] Iorn spit

2 Lock hingenglasses [Looking glasses]

3 Iorn Pots

3 Pair of Pot hooks

1 Iorn Pot hanger

1 sas pan [saucepan]

1 Iorn Skillet

2 Puter Porngers [Porringers]

1 tin funnel

1 Pep Per Bax [Pepper Box]

1 Punsh Boll

1 hack kel [hackle]

1 Pair of fier tonges

1 Grater

2 Pair of sisters [scissors]

2 Candel sticks

1 Parir [sic] of Sheep Shears

1 Bibel

1 testement

1 Prair Book

1 Sermond Book

2 Salters

2 histerry Books

8 Black Bottels

2 Butter pots

5 Chears

1 pair of Stillards

1 pair of iorn wedges

2 files

3 woshen tubs

2 pals

3 piggens

1 tray

1 Bool [Bowl]

5 Baskets

5 Ston Cups

2 Whitglass ____ [torn]

[Second page.]

2 Whit glas Botels

1 Wine Glass

4 Pair of Cards

1 Wollen wheal & Spindel

2 linnen wheals

1 Bell

2 Saddels

2 Bridels

1 pair of Sturrup iorns

3 DiluBs [sic]

1 flax Brak

2 Soop tuBs [sic]

1 Passel of Corn

1 Passl [sic] of Wheat

1 Siprous Cag [Cypress Keg]

1 Passel of Baken

1 Passel of Salt

1 PowDeren tub [sic]

1 Passel of hog lard

1 fat tub

---

[11] Fouts, *William Murfree Tax Receipt Book Hertford County, North Carolina 1768-1770*, c. 1993, 29:#50

1 han mill
1 Small Cag [Keg]
1 Bordar [?]
1 hatchet
1 taper Bit
1 Dowlen Bit
2 Cwopers adds [Cooper's adze]
2 Cwopers howels
2 par of Co/m/pases
1 Ginter [Jointer]
1 Cros iorn
1 rown shave
5 Drawen kniefs
1 Bar [?] of Sklesan waits
1 Gun Barrell an lock
1 Gun
1 sord [sword]
1 Small Passel of pine Staves
6 [?] Sider Barrels
7 hogs/h/ed
1 Pasel of trushoops
1 Pasel of flax onbrok [unbroken]

[Third page.]
1 Meell Sifter
2 Stacks of fodder
4 yards of Cloth
4 Doz. of Candels
1 Paire of fleams
5 Geese
1 passel of Scraps of Leather
1 Passel of flax Brake [broken]
4 old Barrels
1 paire of Carting Hams [Hames]
1 pair of Specksticls [Spectacles]
2 [?] Primers
a Part of one whip saw
7 Silver Dollars

his warren aparel [wearing apparel]
1 Side of lether in tan
1 Soustub
1 Smal passel of oister Shels
1 mil Bag
~~1 Passel of Passel~~
1 passel of pataters
1 Grin Ston
2 Gimblets
2 Chissels
2 orgers [augers]
1 Goug
1 Carpenders adds [adze]
1 Rasser [Razor]
1 froo [froe]
1 vice
1 Pair of nipers
1 Pair of Pinshers
3 Shumaking alls
2 Reap hooks
28 hogs
8 Sheep
2 hammers

### John **PARKER**

State of North Carolina Gates County ss  February Session Court of Pleas and Quarter sessions 1783
The within Inventory was Exhibited into Court on oath by John **PARKER** and was Ordered to be Recorded.          Teste Law **BAKER** CC
    And is Recorded in Book A. Folio 294/95
                    Teste Law **BAKER** CC"[12]

    The only other document in the Estate Record for John[4] **PARKER** is an administrator's bond for John[5] **PARKER** to administer on the estate of John **PARKER**[4], deceased, dated 17 February 1783. The bond was in the sum of £200 and his securities were Stephen **EURE** and Jesse **HARRELL**. All three signed their names.[13] In that same court session, it was ordered that William **BAKER**, George **WILLIAMS**, Jesse **HARRALL** and Seth **RIDDICK**, or any three of them, make a

---

[12]  NCSA, G.041.2194761, Gates County Estates, Record of 1765-1820, Vol. Parker, E.-Parker, M., Folder: Parker, John 1783, Doc. #1049-1052 [Note: Reading this inventory aloud is helpful in determining pronunciation of the phonetic spelling.]
[13]  Ibid., Doc. #1047

division of the estate of John[4] **PARKER** deceased.[14] That division has not been found.

John[5] **PARKER** *(John[4], William[3], Thomas[2], William[1])* appeared on a list of jurors to be called for November Court 1781, and was termed "John **PARKER** Junr." His neighbors, Samuel **EURE**, James **LANDING**, Thomas **BARNES** and Job **UMFLEET** were called to serve on that same jury.[15] His date of birth was no later than 1760, as he had to be 21 years of age to serve on a jury.

John[5] **PARKER** may have had a sister, and brothers named James and Benjamin **PARKER**, but that will be left for others to determine. He first appeared on the Gates County Tax List in 1784, when North Carolina began taxing land, as owner of 237 acres. It is impossible to determine whether he inherited, or purchased this land as the records were in Hertford County.[16]

The first recorded conveyance of land to John[5] **PARKER** was made 13 April 1787, and is abstracted here. "Isaac **PIPKIN** Sheriff of Gates County to John **PARKER** £100..100a. by a ___ Writ of Fi Fa Issued out of Our Inferior Court of Pleas & Quarter Sessions...the 19 [?] day of Feby in the 11th year of our Independence...Commanded that of Goods Chattles Lands & Tenements of the Estate of Charles **VANN** Decd you Cause to be made the sum of Fifty Eight Pounds Two Shillings Current Money of this State...Elisha _____ Senr. Recovered against him for Debt and also the sum of Two pounds nineteen Shillings & Eleven pence which to the said Elisha **COPLAND** Senr was adjuged [sic] and Taxes for his Case in that Sum Expended whereof Jesse **VANN** Admr of Charles **VANN** Decd is _____...begining at a Red Oake on the south side of the Main Sypress [sic] Swamp Standing in William **JONES**es Line then Runing by a Line of Marked Trees to a white oake standing in the patent Line then Runing the Several Courses of the Sd. patent Line to the Main Sypress Swamp thence up the Sd. Swamp with a Line of Marked Trees to the first Station...which Sd. Land is part of a patent Granted to John **NICHOLS** Baring Date the sixth Day of June 1699 Relation being thereunto had doth mor [sic] fully and at Large appear..." Witnesses were Philip **LEWIS** and John **PIPKIN** proved May Ct. 1787, Reg. 12 Aug. 1787.[17]

The following Virginia Patents point out the location of this land. On 20 April 1694, Catherine **LANGSTONE**, "Widow relict of John **LANGSTONE** decd." of Nansemond County, received a patent for 380 acres described as "Land Scituate lyeing & being upon one of the Cypruss branches which Comes out of Sarum Creeke in Nansemond County begining at a Markt white oake in a forke of the Swamp or branch on the Northward side thereof and runs thence Northeasterly twenty five degrees two hundred forty Six poles to a markt pine thence Northwesterly Sixty five degrees two hundred pole to A Markt pine thence Southwesterly twenty five degrees three hundred Eighty Six pole to a Markt pine by the Maine Swamp side thence down the Swamp According to the Courses thereof and bounding thereon to the first Station..."[18]

On 6 June 1699, John **NICHOLLS** received a patent for 249 acres "in the upper parish of Nansemond County at a place called New St. Georges on the North Eastward Side of a Swamp called the cyprus Swamp begining at a pine a Corner tree of Katherine **LANGSTONE**s Standing by the Swamp Side runing thence North Easterly twenty two degrees one hundred Sixty two poles bounding on **LANGSTONE**s line to a white oake, thence Northwesterly fifty three degrees Two hundred fifty four poles to a hiccory thence Southwesterly fifteene degrees one hundred eighty two pole to a red oake Standing in the aforesaid Swamp near the maine rune [?] thence running the Severall Courses of the Said Swamp and bounding thereon to the first mentioned markt pine the said land being due unto the sd John **NICHOLS** by & for the Transportation of five persons...6 June 1699...John **NICHOLLS** Sarah **NICHOLLS** his wife John **NICHOLLS** Ann **NICHOLLS** Mary **NICHOLLS**"[19] These patents place this land to the east of the community of Eure, NC, on NC 137.

On 10 December 1787, Henry **COPLAND** sold Demsey **LANGSTON** 100 acres. It is described as "beginning at a Hickory standing near the Runn of the Sypress Swamp thence Runing by a

---

[14] Fouts, *Minutes of County Court of Pleas and Quarter Sessions Gates County, North Carolina 1779-1786*, c. 1994, 56:#111

[15] Ibid., 36:70

[16] NCSA, C.041.70001, Gates County Tax Lists 1784-1831, [1784-1806,] Charles Eure's Captaincy, p. 6

[17] NCSA, C.041.40001, Gates County Real Estate Conveyances 1776-1788, Vol: A,1; 1:274

[18] VSLA, 8:335

[19] Ibid., 9:190

Line of Marked trees to a Certain bottom of Jno. **PARKER**s line thence with his Line to **ROGERS**es Branch thence Down the branch to the Sypress Swamp thence Down the Sypress Swamp to the first Station which the Said Land was Granted to Richard **OHDOM** [sic] by patten bearing Date the 1st Day of Marh [sic] Anno Domini 1718 Relation being thereunto may more fully appear and Large it Doth & may appear...”[20]  This deed establishes that John[5] **PARKER** owned the same land that has been mentioned as belonging to his father in 1744.

John[5] **PARKER** made his next purchase of land of 100 acres from Thomas and Margret **ROBERTSON** on 18 September 1790.  It is described as “being held by a patten Granted John **LANGSTON** to these presents as by this said Patten Bearing Date the Twentieth Day of July in the year of our Lord Christ Seventeen Hundred Twenty Six all doth and may fully and Largely appear and is Bounded as followeth Vizt, Begining at a corner Tree of Jno. **PARKER**s that usd [sic] in Richard **ODOMOM**s [sic] Patten to be a pine but that by Chance fell down and the present holders of the Land have made Choice of an Oake in its Stead Standing on the Side of Robert **ROGERS**es Branch near the place whereon the aforsaid Pine Stood then Runing John **ODOM**s Line to Stephen **PILANT**s Line So runing Stephen **PILANT**s Line to Thomas **PILANT**s Line then Runing Thomas **PILANT**s line to a Corner of Charles **EUR**s so Runing Charles **EUR**s Line to Sephen [sic] **EUR**s Line and then down Stephen **EUR**s Line to the first Station...”[21]  Thomas **PILAND**’s name will be remembered from Chapter 7.

On 26 January 1795, Elisha **LANDEN** and Levina **LANDEN** sold John[5] **PARKER** 50 acres, described as “Begining in the Little Cypress on Thomas **HARRELL**s Line thence Runing along Said **HARRELL**s line to David **UMPHLET**s line as was then along Said **UMPHLET**s line as was to the Liking Rute [Lickingroot] Branch thence up the Liking Root Branch to a corner of John **PARKER**’s in his Line thence along Said **PARKER**s Line to Haw Tree Branch Israel **BEEMAN**s line thence along the Haw tree Branch Israeel [sic] **BEEMAN**s line to the little Cypress thence down the Little Cypress to the first Station this being the bounderies of one Hundred Acres of land be the same more or Less of this sd. Land so bounded we the aforsaid Elisha & Levina **LANDEN** do Bargain & sell one half unto John **PARKER** his Heirs & assigns for ever the Sd. one half being as by Estimation Fifty acres be the same more or Less being part of a patent Bearing Date the 25th day of March Ano Dom 1743 Granted Unto John **ODOM** Decd....”  Jesse **TAYLOR**, Samuel **GREEN** and Benjeman [sic] (+) **EURE** were witnesses to this deed.[22]

The last recorded purchase of land by John[5] **PARKER** was made 3 February 1796.  Stephen **ROGERS** sold him 100 acres “on the South Side of Cypress Swamp and is bounded as followeth Vizt Begining on the main Cypress swamp at a pine standing in or near the Edge of the Said Swamp thence Near Wt [?] Course by a line of Marked Trees to a Corner Tree Standing in Demsey **LANGSTON**s Line Now along his line to a Corner pine tree of Isaac **LANGSTON**s thence with that Line to a Corner pine of Lewis **SPARKMAN**s & with his Line to the head of /the/ Miry Branch thence down the various Courses of the said Branch to the Main Cypress Swamp thence up the Varcoures [sic] of the Sd. Swamp to the first Mentioned Station with the Said Tract & parcel of Land is part of a Paten Granted to Capt. Henry **BAKER** Bearing Date the 8 [?]th day of July 1730...”  Isaac **LANGSTON**, Kindred **PARKER** and William **UMPHLET** witnessed this deed.

The above deeds account for 587 acres up to 1796.  On 20 December 1802, John[5] **PARKER** sold 1 acre of land to Kindred[6] **PARKER** for the sum of £1 “Current Money of North Carolina.”  It is described as “Beginning at A post Standing on the North Side of the Edenton Roade whereon the said Kindred **PARKER**s House Stands and Runing East to a post Standing on the said Road thence runing North to a Corner post Standing in John **PARKER**s Field thence Runing West to another Corner Post Standing the [sic] said **PARKER**s Field thence Runing South to the first Station Mentioned...” John[5] **PARKER** signed his name, as did the witnesses, James **CRAFFORD**, Reuben[6] **PARKER** and Bray[6] **PARKER**.[23]

John[5] **PARKER**’s full name was “John Baptist **PARKER**.”  He was so named in the Gates

---

[20]  NCSA, C.041.40001, Gates County Real Estate Conveyances 1776-1788, Vol: A,1, 1:323
[21]  Ibid., C.041.40002, 1786-1795, Vol: 2,3, 2:195-196
[22]  Ibid., 3:242-243
[23]  Ibid., C.041.40004, 1803-1810, Vol: 6,7,8, 8:183-184

County Tax List of 1797, as owning 712 acres.[24] The second instance of this name was in August Court 1799, as a juror in the action of Amos **RAYNOR** against Katherine **PILAND**.[25] Middle names, fathers' names, occupations, landmarks, and the designations of "Jr." and "Sr.," were all used to distinguish men of the same given name.

John[5] **PARKER** was dead by 15 May 1810, when his Administrator, Kindred[6] **PARKER**, took an inventory of his estate.[26] On 21 May 1810, Kindred[6] **PARKER**, Richard **BARNES** and William W. **RIDDICK** entered into a bond of £5,000, for Kindred[6] to administer on the estate of John[5] **PARKER**, deceased. All three signed their names.[27]

A Writ of Dower for Clarkey **PARKER**, to have her part of her deceased husband's lands was also made out 21 May 1810, the date of a writ for her year's provisions.[28] On 7 June 1810, her dower was laid off to her as "the ho__ [torn] of the Plantation /& tract of land/ & improvements whereon the the [sic] said John **PARKER** the Husband of the said Clarkey Died Seisd. & possessd. of..."[29] Her portion of the lands amounted to 230 acres, as evidenced by the Tax List of 1811. She retained that land up through 1823.[30]

Clarkey **PARKER** was the daughter of Stephen **EURE**, as evidenced by his will of 3 December 1816, wherein he bequeathed $10.00 to her. His other daughters were Treasy **SPARKMAN**, Penelope **HARRELL** and Mary **LANGSTON**. His will was probated in May Court 1817.[31]

Clarkey **PARKER** was dead by 17 November 1823, as evidenced by Kindred[6] **PARKER**, William W. **COWPER** and Jonathan **WILLIAMS** having entered into an administrator's bond, in the amount of $3,000, for Kindred[6] to be administrator on the estate of Clarkey **PARKER**, deceased.[32] Kindred[6] took the inventory of her estate on 18 November 1823, and made a sale of her personal property 28 November 1823.[33] In November Term, 1824, it was ordered by the Court that Kindred[6] sell all the Negroes belonging to her estate and he did so on 3 January 1825. "1 half Negro Man **JACOB**" was sold to Dempsey **PARKER** for $125.30, Negro Woman **AMA** to Ebron **BRISCO** for $173.05, Negro Girl **CATE** to Dempsey **PARKER** for $250.25, Negro Boy **LUTAN** [?] to Abram W. **PARKER** for $300.06 and Negro Girl **EDITH** to Trecy **PARKER** for $240.00. The total amount was $1,088.66.[34] In an audited account of 16 August 1826, it was noted that H. **HAYS** was paid $4.50, plus $0.54 interest, for making Clarkey's coffin.[35]

Sales of the personal estate of John[5] **PARKER** were made 1 June 1810, by Kindred[6] **PARKER**. Some of the purchasers were Kindred[6], Mary[6], Bray[6], Clarkey, Ruben[6], John, Seth[6] and Elizabeth[6] **PARKER**, for a total of $612.91½.[36]

In August court of Pleas and Quarter Sessions, 1811, it was "then and there Ordered that Kindred **PARKER** Admr. of John **PARKER** decd. Sell Seven Negroes (to wit) **JACOB, AMEY, MARY, SILLA, PEGG, CATE** and **JAMES**, as the Law directs in such cases, in order that an equi-

---

[24] NCSA, C.041.70001, Gates County Tax Lists 1784-1831, [1784-1806,] 1797, Capt. David Lewis' Captaincy p. 205

[25] Fouts, *Minutes of County Court of Pleas and Quarter Sessions Gates County, North Carolina 1794-1799, Vol. I*, c. 1984, 126:#245

[26] NCSA, G.041.2194761, Gates County Estates, Record of 1765-1920, Vol. Parker, E.-Parker, M., Folder: Parker, John 1803, Doc. #1092-1095

[27] Ibid., Doc. #1122-1123

[28] Fouts, *Minutes of County Court of Pleas and Quarter Sessions Gates County, North Carolina 1806-1811, Vol. III*, c. 1985, 111:#656

[29] NCSA, G.041.2194761, Gates County Estates, Record of 1765-1920, Vol. Parker, E.-Parker, M., Folder: Parker, John 1803, Doc. #1173

[30] NCSA, C.041.70001, Gates County Tax Lists 1784-1831, [1807-1831,] 1811, Capt. Abraham Cross' Captaincy, p. 75; 1823, Capt. Asa Odom's Captaincy, p. 285

[31] Almasy, *Gates County, North Carolina Wills 1807-1838, Vol. II*, c. 1985, p. 63-64, Will Book 2:146-147

[32] NCSA, C.041.50011, Gates County Administrator's Bonds 1822-1847, #29

[33] Ibid., G.041.2194760, Gates County Estates, Record of 1765-1920, Vol. Odom-Parker, Folder: Parker, Clarkey 1824, Doc. #1341; #1336

[34] Ibid., Doc. #1339

[35] Ibid., Doc. #1344

[36] NCSA, G.041.2194761, Gates County Estates, Record of 1765-1920, Vol. Parker, E.-Parker, M., Folder: Parker, John 1803, Doc. #1061-1070

table Division may be Made amongst [sic] the legal representatives of the deceased, and that he make a return of his proceedings to this Court hereunto annexed. Teste J **SUMNER**, Clk" The following is an account of those sales:

"A True acct. of Sales of the Negroes belonging to the Estate of John **PARKER** Decd. Sold by the Administrator on the 2nd January 1812 at Six months Credit

| One Negro Man **JACOB** to | Mary & Bray **PARKER** | $390 25½ |
| One Girl **MARY** to | Seth **PARKER** | 310 00 |
| 1 Woman **AMEY** & Child **CATE** | Clarkey **PARKER** | 300 00 |
| 1 Girl **PEGGY** to | Kindred **PARKER** | 90 25½ |
| 1 Girl **PRESILLER** to | Kindred **PARKER** | 130 00 |
| 1 Boy **JAMES** to | Rubin [sic] **PARKER** | 150 1½ |
| Erors [sic] Exceptd. | | $1370 52½ |

Kindred **PARKER** Admr."[37]

Abraham[6], Demsey[6] and Theresa[6] **PARKER** came into May Court 1813, and chose Reuben **PARKER** as their guardian. All three would have had to be at least 14 years of age to make that choice. It was ordered that he give bond and security in the sum of £500 each.[38] The last record of his guardianship was a return for Demsey to February Court 1819.[39]

It was ordered by Gates County Court, on 20 August 1810, that the division of the real estate of John **PARKER** deceased be made and returned to November Court next. That division is transcribed here in full. "Pursuant to an Order of Court Hereunto Subjoined we the Subscribers being Qualified for the purpose of making a Division of the Real Estate of John **PARKER** deced. between his Legitimate Heirs report as followeth Set apart to Kindred **PARKER** Survey No. 10. Containing Forty and Nine Acres Begining at the main Road in William **HUMFLEET**s line thence on His line N33.W.8 po. to a pine Thence N39W35 po Thence N17W.30 po to a post Oak thence N39w10 po. to a Water Oak a Corner in the Lickingroot Branch thence up Said Branch 104 po to a Persemon Tree a Corner thence S19E 120 po to a Stake a Corner of One acre he Bought of his Father on which Stands his Dwelling /House/ thence the Side of Said Acre to the road thence binding said Road to the first Station.

Set apart to Reuben **PARKER** Survey No 9 Containing Sixty Acres Subject to a Deduction of Fifteen Dollars, Begining at a Stake a Corner of an Acre of Ground Set a Part To His Brother Kindred thence N.19.W.120 po. to a Corner Common Tree in the Lickingroot ~~Branch~~ thence up the run to the Intersection of Stephen **EURE**s line thence with his line S 35 E 28 Po. Thence S20 E [?] Elisha **HARRELL**s line 120 pole to abraham **BEEMAN**s Corner thence S3w.12 po. to the road thence binding on said road to the Corner of the Acre lot thence the two Sides of Said Lot to the begining.

Set apart to Seth **PARKER** Survey No. 6 Containing Forty Acres-with Twenty five Dollars to be paid him ~~by~~ Out of Brays Lot & fifteen Dollars Out of Rewbens [sic] lot making forty Dollars, begining at the road in Abraham **BEEMAN**s line thence on his line S3w.6. po thence S 8 w 38 po S20 E36 poles to a poplar thence S40.w 10 poles to a Pine **SMITH**s Corner Thence N 46 w 30 po. Thence N. 53 W.14 po. to a white Oak thence S 46 W. 74 po. to a White Oak-Thence on Thomas **HARREL**s [?] line N30W.39 pole to a Pine William **UNPHET**s [sic] Corner thence N33 W 30 pole to the road thence binding on Said Road to the first Station.

Set a Part to Demsey **PARKER** Survey No. 1 Calld. the House or Middle Division Containing Sixty four Acres Begining at a Water Oak a Corner in **ROGERS**s [sic] Branch thence by a new made line S 38 E. 160 po. to an old Corner water Oak in the Lickingroot thence up the Run 84 po to a Corner Gum thence N 38 w 140 po. to a Corner Gum in **ROGERS**s Branch thence Down Said Branch binding the run to the Begining

Set a Part to Abraham **PARKER** Survey No. 2 Containing Sixty & four Acres, Begining at a Corner Water oak Standing the [sic] Lickingroot Branch thence on William **UMPHLET**s line to an-

37 NCSA, G.041.2194761, Gates County Estates, Record of 1765-1920, Vol. Parker, E.-Parker, M., Folder: Parker, John 1803, Doc. #1059-1060
38 Fouts, *Minutes of County Court of Pleas and Quarter Sessions Gates County, North Carolina 1812-1817, Vol. IV*, c. 1986, 37:#801
39 Ibid., *1818-1823, Vol. V*, c. 1987, 36:#1078

other water Oak Alexander **CARTER**s Corner at the mouth of a Small Branch thence up said branch about Half way where the Water parts & runs into **ROGERS** Branch thence up Said Branch to a Corner Water Oak thence by a new made line S 38 E 160 pole to the beginning

Set apart to Treecy **PARKER** Survey No. 3 Containing Seventy and Six Acres Begining at her Brother Demseys Corner Gum in **ROGERS** Branch Thence S 38 E 140 po to another Gum in the lickingroot thence up Said Branch to the Intersection of Stephen **EURE** line Thence on his line N. 18. w. 54 po. thence N. 45. w. 64 po. to a water Oak Jno. **ODOM**s Corner in a Branch thence Down said Branch to the first Station.

Set apart of Levy **PARKER** Survey No. 4 Containing one Hundred acres Called the **ROB-ERTSON**s Tract begining at a water Oak John **ODOM**s & Stephen **EURE** Corner thence in the The [sic] Head of **ROGERS** Branch thence on Said **ODOM**s line N 67 E 24 po. thence N 43 E 30 po thence N. 27 E 44 po thence N 25 E 14 po thence N 36. E 6 po. thence N 52 E 16 po thence N 67. E 22 po. thence N 74 E. 14 po. thence N 60. E 8 po thence N 74 E. 8 po thence N 83 E 20 pole to a white Oak thence E 20 po thence N 73 E 24 po to a Sweet Gum Col. **BAKER**s Corner Thence on his line S 28 E 31 po to a Post Oak thence S 83 E 114 Pole to a White Oak a Corner of Charles **EURE**s land thence S 65 w. 89 po. thence S 80. w. 34 po. thence S. 67. w. 15 po. to a Gum Stephen **EURE**s Corner thence on his line S. 80 w. 40. po thence N. 75 w. 40 po. thence west 49 po. thence S. 85. w. 61 po Thence S. 74 w. 30. po to the first Station-a Crooked line I I [sic] Pray

Set apart to Mary **PARKER** Survey No. 8 Containing Sixty acres Begining at Levi **LEE**s Corner Gum in the run of the Cypress Swamp running thence with Said **LEE**s line S. 66. w. 60 po. thence S. 71 w. 34. po. to a pine thence S 80 w. 44 po. to a pine by the Fence S. 64 w. 21 po. to a Corner Post Oak thence Running across the Tract S 26. E 80 po to a Corner Gum in the Miery [?] Branch thence Down the run to the run of the Cypruss Swamp thence up Said run to the first Station.

Set apart to Elizabeth **PARKER** Survey No 5 Containing Sixty acres, Begining at a post Oak in /her/ Sister marys [sic] Corner in Levy **LEE**s line thence on his line S 64 w. 31 po thence S. 67 w. 40 po. Thence S. 83 W. 55. po. thence S. 68 w. 48 po to a pine Taylor **CROSS**s Corner thence On his line S. 50. E. 52 po to a Pine Lewis **SPARKMAN**s Corner thence on his line N. 85 E 130 po to a B [sic] Gum in the Mirey Branch thence Down the run of Said Branch to a Gum Mary **PARKER**s Corner thence on her line N 26 w 80 pole to the beginning.

Set apart & Allotted to Bray **PARKER** Survey No. 7 Containg [sic] Seventy and Six acres being the Place he now dwels [sic] Begining at a Red Oak in Levey **EURE**s line Thence on his line N 5 E 92 pole to a Corner Gum in a branch thence up Said Branch Binding The Lands of John **ODOM** 52 po. to a Pine thence leaving Said Branch and running by a line of Trees S. 68. w 60 po thence S 50 w 40 po thence S. 28 w. 48 po. to a pine a Corner in James **GATLING**s line thence S 50. E. 7 Po. to a Pine Said Levy **EURE**s Corner thence on His line S. 80. E. 100 po. to his fence thence S. 87 E. 40 pole to the begining Subject to pay Pay [sic] No. 6. $25. Farewell. Given under Our hands and Seals this 15 of Novr. 1810.  John **ODOM** {Seal} David **LEWIS** {Seal} Thomas **BARNES** {Seal}  Pa. **HEGERTY** Sur. {Seal}"[40]

Kindred[6] **PARKER** *(John[5],John[4],William[3],Thomas[2],William[1])* was born circa 1774. The 1850 Federal Census, enumerated 20 September 1850, shows Kindred, age 76, Prissila, age 65 and Jane **PARKER**, age 23.[41] He was married twice, which becomes evident in determining some of his childrens' ages. He first appears on a marriage bond dated 13 December 1800, with Mary **LANGSTON**. Blake **EURE** was his bondsman. It was noted that he was "of Hertford County" at that time. He next appears on a marriage bond dated 11 June 1820, with "Prissillar" **WILLIAMS**. His bondsman then was Abraham **PARKER**.[42]

His first known land purchase was made 18 February 1800, for 12½ acres from Jesse **TAY-LOR**. It is described as "begining at a black Oak a Corner Tree of Mills **LANDING**s and Jesse **TAYLOR** thence runing a line of Marked trees with Mills **LANDING**s to a Red Oak a Corner tree thence along **TAYLOR**s line to [sic] White Oak a Corner Tree in Jesse **TAYLOR**s line thence along the Said **TAYLOR**s line to Water Oak a Corner tree in Jesse **TAYLOR**s thence along the said **TAY-**

[40]  NCSA, C.041.40005, Gates County Real Estate Conveyances 1811-1812, 1815-1819, Vol: 9,10, 9:26-29
[41]  Almasy, *Gates County, North Carolina Census 1850 & 1860*, c. 1987, p. 81 1850
[42]  Almasy, *Gates County, North Carolina Marriage Bonds 1778-1868*, c. 1987, p. 68

**LOR**s line to the first Station..." John **PARKER**, Whitmill **EURE** and Elisha **HARRELL** witnessed this deed.[43]

The deed for one acre from his father on 20 December 1802 has been mentioned above, as well as the division of his father's land, wherein he acquired another 49 acres, 15 November 1810. On 23 September 1810, Seth[6] **PARKER** sold Kindred[6] 40 acres on the east side of the Edenton Road, "Beginning at a Red oak Standing on the Side of the sd. Road in Abraham **BEEMAN**s line thence up the said road to William **UMPHFLEET** [sic] line thence along the sd. **UMPPHLET**s [sic] Line to Thomas **HARREL**s line as was thence along the said **HARREL**s line to a Corner white Oak of Joseph **SMITH**s thence along the sd. **SMITH** line to a Corner pine of Joseph and Abraham **BEEMAN**s thence along the said **BEEMAN**s to a poplar a Corner of sd. **BEEMAN**s thence Running along the sd. **BEEMAN**s line to the First station mentioned with sd. Track [sic] and parcel of land is part of a paten granted to John **ODOM** Decd. Bairing date 25th Day of March and Adomini [sic] 1743..." The witnesses were Timothy **LANGSTON** and James H (X) **FOWLER**.[44] This parcel is the one received by Seth[6] **PARKER** in the division of his father's lands.

In February Court 1812, it was "Ordered that Kindred **PARKER**, William **UMPHLETT**, Alexander **CARTER** and Bray **PARKER** with their hands work on the Road that leads from John **LEWIS**'s to the Winton Road &c."[45]

On 20 December 1815, Kindred[6] **PARKER** sold Lewis **SPARKMAN** 12½ acres, part of a patent to William **HORN**, dated 22 January 1718. It is described as "begining at Jesse **TAYLOR**s corner a red Oak on **LANDING**s line thence along the sd. **TAYLOR**s line a west course to a Sassafras a corner tree thence along the sd. **TAYLOR**s line to a Water Oak a corner tree, a North cours [sic] thence along the sd **TAYLOR**s line a East course to a Black oak a corner tree thence along **LANDING**s line a South cours to the first station..." Levy **EURE** and Mary (X) **PARKER** witnessed this deed. It was proved in February Court 1816.[46]

On 11 November 1820, William P. **JAMESON** sold Kindred 170 acres for $600.00. It is described as "Beginning at the Ready branch where the Road crosses Said branch, thence down Said branch, to Knotty pine swamp thence down said swamp, to a cypress, a corner tree of Henry **SEARS** thence said **SEARS**'s marked line about a Northwest course to a marked pine a corner tree of Mills **LEWIS**'s thence said **LEWIS**'s line of marked trees, about an East course to the Road, then along the said Road to the first station..." George **WILLIAMS** and William **BYRD** witnessed this deed.[47]

On 16 November 1820, Kindred[6] **PARKER** sold Reuben[6] **PARKER** 101 acres for $550.00. It is described as "Beginning at a water Oak William **UMPHLET**s corner Standing in the lickel [sic] root branch thence up the said branch to a Persimmon tree a corner of Reuben **PARKER** thence along the various courses of said **PARKER**s line to Abraham **BEEMAN**s line thence along Said **BEEMAN**s line to a corner a Poplar stump thence along said **BEEMAN**s line to a pine a corner of Joseph **SMITH** thence along sd **SMITH**s line to a corner white Oak thence along sd. **SMITH**s to Alexander **CARTER**s line corner a white Oak Stump thence along Said **CARTER**s line to William **UMPHLET**s line thence along Said **UMPHLET**s line to the first mentioned Station or Beginning." Wm. M. **HARVEY** and Jno. **BEEMAN** witnessed this deed.[48]

In February Court 1821, it was ordered that Kindred[6] **PARKER** administer on the estate of Timothy **LANGSTON**, deceased, and that he give bond & Security in the sum of $500.00. In August Court of that year, he was appointed Overseer of the road leading from George **ALLEN**'s Shop to **MANNEY**'s Ferry in the room and place of William P. **JAMESON**, deceased.

Kindred[6]'s occupation is revealed in August Court 1823, when it was ordered "that James **BUTTLER**, son of Martha **BUTTLER** be bound an apprentice to him to learn the trade of a cooper. On motion, it was ordered that Kindred[6] **PARKER** be granted administration on the estate of Clarkey

---

[43] NCSA, C.041.40003, Gates County Real Estate Conveyances 1794-1803, Vol: 4,5, 5:104-105

[44] Ibid., C.041.40004, Gates County Real Estate Conveyances 1803-1810, Vol: 6,7,8, 8:184-186

[45] Fouts, *Minutes of County Court of Pleas and Quarter Sessions Gates County, North Carolina 1812-1817, Vol. IV*, c. 1986, 9:748

[46] NCSA, C.041.40005, Gates County Real Estate Conveyances 1811-1812,1815-1819, Vol: 9,10, 10:120-121

[47] Ibid., C.041.40006, Gates County Real Estate Conveyances 1819-1829, Vol: 11-13, 11:82-83

[48] Ibid., 11:71-72

**PARKER**, as previously mentioned.[49] In August Court 1825, he was appointed Overseer of the road in the room of John **BRADY**. Kindred resigned that post in August 1826.[50]

On 15 October 1825, John **BRADY** sold Kindred[6] **PARKER** 50 acres for $175.00. It is described as "Begining at a persimmond tree standing on the side of the old pond [?] a corner of William **SEARS**es thence a direct course to white oak standing in the sd. **SEARS**es line nearly a South est [sic] course thence To a warter oak in a bottom in William P **JEAMESON** [sic] former line thence down the various courses of sd. bottom a line of marked trees to **PETERS** swamp thence a line of marked trees to the main run to a gum a corner tree thence up the main run of sd. swamp to a gum standing in sd. main run oppersit the mouth of **BRADY**s mill swamp thence up the main run of sd. **BRADY**s mill swamp to an ash tree a corner of William **SEARS**es thence along sd. **SEARS**es line of marked trees to a persimmond tree a corner of sd. **SEARS**es thence along sd. **SEARS**es line to the first station or begining..." The witnesses were Conrad **WOLFLEY** and Hy. H. **EURE**.[51]

Kindred[6] **PARKER** was in May Court 1827, and it was ordered that "William **JONES** an infant child son of Elizabeth **JONES**" be bound to him to learn the cooper's trade. In that same Court, it was ordered that **PENEY** and **ABA**, "Colourd Children," be bound apprentices to him, but no occupation was stated. Girls were usually to learn spinning and weaving, or "house business."[52]

He continued to purchase land in Gates County and on 25 May 1829, John **BRADY** sold him another 50 acres, for $160.00. It is described as "Beginning at a poppaw [sic] gum standing in the main run of **PETERSON**'s [sic] swamp in Isaac **PIPKIN**'s line and a corner of Said K. **PARKER**'s line, thence along said **PARKER**'s line to a water Oak a corner of William **SEARS**, thence along said **SEARS** line to a pine a corner in **SEARS** line, thence along a line of marked trees to a water Oak a corner standing near said **BRADY**'s field, thence a line of marked trees to a black gum standing near the edge of said Swamp thence a line of marked trees down the edge of said swamp to a sweet gum a corner tree in the edge of said swamp, thence a line of marked trees near said **BRADY**'s field to a water Oak a corner in said **PARKER**'s line, thence along said **PARKER**'s line to the main run of said **PETERSON**'s swamp, thence up the various courses of the main run of said swamp to the first station..." Wm. H. **GOODMAN** and John **SAUNDERS** witnessed this deed. It was acknowledged in November Court 1830.[53]

The following deed is an excellent example of how very important this category of records can be to the researcher. It is transcribed here in full:

"This Indenture made this 10th day of March in the year of our Lord one thousand eight hundred & Forty between Kindred **PARKER**, Bray **PARKER**, Elizabeth **BRISCO** Abram W. **PARKER** in right of himself also as agent for Seth **PARKER** & likewise as Executor of Reuben **PARKER** deceased all of the County of Gates in the State of North Carolina of the one part & Dempsey **PARKER** of the County & State aforesaid of the other part Witnesseth that for & in consideration of the full & just sum of Ninety dollars to us in hand paid by the said Dempsey **PARKER** at or before the signing & sealing hereof the receipt whereof we do acknowledge hath granted bargained & sold & by these presents do grant bargain & sell unto the said Dempsey **PARKER** his heirs & assigns all & every of our rights & interest to and in a certain tract or parcel of land Situated & being in the County & State aforesaid which said Lands descended to us the said Kindred **PARKER** Bray **PARKER** Elizabeth **BRISCO** Abram W. **PARKER** in right of himself & as agent of Seth **PARKER** & also as Executor of Reuben **PARKER** decsd. as heirs at Law by the death of Treasey **KING** decsd. bounded as followeth to wit: Beginning at a black gum a corner tree of Riddick **GATLING** & the said Dempsey thence running said **GATLING**'s line to a water oak a corner tree of said **GATLING** & the heirs of Mills **EURE** decsd. thence along said heirs of Mills **EURE** decsd. line to a black gum a corner tree in the Licking root branch thence down the said branch to the corner of said Dempsey **PARKER**'s fence

---

[49] Fouts, *Minutes of County Court of Pleas and Quarter Sessions Gates County, North Carolina 1818-1823, Vol. V*, c. 1987, 94:1178; 104:1195; 165:1287; 170:1297

[50] Ibid., *1824-1827, Vol. VI*, c. 1988, 65:1388; 116:1452

[51] NCSA, C.041.40006, Gates County Real Estate Conveyances 1819-1829, Vol: 11-13, 12:122-123

[52] Fouts, *Minutes of County Court of Pleas and Quarter Sessions Gates County, North Carolina 1824-1827, Vol. VI*, c. 1988, 142:1482; 151:1491

[53] NCSA, C.041.40007, Gates County Real Estate Conveyances 1829-1836 Vol: 14,15, 14:241-242

thence to the first station containing by estimation Eighty Acres be the same more or less. To have & to hold unto the said Dempsey **PARKER** his heirs & assigns forever & we the said Kindred **PARKER**, Bray **PARKER**, Elizabeth **BRISCO** & Abram W. **PARKER** for self & Seth **PARKER** & for the heirs of Reuben **PARKER** deceased do hereby warrant & defend the right & interest to & in the said land clear of ourselves & our heirs. In witness whereof we have hereunto set our hands and affixed our seals the day & date first above written.

Signed sealed & delivered in the presence of        Kindred **PARKER** {Seal}

James G **WILLIAMS**                           Bray **PARKER** {Seal}

Ervin **HARRELL**                            Elizabeth her X mark **BRISCO** {Seal}

                                              A. W. **PARKER** {Seal}

                  A. W.**PARKER** agent for S. P. {Seal}

                  A. W. **PARKER** Exr. of R. P. deceased {Seal}"[54]

This single document proves that Kindred[6], Bray[6], Elizabeth[6], Abraham W.[6], Seth[6] and Dempsey[6] **PARKER** are still living, while Treecy[6], who married a **KING**, is now deceased. Elizabeth[6] is now married to a **BRISCO** and their brother, Reuben[6] **PARKER**, is deceased. Seth[6] is living out of the county, as Abraham W.[6] is acting as his agent in this sale.

On 15 November 1842, John **WILLEY**, Trustee, sold Kindred[6] **PARKER** 93 acres of land for $300.00, by virtue of a deed in trust made by Bray[6] **PARKER** on 17 September 1842, to secure a number of debts. It was offered at public sale 29 October 1842, and was the land on which Bray[6] resided. It is described as "Beginning at a black gum standing in Henry M **DAUGHTRY**'s line & corner on Levi **EURE**, thence L. **EURE**'s line to the road leading from Gatesville to Winton thence up the road to a sweet gum a corner on James R. **RIDDICK**, thence a line of marked Trees to a gum standing in the reedy marsh a corner on Henry M. **DAUGHTRY** thence down the branch along the said **DAUGHTRY**'s line to a large pine in the swamp a corner on said **DAUGHTRY** thence down the swamp to the first station..." Hardy and William **CROSS** witnessed this deed.[55]

On that same date, John **WILLEY** sold Kindred[6] **PARKER** all the right and interest of Bray[6] **PARKER** in the lands of Abram W.[6] **PARKER**, deceased, for the sum of $25.00, by virtue of that same deed in trust of 17 September 1842. Lemuel K. **FIELD** and Robert **ROGERS** witnessed this deed.[56] A third deed from John **WILLEY** to Kindred[6] **PARKER**, dated 15 November 1842, sold another 50 acres of land conveyed in that deed in trust from Bray[6] **PARKER** of 17 September 1842, for the sum of $135.00. It is described as "Beginning at a black gum standing in the swamp a corner on Rich[d]. **CURL** thence up the swamp to a cypress in the mouth of **ROGERS** branch a corner on Henry M. **DAUGHTRY**, thence up the branch to a water oak stump a corner on the heirs of Kindred [sic] **PARKER** thence a line of marked trees to red [sic] oak a corner on Rich[d]. **CURL** thence **CURL**'s line to the first station..." Hardy and Wm. **CROSS** also witnessed this deed.[57]

On 10 August 1843, William G. **DAUGHTRY** sold Kindred[6] **PARKER** an unspecified number of acres of land in several different tracts. They are described as "one tract of Land whereon Bray **PARKER** now lives adjoining the Lands of Wm **DAUGHTRY** & others also one tract of Land that the said Bray **PARKER** bought belonging to the Heirs of Asa **ODOM** decd. & also all the said Bray **PARKER**s right and title in all the Lands which said Bray **PARKER** may be entitled to out of the Lands belonging to the Estate of Abram /W/ **PARKER** decd. to wit The Tenson [?] **EURE** tract, the Boon **EURE** tract, the **BLADES** tract and all other Lands to the said estate belonging the same being the tracts of Land that the said **DAUGHTRY** bought at a sheriffs Sale belonging to Bray **PARKER** and sold by the said sheriff by virtue of an execution returnable to Spring term of the Superior Court of Gates 1843 at the instance of Mary **EURE** vs the said Bray **PARKER**..."[58]

On 10 October 1845, Kindred[6] **PARKER** sold the above lands to John **LEE** for $350.00.[59] The one difference noted in this deed is the name "**BRASHER**" appears where "**BLADES**" is written

---

[54] NCSA, C.041.40008, Gates County Real Estate Conveyances 1836-1842 Vol: 16,17, 17:245-246

[55] NCSA, C.041.40009, Gates County Real Estate Conveyances 1841-1847, Vol: 18,19, 18:277-278

[56] Ibid., 18:280-281

[57] Ibid., 18:281-282

[58] Ibid., 19:415

[59] NCSA, C.041.40010, Gates County Real Estate Conveyances 1847-1857, Vol: 20,21, 20:335

in the prior deed description. This is the last land conveyance found for Kindred[6] **PARKER**.

Kindred[6] **PARKER** was dead by August, 1852, as indicated by the following document, transcribed here in full: "State of North Carolina } Court of Pleas & Quarter Sessions

Gates County      }      August Term 1852.

Hardy W. **PARKER** brings into court a paper writing purporting to be the last will and Testament of Kindred **PARKER** deceased wherein he and John F. **PARKER** are appointed executors, and propounds the said Writing for probate as such last will and Testament; and therefore [?] John F. **PARKER** one of the next of kin of said Kindred, and one of his heirs at law enters his Caveat thereto: and it is thereupon ordered that the following issue be submitted to the jury to wit:

Is the paper writing offered for probate or any part thereof, and if so whch [sic] part, the last will and Testament of said Kindred **PARKER** and is the same executed in form to pass real and personal Estate, or either.

And it farther appearing that the following persons to wit, Sarah **BABB**, Seth **PARKER** and wife Elizabeth, James **LAWRENCE** and wife Nancy, Martha Ann **ROGERS** and John F. **ROGERS**, who reside in this state, and the following, to wit, Dixon **HOWELL** and wife Mary, and the Children of Isaac **PARKER** who reside out of the State, are next of kin and heirs at law of said Kindred, and as such interested in the issue and the Court being moved thereby, it is ordered that publication be made in the Old North State published at Elizabeth City, for six weeks before next Term, for said Non-residents giving them Notice of the pendency of this proceeding and that like notice be served on the residents of this state aforesaid – and let this Cause be docketed.

Witness, Nathaniel J. **RIDDICK**, Clerk of the said Court at Gatesville the 3rd Monday of August, in the 77th year of our Independence, Anno Domini 1852 Issued 25 Oct '52. N. J. **RIDDICK**, Clerk." The reverse of this document lists the above names of the Gates County residents and calls John F. **ROGERS** "John Francis **ROGERS**." This order was executed by Asa **HILL**, Sheriff.[60] That notice was published in *The Old North State* in the issue of 2 October 1852.[61]

Kindred[6] **PARKER** made his will 31 December 1851. He gave his daughter Nancy[7] **LAWRENCE**, one feather bed and furniture, which she had already received and $300.00 in cash. He left his wife, Priscilla (**WILLIAMS**) **PARKER**, "the following lands and plantation as a dower, to wit, Beginning in the Mill swamp opposite the south corner of my garden thence a straight line along side of the southern part of my garden to John **BRADY**s line thence my line all round the north part of lands to the first station during her life and at her death I give all the above premises (as dower as aforesaid) to my son Hardy W. **PARKER**." He gave to Hardy W.[7] "all the balance of my plantation and lands (not loaned to my wife) whereon I now live known as the **JIMERSON** lands together with a part of the swamp lands I purchased of James **BRADY**'s heirs to wit: Beginning at a water oak in the **JIMERSON** line thence nearly west to an old poplar stump thence up the swamp to a gum standing side of the John **BRADY** spring thence to a large pine near the south corner of the **BRADY** field thence a strait line to a cypress thence to a cypress at the run of the swamp thence down the swamp to a cypress a corner of John **WILLEY** and the said **JIMERSON** lands thence up the **JIMERSON** line to the First station or beginning to him & his heirs." He named children Sarah[7] **BABB**, John F.[7] **PARKER**, Penelope[7] **BURGESS**, Mary[7] **HOWELL**, Hardy W.[7], Elizabeth[7] and Isaac[7] **PARKER**, with small bequests of a bed, furniture and some stock. Isaac[7] only received $40.00. He directed that all his lands not already given away were to be sold, along with his perishable estate, and any monies arising therefrom were to be equally divided among all his children. The part given to his daughter, Penelope[7] **BURGESS**, was to be shared between the **ROGERS** children and **BURGESS** children. Mary[7] **HOWELL**'s part was to be retained by his executors and paid out to her as needed for her support. Upon the death of her husband, Dixon **HOWELL**, she was to be paid her full share of his estate. He also directed that "three disinterested persons" should value his Negroes and pay his son Isaac[7] **PARKER** his share in cash, or good notes. William L. **BOOTHE** and Riddick **CROSS** witnessed this will. It was probated in November Term, 1852.[62]

---

[60] NCSA, G.041.2194761, Gates County Estates, Record of 1765-1920, Vol. Parker, E.-Parker, M., Folder: Parker, Kindred 1852, Doc. #1651-1652

[61] NCSA, ECONS-2, Vol. XII. Elizabeth City, North Carolina, October 2, 1852. No. 32, p.3, col. 2, item 3

[62] Gates County Will Book 3:156-159

In that same court, the action of Hardy W.[7] **PARKER** vs John F.[7] **PARKER**, the jury declared the will to be authentic and was considered duly proved by the Court. John F.[7] **PARKER** refused to qualify as Executor and "Hardy **PARKER**, the other Executor therein appointed, takes the oath prescribed by law and is duly qualified as Executor thereto."[63]

An inventory of the personal property of Kindred[6] **PARKER** was taken 6 December 1852, and the sales of that property were made 9 December 1852, by both John F.[7] **PARKER** and Hardy W.[7] **PARKER**, his executors.[64] There is no record of any change to John F.[7] **PARKER**'s status as an executor after that November term.

Priscilla **PARKER** submitted her petitions for a year's provisions and dower at February Term 1853. The latter is transcribed here in full:

"State of North Carolina}    Court of Pleas &c

Gates County              } February Term 1853

The Petition of Priscilla **PARKER** against John F **PARKER**, Sarah **BABB**, Seth **PARKER** and wife Elizabeth, Dixon **HOWELL** & Wife Mary, James **LAWRENCE** and Wife Nancy, Martha Ann & John F. **RODGERS**, the children of Isaac **PARKER** deceased, and Hardy W. **PARKER**.

Your Petioner [sic] humbly complaining sheweth unto your worships that Kindred **PARKER**, late of the county aforesaid departed this life in the summer of 1852, having first made a last will and testament, which was duly admitted to probate at the November Term of this court, at which time Hardy W. **PARKER** and John F **PARKER** the executors therein named, took upon themselves the execution of the trust of the said will, by taking the oath prescribed by law.

Your Petitioner further shows your worships that the said Kindred left your petitioner as his widow and relict and being dissatisfied with the provision made for her in the said last will and testament she appeared before the Court of Pleas & Quarter Sessions held for the county aforesaid on the 3rd Monday of February 1853, and signified her dissent to the same.

She further shows your Worships that the said Kindred died seized and possessed of the following tracts of land situate in the county aforesaid in which your petitioner is entitled to dower and thirds that is to say in the **JAMERSON** tract, adjoining the lands of Samuel E. **SMITH**, A. **WOLF-LEY**, John **WILLEY**, John **BRADY** and others containing one hundred and seventy acres. And one other tract called the **BRADY** tract, adjoining the lands of John **WILLEY**, John **BRADY**, and others, containing one hundred and ten acres more or less. Also another tract called the bear garden, containing thirty four and a quarter acres, more or less /adjoining Belver **SEARS** & Henning T **SMITH**/ Also one other tract called the Dempsey **EURE** tract, adjoining Robert M [?] **BALLARD**, O. B. **SAVAGE** and others containing 205 acres more or less. And also an eighth of the Dempsey **PARKER** tract, whereon his widow now lives and her dower.

Your Petitioner further shows, that the above named defendants are the heirs at law of the said Kindred **PARKER**, and that they are all of full age, except, the children of Isaac **PARKER** whose names are unknown, and John F. & Martha Ann **RODGERS**, for whom John F **PARKER** is guardian, who are under the age of twenty one years.

Your petitioner therefore prays that your worships, will appoint some discreet person as guardian, to defend the interest of the said children of Isaac **PARKER** in this suit, And that a writ of dower may issue to the sheriff of said county, commanding him to summon a jury of good and lawful men to lay off and allot, by metes and bounds to your petitioner, her dower and thirds in the lands aforesaid, and put her in possession of the same. That your worships will order copies of this petition with subpoenas to be served upon, the said John F **PARKER**, Seth **PARKER** and wife Elizabeth, Dixon **HOW-ELL** and wife Mary Sarah **BABB**, James **LAWRENCE** and wife Nancy, John F. ~~P Mary E.~~ /Martha A/ **RODGERS**, the children of Isaac **PARKER**, and Hardy W. **PARKER**, commanding them to be and appear &c and that your worships will from time to time be pleased to make such other and further orders and decrees, as the nature of this case may from time to time require And as in duty bound your petitioner will ever pray

W. J. BAKER

---

[63]   NCSA, G.041.2194761, Gates County Estates, Record of 1765-1920, Vol. Parker, E.-Parker, M., Folder: Parker, Kindred 1852, Doc. #1660-1661

[64]   Ibid., Doc. #1697; 1702

Sol. for Petr"[65]

On 24 June 1853, the jury met on the premises and laid off to Priscilla **PARKER** 130 acres of land "beginning at the road gate thence the East Side of the lane to the lot thence round the lot to the North corner of garde [sic] thence South to a Chinquepen tree on a ditch thence a line of marked trees to the run of the Swamp thence along the line of **WOREN** [sic] tract of land to the first Station Giving her the West Side of the /side tract/ including the dwelling house or mansion of the Said Kindred **PARKER** Decd, in which he most generly dwelte [sic] next before and at the time of his death, and all the out houses offices and improvements there unto belonging...and put the Said Priscilla **PARKER** in possession of the Same."[66]

Kindred[6] **PARKER** was called as a juror, appointed as an auditor of accounts of executors and administrators, and to be a commissioner to set apart dower and divide real estate, over a long period of years.

Priscilla (**WILLIAMS**) **PARKER** made an undated will, probated in May Court 1866. She left Sarah Eliza **PARKER**, $25.00, but did not mention her relationship. She loaned to her daughter, Mary **LEE**, wife of Titus J. **LEE**, all the rest of her estate during her natural life. If there was anything left after her decease, it was to go to the children of Elizabeth **PARKER**, wife of Seth **PARKER**. James E. **EVERETT** and Augustus **WOLFLEY** were the witnesses and Mills H. **EURE** was named executor. The last page of the original will shows that Priscilla used an "X" as her mark. In that will, she mentioned her daughter, Mary **LEE**, wife of Titus J. **LEE**. Mary was known to be married to Dixon **HOWELL** in earlier records, and married Titus J. **LEE** 29 October 1859.[67] It follows that Priscilla **PARKER** made her will between that date and October, 1865, when M. H. **EURE** paid the Sheriff taxes on her lands.

An account of sale and inventory of the property of the late "Prissillia [sic] **PARKER** Decd sold by Mills H **EURE** Executor to said Decd" with the terms of sale "Cash in Gold or Silver," was made 11 June 1866, in the amount of $159.73. Her daughter, Mary A. **LEE** purchased a "Beaurow," table, mirror, clock, candle stick, pitcher, five glass tumblers, three dishes and five chickens from that sale.[68]

On 18 May 1868, M. H. **EURE** presented an audited account of Priscilla's estate, transcribed here in full:

"Mills H. **EURE**, Ex'r of Priscilla **PARKER**, dec'd.

In Acc't with Estate of said P. **PARKER**

1866

| | | |
|---|---|---|
| June 11 | To Am't of Acc't Sales of Chattel} Property in specie } | $159.73 |

1866

| | | | |
|---|---|---|---|
| Aug 20th | By Amt. paid A. E. **HALL** for Coffin | 25 | 00 |
| Nov. 25th | " " " M. K. **LAWRENCE** for Services | 10 | 00 |
| May 8th | " " " **EDWARDS & EURE** for burial Cloths | 25 | 47 |
| Aug. 20th | " " " S. E. **SMITH** Auctioneer | 5 | 00 |
| " 30 | " " " Tom **PARKER** for diging Grave | 1 | 00 |
| " 20 | " " " Exum **GREEN** for Services | 1 | 00 |
| 1867 | | | |
| Aug.23 | " " " M. L. **EURE** for writing Will | 5 | 00 |
| 1866 | | | |
| " 25 | " " " O B **SAVAGE** Med. Acc't | 11 | 00 |
| Octo 6th | | | |
| 1865 | " " " Mary **CARTER** making S___ [?] | 1 | 00 |
| " " | " " " Shff. Taxes for year 1865 | | 53 |

[65] NCSA, G.041.2194761, Gates County Estates, Record of 1765-1920, Vol. Parker, E.-Parker, M., Folder: Parker, Kindred 1852, Doc.#1641-1643;Doc. #1672-1675
[66] Ibid., Doc. #1690-1691
[67] Almasy, *Gates County, North Carolina Marriage Bonds 1778-1868*, c. 1987, p. 59
[68] NCSA, G.041.2194762, Gates County Estates, Record of 1765-1920, Vol. Parker-Pierce, Folder: Parker, Priscilla 1866, Doc. #221-223

1867

| Apl. 11 | " " " Wm. H. **LEE** – Med. Acc't | 20 | 00 | |
|---|---|---|---|---|
| Feb. 8 | " " " H. C. **WILLY** [sic] " " | 13 | 00 | |
| | " 5 per cent. Com's on $302.73 whole } | | | |
| | amt. of receipts, & expenditures & Legacy } | 15 | 14 | |
| | " Am't paid Clerk for probate of Will | 1 | 00 | |
| | " " " " " Acc't Sales & Inventory | | 40 | 134.54 |
| 1868 | | | | $25.19 |
| May 18 | By am't of Legacy paid to} | | | |
| | Sarah E. **PARKER** _ _ _} | | | 25 00 |
| | Bal. due Estate – M E **L**. Legatee | | | 19 |
| | M H. **EURE** Extor"[69] | | | |

These families are easily traced in Gates County records from this point forward. No further information included here.

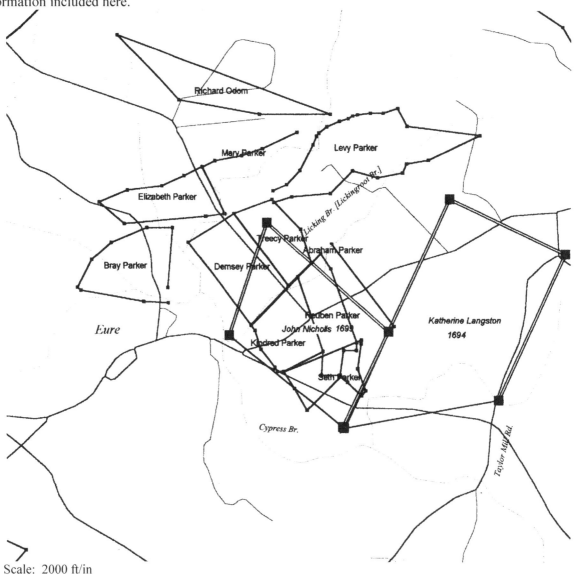

Scale: 2000 ft/in

Map depicting 1810 division of land of John[5] **PARKER** in Gates County. Richard **ODOM** patent is incomplete and not accurately placed on this map. **NICHOLLS** and **LANGSTON** patents are delineated with double lines.

---

[69] NCSA, G.041.2194762, Gates County Estates, Record of 1765-1920, Vol. Parker-Pierce, Folder: Parker, Priscilla 1866, Doc. #217

## John F.[7] **PARKER** *(Kindred[6],John[5],John[4],William[3],Thomas[2],William[1])*

John F.[7] **PARKER** was the eldest son of Kindred[6] and Mary (**LANGSTON**) **PARKER**, born between 1809 and 1811. He is called "John Frank **PARKER**" in a Bible record.[1] He appeared on a marriage bond with Elizabeth **CARTER**, dated 7 November 1857. James E. **EVERETT** was his bondsman.[2] No record of any previous marriage for him has been found. Elizabeth J. **CARTER** was born September 1834.[3]

An Application for Letters of Administration on the Estate of Jno. F.[7] **PARKER** was made by Jno. J. **GATLING**, Public Administrator, on 1 December 1885. He stated that "the estate was worth about $1,000.00 and that Eliz. **PARKER**, widow of dec'd, Kindred **PARKER**, Thos. **PARKER**, Sallie **PARKER**, __[blank]__ **PARKER** & Sue **PARKER**, the last two minors without guardian, under 21 yrs. of age and Willis **HOFFLER**s wife __[blank]__ **PARKER** are entitled as heirs and distributees thereof."[4]

The account of sales and inventory of the property of John F.[7] **PARKER** was made 18 December 1885. Most items were purchased by the widow, Thomas J.[8] and Kindred[8] **PARKER**. The account was returned to court 15 November 1886.[5]

The petition for dower made by Elizabeth J. **PARKER** is undated. It went to Superior Court as a Special Proceeding and is transcribed here in full, though nearly illegibly faint:

"Elizabeth J. **PARKER**, widow

Against                              } Petition for Dower.

Willis J. **HOFLER** & wife __[blank]__ **HOFLER** Kindred **PARKER** T. J. **PARKER** Sallie **PARKER** C. V. **PARKER** and Sue **PARKER** the last three minors by their Guard [sic] ad litem Willis J. **HOFLER** heirs at law of John F. **PARKER**

The plaintiff above named for complaint alleges: That she is the widow of John F. **PARKER** who died intestate in Gates County some time during the year 1885, leaving him surviving the __[illegible] defendant Mary **HOFLER** and the other defendants **PARKER** his children and only heirs at law.

That her said husband died seized and possessed of the following lands in Gates County:

1. The House [?] Tract adjoining the lands of Riddick **EURE**, Hardy **PARKER** B. B. **LEE** and others and containing (150) One Hundred & fifty acres. (over) [End of page.]

2. The Bear Garden tract adjoining the lands of James O. **EURE** Dr. R___ **SAVAGE** and others and containing (105) One Hundred and five acres.

3. A tract of Swamp land lying on Sarem Creek containing about (70) acres.

That she desires to have her Dower allotted to her in the said lands.

Wherefore she prays that a Writ of Dower may issue Commanding the Sheriff of Gates County to summon a jury of _____ persons qualified to act as Jurors and connected with the parties neither by blood nor marriage and entirely disinterested to view the said lands and to allot and set apart to her one third thereof in value in proper metes and bounds so as to include the Dwelling House and all other out houses buildings & improvements thereon, for the term of her natural life and that they report their proceedings thereon in due form of law. L. L. **SMITH**, Atty. for Pltff."[6] This document is undated, but the Order for Dower was made 8 February 1886, and the following was made only four

---

[1]  Almasy, *Gates County, North Carolina Census 1850 & 1860*, c. 1987, p. 20  As of 9 August 1850, John F. Parker is listed as 39 years of age.  Gates County Historical Society, *Bible Records of Gates County, N. C.*, c. unknown, p. 147.  This page shows "John Frank Parker was born in 1809 and died April 6, 1885."  The publication date of the Bible is 1851, thus it is not a contemporaneous record and was transcribed in narrative form.

[2]  Almasy, *Gates County, North Carolina Marriage Bonds 1778-1868*, c. 1987, p. 68

[3]  Powell, David, *1900 Gates County Census*, c. 1994, p. 49

[4]   NCSA, G.041.219761, Gates County Estates, Record of 1765-1920, Vol. Parker, E.-Parker, M., Folder: Parker, John F. 1886, Doc. #1292

[5]  Ibid., Doc. #1321-1324

[6]  Ibid., Doc. #1382-1384

days later.[7]

On 12 February 1886, a jury was qualified by D. E. **RIDDICK**, Sheriff of Gates County, "to set apart and allot to Mrs. Eliz. J. **PARKER** widow of John F. **PARKER** Dec'd. /her Dower/" which is described as "to the best of our knowledge and belief one third in value of the lands of the Said John F. **PARKER** dec'd. To Wit-Begining on the land of R B G **COWPER** at a ditch, thence along the said ditch nealy an East Coarse [sic] to a Pine Tree thence along the said line to a Forked Pine thence said line to a Poast Oak at a Branch, thence down the Said Branch adjoining the lands of Hardy W **PARKER** and others nearly South West to a Water oak Stump on Boon **FELTER**s [**FELTON**s] land /thence/ a Northerly course to Jack **LEE**s land to a Branch, thence up the Said Branch to the first Station including the House and all out buildings, to have and hold the same free from all incumberance whatever during the term of her natural life. Signed and Sealed this the 12th day of Feb 1886. James his X mark **MULLEN**, {Seal} Thos his X mark R **EURE** {Seal} J. H. **HOFLER** {Seal} Jury Witness D E. **RIDDICK** Shiff"[8] The "account final" of the estate of John F.[7] **PARKER** was returned to court 6 June 1887, by Jno. J. **GATLING**, Public Administrator.[9]

Several receipts to John J. **GATLING**, Public Administrator of John F.[7] **PARKER**, deceased, appear in his estate records. One was from Elizabeth J. **PARKER**, undated, for the "sum of $20.00 it being the amt paid by Amos **CULLENS** for the rent for 1885 of the Bear Garden place-in part payment of the balance due me on my years allowance, as per report of Commissioners."[10] On 3 August 1886, another receipt from Elizabeth was for $87.75, for payment of a "bal due on my years provision." It was signed "Eliz J. her X mark **PARKER**, and witnessed by Kindred[8] **PARKER**.[11] On 6 June 1887, John R. **WALTON** made a receipt to **GATLING**, as administrator of John F.[7] **PARKER**, for "$3.00 for tuition of daughter Susie."[12]

In Spring Term, 1889, the Norfolk & Carolina Rail Road Company vs. Elizabeth J. **PARKER** and others, heirs-at-law of John F.[7] **PARKER**, had their case on appeal. Part of the testimony was "These witnesses said that part of the land had been cut off from the main farm & would have to be cultivated & fenced to themselves & the farm had been cut in two by the road and injured from three hundred to $500.00. All the evidence tended to show that the road bed was not completed, but was then in process of construction. Kindred[8] **PARKER**, one of the defendants, was introduced as a witness & was allowed to testify, after objection by plaintiff, that the agents of the plaintiff company had torn down his fence in constructing their road & had failed to put it up again & that to enclose his land after the construction of the road, would require more fencing & greater cost, and the plaintiff excepted to all this testimony /except/ that it would take more to fence the land." This was one of the objections offered. Another was that "The same witness testified that the road bed was thrown up considerably above the surface of the land at a point back of the house & that the plaintiff had not made a crossing, which was necessary for the farm. To this evidence, as to the crossing, the plaintiff objected. The Court then asked the witness if he had demanded of the railroad a crossing at that point & the witness replied that he had, & that the company had failed to make it. The objection was then overruled & the plaintiff excepted. Defendants counsel asked the witness if the land had been injured as to its drainage-he replied it had been damaged as to the drainage & as an instance of it his mule in attempting to cross the rail-road /bed/, had been stuck in the mud & had to be cut out & this occurred also by reason of their refusal to construct crossings after being requested to do."

Though the railroad was then called "Chowan & Southern Railroad Company" vs. E. J. **PARKER** and others, an order was filed 8 October 1890 and the suit was appealed to the Supreme Court, where the decision went against the railroad, and was put back to Superior Court. The defendants were Elizabeth J. **PARKER**, Willis **HOFLER** & wife Mary A.[8], Kindred[8] **PARKER**, Sallie[8] **PARKER**, Caroline[8] **PARKER** and Sue[8] **PARKER**. The jury found in favor of the defendants and

---

[7] NCSA, G.041.219761, Gates County Estates, Record of 1765-1920, Vol. Parker, E.-Parker, M., Folder: Parker, John F. 1886, Doc. #1389-1390
[8] Ibid., Doc. #1385-1386
[9] Ibid., Doc. #1320
[10] Ibid., Doc. #1307
[11] Ibid., Doc. #1296-1297
[12] Ibid., Doc. #1302-1303

assessed their damages as $375.00, with interest from 8 April 1889. Thomas J.[8] **PARKER** was also named as a defendant in this suit.[13] This land is located on County Road 1217, at Sarem, where the railbed still exists. The tracks were removed several years ago.

Mary Ann[8] **PARKER** was born 2 September 1858 and married Willis **HOFFLER**. Kindred[8] **PARKER** was born 24 March, 1860, and died unmarried 5 January 1928. Thomas Jefferson[8] **PARKER** was born 12 October 1861.[14] He married Ida **MULLEN**, daughter of James and Polley **MULLEN**, 25 January 1893.[15] Sallie[8] **PARKER** was born 23 November 1863, and died 19 January 1942. Caroline Virginia[8] **PARKER** was born 1 June 1868, and died 26 July 1937. Susan[8] **PARKER** was born 28 November 1872.[16]

ൠൠൠൠൠൠൠൠൠൠൠൠൠൠൠൠൠൠൠൠൠൠൠൠൠൠൠൠൠൠൠൠൠൠൠൠൠൠൠൠ

Isaac[7] **PARKER** *(Kindred[6],John[5],John[4],William[3],Thomas[2],William[1])*, was most likely the son of Kindred[6] and Mary **(LANGSTON) PARKER**. He is mentioned as being deceased in the 1853 petition of Priscilla **PARKER**. No further information.

Sarah[7] **PARKER** *(Kindred[6],John[5],John[4],William[3],Thomas[2],William[1])*, daughter of Kindred[6] and Mary **(LANGSTON) PARKER**, has been mentioned in previous documents as "Sarah **BABB**." She was born circa 1807 and was 43 years of age in 1850. The children listed in that census with her were William K.[8], age 14, Thomas W.[8], age 12, Alice O.[8], age 10, Lewis H.[8], age 8, and "Gabrella"[8] **BABB**, age 5.[17] Her marriage date is estimated here to be circa 1835 and she married William **BABB**, a widower.

William **BABB** made his will 25 July 1849, naming his beloved wife, Sarah **BABB**, to whom he loaned his "negro man **TOM** and a Girl by the name of **LUCINDY**" during her life, and all the land whereon he then lived. He bequeathed to his daughter, Sarah Ann **RUSSELL**, wife of Demsey **RUSSELL** 10 Shillings, and to daughter Margaret E. **MARCH**, wife of John B. **MARCH**, "one beauro and one family bible which was her mothers." His two grandchildren, Almedia Lucrecy and James Thomas **BAKER**, children of Blake **BAKER**, Jr., received $50.00 each. He named all his other children as James B. **BABB**, John C. **BABB**, Wm. K. **BABB**, Thomas W. **BABB**, Lewis H. **BABB**, Jane **COLLINS**, wife of Miles **COLLINS**, Mary Susan **BAKER**, wife of Blake **BAKER**, Jr., Margaret E. **MARCH**, wife of John B. **MARCH**, Alsey Ailery [sic] **BABB**, and "Gaberiellar" **BABB**. He appointed his friend, Edwin **SMITH**, as his executor. The will was exhibited into February Term, 1850, with a caveat of Sarah **BABB** et als vs Dempsey **RUSSELL**. A jury declared the will valid and Edwin **SMITH** refused his appointment, at which time John F.[7] **PARKER** was appointed administrator, with the will annexed.[18]

Sarah[7] **BABB** made her will and codicil 18 March 1855. It was exhibited into May Court 1855, by her executor, John F.[7] **PARKER**, and proved by Augustus **WOLFLEY**. She was "of sound mind but feeble in health," and named her children as Wm. K. **BABB**, Allice Olivia **BABB**, Thos. W. **BABB** and Lewis Henry **BABB**. She left to the latter two sons "one negro man named **TOM** which negro I drew from my fathers estate." The other witness to this will was Hardy W.[7] **PARKER**.[19]

Penelope[7] **PARKER**, *(Kindred[6],John[5],John[4],William[3],Thomas[2],William[1])* daughter of Kindred[6] and Mary **(LANGSTON) PARKER** was born circa 1815 and was 35 years of age in 1850.[20] Her first husband was Robert **ROGERS** who died in the latter part of 1846. Penelope[7], called "Pennina" in the court order, was granted administration on the estate of Robert **ROGERS** in a bond of $10,000, in November Court 1846. Kindred[6] and John F.[7] **PARKER** were two of the sureties on that bond.[21] They had three known children. One son was James[8], another was named John F.[8] and

---

[13]   NCSA, G.041.219761, Gates County Estates, Record of 1765-1920, Vol. Parker, E.-Parker, M., Folder: Parker, John F. 1886, Doc. #1325-1381

[14]   Gates County Historical Society, *Bible Records of Gates County, N. C.*, c. unknown, p. 147

[15]   Powell, David, *Late Nineteenth Century Gates County Marriages from 1883 to 1900*, c. 1997, p.112, 1893-021

[16]   Gates County Historical Society, *Bible Records of Gates County, NC*, c. unknown, p. 147

[17]   Almasy, *Gates County, North Carolina Census 1850 & 1860*, c. 1987, p. 41, 1850 Census

[18]   Almasy, *Gates County, North Carolina Wills 1838-1867, Vol. III*, c. 1987, p. 59, 3:127-129

[19]   Ibid., p. 80, 3:181-183

[20]   Almasy, *Gates County, North Carolina Census 1850 & 1860*, c. 1987, p. 30, 1850 Census

[21]   NCSA, C.041.30003, Gates County Court Minutes 1827-1850, pp. not numbered, November Court 1846,

their daughter was Martha Ann[8] **ROGERS**.[22] James[8] **RODGERS** was mentioned as being represented by his guardian in a deed from W. J. **BAKER** to James R. **RIDDICK**, dated 16 December 1848. Penelope[7] and James[8] had exhibited a petition to sell this 360 acres of land & pay debts, in April, 1848. This deed was witnessed by John F.[7] **PARKER**. It was proved by him in May Term, 1857.[23]

James[8] **RODGERS** was deceased by November, 1849, as evidenced by the following order of Court: "It is ordered that letters of administration on the Estate of James **RODGERS**, deceased, be granted to Henry C. **WILLEY**, upon his entereing into Bond in the sum of Two Thousand Five Hundred Dollars with John **WILLEY** and Hardy **CROSS** as Securities. Which Bond is accordingly executed and the said **WILLEY** duly qualified as the administrator of said **RODGERS** by taking the oaths in such case made and provided."

In that same Court, the following order changes that status: "It is ordered that the letters of administration upon the Estate of James **RODGERS**, deceased, which were granted to Henry C. **WILLEY**, during the present Term, be revoked, and that the Bond entered into by him, as the administrator of said deceased be declared Null and Void. It is further Ordered that letters of administration upon the Estate of the said James **RODGERS** be committed to Penelope **RODGERS** upon her entering into Bond in the sum of Twenty five Hundred Dollars with John F. **PARKER** and Kindred **PARKER** as her sureties. Which said Bond is accordingly executed and the said Penelope **RODGERS** duly qualified as the administratrix of the said James by taking the oath prescribed by law."[24]

She appeared on a marriage bond, as Penelope **ROGERS**, with Edward W. **BURGESS** on 20 June 1850. Alfred M. **RIDDICK** was his bondsman.[25] Neither of them appear in the 1860 U. S. Census. No further information.

Elizabeth[7] **PARKER**, *(Kindred[6],John[5],John[4],William[3],Thomas[2],William[1])* daughter of Kindred[6] and Mary **(LANGSTON) PARKER**, was born circa 1819-1820 and was 30 years of age as of 7 August 1850, as she was living with her husband and mother-in-law on that date.[26] She appeared on a marriage bond with Seth **PARKER**, dated 3 March 1849. His bondsman was Elisha (X) **HARRELL**.[27] Seth[7] **PARKER** was the son of Reuben[6] and Judith **(BEEMAN) PARKER**.

This family appears in the 1870 Federal Census next door to Elizabeth[7]'s brother, John F.[7] **PARKER**. Seth[7] is listed as 50 years of age and Elizabeth[7] is listed as 55, which is probably in error. The children listed with them are Hardy[8], age 15, Mary[8], age 12 [?] Caroline[8], age 13 and Langston[8]**PARKER**, age nine.[28] They do not appear in the 1860 Census and may have had other children.

Nancy[7] **PARKER**, *(Kindred[6],John[5],John[4],William[3],Thomas[2],William[1])* daughter of Kindred[6] and Priscilla **(WILLIAMS) PARKER** left few records. A Nancy **LAWRENCE** appears in the 1860 Federal Census as age 36, living in the household of Thomas **UMPHLET**. The family next door contains a James **LAWRENCE**, age 56, and "Kendrid" **LAWRENCE**, age 18.[29] This is obviously a misspelling of the name "Kindred." It was Nancy[7] **(PARKER) LAWRENCE** who was residing with the **UMPHLET** family on that date was the mother of Kindred **LAWRENCE** Her date of birth would have been circa 1824. No further information.

Mary[7] **PARKER**, *(Kindred[6],John[5],John[4],William[3],Thomas[2],William[1])* daughter of Kindred[6] and Priscilla **(WILLIAMS) PARKER**, has been mentioned as "Mary **HOWELL**, wife of Dixon **HOWELL**," in several previous documents. No record of this marriage has been found. They resided in Gates County as of 10 August 1850, as found in the Federal Census enumeration of that date.

---

sixth page of that court.

[22]   NCSA, G.041.2194761, Gates County Estates, Record of 1765-1920, Vol. Parker, E.-Parker, M., Folder: Parker, Kindred 1852, Doc.#1707 John F. and Martha Ann Rogers are named in a guardian account with John F. Parker, Feb. 1858

[23]   NCSA, C.041.40011, Gates County Real Estate Conveyances 1857-1861, Vol. 22:50-51

[24]   NCSA, C.041.30003, Gates county Court Minutes 1827-1850, [1842-1850] November Court 1849

[25]   Almasy, *Gates County, North Carolina Marriage Bonds 1778-1868*, c. 1987, p. 15

[26]   Ibid., *Gates County, North Carolina Census 1850 & 1860*, c. 1987, p. 16, 1850 Census

[27]   Ibid., *Gates County, North Carolina Marriage Bonds 1778-1868*, c. 1987, p. 69

[28]   U. S. Federal Census, 1870 Gates Co., NC, Series: M593, Roll 1139, Hall Twp., p. 6

[29]   Almasy, *Gates County, North Carolina Census 1850 & 1860*, c. 1987, p.110, 1860 Census

Dixon **HOWELL** is listed as 27 years of age and born in Virginia.  Mary **HOWELL** is listed as age 24 and born in North Carolina.[30]  Her date of birth would have been circa 1826.  They removed to another area, most probably in Virginia, between 1850 and 1852, when her father died.

She apparently returned to Gates County as she appears on a marriage bond with Titus J. **LEE**, dated 28 October 1859.  The marriage was performed by O. B. **SAVAGE**, J. P., 29 October 1859.[31]  There were no children of this marriage.  Titus J. **LEE** made his will 24 August 1864, "being in sound mind but wounded in body."  He left his wife, Mary A. **LEE**, all his estate and after her death it was to go to his friend, Mills H. **EURE**.  The will was proved in February Term, 1866, by the witnesses, O. B. **SAVAGE** and W. T. **RIDDICK**.  Mary A. **LEE**, widow, dissented from all the provisions of her husband's will, by her attorney, Jas. W. **ROBERTS**, which was allowed by the court.[32]  No further information included here.

Hardy W.[7] **PARKER**, *(Kindred[6],John[5],John[4],William[3],Thomas[2],William[1])* son of Kindred[6] and Priscilla (**WILLIAMS**) **PARKER**, was born circa 1826, and was probably a fraternal twin to his sister, Mary[7].  He appears in the Federal Census of 1850 as 24 years of age and his occupation was "Blacksmith."[33]

Hardy W.[7] **PARKER** resided in Bertie County, NC, and enlisted there in Company F, 5th Infantry Regiment[34] of the Confederate States Army 1 July 1861, where he mustered in as a First Sergeant.  He was age 35 and a farmer.  He was wounded in action at **GAINES'** Mill, VA, 27 June 1862, and died of those wounds at Richmond, VA, 14 July 1862.[35]

He never married and died without issue.  He made his will 5 September 1861, in Fairfax County, VA, stating that he was "now in the Army of the Confederate States of America."  He directed that all his debts be paid by his executrix, selling as much of his estate as was necessary.  The remainder was bequeathed to his mother, who was also appointed his executrix.  This will was exhibited into Gates County August Court 1862.[36]

In an audited account of Hardy W.[7] **PARKER**'s estate, settled 16 November 1863, she paid "Taxes for 1861," on 1 January 1862.[37]  Priscilla **PARKER** made an inventory of the bonds notes and accounts belonging to his estate on 10 August 1862 and made sales of his property and effects 5 November 1862.[38]

On 16 February 1863, there was a further account of sales of the Estate of Hardy W.[7] **PARKER**.  This sale consisted of assorted lumber, corn and real estate.  The tracts described as "The Home track [sic] of land" and "the **ELLICE** " " " " were sold to Aug. **WOLFREY**; the "Dempsey **EURE** track of land" was sold to Wm. **MATHEWES** and the "**GREEN** " " " " was sold to Thos. W. **BABB**.[39]

〰〰〰〰〰〰〰〰〰〰〰〰〰〰〰〰〰〰〰〰〰〰〰〰〰〰〰〰〰〰〰〰〰〰〰〰〰〰〰〰〰〰

Bray[6] **PARKER** *(John[5],John[4],William[3],Thomas[2],William[1])* was born in May 1784.[40]  No estate records have been found for him, but he died some time after 1860.[41]  Gates County Court Minutes have not been searched for records of his death after May Court 1861.  He owned no assets then.  The Tax Lists for 1858 and 1859 have been searched and he was not listed then, though still living as

[30]  Almasy, *Gates County, North Carolina Census 1850 & 1860*, c. 1987, p. 21, 1850 Census

[31]  Almasy, *Gates County, North Carolina Marriage Bonds 1778-1868*, c. 1987, p.59

[32]  Almasy, *Gates County, North Carolina Wills 1838-1867, Vol. III*, c. 1987, p. 138, 3:338-339

[33]  Almasy, *Gates County, North Carolina Census 1850 & 1860*, c. 1987, p. 24, 1850 Census

[34]  *The Roster of Confederate Soldiers 1861-1865, Volume XII, Oadneal, Alfred N. to Rand, William H.*, Edited by Janet B. Hewett, c. 1996, p. 140

[35]  NC State Division of Archives and History, *North Carolina Troops 1861-1865 A Roster* Compiled by Weymouth T. Jordan, Jr., Unit Histories by Louis H. Manarin, Vol. IV, Infantry, Second printing, 1989, pp. 206, 730

[36]  Almasy, *Gates County, North Carolina Wills 1838-1867, Vol. III*, c. 1987, p. 118, 3:292

[37]  NCSA, G.041.2194761, Gates County Estates, Record of 1765-1920, Vol. Parker, E.-Parker, M., Folder: Parker, Hardy W. 1862, Doc. #516-518

[38]  Ibid., Doc. #519-524

[39]  Ibid., Doc. #526-527

[40]  Gates County Historical Society, *Bible Records of Gates County, NC*, c. unknown, p.140

[41]  U. S. Federal Census 1860, M653, Roll: 898, Hall Township, p. 17, Bray and Nancy Parker are listed with their son, William.

shown by the 1860 Federal Census records. He was definitely deceased prior to 14 August 1869, as Elisha and Elizabeth **PARKER**, and Mildred **LEE** sold to Penelope **PARKER** their interest "in a certain tract of land known as the Bray **PARKER** tract," on 14 August 1869. It was entered into the Probate Court 29 July 1872.[42]

Bray[6] **PARKER** appeared on a marriage bond with Nancy **WILLIAMS**, dated 22 January 1806. Timothy **LANGSTON** was his bondsman.[43] Nancy was born 12 July 1784, to Jonathan and Mildred **WILLIAMS**.[44] This is confirmed in a bond dated 13 July 1816, given by "H. **WILLIAMS**, Bray **PARKER** & Wife, Priscilla **WILLIAMS** and Levi **ROGERS** & Wife," warranting an equal share in the five Negroes left to the daughters of Jonathan **WILLIAMS** in his will. They were Polly **WILLIAMS**, Milly **ARLINE**, Nancy **PARKER**, Priscilla **WILLIAMS** and Elizabeth **ROGERS**. Milly **ARLINE** had predeceased her father and the bond would "make Over and Secure to the Heirs of Milley **ARLINE** all the Interest in Said Negroes /She/ the Said Milly **ARLINE** would have been Entitled to in case She had Survived her Father." The witnesses were George **WILLIAMS** and Philip **ROGERS**.[45]

On 2 December 1811, Bray[6] **PARKER** sold Levy **EURE** five acres for £6..15. It is described as "Being in the county of Gates begining at a red oak stump on the South side of the road running my own line to the road thence running up the sd road to my own line again thence along my own line East course to the first station it being part of a pattern granted unto Richard **ODOM** which Bears Date the 1st day of March 1718. ... Bray **PARKER** ackd." Charles **EURE** and Mary her X mark **TAYLOR** witnessed this deed. It was acknowledged in February Court 1816, and registered 12 June 1816.[46]

On 29 February 1836, Bray[6] **PARKER** sold Nannah **HUMPHFLET** "Forty or Fifty acres" for $30.00. It was "known by the name of the **STALLINGS** tract, and the said Bray **PARKER** do warrant & defend all such right as ~~I the said~~ George M **MULLEN** warranted to the said Bray **PARKER** and no other." Wm. L. **BOOTHE** was the sole witness.[47]

On 24 November 1837, Rodon **ODOM** sold Bray[6] **PARKER** 22 acres for $31.87½. It is described as "Beginning at a large pine corner on said Bray **PARKER** & John **GATLING**, thence S 82½° E. 95 poles to the road, thence along the __[blank]__ 37½ poles to a sweet gum corner on said **ODOM** & John **GATLING**, thence N 31° E. along said **GATLING** to the first Station..." Wm. L. **BOOTHE** was the sole witness and it was proved on his oath in November Court 1838.[48]

Beginning in late 1842, Bray[6] **PARKER** apparently went deeply into debt as shown by the deeds in trust for his lands mentioned in Chapter 8. As he was incapable of repaying those debts, his property was sold, including his interest in his brothers' and sister's estates. On 19 December 1842, James R. **RIDDICK**, Sheriff of Gates County, sold William G. **DAUGHTRY** "the land whereon Bray **PARKER** now lives, and also one tract of land which the said **PARKER** bought belonging to the heirs of Asa **ODOM** deceased & also his right & title in all the lands which said Bray **PARKER** may be entitled to out of lands belonging to estate of Abram **PARKER**, to wit, the Tinson Y. **EURE** tract, the Boon **EURE** tract, the **BLADES** tract, & all other lands to the said estate belonging the property of the said Bray **PARKER** for want of goods and chattels, and did duly advertise and expose the same at public sale before the Court house door..." This property was sold to pay an execution against Bray[6] in the amount of $460.00 damages and $97.43 costs, brought by Mary **EURE**.[49]

On 7 April 1846, Bray[6] **PARKER** sold to Henry L. **EURE** for $275.00 "all my interest right title & Estate in and to all and singular the personal estate left at his death by the late Dempsey **PARKER** of said County and transmitted to his representatives together with all charges in action and rights of any [?] kind possessed by the sd intestate Dempsey **PARKER** at the time of his decease be-

---

[42] Gates County, NC Deed Book 23:934

[43] Almasy, *Gates County, North Carolina Marriage Bonds 1778-1868*, c. 1987, p. 66

[44] Gates County Historical Society, *Bible Records of Gates County, NC*, c. unknown, p.140

[45] NCSA, C.041.40005, Gates County Real Estate Conveyances 1811-1812,1815-1819, Vol: 9,10, 10:242

[46] Ibid., 10:117

[47] NCSA, C.041.40008, Gates County Real Estate Conveyances 1836-1842, Vol: 16,17, 16:85

[48] Ibid., 16:329-330

[49] NCSA, C.041.40009, Gates County Real Estate Conveyances 1841-1847, Vol: 18,19, 18:488-489

ing my entire distributive share in said intestate Estate." It was witnessed by John **RIDDICK** and Geo. W. **SMITH**.[50] The last time Bray[6] **PARKER** appears on the Gates County Tax list is in 1842, in Hall District.[51]

The children of Bray[6] and Nancy **(WILLIAMS) PARKER** were Mildred[7], born 6 February 1807; Elisha[7], born 18 April 1809; Rasco[7], born 20 March 1811; Rosella[7] (or Rosetta,) born 25 March 1815; William[7], born 7 [?] July 181_; Levi[7] and Elizabeth[7], born 8 February 1818; Charity[7], born 6 June 1821; Jane[7], born 4 February 1824, and Penelope[7] **PARKER**, born 10 December 1827. These names and dates were taken from a Bible record, with the exception of William[7] **PARKER**.[52] Apparently the name and birth year are illegible in that Bible, but the Census record "fills in the blanks." That census was enumerated 14 August 1850. He was listed as 35 years of age. Bray[6] **PARKER** appears there as 65 years of age, with Nancy at 64 years.[53]

Levi[7] **PARKER**, son of Bray[6] and Nancy **(WILLIAMS) PARKER**, was born 8 February 1818, as mentioned above. He appears in the U. S. Federal Census of 1850, as 33 years of age, with Elizabeth **PARKER**, age 36, John[8], age 9, Isaac[8], age 6, Abram[8], age 4 and George[8], age 3 months.[54]

Elisha[7] **PARKER** was appointed Special Administrator on the estate of Levi[7] **PARKER** 20 December 1853. He and O. B. **SAVAGE** entered into an administration bond of $200.00.[55] An inventory and sales of his estate was made 4 January 1854, by his administrator.[56] No further information.

The following deed of gift may well indicate an approximate time of death for Bray[6] and Nancy. On 18 December 1860, John **LEE** to Penelope **PARKER** & William J **PARKER**, "...for & in consideration of the natural love he the said **LEE** hath & beareth towards /the/ said Penelope & William J. **PARKER** he the said **LEE** hath this day given & granted unto the said Penelope & William J. **PARKER** & to their heirs forever, all that tract of land & plantation whereon the said Penelope & William J. **PARKER** now lives & known as the Bray **PARKER** place upon condition however that the said Penelope & William J. **PARKER** do maintain or cause to be maintained the two old folks, to wit, Bray **PARKER** & Nancy **PARKER** their life time in as good, comfortable & decent a manner as they have heretofore done or as they are able to do all other matters & things notwithstanding...

John his (X) mark **LEE**

Signed, sealed & delivered in the presence of

Witness Elisha **PARKER** John F. **PARKER**

County Court Clerk's office June 12th. 1861.

The foregoing deed of Gift from John **LEE** to Penelope **PARKER** and Wm. J. **PARKER** was this day exhibited before me and proved by the oath of John F. **PARKER** one of the subscribing witnesses thereto therefore let the same be registered. Jno. R. **WALTON** P. R. Test Henry L. **EURE** C. C. Clk."[57] The probate date of this deed, only six months after it was executed, may be of the significance indicated above.

〰〰〰〰〰〰〰〰〰〰〰〰〰〰〰〰〰〰〰〰〰〰〰〰〰〰〰〰〰〰〰〰〰〰〰〰〰〰〰〰〰

Elizabeth[6] **PARKER** *(John[5],John[4],William[3],Thomas[2],William[1])* was born circa 1785. She appears on a marriage bond with Ebron **BRISCO**, dated 29 May 1819. His bondsman was Timy. (X) **BRISCO**.[58] On 17 November 1829, Abram[6] **PARKER** entered into an administrator's bond on the estate of Ebron **BRISCO** in the amount of $1,000, with Dempsey[6] **PARKER** and John **BEEMAN** as his bondsmen.[59] In 1850, she is listed in the U. S. Federal Census as Elizabeth **BRISCOE**, age 65,

---

[50] NCSA, C.041.40009, Gates County Real Estate Conveyances 1841-1847, Vol: 18,19, 18:488-489;19:354-355

[51] NCSA, C.041.70002, Gates County Tax Lists 1832-1851, [1842-1851] 1842, p. 9

[52] Gates County Historical Society, *Bible Records of Gates County, NC*, c. unknown, p.140

[53] Almasy, *Gates County, North Carolina Census 1850 & 1860*, c. 1987, p.23, 1850

[54] Ibid., p. 83, 1850

[55] NCSA, G.041.2194761, Gates County Estates, Record of 1765-1920, Vol. Parker, E.-Parker, M., Folder: Parker, Levi, Doc. #1914-1915

[56] Ibid., Doc. #1917

[57] NCSA, C.041.40011, Gates County Real Estate Conveyances 1857-1861, Vol:22, 22:719

[58] Almasy, *Gates County, North Carolina Marriage Bonds 1778-1868*, c. 1987, p.23

[59] NCSA, C.041.50011 Gates County Administrators' Bonds 1822-1847, 1828-1835 #23

living with Richd. **BRISCOE**, age 25.[60] Elizabeth[6] never remarried.

The known children of this couple are John[7], Richard[7] and Lavinia[7] **BRISCOE**, as evidenced by the order of Gates County Court 18 August 1834, for Jethro **HARRELL** to be their guardian. He entered into bonds of $400.00 with Abram W. **PARKER** and Elisha **HARRELL** as his bondsmen.[61]

John[7] **BRISCOE** was born in 1820, as shown by the 1850 U. S. Federal Census, and appears on a marriage bond with Judith **SAVAGE**, dated 13 January 1847, with Richard D. **BRISCOE** as his bondsman. His brother, Richard D.[7] **BRISCOE**, appears on a marriage bond with Mary E. **SAVAGE**, dated 7 January 1854, with Hardy W.[7] **PARKER** as his bondsman.[62] Lavinia[7] **BRISCOE** appears on a marriage bond with Wm. **HARRELL**, of Mills **HARRELL**, dated 23 December 1848. Wm. L. **BOOTHE** was his bondsman.[63]

Elizabeth[6] (**PARKER**) **BRISCOE** made her will 25 May 1863, naming her son, R. D.[7] **BRISCOE** as her executor. She directed that after all debts and funeral expenses were paid, that her property be equally divided between "my son R. D. **BRISCOE**, Lavenia **HARRELL** and Penelope **BRISCOE**, daughter of John W. **BRISCOE**." The witnesses to this will were H. C. **WILLEY** and Mills. K. **LAWRENCE**. She used a mark of "X" as her signature. The will was exhibited into August Court 1863.[64] No further information.

Reuben[6] **PARKER** *(John[5],John[4],William[3],Thomas[2],William[1])* was born circa 1787. He first appears on the Gates County Tax Lists in 1808, with one poll, which would indicate that he had reached the age of 21 years. He listed no land until 1811, after the division of his father's estate, and then had 65 acres.[65] It appears that the only other land he acquired was that 101 acres purchased of his brother, Kindred[6] **PARKER**, 16 November 1820. His last listing in the Gates County Tax Lists is found for the year 1835, when he owned 167 acres of land, with no polls.[66]

He was circa 23 years of age in 1810, when it was ordered by the Court that Abraham[6] and Demsey[6] **PARKER** be bound apprentices to him, "to learn the Trade or business of a Cooper &c."[67] His guardianship of Abraham[6], Demsey[6] and Theresa[6] **PARKER**, in May of 1813, has been previously mentioned in Chapter Eight.

Reuben[6] **PARKER** appears on a marriage bond dated 13 March 1813, with Judith **BEEMAN**. Whitmel **EURE** was his bondsman.[68] Judith **BEEMAN** was nee Judith **EURE**, daughter of Charles and Selea **EURE**, as evidenced by the will of Charles **EURE**, made 26 January 1811, mentioning his daughter, Judith **BEEMAN**.[69] She appears on a marriage bond dated 2 March 1809, with David **BEAMAN**. Whitmill **EURE** was also his bondsman.[70] David **BEEMAN** made his will 12 December 1809, exhibited into February Court 1810 by his executor, Abraham **BEEMAN**.[71]

On 17 November 1820, Reuben[6] and wife Judith **PARKER** sold 15 acres to John **BEEMAN** for $195.00. It is described as "Beginning at a corner of Abraham **BEEMAN** in Lewis **SPARK-MAN**s line, thence along sd **SPARKMAN**s to Levi **EURE**s line thence along said **EURE**s line to Abraham **BEEMAN**s line, thence along sd. **BEEMAN**s the various courses to the first station... Reuben **PARKER** Judith her X mark **PARKER**." They acknowledged this deed in open Court November 1820. Witnesses were Jas. **RIDDICK** and Levi **EURE**.[72]

Reuben[6] **PARKER** made his will 26 November 1834, probated in February Court 1836. He

---

[60] Almasy, *Gates County, North Carolina Census 1850 & 1860*, c. 1987, p. 21

[61] NCSA, C.041.30003, Gates County Court Minutes 1827-1850, pages not numbered, first page of August Court 1834

[62] Almasy, *Gates County, North Carolina Marriage Bonds 1778-1868*, c. 1987, p. 13

[63] Ibid., p. 39

[64] Almasy, *Gates County, North Carolina Wills 1838-1867, Vol. III*, c. 1987, p. 136, Will Bk. 3:331

[65] NCSA, C.041.70001, Gates County Tax Lists 1784-1831, [1807-1831] 1808:29;1811:75

[66] NCSA, C.041.70002, Gates County Tax Lists 1832-1851, [1832-1841] 1835:104

[67] Fouts, *Minutes of County Court of Pleas and Quarter Sessions Gates County, North Carolina 1806-1811 Vol. III*, c. 1985, 115:#661

[68] Almasy, *Gates County, North Carolina Marriage Bonds 1778-1868*, c. 1987, p. 69

[69] Ibid., *Gates County, North Carolina Wills 1807-1838, Vol. II*, c. 1985, p. 52, Will Bk. 2:122-123

[70] Ibid., *Gates County, North Carolina Marriage Bonds 1778-1868*, c. 1987, p. 5

[71] Ibid., *Gates County, North Carolina Wills 1807-1838, Vol. II*, c. 1985, p.23, Will Bk. 2:52-53

[72] NCSA, C.041.40006 Gates County Real Estate Conveyances 1819-1829 Vol: 11-13, 11:70

directed that his wife, Judith **PARKER**, should have $175.00 to buy provisions for the support of her and his children for one year. He also lent to her his land on the North side of the road, binding on the lands of Mrs. Lucrecia **BEEMAN** and Mrs. Priscilla **HUMPHLET**. This land was left to his son, Seth[7] **PARKER**, after Judith's death. His daughters, Sophia[7], Martha[7], Nancy[7] and Cinthia[7] **PARKER**, his youngest, were to have all the balance of his lands, except his right & interest to and in the lands of Treacy **KING**, deceased. That interest was to be sold and the proceeds were to be added to his account of sales and divided accordingly. He named his brother, Abram W.[6] **PARKER**, to be his executor. Wm. L. **BOOTH** and D. **SPARKMAN** witnessed his will.[73] Treacy[6] **KING** was Reuben's sister who died between 1832-1834. She will be treated here at a later time.

Abram W.[6] **PARKER**, Executor of Reuben[6] **PARKER**, took the inventory and made a sale of his property on 26 February 1836.[74] The division of his lands was made 1 March 1838 and was returned to August County Court. It is transcribed here, in full:

"State of North Carolina Gates County} February Term 1838. It was then and there ordered that William L. **BOOTHE**, Peter **PILAND** Dempsey **SPARKMAN** & Mills **SPARKMAN** be appointed commissioners to divide the lands of Reuben **PARKER** decsd. among the rightful heirs of said decsd. and make a report to the next term. Test W. G. **DAUGHTRY** Clk.

Pursuant to the annexed order we your Commissioners proceeded to set apart to the lawful heirs of Reuben **PARKER** decsd. or to divide the land in reference to the will of said deceasd. The whole by survey, contains One hundred and fourteen acres. Lot No 1 which is a part of the plot below, was drawn by Syntha **PARKER**, bounded as follows. Beginning at a white oak at the fence corner on Lot No. 2. thence N25° W. a straight line of marked trees to a small gum in the branch, corner on Dempsey **PARKER**, thence up the branch its various courses to a large pine corner on Mills **EURE**, thence N 28° E. a line of marked trees to a pine, corner, thence S. 42° W. 76 poles to the first station, containing 32 acres. Lot No. 2. which is the ballance of the first plot, was drawn by Martha **PARKER**, bounded as follows. viz. Beginning at a white oak corner on Lot No. 1. running thence S 42° W. 92 [sic] to a stump corner on M. **EURE**, thence N 30° W. 67 poles to a water oak, corner in the branch, thence up the branch its various courses to a gum, corner on Dempsey **PARKER** & Lot No. 1. thence S 25° E. a straight line of marked trees to the first station, containing 37 acres. Lot No. 3. which is a part of the plot below was drawn by Ann **PARKER** bounded as follows, viz. Beginning at a large white oak at the road, thence S 31½° E. to a small gum corner, thence N 50° E. a line of marked trees to a large oak, thence S 56½° E. 14½ poles to a poplar, thence S 44° E. 30 poles to a pine corner on Mrs. **BEEMAN** thence N 20° E. 17 poles to a gum N 34° W. 16 poles to [sic] poplar, thence N 7° W. 20½ poles to a post oak, thence N 6° E. 19 poles to a oak, thence N 12° E. 15 poles to road, thence down the road to the first Station, containing 22 acres. Lot No. 4, which is the ballance of the above plot was drawn by Elisha **HARRELL**, bounded as follows. Beginning at a large oak at the road, thence S 31½° E. a straight line to a small gum corner on Lot No. 3. thence S 50°. W. a line of marked trees to a sweet gum, corner on Dempsey **PARKER**, thence N 42° W. 8 poles to red oak, thence N 32 W. 48 poles to red oak thence N41½° W. 15⅛ poles to the road thence along the road to the first station, containing 23 acres. We your commissioners also further adjudge that in order to effect the division equal Lot No 1 have 32 acres- Lot No. 2 have 37 acres.- Lot No 3. have 22 acres-& Lot No 4 have 23 acres. Given under our hands and seals this 1st. day of March 1838. Wm. L. **BOOTHE**, D. **SPARKMAN** Mills **SPARKMAN** Allen **SMITH** Co S. Proved August Court 1838."[75]

There are extant guardian accounts of William W. **COWPER** as the only known guardian of the children of Reuben[6] and Judith **PARKER**. They began in 1838, with "Scynthy", Nancy, Seth and Martha **PARKER**. The final account for Seth **PARKER** was in February Court 1842.[76]

Elisha **HARRELL** married Sophia[7] as evidenced by the above division and a petition to the

---

[73] Almasy, *Gates County, North Carolina Wills 1807-1838, Vol. II*, c. 1985, p. 162, Will Bk. 2:367-368

[74] NCSA, G.041.2194762, Gates County Estates, Record of 1765-1920, Vol.: Parker Pierce, Folder: Parker, Reuben 1836, Doc. #275;280-283 Record of sales appears to be incomplete.

[75] NCSA, C.041.40008, Gates County Real Estate Conveyances 1836-1842, Vol: 16,17, 16:315-316

[76] NCSA, C.041.2194762, Gates County Estates, Record of 1765-1920, Vol. Parker-Pierce, Folder: Parker, R. 1838, Doc. #232-240; 1845, Doc. 243-251; Reuben 1836 , Doc. #279;284-305

court in 1844, concerning another family member.[77] She was born circa 1814, and they had William[8], age 9, and Mariah[8] **HARRELL**, age 2, by 1850.[78]

Martha[7] **PARKER** appears on a marriage bond with Joseph **EURE**, dated 9 June 1840, with Washington **HARRELL** as his bondsman.[79] They appear in the 1850 Federal Census, next door to Elisha and Sophia **HARRELL**, with children Emiline[8], age 4, Henry[8], age 2, and Parker[8] **EURE**, age 3/12. Martha[7] **PARKER** was born circa 1821.[80]

Seth[7] **PARKER** was born circa 1822 and married his first-cousin, Elizabeth[7] **PARKER**, daughter of Kindred[6] **PARKER**. Their family is found on page 102.

Nancy[7] **PARKER** appears on a marriage bond with Francis **LANGSTON**, dated 6 October 1849, with William S. **BOOTHE** as his bondsman.[81] This couple appears in the U. S. Federal Census for 1860 with children Mary[8], age 7, Emeline[8], age 5, Priss[8], age 3 and Isaac[8] **LANGSTON**, age 1. Nancy[7] **PARKER** was born circa 1823-1826.[82]

Cynthia[7] **PARKER**'s name is spelled in numerous ways, from Cinthy to Scyntha, and in the 1850 Federal Census it appears as "Scynitha." She appears on a marriage bond with Richard **SAUN-DERS**, dated 18 March 1850, with Henry **CARTER** as his bondsman.[83] Cynthia[7] **PARKER** was born circa 1828.[84]

On 29 August 1849, Judith **PARKER** made the following deed to Seth[7] **PARKER**, described as "for and in consideration of the Love and affection which she the said Judith **PARKER** has for her son Seth **PARKER** as well as the further consideration of the sum of one dollar to me the said Judith in hand paid by the said Seth **PARKER** the receipt whereof I do hereby acknowledge (and also the further consideration that the said Seth **PARKER** hath promised to support me the said Judith **PARKER** during my life to live with the said Seth **PARKER** as one of the family I [?] have bargain [sic] conveyed and by these presents do give, grant bargain sell convey and confirm unto the said Seth **PARKER** his heirs executors administrators assignees [?] for ever followearing [sic] property to Wit. All my dower right title and Interest in the tract of land wherin [sic] I now live bounded by the land of the said Seth **PARKER** Joseph **EURE** and others containing by estimation sixty [60] acres be the same more or less and known as the land whereon Reuben **PARKER** formerly lived also one bay mare and cart wheel and gear..." It was signed "Judith her X mark **PARKER**" and the witnesses were Na. **SMITH** and Titus J. **LEE**. It was proved in November Term 1849.[85]

She was living with Seth[7] **PARKER**, and his wife Elizabeth[7], at the enumeration of the U. S. Federal Census on 7 August 1850, and was listed as 60 years of age.[86] She does not appear in the 1860 Census.

ロロロロロロロロロロロロロロロロロロロロロロロロロロロロロロロロロロロロロロロロロロロロロロ

Seth[6] **PARKER** *(John[5],John[4],William[3],Thomas[2],William[1])* was born circa 1789. The deed from Seth[6] to Kindred[6] **PARKER**, for his share of his father's lands, was made 23 September 1810, as previously noted. It would be necessary for him to be 21 years of age to make such conveyance.

On 21 July 1823, Seth[6] **PARKER** sold 70 acres of land to Jesse **LEE**. It is described as "Beginning at Ruth **PARKER** dividing [sic] thence running to **ODOM**s corner thence adjoining Henry **COPELAND** land thence runing to **BARNES**'s line & from thence to the beginning..." Abram W.[6] and Bray[6] **PARKER** witnessed this deed, proved in November Term 1823.[87]

On 20 July 1824, William **SEARS** sold 41 acres to Seth[6] **PARKER**. It is described as "Be-

---

[77] NCSA, C.041.2194762, Gates County Estates, Record of 1765-1920, Vol. Parker-Pierce, Folder: Parker, R. 1838, Doc. #259-262

[78] Almasy, *Gates County, North Carolina Census 1850 & 1860*, c. 1987, p. 25, 1850 Census

[79] Ibid., *Gates County, North Carolina Marriage Bonds 1778-1868*, c. 1987, p. 28

[80] Ibid., *Gates County, North Carolina Census 1850 & 1860*, c. 1987, p. 25, 1850 Census

[81] Ibid., *Gates County, North Carolina Marriage Bonds 1778-1868*, c. 1987, p. p. 56

[82] Ibid., *Gates County, North Carolina Census 1850 & 1860*, c. 1987, p. 119, 1860 Census

[83] Ibid., *Gates County, North Carolina Marriage Bonds 1778-1868*, c. 1987, p. 82

[84] Ibid., *Gates County, North Carolina Census 1850 & 1860*, c. 1987, p. 14, 1850 Census. Richard Saunders was listed as a "Laborer" and they were living in the family of Henry and Nancy Carter.

[85] NCSA, C.041.40010, Gates County Real Estate Conveyances 1847-1857 Vol:20,21, 20:279

[86] Almasy, *Gates County, North Carolina Census 1850 & 1860*, c. 1987, p. 16

[87] NCSA, C.041.40006, Gates County Real Estate Conveyances 1819-1829 Vol: Vols. 11-13, 11:256

gining at a post oke [sic] in David E **SUMNER**s line thence running nearly a west course a line of marked trees to Seth **PARKER**s line thence along Said **PARKER**s line to Jonathan **PARKER**s line to Kinchen **NORFLEET**s line thence to Nancy **PARKER**s line thence Said Nancy **PARKER**s line to the first Station..." Kindred⁶ **PARKER** and Hy. H. **EURE** witnessed this deed, proved in February Court 1826.⁸⁸

On 18 February 1826, Seth⁶ **PARKER** sold 25 acres to Nancy **PARKER**. It is described as "begining at a b/l/ack gum on Henry **WILLIAMS** line thence runing nearly a South Course to Kinchan **NORFLETT**s line thence along said **NORFLETT** to Nancy **PARKER**s line thence along Said Nancy **PARKER** line to Henry **WILLIAMS** thence along Said **WILLIAMS** to the first station..." James **SIMPSON** and Demsey **VANN** witnessed this deed, proved in February Court 1826.⁸⁹ On the same day, Nancy **PARKER** sold Seth⁶ **PARKER** 15 acres. That land is described as "Begining at a red oak a corner tree on said Seth **PARKER**s line adjoining the line of Levy **CREECEY** runing a south course to a line of marked trees to a corner tree a black gum on Nancy **PARKER**s land thence nearly an east Course to a Gum a corner tree on James **SIMPSON**s Land thence along a line of marked trees on said **SIMPSON**s line to a pine a corner tree on Hillery **WILLEY**s line thence a line of marked trees to the first station..." James **SIMPSON** and Demsey **VANN** also witnessed this deed, proved in February Court 1826.⁹⁰

On 20 February 1826, Seth⁶ **PARKER** sold 60 acres to Henry G. **WILLIAMS**. It is described as "begining at warter [sic] Oak Jonathan **PARKER**s Corner thence along sd. **PARKER**s line to Hillery **WILLEY**s Corner a sweet gum thence along sd. **WILLEY**s line to Levi **CREECE**s corner a pine thence along sd. **CREECE**s line to Hillery **WILLEY**s line thence along sd. **WILLEY**s line to James **SIMPSON** corner a pine thence along sd. **SIMPSON** line to a corner of Nansey **PARKER** a Sweet gum thence a direct Course to a black gum standing in the main run of the swamp thence along sd. Nancy **PARKER**s line to the first Station or begining..." D. **WILLIAMS** and Jonathan **WILLIAMS** witnessed this deed, proved in February Court 1826.⁹¹

All the above deeds state that Seth⁶ **PARKER** was "of Gates County." He appears in the Gates County Tax Lists for 1823-1825, but not thereafter.⁹² It is probable that 1826 is the year that he removed to Tennessee. On 10 March 1840, the heirs at law of Treasey⁶ **KING** sold their right to her lands to Dempsey⁶ **PARKER**, as previously mentioned. Abram W.⁶ **PARKER** was "agent of Seth **PARKER**" at that time.

On 23 December 1846, Seth⁶ **PARKER** "of the state of Tennessee" sold to William **BABB** "all his right title and interest to & in the following tracts of land, as one of the heirs at law of Dempsey **PARKER** deceased late of the said county of Gates, to wit the tract of land on which the said Dempsey **PARKER** lived at the time of his death and which he the said Dempsey **PARKER** purchased of Elisha **EURE**, John **SPARKMAN** and Hillery **TAYLOR** as will more fully appear by reference to their deed which said tract contains about two hundred acres...and is subject to the Dower of Chitty **PARKER** the widow of the said Dempsey and also the tract of land situate in the said county known as the **JONES** Plantation, one third of which the said Dempsey **PARKER** bought of John **JONES** to whom it descended from Henry **JONES** Senr & Henry **JONES** Jur: [sic] which said tract of land and the interest of the said Dempsey **PARKER** therein is particularly described in a deed made by the said John **JONES** to the said Dempsey **PARKER** bearing date the 8ᵗʰ of February 1838 and of record in the registers Office of said county in Book No 16 page 235, 236, and the interest of Hardy C. **JONES** in thirty eight acres of the said tract of land purchased by the said Dempsey as will fully appear by reference to the deed of James R **RIDDICK** Sheriff of [sic] recorded in the registers Office of Gates County in Book No 17 page 403 404 & 405.

To have & to hold all my right title & interest in the premises herein conveyed (being and interest of One sixth as one of the Heirs at law of the said Dempsey **PARKER**)..." Will J. **BAKER** wit-

---

⁸⁸ NCSA, C.041.40006, Gates County Real Estate Conveyances 1819-1829 Vol: Vols. 11-13, 12:88
⁸⁹ Ibid., 12:105-106
⁹⁰ Ibid., 12:109-110
⁹¹ Ibid., 12:117-118
⁹² NCSA, C.041.70001 Gates County Tax Lists 1784-1831 [1807-1831] pp. 276;294;316

nessed this deed, proved in November Term 1848.[93]

Seth[6] **PARKER** sold William **BABB** yet more of his right, title and interest or estate as an heir of the late Dempsey[6] **PARKER** on that same date. It is described as "the tract known as the Old place bounded by the lands of Riddick **GATLING**, John **LEE** & others containing by estimation one hundred & fifty acres more or less, the Dempsey **EURE** tract adjoining the lands of Robt H **BALLARD** John **RIDDICK** and others containing by actual survey Two hundred and five acres the **SMITH** place containing by estimation fifty acres and bounded by the lands of Mills **SPARKMAN** and heirs [?] James **CARTER** Judith **SAVAGE** & others and the James **HARRELL** tract adjoining the lands of James R **RIDDICK** Reuben **HARRELL** and others & lying on the waters of Sarum Creek and supposed to containe seventy five acres...in fee simple forever and I the said Seth **PARKER** do more over by these presents authorise and impower him the said William **BABB** to demand secure sue for and recover of the Clerk & Master in Equity of the County aforesaid or of the assurities [?] to his Official bond all and every part of my right and interest to and in the before described premises herein before conveyed..." Wm. J. **BAKER** also witnessed this deed, proved in November Term 1848.[94] No further information on this Seth **PARKER**.

ᴦᴜᴦᴜᴦᴜᴦᴜᴦᴜᴦᴜᴦᴜᴦᴜᴦᴜᴦᴜᴦᴜᴦᴜᴦᴜᴦᴜᴦᴜᴦᴜᴦᴜᴦᴜᴦᴜᴦᴜᴦᴜᴦᴜᴦᴜᴦᴜᴦᴜ

Mary[6] **PARKER** *(John[5],John[4],William[3],Thomas[2],William[1])* is estimated here to have been born circa 1790. She married James **GOODWIN** as evidenced by the abstract of the following deed: 12 January 1839 James and Mary **GOODWIN** his wife to Dempsey **PARKER** 1/9 of 80 acres $10.00 "...all our right and Interest to and in a certain tract or parcel of land lying and being in the County of Gates (NC) Aforesaid which land descended to the said Mary **GOODWIN** one of the heirs at Law by the death of Terese **KING** wife of Jno. **KING** and bounded as follows To wit Beginning at a water oak in Riddick **GATLING** line Thence running said **GATLING** line to a black gum a corner of said **GATLING** and said D. **PARKER** Thence D. **PARKER**'s to a corner of Reuben **PARKER**'s heirs and D. **PARKER** in the Lickaroot [sic] branch thence up the branch to a corner a black gum a corner of Mills **EURE**'s heirs thence said M. **EURE**'s heirs line to the first station Containing in the whole about Eighty Acres more or less and the said Mary being a ninth heir (ie) taking one ninth of the /said/ land ..." Jas. his X mark **GOODWIN** Mary her X mark **GOODWIN** Witnesses Wm L. **BOOTHE** Jesse **PILAND** Proved by WLB August Ct. 1839.[95]

Mary[6] **(PARKER) GOODWIN** was dead by November, 1846, as evidenced by the order of the court issuing letters of administration on the estate of Mary **GOODIN** [sic] to James **GOODIN**. He entered bond in the sum of $1,000.00, with S. W. **WORRELL** and Will **GOODIN** as his securities, and qualified as her administrator.[96] She died without issue. No further information.

Levi W.[6] **PARKER** *(John[5],John[4],William[3],Thomas[2],William[1])* was born circa 1791. He first appears in the Gates County Tax Lists in 1811, when Kindred **PARKER** listed 100 acres "for Levi **PARKER**." Levi listed that 100 acres in his own right from 1812 through 1819.[97] He most likely married in North Carolina, then removed to Pickens County, AL, before 1827.

On 15 May 1832, he made the following power of attorney: "The State of Alabama Pickins County} To all whom it may concern. Know ye that I Levi W. **PARKER** of the County and State aforesaid have this day constituted made & appointed Randal **SHERROD** of Edgecomb County N. Carolina (at present in the County and State first above written) my true, sole & lawful attorney, to do transact & perform for me, all & whatsoever matter or thing I might, could, would, should or ought to do in the State of North Carolina, and the same to do & perform in as ample & full a manner as if I were present, acting for myself, but more especially to make titles to a certain piece tract or parcel of land lying in the County of Gates North Carolina which I sold to my brother Abraham **PARKER**, and to receive all monies due me from said Abraham **PARKER** for said land, as also to receive & do all

---

[93] NCSA, C.041.40010, Gates County Real Estate Conveyances 1847-1857 Vol: 20,21, 20:157-158

[94] Ibid., 20:158-159

[95] NCSA, C.041.40008, Gates County Real Estate Conveyances 1836-1842, Vol: 16,17, 17:87

[96] NCSA, C.041.30003, Gates County Court Minutes 1827-1850, 4 vols., November Court 1846, pages unnumbered

[97] NCSA, C.041.70001, Gates County Tax Lists 1784-1831 [1807-1831] pp. 75;92;108;124;142;160; 177;196;213

things else that may be necessary to receive from my Brother Kindred **PARKER** Administrator of my deceas[d] Mother Clarkey **PARKER** all monies that may be due & coming to me as one of her heirs & representatives, my wish is not only to give said Randal **SHERROD** the power here especially delegated but to make him my general attorney in said State of North Carolina, and do hereby give & grant him full power in law or Equity to become the same. In Testimony whereof I have hereunto set my hand & seal this 15th day of May A. D. 1832. Signed sealed & delivered in the presence of [sic] L. W. **PARKER**

The State of Alabama Pickins County} Personally appeared before me Francis W. **BOSTICK** Clerk of the County Court for the County of Pickens in the State aforesaid the within named Levi W. **PARKER** who acknowledged that he signed, sealed & delivered the within Power of attorney to the within named Randal **SHERROD** for the purposes therein expressed on the day and date therein mentioned. Given under my hand and private seal, there being no seal of office, at office this 15th day of May A. D. 1832. attest Francis W. **BOSTICK** Clerk" This document was certified by George H. **FLOURNY**, Judge of the County Court of Pickens County, and recorded by the clerk on the same day. It was exhibited into Gates County Court and ordered to be registered in November 1832.[98]

On 2 August 1832, Randol **SHERARD** of Edgecomb County, NC, as agent for Levi W. **PARKER**, sold the land mentioned in the above power of attorney to Abram[6] **PARKER** for $110.00. It is described as "Beginning at a corner water oak in the branch, a corner of Mills **EURE** & others, thence running said **EURE**s line of marked trees an East course to Dempsey **EURE**'s line, thence said D. **EURE**'s line of marked trees to a corner white oak, Benjamin **WYNNS** corner thence said **WYNNS** line of marked trees near a North course to John **SPARKMAN** line, thence down said **SPARKMAN**s line of marked trees near a South course to the first Station or beginning, containing by estimation One hundred acres, be the same more or less..." This deed was witnessed by John **SPARKMAN** and Kindred **PARKER**, proved and ordered to be registered in February County Court 1836.[99] This land is his share in the division of his father's real estate, known as the "**ROBERTSON**s Tract." The recorder of this deed consistently wrote the name "Randol" as "Randolph," and just as consistently erased the letters "ph."

Levi W.[6] **PARKER** and his family appear in the 1850 U. S. Federal Census for Pickens County, AL. They are listed as Levi W., age 56, Farmer, born in NC; "Clamilia," age 43, born in NC; Randel, age 23, Farmer born in AL; Elmirah, age 20, born in AL; Redden, age 16, Farmer, born in AL; William, age 15, Farmer, born in AL; James, age 10, born in AL, and "Tersecia," age 5, born in AL.[100] "Tersecia" was "Theresa."

Levi W.[6] **PARKER** and his family also appear in the 1860 U. S. Federal Census for Pickens County, AL. They are listed as Levi W., age 65, Farmer, born in NC; Clementine, Housewife, age 52, born in NC; Elmira, age 23, Domestic, born in AL; Warren, age 19, Farmer, born in AL; Theressa, age 15, born in AL.[101] The Randol **SHERARD** of Edgecombe County, who was attorney for Levi W.[6] **PARKER**, was probably his father-in-law, as he named his eldest son "Randel." The discrepancies between these two records are unexplained. Only Clementine, Elmira and a Jane **PARKER**, age 25, appear in the 1870 U. S. Census.[102] No further information.

Theresa[6] **PARKER** *(John[5], John[4], William[3], Thomas[2], William[1])* is estimated here to have been born circa 1794. Her name has undergone numerous spelling variations in the few records in which she appears. She received 76 acres in the division of her father's land and listed 75 acres, for tax purposes, between 1824 and 1830.[103] This land is mentioned in other records. She appears on a marriage bond with John **KING**, dated 19 January 1830, with Henry **PUGH** as his bondsman.[104]

Theresa[6] (**PARKER**) **KING** was dead by the time her brother, Reuben[6] **PARKER**, made his

[98]  NCSA, C.041.40007, Gates County Real Estate Conveyances 1829-1836 Vol: 14,15, 14:489-490

[99]  Ibid., 15:345

[100]  1850 U. S. Federal Census, Pickens Co., AL, #M432-13, p. 30B, transcribed by Elsie Burton, proofread by Clayton Burton for http://ftp.rootsweb.com/pub/usgenweb/al/pickens/census/1850/pg0025a.txt

[101]  1860 U. S. Federal Census, Pickens Co., AL, Bridgeville PO, M653, Roll: 20 , p. 763B

[102]  1870 U. S. Federal Census, Pickens Co., AL, Bridgeville PO, M593, Roll: 36, p. 173B

[103]  NCSA, C.041.70001, Gates County Tax Lists 1784-1831 [1807-1831] pp. 307;325;344;358; 379;398;419

[104]  Almasy, *Gates County, North Carolina Marriage Bonds 1778-1868*, c. 1987, p. 54

will 26 November 1834. No further information.

Abraham W.[6] **PARKER** *(John[5],John[4],William[3],Thomas[2],William[1])* was born 13 February 1796.[105] In November Court 1826, it was ordered that Abraham[6] **PARKER** be appointed guardian to William **JOHNSON**, son of Esther **BLADES** and that he give bond and security in the sum of $300.00, with Demsey **EURE** & Reuben[6] **PARKER** as securities. He was also granted a "Certificate for licence to sell Spirituous liquors by the small measure at the Cross roads for one year."[106] The **PARKER, BLADES** and **JOHNSON** relationships, if any, are undetermined at this time. The "Cross roads" has been known as **PARKER**'s Cross Roads and is now known as "**BALLARD**'s Cross Roads." He continued to renew that license for several years.

On 9 December 1826, Andrew **JOHNSON** sold Abraham W.[6] **PARKER** 130 acres for $200.00, described as "beginning at /the/ run on the West side of **COLE**s Creek thence a N. West course to Edward **PILAND**s line thence along said **PILAND**s line to Mrs. **LEWIS** land thence down the Ferry road nearly a South course to Samuel **EURE**s land thence along his line to **COLE**s Creek Run thence up **COLE**s /Creek/ Run to the first Station..." This deed was witnessed by Isaiah **MAT-THEWS** and Wm. L. **BOOTHE**.[107]

On 2 August 1827, Andrew **JOHNSON** sold Abraham W.[6] **PARKER** 27½ acres of land for $121.24, described as "Beginning at a red oak of Uriah **EURE**'s line thence along said **EURE**s line near a west course to David **LEWIS** line thence down said **LEWIS** line to the run /of the/ Licking root Branch thence down the run of said Branch to A Black gum of Abram W **PARKER**s line thence up said **PARKER**s line to the first Station..." This deed was witnessed by Henry **CARTER** and John his X mark **SPEIGHT**, Jur.[108] Both these deeds were proved in August Court 1827.

Abraham W.[6] **PARKER** appears on a Gates County marriage bond with Mary **CROSS**, dated "1830." The day and month were left blank by the Clerk. Wm. E. **PUGH** was his bondsman. She previously appeared on a marriage bond with David **CROSS** 22 November 1825, as Mary **EURE**.[109]

Mary **CROSS** was the daughter of Mills **EURE**, as evidenced by the suit in May Court 1837 of "Mrs. Louisa **EURE** & others vs Nathanil **EURE**," in which Abm. W. **PARKER** and wife Mary were named. The issue to be tried was "whether the paper writing offered for probate as the Last wills and Testaments of Mills **EURE** of [sic] Either of them be the Last will & Testament of the said Mills dec[d] Executed in due form of Law To pass reale or personal estate." The jury determined that neither one was his last will and Testament.[110]

In February Court 1831, Abram W.[6] **PARKER** was appointed guardian to Wm. **JOHNSON** for a second time. He offered John **BEEMAN** and John **RIDDICK** as his securities in the sum of $400.00. He was appointed guardian to Emmy, Armesia, Henry, Mary and Mills **EURE**, Orphans of Lewis **EURE**, at the same time. His securities were John **BEEMAN** and Mills **EURE** in the sum of $3,000.00.[111]

Abraham W.[6] **PARKER** made his will 10 June 1837. He named his wife, Mary **PARKER**, as his executrix and bequeathed his entire estate to her alone. He died 29 November 1840, and is buried in the **BALLARD** Cemetery in Gates County.[112]

Abram W.[6] **PARKER**'s will came up on the Appearance Docket for February Court 1841. It was termed "The Executrix of A W **PARKER** vs The Distributees & heirs at law of A W **PARKER**} Issue notice to defendants." The issue was "Whether the paper writing offered for probate be the last will an [sic] Testament of of [sic] A W **PARKER** and executed with the formality required by law to pass real & personal estate. The following Jury to wit Timothy **WALTON** Jethro D **GOODMAN**

---

[105] NCSA, Pre-1914 Graves Index, Gates County, Gatesville, NC, Ballard Cemetery. David Powell, of Eure, NC, reported this name as "Bram Parker" inscribed on the gravestone.

[106] Fouts, *Minutes of County Court of Pleas and Quarter Sessions Gates County, North Carolina 1824-1827, Vol. VI*, c. 1988, 125:#1463

[107] NCSA, C.041.40006, Gates County Real Estate Conveyances 1819-1829 Vol: 11-13, 13:73-74

[108] Ibid., 13:67-68

[109] Almasy, *Gates County, North Carolina Marriage Bonds 1778-1868*, c. 1987, p. 66; p. 19

[110] NCSA, C.041.30003, Gates County Court Minutes 1827-1850, May Ct. 1837, 8th page. Pages unnumbered.

[111] Fouts, *Minutes of County Court of Pleas and Quarter Sessions Gates County, North Carolina 1828-1831..., Vol. VII*, c. 1990, 101:# 137

[112] NCSA, Pre-1914 Graves Index, Gates County, Gatesville, NC, Ballard Cemetery.

Dempsey **KNIGHT** Anthony **MATTHEWS** Solomon **ROUNTREE** Jethro S **HASLET** Edward **RIDDICK** Samuel **HARRELL**, Oliver H **SAVAGE** Etheldred **CROSS**, Wm. **JONES** & John **BRADDY** being Sworn and empanelled say that the paper writing offered...is the last will and Testament of Abram W **PARKER** and properly executed to pass real and personal estate.

The defendants being dissatisfied with the Judgment prayed for and obtained an appeal to the next Sup Court of law to be held for the County of Gates at the Court House in Gatesville on 1st. Monday after the 4th. Monday in Sept. next giving Henry **GILLIAM** & Whitl. **STALLINGS** security for the same in the sum of One thousand dollars." W. G. **DAUGHTRY**, Clerk of the County Court, certified that the above was a true and correct transcription from the records of his office, dated 10 September 1841.[113] An appeal bond to pay costs and charges if the appeal failed had been signed by Kindred[6], Bray[6] and Demsey[6] **PARKER**, along with Henry **GILLIAM** and Whitm̲i̲l̲ **STALLINS**, 19 May 1841.[114]

Mary **PARKER** was granted an Administration Bond in the sum of $60,000 to be administrator "Ruduete" Lite [Pendente Lite] of Abm W **PARKER** 15 February 1841. Mary **PARKER**, Nathl. **EURE**, John **WILLEY** & Cyprian **SMITH** [signed Sipha **SMITH**,] all signed that bond.[115]

In an undated document, concerning the "Executors of A W **PARKER** vs The heirs & distributees of A W **PARKER**," Kindred[6] **PARKER** made oath that Jesse "**LAW**" [may be "**LEE**"] "is a material witness for the defendants, but is confined at home by severe sickness. He stated that he expects to prove by the witness that he heard A W **PARKER** say he had made a last will and testament in which he made distributions of his estate entirely different from the distribution that has been made in the paper writing offered for probate as his last will & testament ~~That this affidavit is~~ That this conversation took place between the witness & A W **PARKER** shortly before the death of said **PARKER**..."[116]

The previous affidavit appears to have been made at about the same time as the following: "Mary **PARKER** vs The Heirs at Law of Abraham W **PARKER** Superior Court Spring Term 1842 Kindred **PARKER** one of the Defendants in the above named case maketh oath that Jno D **PIPKIN** as he thinks & is advised is a material a [?] witness for him that he can not safely come to trial without the benefit of his testimony, that he has been summoned & does not attend and that he is not kept away by his consent or contempt [?] The Defendant expects to prove by the witness that __[?]__ he had a conversation with the supposed Testator /A W **PARKER**/ in which he said he intended to make a will in which he should have a thousand Dollars to carry on the suit between **GILLIAM** & himself- & that he intended his [?] said will to give Jno F **PARKER** son of Kindred **PARKER** a considerable part of his estate-This affiant further maketh oath that this affidavit is not made for delay but for the causes as set forth. Kindred **PARKER** Sworn to in open Court H. **GILLIAM** Clk

This affiant further maketh oath that he expects to prove by Jesse **LAW**-That A W **PARKER** the supposed Testator told him about two months before his death that he [sic] **PARKER** had made a will in which he had given Jno F **PARKER** a considerable part of his land & other property & that he had given legacies to others of his family & that if he **PARKER** were to die then such a will would be found in his House. Kindred **PARKER** Sworn to in open Court H. **GILLIAM** Clk"[117]

This controversy appears again in the November 1842 term of Gates County Superior Court, where the issue was still whether or not the paper writing offered for probate was the last will and testament of Abm. W.[6] **PARKER**. The jurors were Wm. F. **BENNET**, Thomas **RIDDICK**, Riẕup **RAWLS**, I. [?] H. **RIDDICK**, Jesse **EASON**, James H. **PARKER**, Henry **GOODMAN**, Riddick **LASSITER**, Adam **RABY**, Harry **BOOTH**, Henry **HOFFLER** & Wm. H. **GOODMAN**, who agreed that it was. It was then ordered to be admitted to probate.[118]

---

[113] NCSA, G.041.2194760, Gates County Estates, Record of 1765-1920, Vol. Odom-Parker, Folder: Parker, Abraham W. 1839, Doc. #1146-1147

[114] Ibid., Doc. #1151

[115] NCSA, C.041.50011 Gates County Administrators' Bonds 1822-1847 [1836-1847] #100

[116] NCSA, G.041.2194760, Gates County Estates, Record of 1765-1920, Vol. Odom-Parker, Folder: Parker, Abraham W. 1839, Doc. #1032

[117] Ibid., Doc. #1034

[118] Almasy, *Gates County North Carolina Wills 1838-1867, Vol. III*, c. 1987, pp. 23-24, Will Bk. 3:40-42

Abraham W.[6] **PARKER** took several deeds in trust from various people. He was a merchant in Gates County, as evidenced by a 21-page inventory and sale of his goods 10 March 1841.[119] The deeds in trust secured payment of his customers' debts. He purchased 200 acres of Dempsey **EURE**'s land on 14 December 1833, from Samuel **EURE**, trustee, by a deed in trust to secure debt, dated "10"[120] [sic] September 1832. This land adjoined "the lands of Abram W. **PARKER**, Mills **EURE**, Elisha **HARRELL**, John **BEEMAN**'s heirs, Dempsey **SPARKMAN**, James **BROWN** & Benjamin **WYNNS**, it being the tract of land whereon the said Dempsey **EURE** now lives..." This deed was witnessed by Peter **EURE** and J. **WILLEY**, who proved it by his oath in February Court 1836.[121]

This is the same land that appears in the following petition: "State of North Carolina Gates County} November Sessions 1842 The Petition of Mary W. [sic] **PARKER** to the worshipful Justices of the Court aforesaid

Humbly complaining shews unto your worships, that she is tenant in common of a certain tract or parcel of land situate, lying and being in the county aforesaid, bounded by the lands of the heirs and devisee of Abram W. **PARKER** decd., Mills **EURE**, Elisha **HARRELL** John **BEMAN**'s heirs, Dempsy **SPARKMAN**, James **BROWN** and Benjamin **WYNNS**, it being the same tract of land which conveyed by Samuel **EURE** trustee &c to Abram W. **PARKER**, by deed bearing date the 14 Decr. 1833, with one Dempsy **PARKER**. She shews unto your worships that she is entitled to one undivided half or moiety of said /tract of land in fee simple/ by devise from her late husband Abram W. **PARKER**, and that said Dempsy **PARKER** is entitled to the other moiety. She further represents that she is desirous of having the said land divided and her share allotted to her in severalty. She therefore prays your worships to appoint five commissioners to divide the aforesaid land, agreeably to the Act of the General Assembly in such case made and provided. May it please your worships to grant all proper process and for such other further and general releif as the nature of ~~you~~ her case requires and your petitioner as in duty bound will ever pray &c David **OUTLAW** Atto for Pet[r]. Commissioners William W. **COWPER**, Peter **PILAND**, Riddick **GATLING**, Mills **DAUGHTRY**, Joseph **GATLIN**"[122]

That division was made 20 February 1843. Demsey[6] **PARKER** was allotted 205 acres and Mary Ann **PARKER** was allotted 77 acres. Demsey[6]'s lot was valued at $410.00 and he paid over to Mary Ann $70.25, making each share $339.75.[123]

There was a petition made to the Court by Demsey[6] **PARKER** in February Term 1843. He had filed a petition against Abram W.[6] **PARKER**, in August 1840, for damages he sustained by the overflowing of his lands [by a millpond,] but it was abated by Abram[6]'s death. He stated that Mary had qualified as executrix to Abram[6]'s will and had "intermarried with Robert H **BALLARD**," and that Abram[6]'s estate had "come to the hands of said Robert H & wife Mary, to the amount of twenty thousand dollars" and he wanted the suit revived.[124]

It appears that Abram W.[6] **PARKER** died rather suddenly as he had put in his answer to that earlier petition in November Court 1840.[125] He listed 1,487 acres of land for taxes in 1840.[126]

Mary **PARKER** appears on a marriage bond with Robert **BALLARD**, dated 15 February 1843, with Thomas **RIDDICK** as his bondsman.[127] She was born 17 March 1799, and died 2 January

---

[119] NCSA, G.041.2194760, Gates County Estates, Record of 1765-1920, Vol. Odom-Parker, Folder: Parker, Abraham W. 1839, Doc. #1161-1182

[120] NCSA, C.041.40007, Gates County Real Estate Conveyances 1829-1836 Vol: 14,15, 14:422 This deed is dated 19 September 1832. Abram W. Parker held 12-month "notes of hand" against Dempsey Eure for $989.71, bearing interest from 15 May 1832, and $23.47 from 1 January 1832. He also included slaves named Jim and Mary.

[121] NCSA, C.041.40007, Gates County Real Estate Conveyances 1829-1836 Vol: 14,15, 15:347

[122] NCSA, G.041.2194760, Gates County Estates, Record of 1765-1920, Vol. Odom-Parker, Folder: Parker, Abraham W. 1839, Doc. #1192

[123] Gates County, NC Deed Book 18:387

[124] NCSA, G.041.2194760, Gates County Estates, Record of 1765-1920, Vol. Odom-Parker, Folder: Parker, Abraham W. 1839, Doc. #1047;1051

[125] Ibid., Doc. #1050

[126] NCSA, C.041.70002, Gates County Tax Lists 1832-1851 [1832-1841] John Matthews Captaincy, p. 260

[127] Almasy, *Gates County, North Carolina Marriage Bonds 1778-1868*, c. 1987, p. 4

1869.  She is also buried in the **BALLARD** Cemetery.[128]

The following petition specifies a number of Abram W.[6] **PARKER**'s purchases after making his will.  "Kindred **PARKER** & others heirs at Law of Abram W & of Dempsey **PARKER** & Mary **GOODWIN**  To the Court}  Pet for sale of Land

North Carolina }  In Equity

Gates County   }                     Spring Term 1846

To the Honbl. the Judge of the said [?] Court.

The petition of Bray **PARKER**, Elisha **PARKER**, Kindred **PARKER**, Seth **PARKER**, Elizabeth **BRISCOE**, Levi **PARKER**, Seth, Sophia, Martha, Cynthia & Nancy **PARKER** Sheweth your Honor that Abram W **PARKER** late of said county, having made a last will and testament in due form of law to pass real estate departed this life in the year 1839 [sic] leaving your petitioners Bray, Kindred, Seth & Levi **PARKER** /brothers/ Elizabeth **BRISCOE** a Sister; and your petitioners Seth, Sophia, Martha, Cynthia & Nancy **PARKER** the nephew and nieces of said Abram W & children of Reuben **PARKER** a brother of said Abram W, who died in the lifetime of said Abram W; and also Demps/e/y **PARKER** & Mary **GOODWIN** a brother & sister of said Abram W. his only heirs at law.  That the said Abram W after the making of a last will and testament purchased the following pieces or parcels of land of which he died seised, to wit, one tract purchased by the said Abram W. of William **JOHN-SON**, beginning at a red oak stump inside of the field of Mary **CULLENS** at the corner of said field on the Sarum Creek road, thence down the said **CULLENS**' line to the run of the branch, thence down the run of said branch to a maple a corner of Abram W. **PARKER**, thence the said **PARKER**s line of marked trees to a small post oak a corner tree on Sarum Creek road, thence the road to the first Station containing thirty acres more or less:  One other tract of land purchased by the said A. W. **PARKER** of Demps/e/y **SPARKMAN**, beginning at a large pine a corner of Jethro **EURE** and Boon **EURE**'s land, thence N68W a line of marked trees to a pine, a corner of said Boon **EURE** & Wiley **CARTER**, thence S2E26 poles to a black gum in the branch a corner of said **CARTER**, then S68E111 poles to a small pine a corner tree, thence N3W to the first station containing sixty and one fourth acres:  One other tract of land purchased by the said Abram W of Ezekiel & Nancy **LASSITER**, Known as as [sic] the **SPIVEY** Pattent, adjoining the lands of the said A W **PARKER** & others and lies on Chowan River, out of which tract of land Moses **SPIVEY** left to James **BROWN** by will one hundred acres, which lands belong to the said Nancy **LASSITER** and the heirs at law of the said James **BROWN**, the said:  One other tract of land purchased by the said A W **PARKER** of Elizabeth **PARKER** it being a tract of land give_ by Moses **SPIVEY** to James **BROWN** the father of said Elizabeth, and bounded by the lands of William G **DAUGHTRY**, **BENNETS** Creek and thence through the River Pocoson to Chowan River, thence up the River to the mouth of Sarum Creek, thence up the said Creek to the mouth of herring Creek, thence the said A W **PARKER**'s line to **COLE** Creek, commonly called new Bay, [?] containing one hundred acres more or less:  And one other tract of land purchased by /of/ Boon **EURE** & Nancy **EURE** by the said A W **PARKER** and bounded as follows to wit, beginning at a pine Stump a corner of David C **CROSS**' land at a red Oak, thence said **CROSS**' line to Reuben **PILAND** line, thence said **PILAND**'s line to a pine Stump, a corner tree of said **PILAND** & A W **PARKER**'s land and Martha **TAYLOR**'s land, thence said **TAYLOR**'s line to A W **PARKER**s line, thence said **PARKER**'s line nearly a north course to a pine Stump a corner of the Said **EURE** & A W **PARKER**, thence the said **PARKER**s line runs a west course to the first station containing fifty acres more or less;* [sic] which said several pieces of land upon the death of the said A W **PARKER** descended to the following persons, in the following proportions as the heirs at law of the said Abram W., to wit:  to Bray, Kindred, Seth (the elder) /Levi/ & Dempsey **PARKER**, Elizabeth **BRISCOE** & Mary **GOODWIN** all of whom are the brothers and sisters of the said A W **PARKER**, to each of them one undivided eighth part, and your petitioners Seth, Sophia, Martha, Cynthia and Nancy **PARKER** the children of Reuben **PARKER** deceased who died in the life time of the said A W **PARKER**, and who was a brother of the said A W **PARKER**, one eighth part of the whole.  They shown [sic] your Honor that the said Bray since the death of said A W **PARKER** has conveyed his undivided eighth part to John **WILLEY** by deed of trust, who has duly conveyed the same to your petitioner Elisha **PARKER**; and that Seth **PARKER** (the elder) has conveyed his undivided eighth

---

128  NCSA, Pre-1914 Graves Index, Gates County, Gatesville, NC, Ballard Cemetery.

part to your petitioner Kindred, whereby your petitioner Kindred has become the owner of two eighths:

They further show your Honor that since the death of the said Abram W **PARKER**, the said Dempsey **PARKER** and Mary **GOODWIN** have died intestate and without issue whereby their interest in said lands have descended to your petitioners Bray, Kindred, Seth & Levi **PARKER** and Elizabeth **BRISCOE**, who are the brothers and sister of the said ~~Abram~~ Dempsey **PARKER** & Mary **GOODWIN** to each one undivided sixth part, and to your petitioners Seth, Sophia, Martha, Cynthia & Nancy **PARKER** the children of the said Reuben **PARKER** also one sixth:

Your petitioners show your Honor that nearly all of said land is unimproved, and much of it is swamp land and that actual partion [sic] of the same would not be made among them according to their respective rights without greatly disparaging the value of the whole: they therefore pray your Honor to order and decree a sale of the same upon such terms as to your Honor shall seem right; and that your Honor will direct the proceeds of said sale to be divided as follows to the said Elisha who claims under the said Bray one eighth of the whole, to said said [sic] Bray as the heir at law of the said Dempsey & Mary **GOODWIN** ~~two~~ /one/ sixth of two eighths, to the said Kindred two eighths & one sixth of two eighths, to Elizabeth **BRISCOE** ~~two~~ /one/ eighth and one sixth of two eighths, to Levi **PARKER** one eighth & one sixth of two eighths and to Seth, Sophia, Martha, Cynthia & Nancy **PARKER** the children of Reuben, one eighth & two sixth [sic] of one eighth.

And your petitioners will ever pray.

Aug. **MOORE**

Sol for petitioners

John **MATHEWS** [sic] makes oath that ~~they~~ /he/ ~~are~~ /is/ acquainted with the lands described in the foregoing petition and that the same cannot be divided among the petitioners without greatly disparaging their value; and that the proceeds of the sale would be of more value to the petitioners than an actual division of the lands.  John  W [?] **MATTHEWS**

Sworn to before me

Will J **BAKER** clk

Superior Court  }

of Gates County}

*And a tract of land which James **BROWN** formerly lived adjoining the lands of Elisha **PARKER**, Etheldred **RIDDICK**, Dempsey **SPARKMAN** & Levi **EURE** containing one hundred acres more or less.  And also another tract adjoining the lands of James **CARTER** and the lands of the heirs of Lewis **SPARKMAN** & containing twelve acres more or less"[129]

〰〰〰〰〰〰〰〰〰〰〰〰〰〰〰〰〰〰〰〰〰〰〰〰〰〰〰〰〰〰〰〰〰〰〰〰〰〰〰〰〰〰〰〰

Demsey[6] **PARKER** *(John[5],John[4],William[3],Thomas[2],William[1])* was born circa 1798-1799.  The last record of the guardian account of Reuben[6] **PARKER** for Demsey[6] **PARKER** was in February 1819, which indicates that he had come of age.[130]

The first purchase of land for Demsey[6] **PARKER** was from John **BEEMAN** for 130 acres on 24 September 1827.  It is described as: "Begining at the run of the big swamp in the fort Island Road, thence to a Corner pine standing in John **SPARKMAN**'s line thence along said **SPARKMAN**'s line to a Corner Oak ~~thence~~ Thence said **SPARKMAN**'s line S. to a corner pine thence along said **SPARKMAN**'s line E. to a Corner pine thence Said **SPARKMAN**'s line S. to a Sassafras a corner, thence along said **SPARKMAN**'s line to David **LEWIS** ~~LEWIS~~ line thence said **LEWIS** line to road that leads immediately from Gates Court House to Winton thence a Cross [sic] the Road to the run of the aforesaid Swamp thence up the swamp to the first Station..."  Witnesses to this deed were W. L. **BOOTH**, Wm. W. **COWPER**  "The Conditions of the above obligation is such that if the said John **BEEMAN** do pay or cause to be paid unto Dempsey **PARKER** the just sum of eight hundred dollars on or before the 25th December next the obligation is to /be/ void  Reg. Feb. Ct. 1828"[131]

---

[129]  NCSA, G.041.2194760 Gates County Estates, Record of 1765-1920, Vol. Odom-Parker Folder: Parker, Abraham W. 1839 Doc. #1039-1044

[130]  Fouts, *Minutes of County Court of Pleas and Quarter Sessions Gates County, North Carolina 1818-1823, Vol. V,* c. 1987, p. 36:#1078

[131]  NCSA, C.041.40006 Gates County Real Estate Conveyances 1819-1829 Vol: 11-13  13:159

**Chapter 9**: Descendants and siblings of Kindred[6] **PARKER** *(John[5],John[4],William[3],Thomas[2],William[1])*

Demsey[6] **PARKER** married Chitty **JONES**, widow of Henry **JONES**, by February 1833, as evidenced by the will of that Henry **JONES**, and later records. Chitty was born circa 1799-1800.

Henry **JONES** made his will 7 November 1831, and it was probated in November Court of that year. After the payment of his debts, he lent his wife, "Chitty" **JONES**, all the land and plantation whereon he then lived, known by the name of the **VOLENTINE** land, two Negro men, named **DAVY** and **ABRAM**, and one Negro woman, named **AMY**. He gave her "one gray mare, geer and gig, four cows and calves; one feather bed and furniture of the first choice," and the use of a tract of land called the "**RALLS** tract during her natural life or widowhood." He split the George **LAW-RENCE** tract between his sons, John and Hardy **JONES**. This land adjoined Miles **PARKER** and Lewis **EURE** and contained 600 acres.

He left to his daughter, Louisa **JONES**, "all that tract of land called known by the name of the **RAWLS** tract of land a part of which lies in the County of Gates and State of N. C. & a part being in the County of Nansemond and State of Virginia being the desire [sic] tract lent to my wife Chitty **JONES** during her natural life or widowhood containing three hundred and sixty six acres..." He also named his son, Henry **JONES**, to receive the "**VOLENTINE**" land after the death or widowhood of his wife. He appointed his wife and friend Elijah **HARE** as executrix and executor to his will, both of whom renounced their rights of executorship. William **LEE** was appointed administrator, with the will annexed, under bond of $8,000.[132]

The following decree was handed down in February Court 1833: "Chitty **PARKER** & her husband D. **PARKER** vs Henry **JONES** admr.} Decree This cause coming on to be heard upon the petition and report of the Jury, the Court doth declare that the said Chitty is not as comfortably provided under the will of her late husband Henry **JONES** as she would have been had the said Henry died intestate. The Court doth therefore order adjudge and decree the said Chitty to have a tract of land of which the said Henry died Seized Caled [sic] the **VALENTINE** tract, during the term of her natural life, in full of her right of dower in the real estate of the said Henry. And the Court doth further adjudge and decree the said Chitty to be possessed absolutely of the following personal estate of the said Henry (to wit) negro man **DAVID**, man **ABRAM**, woman **AMY** & old woman **PLEASANT** one Gray mare & gig & harness four cows & calves four ewes & lambs one feather bed & furniture. And that she pay to the administrator of the said Henry the sum of two hundred and twenty eight dollars as soon as the negroes shall be placed in the possession of the said Chitty & that each party pay one half of the Costs"[133]

On 5 December 1835, Elisha **UMPHFLET** sold Dempsey **PARKER** his interest in 6¼ acres, "Beginning at a corner pine the haw tree branch a corner of Reuben **PARKER** decsd. thence along said **PARKER**'s line to Penny **CARTER**'s line, thence down her line to the run of the little Cypress, thence up the run of said Cypress, to the mouth of the haw tree branch, thence up said branch to the first station, or beginning." Witnesses were A. W. **PARKER** and Nathan **SMITH**.[134]

On Tuesday, 19 August 1834, "Demsey **PARKER** Came into Court relinquished the Guardianship of Louisa **JONES** orphan of Henry **JONES** decd. wheupon [sic] it was ordered that Henry **GILLIAM** be appointed that he enter into Bond with James R. **RIDDICK** & James **BOOTH** Secuities [sic] in the sum $2000."[135] No reason for this change appears in the records.

On 8 February 1838, John **JONES** sold to "Dempsey **PARKER** (of John,)" 300 acres. "all right and interest of the said John **JONES** to & in a certain plantation & lands...known by the name of the Henry **JONES** plantation it being the same right that descended to the said John **JONES** as an heir at law by the death of Henry **JONES** Sr. decsd. and Henry **JONES** Jr. decsd. the said lands and plantation being at this time /the/ dower of Mrs. Chetta **PARKER**...Beginning in the run of the Cypress Swamp adjoining the lands of James **SUMNER** thence to a post oak, Thence to a black gum, thence to a pine in **SUMNER**s line Thence to a maple a corner of Miles **HOWELL**, Harrison **HARE** & Dempsey **PARKER**, thence to a sweet gum Harrison **HARE**'s line, thence to a maple in said **HARE**'s line, thence to a pine, thence said line to another pine, thence to a white oak, thence to a pine

[132] Almasy, *Gates County North Carolina Wills 1807-1838, Vol. II*, c. 1985, p. 132-133, Will Book 2:293-295
[133] NCSA, C.041.30003 Gates County Court Minutes 1827-1850, 4 vols., Feb. Ct., 1833
[134] NCSA, C.041.40008 Gates County Real Estate Conveyances 1836-1842 Vol: 16, 17 16:8
[135] NCSA, C.041.30003 Gates County Court Minutes 1827-1850, 4 vols., Aug. Ct., 1834

a corner of Harrison **HARE** & Elijah **HARE**, thence to a dead pine a corner of D. M. **SAUNDERS** E. **HARE** and D. **PARKER**, thence to a Catawba tree, thence D. M. **SAUNDERS** line & David **HOWELL**'s binding on the Creek to the Cypress swamp, thence to the first station...and the said John **JONES** owning one third part (that is to say) after the death of Mrs. Chetta **PARKER**, aforesaid... John his X mark **JONES**." Witnesses to this deed were Elisha **PARKER** and James his X mark **SUMNER**. Proved February Court 1838.[136]

On 17 February 1838, James R. **RIDDICK**, Sheriff, sold to Dempsey **PARKER** "of John," 28 acres of land described as "by virtue of one certain writ of Fi Fa issued from the Gates County Court November term 1837...for costs and charges on a certain malicious prosecution brought vs one Miles **HOWELL** by Hardy **JONES** which **JONES** failed to prosecute...ordered that said Hardy **JONES** should pay the cost of said endictment...which writ was directed to the sheriff of Gates County against the goods, & chattles, lands & tenements of Hardy **JONES**...returnable on the third Monday in February in the year of our Lord one thousand eight hundred & thirty-eight...I did by virtue thereof enter upon & levy the aforesaid writ of Fi. Fa. on a certain tract of land...as the property of said Hardy C. **JONES**...which tract of land is a part of said Hardy C. **JONES** lot of land in the plantation whereon Henry **JONES** deceased lived & died...did duly advertise & expose the same...on this 3rd Monday 17th day of February one thousand eight hundred & thirty-eight when and where the aforesaid party Dempsey **PARKER** of John appeared & bid for the said Twenty-eight acres of land the sum of Fourteen dollars & Twenty-eight cents... Acknowledged Feb. Co. Ct. 1841."[137]

On 8 August 1839, Lavinia **SMITH** sold to Dempsey[6] **PARKER** six and one-quarter acres of land for $16.00. It was "all her right & interest to & in a certain tract of land lying in Gates County and known by the name of the Joseph **SMITH** Old place it being the same land that descended to the said Lavinia as an heir at law by the last Will & Testament of Joseph **SMITH** decsd. bounded as follows Viz. Beginning at a pine in the Haw-tree branch a corner of Reuben **PARKER** decsd., thence along said **PARKE**'s [sic] line to Penny **CARTER**'s line, thence down her line to the run of the little Cypress, thence up the run of said Cypress to the mouth of /the/ Haw-tree branch, thence up the said branch to the first station, containing in the whole of the Old place Fifty acres, and about six & a fourth acres to said Lavinia's share (more or less)..." Lavinia her X mark **SMITH** Witnesses were Willis **CROSS**, William H. **CROSS**.[138]

On 19 June 1843, James **HARRELL** sold to Dempsey[6] **PARKER** 75 acres described as "Beginning at a pine a corner tree at the head of the middle pocoson thence running a South west course along a line of marked trees to the head of Sarum creek to a black gum a corner tree, thence along down the said creek to a mark [sic] cypress a corner tree on the upper side of a gut, thence along a line of marked trees to a large forked gum a corner tree in the said pocoson, thence up the pocoson to the first station..." Witnesses were P. **HARRELL** and Mills **SPARKMAN**.[139]

Demsey[6] **PARKER** was dead by 19 March 1846, as evidenced by the special administration granted Will J. **BAKER**, he having produced a power of attorney from Chittey [sic] **PARKER** to empower him to act for and in her stead "upon his entering into bond in the sum of Five thousand dollars with Thomas **RIDDICK**, Dempsey **SPARKMAN** & Richard B. **BAKER** his securities." That bond was entered the same day.[140]

Chetty **PARKER** submitted a Petition for Dower to the Court, transcribed here in full: "North Carolina Gates County Court of Pleas & Quarter sessions May Term 1846 To the worshipful, the Justices of the said Court: The petition of Chitty **PARKER**, widow of Dempsy **PARKER** late of said county, against Kindred **PARKER**, Levi **PARKER**, Bray **PARKER**, Elizabeth **BRISCO**, Elisha **HARRELL** & wife, Joseph **EURE** & wife, Seth **PARKER** /Nancy **PARKER**,/ ~~Cynthia & Nancy~~ /W W **COWPER**/ Guardian to Cynthia ~~& Nancy~~ **PARKER** Orphants of Rubin [sic] **PARKER** deceased & Seth **PARKER** Senr.

---

[136] NCSA, C.041.30003 Gates County Court Minutes 1827-1850, 4 vols., Feb. Ct. 1833

[137] NCSA, C.041.40008 Gates County Real Estate Conveyances 1836-1842 Vol: 16, 17, 17:403-405

[138] Ibid., 17:106-107

[139] NCSA, C.041.40009 Gates County Real Estate Conveyances 1841-1847 Vol: 18,19, 18:426-427

[140] NCSA, G.041.2194760 Gates County Estates, Record of 1765-1920, Vol. Odom-Parker

Folder: Parker, Dempsey 1846, Doc. #1969;1972

Your petitioner respectfully showeth unto your worships that the said Dempsey **PARKER** departed this life since the last term of this court without having made a last will and testament seized and possessed of the following tracts or parcels of land lying and being in the said County of Gates to wit: The "Home place" at which he resided in his life time adjoining the lands of Dempsy **SPARKMAN** the Devisees of David **LEWIS** & others.

The **SMITH** tract, adjoining the lands of Penny **CARTER**, heirs of Mills **SPARKMAN**, Charney **UMPHLET** & others

The "Old place" adjoining the lands of Riddick **GATLING**, John **LEE**, Robt H **BALLARD** & others

The tract known as the James **HARRELL** land lying on Sarum Creek and adjoining the lands of J R **RIDDICK** & others.

The Dempsey **EURE** tract, bounded by the lands of Robt H. **BALLARD** John **RIDDICK** Elisha B. **HARRELL** & others.

Your petitioner shows unto your worships that she is entitled to her Dower in the said lands and prays your worships to order a writ of Dower to issue to the Sheriff of the said County of Gates, Commanding him to summon a jury of twelve disinterested freeholders of said County connected with the said parties neither by consanguinity or affinity who shall view the same & allot and assign unto your petitioner one third part of the lands of which the said D **PARKER** so as aforesaid died seized, and that they make due return of the [?] manner in which they have executed this writ.

Your petitioner further prays your worships to direct a copy of this petition to issue with [?] a subpoena to be served [?] upon the said defendants at least ten days before the next term of this court. As in duty bound your petitioner will ever pray  Will J **BAKER** sol for Petitioner"[141]

In May Term 1846, Chetty **PARKER** petitioned the Court for her year's provisions. They were allotted to her 19 June 1846, and consisted of the following items: "70 Bbls. corn, 2,000 lbs. bacon, 4,000 lbs. fodder, 30 lbs. coffee, 100 lbs. brown sugar, 20 lbs. loaf Do., 12 Gallons molasses, 2 Bbls. flour, 10 Bushels sweet potatoes, 5 Do. Do. Do. plantains [plantings,] 4 Bbls. fish, 5 bushels Salt, 10 Do. pease, 1 Cow & calf, 1 Beef cattle, 2 Sows & pigs, 4 Head Sheep, 4 lbs. pepper, 2 lbs. Spice, 2 lbs. tea, 1 Bbl. brandy, 1 Bbl. vinegar, 100 lbs. picked cotton, 20 lbs. flax, 2 stands lard, 1 bed & furniture, 25 lbs. tallow, 1 wheel & Cards." Not all the items were on hand and she was provided with $219.18 to buy what was lacking.[142]  That sum was paid to her by W. J. **BAKER**, administrator of Dempsy[6] **PARKER**, per his account current with the estate on 24 July 1847.[143]

Chetty **PARKER**'s dower in her deceased husband's land was laid off to her 17 September 1846.  Thomas **RIDDICK**, Sheriff, attended by Allen **SMITH**, County Surveyor, and a jury consisting of Solomon **ROUNTREE**, John S. **ROBERTS**, Cordy Y. **SAVAGE**, John **BROWN**, James **BROWN**, Willis R. **HAYS**, Reuben **PILAND**, William G. **DAUGHTRY**, Andrew **EASON**, Robert **HAYS**, Gordon **HINTON** and Robert H. **BALLARD**, freeholders.  They laid off to her "the part or portion of the said plantation on which said Dempsy **PARKER** desd lived & died, included and comprised in the following limits and bound [sic] to Wit:  Beginning at a red oak on the Fort Island road near the Common School House, thence up the road to the little Cypress corner on Mills **SPARKMAN**s heirs-thence up sd. Swamp binding Dempsey **SPARKMAN** and the David **LEWIS** Land keeping [?] the road leading from Gatesville to Winton to the run of Robert **BALLARD**s Mill pond & corner on sd **LEWIS** & Martha **TAYLOR** thence up the run of sd. Mill pond to the corner on Lewis **EURE**s heirs & Judith **SAVAGE** thence William /H/ [?] **SAVAGE** heirs line to the first station containing Two hundred Acres be the Same more or Less – it being the tract on which the sd. Dempsy **PARKER** lived and died on including the dwelling House or mansion of Said Decd. in which he most generally dwelt-next-before and at the time of his death: and all the out Houses, buildings offices and improvements thereunto belonging..."  She was put in possession of the same on that day.[144]

On 7 December 1857, John F.[7] **PARKER** sold his interest in 500 acres of land to Chetty

---

[141]  NCSA, G.041.2194760 Gates County Estates, Record of 1765-1920, Vol. Odom-Parker Folder: Parker, Dempsey 1846, Doc. #1996-1997
[142]  Ibid., Doc. #1984;1992
[143]  Ibid., Doc. #2000
[144]  Ibid., Doc. #1954-1955

**PARKER** for $350.00. It is described as "...all my Right & interest to & in the lands & plantation known as the Henry **JONES** place lying & being in Said County of Gates & bounded on the West by Somerton Creek on the South by the lands of Wm. **JERNIGAN** on the East by the lands of Jas. E. **HOWELL** & the lands formerly belonging to Elijah **HARE** Decd. & on the North by the lands of Nathan **SPIVEY** & containing in the entire tract about Five hundred acres, more or less, the said John F. **PARKER** owning & claiming title to said premises as follows to Wit: one third of the entire tract, in Right of Nathan **SPIVEY** and Wife Louisa **SPIVEY** one sixth of one third owned by Dempsey **PARKER** decd. Which descended to Levi / **PARKER**/ (of Alabama) as an heir at law of the said Dempsey Decd. also one sixth of said decds. third Which descended to Bray **PARKER** as an heir at law of said Dempsey Decd. & purchased at a Sheriffs sale by one David Rice **BEST** of Hertford County & State aforesaid." It was signed by John F. **PARKER** and witnessed by W. L. **BOOTHE**, who proved it in February Term 1858.[145]

On 30 October 1853, John F.[7] and Hardy W.[7] **PARKER**, Executors of Kindred[6] **PARKER**, deceased, had sold 300 acres to Chetty **PARKER** as "all the right & interest the sd. Kindred **PARKER** was intitled to by Law from the death of his brother Dempsey **PARKER** of the land above mentioned, land on Elijah **HARE**, Nathan **SPIVEY** and wife on Somerton Creek...300 acres being the land Henry **JONES** lived and died on known as the **JONES** plantation being 1/6th part that Dempsey **PARKER** owned..." The witnesses were Augustus **WOLFLEY** and W. L. **BOOTHE**. It also was proved in February Term 1858.[146]

Chetty **PARKER** was dead by 28 June 1862, as evidenced by the bond of that date, in the amount of $15,000.00 for a Special Administration to Quinton **BRADY** who was appointed administrator on her estate. His bondsmen were John **BRADY** and Richard H. L. **BOND**.[147] An inventory and sale of her property was made 9 July 1862, and the total of sales was $1,320.86.[148]

At some point during the intervening five years, John F.[7] **PARKER** became administrator De bonis non on the estate of Chetty **PARKER** before 8 January 1867. The officers of the Court had decreed a judgment against him in the sum of $36.65, for costs and charges, in that office.[149]

The following petition for sale of land includes all the heirs of Chetta **PARKER** and is transcribed here in full: "State of North Carolina Gates County} Court of Equity Spring Term 1867 To the Honorable, the Judge of said Court, The petition of Robert H. **SAUNDERS**, Mary A. **BRADY**, Lucy L. **TURNER**, and Chetta and James T. **SPIVEY** by their guardian Nathan **SPIVEY**; Richard D. **BRISCOE**, Lavenia **HARRELL**, Mills K. **LAWRENCE** and wife Penelope; John F. **PARKER**, & Rufus **HARRELL** and Maria **HARRELL** by their next friend Elisha **HARRELL**; Thomas W. **BABB**, Lewis **BABB**, Virginia and William **BABB** heirs at law of William K. **BABB** /by their next friend Thos W. **BABB**/ John **BROWN** and wife Alice; Blake **BAKER** and wife Sousan, [sic] Jane T. **BAKER** and Almeta **BAKER**, heirs at law of Almeta **BAKER**, /by their next friend Blake **BAKER**/ John B. **MARCH** and wife Margarett, John E. **BABB**, Miles **COLLINS** and wife Jane, Thomas **RUSSELL**, __[blank]__ **RUSSELL** and __[blank]__**RUSSELL** heirs at law of Sarah **RUSSELL** by their next friend Dempsey **RUSSELL**, respectfully showeth unto your Honor that they are tenants in Common of a tract of land situate in Gates County adjoining the lands of James **JERNIGAN** and others, /known as the **JONES**' place/ Containing by Estimation three hundred Acres, That their interests in the said tract of land are as follows, the said Robert H. **SAUNDERS** Mary A **BRADY**, Lucy L. **TURNER**, Chetta **SPIVEY**, and James T. **SPIVEY** being heirs-at _ law, in right of their Mother, to Chetta **PARKER** are Entitled to four fifths of the Entire tract of land, the other petitioners representing the heirs-at-law of Dempsey **PARKER** are Entitled to the remaining one fifth of said tract of land in the following proportions: Richard D. **BRISCOE**, Lavinia **HARRELL** and Penelope wife of Mills K. **LAWRENCE** being heirs-at-law of Elizabeth **BRISCOE** are Entitled to one third of the said one fifth; John F. **PARKER**, Rufus **HARRELL** and Maria **HARRELL** the last two in right of their

---

[145] NCSA, C.041.40011 Gates County Real Estate Conveyances 1857-1861, Vol: 22:153-154

[146] Gates County, NC, Deed Book 22:167

[147] NCSA, G.041.2194760 Gates County Estates, Record of 1765-1920, Vol. Odom-Parker Folder: Parker, Chetta 1862, Doc. #1291

[148] Ibid., Doc. #1294

[149] Ibid., Doc. #1324

Mother –[blank]—are Entitled to one third of the said one fifth, the said John F. **PARKER** being Entitled to four fifths of the said one third of one fifth, ~~and~~ and the said Rufus **HARRELL** and Maria **HARRELL** to the other fifth of a third of said one fifth: the said Thomas W. **BABB**, Lewis **BABB**, Virginia and William **BABB** heirs-at-law of William K. **BABB**, Alice wife of John **BROWN**, Sousan wife of Blake **BAKER**, Jane T. **BAKER** and Almeta **BAKER** heirs-at-law of Almeta **BAKER**, Margarett wife of John B. **MARCH**, John E. **BABB**, Jane wife of Miles **COLLINS**, Thomas **RUSSELL** ___ ___[blank]_____ heirs-at-law of Sarah **RUSSELL** are Entitled to the other one third of the said one fifth.

Your petitioners further shew that ~~they desire that~~ they desire to have partition of said land made amongst them according to their respective right and interests therein, but that owing to the size of the said tract of land, the number of the parties interested, the nature and quality of the soil, and other causes, it is impossible that actual partion [sic] thereof can be made without serious injury to the parties interested. Your petitioners therefore pray your Honor to order a sale of said land, on such terms as your Honor shall deem just and reasonable and that the proceeds of the sale may be divided among them according to their respective shares and interests in the said land, and may be paid to, or secured for them, according to law, and the Course of this Honorable Court. And your petitioners, as in duty bound will ever pray, M. L. **EURE** Solicitor for the Petitioners North Carolina Gates County} In Equity __[blank]__ makest outt [sic] that they are well acquainted with the tract of land described in the foregoing petition, and that owing to the size of the said tract, the quality of the soil, and the number of persons Entitled to shares therein they do not believe that actual partion of the same could possibly be made without serious injury to the parties. Sworn to and subscribed before me at Office this the 3rd day of April AD 1867. C. M.E." The decree for sale of the land was handed down in Spring Term 1867.[150]

On 19 August 1867, M. K. **LAWRENCE** bid $560.50 for "the Chetta **PARKER** tract," in a report of a sale of land to be made under a decree of the Court of Equity in Spring Term 1867. The decree was made on behalf of John F.[7] **PARKER** and others mentioned in a petition for sale of land.[151] The Court ordered that the whole of the purchase money be paid out to the heirs at Fall Term 1870. Claudia and Andrew **BRADY** are mentioned as heirs, "in right of their Mother the said Mary," and are the only ones who do not appear in the 1867 petition.[152] No further information.

---

[150] NCSA, G.041.2194760 Gates County Estates, Record of 1765-1920, Vol. Odom-Parker Folder: Parker, Chetta 1862, Doc. # 1327-1331
[151] Ibid., Doc. #1319
[152] Ibid., Doc. #1314

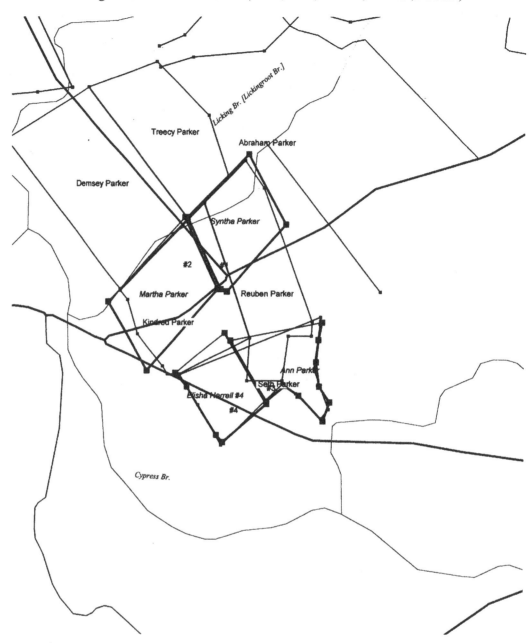

Scale:  1000 ft/in
Map depicting the 1838 division of land of Reuben[6] **PARKER** shown in bold, with names of heirs in italics.

## Peter[3] PARKER *(Thomas[2] William[1])*

The ancestry of Peter[3] **PARKER** *(Thomas[2] William[1])* was previously noted in Chapter Seven, page 70. He owned land in Isle of Wight and Nansemond Counties, VA, as well as Chowan County and present-day Hertford County, NC, as will be shown. Bertie County was formed from Chowan in 1722, thus Chowan records include both counties until that year. Hertford was formed from Bertie, Chowan and Northampton in 1759.[1]

John and Mary **EARLY** sold a parcel of land to John[4] and Peter[3] **PARKER**, of Nansemond County, VA, 1 November 1700, for 900 pounds of tobacco. The book in which this deed appears is a copy of an earlier book wherein the clerk reproduced what was left of a deteriorating record. This land is described as a "parcell of land situated in the prect of Chowan butted bounding (tore out) [sic] ___kd pine on the river side at a Short Branch at the upper end of the old field and so running down the river South & West 200 poles to a markd pine thence east & South 320 poles to a markd pine, thence north and by east 200 poles to a markd pine thence west and __ by No. 320 poles to the first station, as is amply express_t_ by the plat of the said land bearing date 3rd of June 1699..." Any witnesses' names are lost. The metes and bounds expressed in this deed plot out to 400 acres. It was ordered to be registered 19 July 1701.[2] As the Chowan River runs roughly north and south, this land appears to be on the east side of it. No record has been found of the 1699 patent to John **EARLY**.

The majority of John **EARLY**'s lands were on the west side of the Chowan River, on or near Wiccacon Creek, by 1713. On 1 July of that year, he was granted four parcels of land, for a total of 2,151 acres, all on Wiccacon Creek. The first of those patents contained 486 acres, described as "lying on ye main Branch of Wicacoane [sic] Creek Commonly called Bear Swamp, Beginning at a pine near the head of Goodwater branch running thence So 200 pole to a poplar then So. 55[d]. Wt 94 pole thence So. 100 pole to a red Oak, then Et. 120 pole to a pine then No. 28[d] Et. 160 pole to a red Oak, then So. 40[d] Et. 96 pole to a White Oak, then So. 75[d]. Et. to a pine on fugo [sic] branch, thence by ye meanders of Wicacoane Creek, Horse Swamp, & Good Water branch to ye first Station..."[3] This patent will be mentioned again.

On 15 May 1697, the Lords Proprietors of North Carolina granted 640 acres to Lewis **WILLIAMS** in Chowan Precinct. It is described as "Beginning at a pine Standing by the side of Chowan River, thence East 31.d. South 320 po. to a live Oak, S. 37d. West 320 po. to a red Oak West 37d. North 320 po. to a red Oak Standing by the side of the aforesaid River, then up the River to the first Station..."[4] This patent was assigned to "Jon." **WHITE** by Lewis **WILLIAMS**, and his wife Mary, 9 September 1700.[5]

On 1 March 1700/01, Jon. and Sarah **WHITE** sold 240 acres of that land to William **WILLIAMS**. It was described as the "uppermost 200 & 40 Acres beginning at the uppermost side Line and running down the River to a marked Hiccory for Br_ed_th thence from the River /Side/ being 37d South to the h_ed_ Line so running as the Line directs to the first Station..." It was registered 19 July 1701.[6]

On 25 October 1706, William and Susannah **WILLIAMS**, of Isle of Wight County, VA, sold to Peter[3] **PARKER**, of the Upper Parish of Nansemond County, VA, 240 acres for 2,800 pounds of tobacco. It was on the east side of Chowan River and is described as "beginning at a marked pine standing by ye River & is running Down ye River for Breadth to a Marked Hickery Thence from the River Side Running East to a Marked Hickery a Corner tree of ye head line & so along ye head to the next Corner tree & from thence to ye first station...it being part of a Patent of 640 acres to Lewis

[1] Corbitt, David Leroy, *The Formation of the North Carolina Counties 1663-1943,* c. 1950, p. 25;122

[2] Chowan County, NC, Deed Book C#2:5

[3] NCSA, S.108.160.1M, Secretary of State Land Grant Record Books 1693-1960, Vols. 1-4, 1:202, File #174; File 116; 1:203, File #117, File #175, hereafter NC Land Grants

[4] Ibid., 1:84, File #39

[5] Chowan County, NC, Deed Book W#1:13, courtesy of Weynette Parks Haun, Durham, NC.

[6] Ibid., W#1:21

**WILLIAMS** dated __ May 1697, which Patent is now in possession of John **WHITE** Sen. and by a conveyance secured to me from sd. **WHITE** bearing date 1 March 1700...” Witnesses were Jno. **PARKER**, Robt. **SCOTT** and Humphrey **MARSHALL**.[7]

On 9 December 1706, Peter[3] **PARKER**, with consent of his wife Elizabeth, sold Robert **SCOTT** of Isle of Wight County, VA, 100 acres he formerly purchased of Thomas **MANDEW**. It is described as “lyeing & being upon ye South side of the Maine Blackwater Swamp, it being part of a pattent formerly granted to Thomas **MANDEW** bearing date ye 28th of October 1702. The sd Land joines upon a Swamp called Nottoway Swamp...Begining att a marked Hickory standing in or near the Line from thence to a marked Gum, a Line tree of the pattent, & soe along the sd Line to a marked White Oak, a Corner tree of the pattent standing by ye side of a Branch called ye Indian pond Branch & soe downe ye sd Branch to ye aforesd Nottoway Swamp & soe along ye various courses of ye Run of ye Swamp to a marked Gum standing by ye side of ye Run & from thence by a Line of marked Trees to ye first station...” It was signed by “peter his P mark **PARKER**,” and “Eliza her E mark **PARKER**.” This deed was witnessed by William **SCOTT**, Jr., and Robert **RICKS** [or **HICKS**,] and acknowledged by Peter **PARKER** on that same date. There was a third witness, but the name is illegible. A power of attorney from Elizabeth **PARKER** to Wm. **BUTLER** [or **BUFFER**] was also ordered to be recorded. It was witnessed by John his J mark **ROBERTS** and Thomas his T:R mark **ROBERTS**.[8]

Peter[3] **PARKER** had purchased this parcel of land in Isle of Wight County, VA, from Thomas **MANDEW** 9 June 1704, as being “of Nansemond County.”[9] Peter[3] had been in Chowan Precinct of Albemarle County, in North Carolina, since 1700, but he still owned at least two parcels of land in Nansemond County in 1706, thus was apparently considered as “of Nansemond.”

On 20 October 1712, William (W) **PADGETT** gave Treddell **KEEFE** a power of attorney to acknowledge a deed to Peter **PARKER** for 250 acres of land on the “West side of Chowan River at the lower corner of Charles **GAFFIN**s land and running with ye sd. land No. by West 308 po. to a pine No. East 320 po. to Patrick **LEWIS** Corner tree & thence along ye River to first station...” It was witnessed by Wm. **CRAWFORD** and Thomas **MANDEW**.[10]

There were 64 tithables on the Indian Town List of 12 January 1712/13, in Chowan County. This list appears to have been taken in much the same manner as the later census in that each individual is listed in the sequence of his residence. The following names from that list are known to have lived in the northwestern end of present-day Chowan County, between Catherine Creek and Indian Town Creek: “Jno. **SUMNER** & Ja: **SUMNER** 2; George **WHITE** 1; Jno. **WHITE** Junr. 1; Wm. **COPELAND** 1; Tho. **PARKER** 1; Jno. **WELCH** 1; Peter **PARKER** Senr/ 1; Jno **PARKER** and Peter **PARKER** Junr } 2; Jno **WHITE** Senr 1; Richd. **SOWELL** 1; Jno **JORDAN** 1 and Moses **FFOXWORTH** [sic] 1.” William **CRANFORD** was the Constable appointed to take that list.[11] His signature on this document is “**CRANFORD**,” but his name appears in many records as “**CRAWFORD**,” and even “**GRANFIELD**.”

On 19 May 1713, William **WILLIAMS** of “the Isle of White [sic] County” in VA appointed Wm. **CRAWFORD** his attorney to acknowledge a sale of land to Peter **PARKER**. It was witnessed by W. **BRATTLE** and Peter **PARKER**. The deed itself mirrors the one he and his wife, Susannah, made 25 October 1706, with some minor differences in the land description. It was described as “begining at ye uppermost side line and running ye River for breadth to a Marked Hickery near ye River Side, thence, unto ye woods E37°S to ye head line so turning as ye line directs to ye first station...” The witnesses to this deed were W. **BRATTLE** and Peter **PARKER**, Jr.[12] This deed may well have been a replacement for the earlier one, perhaps lost or destroyed during the turmoil of the Tuscarora War.

---

[7] Chowan County, NC, Deed Book W#1:76
[8] Isle of Wight County, VA, Deed Book 2, 1704-1715, 2:61-62
[9] Ibid., 1:421
[10] Chowan County, NC, Deed Book W#1:137
[11] NCSA, C.C.R. 190, Taxes & Accounts-Chowan County 1679-1754
[12] Chowan County, NC Deed Book W#1:166

**Chapter 10**: Peter[3] **PARKER** *(Thomas[2], William[1])*

Peter[3] **PARKER** was granted 260 acres on 27 August 1714.  It is described as "lying on ye No. Et. Shore of Chowan Beginning at a pine on ye. River pocoson then along ye. same 120 pole, then So. 70 Et. 20 pole, then So 55 Et. 40 pole, then So. 10. Et. 24 pole, then So. 65 E. 16 pole, then Wt. 72 pole, then So. 10 Wt. 28 pole, then So. 40 Wt 10 pole, then So. 15 Et. 26 pole, then So. 48 pole, then So. 17 Et. 88 pole to a Juniper, then Et. 48 pole to a red Oak, then So. 55 Et. 26 pole to a pine on ye head of ye. long branch Jams. **FLEMING**'s Corner tree, then along ye. same branch 320 pole to another pine, Jams **FLEMING**'s Corner tree, then along his line No. 75 Wt. 174 pole to ye. first Station..."[13]

A patent issued to James **FLEMING**, also on 27 August 1714, contained 600 acres "lying in Chowan precinct, begining at a Hiccory on Stopping Creek pocoson, then So 30 Et. 160 pole to a pine, then So. 60 Et. 80 pole to a Hiccory, then Et. 60 pole to a red Oak, then So. 40 Et. 48 pole to a red Oak, then So. 60. Et. 72 pole to ye center of two red Oaks & a wt. Oak by ye head of Beechy Swamp, thence along ye. said Swamp So. 30 Wt. 106 pole to a white Oak, then So. 45 Et. 106 pole to a white Oak Wm. **COPELAND**s Corner tree, then No. 45 Wt. 90 pole to a pine on ye. upper end of ye. long branch, then through ye. branch 30 pole to a pine, then No. 40 Wt. 64 pole to a pine in ye. River pocoson, then along ye. pocoson by Various Courses to a pine in Stopping Creek Marsh, thence along ye. sd. Marsh & Creek to ye. first station..."[14]  This patent contains defective metes and bounds, thus does not lend itself to being plotted.  It does, however, help to place Peter[3] **PARKER**'s adjoining land.  William **COPELAND**'s holdings were on Sandy Run, as evidenced by his 1,040-acre grant of 9 December 1712.  It adjoined Sandy Run, Beaver Dam Swamp and Bear Swamp.[15]

On 20 July 1714, Thomas **GARRETT**, Sr., sold 100 acres to Isaac **ZEHENDER**.  It is described as "bounding on ye South on Stopping Creek to the West Kathren Creek to ye East on Warrick Swamp & to ye North by a line of marked trees running from a White Oak on Katherine Creek to a fork'd poplar on Warrick Swamp Including ye Indn. Old Field, being part of a Greater tract of 330 acres granted to me sd Thos. **GARRETT** .by patent dated 10 December 1712..."[16]

On 18 January 1714/15, John **EARLY** and his wife, Mary, sold Peter[3] **PARKER** 200 acres of land "at ye upper side of ye White Oak swamp on Wickacone creek, joining Fugoa Branch and the Creek..."  It was witnessed by William and Kath. (X) **CRAWFORD**.[17]

On 16 July 1716, Peter[3] **PARKER**, Senr. gave his power of attorney to his friend John **NAIRNE** to acknowledge a deed to Richard **WILLIAMSON** for 250 acres of land.  Witnesses were Richd: (R) **SOWELL** and Thos: (T) **RODGERS**.  That land is described as "One Certain Messuage & Tract of Land Scittuate lying & being butted & bounded on ye West Side of Chowan River Containing Two hundred & fifty acres which was Survey'd by Collo: Edwd: **MOSELEY** for Wm: **PAGETT** July 3d. 1707 & Assigned to me by the Sd. **PAGETT** 18th: March 1709 begining at Chas. **GAVIN**s Corner tree thence Runing W by [?] N? [sic] 308 Pole to a pine yn: N. E. 320 Pole along Pat **LAUGHLY**'s Line Corner tree on Chowan River thence along ye River to the first Station..."  It was signed by Petr: (P) **PARKER** Senr: and the same witnesses who appear on the power of attorney.[18]

John **NAIRNE** resided on the west side of Chowan River when he was appointed attorney for Peter[3] **PARKER**.  It appears that Peter[3] had already moved to the eastern side by that time.  His name, next to that of [Wi]ll **CRANFORD**, appears on a list of tithables from [Sa]lmon Creek/Wickacon [sic] district, with one tithable and the notation of "gone away."  That list is identified as "c. 1717," which is more probably 1716.[19]

On 17 April 1716, John **JACKSON** of Chowan sold Nicholas **FERRELL** 100 acres on the "north side of Chowan River...Beginning at **BALLARD**s Bridge and so Running to the long branch bridge for length and from thence to Jno. **WHITES**s Junr. to be his bounds for breadth..."  Robert

---

[13] NC Land Grants 1:236, File No. 164

[14] Ibid., 1:226, File No. 142

[15] Ibid., 8:303, File No. 1022

[16] Chowan County, NC, Deed Book W#1:179-180, courtesy of Weynette Parks Haun.

[17] Hofmann, Margaret M., *Chowan Precinct North Carolina Genealogical Abstracts of Deed Books 1696 to 1723*, c. 1976, 83:644, Deed Book B#1:45

[18] Chowan County, NC, Deed Book B#1:329

[19] NCSA, C.C.R. 190, Taxes & Accounts-Chowan Co. 1679-1754

**Chapter 10**: Peter[3] **PARKER** *(Thomas[2], William[1])*

**HOLLBROOK** and Petr his P mark **PARKER** witnessed this deed.[20]

A 1717 Tax List shows Peter[3] **PARKER** in Chowan, with 1,000 acres and two tithables. His neighbors are John **WHITE**, Sr. and Junior, Nic. **FERRILL** and Samuel **PADGET**.[21] This definitely places him on the east side of Chowan River. Nine hundred of the 1,000 acres are accounted for by calculating the number of acres in his patent, purchases and sales. On 14 8ber [October] 1717, Peter[3] and Elizabeth **PARKER** sold the 260-acre grant to Jno. **WELCH**. Both signed with their usual marks. Aaron **OLIVER** and Jean her J mark **PARKER** witnessed this deed...[22]

Peter[3] **PARKER** is estimated here to have been born circa 1645. He was married to Elizabeth well before December, 1706, when he and Elizabeth sold the land in Isle of Wight County, VA. He made his will in Chowan Precinct of Albemarle County on 5 September 1716. It was proved in court 22 April 1720. It is transcribed here in full:

"In y[e] name of god amen I Peter **PARKER** of Chowan p[r]c[t]. of y[e] County of Albermarle in y[e] Province of N[o]. Carolina being sick and weak of body but of /Sound &/ perfect memory thanks to Almighty god for y[e] Same and calling to mind the mortallity & Frailty of mankind & that it is appointed for all men once to dye I therefor doe hereby constitute & ordaine this to be my last will [sic] Testam[t]. in manner and [sic] following. First I recomend my soul into y[e] hands of almighty god that gave it hopeing thro y[e] merits of my blessed redeemer to receive a joyfull resurrection at y[e] last day, my body to be buried in such Christian like maner as to my Exco[rs]. hereafter named shal seem meet, and as touching such worldly Estate as it hath pleased almighty god to be stow on me in this transitory world I dispose y[e] same in manner & form following.

Imp[s]. to my Eldest son John **PARKER** I give & bequeath that plantation where on he now lives with all y[e] land adjoining thereunto above y[e] deep run branch to him & his heirs for ever one mare he has now in possession with her increase. Item to my Son Thomas **PARKER** I give & bequeath that plantation whereon I now live with all y[e] remaing part of my land adjoining thereunto below y[e] deep run to him & his heirs forever & three Cows & Calves to be paid him out my Stock and one young mare now in y[e] woods w[th] all her increase for ever and to [sic] at age & take his legacies & land in possession at y[e] age of Eighteen years old if his mother Lives & if She Should dye to be like quallified at y[e] age of Sixteen years old. Item to my Son Joseph **PARKER** I give & bequeath a parcell of Land containg 240 Acres w[ch]. I bought of John **EARLY** lying on y[e] west side of y[e] main branch of Wickacone Creek adjoining to y[e] wh[t]. oake swamp to him & his heirs for ever & 3 cows & calfes to be pd. him out of my stock and one young mare that his Cousin Peter **PARKER** has now in possession with all there increase for ever except y[e] fourth Colt which y[e] mare brings w[ch] ye above mentioned Peter **PARKER** is to have for his trouble in looking after y[e] S[d] Mare and my desire is that my son Jos. should be at age to posses as above mentioned. My land at y[e] Elm Swamp which I sold to Joseph **THOMAS** I desire he may Enjoy he ~~pay~~ & his heirs forever he paying twelve hundred pounds of Tobacco to my Exe[crs]. here after named or to my Children already mentioned. And as for my plantation whereon I lived in Virginia if sold or rented I desire y[e] produce /thereof/ to be equally devided amon'st my three ~~Children~~ Sons already named. To my Daughter Mary **PARKER** I give 3 Cows & Calfes to be paid out of Stock at y[e] day of Marridge or at the age of Sixteen. To my Daughter Ann **PARKER** I give 3 Cows & Calves to be p[d]. out of my Stock at y[e] day of Marrige or at y[e] age of Sixteen. I Desire my well beloved wife Eliz: **PARKER** should have y[e] Priviledge of all my moveable Estate and make use of & live on dureing her Widdow hood and before y[e] Day of her Marridge or at her decease w[ch]. shall first happen desire my hole moveable Estate should be equally devided Amongst all my Children above mentioned my Eldest Son John **PARKER** excepted Notwithstanding if my wife should marry I desire she may have a Childs part. To Eliz. **CRANFORD** I give y[e] first cow calfe either of my cows brings w[ch] is now in y[e] Possession of Wm. **CRANFORD** w[th]. all her increase forever. Lastly I constitute appoint and ordain my Eldest Son J[n]o. **PARKER** to be whole Executor of this my last will & Testam[t]. utterly Renouncing Revokeing makeing void all former will or wills by be [sic] formerly made Rattifying this and [?] confirming this only & no other to be my last will and Testam[t]. In Witness

---

[20] Chowan County, NC, Deed Book B#1:271
[21] Haun, *Old Albemarle County North Carolina Miscellaneous Records 1678 to ca 1737*, c. 1982, 97:#275
[22] Chowan County, NC, Deed Book B#1:504

whereof I have hereunto sett my hand & fixed my Seal this 5th day of septem[br]. in y[e] year of our Lord
1716                             Peter **PARKER**
Signed Sealed publi*sed* and                              }
Acknoleledged [sic] in y[e] presence of us }
Sam[ll]. **BOREMAN** [BOZEMAN] John **WOLCH** [WELCH]
Peter **PARKER** Junr                                    Proved att Chowan Apr[ll]: court 1720
                                                         Letters granted Aprill ye 22/1720"[23]

This will was transcribed from the original into Chowan County Will Book Two, some time after 22 April 1720.  This fact accounts for the signatures, as opposed to the usual marks used by Peter **PARKER** and Peter **PARKER**, Jr.  The original does not appear to be extant.  Samuel **BOZEMAN** will be shown to be a neighbor of Peter[3] **PARKER** in a discussion of his eldest son, John[4] **PARKER**.

John[4] **PARKER** *(Peter[3], Thomas[2], William[1])* first appears in Nansemond County, VA, records 29 October 1696, with a patent for 87 acres next to Peter[3] **PARKER**.[24]  His birth is estimated here to have been circa 1675.  He is the eldest son of Peter[3] **PARKER**, and moved to Chowan County, NC, with his father in 1700.

All the other children mentioned in Peter[3] **PARKER**'s 1716 will were under the age of 16, when he made the will.  John[4] was probably the son of an earlier wife.  An at least 25-year gap in age between John[4] and the other children makes that a likely premise, even though he is referred to as Elizabeth's "son" in a deed from Joseph **THOMAS** to Lemuel **BASS**, dated 23 March 1729/30.  That deed was for 175 acres of land on the south west side of Oropeak Swamp, plus 14 acres "purchased of Elizabeth **PARKER** & John **PARKER** her son."  It is described as beginning "at a marked gum standing on the side of Oropeak swamp, in the mouth of a small branch, thence running up the said branch along a line of marked trees to a poplar, it being a line tree of John **BATTLE**s, thence running down the sd. line to a marked white oak standing on the west side of Oropeak swamp, it being a corner tree of John **BATTLE**s line, running up the said swamp to the first station.  The sd. land is commonly called & known by the name of "Little Neck..."[25]  That "small branch" on the west side of Oropeak swamp, was Elm Swamp, as evidenced by a Virginia patent to Patrick **WOOD**, for 258 acres in Nansemond County, dated 28 October 1702.  It is described as "on both sides of a Swamp called the Elm*e* Swamp it being a branch of the main *C*oropeak Swamp begining at a white Oake standing in John **BATTAILE**s [sic] Line..."[26]  Peter[3] **PARKER** mentioned the land at Elm Swamp in his will.  His deed to Joseph **THOMAS**, and the one from Elizabeth and John[4] **PARKER**, were recorded in Nansemond County, making the original wording unavailable.

On 30 August 1714, John[4] **PARKER** was granted 376 acres in Chowan Precinct.  It is described as being "on ye No. Et. side of Chowan River, beginning at a pine in Thos. **PARKER**s line, then So. 10 Et. 40 pole to a pine then No. 70 Wt. 70 pole to a pine in Jno. **JORDAN**s line, then No. 50 Et. 12 pole to a White Oak, then No. 80 Et. 100 pole to a pine Jno. **JORDAN**s Corner tree, then No. 30 Et. 172 pole to a pine then No. 92 pole to a pine, then No. 65 Wt. 68 pole to a pine then So. 80 Wt. 52 pole to a pine on Wm. **COPELAND**s line, then along his line So. 10 Wt. 82 pole to another pine his corner tree then Wt. 190 pole to ye. Center of two pines in Thos. **PARKER**s line then along his line to the first station..."[27]

On 19 January 1715/16, he was granted another 96 acres, described as "Beginning at a White Oak Peter and Thomas **PARKER**s corner tree, then along Peter **PARKER**s line So. 70 Wt. 483 poles to a Black Oak, yn. S. 35 Wt. 80 poles to a Pine Saml. **BOUZMAN**s corner tree, then along his line S. 75 E. 36 poles to a Gum, then S. 8 E. 112 poles to a pine a corner tree of **BOAZMAN**s and Richard **SHOWLES**'s then along **SHOWLES** line So. 40 E. 62 poles to a pine, yn. No. 67 E. 30 poles to a pine, then No. 28 Wt. 12 poles to a red oak, Thomas **PARKER**s corner tree, thence along his line to

---

[23]  NCSA, Chowan Co., SS 875, Will Book 2, p. 229
[24]  See Chapter 7, page 70, for a description of that patent.
[25]  Chowan County, NC, Deed Book H#1:15
[26]  VLOP, 9:478
[27]  NC Land Grants, 1:239, File No. 176

ye. first Station..."[28]

On 16 August 1716, John **PETTEVER** was granted 640 acres of land lying in both Chowan and Perquimans Precincts, described as "beginning at a Cypress at the head of ye. Indian Town Creek Robt. **WILSON**s corner tree yn. down ye. Creek Swamp 68 poles to a maple John **WHITE**s corner tree then along the several courses of his lines to a pine John **PARKER**s corner tree, then along his line to a pine on Sandy run thence the meanders of the Said Swamp to the Pocoson So along the Pocoson to a pine in Robert **WILSON**s line, then along his line to the first station..."[29] The precinct [county] boundaries were very indefinite in this era and all of this land lies in what is now Chowan County.

This description places at least one of John[4] **PARKER**'s holdings near Sandy Run and near the head of Indian Town Creek, in Chowan County. Indian Town Creek has also been known as "**DILLARD** Creek, among other names."[30] It currently shows on some modern maps as "Indian Creek." The name "Indian Town Creek" has been easily confused by some researchers with another stream named "Old Town Creek." The latter creek is north and west of the former and lies in Gates County, instead of Chowan.

John[4] **PARKER** witnessed several deeds between family members in 1717-1719, and they will be discussed at a later time. On 20 July 1717, Moses **FOXWORTH** was granted 240 acres of land in Chowan precinct, described as "beginning at a pine in John **JORDAN**s line then along his line No. 50d E. 154 pole to a pine then S. 61d E. 96 pole to a White Oak then S. 35d E. 24 po. to a pine John **JORDAN**s corner tree, then No. 33d e. 220 pole to a poplar, then No. 35d Wt. 24 pole to a pine, then S. 64d Wt. 64 pole to an Oak then No. 24d Wt. 66 pole to a pine John **PARKER**s corner tree, then S. 46d Wt. 120 po. to a pine, then S. 65d Wt. 152 pole to a pine in Thomas **PARKER**s line, then S. 85 Wt. 52 po. to a red Oak a corner tree of the Said **PARKER**s, then S. 28d E. 12 pole, then S. 65d Wt. 20 pole to a pine John **PARKER**s corner tree, then S 40d Et 84 pole to the first Station..."[31] This patent establishes Moses **FOXWORTH** as another neighbor to John[4] **PARKER**.

On 14 February 1723/24, Moses and Martha **FOXWORTH** sold John **OVERTON**, of Nansemond County, VA, 100 acres of land on Hogg Yard Branch and the head of Indian Town Creek. The witnesses were John[4] **PARKER**, who signed his name, and Joseph **PARKER**, who used the mark "Ŧ" as his signature.[32] This man is Joseph[5] **PARKER**, one of the sons of John[4] **PARKER**. He will be mentioned again.

John[4] **PARKER** is shown in a listing of landowners for 1720, the year his father died, with a total of 1,040 acres of land. It was listed as being in Chowan County, with 240 acres on "wickacorn Creek," and 200 acres on "East Side Chown: River," both held by deeds. The remaining 600 was on "Stumpy Creek," held by patent.[33] The other children in the family were not yet old enough to claim their bequests of land given them in their father's will, thus their lands were listed under John[4] **PARKER**'s name.

On 8 June 1738, John[4] **PARKER** purchased an unknown number of acres from Jane **PARKER**, widow of Thomas **PARKER**, deceased, and her son Will **PARKER**. Much of the description of this deed is missing, but it was located on the south side of Poplar Run, beginning at the mouth of a branch, formerly the line of Frank **PARKER**, and adjoined John[4] **PARKER** and a landmark called the "halfway place," then back to Poplar Run. Jane's signature is missing, but Jas. **WILLIA[MS]**, Jas. **PARKER** and Martin (M) **NOWEL** witnessed this deed.[34]

On 29 December 1738, Jane and her son Francis **PARKER**, sold fifty acres to John[4] **PARKER**. This deed is also missing important landmarks, but does mention a man named "Charles,"

[28] NC Land Grants, 1:239, File No. 176, 8:295, File No. 1360

[29] Ibid., 8:271, File No. 957

[30] Powell, William S., *The North Carolina Gazetteer, a Dictionary of Tar Heel Places*, c. 1968 by UNC Press, p. 143

[31] NC Land Grants, 8:154-155, File No. 713

[32] Chowan County, NC, Deed Book C#1:439

[33] NCSA, C.024.99011, Chowan County Miscellaneous Papers, Vol. XIX- No dates, p. 70; Lists of Acreage 1697-1720, NCSA, C. C. R. 187, courtesy of NCSA

[34] Chowan County, NC, Deed Book W#1:387

[who is most likely Charles **JORDAN**,] Mat. **GUMBS** and a "pond." Jos. **COCKRIL**, Jos. **PARKER** and Jas. **FARLER** witnessed this deed.[35]

An order of Vestry dated 12 March 1742, named John **PARKER** and John **CHAMPEN** as processioners for the "district from the Indian town Creek on which **BALLARD**s bridge stands to Warwick Swamp and so to the bounds of pequimons..." On 4 June 1743, the land of John **CHAMPEN** was processioned with Edward **WELCH** and John **ARLINE** present. John[4] **PARKER**'s land was next, with Peter **PARKER** present.[36]

John[4] **PARKER**'s date of death is unknown, but he appears to have had a son, John[5] **PARKER**, who was dead by October 1747. One of his children was Elisha[6] **PARKER**, who was at least of 14 years of age in October 1747. He came into that court and prayed to choose his own guardian.[37] The court minutes contain several blanks, but the missing names are provided in John[5]'s estate records. Thomas **GARROT**, John **LEWIS** and Ephrim **BLANCHARD** entered into a guardian bond in the sum of £100, "the ___ Day of October anno Dom 1747." The purpose of this bond was for Thomas **GARROT** to be qualified as guardian to Elisha[6] **PARKER**, son of John[5] **PARKER**, deceased.[38] It is curious that James[5] **PARKER** had signed a note promising to pay Elisha[6] **PARKER** the sum of £200 a very short time prior to the date of the guardian bond. No reason for the note has been found. It will be mentioned again.

John[5] **PARKER** had another son, named Peter[6] **PARKER**, as evidenced by the 1750 Tax List for Perquimans County. Peter[6] **PARKER** appears on that list with his "brother Elisha," for a total of two polls in the district of Thomas **WEEKES**.[39] Peter[6] was apparently the elder of the two and Elisha[6] was at least of 16 years of age to be taxable. Both Peter[6] **PARKER** and Elisha[6] **PARKER** appear again, on a Militia List for Perquimans County in 1754.[40]

Elisha[6] *(John[5], John[4], Peter[3], Thomas[2], William[1])* **PARKER** appears on a Chowan County marriage bond with Rebecka **WARREN** on 13 November 1752. Charles **BLOUNT** was his bondsman.[41]

In Perquimans County April Court 1753, Elisha[6] **PARKER** came into court and prayed for letters of administration on the estates of Sarah and James **WARREN**, orphans of Abraham **WARREN**, deceased. His request was granted and it was ordered that he give security in the sum of £50 Proclamation Money. That security was provided by Charles **BLOUNT** and Edward **HALL**.[42] It is most likely that Abraham **WARREN** was the father of his wife, Rebecka. No further information.

James[5] and Joseph[5] **PARKER** *(John[4], Peter[3], Thomas[2], William[1])* appear to be John[4] **PARKER**'s sons. James[5] **PARKER** first appears with a John **PARKER** as a witness to the will of John **WELCH**, 23 April 1730.[43] His birth is estimated here to have occurred circa 1709. He married Elizabeth **WALLIS**, as will be shown.

On 10 November 1740, James **COPELAND** sold Thomas **WARD** 220 acres in Chowan County. That deed was witnessed by James[5] **PARKER** and Peter **PARKER**.[44] On 12 October 1754, James[5] **PARKER**, Sr., executed four deeds to four cousins. The first is extracted here. "To all people to whom these present Shall come I James **PARKER** Senr do Send Greeting Know ye that I the Said

---

[35] Chowan County, NC, Deed Book W#1:386

[36] Haun, *Chowan County, North Carolina Miscellaneous Papers 1685-1744, Book I*, c. 1993, 111:#440-441

[37] Haun, *Chowan County North Carolina County Court Minutes (Court of Pleas & Quarter Sessions) 1735-1738:1746-1748, Book II*, c. 1983, 112:#181

[38] NCSA, G.024.1750499, Chowan County Estates, Record of 1728-1951, Vol. O'Malley-Parrish, Folder: John Parker, 1747, Doc. #1095. There are no signatures, nor witnesses, on this document.

[39] Scanned from original photocopies of the archival documents, NCSA, Perquimans Co. Tax Records, Taxables, 1750-1753, by Harold Colson, http://perqtqax.homestead.com/files/1750listweekes2.jpg

[40] Ibid., NCSA Military Collection, TR 1-49, Militia Muster Roll, Perquimans County, North Carolina, http://perqtax2.homestead.com/files/militia1.jpg

[41] Chowan County, NC, Marriage Bonds 1741-1868, P-R contributed to Chowan NC GenWeb Project by Dayle Noble Biba, http://www.rootsweb.com/~ncchowan/chdnbmarrs-p.htm Hereafter, Chowan Co. Marriage Bonds

[42] Haun, *Perquimans County North Carolina County Court Minutes 1738 thru 1754, Book II, (with Deeds 1735 thru 1738,)* c. 1987, 105:#234-51

[43] NCSA, NC SS Wills, Chowan County

[44] Chowan County, NC, Deed Book A#1:15

**Chapter 10**: Peter[3] **PARKER** *(Thomas[2], William[1])*

James **PARKER** in the County of Chowan in the province of North Carolina planter for and in Consideration of the Love and Good will which I have and do bear toward my Loving Cousin Job **PARKER** son of Joseph **PARKER** Deceased, of the afsd County I have given and granted & by these presents do give and grant unto the said Job **PARKER** his heirs Exrs. admrs. and Assigns or any of them for ever all my whole Right title and Interest from me my heirs Executors Admrs. & assigns or any of them one messuage or tract of Land Containing one hundred and forty acres Lying in the afsd County bounding on the East side of Chowan River and Joining on the south side of Jacob **PARKER**s land being part of a patent belonging to the sd James **PARKER** Containing 600 acres...this 12th Day of 8ber in the year of our Lord 1754. James **PARKER** Signed Seald & Delivered in the Presence of us} Thomas **PARKER** Jesse **COPLAND** Michael his W mark **WELCH**" This deed of gift was proved by the oath of Jesse **COPLAND** in January Court 1755, registered 25 January 1755.[45]

The second deed of that date was given to his "Loving Cousen Joseph **PARKER**. It is described as "one Messuage or tract of Land Containing one hundred Acres of Land in the aforesaid County bounding on the East end of Job **PARKER**s Land on the South side of Jacob **PARKER**s Land being part of a Patent belonging to the said James **PARKER** Containing Six Hundred Acres..."[46] This deed bears the same witnesses and registration date as the one to Job **PARKER**.

The third deed in this series was given to his "Loving Cousen Jacob **PARKER** son of Joseph **PARKER** Deceased," and is described as "one Messuage or tract of Land Containing one hundred Acres of Land Lying in Chowan County on the East side of Chowan River and Joining on the Indian Landing Land [?] being part of a patent belonging to the said James **PARKER** Containg [sic] four hundred Acres..." This deed is represented as being signed "Jas. **PARKER**," instead of his usual signature of "James **PARKER**."[47] These deeds are not originals, but copies of them made by the Register of the county.

The fourth deed was given to his "Loving Cousen Nathan **PARKER**," and is described as "one messuage or tract of Land Containing one hundred and fifty Acres Including part of the marsh Lying in Chowan County and being [sic] at a pine on the head of Middle brech [sic] [branch] thence So E: 40 pole to a pine then fifty Degrees W 124 poles to a Gum so taking the Courses of the patent to the head Line being part of a patent belonging to the said James **PARKER** Containing four hundred Acres..." This deed is the most significant of the four in that not only James **PARKER** signed it, but so did Eliza her E mark **PARKER**. Witnesses were Thos. **PARKER**, Jesse **COPLAND** and Michael his W mark **WELCH**.[48] It will be mentioned again.

On 13 January 1755, a fifth deed was given to his "Loving Cousin Mary **CANNON** and Jeremiah **CANNON** her Husband weaver." It is described as "one messuage or tract of Land Containing one hundred and fifty acres including part of the Marsh Joining thereto formerly known by the name of the Indian Landing on the Northest side of Chowan River and bounding on the South West Side of Nathan **PARKER**s land being part of a patent belonging unto the said James **PARKER** Containing four hundred Acres ..." It was witnessed by Thomas **FARMER**, Jesse **COPLAND** and Nathan **PARKER**, registered 25 January 1755.[49]

On 1 September 1767, Nathan **PARKER** was "of county of North Hampton, North Carolina," and he sold 100 acres of that land to Jacob **PERREY**, Jr., of Perquimans County. It is described as "beginning at Stumpy Creek at the mouth of a branch known by the name of the Deep Branch, then up said branch by its various courses to John **DONEN**s line that was formerly then turning said John **DONEN**s line to the center of three white oaks standing in a small branch, Jeremiah **CANNON**s corner trees, down his line to the marsh through said marsh in a direct course with the aforesaid lines to the afsd. Stumpy Creek, up said Creek by its various courses to first station..." This deed was signed by Nathan **PARKER** and witnessed by Jacob his JP mark **PERRY**, Jeremiah **CANNON** and Ruth her

---

[45] Chowan County, NC, Deed Book G#1:326-327
[46] Ibid., G#1:329-330
[47] Ibid., G#1:331-3322
[48] Chowan County, NC, Deed Book, G#1:332-333  N.B.  Copies of all five of these deeds are courtesy of George P. Bauguess.
[49] Chowan County, NC, Deed Book, G#1:328-329

W mark **LILLY**. An additional note appears at the end of this deed and it states that "This Withen Deed of Seal being Part of A Patten granted to John **PARKER** bearing Deat July the first Day Ano: Dom: 1713." It was proved in October Court 1767, but not registered until 25 July 1769.⁵⁰

No record of the 1 July 1713 patent to John⁴ **PARKER** has been found. This parcel of land appears in the records once again, on 30 August 1784. On that date, John **WHITE**, of Perquimans County, sold it back to Nathan **PARKER** of Northampton, described as "100 acres...part of a tract of land granted to John **PARKER** for 400 acres July 1, 1713 and by the said John **PARKER** son & Heirs [sic] James **PARKER**, Conveyed to Nathan **PARKER** in a deed baring date 12 Oct. 1754 and by said **PARKER** conveyed to Jacob **PERRY** in a deed dated 1 September 1767 and by said **PERRY** conveyed to John **WHITE** by deed of 10 June 1775..." The only difference in the bounds is that the "three white oaks in a small branch" then stood in Joseph **CANNON**s line. John and Huldah **WHITE** signed this deed and it was witnessed by Jos. **SCOTT** and Elial **GRIFFIN**. It was proved in March Court 1785, but not registered until 27 September 1786.⁵¹

This deed conclusively proves that James⁵ **PARKER** is the son of John⁴ **PARKER**. It will be noted that John⁴ **PARKER** was given "that plantation where on he now lives with all yᵉ land adjoining thereunto above yᵉ deep run branch" by his father, Peter³ **PARKER**. His 1713 patent appears to adjoin that land. The "Joseph **PARKER** Deceased," mentioned in the previous deeds, was also mentioned in Peter³ **PARKER**'s will, as one of his sons. Children of Joseph⁴ **PARKER** and John⁴ **PARKER** were indeed "Cousins."

On 25 March 1752, Lord **GRANVILLE** granted John **WALLIS** 321 acres in Chowan County, joining Luke **WHITE**, Wm. **HERRON**, Saml. **WOODWARD** and a fork of Poly Bridge Swamp. James **PARKER** was one of the "sworn chain carriers" during the survey of that land.⁵² Chain-carriers were almost always family members, or very close and trusted friends.

John **WALLES** made his will in Chowan County, transcribed here in full. "Know all men That I John **WALLES** Being of Sound and perfect memory Doth Apoint and Ordain this to Be my Last Will and Testament In manner and form following

Item  I Bequeath my Body To the Earth To be Bury'd in a Desent and Christian Like Manner and my Soul I Recommend To God in hopes of a Joyefull Resurection.

Item  I Give To my Granson John **PARKER** son of my Daughter Elizabeth **PARKER** all that Track and parcel of Land that I purchace'd and Bought of Moses **WOOD** and arnold **WHITE** Laying in perquimons County I Say to him and his Heirs for Ever.

Item  I Give to my Grandaughter Lydia **PARKER** Daughter of Elizabeth **PARKER** the Bed my Wife Lay on in her Late Sickness.

Item  I give to my Gran Children James **PARKER** Samuel **PARKER** and Enock **PARKER** Sons of Elizabeth **PARKER** Each of them one young Heffer or Cow

Item  I Give to my Daughter mary **PARKER** all the Rest of my Lands and tenements Not afore mention'd afore I Say to the Said mary **PARKER** and her Heirs for Ever Lawfully Begot of her Body

Item  I Give to my afore Said Daughter mary **PARKER** all my hogs Horses Cattle Sheep House Hold furniture Debts Bonds With all the Rest of my Estate Let it Be of What Kind or Quality So Ever I Say to the Said mary **PARKER**s own proper use

Item  I Leave my Son /in Law/ Peter /**PARKER**/ my hould and Sole Executor to this my Last Will and ₮ testament as Witnes my hand and Seal this twenty Six Day of October in the year of our Lord one thousand Seven hundred and fifty Six        John his ₊ mark **WALLES**

Signed and Seald in the presence of } of [sic] Wm. **BOYD** Jurat  Mary her W mark **LONG**  John his ₊ mark **SIMSON**"⁵³  There is no date of probate on this will. This will appears to be what is known as a "Quaker will," as opposed to one made by a member of the Church of England. The latter usually begins "In the name of God Amen."

⁵⁰ Chowan County, NC, Deed Book, N#1:63
⁵¹ Ibid., S#1:265
⁵² Hofmann, Margaret M., *The Granville District of North Carolina 1748-1763, Abstracts of Land Grants, Volume One*, c. 1986, p. 48:#447
⁵³ NCSA, SS Wills, Chowan Co., John Walles 1756

**Chapter 10**: Peter[3] **PARKER** *(Thomas[2],William[1])*

John **WALLES** named the children of Elizabeth **PARKER** as John[6], Lydia[6], James[6], Samuel[6] and Enock[6] **PARKER**, and stated that his daughter Mary was married to Peter[5] **PARKER**. The actual reason for John **WALLES'** omission of James[5] **PARKER**'s name as the other parent of his grandchildren will forever remain unknown. James[5] may have fallen out of favor with him when he made those five deeds of gift to his cousins, as that would diminish his daughter's and grandchildren's possible inheritance. It will be noted that Elizabeth **PARKER** signed the deed to Nathan **PARKER** on 12 October 1754, and all the deeds called James[5] "Sr." One of the grandchildren was named James **PARKER**, thus the "Sr." distinguished him from his son. There can be little doubt that James[5] **PARKER** married Elizabeth **WALLES** some time prior to 1752, when John **WALLES** received the land grant mentioned earlier.

On 31 January 1760, James[5] **PARKER** sold 188 acres of land to Charles **COPELAND**. It is described as "beginning at a pine William **COPELAND**s Corner Tree Then Southward by a line of marked trees across the ridg [sic] to a pine in Uriah **HUTSON**s line Bryant **BYRUM**s Corner Tree then up **HUTSON**s line by its Various Courses to a pine a Corner Tree in the head line then Northward with the sd. head line which is now John **ROBENSON**s line by the various Courses of the patten to a Corner Tree on Sandy Run in William **COPELAND**s head line then with the sd. **COPELAND**s line to the first station..." The witnesses were Bryant his B mark **BYRUM** and Joseph his + mark **COPELAND**. It was proved by the affirmation of Bryant **BYRUM** in October Court 1760, and was registered in February 1767, after the death of James[5] **PARKER**.[54]

On that same date of 31 January 1760, James[5] **PARKER** also sold 188 acres to Bryant **BYRUM**. It is described as "begining at a pine William **COPELAND**s Corner Tree near Sandy Run Then along ye sd. **COPELAND**s Line to David **WELCH**es line then along ye sd. **WELCH**es Line to a pine a Corner Tree on Abraham **GUMBRE**s then along **GUMBRE**s line to the aforsd. Bryant **BYRUM**s own line then along his Line to uriah **HUTSON**s line then along **HUTSON**s line to a pine a Corner tree in ye sd. **HUTSON**s line then Northward across the ridg By a line of marked Trees to the first station Near Sandy Run." This deed was witnessed by Charles his C mark **COPELAND** and Joseph his + mark **COPELAND**, proved in the same court as the previous deed and registered in "Feby ___ ."[55] These two parcels constitute the grant to John[4] **PARKER** of 376 acres on 30 August 1714.

James[5] **PARKER** was dead by 29 July 1766. On that date James **SUMNER**, Hardy his H mark **HURDLE** and Jacob **JORDAN** entered into an administration bond in the sum of £200 for James **SUMNER** to administer on the estate of James **PARKER** deceased. In November Superior Court of 1766, one Elisha **PARKER** complained of James **SUMNER**, Esquire, administrator of James[5] **PARKER**, in a plea for £200 "unjustly detained from him." James[5] **PARKER** had signed a note to Elisha for the £200 on 26 September 1747, in Perquimans County, and refused to repay it when requested, as did James **SUMNER**, after his death.[56] No resolution of this conflict has been found.

The named children of James[5] and Elizabeth (**WALLIS**) **PARKER** were John[6], Lydia[6], James[6], Samuel[6] and Enoch[6] **PARKER**. There appears to be an older son, named Amos[6] **PARKER**, who was possibly from an earlier marriage. He will be mentioned again.

At least one of James[5] **PARKER**'s sons was still a minor as of December 1768. Between 20 and 24 December of that year, it was ordered in Chowan County Court that "Samuell [sic] **PARKER** orphan of James **PARKER** deceased be bound unto David **WELCH** to learn the trade of a Cordwainer untill he arrives at the age of twenty /one years/ he being now nineteen years of age."[57] This record takes the date of the marriage of Elizabeth **WALLES** and James[5] **PARKER** back to at least 1748-1749, if not a number of years earlier.

There was an earlier Samuel **PARKER** living in the vicinity of James[5] **PARKER** by 1750, as

---

[54] Chowan County, NC, Deed Book L#1:212

[55] Ibid., 1:222

[56] NCSA, C.R.024.508.79, Chowan County Estates Records 1728-1951, Orindell-Parker, Peter, Folder: Parker, James 1766

[57] NCSA, C.024.30007, Chowan County Court Minutes & Ref. Docket, P & Q Sessions 1762-1772, pages not numbered

evidenced by a deed from Charles **COPELAND** to Samuel **PARKER** for 220 acres of land for 15 Shillings, "lying in the fork of sandy run Swamp...beginning at the run at a pine William **COPELAND**s head line then along sd. head line to a pine corner tree of Thomas **WARD**s land and John **WHITE**s land then along a streight line to Sandy run Swamp again then up sd. Swamp to first station..." It was witnessed by Wm. **COPELAND**, Senior and Junior.[58] (See the above deed from James[5] **PARKER** to Charles **COPELAND** for neighboring landowners.)

That Samuel **PARKER** made his will 24 February 1760, probated in December Court 1769. It was copied from the original as Samuel "**PARKS**," as well as the rest of his family members' names. That original will is no longer extant. Samuel used a mark of "X" instead of a written signature. James **NORFLEET** was the clerk who copied this will into the current book and may have misread the name. The following evidence lends weight to that conclusion. The 1750 deed from Charles **COPELAND** to Samuel **PARKER** mentions that the 220 acres was "lying *in the fork of sandy run Swamp*," and Samuel "**PARKS**" left to his son, John "**PARKS**," "one hundred acres of land on the south East of the manor plantation *in the Bend of Sandy run swamp*." This appears to be the same property. He also left his estate to his wife, Elizabeth for life, then to be divided among his five children, giving son Daniel "one fifty [sic] acres of land," the manor plantation consisting of 70 acres to son Samuel, and beds, furniture and spinning wheels to daughters Mary and Elizabeth. The witnesses to this will were E. **CUMMINGS**, Nathan **PARKER** and Jeremiah **CANNON**.[59]

His relationship to James[5] **PARKER** is undetermined, but James[5] **PARKER** did name a son Samuel, as previously proved. Their deaths occurred about six years apart. He most probably was yet another son of John[4] **PARKER**.

On 20 March 1780, John[6] **PARKER** of Perquimans County and Nathan[5] **PARKER** of Northampton County made a deed of gift to their "loving kinsman Samuel **PARKER** of the county of Chowan," of 100 acres "on the South side of Middle Creek Swamp and joining **WHITE**s line, thence by its various courses to the made road, thence up the said road, thence to the said swamp, thence to the first station, being part of a patent granted to John **PARKER** containing four hundred acres..." It was signed by John[6] his J mark **PARKER** and Nathan[5] **PARKER**. Jonathan **JORDAN** was the witness and proved the deed in June County Court 1780.[60]

On 10 September 1791, Samuel[6] **PARKER** *(James[5],John[4],Peter[3],Thomas[2],William[1])* sold eight acres of that land to Nathan[5] **PARKER**, described as "Beginning in a Branch known by the name of the Deep Branch in the Pattent Line of said Nathan **PARKER**s Line thence down said Branch to the Second Small Branch or Bottom that makes out of said Deep Branch on the east side thence along a Line of Marked Trees Easterly to the Patten Line divides between the said Land and the land that was formed by Drennings [sic] now **CANNON**s thence down said Pattent Line to the first Station it being part of a tract of Land granted to John **PARKER** for 400 acres in a pattent bearing date July 1st 1713..." It was signed by Samuel his S mark **PARKER** and witnessed by John **TOPPING**, Jacob **JORDAN**, Jr. and Edward **WELCH**.[61]

Samuel[6] **PARKER** made his will in Chowan County 2 October 1810, probated in March Court 1811. It is transcribed verbatim here: "In the Name of God amen I Samuel **PARKER** of the County of Chowan & State of NoCarolina-Being weak in body but of Sound & purfecet Memory thanks be to God for the Same Colling to mind that it is appointd for all men Once to Diy I thurefore do make and ordain this my Last Will and Testament in the maner as followeth Vy [sic]

1  Its my Will and desire that all of my Just Debts Feuneral Expenes be paid by my Exutors here after mention

2  its my will and Desire that my wife Silva **PARKER** Shall have the use of all the plantion & Bilding thureon with the priviledgs of the woodling land To suport the Sam with timber during the time Shee remains to be my Widdow And No longer

---

[58] Chowan County, NC, Deed Book C#2:163
[59] NCSA, C.024.80005, Chowan County Record of Wills 1768-1799; 1807-1841, Vols. B,C, B:124-125, courtesy of Weynette Parks Haun
[60] Chowan County, NC, Deed Book R#2:354
[61] Ibid., S#2:213

3  I Give and bequath to my Son John **PARKER** All my Lands to him & his Hirs of his body lawfully Begotton for Evr

4  Its my will and desire that my beloved wife Shall Have the use of all my parishable property for the Suport of her Self and Children While Shee remains To be ny [sic] Widdow and No longer

5  Its my will and Dieser [sic] that if my Wife Should marry again that then all my purishable property Shall be Equally devided betwen hir & my four Daughtors namley Lyda Kiziah Nancey Silva

And I give and bequath unto my Daughtor Elezebth **HARRELL** two Dollars or the Value of it beside what Shee Has all ready Had

I do hereby appoint my beloved Wife Silva **PARKER** and Son John **PARKER** my To [sic] be my holey and Soley Executors to See this My last will and testament fulley Complideed with Uttrley revoking disonulling all others wills And testaments formaley made by me Pronouncing & Confirming this and no other to be my last Will and testament in Witness Whareof I have Here unto Set my Hand and fixed my Seal This Second day of October in the year of our Lord 1810

Samuel his XS  mark **PARKER**

Sined Selead in The presents of Miles **WELCH** Jurt. [Jurat] Peminah her X mark **FULLENTON**-proved March Term 1811  John **PARKER** Qualified"[62]

There is a copy of this original will in the same file.  The only differences between the two appear to be spelling corrections.  The names "Silva" and "Elezebth" are corrected to "Silvia" and "Elizabeth **PARKER**."  "Peminah **FULLENTON**" has been changed to "Peninah **FULLINGTON**" in the copy made by James **NORFLEET**, the clerk of court.

The date of marriage of Samuel[6] and Silvia **PARKER** is unknown.  Their known children were Elizabeth[7], who married a **HARRELL**, and Lyda[7] [Lydia,] Kiziah[7], Nancey[7], and Silva[7].

Enoch[6] **PARKER** *(James[5],John[4],Peter[3],Thomas[2],William[1])* and his family were Quakers.  He was "of Little River" on 15 July 1778, when he was received by request into Pasquotank Monthly Meeting.  On 21 April 1779, he requested a certificate to Perquimans Monthly Meeting to marry.  On 14 March 1806, Enoch[6] produced a certificate from Piney Woods Monthly Meeting and was reported married to Elisabeth **PERISHO** 14 November of that year.[63]  He died in Chowan County by 14 March 1808, as evidenced by the administration bond entered into by Elizabeth her X mark **PARKER**, with Jacob **CULLENS** and Ephraim **ELLIOTT** as bondsmen, in the sum of £600.  In September Term of Chowan County Court 1810, it was ordered that John **FULLINGTON**, Thomas **BROWNRIGG** and Job **LEARY**, Esquires, audit and settle Elizabeth's accounts on Enoch[6]'s estate and divide the estate among the heirs.  That order was carried out 27 November 1810, and the shares of the estate were divided among Elizabeth, Francis **MING**, in right of his wife, Mary Sarah[8], and Ruth[8] **PARKER**.[64]

John[6] **PARKER** *(James[5],John[4],Peter[3],Thomas[2],William[1])* is listed in the Quaker records as being married to Jael, whose maiden name is unknown.  Their children, born after they became members of **SUTTONS** Creek Monthly Meeting, were Ruth[7], born 25 May 1779; Penina[7], born 22 July 1781; Sarah[7], born 16 January 1784 and Seth[7] **PARKER**, born 27 July 1788.[65]

Ruth[7] **PARKER** married Samuel **BUNDY** on 17 January 1799, at **SUTTONS** Creek Meeting House.  Penina[7] **PARKER** married Nathan **NICHOLSON** 16 May 1799, in the same place.  Seth[7] **PARKER** was dismissed for "marrying contrary to discipline" on 12 July 1806.  His wife's name was not mentioned.[66]

John[6] **PARKER** made his will in Perquimans County on 4 October 1800, probated in February Term 1803.  In that will, he mentioned having made a deed of gift of land on the same date to grandsons Nathan[8] **BUNDY** and John[8] **NICHOLSON**.  He bequeathed his manor plantation to his son, Seth[7] **PARKER**, with the woodland on the eastern side of the fork Swamp and his lands lying in

---

[62]  NCSA, Chowan County Wills, C.R.024.801  The reverse of this document shows "Samuel Parkers Last Will &c March 1811  Recorded in Book B Page 304 and 305  James Norfleet Clk."

[63]  Hinshaw, William Wade, *Encyclopedia of American Quaker Genealogy, Vol. I, North Carolina*, c. 1936, p. 160; p. 199

[64]  NCSA, Chowan County Estates Records, C.R.024.508.79, Folder:  Parker, Enoch 1808

[65]  Hinshaw, William Wade, *Encyclopedia of American Quaker Genealogy, Vol. I, North Carolina*, c. 1936, p. 186

[66]  Ibid., p. 199

the woods about "pine Glade."  In case of his decease, it was to go to grandson Nathan[8] **PARKER**, son of his son John[7] **PARKER**.  His beloved wife, Jail, was to have the use of the said plantation lands, buildings and improvements, until son Seth[7] should reach the age of 20, then to have her choice of one-half, divided by his path, or road, straight from the house out to the public road, during her natural life.

His daughter, Sarah[7] **PARKER**, was bequeathed 50 acres, joining the part given to grandson Nathan[8] **BUNDY**, but if he died without heir, then to grandson Noah[8] **PARKER**, son of his son John[7] **PARKER**.  His son John[7] **PARKER** and son-in-law, Samuel **BUNDY** were named as his executors. John[6] used the mark "ɟ" as his signature.  Witnesses were Silas **HASKET**, William **HASKET** and John **POOL**.[67]

Amos[6] **PARKER** *(James[5],John[4],Peter[3],Thomas[2],William[1])* was married to Mary **FARLEE**, daughter of James and Rachel **FARLEE**, prior to 12 January 1750/51, as evidenced by the will of James **FARLEE** of Chowan County, on that date.  He named his wife, Rachel, his daughter Mary **PARKER**, sons Samuel and James, daughters Sarah and Christian.  Samuel **FARLEE** was bequeathed all his lands, except the "old plantation" in Chowan County, which went to Rachel during her natural life.  After her decease, it then went to Samuel.  Amos[6] **PARKER** was a witness to this will.[68]  He continued to be associated in the records with this family as long as he was in Chowan County.

On 28 February 1756, Samuel **FARLEE** sold Amos[6] **PARKER** 450 acres in Chowan, described as "part of a parcel or tract of land sold...to Richard **GARRETT** by afsd. Saml. **FARLEE** and then conveyed by Richd. **GARRETT** to the afsd. Saml. **FARLEE** as by his deed of release dated 11 December 1755...beginning at a bridge called **BALLARD**s Bridge and so running up the swamp as to contain the sd. quantity 450 acres of land on the Esrn. side of the main road."  Witnesses were Michael his M mark **WELCH**, Christian **FARLEE** and Mary **PARKER**.[69]

On 31 August 1761, Amos[6] **PARKER** and Mary **PARKER**, his wife, of Chowan Province, sold William **HARPER** of same 100 acres for £30 "Proclamation Money Beginning at the head of a Branch commonly none [sic] by the name of the Spring Branch then down said Branch to the land of David **WELSH** then along the said **WELSH**es line to a Branch commonly none by the name of the Popler Run then up the said Popler Run to the land of the aforesaid David **WELCH** then by his line to the land of James **PARKER** then by his line to the first station, the aforesaid land being taken out of a larger tract of land belonging to James **PARKER**..."  Both Amos[6] and Mary signed this deed.  Witnesses were William his W mark **BOND** and Evan **SKINNER**.[70]

Amos[6] **PARKER** was "of Chowan" in 1761, but appears on a tax list for Perquimans County in 1764, 1765 and 1771.  He does not appear on the Perquimans list for 1772, so probably moved to Northampton County at that time.  In the above tax list for 1771, he lists four taxables as himself, sons Samuel and Henderson, with "Apprentice Enoch **PARKER**."[71]  The Chowan/Perquimans County line appears to have been very indistinct for many years, making the same person appear to be in two different counties without ever moving.

In the above Perquimans tax list of 1765, Amos[6] **PARKER** appears with "Son Saul," which most probably was an abbreviation for "Samuel."

They had moved to Northampton County, NC, before 20 May 1775, as Amos[6], Nathan, Joseph, Jonathan, Jacob and Samuel **PARKER** were on a list for commanding officer of the Militia, Col. Allen **JONES**.[72]

---

[67]  LDS Microfilm #19552 pt. 4, Perquimans County Probate Records, Wills 1761-1941, Will Book E 1793-1817, p. 185

[68]  NCSA, NC Wills, S. S. Chowan County, James Farlee 1750

[69]  Chowan County, NC, Deed Book H#1:218

[70]  Ibid., L#1:17

[71]  Scanned images of copies of original documents, NCSA, Perquimans Co. Miscellaneous Records, Jury Lists, 1762-1768; Perquimans Co. Tax Records, Taxables, 1771; Record Series G. A. 11.1 [1772] http://perqtax5.homestead.com/files/1771list20.jpg; http://perqtax.homestead.com/files/1772list19.jpg., made by Harold Colson

[72]  Hinshaw, William W., *Encyclopedia of American Quaker Genealogy, Vol. I, North Carolina*, c. 1936, p. 250

**Chapter 10**:  Peter[3] **PARKER** *(Thomas[2],William[1])*

Amos[6] **PARKER** made his will 24 March 1799, in Northampton County, naming wife Mary, daughter Mary[7] **BROWN**, Henderson[7] **PARKER**, James[7] **PARKER**, grandson Daniel[8] **PARKER**, and daughters Martha[7] **PARKER**, Salley[7] **JACKSON** and Penonne[7] [?] **NEWSOM**.  The witness to this will was Josiah **PARKER**.  It was probated in March Court 1800.[73]  The Quaker records by William Wade **HINSHAW** list Amos[6] as "d. 12-1-1804," which appears to be in error.[74]

That same source lists Mary **PARKER** as having died on 4 September 1812, with Samuel[7] **PARKER** dead 2 June 1790; Tamur[7] **BURGES** dead on 20 December 1809 and Martha[7] **PARKER** dead "18 [sic]-9-1824."  Reading of the original records may clarify any discrepancies.

Mary[7] **PARKER**, "Jr.," was reported married to Josiah **BROWN** on 20 June 1795, at Rich Square Monthly Meeting.  Further research on the family of Amos[6] **PARKER** is being pursued by others.

It will be remembered that Peter[5] **PARKER** *(John[4],Peter[3],Thomas[2],William[1])* was married to Mary **WALLES** prior to 8 October 1755, as he was mentioned as her husband in a deed of gift from John **WALLES** to his daughter, Mary **PARKER**, wife of Peter **PARKER**, for 200 acres of land whereon he lived.  That land is located on the south side of **BALLARD**'s Creek.  He retained "full power privilege benefit & behoof of the plantation lands during his natural life."  This deed was witnessed by Thos. (I) **HOLLIDAY** and Joseph **BARKER**, then acknowledged by him in April Court 1756.[75]  On 10 December 1755, John **WALLES** gave his nephew, Isaac **WILLIAMS**, 100 acres, described as "where the said Isaac **WILLIAMS** now lives...bounding on **WHITE**'s line and on **BARBER**s line on **BOYCE**s line & on **WALLIS**' line..."  Wm. **BOYD**, Peter **PARKER** and Isaac (I) **SPEIGHT** were witnesses.[76]

John **WALLACE** was dead by 26 October 1765, the date of a deed for 300 acres from Isaac **WILLIAMS** and Ann his wife, and Peter **PARKER** and Mary his wife, to William **BOYD**.  It is described as "whereas the said John **WALLACE** did in his life time devise unto the sd. Isaac **WILLIAMS** and Ann his wife Peter **PARKER** & Mary his wife a certain tract in Chowan County...joining the lands of James **WHITE**, Richard **GLAUGHANGN** [sic,] Samuel **WOODWARD**, William **BOYD** and Ganston **DESHAN** being a tract of land taken by the afsd. **WALLACE** Decd. of the Earle of Granville agents bearing date 25 Mar. 1752...300 acres in Fee Tail...35 pounds Sterling money of Gr. Brit..."  Elisha **PARKER** and Philip **PARKER** were witnesses to this deed.[77]

Peter[5] **PARKER** *(John[4],Peter[3],Thomas[2],William[1])* was married to Mary **WALLES**, daughter of John **WALLES**, prior to 8 October 1755, as previously noted.  That marriage date was most likely sometime in 1744.  As John **WALLES** named the children of his other daughter, Elizabeth **PARKER**, in his 1756 will, but none of those of Mary **PARKER**, it can be presumed that they had not produced any heirs at that time.

That changed over time and Mary (**WALLES**) **PARKER** died prior to 1785, when Peter[5] **PARKER** made his will, transcribed here in full:

"In the Name of God amen I Peter **PARKER** of Chowan County and Province of North Carolina Being of Sound and Perfect mind and memory Bless'd be God Do this third Day of July in the year of our lord 1785 Do make and publish this my last Will and Testament In maner and form 1 Following that is to Say first I Give and Bequathe unto ~~both~~ my Son Elisha **PARKER** five Shillings Specia he have/ing/ all Redy ReSeved a Sefisant part of My Estate

2  I Give and bequath unto my Son Peter **PARKER** one Negrow Woman Named **PLESANT** provided he the Said Peter **PARKER** give to my Son Seth **PARKER** the first Child that the Said Negrow Woman Shuld Bring to Be Deliverd to thim [sic] the Said Seth **PARKER** at the adge of two years old or in Lieu? their of twenty pounds Specia Like wiSe to pay to my Daughter Rodith **PARKER** Tenn pounds Specia Which I give unto him and hur? heirs for Ever.

---

[73]  Hofmann, Margaret M. *Northampton County, North Carolina 1759-1808 Genealogical Abstracts of Wills*, c. 1975, p. 108, Will Book 2:196

[74]  Hinshaw, William Wade, *Encyclopedia of American Quaker Genealogy, Vol. I, North Carolina*, c. 1936, p. 222

[75]  Chowan County, NC, Deed Book H#1:132

[76]  Ibid., H#1:160

[77]  Ibid., L#1:135

3   I Give and be quathe unto my Son Willis **PARKER** one Negrow garl **BRIDGET** Provided that the Said Willis **PARKER** give unto my Son ISaack **PARKER** the first Child that the Said Negrow woman Shuld Bring to Be Delved to the Said ISaack **PARKER** at the adge of two years old or in Li/e/w their of the Sum of twenty pounds Specia to him the Said Isaack **PARKER** /to/ all to pay & Pay to my daughter Rodath **PARKER** the Sum of ten Pounds Specia Which I give unto Them and heir [sic] heairs for Ever

4   I Give and be quath unto my Daughter Sele **PARKER** one Negrow garl Named **PEG** Which I give unto hur and hur heairs for Ever

I give and be quath unto Daughter Seley **PARKER** one Fether Bed and furnertur Which I give unto hur and hur heairs for Ever

5   I give and be quath unto my Son Willis **PARKER** one fether Bed and funurtur? Which I give Unto him and his heairs for Ever

6   I Give and be quath unto my Son Daughter Roade/th/ **PARKER** one fether bed and furnertuer? Which I Give to hur and hur heairs for Ever

7   I Give and Bequath unto my Son Seth **PARKER** one Desk and all my Shoe makers tools all Which I give unto him and his heairs for Ever

8   I Give and Bequath unto my Son ISaack **PARKER** one ovel Table and and [sic] all my Carpen [sic] tools all which I Give unto him and his heairs for Ever.

9   I Give and Bequath unto my Son Peter **PARKER** one Lardg Chest and all my Coopers Tools all Which I give unto him and his heairs for Ever.

10   and all the Remainder part of my hole EState to be Equely Devided amongst Six of my Children Namly Seth **PARKER** and Peter **PARKER** and ISaack **PARKER** Willis **PARKER** and Seley **PARKER** and Rodah **PARKER** all which I give unto them and their heairs for Ever.

and I hear By make and ordain my Son Peter **PARKER** and my frind Jacob **JORDAN** Executors of this my last will and testament in Whear of I the Said Peter **PARKER** have to this will and Testament Set my hand and Seal this Day and year above Written.

**MEREDET** [sic]                                          Peter **PARKER**   {Seal}
Miriam **THOMPSON**

[Reverse of document:]   Peter **PARKER**s Will Proved June Court 1789  Recorded in Book B folio (99) & 100  Jas **NORFLEET** clk"[78]

The inventory of the estate of Peter[5] **PARKER** is not dated, but the account of sales is dated 8 July 1789, and signed by his executor, Peter[6] **PARKER**.  Some of the purchasers at that sale were Elisha, Isaac, "Petter," Willis and Seth **PARKER**.[79]

Elisha[6] **PARKER** *(Peter[5],John[4],Peter[3],Thomas[2],William[1])* was apparently Peter **PARKER**'s eldest son.  As he stated that Elisha[6] had already received a sufficient part of his estate, and he mentioned no land in his will, it appears that he may have given his lands to him prior to writing that will. No recorded deed of gift has been found.

Elisha[6] **PARKER** was granted a tract of 232 acres of land in Chowan County on 10 December 1790.  It is described as being "on the south east side of **BALLARD**s Bridge Creek beginning at a Cypress on a small Drean [Drain] that makes out of Said Creek & running S10W42 po. to the mouth of a Deep Branch then up the Branch by the Various Courses 84 po. to a pine then up said Branch 40 po. to another pine then S4E58 po. to a pine at the road Side by the Head of the rooty Branch then down the Various Courses of Said Branch 364 po. to Miss Ann **EARL**s line then Along her line North twenty five West 348 po. to **BALLARD**s Bridge Creek then along down the Creek to the first Station..."  It was registered 28 June 1791.[80]

Elisha[6] **PARKER** made his will 4 January 1828, probated June Term, 1830.  It is transcribed here in full:

"In the name of God, I Elisha **PARKER** of Chowan County and State of North Carolina, be-

---

[78]  NCSA, Chowan Co. Wills, C.R.024.801, Peter Parker 1785
[79]  NCSA, G.024.1750499, Chowan County Estates, Record of 1728-1951, Vol. O'Malley-Parrish, Folder:  Peter Parker, 1789, Doc. #1247-1248; #1245-1246
[80]  Chowan County, NC, Deed Book S#2:50

ing of Sound and perfect mind and and [sic] Memory, and calling to mind the uncertainty of this life, do this fourth day of January one thousand eight hundred and Twenty eight make and publish this my last Will and Testament, in the following manner viz first, I give and bequeath unto my beloved Wife Elizabeth **PARKER**, my Negroe Woman **FRANKEY**, for ever. I moreover loan to my ~~Negroe~~ Wife Elizabeth dureing her natural life, my Negroe Slaves, **ISAAC**, Negroe Boy **JERRY**, **CELEA**, & **EDNEY** and the part of the Plantation whereon I now live, begining at the Mill, and running from thence to the head of the branch thence along the Orchard fence to the Pond, thence along the Pond fence, to the far Corner of the new Ground, thence along the New Ground fence to the Branch, & thence round to the Mill, with the use of all the Houses, except the Shed Room, in the West end of the Dwelling House, The Still and Still Works, Cyder Works & Canoe together with the use of Timber and fire Wood, for the use of the Plantation. I also give unto my wife Elizabeth, two feather Beds, & Bedsteads, all the House hold and Kitchen furniture except what may be herein after divided, all the weaving Spinning and plantation Utensils, the two old Mules, two Yoke of Oxen, all the Carts, & the new Wheels, the Riding Chair, & Harness, her Choice of Six Cows and Calves, or yearlings, Stocks of Bees, all the Sheep & Hoggs, all the Corn & fodder, and the provisions of every kind that are laid in for this year, the Grind Stone, & hand Mill, and should it so happen, that my Wife does not leave a Will, at her Death then and in that Case, It is my Will, that all the aforesaid property be equally divided betwen my Children, Jacob **PARKER** Elizabeth **PARKER** Sarah **PARKER**, and Peter **PARKER**, Secondly, I give unto my Daughter Mariam **WOODWARD**, five Shillings.

Thirdly, I give unto my Son Job **PARKER** five Shillings; fourthly, I give unto my Son Jacob **PARKER**, One hundred Acres of Land on the Pitch old point Ridge, My Negroe Man **JACOB**, one feather Bed and Bedstead, one fourth part of the Cattle not divided to my Wife and the Gun with the Iron Ram Rod & fourth part of the Bees not heretofore divided. Fifthly, I give unto my Daughter Elizabeth **PARKER**, my Negroe Woman **MARY** and all her Children with their increase, but She is not to have **EDNEY** untill after my Wifes Death. I give /her/ also after my Wifes Death, the Loom and one half of the Spinning Wheels. I give and bequeath unto my Said Daughter Elizabeth, one Feather Bed and Bedstead with the furniture, my year old Colt, and one fourth of the Cattle not devised to my Wife and one fourth part of the Bees not divided to my Wife. Sixthly, I give unto my Daughter Sarah **PARKER**, my Negroe Woman **SILLAH** and her Children with their Increase one feather Bed & Bedstead with the Furniture; one fourth part of the Cattle and Bees, not devised to my Wife and a Colt to be raised. I also give unto my Daughter Sarah after my Wifes Death, the Spinning Machine, and one half of the Spinning Wheels; Seventhly, I Give unto my Son Peter **PARKER**, one hundred and ninety two Acres of Land lying on Indian Creek, being the residue of the Land, not heretofore devised to my Son Jacob **PARKER** Reserving to my Wife the privilage herein before mentioned. I Give him also, one fourth part of the Cattle & Bees not divised to my Wife, and the Gun with the back Catch, I likewise give unto my Son Peter **PARKER**, my Negroe Woman **CELIA**, and Negroe Boy **GERRY**, after the Death of my Wife. As I have not mentioned it before in my Will, I do now give unto my Son Jacob **PARKER**, my Negroe Man **ISAAC**, after the Death of my Wife. I Give also unto my Son Peter **PARKER**, the use of the Shed Room in the West end of the House lastly I do hereby appoint my Son Jacob **PARKER** and my Friend Charles E. **JOHNSON** Executors of this my last Will and Testament. In Witness whereof I Elisha **PARKER** have to this my last Will and Testament, Set my hand and affixed my Seal, the day and Year above Written.

Elisha **PARKER** {Seal}

Signed Sealed & published and declared by the Said Elisha **PARKER** the Testator, ~~to be his~~ as his last Will & Testament in the presence of us, who were present at the time of Signing & Sealing thereof
W^m..**PRIVETT**. Jurat}
Saml. **PRIVETT**. Jurat}
The foregoing Will was exhibited in Open Court at June Term 1830, proved by the Oaths of W^m.. **PRIVETT** and Samuel **PRIVETT** the Subscribing Witness's to the Same & Ordered to be Recorded. Test Edm^d. **HOSKINS**, Clk."[81]

The total of 292 acres of land that Elisha[6] **PARKER** bequeathed to his two sons, Jacob[7] and

---

[81] NCSA, C.024.80005, *Chowan County Record of Wills 1768-1799; 1807-1841, Vols. B, C*, C:151-152

Peter⁷ **PARKER**, appears to include the 1791 patent, plus at least 60 more acres of land.  That may be the land his father gave him, prior to writing his will.

Newspapers are often a rich source of information on our ancestors that is otherwise unavailable.  A case in point is the obituary of this Elisha⁶ **PARKER**, transcribed here in full:  "Died, On Friday the 3_th ult. [30 April 1830] Mr. Elisha **PARKER**, in the 86ᵗʰ year of his age, after a long and tedious indisposion, a respectable and industrious farmer of this County.  Mr. **P.** was one of the few remaining relics of the revolution."⁸² Further research may reveal documentation of his Revolutionary War military service.  This notice places his birth circa 1745.

Peter⁷ **PARKER** *(Elisha⁶,Peter⁵,John⁴,Peter³,Thomas²,William¹)* appears on a marriage bond in Perquimans County with Elizabeth **SKINNER** on 26 March 1833.  His bondsman was James L. **BUNCH** and witness was John **WOOD**.⁸³

Peter⁷ **PARKER** was dead by 15 February 1839, the date of a special administrator's bond for Jacob⁷ **PARKER** to administer on the estate of Peter⁷ **PARKER**, deceased, in the sum of $4,000.00.  Thomas **SATTERFIELD** and John M. **JONES** were his bondsmen.⁸⁴

In the account of sales of Peter⁷ **PARKER**'s estate, there is a list of notes that belonged to the heirs of John **BONNER**, deceased, to their guardian Peter⁷ **PARKER**.  The earliest is dated 2 January 1837.⁸⁵ His relationship to John **BONNER**, if any, is unknown to the writer.

The petition of Elizabeth **PARKER** for dower in Peter⁷ **PARKER**'s lands was filed in May Term 1839.  It describes the Chowan and Perquimans lands that he owned and states that Jacob⁷ **PARKER** has been appointed administrator, "and that the said Peter died leaving an only Daughter Ann his heir at law," and asks that dower be allotted to her.

There were two orders for dower of Elizabeth **PARKER**, widow of Peter⁷ **PARKER**.  Both are included here:  "State of North Carolina } Chowan County Court} August Term, 1839.

To the Sheriff of Chowan County, Greeting:
Ordered, That the Sheriff summon a Jury to lay off and set apart by metes and bounds to Elizabeth **PARKER**, Widow of Peter **PARKER** deceased her dower in the lands of her said deceased husband, "situated lying and being in the County of Chowan adjoining the lands of Charles E. **JOHNSON** and others containing about two hundred and Ninety Six Acres, in and upon which said tract of land Elizabeth the Widow of Elisha **PARKER** deceased has her dower-(said Elisha having been the father of the late Peter")  [sic] and make report
Issued 19ᵗʰ September 1839.  Test John **BUSH** Clk  By T. V. **HATHAWAY** Dy Clk"  Report filed 2 Novr. 1839"

"State of North Carolina }
Chowan County Court    }  August Term, 1839.

To the Sheriff of Perquimons County, Greeting:
Ordered, That the Sheriff summon a Jury to lay off and set a part by metes and bounds to Elizabeth **PARKER**, Widow of Peter **PARKER** deceased her dower in the lands of her said deceased husband, "situated lying and being in the County of Perquimons ~~adjoining~~ bounded /by/ the lands of Humphry **ELLIOTT**, Humphry **ALFIN**, Francis **ELLIOTT** and others, containing three hundred and twenty nine & a half Acres more or less."  [sic] and make report.
Issued 5ᵗʰ. September 1839.  Test John **BUSH** Clk  By T. V. **HATHAWAY** Dy. Clk"⁸⁶

The first of these, for the 296 acres in Chowan County, indicates that Elizabeth **PARKER**, widow of Elisha⁶, was still living at that time.  The second, in Perquimans County, makes no mention of her, thus Peter⁷ **PARKER** had probably acquired that land by purchase instead of inheritance.

---

⁸² NCSA, EdEGw-2, Edenton Gazette Jan. 12, 1819-Dec. 21, 1831, Vol. XXVI. No. 19. Edenton, N. C. Thursday Morning, May 6, 1830.  Whole No. 1219.  Third page, fifth column.
⁸³ NCSA, An Index to Marriage Bonds Filed in the NCSA, Groom List, Parish, John R., Fiche #30, Record: 07701077, Bond #000105681, courtesy of Weynette Parks Haun.
⁸⁴ NCSA, G.024.1750499, Chowan County Estates, Record of 1728-1951, Vol. O'Malley-Parrish, Folder: Peter Parker, 1839, Doc. #1258-1259
⁸⁵ Ibid., Doc. # 1318-1319;1322-1325
⁸⁶ NCSA, G.024.1750499, Chowan County Estates, Record of 1728-1951, Vol. O'Malley-Parrish, Folder: Peter Parker, 1839, Doc. #1271-1272; 1273

**Chapter 10**: Peter[3] **PARKER** *(Thomas[2],William[1])*

The report of the commissioners for Chowan County who laid off the dower lands to Elizabeth **PARKER**, on 2 November 1839, is described as "The following parcel of land lying On the South Side of the main Road; to be bounded as follows. – viz: Beginning at the line which divides the lands of Charles E **JOHNSTON** & the land intended as the dower, at the West corner of the same and running the various Courses of the line a South Eastly [sic] Course to a Sufficicient distance so as to Include the Cleared land and the courses of the main Road, to make One Third of all the land, which Peter **PARKER** died siesed [sic] and possessed of in the County of Chowan and which If surveyed, is to be laid out by meets and bounds. We also give to said Widow, the room in the dwelling house, which belonged to Peter **PARKER** at the time of his death."[87]

The report of the Commissioners for Perquimans County contains a slightly better description of that land. It is described as "Begining at a Red oak in Humphry **ELLIOTT**s corner and Running said **ELLIOTT**s line to Humphry **ALPHIN**s line and along said **ALPHIN**s line to a Forked perseman [sic] Tree, thence through the plantation to a white oak nearly South westerly Course & thence the same Course to the lands of the Heirs of John **GOODWIN** Decd then along said line to Job **GOODWIN**s Corner, thence along Jobs line to Samuel **SMITH** line & thence along Humphry **ELLIOTT**s line to the said Red oake the first Station...26th of October 1839..."[88] An inventory and sales of estate for Peter[7] **PARKER**, dated 7 March 1839, mentions "The Ballyhack plantation," which is the parcel located in Ballahack District of Perquimans County.[89]

A petition by Elizabeth **PARKER** and Ann F.[8] **PARKER** for division of slaves of Peter[7] **PARKER**, in November Term 1840, shows that Sarah Ann[8] [sic] **PARKER** died, but no dates are included. Administration on her estate was granted to Wm. R. **SKINNER** "at this term of Court," thus her death most likely occurred a very short time previous to that date. The remainder of this document refers to her as Sarah Elizabeth[8] **PARKER**. Elizabeth and Ann F.[8] **PARKER** request that they each be given half the slaves due from Peter **PARKER**'s estate to Sarah Elizabeth[8], as the only distributees.[90]

On 3 November 1840, William R. **SKINNER** entered into an administration bond on the estate of Sarah Elizabeth[8] **PARKER** in the sum of $1,000.00. Jacob[7] **PARKER** was his bondsman.[91] The above petition was entered into that same court.

On 4 November 1839, William R. **SKINNER** entered into a guardian bond in the sum of $10,000.00, and was appointed guardian to Ann F.[8] **PARKER**, orphan of Peter[7] **PARKER**. His bondsmen were James C. **SKINNER** and Burton W. **HATHAWAY**.[92] He made returns on her account from 1840 through 1847.[93]

On 10 November 1846, Jonathan **WHITE** was appointed and entered into a guardian bond in the sum of $5,000.00 to be guardian to Ann F.[8] **PARKER**, in Perquimans County Court. His bondsmen were Jeptha **WHITE** and Nathan **WINSLOW**. There were certifications of his guardian bonds in November Term, 1849, February Term, 1853, and 31 July 1855.[94] No further information included here.

Willis[6] **PARKER** *(Peter[5],John[4],Peter[3],Thomas[2],William[1])* appears on a Chowan County marriage bond with Elizabeth **TOPPING** 24 May 1790, with Abraham **NORFLEET** as his bondsman.[95]

He made his will in Chowan County, transcribed here in full: "In the name of God Amen I Willis **PARKER** being of sound mind and memory but Calling to mind the mortality of my body and knowing that it is appointed for all men one [sic] to die, do make ordain and Constitute this to be my

---

[87] NCSA, G.024.1750499, Chowan County Estates, Record of 1728-1951, Vol. O'Malley-Parrish, Folder: Peter Parker, 1839, Doc. #1290-1291

[88] Ibid., Doc. # 1274-1275

[89] Ibid., Doc. #1311-1317

[90] Ibid., Doc. #1334-1335

[91] NCSA, G.024.1750499, Chowan County Estates, Record of 1728-1951, Vol. O'Malley-Parrish, Folder: Sarah Elizabeth Parker, 1840 (?) Doc. #1429

[92] Ibid., Doc. #1288-1289

[93] Ibid., Doc. #1354-1362

[94] Ibid., Doc. #1367-1369

[95] Chowan County, NC, Marriage Bonds, http://www.rootsweb.com/~ncchowan/chdnbmarrs-p.htm

last Will and Testament in writing. To wit

First, I lend to my wife Elizabeth **PARKER** the Plantation where I live on and all of my Perishable property during her natural life and after her decease the said land to my Son John **PARKER** to him and to his heirs forever. – by Paying to my daughters Mary **JONES**, Sarah **PARKER** and Elizabeth **PARKER** the Sum of Twenty five Dollars each to them and their heirs forever, and lastly I give the residue of property to my Surviving heirs to Share and Share alike to them and to their heirs forever.

I hereby nominate my Son John **PARKER** my Executor to this my last will and Testament. In testimony whereof I have hereunto Set my hand and Seal affixed [sic] my Seal this 30th.. December 1842.

Willis PARKER {Seal}

Signed Sealed and in presence off Tho.ˢ.. **SATTERFIELD** Jesse **PARKER**."⁹⁶ [No probate date recorded.] A notice was given 5 April 1847, to all creditors and debtors of the estate of Willis **PARKER** that John **PARKER** had qualified as his executor in February Term, 1847.⁹⁷

Isaac⁶ **PARKER** *(Peter⁵·John⁴, Peter³, Thomas², William¹)* appears on a Chowan County marriage bond with Betsey **SMALL** 20 March 1795. His brother, Seth⁶ **PARKER** was his bondsman⁹⁸ No further information.

Seth⁶ **PARKER** *(Peter⁵·John⁴, Peter³, Thomas², William¹)* appears on a Chowan County marriage bond with Elizabeth **PRICE** on 28 September 1791. His brother, Isaac⁶ **PARKER**, was his bondsman.⁹⁹

Seth⁶ **PARKER**, Sr., made his will in Chowan County, transcribed here in full:

"In the Name of God, Amen. Chowan County, August the 24th 1820.

I Seth **PARKER**, Senior, am weak in Body but Sound in mind and memory. Thanks be to Almighty God for the Same, and as its appointed for all men once to die, I make and ordain this to be my last Will and Testament in a manner underneath mentioned, viz. 1st. I recommend my soul to Almighty God to take to himself to deal as he sees fit, and my Body to the dust of the earth to be buried in a Christian like manner by the care of my Executors and Friends that I leave behind. And of this world's Goods, as the Lord has blessed me with in this life, I leave as followeth: 2d. I give and bequeath unto my dear beloved wife Elizabeth **PARKER**, one Negro Man **SAM**, one Mare, her choice, one Yoke of Oxen and Cart, one Horse Cart, one Riding Chair, Three Cows and Calves, Three Ewes and Lambs, Three Stocks of Bees, Two Sows and Pigs, one Plough and Geers, Two Axes, Two Weeding Hoes, and all my Household and Kitchen Furniture, she making no waste of the same, she only to live on during her widowhood, and if she never marries, to her natural life. 3d. I give and bequeath unto my Son Jesse **PARKER**, one Negro Man named **MOSES**, to him the said Jesse **PARKER**, to him and his heirs /and/ [sic] forever. 4th. I give and bequeath unto my Daughter Elizabeth **PARKER** one Negro Man named **DAVE** to her the said Elizabeth **PARKER**, to her and her heirs /and/ forever. 5th. I give and bequeath unto my Daughter Mary **PARKER**, one Negro Man **MAYOR**, to her the said Mary **PARKER**, to her and her heirs and forever. 6th. I give and bequeath unto my son Nathaniel **PARKER**, one Negro Man **SAM**, after the death of my wife, to him the said Nathaniel **PARKER**, to him and his heirs and forever. 7th. I give and bequeath unto my two younger Children, Seth **PARKER** and Sarah **PARKER**, all the rest of my Estate, to be Sold and equal divided betwixt the Two Children, and if they have not enough to make them equal with my other children, the Negroes must be valued, and they must pay in proportion to make them all good alike. Last of all I appoint my son Jesse **PARKER** and my Brother Willis **PARKER** my sole Executors to this my last Will and Testament, conforming, [sic] declaring this and no other to be my last Will and Testament in manner as above said. As witness I hereunto set my hand and Seal, the day and date above written.

his mark

Signed, Sealed, in presence of us.                    Seth  + **PARKER**

---

⁹⁶ NCSA, C.024.80005, Chowan County Record of Wills 1768-1799; 1807-1841, Vols. B,C Vol. C, 1807-1841, C:278

⁹⁷ NCSA, G.024.1750499, Chowan County Estates, Record of 1728-1951, Vol. O'Malley-Parrish, Folder: Willis Parker, 1847, Doc. #1518

⁹⁸ Chowan Co. Marriage Bonds, http://www.rootsweb.com/`ncchowan/chdnbmarrs-p.htm

⁹⁹ Ibid.

**Chapter 10**:  Peter[3] **PARKER** *(Thomas[2],William[1])*

Abs[m]. H. **PRITCHARD**.
Charles **O'NEAL**.

The foregoing Will was exhibited in open Court at December Term /1820/ proved by the oath of Abselom H **PRISHARD**, one of the Subscribing witnesses to the Same, and ordered to be recorded. Test.  Henry **WILLS**, Clk."[100]

An account of the sales of the estate of Seth[6] **PARKER** by his executors is dated 27 December 1820.  Purchasers included the widow, Willis[6], Nathaniel[7] and Jesse[7] **PARKER**, with several neighbors.[101]

Seth[6] **PARKER** mentioned his two "younger children" in his will.  Both were minors at the time of his death.  On 12 March 1823, Willis[6] **PARKER** entered into a guardian bond in the amount of £600 [sic] to be appointed "guardian to Seth and Sarah **PARKER**, orphans of Seth **PARKER**, deceased."  His bondsmen were Henry **ELLIOTT** and William **BIRUM**.[102]  In March Term, 1823, a division of the estate was made, naming Nathaniel[7], Seth[7], Jr., Sarah[7], Jesse[7] and Elizabeth[7] **PARKER**, and Allen **SMALL**, in right of his wife Mary[7].[103]  No further information.  The excellent records of Chowan County will facilitate further tracing of these families.

௫௫௫௫௫௫௫௫௫௫௫௫௫௫௫௫௫௫௫௫௫௫௫௫௫௫௫௫௫௫௫௫௫௫௫௫

Joseph[5] **PARKER** *(John[4],Peter[3],Thomas[2],William[1])* was a witness to the 14 February 1723/24 deed from Moses **FOXWORTH** and wife to John **OVERTON**, as previously noted.  It is estimated here that he was born circa 1702-1703.  He married Sarah **WELCH** some time prior to 1730.

John **WELCH** made his will in Chowan Precinct in the County of Albemarle on 23 April 1730.  He bequeathed to his wife Elizabeth the plantation whereon he then lived, then to his eldest son, Edward **WELCH**, who was to be permitted to live thereon.  He bequeathed to his "eldest daughter Sarah the plantation whereon she now lives that I had of James **MAGLOHAN** with 150 acers of land belonging to it to her and her disposing."  His son John **WELCH** was bequeathed the plantation he had purchased from Nathan **MIERS** on the side of Cock Fighting Branch and son James was to have a parcel of land beginning at the mouth of the Great Pine Branch to its head, then down Cock Fighting Branch to the mouth, then down Poppler Run to the swamp.  This will was witnessed by John **PARKER**, Benjamin **EVANS** and James **PARKER**.[104]  It was proved in Chowan County Court 21 January 1730/31, by the first two witnesses.[105]

The phrase "the plantation whereon she now lives," implies that Sarah was no longer living at home, but was then married and living on the James **MAGLOHAN** property.  Her husband was Joseph[5] **PARKER**, as proved by the following undated petition transcribed here in full:
"Chowan}
precinct  } ss  To the Worship[l] the Justices in Court
Now Setting

The Petition of Joseph **PARKER**
Sheweth

That John **WELCH** of S[d] Precinct about the year 1730 made his last Will in Writing and therein appointed his wife Elizabeth his Execut[rx]. and in the same year dyed leaving four Children and several Legacys to them by the s[d] Will

That Elizabeth applyed for Ltres Testamentary but as your Petit[r] is inform'd never took them Out of the Secretarys Office, nor paid the Legacyes left

That about Two years past the said Elizabeth dyed without Will or Other Disposition of the said Estate

[100]  NCSA, C.024.80005, Chowan County Record of Wills 1768-1799; 1807-1841, Vols. B,C Vol. C, 1807-1841, Vol. C, 1807-1841, C:91-92
[101]  NCSA, G.024.1750499, Chowan County Estates, Record of 1728-1951, Vol. O'Malley-Parrish, Folder:  Seth Parker, 1820, Doc. #1484-1487
[102]  Ibid., Doc. #1494
[103]  Ibid., Doc. #1482
[104]  NCSA, SS Wills, Chowan County
[105]  Haun, *Chowan County North Carolina County Court Minutes Pleas & Quarter Sessions 1730-1745*, c. 1983, 4:#9

That the Eldest son named Edward **WELCH** has Enter'd on the said Estate without Administering thereon According to Law and Embe<u>ze</u>ls the same.

That your Petit[r] having Intermarried with Sarah **WELCH** Eldest Daughter of the said John & Elizabeth Out of the Tender regard he has to the said Orphans as yet remaining Unprovided for. And to prevent further Embezelments of the said Estate prays Administration thereof

And he will pray &c

Tho **JONES** <u>pr</u> petit[r"106]

Although this document is undated, it is proved to have been created some time in the year 1737, as it was read in July Court and it was then ordered to summon Edward **WELCH** to appear at the next court to "shew Cause if any he hath why ye sd **PARKER** should not have Letters of Adm<u>mn</u>: on the said Estate."[107] In October Court of that year, the petition was again continued "for a Summons to issue for John **WALSH** [sic] to appear at ye next Court &ca."[108] The administration was finally granted to Joseph[5] **PARKER** in January Court 1737/38.[109]

His next appearance is on a Chowan County Tax List for 1739. He was listed with one tithable [poll] next to John[4] **PARKER**, who had five.[110] The tax for that year was 10 Shillings on each tithable person in St. Paul's Parish.[111]

The last reference found for this Joseph **PARKER** is a list of masters, mistresses and overseers taken by John **COFFIELD**, Constable, in his district and sworn to before Timy. **WALTON** on 25 October 1762.[112] Joseph's name appears next to Jeremiah **CANNON**, which places him near **CANNON**'s Ferry and Holiday Island. No further information.

---

[106] NCSA, C.024.50005, Chowan Inventory of Estates, 1795-1811; Accts & Sales of Estates, 1707-1790; Civil Suits, Gen. Court & Court of Admiralty, 1706-1740. This petition appears under Civil Suits, within the last one-quarter of the reel. There are no page numbers to reference.

[107] Haun, *Chowan County North Carolina County Court Minutes (Court of Pleas & Quarter Sessions) 1735-1738:1746-1748, Book II*, c. 1983, 46:#75

[108] Ibid., 50:#82-445

[109] Ibid., 53:#87

[110] NCSA, C.C.R. 190, Taxes & Accounts 1679-1754, Tax Lists-Chowan

[111] Fouts, *Vestry Minutes of St. Paul's Parish Chowan County, North Carolina 1701-1776, Second Edition*, c. 1998, 36:#85

[112] NCSA, C.R.024.701.2, Chowan County Taxables 1717-1769

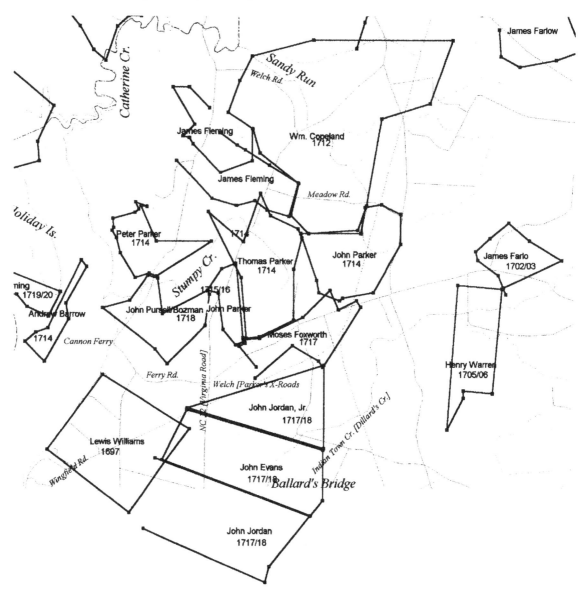

Scale:  0.76 mi/in

Map depicting approximate placement of 1714 land grants to Thomas[3], Peter[3] and John[4] **PARKER** in Chowan County, North Carolina.

## Thomas[4] PARKER *(Peter[3],Thomas[2],William[1])*

Thomas[4] **PARKER** *(Peter[3],Thomas[2],William[1])* was under 16 years of age when he inherited the land whereon his father lived, "with all y[e] remaining part of my land adjoining thereunto below y[e] deep run." The number of acres was not mentioned in Peter[3] **PARKER**'s 1716 will, but is revealed in a deed made from Thomas **PARKER**, of Bertie County, to Joseph **PARKER**, of Chowan County, 30 August 1740. It was 640 acres, sold for £225 and described as "lying on the East Side of Chowan River beginning at the River bank at a Pidg Hickery but Now is washed Down and a Stake set up Deviding between the Said Land and old John **WHITE**s land that was then and So running out from the River by a Line of Marked Trees to a marked White Oak a Corner tree Standing in the Long Branch Then along the head line by its Various Courses to Stumpty Creek Swamp then Down the said Creek by its Various Courses to the River then the River by its Various Courses to the first Station..." The witnesses were John **PARKER**, Thomas **HEARENDEN** and James **PARKER**. It was proved 7 April 1744, by Thomas **HEARENDEN**.[1]

Thomas[4] **PARKER**'s year of birth is estimated here to have been circa 1704. His first recorded purchase of land in Bertie County was from Henry and Mary **ROADS**, "of Onsloe Precinct," 9 March 1731/32. He was then termed as "of Chowan." Thomas[4] **PARKER** paid £130 current money of North Carolina for 400 acres of land described as being "on a Place Called the Cypruss Swamp beging [sic] at a Cyprus standing in the Swamp and Runing on a Strait Course to a pine standing in the Head Line being a Corner tree Betwixt John **BRYAN** and The aforesaid Henry **RODES** and so along the Head Line to a Markt Poplar standing in Tumbling Branch being the Corner tree of the head Line and so down to the Cyprus Swamp to an Elmn standing in the Swamp the Lower Corner tree on the Swamp..." It was witnessed by John **PARKER**, Joseph **PARKER** and James **PARKER**, and was proved 28 March 1740.[2]

On 10 February 1741/42, Thomas[4] **PARKER** purchased 640 acres of land in Bertie Precinct from John **GRAY** for £110. It is described as being "on the West side of Chowan River in St. John's Neck begining at an Elm John **BRYAN**s Corner on the Cypruss Swamp: then along his Line So.. 60[d].. E: 280 pole to a Poplar in Tumbling Branch then No. 8[d]. Et: to a pine in the Head of Femur Branch to Chinkapen Creek then down Chinkapen Creek to the mouth of Cyprus Swamp: thence the windings of the Swamp to the first Station..." John **FREEMAN** and John **WILSON** witnessed this deed and it was proved in February Court 1741/42.[3] This land is located northwest of the community of Colerain, near **GLOVER**'s Crossroads and very near the Bertie/Hertford border.

On 7 April 1742, Thomas[4] **PARKER**, Turner, sold James **FREEMAN**, Planter, 166 acres of land for £33. It is described as "being in St: Johns Neck in Bertie county afores[d]. and Where the s[d] **FREEMAN** Now Dwells Containing by Estimation one Hundred And Sixty Six Acres (More or Less) Butted and Bounded as follows (To wit) Begining at a Live Oak at the Run of Cyprus Swamp Near the mouth of Tumbling al[s] [alias] Gumbling Branch Runing thence up the said Run Various Courses to an Elm Thence South 122 pole to a pine in the Head Line of the Survey thence S:60 E: 158 pole to a pine in Tumbling Branch thence Down the s[d] Branch N. 116 pole to a Poplar thence N. 10 W: 30 pole to a pine Thenc [sic] N: 5 E: 124 pole to the first station as admeasured by John **WYNNS** Deputy Surveyor..." Witnesses were James his ╪ mark **AVERITT** and John **SOWELL** and it was proved in May Court 1743.[4]

On 27 April 1742, Thomas[4] **PARKER**, Turner, sold John **FREEMAN**, Carpenter, 290 acres of land for £60. It is described as "being in St. Johns Neck in Bertie County & where the s[d] **FREEMAN** now Dwells...begining at a Marked Live Oak at the Run of Cypress Swamp Near the Mouth of Tumbling (als: Gumbling) Branch Runing thence Down Cyprus Swamp & up Chinkapen Swamp Run Various Courses to a Cyprus **BUNCH**es Now Corner: thence S[o]. 35: West a Cross Fumur Branch 172

---

[1]  Chowan County, NC, Deed Book A#1:228-229
[2]  Bertie County, NC, Deed Book F:14-15, courtesy of Jim Sizemore of Gatesville, NC
[3]  Ibid., F:314-315, courtesy of Jim Sizemore
[4]  Ibid., F:423-424, courtesy of Jim Sizemore.

Pole to a pine then Sᵒ. 80 Wᵗ. 158 pole to a pine in Tumbling Branch thence Down sᵈ Branch Nᵒ. 116 pole to a poplar Thence N. 10 Wᵗ. 30 pole to a pine thence No 5 E: 124 pole to the first Station as admeasured by John **WYNNS** Deputy Surveyor...” Witnesses were John ꝉ **WELLS**, Bennet his + mark **BAKER** and John **SOWELL**.  It was proved in May Court 1742, by the oath of John **SOWELL**.[5]

On 24 February 1747/48, Thomas⁴ **PARKER**, “Wheelwright,” sold another 150 acres of land to John **FREEMAN**, Wheelwright, for £25.  It is described as lying on the north side of Barbaque Swamp...begining at a cyprus on the North Side of Barbique Swamp running North 20 Eᵗ. 40 pole to a pine in Thomas **MC CLENDON**’s former Line thence Along Said Line No 68 West 80 pole to A pine thence North 50 pole to the Center of three Oaks thence West 180 pole to A live Oak in a Branch on **GREEN**s Line, thence Sᵒ. 112 pole to Barbique Swamp thence Along the Swamp Easterly 240 poles to the first Station Togeather with A Grist Water Mill Standing on the Said Barbique Swamp and Also one Acre of Land lying on the South Side of the run of the Said Barbique Swamp Laid for the use of the Aforesaid Mill which Said Land & Mill we the Said Thomas **PARKER** and John **FREEMAN** bought of Elias **STALLINS** as may Appear by his Deed now on record...”  Witnesses were Benjⁿ. **WYNNS** and Richard his R B mark **BROWN**, proved in May Court 1748.[6]

On 7 August 1752, Robert **WARREN**, of Duplin County, sold 213 acres of land to Thomas⁴ **PARKER**, of Bertie, for 40 Shillings.  It is described as “Beginning at a Cyprus standing on [?] the Cyprus Swamp it being a Corner tree Between John **DAVIS** and Henry **ROADS**, then along their Line to a small Black Oak another of John **DAVIS**’s Corner trees, then along his head Line to a Lightwood Limb being in the ground, being in the Center of three Pines, then by a Line of markt trees to a Pine standing in a Bottom, that Issues out of a branch of the Cyprus Swamp then Down the said Bottom to the said branch, then Down the said branch to the said Swamp, then Down the said Cyprus Swamp to the first Station...”  Witnesses were John **FREEMAN**, Richard **RANER** and Lazarus his L mark **GARRET** and it was proved in May Court 1753.[7]

His final land transaction was made on 10 January 1761, when Thomas⁴ **PARKER**, “blacksmith,” sold 100 acres of land to Hardy **HUNTER**, “Wheel right,” for £21.  It is described as “Beginning on the East Side of Chincop__ Swamp whereon Samuel **OSTEEN** [?] Did live Containing One Hundred Acres, at a pine Edward **BRYANT**s Corner Tree running thence south One Hundred and Ninety pole to a Hickory South Seventy Degrees West Eighty Eight pole to the Corner of two Cyprusses and two Gums on Chincopin swamp thence Down Said Swamp to the first Station...”  Witnesses were William **RICE** and Job **HUNTER** and it was acknowledged by Thomas⁴ **PARKER** in July Court 1761.[8]

Thomas⁴ **PARKER** made his will 27 December 1761, in Bertie County.  It is transcribed here in full: “In the name of God Amen I Thomas **PARKER** of the County of Bertie being weak in body but of Perfect Memory Considering the uncertainty of this Frail and Mortal life do make this my last will and testament in manner and form Following  Vizt first and Principally I recommend my Soul to the almighty when he Shall See fit to Call for it out of this Mortal Body, and as for my Worldly Estate after my Funeral Charges and Just Debts being Paid I Give Devise an[d] Dispose of In the Manner hereafter Mentioned

Imprimis – I Give Devise and bequeath unto my well beloved Son Abraham **PARKER** Two hundred and Fourteen Acres of wood Land Situate in the County of Bertie and on the west Side of Cypress Swamp to the Said Abraham his Heirs and assigns forever

Item I Give Devise and bequeath unto my well beloved Son Peter **PARKER** the Plantation whereon I now Live Containing Two hundred and Twenty Acres being one Half of the Land belong [sic] to the Plantation to the Said Peter his Heirs and assigns forever

Item I Give Devise and bequeath unto my well beloved Son Jacob **PARKER** Two hundred and Twenty Acres of wood Land being the one Half of the Land belonging to the Plantation whereon the Said Thomas **PARKER** Lived and in Bertie County to the Said Jacob his Heirs and assigns forever

---

5  Bertie County, NC, Deed Book, F:353, courtesy of Jim Sizemore.
6  Ibid., G:119-120, courtesy of Jim Sizemore.
7  Ibid., G:496-497, courtesy of Jim Sizemore.
8  Ibid., K:82, courtesy of Jim Sizemore.

Item I Give and bequeath unto my Son Isaa[c] **PARKER** Tenn Pounds Proclamation Money to be paid by his three Brothers Vizt. Peter Abraham and Jacob **PARKER**s My will and Desire is that my son Peter Shall pay unto the Said Isaac in part of Said Tenn Pounds five Pounds the other Brothers Vizt Abraham and Jacob Fifty Shillings Each to the Said Isaac his heirs Exec[rs] adm[rs] or assigns

I Give and bequeath unto my Daughter Elizabeth **PARKER** one Puter Bason being the Largest in the Family to the said Eliz[th] her heirs Exec[s] Adm[s] or assigns

I Give and bequeath unto the three Brothers before Mentioned Peter Abraham and Jacob **PARKER** one Puter Bason to Each of them to them their Heirs Exec[s] adm[s] or assigns

I Give and bequeath unto my well beloved wife Hannah **PARKER** Two Cows also Tw[o] Sows and Piggs to the Said Hannah her heirs Exec[s] Adm[rs] or assigns

Item I Give and bequeath further to my Sons Vizt Abraham and Jacob **PARKER**s one feather Bed to Each of them with furniture to them their Heirs Exec[rs] adm[rs] or assigns

I Give and bequeath unto my son Peter one Feather Bead with Furniture to the Said Peter **PARKER** his heirs Ex[rs] adm[rs] /or/ assigns also my wi[ll] and Desire is that my Two Daughters Vizt Eliz[th] and Mary **PARKER**s Shall have Each of them one Feather Bead and Furniture to them & their heirs & Exec[s] adm[s] or assigns

Item I Give and bequeath unto my three Sons Vizt Peter Abraham and Jacob **PARKER**s all my Tools belonging to my Shops to be Equally Divided between them

Item my will and Desire is that the Residue of Cattle not Mentioned Shall be Given to my Daughter Elizebeth to her and her heirs Exec[s] Adm[s] or assigns

Item I Give and bequeath to my Son Abraham and my Son Peter Each of them a New Chest to them their heirs Exec[s] Adm[s] or assigns

Item I Give and bequeath unto my son Jacob one Case of Bottles to the Said Jacob his heirs Exec[s] adm[s] or assigns

Item I further Give and bequeath unto my well beloved wife Hanna[h] **PARKER** one Case of Bottles to the Said Hannah her hei[rs] Exec[s] adm[s] or assigns

Item I further Give and bequeath unto my Daughter Elizebeth **PARKER** one Riding Mar[e] to Said Elizebeth her heirs Exec[s] adm[s] or assigns

Item my will and Desire is that the Residue of my Personal Estate not before Mentioned Shall be Equally Devided between my three Sons Vizt Peter Abraham and Jacob **PARKER**s them their Heirs Exec[s] adm[s] or assigns

Lastly I ordain Nominate Constitute and appoint my Trusty Friends Vizt. John **FREEMAN** Jacob **LASSITER** & John **MEASELLS** to be my whole and Sole Executors to this my Last Will and testament hereby Revoking all other will or wills by me made In Witness whereof I the Said Thomas **PARKER** being of Perfect mind & memory hath hereunto Set my hand and Seal the 27 Day of December Anno Dom 1761      Thomas [?]**PARKER**
Signed Sealed Published and Delivered in Presents of}
James [?] **HENNEFORD** Simon **VANPELT** Senr James **FREEMAN**"[9]

  This will is from the Will Book in Bertie County Court House, Windsor, NC, and is not the original. The "signature" of Thomas **PARKER** appears more as "peter" than Thomas, but has been verified from the original to be "Thomas."

  There is no date of probate on this will, but Thomas[4] **PARKER** was dead by April 1762, as evidenced by it being exhibited into that court and proved by the oath of Simon **VANPELT**. An inventory of his estate was exhibited into that same court by Jacob **LASITER**. In July Court 1762, it was ordered that Jacob **LASSITER** be permitted to sell so much of the estate of Thomas[4] **PARKER** as would be sufficient to discharge his debts.[10]

  Hannah **PARKER** was most likely a **FREEMAN** by birth, though there is no known marriage record for this couple. John **FREEMAN** sold 50 acres of land in Chowan Precinct to James **SUMNER** 10 October 1740. It lay on the west side of Warrick Swamp, at the mouth of Walnut

---

[9] Bertie County, NC, Will Book A:16-19
[10] Haun, *Bertie County North Carolina County Court Minutes 1740 thru 1743; 1758 thru 1762, Book II*, c. 1977, 94:#574-575;97:588

Branch, Deep Branch and Fox Branch.[11]  This is the neighborhood of Peter[3] **PARKER**.  John **FREEMAN** witnessed the deed from John **GRAY** to Thomas **PARKER** in Bertie County 11 August 1741.  They appear together in other records as well.  No further information included here.

ꕔꕔꕔꕔꕔꕔꕔꕔꕔꕔꕔꕔꕔꕔꕔꕔꕔꕔꕔꕔꕔꕔꕔꕔꕔꕔꕔꕔꕔꕔꕔꕔꕔꕔꕔꕔꕔꕔ

Joseph[4] **PARKER** *(Peter[3],Thomas[2],William[1])* was also under 16 years of age when Peter[3] **PARKER** made his will.  His year of birth is estimated here to have been circa 1706.  Peter[3] bequeathed to Joseph[4] the 240 acres he had purchased of John **EARLY** "lying on y[e] west side of y[e] main branch of Wickacone Creek adjoining to y[e] wht. oake swamp."  This parcel is part of the 1713 patent to John **EARLY** for 486 acres, sold to Peter[3] in 1714, and mentioned in the previous chapter.

On 15 May 1734, Joseph[4] **PARKER** of Chowan Precinct in the County of Albemarle sold 200 acres of land to James **MAGLOHON**, of Bertie Precinct of the same county, for £40.  It is described as "All That Part & Parcell of Land Lying in Bertie precinct aforesaid Begining at the Upper side of the Mouth of the white Oak on Wiccacon Creek Swamp Then up the said White Oak Swamp to the Head Line of the Main survey Then with the said Line to fago Branch Then Down the said Branch to Wiccacon Creek Then down the said Creek and Swamp to the first station..."  It was signed and acknowledged by Joseph[4] **PARKER**, and witnessed by John his X mark **WHITE**, Jr., and Nicholl̲as̲ **FAIRLESS**.[12]  This name has also been spelled "**FERRELL**" and "**FERRILL**," in earlier records.  This parcel will be recognized as the one given to Joseph[4] in his father's will.

An order of Vestry dated 12 March 1742, named John **PARKER** and John **CHAMPEN** as processioners for the "district from the Indian town Creek on which **BALLARD**s bridge stands to Warwick Swamp and so to the bounds of p̲e̲quimons..."  On 7 May 1743, the land of Thomas **HOLLADAY** was processioned with Joseph **PARKER**, Charles **JORDAN** and Ed. **JORDAN** present.  Joseph[4] **PARKER**'s land was processioned with the same witnesses.[13]  Thomas **HOLLADAY** owned part of the land now known as "Holiday Island," in Chowan River, which aids in locating the lands of Joseph[4] **PARKER**.

On 16 September 1738, Franc̲e̲s **THOMAS** made his will in Chowan County.  He named sons Stephen, Frances, John, William and daughter, Elizabeth **THOMAS**, and his wife Mary.  His executors were Joseph **PARKER** "ye Son of Elizabeth **PARKER**," James **PARKER**, Thomas **WARD** Jr. [?] and John **RICE**.  No connection has been made between this man and the Joseph **THOMAS** to whom Peter[3] had sold land prior to 1716.  He lived on a plantation called "the forck of the Duckinstool," which he bequeathed to son Thomas, along with a plantation that had been settled by Benjamin **EVANS**.  This will was witnessed by John **JORDAN**, Edmond his X mark **CONELL** and James **WILLIAMS** and proved 19 January 1739/40.[14]

Joseph[4] **PARKER** may have had other land transactions in Chowan County, but they do not appear to have survived.  He made his will 15 November 1749, in Chowan County.  It is transcribed here in full:

"In the Name of God Amen I Joseph **PARKER** Senr. of the Province of North Carolina In the County of Chowan being sick and weak In body but of Sound and perfect memory thanks be to God for the Same and Calling to mind the mortality and frailty of Man and that it is appointed for all men once to Dye I Doe therefore hereby Constitute appoint and ordain this to be my Last Will and testament In Manner and form following first I Recommend my Soul Into the hands of almighty God that gave it and my body to be buried in Such Christianlike manner as the Executors hereafter Named Shall Deem meet and as to what Ever worldly estate as it hath pleased God to bestow on me In this transitory world I Dispose of the Same In manner and form following///

Item  I give and bequa̲t̲h unto my eldest Daughter Mary **CANNON** one hundred and fifty acers of land known by the name of the Ingen landing begining at the R̲ever aposite and against the line trees upon the Est Side following out to the head line to her and the heirs of her body lawfully begotten for Ever///

---

[11]  Haun, *Chowan County, North Carolina Deed Books: W-1 1729-1738;C-2 1739-1740;D 1748-1806 and various earlier & later dates Vol. I*, c. 1998, 103:#525
[12]  Bertie County, NC, Deed Book D:82-83
[13]  Haun, *Chowan County, North Carolina Miscellaneous Papers 1685-1744, Book I*, c. 1993, 111:#440
[14]  NCSA, SS Wills, 1663-1789 Francis Thomas 1738

Item  I give and bequath unto my Daughter Ruth **PARKER** two [?] Cows and Calfs to be Delivered unto her at my Decease and one feather bed a boulster one Sheet and one blankit to be Delivered unto her at her mothers Death or marige to her and her heirs for Ever.///

Item  I give and bequath unto my eldest Son Nathan **PARKER** the Plantation lying upon S_____ Creeak [about three words missing] Deceased formerly lived [line missing] C_____ by estimation [?] ___acers more or less and one bay hors named Spiser to him and his heirs for ever///

Item  I give and bequath unto my Son Joseph **PARKER** one hundred acres of land Runing a Cross the head of the land whereon he now liveth to him and his heirs for Ever and one Small gun and Shuemakers tools to be Delivered to him at the age of twenty years or marige and fifty acres of land lying in bear Swamp and one Sow and picks to be Delivered unto him at the age of Sixteen years to him and his heires for Ever.//

Item  I give and bequath unto my Son Jacub **PARKER** one hundred acers of land begining upon the Rever and goining upon the Ingen landing land and [torn] the Rever and fifty acers of land lying in bear Swamp and Coopers tooles and one Sow and picks to be Delivered him at the age of Sixteen years to him and his heirs for Ever///

Item  I give and bequath unto my Daughter Penina **PARKER** two Cows and Calfs to be Delivered unto her at the age of Sixteen years or marige to her and her heirs for ever//

Item  I give and bequath unto my Son Jobe **PARKER** the maner Plantation whereon I now liveth Containing one hundred and twenty acres of land to him and his heirs for Ever but if he Duyes without heire It is to fall to Jacub **PARKER** his brother and his heirs for Ever//

Item  My will and Pleasure is that my well beloved wife Ruth **PARKER** Shall have my horse Called Dimond and the Side Saddle at her Disposall for Ever and all the Remainder of my Stock Cattell hoges Sheep and a horse and housall [sic] goods untell her Death or marige and then for my Daughter Penina **PARKER** to have fifty Shillings Virginia Correncee or to the Value In Good or Chattells and then the Rest to be Equally Devided beteen my wife and six youngest Children namely Ruth Nathan Joseph Penina Jacub and Job for ever  Lastly I Constitute apoint and ordain my well beloved wife Ruth **PARKER** and [torn-Richard **PARKER**] to be my Whole Executors of this my last will and testament utterly Renounceing and Revoking and making Void all former will or wills by me formerly made Ratifying and Confirming this only and no other to be my last will and testament In witness whereof I have here unto Sett my hand and Seal this fifteenth day of November and in the year of our lord one thousand Seven hundred and forty Nine          Joseph **PARKER**
Signed Sealed Pronounced and Declared In the presents of Us.
Jereremiah [sic] **CANNON** affirmed  Mary **CANNON**

North Carolina  Chowan County  At a Court held for the said County, at the Court-house in Edenton, the third Thursday in [15] January Anno Dom 1749/50

These may certify that Jeremiah **CANNON**, one of the subscribing Evidences to the within Will, appeared in open Court, and Being a Quaker, affirmed, in due Form of Law, that he was present, and saw Joseph **PARKER** sign, seal, publish and declare the Within, to be and contain his last Will and Testament, and that the said Joseph **PARKER** was Then and at that Time of sound and disposing Memory; and that he also saw Mary **CANNON** the other subscribing Evidence sign her Name thereto at the same Time.  Then also appeared Richard **PARKER**, Executor, in open Court, and took the Executors Oath in due Form of Law.  Ordered that the Honble. Nanthaniel **RICE** Esq. Secretary of this Province, or his Deputy, have Notice thereof, that Letters Testamentary may issue thereon as the Law directs. Test, Will **MEARNS** C. C.”[15]

The birth dates for the children of Joseph[4] **PARKER** *(Peter[3],Thomas[2],William[1])* and his wife, Ruth, are found in the genealogical papers of John T. **CHAPPELL**, a Quaker missionary in China. They are Mary[5], 29 August 1729; Ruth[5], 21 August 1731; Nathan[5], 2 November 1733; Joseph[5], 7 May 1736; Jacob[5], 2 July 1740; Penina[5], 1 March 1744 and Jobe[5], 9 November 1749.[16]

---

[15]  NCSA, NC Wills, Vol. XXIII, p. 53
[16]  Courtesy of Karl William Parker, a descendant of this family.  The dates from these papers are very specific and were possibly taken from a family Bible record, though that cannot be confirmed.

**Chapter 11**: Other descendants of Peter[3] **PARKER** *(Thomas[2],William[1])*

Even though Joseph[4] **PARKER** was not a Quaker, all his children were of that faith. Mary[5] **PARKER** *(Joseph[4],Peter[3],Thomas[2],William[1])* was reported married to Jeremiah **CANNON**, at Perquimans Monthly Meeting, on 6 February 1748.[17]

In Chowan County October Court 1760, the petition of Jeremiah **CANNON** praying to keep a ferry from his plantation on Chowan River, was read and granted. On the motion of Mr. William **CUMMING**, Attorney, that a public road be laid out from Jeremiah **CANNON**'s ferry on Chowan River, to the most convenient place of the Virginia Road leading to the Edenton Road, it was ordered that Charles **JORDAN**, Jacob **JORDAN**, James **PARKER**, Amos **PARKER**, David **WELCH**, Nathan **PARKER**, Thomas **FARMER**, Jesse **COPELAND**, Michael **WELCH**, Bryant **BYRAM**, John **JORDAN** Senr. and John **GORDAN** [sic] Junr. be appointed a jury to lay out the same, and make return thereof. It was then ordered that Jeremiah **CANNON** be allowed the sum of one Shilling and four pence Proclamation Money for a "Man & Horse & Eight Pence Procln. Money for a foot Person to be carried over from his Plantation to **SUMNER**s ~~ferry~~ Island on Chowan River."[18] That island is now known as "Holiday Island" and the **CANNON** Ferry Road intersects with NC State Road 32 at the community of **WELCH**, in Chowan County.

Jeremiah **CANNON** outlived his first wife, Mary[5] **PARKER**, and married again as evidenced by his will made 3 March 1779. He gave to his wife, Rachel **CANNON**, "all the Right and title which I have by Entermarying with her in the lands and plantation formerly belonging unto her former Husband John **SMITH** lying in perquimans County." His daughter Sarah married Benjamin **ARNOLD** and Jeremiah bequeathed to her 400 acres of land in Northampton County, and "bounded upon Hunting quarter Swamp as my Deeds from Robert **HOUSE** and John **GRIFFITH** Shall more fully Set forth..." He mentioned his son Jacob **CANNON** and bequeathed to his son, Joseph **CANNON**, the land whereon he lived and 50 acres in bear Swamp in Perquimans County. He named his son Joseph to be his executor.

It appears from another article of this will that Rachel had children of her own and that Jeremiah made an agreement of distribution of property with her 29 February 1765. Mary[5] had obviously died before that date. This will was probated in June Court 1779. It was not signed, nor were there any witnesses recorded.[19] The children of Jeremiah and Mary[5] **CANNON** appear to have been Sarah[6], Joseph[6] and Jacob[6] **CANNON**.

Ruth[5] **PARKER** *(Joseph[4],Peter[3],Thomas[2],William[1])* was born 21 August 1731. In her father's will, she was termed Ruth "**PARKER**," thus it would appear that she was not married by that date. That is not always the case, but Joseph[4] **PARKER** did call his daughter Mary[5] by her married name. No record of marriage has been found for this woman.

The widow of Joseph[4] **PARKER** was also named Ruth. She was reported married to Thomas **FARMER** at Perquimans Monthly meeting 5 February 1755.[20] When he made his will 18 October 1760, he stated that he was "old and feeble but of perfect memory and Sound Judgment." He named his six children, who were John, Mary, William, Ann, Joseph and Thomas **FARMER**. Caleb **ELLIOT** and Jeremiah **CANNON** were named as his executors.[21] These are all common names in the various **PARKER** families, but most probably did not derive therefrom, in this instance.

On 2 March 1756, Caleb **ELLIOTT**, of Perquimans County, sold 90 acres of a tract in Chowan County to Ralph **BUFKIN**. One of the witnesses was one Jos. **FARMER**.[22] He would most probably have been at least of 21 years of age, which would preclude his being the son of Ruth[5] **PARKER**, daughter of Joseph[4] **PARKER**. It is more likely that a man who described himself as "old and feeble," with grown children, would have married an older woman rather than one nearly the age of his own daughters. In January, 1762, it was ordered in Chowan County Court "that Thomas **FARMER** an infirm Man Seventy years of age be recommended to the Assembly to be exempt from

[17] Hinshaw, William W., *Encyclopedia of American Quaker Genealogy, Vol. I, North Carolina*, c. 1936, p. 66
[18] NCSA, C.024.30002, Chowan County Court Minutes 1755-1772, 1755-1761, p. 523
[19] NCSA, Chowan Co. Wills, C.R.024.801  Jeremiah Cannon 1779
[20] Hinshaw, William W., *Encyclopedia of American Quaker Genealogy, Vol. I, North Carolina*, c. 1936, p. 66
[21] NCSA, Chowan Co. Wills, C.R.024.801.  Thomas Farmer 1760
[22] Chowan County, NC, Deed Book H#1:166, courtesy of Weynette Parks Haun.

paying Taxes." Thomas **FARMER** was dead before October Court 1762, when it was ordered that Caleb **ELLIOT**, executor, sell the perishable estate of the deceased.[23]

Ruth **FARMER** was chosen by Penina[5] and Job[5] **PARKER** to be their guardian in October Court 1762, with Joseph **PARKER** and Jeremiah **CANNON** as her bondsmen.[24] Her guardian bonds for them were entered into on 2 November 1762, in the sum of £100 each. The mark of Ruth **FARMER** appears as "RF."[25] On 27 April 1767, she was discharged from that duty "the parties being of Age & Satisfied."[26] Penina[5] **PARKER** would have been of age on that date, but Jobe[5] would have only been 17 years of age, assuming his date of birth to be correct. That date may well be in error and was possibly 11 November 1745, instead of 1749.

Nathan[5] **PARKER** *(Joseph[4],Peter[3],Thomas[2],William[1])* was born 2 November 1733. He was "liberated to marry" Sarah "**FARLER**" 7 August 1754.[27] The spelling of this name appears to be in error.

James **FARLEE** made his will 12 January 1750/51, wherein he named his wife, Rachel, sons Samuel and James, and daughters Mary **PARKER**, Sarah and Christian **FARLEE**. He appointed John **CAMPBELL**, of Bertie County, as his sole executor. This will was witnessed by William **BOYD**, Jr., Amos **PARKER** and John his [shape of new moon] mark **BACKCUS**.[28] Sarah **FARLEE**, not "**FARLER**," became the wife of Nathan[5] **PARKER**.

Nathan[5] was almost 22 years of age in October Court 1755, when the following entry was made on the record: "The petition of Joseph **PARKER** Jacob **PARKER** and Elizabeth ~~**PARKER**~~ **WELCH** Infants ~~praying that~~ praying that Jeremiah **CANNON** & Nathaniel **PARKER** may be appointed their Guardians Ordered that they be Appointed their guardians and give Security in the Sum of fifty pounds Each."[29]

On 25 October 1755, the Vestry of Saint Paul's Parish met at **CONSTANT**'s Chapel and divided the parish into cantons, or districts, and appointed two freeholders to procession the bounds of all the land in the parish. It was ordered that William **COUPLAND** and Nathan **PARKER** "do Procession All The Lands Included between The Sandy Run and Indian Town Creek, Chowan River and Perquimons."[30] These bounds include the lands of the late Joseph[4] **PARKER**, Nathan[5]'s father.

On 12 October 1754, Nathan[5] **PARKER** received the deed of gift of 150 acres from his cousin, James[5] **PARKER**, as previously mentioned. He had already received an unknown number of acres from his father, lying on Stumpy Creek. Before 1 September 1767, he had moved to Northampton County, as evidenced by a deed from him to Jacob **PERREY**, Jr., on that date. It was for 100 acres beginning at "Stumpy Creek at the mouth of a branch known by the name of the Deep Branch, then up said branch by its various courses to John **DONEN**s line that was formerly then turning said John **DONEN**s line to the center of three white oaks standing in a small branch, Jeremiah **CANNON**s corner trees, down his line to the marsh through said marsh in a direct course with the aforesaid line to the afsd. Stumpy Creek, up said Creek by its various courses to the first station..." Witnesses were Jacob his JP mark **PERRY**, Jeremiah **CANNON** and Ruth her W mark **LILLY**. The following notation appears at the end of this deed: "This Withen Deed of Seal being Part of A Patten granted to John **PARKER** bearing Deat July the first Day Ano: Dom: 1713. October Court 1767. Registered 25 July 1769."[31] There is a possibility that Ruth **LILLY** was Nathan[5] **PARKER**'s sister, but it has not been pursued by this writer.

---

[23] NCSA, C.024.30002, Chowan County Court Minutes, 1755-1772,[1761-1766,] p. 33;p. 87

[24] NCSA, C.024.30007, Chowan County Court Minutes & Reference Docket, Pleas & Quarter Sessions 1762-1772, pages not numbered

[25] NCSA, G.024.1750499, Chowan County Estates, Record of 1728-1951 Vol. O'Malley-Parrish, Folder: Parker, Joseph 1750's, Doc. #1173-1174;1177-1178

[26] NCSA, C.024.50050, Chowan County Orphan Court Docket 1767-1775, p. 4

[27] Hinshaw, William W., *Encyclopedia of American Quaker Genealogy, Vol. I, North Carolina*, c. 1936, p. 66

[28] NCSA, NC Wills, S. S. Chowan County, James Farlee 1750

[29] NCSA, C.024.30002, Chowan County Court Minutes 1755-1772, [1755-1761,] p. 405

[30] Fouts, *Vestry Minutes of St. Paul's Parish, Chowan County, North Carolina 1701-1776, Second Ed.*, c. 1998, p. 79:#177

[31] Chowan County, NC, Deed Book N#1:63

On 18 September 1767, Nathan[5] and Sarah (**FARLEE**) **PARKER** produced certificates from Perquimans Monthly Meeting in Rich Square Monthly Meeting, in Northampton County. He was chosen overseer for Rich Square 16 November 1771. Nathan[5] and family requested a certificate back to Perquimans Monthly Meeting 18 December 1784, when they moved back to Chowan County.[32]

On 24 November 1790, Nathan[5] **PARKER** was granted 50 acres in Chowan County, on the east side of Chowan River. It began at a cypress on the north side of the mouth of Stumpy Creek and running up the river 120 poles to a pine near the river, then south 50 degrees east 130 poles to the creek, then down the various courses of Stumpy Creek to the first station.[33]

On 10 September 1791, Samuel[6] **PARKER** of Chowan sold to Nathan[5] **PARKER**, of the same county, eight acres for £8, described as "Beginning in a Branch known by the name of the Deep Branch in the Pattent Line of said Nathan **PARKER**s Line thence down said Branch to the Second Small Branch or Bottom that makes out of said Deep Branch on the east side thence along a Line of Marked Trees Easterly to the Patten Line divides between the said Land that was formed by Drennings now **CANNON**s thence down said Pattent Line to the first Station it being part of a tract of Land granted to John **PARKER** for 400 acres in a Pattent bearing date July 1st 1713... Samuel his S mark **PARKER**." Witnesses were John **TOPPING**, Jacob **JORDAN**, Junr. and Edward **WELCH**.[34] This is part of the parcel given to Samuel[6] by John[6] and Nathan[5] in 1780, as mentioned before.

On 22 August 1794, John **AVERY** and Penninah his wife sold Nathan[5] **PARKER** 50 acres of land in Chowan, described as "part of a tract of land formerly belonging to Jesse **COPELAND** deceased and by his son in law John **WINSLOW** and Charity **WINSLOW** said Jesse **COPELAND**s Daughter Conveyed to John **AVERY** and Penninah his wife by a deed bearing date the 11 September 1786...Begining on the East side of Chowan River at a Red Oak and Runing up the River ten Chain then S70½E to the head line then S35W to the Corner then the Various Courses thereof Binding on John **BROWNRIGG**s Line down to the River to the first station... John his A mark **AVERY**, Penninah **AVERY**." Witnesses were Rogr [?] **FORD** [?] Jos. **PARKER** and John **HARRILL**.[35]

Nathan[5] **PARKER** had been an elder in his faith for 27 years when he died 28 April 1797.[36] He made his will 9 September 1795, transcribed here in full: "To all to whom these presents shall be read, heard or understood, Know ye that I Nathan **PARKER** of Chowan County and State of North Carolina being of perfect mind and sound Judgment do this 9th day of the Ninth month in the year of our Lord One thousand seven hundred and ninety five do make and ordain this to be my last will and testament in manner and form following, that is to say It is my will that all my Just [?] debts and funeral Expences be discharged by my Executors here after named. Secondly my will and desire is that my loving wife Sarah **PARKER** do have the use of all my lands lying in this County of Chowan during her life. Thirdly I give and bequeath unto my daughter Rachael **WOOTTEN** ten Silver dollars. 4th. I give and bequeath unto my son in Law Arthur **WOOTTEN** the Sum of five shillings to him and his heirs. 5th. I give and bequeath unto my daughter Sarah **ELLIOTT** my plantation and all my land lying in North hampton [sic] County which I bought of Charles **COUNSIL** to her and her heirs forever upon her special trust that she pays to my son Jonathan **PARKER**s two Daughters named [?] Leah and Miriam **PARKER** the sum of Fifty pounds Virginia Money equally divided between them and delivered to them as they may arrive to the age of twenty years to them and their heirs forever 6th. I give and bequeath unto my said daughter Sarah **ELLIOTT** my plantation and Land which I bought of John **AVERY** in Chowan County to her and her heirs forever after the death of my wife. 7th. I give and bequeath unto my daughter Lydia **ELLIOTT** my plantation whereon I now live and all my land being in this County to her and her heirs forever after the death of my wife upon her Special trust that she pays to my daughter Rachaels son Jonathan **WOOTTON** the sum of fifteen pounds Virginia Money delivered to him after the death of my wife to him and his heirs forever. Eigh<u>tl</u>y My will and desire is that my two Grandsons namely Jonathan **WOOTTEN** and Nathan **WOOTTEN** do have two full years schooling and the Expence be paid out of my Estate by my Executors hereafter named. 9th.

---

[32] Hinshaw, William W., *Encyclopedia of American Quaker Genealogy, Vol. I, North Carolina*, c. 1936, p. 250

[33] Chowan County, NC, Deed Book S#2:45

[34] Ibid., S#2:213

[35] Ibid., S#2:380

[36] Hinshaw, William W., *Encyclopedia of American Quaker Genealogy, Vol. I, North Carolina*, c. 1936, p. 15

My will is that my loving wife Sarah **PARKER** may have the use of all the remainder of my Estate during her life or till marriage, if she should not marry my will is that all the remaining part of my Estate be equally divided at the time of her Death between my two Daughters Sarah **ELLIOTT** & Lydia **ELLIOTT** yet if she should marry my will is that all the remaining part of my Estate be equally divided between my wife and my afore mentioned two Daughters Sarah & Lydia **ELLIOTT** to them and their heirs forever 10th and Lastly I hereby make and ordain My Brother Job **PARKER** and my Cousin Joseph **PARKER** Executors of this my last will and testament in manner and form abov [sic] said  In Witness wherof I the said Nathan **PARKER** have to this my last will and testament set my hand and seal as above Written                    Nathan **PARKER**

Signed Sealed and deliverd in presence of Jos **LIVETT**  Jut [Jur [?] Jos **SCOTT** Jr

The above and foregoing will was exhibited and proven in open court at June Term 1797 by the oath of Jos **LIVETT** a subscribing Witness thereto at the same time Jos **PARKER** one of the within named Executors appeared and took the necessary oaths for his qualification, ordered that letters testamentary issue thereon  Jas **NORFLEET** clk"[37]

Two of Nathan[5] and Sarah **PARKER**'s children predeceased them, thus are not mentioned in this will.  Jonathan[6] **PARKER** was born 1 April 1755.  Rachel[6] was born 17 April 1759.  Ruth[6] was born 6 February 1762, and died 21 April 1779.  Sarah was born 13 February 1767.  Nathan[6] was born 30 January 1770, and died 12 June 1784.  Lydia[6] was born 16 May 1772.[38]

Rachel[6] **PARKER** was married to Arthur **WOOTEN**, at Rich Square Meeting House 16 February 1783.[39]

Lydia[6] **PARKER** was reported married to Exum **ELLIOTT** 4 August 1790, in Perquimans Monthly Meeting.[40]  She was married for a second time, as Lydia **ELLIOTT**, to William **MURPHY** who appeared on a Chowan County marriage bond with her dated 2 October 1797. James **BRINN** and Wm. **NORFLEET** were his bondsmen.[41]

On 10 August 1805, William **MURPHRY** and wife sold William **WARD** an unspecified number of acres "for and in consideration of the Sum of Forty five Dollars to be paid to Sarah **PARKER** Widow of Nathan **PARKER**, yearly for and during the Natural life of Sarah **PARKER**, it being for the rent of the old Plantation to be paid by the sd. William **WARD**" on a "Certain tract or parcell of land whereon Exum **ELLIOTT** last lived on-at or before his death.  It being the said William **MURPHRY** & Lydia **MURPHRY**s his wifes Dower with all necessary buildings thereunto belonging and he the sd. Wm. **WARD** is to rent out the sd. Plantation after the Experation of Four years and to pay all that he gets over $45 for his Trouble unto the said William **MURPHRY** or his heirs or assigns for and during the Natural life of Sarah **PARKER**, then to be Void..."  This deed was signed by William **MURPHRY** and Lydia her X mark **MURPHRY**, and witnessed by Humphrey **WARD**.[42]  Sarah **PARKER** died 10 May 1813.[43]  No further information.

Joseph[5] **PARKER** *(Joseph[4], Peter[3], Thomas[2], William[1])* was born 7 May 1736.  He received a total of 150 acres of land in his father's will, then another 100 from his cousin, James[5] **PARKER**, in 1754.

On 28 December 1764, Joseph[5] **PARKER** gave a deed of gift "for divers Good Causes and Considerations, but more Especially for the love and Good will I do Bear and have to my well beloved brother, Job **PARKER**," of 100 acres described as being "on the North East Side on chowan river and bounded as followeth beginning at a pine a corner tree on the South East Side of said Job **PARKER**'s land Joining upon Thomas **HOSKINS** land then running by a direct line to a poplar a Corner tree in the long Branch then along said Branch by Various courses to a Gum a Corner tree in Said Branch then along a line of marked trees to the East Side of Sd. Job **PARKER**'s land then along said **PARK-**

---

[37]  NCSA, C.024.80004, Chowan County Wills, Record of 1760-1772; 1785-1794, Vol. 1, A, A:284-285

[38]  Hinshaw, William W., *Encyclopedia of American Quaker Genealogy, Vol. I, North Carolina*, c. 1936, p. 223

[39]  Ibid., p. 250

[40]  Ibid., p. 66

[41]  Chowan County, NC, Marriage Bonds, 1741-1868, contributed to the Chowan NC GenWeb Project by Dayle Noble Biba at http://www.rootsweb.com/~ncchowan/chdnbmarrs-m.htm#M

[42]  Chowan County, NC, Deed Book C#2:231

[43]  Hinshaw, William W., *Encyclopedia of American Quaker Genealogy, Vol. I, North Carolina*, c. 1936, p. 223

ERs line to the first station it being part of a Pattern Granted to Lewis **WILLIAMS** for 640 acres Bearing date May 15th 1697...” Joseph[5] signed his name and this deed was witnessed by Wm. **COPELAND**, Nathan **PARKER** and Josiah **COPELAND**.[44] This land is easily recognized as having been purchased from William and Susannah **WILLIAMS** in 1706, by his grandfather, Peter[3] **PARKER**.

This deed was mistakenly recorded in a Chowan County Will Book, which has been misleading to other researchers in that they believed it to be an actual will. It was literally lost to the parties involved, for nearly 11 years later, it was rewritten with some interesting differences. It is abstracted here. On 2 June 1775, “Joseph **PARKER** of the County of Northampton & province of North Carolina to Job **PARKER** of the County of Chowan...for and in Consideration of £30...100 Acres being part of a Tract of Land granted to Lewis **WILLIAMS** by Patent for Six hundred and forty Acres bearing Date May the 15th day 1697 & bounded as followeth begining in a line that divides between sd. Job **PARKER**’s Land and Thomas **HOSKINS**’s that was formerly over half a Mile from the River in a small pond, known by the name of the Perseman pond at three pines at the sd. Job **PARKER**’s corner then along **HOSKINS**’s line to a corner a poplar in the long branch then along the head line by its various courses to another corner in Jacob **JORDAN**’s line then turning towards the River along the Patent line to a corner near the head of the little House neck Branch then along a line of marked Trees to the first Station...” Josiah **COPELAND**, Nathan **PARKER** and Jacob **PARKER** witnessed this deed.[45]

Joseph[5] **PARKER** and Jacob[5] **PARKER** produced certificates in Rich Square Monthly Meeting, “of unity & clearness in relation to marriage,” dated 6 February 1765. On 17 January 1767, Joseph[5] **PARKER** requested a certificate to Isle of Wight County, VA, to marry. Sarah, wife of Joseph[5], produced a certificate from Western Branch Monthly Meeting, dated 23 July 1768.[46] Sarah’s maiden name is unknown to this writer.

Joseph[5] **PARKER** made his will in Northampton County, NC, 2 February 1792, probated in June Court of that year. He named his wife, Sarah, and bequeathed to his son Jeremiah[6] the plantation whereon Matthew **GRIFFIN** and John **NURNEY** formerly lived. He had purchased this land from William **WILLES** and said **NURNEY**, although the deed was taken of said **GRIFFIN**. He bequeathed 245 acres of land to son Josiah[6] “the plantation whereon I now live and all the land I bought of Thos. **HAYS** and John and Matthew **GRIFFIN**.” Josiah[6] was to bear the expense for a framed house for Joseph[5]’s son, Alexander[6] **PARKER**. He bequeathed to Alexander[6] the land he had purchased of John **HAYS**, John **LEMMON** and John **PARKER**, and mentioned a daughter, Judith[6] **PARKER**. His executors were to be Josiah[6] **PARKER** and cousin Isaac **PARKER**. Jacob **PARKER** and Rhoda (X) **JORDAN** were witnesses.[47]

Records of Rich Square Monthly Meeting show that Joseph[5] **PARKER** died 8 April 1792, and Sarah died 14 March 1804. The births of their children are listed as Jeremiah[6], born 25 January 1767 [?]; Josiah[6], born 4 October 1769; Alexander[6], born 24 September 1771, and Judith[6], born 4 September 1776.[48]

Jeremiah[6] **PARKER** requested a certificate to Welles Monthly Meeting 20 June 1789, to marry. This date is in doubt, as Jeremiah **PARKER** was reported married to Keron **NEWBY** on 6 May 1789, in Perquimans Monthly Meeting. On 1 April of that year, Jeremiah produced a certificate from his monthly meeting, to marry, and Keran **NEWBY** requested a certificate to Rich Square Monthly Meeting.[49] Their children were listed as Sarah[7], born 10 January 1790; Robert[7], born 13 March 1792; Jemima[7], born 27 January 1795; Richard[7], born 14 October 1797; Catharine[7], born 28 June 1800; Mary[7], born 9 June 1803, died 5 November 1805, and Isaac[7], born 22 September 1806. On 21 May 1814, Jeremiah[6] **PARKER** was recommended an elder, along with his wife, Keren

---

[44] Chowan County, NC, Will Book B:98-99

[45] Chowan County, NC, Deed Book Q#1:269

[46] Hinshaw, William W., *Encyclopedia of American Quaker Genealogy, Vol. I, North Carolina*, c. 1936, p. 250

[47] Hofmann, Margaret M., *Northampton County, North Carolina 1759-1808, Genealogical Abstracts of Wills*, c. 1975, p. 78, Will Book 2:11

[48] Hinshaw, William W., *Encyclopedia of American Quaker Genealogy, Vol. I, North Carolina*, c. 1936, p. 223

[49] Ibid., p. 66

**PARKER**. They, along with their children, Robert[7], Jeremiah[7], Richard[7], Jemima[7], Catharine[7] and Isaac[7], requested a certificate from Rich Square Monthly Meeting to White Water Monthly Meeting, Wayne County, Indiana.[50] No further information.

Josiah[6] **PARKER**, son of Joseph[5], married Martha **PEELE**, at Rich Square Meeting House 21 March 1792.[51] Their children are also listed. The first child was Samuel[7], born 20 February 17—[torn]; Joseph[7], born 26 February 17—[torn], died 1 December 17—[torn]; Rebecca[7], born 4 January 17—[torn]; William[7], born 5 December 1800; Nathan[7], born 30 July 1805; Julia[7], born 18 August 1806; Martha[7], born 29 December 1809, and Phebe May[7], born 14 January 1813.[52]

Alexander[6] **PARKER**, son of Joseph[5], requested a certificate from Rich Square Monthly Meeting to Jack Swamp Monthly Meeting, to marry 20 December 1794. He produced that certificate in Jack Swamp 3 January 1795, and was reported married to Mary **HICKS** 7 February 1795. Alexander[6] **PARKER** died 1 October 1814. His family is listed as child Mary[7], born 28 February 1796; Sarah[7], born 6 May 1798; Judith[7], born 27 July 1800; Mildred[7], born 2 October 1802; Elizabeth[7], born 6 March 1805; Rebecca[7], born 2 November 1807 and Joseph[7], born 2 June 1811.[53]

Judith[6] **PARKER**, daughter of Joseph[5] of Northampton County married William **COPELAND** at Rich Square Meeting House on 25 March 1795.[54] No further information on these families included here.

Jacob[5] **PARKER** *(Joseph[4],Peter[3],Thomas[2],William[1])* was born 2 July 1740, in Chowan County. He was bequeathed a total of 150 acres in his father's will in 1749/50. On 12 October 1754, his cousin James[5] **PARKER**, made a deed of gift to him for 100 acres, as previously mentioned.

He was still of Chowan on 16 August 1763, when he sold Jeremiah **CANNON** 60 acres of that last parcel for £40. It is described as "Lying and bounding upon the East side of Chowan River being part of a pattent granted to John **PARKER** bearing date July 1st 1713 bounded as followeth Beginning at a pine in the River bank and upon the south side and joining upon a Branch known by the name of the White Oak Branch thence along a line of new marked trees to a pine an old pine tree Standing near said Branch being a dividing line between said Jacob **PARKER** and Job **PARKER** then along said line to a pine a corner tree between said Jacob **PARKER** and Thos **HOSKINS** land then along a direct line of marked trees to a pine a corner tree between said Jacob **PARKER** and the aforesaid Jeremiah **CANNON** land then along a line of marked trees on the south side of said Jeremiah **CANNON** and to the aforesaid River then along said River to the first station, not debaring the said Job **PARKER** of vent for his water in the afsd. Branch..." William **COPELAND** and Nathan **PARKER** witnessed this deed.[55]

Jacob[5] **PARKER** removed to Northampton County, NC, and married Rhoda **DRAPER** 8 September 1765, as recorded in Rich Square Monthly Meeting.[56] Their children are listed as Abigail[6], born 22 February 1766; Isaac[6], born 2 November 1769; Jacob[6], born 9 April 1771; Peninah[6], born 19 July 1776; Joseph[6], born 11 May 1778; Micajah[6], born 4 November 1780; Benjamin[6], born 22 March 1783; Jesse[6], born 12 July 1785, and George[6], born 13 January 1788.[57] No further information.

Peninah[6] **PARKER**, married Jonathan **BLANCHARD** at public meeting on 21 June 1789. Isaac[6] **PARKER**, married Sarah **PEELE** at Rich Square Meeting House on 20 March 1793. Jacob[6] **PARKER**, married Faith **JUDKINS** on 1 October 1794. Abigail[6] **PARKER** married James **JUDKINS** at Rich Square Meeting House 21 January 1801. Joseph[6] **PARKER** married Margaret **JUDKINS** at Rich Square Meeting house 21 October 1801.[58] No further information.

Micajah[6] **PARKER** requested a certificate to Short Creek Monthly Meeting, in Jefferson County, Ohio, 20 April 1805. His brother, Joseph[6] **PARKER**, made the same request on 20 July of

---

[50] Hinshaw, William W., *Encyclopedia of American Quaker Genealogy, Vol. I, North Carolina*, c. 1936, p. 223;250;251

[51] Ibid., p. 250

[52] Ibid., p. 223

[53] Ibid., p. 250; 222

[54] Ibid., p. 250

[55] Chowan County, NC, Deed Book L#1:66

[56] Hinshaw, William W., *Encyclopedia of American Quaker Genealogy, Vol. I, North Carolina*, c. 1936, p. 250

[57] Ibid., p. 222

[58] Ibid., p. 250

that year. Micajah[6] returned the certificate granted to him in 1805, on 15 February 1806. Faith **PARKER**, and her daughters, were granted a certificate to Short Creek 15 March 1806. Jacob[6], Jr., and his family were granted a certificate to Short Creek 21 June of that year.[59]

On 18 June 1808, Jacob[5] **PARKER**, Sr., with wife Rhoda and son George[6], was granted a certificate to Short Creek Monthly Meeting, Jefferson Co., OH.[60]

On 22 November 1808, Micajah[6] **PARKER** married Julia **PEELE** at Rich Square Meeting House. On 15 September 1810, Micajah[6] requested a certificate to Short Creek Monthly Meeting, in Jefferson County, Ohio, and Julia and their daughter, Elizabeth[7] **PARKER**, were granted a certificate to the same place. Some of the other children of this couple are revealed when Julia **PARKER**, with minor children Elisabeth[7], Isaac[7], Sarah[7], Jane[7] and Rhoda[7] were all received on certificate from Short Creek Monthly Meeting on 20 September 1823. Their daughter, Elizabeth, married John **PEELE** at Rich Square Meeting House on 25 November 1835.[61] Elizabeth[7] **PARKER**, daughter of Micajah[6] and Julia, was born 18 August 1809. Julia **PARKER** died 13 August 1863, in Northampton County.[62] No further information.

Isaac[6] **PARKER**, with his wife, Sarah and their children, Mary[7], John[7], Rhoda[7], Martha[7] and Abigail[7], also removed to Short Creek upon being granted a certificate 18 June 1808.[63] No further information.

---

[59] Hinshaw, William W., *Encyclopedia of American Quaker Genealogy, Vol. I, North Carolina*, c. 1936, p. 251

[60] Ibid., p. 251

[61] Ibid., p. 251

[62] Ibid., p. 223

[63] Ibid., p. 251

**Chapter 12**: Jobe[5] **PARKER** *(Joseph[4], Peter[3], Thomas[2], William[1])* and some of his descendants

## Jobe[5] PARKER *(Joseph[4], Peter[3], Thomas[2], William[1])*

Jobe[5] **PARKER** *(Joseph[4], Peter[3], Thomas[2], William[1])* was supposedly born 9 November 1749, but that date has been questioned in the previous chapter. He received 120 acres of land in his father's will, and another 140 acres from his cousin, James[5] **PARKER**, in 1754. His name is spelled both "Jobe" and "Job," in the various records in which he appears. On 28 December 1764, Joseph[5] **PARKER** gave a deed of gift of 100 acres of land to his "beloved brother," Job **PARKER**.[1] He continued to acquire land throughout his lifetime. He, too, was a Quaker.

On 1 August 1770, Job[5] **PARKER** was disowned for "marrying out of society," in Perquimans Monthly Meeting.[2] His first wife's name is not mentioned in the Quaker records, but it is revealed in a Chowan County deed from Job **PARKER** to Joseph and Elizabeth Margaret **MEREDITH**, of Hampton, VA. This deed is incorrectly listed in the Chowan County Grantee Index as "James **MC CULLOCH** To Mary **MC CULLOCH**." It is extracted here:

"Whereas in consideration of a decree of the high Court of Chancery in Great Brittain, James **MC CULLOCH** of Camrly [?] in the kingdom of Ireland esquire became possessed as surviving trustee of the principal of £797.12.1 Sterlg new South sea Annuity the 25th. day of October 1755 which sum he held in trust to pay the dividends and interest thereof to Mrs Mary **MC CULLOCH** wife of Henry **MC CULLOCH** esquire formerly secretary of the province of North Carolina for her life for her separate use and after her death to pay such dividends and interest to the said Henry **MC CULLOCH** for his life in case he should survive her an [sic] after the death of the survivor of them then the principal to be divided among the children of the said marriage and whereas the children of the said marriage were Henrietta May **MC CULLOCH** (now married to Mark **BROWNRIG**) Dorothy Beresford **MC CULLOCH** now married to Jordan **WHITE**, Elizabeth Margaret **MC CULLOCH** (now married to Joseph **MEREDITH** of Hampton in Virginia) and Penelope **MC CULLOCH** who married Job **PARKER** under mentioned and di/e/d in the year 1772 having one child who after wards died, and whereas by the death of the said James **MC CULLOCH** the arrears of the said principal sum dividends and interest came into the hands of William **MC CULLOCH** of the City of Doublin [sic] esquire as representative of the said James **MC CULLOCH** his brother and a considerable part of the money yet remains due by an account stated by the said William **MC CULLOCH** that on the 20th of April 1776 there was due the sum £1309.16.3) and the said Job **PARKER** undermentioned conceives himself entitled to receive his wifes share of the principal sum, dividend and interest due at the time of her death, the said Job **PARKER** doth therefore for and in consideration of the sum of one hundred and fifty pounds currant mony of Virginia to him in hand paid by the said Joseph **MEREDITH** (husband of the above mentioned Elizabeth Margaret) at or before the sealing or delivery of these presents (the receipt whereof he doth hereby acknowledge and thereof and therfrom entirely acquit and discharge the said Joseph **MEREDITH** and Elizabeth Margaret his wife and also for divers good causes and considerations him hereunto moving, grant bargain and sell assign and set over to the said Joseph **MEREDITH** and Elizabeth Margaret his wife all the share, interest, concern of him the said Job **PARKER**, either as husband of the said Penelope or as representative of the child of him and the said Penelope above mentioned or any part thereof and all the estate, right, title, claim and demand whatsoever which he hath in & to the same or any part thereof, to have and to hold... In witness Whereof the said Job **PARKER** hath hereunto set his hand and affixed his seal the twenty eighth day of March in the year of our Lord one thousand seven hundred and eighty six.

Job **PARKER** (Seal)

sealed & delivered in the
presence of H. **BOND**} State of North Carolina} March term 1786
E. **NORFLEET**     } Chowan County     } Present the worshipfull Justices
The within deed was duly proved by Henry **BOND** one of the subscribing witnesses. Ordered that it may be registered. Test Lott **BURNSTIE** [?] C. C.

---

[1]  Chowan County, NC, Will Book B:98-99
[2]  Hinshaw, William W., *Encyclopedia of American Quaker Genealogy, Vol. I, North Carolina*, c. 1936, p. 66

Registered Wm.. **RIGHTON** Regr."[3]

Penelope **PARKER**'s estate was still in the legal system as of 26 March 1788, when Joseph **MEREDITH** submitted the following document: "Inventory of Penelope **PARKER**'s estate according to my Calculation is four Hundred and Twenty Seven pounds one Shilling & Nine pence three farthings Sterling money and now in the hands of William **MC CULLOCH** Esqr. of the City of Dublin. March 26th. 1788." Joseph **MEREDITH** was Penelope's administrator.[4]

Penelope **PARKER** was more likely dead late in 1771, as Job[5] **PARKER** "condemned his outgoings" and was reinstated in Perquimans Monthly Meeting on 1 January 1772.[5] Job[5] requested a certificate to Rich Square Monthly Meeting, to marry, on 2 August 1775. He married Isabel **PEELE** at Rich Square Meeting House, on 20 August 1775.[6]

As of 1764, Job[5] **PARKER** owned 360 acres of land. On 6 October 1789, Jonathan **JORDAN** sold him 170 acres, described as "beginning at the Mouth of A Branch makeing out of Stumpey Creek Swamp Known by the name of the Meeting house Spring Branch So up the said Branch to a line of Marked Trees, so along the said line a Cross the Main Road to a White Oak Standing on the Side of an Old field then thro the old field to a red oak from thence along a line of marked trees to a Pine in Edward **WELCH**es line thence along his line to Poplar Run, thence down said run to Stumpey Creek Swamp then down the Swamp to the first station..." It was signed by Jonathan **JORDAN** and Mary **JORDAN** and was witnessed by Jacob **CULLINS**, James his X mark **WOODWARD** and Rachel her X mark **WOODWARD**.[7]

On 6 March 1791, John[6] **PARKER** of Perquimans County, sold 300 acres to Job[5] **PARKER** of Chowan county. It is described as being "in County of Chowan beginning on the East side of Middle Creek Swamp at a bottle Ended black Gum in Samuel **PARKER**s Line thence along said Line nearly East to the main Road thence Slanting a Cross the said Road to a pine Thence the Courses of the Road Southerly 120 pole to a Black oak thence S20E53 pole to a pine thence S47E36 Pole to an old pine Stump on the South East side of the Pynewoods Road Jacob **JORDAN**s line. Thence N47E146 Pole to the Centre of two Pine and an oak thence South East by a line of Marked Trees a Cross the Pynewoods Road to a Corner a Dead pine Standing in the Lowgrounds thence Nearly North East to a Corner in the Edge of the lowgrounds Near the Corner of Edward **WELCH**es Old plantation Thence nearly West to a Red oak in an old field thence to a white Oak near the Branch thence by a line of marked trees near the Same Course to Middle Creek thence down the said Swamp to the first station..." This John **PARKER** used the mark of "J." It was witnessed by Jacob **JORDAN** Junr., Moses **HOBBS** and William **HIRBY**.[8]

Just six days later, on 12 March 1791, John **TOPPING** sold Job[5] **PARKER** 62 acres for 100 "Spanish Mill'd Dollars." It is described as beginning "on west side of Long Branch at a Pine thence nearly a west Course to a large pine a Corner tree thence nearly No. by a line of marked Trees to a Corner the tree go an [sic] Thence nearly east to a post oak thence to a Red Oak thence to a forked pine thence to the sd. long branch near the going over place thence down the said branch to the first station adjoining the Lands of John **BROWNRIGG**, John **LAVEY** and Thomas **MING**." Witnesses were Jacob **JORDAN** Junr., Willis **GRIFFIN** and John **FULLENTEN**.[9] John **TOPPING** sold Job[5] another three acres 19 June 1793. Nathan[5] and Joseph **PARKER** witnessed that deed and it was proved in June Term, 1796, by the affirmation of Nathan[5] **PARKER**.[10]

On 9 December 1796, Joseph **JORDAN** sold Job[5] **PARKER** 60 acres in Chowan County, described as "Beginning at a Black Gum said **PARKER**s and **CANNON**s Corner tree in the long Branch thence down the middle of the Branch 25 chain to a poplar said **PARKER**s and **MING**s Corner tree thence continuing down the Branch 7¾ Chain to two ash's a gum and buck Beach in the Branch oppo-

---

[3]  Chowan County, NC Deed Book R#2:484-486

[4]  NCSA, G.024.1750499, Chowan County Estates, Record of 1728-1951, Vol. O'Malley-Parrish, Folder: Parker, Penelope 1788, Doc. #1240-1241

[5]  Hinshaw, William W., *Encyclopedia of American Quaker Genealogy, Vol. I, North Carolina*, c. 1936, p. 66

[6]  Ibid., p. 66;250

[7]  Chowan County, NC, Deed Book S#2:168

[8]  Ibid., S#2:206

[9]  Ibid., S#2:202

[10]  Ibid., U#1:74

site the mouth of a small branch then up the small branch joining Bond **JAMISON**s land 20¾ Chain to a pine at the head of the branch thence N4dE34 Chain to a Red oak in Jacob **JORDAN**s line thence N45W to the first station..." Trecey her X mark **JAMISON** and Jos. **PARKER** witnessed that deed.¹¹

On 20 August 1800, Job⁵ **PARKER** sold 50 acres to John **FULLENTON**, described as "Beginning on the west side of Long Branch at a marked pine, adjoining the land of Thomas **BROWNRIGG**, thence nearly a W. course, by a line of marked trees to a pine, a Corner thence nearly No. by a line of marked trees, thence nearly E to a post oak, a red oak, a forked pine thence to the said Long branch near the crossing place adjoining Wyley **MING**s land thence down the long branch to the first station..." David **WELCH** and John **HARRELL** witnessed this deed.¹²

On 26 September 1801, Jacob **JORDAN** sold Job⁵ **PARKER** his interest in the grist and saw mills built by Jacob **JORDAN**, Esquire, deceased, described as built "a Cross the North East prong of **BALLARD**s Creek Swamp adjoining the lands of Henry **EALBANKS** & Nicholas **STALLINGS** Esqr. decd. with 1 acre of land at each end of the dam which was laid off by a Jury of Men..." Thos. **BROWNRIGG** and Jno. **LEARY** witnessed this deed.¹³

On 25 February 1802, Jacob **JORDAN** disposed of more of his lands by selling Job⁵ **PARKER** 226 acres in Chowan, described as "begining in the run of the swamp at **JORDAN**s Bridge thence up sd run the various courses thereof to the Mouth of the Hog Yard Branch thence up sd branch the various courses to the head thence by a line of marked trees to the corner a dead pine Nathan **JORDAN**'s & Jacob **JORDAN**s corner tree thence N42W274p to the Road thence along the road an Eastrd:ly course to the Duck Pond Pond [sic] Branch thence down the various courses of the run to the run of the swamp thence up the various courses of the run to the first station..." James **CHAPPELL** and Miles **HOBBS** witnessed this deed.¹⁴

Several of these purchases will be recognized in Job⁵ **PARKER**'s last will and testament, made 11 February 1812, probated December Term of that year.  It is transcribed here in full:

"To all to whom these presents may come, know ye that I Job **PARKER** of the County of Chowan and State of North Carolina now living at Harmony Hall being weak in body but of sound and perfect understanding as heretofore, thanks to ___ do Constitute and appoint this and no other to be my last will and testament in manner and form following

First-First of all it is my will and desire that all my just debts be discharged by my Executors hereafter named out of the rents of my fisheries and the old plantation on the river and long neck field, except a fourth part of said rent which is for my son Joseph **PARKER**.

Secondly-It is my will and desire that my daughter Martha should have sufficient schooling to fit her for common business and the expences paid out of my Estate.

Thirdly-I give to my beloved wife, Isabel **PARKER** one bed and furniture, six chairs, one chest, one horse and riding chair, one cow and calf, two ewes and lambs, all of her own choice, also all the rents of the minor children's land until they arrive at the age of twenty one.  Except the land or any part thereof should be sold.  I also lend to my said wife as long as she remains to be my widow all the perishable part of my Estate (Except what is hereafter given to my children.)  I also lend to her while she remains to be my widow my plantation land where I know live.

Fourthly-I give and bequeath to my son Joseph **PARKER** my plantation and land which I bought of Jonathan **JORDAN** also the land where Joseph **SCOTT** formerly lived adjoining Samuel **PARKER**'s land thence from his Corner tree a small pine standing on the East side of the Virginia road an East course no further than to the pinewoods road, two hundred and fifty acres be the same more or less to him and his heirs forever.

Fifthly-I give and bequeath to my son Job **PARKER** all my land lying on the west side of the Virginia road (between the lines of **CANNON**s land and William **RIGHT**s) down to the long branch from thence over the west side of the long branch between **CANNON**s and Issac **BARBER**s lines as far as

---

¹¹  Chowan County, NC, Deed Book, U#1:324

¹²  Ibid., B#2:162

¹³  Haun, *Chowan County, North Carolina Deed Books: W-1 1729-1738 C-2 1738-1740 D 1748-1806 and various earlier & later dates, Vol. I*, c. 1998, 48:#263, Deed Book W#1:475-476

¹⁴  Ibid., 49:#264, Deed Book W#1:476-477

the East end of the long neck field when he comes to the age of Twenty-one years to him and his heirs forever.

Sixly-I give and bequeath to my son Elias T. **PARKER** my plantation at cross roads and the land thereunto belonging which I bought of Jordan **WHITE** with all my land that lies between the Virginia Road and pinewoods road as far as to Joseph **PARKER**'s line and also twenty acres on the East side of pinewoods road adjoining him and one horse and saddle and my knife of instruments to him and his heirs, forever.

Seventhly-I give and bequeath to my son Jacob N. **PARKER** my plantation at Harmony Hall and all my land adjoining it as far as the pinewoods road except what is already given to my son Elias one horse and saddle, one marble mortor and one herb still to him and his heairs forever.

Eighthly-I give and bequeath to my four sons Joseph, Job, Elias, and Jacob **PARKER** on their especial trust that neither of them shall sell or dispose of his part in any manner whatever, except it be from one to any other or others of them same brothers without it is by the free concent of all the four heirs-all my land and fisheries on Chowan River as far as to the East end of the long neck field by a line North and South from **BARBER**s line to **CANNON**s line each of them share and share alike to them and their heirs forever.

Ninethly-I give and bequeath unto my daughters [sic] Pharaba **GRANBERY** one large Book The Select Works of William Penn with such other articles as she has already received to her and her heirs forever.

Tenthly-I give and bequeath to my daughter Penanah **MOORE** one feather bed, furniture and such other articles as she has already received to her and her heirs forever.

Eleventhly-I give and bequeath to my two younger daughters Isabel and Martha **PARKER** each one feather bed and furniture, one cow and calf, two ewes and lambs one linin wheel to each the full number of articles above mentioned in this paragraph to them and their heirs forever. I also give to my three youngest daughters, Sarah, Isabel and Martha after the marriage or decease of my wife Isabel **PARKER**, all the perishable part of my Estate which I lint to her that is then remaining to each of them three, share and share alike to them and their heirs forever.

Twelvethly-I give to my son Job **PARKER** one younger mare bridle and saddle-the bridle and saddle is now in his possescion, one hoan and racor to him and his heirs forever.

Thirteenthly-I also give to my son Joseph **PARKER** my best walking stick to him and heirs forever.

I further more authorise my executors /by and with the conscent of my wife and children/ to sell and dispose of my lands and purchase elsewhere so as might be to their advantage.

It is my will and desire that my beloved wife Isabel **PARKER**, Joseph **MOORE**, Joseph **PARKER** and Thomas **GRANBERY** to be my whole and Sole Exceculors of this my last will and testament, entirely revokeing and disallowing all former will or wills made by me confirming this and no other to be my last will and testament. Whereunto I have set my hand and seal this Eleventh day of the Second Month 1812.                 Job **PARKER** {Seal}

Signed, sealed, and acknowledged in the presence of William **BAINES**, Jun. John (X) **PERISHO**

The above and foregoing will was proved at December term 1812 by William **BAINES** at the same time Joseph **MOORE** and Thomas **GRANBERY** two of the Executors therein named qualified as such to.   James **NORFLEET** CSC"[15]

Job[5] **PARKER** was dead before 21 December 1812, the date the inventory of his personal property was taken by one of his executors, Thos. **GRANBERY**, and affirmed by Joseph **MOORE**, the other executor. It was not exhibited into court until March Term, 1813, probably because he died so late in the court session.[16]

It has long been said that Job[5] **PARKER** was a "doctor." His will and the inventory of his estate, transcribed here in full, seems to bear that out:

"A True and perfect Inventory of the Goods and Chattles &c of Job **PARKER** Deces[d] taken 21 December 1812

| 5 Beds & furniture | 1 Tribute. 1 Grid Iron |

---

[15]  NCSA, Chowan Co., NC, Wills
[16]   NCSA, G.024.1750499, Chowan County Estates, Record of 1728-1951, Vol. O'Malley-Parrish, Folder: Parker, Job 1812, Doc. # 1088-1090

3 Walnut Tables
4 Pine Tables
1 Doz. Windsor Chairs
3 Chests, 6 Walnut Chairs
1 Clock. 6 Flag bottomed Chairs
1 Desk. 1 Small Looking Glass
1 Sugar Canister. 1 Candle Stand
2 Guns, 2 p[r] Tongs. 1 Shovel
1 old Trunk
6 Volumes Medical Reopository [sic]
3  do  Clais'n [sic] on Quakerism
1 Buchn family Phisician
1 John Griffats Journal
1 Job Scotts  do
1 John Woolmans  do
1 Defence of Quakerism
1 Book Laws of N York
1 Selects [?] Work of W Pen.
1 Large Bible
1 Salmons Geography
1 Principals Religion
1 Sewils History
1 Foxes Journal
2 Testaments
1 Barkley Apollogy
A number of old Books
and small Pamphlets
3 Slates
Sundry Bottles. Vials &c}
Contain[g] diffe[d] kinds Medacines}
2 p[r] And Irons 1 Spider
4 Iron Pots, 2 Dutch Ovens
1 Bell metal Skillet
1 Iron ditto. 3 pr Pot Hooks
2 Pot Trammels. 1 Tea Kettle
1 p[r] Waffle Irons

1 p[r]. Sheep Sheers
2 Razors. 1 Hone 1 Strop.
1 shaving Box
1 Herb Still:
1 Pocket Knife & Instruments
3 Taper Bitts, 3 Augers,
3 Hand Saws. 1 Drawg. Knife
1 Iron Wedge. 4 Irom Bolts
2 Hammers. 2 Planes,
2 Iron Chains
1 Guaging Rod. 1 Box Trumpery
2 Grubbing Hoes
5 Weeding   do
1 Hilling     do. 5 Axes
3 plows, 1 p[r]. Traces
5 Clevy Irons. 2 Cross cut Saws

1 Griddle. 4 Washing Tubs
1 Pale. 3 Piggins
4 Pewter Dishes.
7  do  Plates.
6  do  Basons
4 Bread Treys.
1 trashing [sic] Machine.
1 Coffee Mill. 2 Meal Tubs
1 Fat Tub. 2 Sugar Tubs.
1 Loom &c. 1 Lining wheel.
1 Wooling ditto
1 Seine Chest, Some Rope}
 Corks, Sinkers &c          }
3 p[r]. Small Scales
2 p[r]. Large ditto
1 Corner Beaufat.
5 Dishes. 1 doz large Plates
1½ doz. Small ditto
1½ doz. Cups & Saucers.
3 milk Pots. 1 Tea Pot.
1 Coffee ditto. ½ doz. Wine Glasses
½ doz. Tumblers. 1 Glass Bowl
2 Mugs, 2 pitchers, ½ doz. Bowls,
3 Salts: 1 Cruit, 3 Peppers
1 Tea Water, 3 Small ditto
½ doz Silver Tea Spoons
¾ doz.  do    do    do  old
1          do Butter Boat
1½ doz. White metal Table Spoo/ns/
½  "   Large Knives & forks
½  "   Small    do        do
4 Stone Jugs.  3 do. butter Pots
1 Stone Pitcher.  2 old Cases}
  & Some Bottles . . . . .      }
4 Candle Sticks
2 p[r]. Cotton Cards
1 p[r]. Wool    do

9 Sheep
17 Hogs now fattening to Kill this Season}
4 Sows, & 4 Small Hogs
1 Small Batteau
Supposed to be about 75 Blls Corn
2 Stacks of Oats
700 [lb] Fodder
Sundry accots amount to
£48.9.2
  2.3.9 vs. Seth **WOOD**
£50.12.11
Isaac **WARD**s Note for   £  8. 0.0
Nathan **JORDAN**s do "    50. 0.0
James **BYRAM**s    do "   18.11.0
Miles **STALLINGS** do "   20. 0.0
Morning **JORDAN**s do      6. 0.0

| | | |
|---|---|---|
| 2 Scythes & Cradles. 2 Reep Hooks | | £103..11..0 |
| 1 Sett Shoemakers Tools, Lasts &c | Cash on hand $10 | 5. 0.0 |
| 2 Chizzles.  2 Gouges. | | |
| 2 Grind Stones | | |
| 1 Hand Mill | | |
| 1 doz. Cyder Barrels in bad order | | |
| 1      ditto    Hhd. 2 old Barrels | | |
| 1 Bell mettel Mortear | | |
| 1 Marble ditto | | |
| 2 ox Carts. 2 ox Yokes | | |
| 2 Riding Chairs. 1 Sett Harness | | |
| 1 Womans Saddle | | |
| 1 Mans      ditto, 2 Bridles | | |
| 1 Wheat Fan. 1 Wheat Stand | | |
| 4 Cypress Stands | | |
| 10 Bushels Salt | | |
| 3  ½ bus. Measures | | |
| 6 Baskets, 4 Bells | | |
| 2 Yoke of oxen | | |
| 4 Cows. 2 Heifers, 3 Calves | | |
| 1 Grey Horse | | |
| 1 Mare and Colt | Tho[s] **GRANBERY** } Execu[r] | |
| 1 Two year old Filly | affir[d.] Joseph **MOORE**"[17] | |

Joseph[6] **PARKER** *(Job[5], Joseph[4], Peter[3], Thomas[2], William[1])* was born 12 September 1776, in Chowan County. On 18 January 1800, he produced a certificate to marry, and of membership, from Piney Woods Monthly Meeting, Perquimans County, in Pasquotank Monthly Meeting. He married Elisabeth **MORRIS**, at a meeting place near Newbiggin [sic] Creek, 9 March 1800. She was born some time in January, 1782, the daughter of Aaron and Miriam **MORRIS**.[18]

Joseph[6] **PARKER**, of Pasquotank County, sold his one-quarter interest in the "River Plantation as bequeathed in my father Job **PARKER**'s last will, lying and being in the County of Chowan" to Job **PARKER** on 2 February 1816.[19]

Their children were recorded in Pasquotank Monthly Meeting as Mary[7] **PARKER**, born 2 April 1802, "at 12:30 A. M.," and died 21 December 1832. Their first son, Aaron[7] **PARKER**, was born 10 June 1804, at 5:00 A. M., and died 15 August 1807, aged three years, two months and five days. Job[7] **PARKER** was born 4 May 1806, and died 4 November of the same year. Margaret[7] **PARKER** was born 28 August 1807. Isabella[7] **PARKER** was born 1 October 1809.

John Peele[7] **PARKER** was born 4 December 1812, and died 7 September 1817. Ann Robinson[7] **PARKER** was born 28 July 1815, and died 13 March 1836. Jane[7] **PARKER** was born 21 February 1818, and died 22 September 1823. Joseph Robinson[7] **PARKER** was born 22 February 1820, and "died the same day." Joseph[6] **PARKER** died in July, 1865, aged nearly 89 years. Elisabeth, his first wife, predeceased him by many years, dying 7 March 1827.[20] He had married Martha **WHITE** on 10 May 1838, at Piney Woods Meeting House.[21]

Mary[7] **PARKER**, daughter of Joseph[6] and Elisabeth, married William **WILSON**, at Newbegun Creek Meeting House, 19 January 1824. Her sister, Margaret[7] **PARKER**, married Elias **WHITE** on 24 March 1830. Isabella[7] **PARKER** married Joseph **ELLIOTT** 23 March 1831, and Ann Robin-

---

[17]   NCSA, G.024.1750499, Chowan County Estates, Record of 1728-1951, Vol. O'Malley-Parrish, Folder: Parker, Job 1812, Doc. #1088-1090
[18]   Hinshaw, William W., *Encyclopedia of American Quaker Genealogy, Vol. I, North Carolina*, c. 1936, p. 113
[19]   Chowan County, NC, Deed Book G#2:209
[20]   Hinshaw, William W., *Encyclopedia of American Quaker Genealogy, Vol. I, North Carolina*, c. 1936, p. 113;160
[21]   Ibid., p. 66

son[7] **PARKER** married Aaron **ELLIOTT** 30 October 1833. All these marriages were entered into in the same meeting house.[22]

Joseph **ELLIOTT**, son of Thomas and Abigail **ELLIOTT**, was born 18 January 1803 and died the latter part of 1834. The children of Joseph and Isabella[7] **ELLIOTT** were William Lancaster Bailey[8] **ELLIOTT**, born 16 January 1832, and Joseph Parker[8] **ELLIOTT**, born 7 December 1833.[23]

The above reference to Joseph Robinson[7] **PARKER**'s death is in error. He was granted a certificate from Pasquotank Monthly Meeting to Dartmouth Monthly Meeting, Massachusetts, 17 April 1841, where he attended college. On 16 November 1844, he was received in Pasquotank on certificate from Dartmouth, endorsed by Milford Monthly Meeting, Wayne County, Indiana. He requested a certificate to Piney Woods Monthly Meeting, to marry, on 17 June 1848. Margaret A. **PARKER** was received in Pasquotank, on certificate from Piney Woods, 21 April 1849.[24]

Margaret Ann **PARKER** was recorded as daughter of Thomas and Nancy **NEWBY**, born 3 July 1830, in Perquimans County. Their children were listed as John Newby[8] **PARKER**, born 27 September 1849; Mary Elizabeth[8] **PARKER**, born 25 February 1852, died 11 September 1854; Joseph Wilson[8] **PARKER**, born 14 November 1854; Edward Peele[8] **PARKER**, born 6 April 1857; Margaret Morris[8] **PARKER**, born 10 August 1859, died 14 September 1864; William Thomas[8] **PARKER**, born 2 November 1861; Sarah Isabella[8] **PARKER**, born 30 April 1864, died in April 1881, at Friends School, Providence, Rhode Island.[25]

Joseph Robinson[7] **PARKER** married secondly Deborah Ann **PEELE** at Rich Square Monthly Meeting on 3 March 1869. She was reported to be the daughter of James and Ruth **PEELE**. Their only known child was James Peele[8] **PARKER**, born 30 May 1875.[26] Joseph Robinson[7] **PARKER** was a County Commissioner for Perquimans County in 1870.[27]

Martha[6] **PARKER** *(Job[5],Joseph[4],Peter[3],Thomas[2],William[1])* has left little in the way of records, but she is mentioned in those of other family members. She was dead before February 1845, had married a man with the surname of **WHITE**, and left one son named Gabriel **WHITE**, who was under age on that date.[28]. She may have been the Martha **PARKER** who was disowned by Perquimans Monthly meeting on 4 December 1825, for marrying contrary to discipline.[29]

Job[6] **PARKER** *(Job[5],Joseph[4],Peter[3],Thomas[2],William[1])* was disowned by Perquimans Monthly Meeting on 6 December 1817, for hiring slaves.[30] No record of reinstatement has been found for him. He and Jacob N.[6] **PARKER** appeared on a guardian bond 11 June 1827, and again on 21 March 1831, for Job[6] to be guardian of John Franklin[7] **PARKER**, orphan of their brother Elias T.[6] **PARKER**. He had failed to renew the former bond and was summoned to court to show cause on the third Monday in March of 1831. He was summoned again, for the same purpose, in March of 1834.[31] Job[6] **PARKER** was born circa 1794, as he was listed in the 1850 Chowan County Federal Census as age 56 and a farmer. His family is listed as Mary, age 37; Thomas[7], age 16; Mary[7], age 15; Joseph[7], age 10; William[7], age 8, and Martha[7], age 1.[32] He appears again in the 1860 Chowan County Census as age 66, with Mary, age 45; Joseph[7], age 22; Mary[7], age 22 [?] William[7], age 18, and Adaline[7], age 5.[33] He does not appear in the 1870 Census. No further information.

---

[22] Hinshaw, William W., *Encyclopedia of American Quaker Genealogy, Vol. I, North Carolina*, c. 1936, p. 160

[23] Ibid., p. 98

[24] Ibid., p. 160

[25] Ibid., p. 15

[26] Ibid., p. 252; p. 15

[27] U. S. Federal Census, Chowan County, NC, 1870, M593, #1154, p. 35, Belvidere Twp., Family #253

[28] NCSA, G.024.1750499, Chowan County Estates, Record of 1728-1951, Vol. O'Malley-Parrish, Folder: John Franklin Parker, 1845 Doc. #1155-1156

[29] Hinshaw, William W., *Encyclopedia of American Quaker Genealogy, Vol. I, North Carolina*, c. 1936, p. 66

[30] Ibid., p. 66

[31] NCSA, G.024.1750499, Chowan County Estates, Record of 1728-1951, Vol. O'Malley-Parrish, Folder: Parker, Elias T., Doc. #0890; 0892; 0886; 0884

[32] U. S. Federal Census, Chowan County, NC, 1850, M432, #625, p. 87, "Dist. above Edenton," Dwelling #125

[33] Ibid., 1860, M653, #893, p. 44, "Dist. above Edenton,: Dwelling #362

**Chapter 12**: Jobe[5] **PARKER** *(Joseph[4],Peter[3],Thomas[2],William[1])* and some of his descendants

Elias T.[6] **PARKER** *(Job[5],Joseph[4],Peter[3],Thomas[2],William[1])* was also disowned by Perquimans Monthly Meeting on 4 December 1819, for hiring slaves.[34] He married Margaret **TOWNSEND**, daughter of Josiah **TOWNSEND**, 8 June 1820, in Perquimans County.[35] He died 6 March 1825, in Chowan County, as stated in a petition for dower by his wife, Margaret W. **PARKER**. He owned approximately 300 acres of land, adjoining the lands of Ephriam **ELLIOTT**, Joseph **CANNON** and Jacob[6] **PARKER**.[36] That dower was laid off to her 24 March 1825, and is described as "All The land in the square where the Dwelling House stands, and On the west side of the Virginia Road between the ferry road & Virginia Road a Piece beginning on the main road at an red Oak and running a straight course a cross the field to a Maple then straight to **CANNON**s line, Also a Piece lying On the east side of the Virginia Road and North side of the ferry Road, beginning On the ferry Road at a Pine running No. to a Pine a corner tree then a straight line to the <u>v</u>irginia Road to an Oak in the branch **TROT-MAN**s line."[37]

On 15 March 1825, Jacob N.[6] **PARKER**, Ephraim **ELLIOTT** and Job[6] **PARKER** entered into an administration bond, in the amount of $1,825.00, for Jacob N.[6] **PARKER** to administer on the estate of Elias T.[6] **PARKER**, deceased.[38] Job[6] **PARKER** became guardian to his only child, John Franklin[7] **PARKER**, as previously stated.

John Franklin[7] **PARKER** *(Elias T.[6],Job[5],Joseph[4],Peter[3],Thomas[2],William[1])* was the only child of Elias T.[6] and Margaret W. **PARKER**. He was dead by 10 May 1838, the date of an administration bond in the sum of $2,000.00 for Robert A. **GORDAN** to administer on his estate. James R. **BURBAGE** and Thomas **CLARK** were his bondsmen.[39]

The following petition reveals a great deal about John Franklin[7] **PARKER**'s family and is included here in full:      "North Carolina }

To Febry Term 1845Chowan County}  Court of Pleas & Quarter Sessions

To the worshipful the Justices of the said Court

The petition of Joseph **PARKER**, Benjamin **ALBERTSON** & wife Sarah, Peninah **MOORE**, and of Gabriel **WHITE** an infant by his guardian William C ____, [?] shew your worships that Elias **PARKER** late of said County died sei<u>s</u>ed in fee of a certain piece or parcel of land lying and being in said County adjoining the lands of Joseph **CANNON**, William **BUSH** and the lands belonging to the heirs of Jacob N **PARKER**, containing three hundred & fifty six acres by actual Survey, and is known as **PARKER**s Cross Roads-that the said Elias at the time of his death left an only child & heir at law by the name of John Franklin **PARKER**, to whom said lands did descend in fee. That said /John/ Franklin **PARKER** has since died an infant intestate and without issue, leaving your petitioners Joseph, Sarah & Peninah, and Pherebe **GRANBERY**, Job **PARKER** Jacob N **PARKER** and Isabella **TOWNSEND** his paternal uncles and aunts, and your petitioner Gabriel the infant child of Martha **WHITE** who was also a paternal aunt, his only heirs at law. That the said Isabella<u>h</u> **TOWNSEND** has since the death of said /John/ Franklin also departed this life intestate leaving an only child Maria her heir at law to whom her undivided /interest/ in said lands descended-that said Maria<u>h</u> has also died intestate and without issue leaving the aforesaid persons (except her mother Isabella) her only /maternal/ heirs at law. Your petitioners further shew your worships that said Phereba **GRANBERY** & Job **PARKER**, or some person acting for said Job, have sold their undivided interest in said land to Henry **CANNON** of said County, and the said Henry **CANNON** has also, since the death of Jacob N **PARKER** purchased his undivided interest in said lands, whereby the said Henry has become a tenant in common with your petitioners. Your petitioners shew your worships that they are anxious to divide said lands or to sell the same, and with that view they have proposed to said Henry, by their request to

---

[34] Hinshaw, William W., *Encyclopedia of American Quaker Genealogy, Vol. I, North Carolina*, c. 1936, p. 66

[35] Fouts, *Abstracts from the Edenton Gazette and North Carolina General Advertiser Edenton, North Carolina 1820-1821, Volume IV*, c. 1996, 34:#194 Monday, 12 June 1820 edition, marriage announcements

[36] NCSA, G.024.1750499, Chowan County Estates, Record of 1728-1951, Vol. O'Malley-Parrish, Folder: Parker, Elias T., Doc. #0877-0878

[37] NCSA, G.024.1750499, Chowan County Estates, Record of 1728-1951, Vol. O'Malley-Parrish, Folder: Parker, Elias T., Doc. #0876

[38] Ibid., Doc. #0888

[39] NCSA, G.024.1750499, Chowan County Estates, Record of 1728-1951, Vol. O'Malley-Parrish, Folder: John Franklin Parker, 1845 (?) [sic,] Doc. #1161

sell to him their undivided interest in said lands upon the same terms which he gave for the shares which he has purchased, which your petitioners allege was sold upon _entenable [?] terms, or to divide the same upon some principle of justice and equality. All of which the said Henry refuses to accede to, but has taken possession of the entire tract and is enjoying the profits of the same.

Your petitioners pray your worships to appoint competent commissioners to divide said lands between them and the said Henry according to their respective rights; and that said Henry may answer on oath the allegations in this petition. And may it please your worships to order a copy of this petition & _____ to be served upon the said Henry to be &c          Aug. **MOORE** Sol for petitioners"[40]

An order to make that division was issued 3 February 1845, and the division was made into seven shares on 11 February 1845. Henry **CANNON** received lots one through three; George W. and Annette **PARKER** received lot four; Joseph R. **PARKER** received lots five and six, and Gabriel **WHITE** received lot seven.[41] This land lies at the intersection of Ferry Road, Ryland Road and NC 32. It was called "**PARKER**'s Cross Roads" in 1845, but is now known as the community of "**WELCH**," or "**HUTSON** Corner," on current maps.

Jacob N.[6] **PARKER** *(Job[5], Joseph[4], Peter[3], Thomas[2], William[1])* was disowned by Perquimans Monthly Meeting, on 6 June 1818, for hiring slaves and "gross language."[42] He appeared on a Gates County marriage bond with Harriet **OUTLAW** 20 December 1824, with Nathan **CULLIN** as his bondsman.[43] Harriet was the daughter of George and Christian **OUTLAW** of Gates County.[44]

Jacob N.[6] **PARKER** first appears in Gates County on the Tax List for 1826, listing 1,026 acres of land in James **ROUNTREE**'s district.[45] That district lies in the area well known as Indian Neck, between Catherine Creek and **BENNETT**'s Creek. At that time, the watercourse now known as **TROTMAN** Creek was considered and called "Catherine Creek."

On 13 February 1828, Jacob N.[6] and wife Harriet E. **PARKER**, of Chowan County, sold 273 acres of land to Seth W. **ROUNTREE**, of Gates County, for $1,013.75. This land lies in Gates County and is described as "Beginning at Boar swamp Noah **ROUNTREE**'s corner in Daniel **EURE**s line thence S48.E 16 poles Thence S41 E 11 poles thence S 48. E 47 poles thence S 35 E 65 poles to a gum stump Daniel **EURE**s corner thence N 29 E 35 poles thence N 22 E 38 poles thence N 30 E 8 poles to a red & post Oak Isaac **HYATT**s corner thence S 85 E 32 poles thence N 83 E 12 poles thence S 80 E 58 poles to the Indian Cave thence S 55 E 75 poles to the catherine Creek thence down said Creek to the mouth of Bare [sic] swamp thence up said swamp to the first Station..." Both signed their names, with Harriet signing hers as "Harriet E G **PARKER**." This deed was witnessed by Jos. T. **GRANBERY** and Saml. **RIDDICK**.[46]

On 14 February 1839, Jacob N.[6] and wife Harriet E. **PARKER**, of Chowan County, sold 280 acres of land to Noah **ROUNTREE** for $1,350.00. This land also lies in Gates County and is described as being "Bounded on the West by Catharine Creek on the North by the land of John **WHITE** and others on the East by Joseph **FEARLESS** and Seth **SPIVEY** and on the South by the old mill pond...being a tract of land formerly belonging to George **OUTLAW** deced. ..." J. **RIDDICK** and Nathaniel **WOODWARD** witnessed this deed.[47]

He made his will, 12 January 1842, and died shortly thereafter. It is transcribed here in full: "State of North Carolina}

Chowan County}          In the name of God. Amen:

---

[40] NCSA, G.024.1750499, Chowan County Estates, Record of 1728-1951, Vol. O'Malley-Parrish, Folder: John Franklin Parker, 1845 (?) [sic,] Doc. #1155-1156

[41] Ibid., Doc. #1151-1152

[42] Hinshaw, William W., *Encyclopedia of American Quaker Genealogy, Vol. I, North Carolina*, c. 1936, p. 66

[43] Almasy, Sandra L., *Gates County, North Carolina Marriage Bonds 1778-1868*, c. 1987, p. 67

[44] NCSA, C.041.30005, Gates County Minutes, Court of Equity 1808-1867, Vol: 2 vols, 1808-1830, pages not numbered, on the second Monday after the fourth Monday in September 1816, Harriet and George Outlaw were represented by their guardian, Timothy Walton, in a suit by Christian Outlaw, widow of George Outlaw.

[45] NCSA, C.041.70001, Gates County Tax Lists 1784-1831, p. 341

[46] NCSA, C.041.40006, Gates County Real Estate Conveyances 1819-1829, Vol: 11-13, 13:113-114

[47] NCSA, C.041.40008, Gates County Real Estate Conveyances 1836-1842, Vol: 16,17, 17:139-140

**Chapter 12**: Jobe[5] **PARKER** *(Joseph[4], Peter[3], Thomas[2], William[1])* and some of his descendants

I Jacob N. **PARKER** of the state and county afore said being in perfect mind and memory tho weak in body do make and ordain this my last will and testament in the following manner viz:
Item 1  I Lend to my to my [sic] wife Harriet E. **PARKER** during her /natural/ life all the Land lying on the south side of the new road up to the first cross-ditch except one acre the family burying ground and that I reserve for the benefit of the family  also the **JORDAN** Tract with the priviladge of fire wood and rail timber.  I also lend unto my wife all the House hold & Kitchen furnature that She may wish to retain also my Baroche and Horses also my Double gig and Harness during her life or widow Hood, and if she should marry then it is my will that all the articles named in the above Item and the proceeds arising there from to be eaqually divided between my wife and Children
Item 2.  I Give and bequeath unto my wife Harriet E. **PARKER** one hundred and fifty Barrels corn, ten Thousand pounds of Fodder ten Bushels of Peas Threethousand [sic] pounds of Pork or its equivo-lent in Bacon and one barrel of Lard, Two sows & Pigs choice sixteen Shoats Stock of Geece, two Mules and two Horses choice, one yoke of Oxen, Two Cows & Calves, two young heifers and two young Steers her choice, two Horse carts and one Ox Cart and Wheels her choice.  One waggon and Harness and all the Ploughs and geer, two Spades, two Grubbin Hoes, all the weeding and hiling hoes Six axes choice also my Brandy Still and 1 Wheat Fan.
Item 3.  I Lend unto my wife during her life my Cotton Gin
Item 4  I give unto my Son George my percussion Gun with the apparus [sic]
Item 5  It is my desire that my executor or Executors to sell the plantation where I now live on such a credit as he or they may think proper.  Subject to the Incumberence on it.  Except one acre of Land whereon my Still-house Stands and that I leave unto my Wife ~~my~~ during her life.
Item 7} [sic]  I also loane unto my wife my **JORDAN** land during her life and after the death of my wife, I wish it sold and the proceeds Equally divided between my children.
Item 8  My will and desire is that all the rest of my lands (viz.) the **BOYCE** tract fifty acres near John **BYRUM**s my mill with the four acres of Land attached to her with all the apparatus, also my I/n/terest in a Track of Land formerly belonging to John F. **PARKER** also part of a lot in the Town of Edenton and all my Interest in Bell Grade fishing, also one fourth part of the **PARKER** Fishery reserveing to my wife the offil during her life to be sold by my Executor on such Credit as he may think proper
Item 9  It is my will and desire that my Executor sell all my chattle property which is not Loaned or given away.  also the following Negroes, **BEN**, **SILAS** and **JERRY** and if any more should be to be Sold to pay my Debts, then Sell Such as my Wife and Executor may think Propper, Either at public or private sale the Bl [sic] of the negroes to be kept in common stock and Such of them as my wife may not need on the Plantation for the support of her and her children, and in raising the young negros may be hired out, and the proceeds Eaqually divided between my wife and Children, and in Case my wife should marry, then the negros to be Eaqually divided between my wife and chrilden [sic], it is also my will that when my son George arrives at at [sic] the age of twenty one or my daughter Ann Mariah should marry, then an Equal Division.
Item 10}  I give unto my wife One hundred Dollars to be raised out of my Estate.  I also give unto my wife my Silver Watch.
I hereby do appoint my friend Josiah T. **GRANBERY** Executor to this my last Will and Testament, and I further appoint my Friend Josiah T. **GRANBERY** Testamentary Guardian to my Children in Witness whereof I have set my hand and Seal this the 12 of January 1842
Signed Sealed and delivered in the presence of}
John **BUSH** James J. **CANNON**}                                    Jacob N. **PARKER** {Seal}
The foregoing Will was exhibited in open Court at February Term 1842 proved by the Oaths of John **BUSH** and James J. **CANNON** the subscribing Witnesses thereto and ordered to be Recorded - and at the same time Josiah T. **GRANBERRY** the Executor therein mentioned appeared and qualified by takeing the Oath prescribed by Law.  Ordered that letters testementory issue.  Test H. T. [?] **HATHAWAY** Clk"[48]

Jacob N.[6] **PARKER** made his will 12 January 1842, and was dead before 1 February 1842, the date of the inventory of the bonds and money found by Jos. T. **GRANBERY**, his executor.  An Inventory and account of sales of his property was sold by his executor on the 11th, 23[d], and 24th of

---

[48]  NCSA, C.024.80005, Chowan County Record of Wills 1768-1799; 1807-1841, Vols. B,C, C:230-233

February 1842, on a credit of six months. The only item sold on the 11th was the one half interest in the "Belgrade Fishing apparatus and leads." It was purchased by John L. **WORD** [**WARD**] and James **CANNON** for $950.00. Harriet E. **PARKER** purchased "The Plantation whereon Dec[d] resided" for $1,000.00. All the property sold for a total of $4,900.27. This sale is unusual in that she and Job[6] were the only purchasers bearing the **PARKER** surname.[49]

On 1 March 1842, Harriet **PARKER,** of Chowan County, sold 450 acres of land in Gates County, "in the part called the Indian neck," to Noah **ROUNTREE** for $1,010.00. It is described as "Beginning at a corner in the Boar swamp then running West on the said **ROUNTREE**'s line to the Juniper swamp, thence along the swamp to Abel **ROGERSON**'s line thence along said **ROGERSON**'s line to the place called Cat hole in Catharine creek, thence up the creek , to the be/a/ver dam & Seth W. **ROUNTREE**'s corner, thence up the run of the swamp to the first station..." Seth W. **ROUNTREE** and N. **NIXON** witnessed this deed.[50]

Jacob N.[6] and Harriet E. (**OUTLAW**) **PARKER**'s children were George W.[7] and Ann Mariah[7] **PARKER**. She is termed "Annette" in the petition for division of the lands of John Franklin[7] **PARKER**.

George W.[7] **PARKER** *(Jacob N.[6],Job[5],Joseph[4],Peter[3],Thomas[2],William[1])* is listed as "G. W. **PARKER**" in the 1850 Chowan County Federal Census as age 20 and employed as a teacher.[51] In the 1860 Census, he appears as G. W. **PARKER**, age <u>4</u>0, with Elizabeth, age 36, Mary[8], age 8, and Thomas[8], age 5.[52] No further information.

Pheraby[6] **PARKER** *(Job[5],Joseph[4],Peter[3],Thomas[2],William[1])* was dismissed from Perquimans Monthly Meeting on 4 January 1806, for marrying out of society.[53] No marriage record for her has been found, but she appears to be the wife of Thomas **GRANBERY**, one of the executors to her father's will. She appears to have been still living as of February, 1845, the date of the petition for the division of lands of John Franklin **PARKER**. No further information.

Peninah[6] **PARKER** *(Job[5],Joseph[4],Peter[3],Thomas[2],William[1])* was married to Joseph **MOORE** some time before 11 February 1812, as she is termed "Penanah **MOORE**" in her father's will. Joseph **MOORE** was named one of his executors, as was Thomas **GRANBERY**. No further information.

Isabel[6] **PARKER** *(Job[5],Joseph[4],Peter[3],Thomas[2],William[1])* was one of Job[5] **PARKER**'s younger daughters. She was dismissed as Isabel **PARKER**, "now **TOWNSEND**," from Perquimans Monthly Meeting on 6 June 1812, for marrying contrary to discipline. Her husband's given name is unknown at this time. Isabel[6] **PARKER** died between May 1838 and February 1845, as evidenced by that same 1845 petition. She left a daughter, Maria[7], who was also deceased by February, 1845. No further information.

Sarah[6] **PARKER** *(Job[5],Joseph[4],Peter[3],Thomas[2],William[1])* was reported to Perquimans Monthly Meeting as married to Benjamin **ALBERTSON** on 4 November 1809.[54] They were also still living as of February 1845, as previously noted. No further information.

Martha[6] **PARKER** *(Job[5],Joseph[4],Peter[3],Thomas[2],William[1])* married a **WHITE**, but his given name is unknown at this time. Their only known child was Gabriel[7] **WHITE**, who received lot seven in the division of John Franklin[7] **PARKER**'s real estate. No further information.

The map on the following page lists the property owners along "two and one half miles and Seven Chains" of the eastern shore of Chowan River in Chowan County, NC. They are in order from the top: Thomas **BROWNRIGG**, Sarah **PARKER**, William **MURPHEY**, William **JACKSON**, Wiley **MING**, Job **PARKER**, Jacob **PARKER** and **CANNON**. This map was graciously brought to the author's attention by Mr. George **STEVENSON**, Private Collections Archivist, at the North Carolina State Archives, in Raleigh, NC.

---

[49] NCSA, G.024.1750499, Chowan County Estates, Record of 1728-1951, Vol. O'Malley-Parrish, Folder: Jacob N. Parker 1842, Doc. #0962-0964; Doc. #965-968

[50] NCSA, C.041.40009, Gates County Real Estate Conveyances 1841-1847, Vol: 18,19, 18:206-207

[51] U. S. Federal Census, Chowan County, NC, 1850, M432, #625, p. 104, "Dist. above Edenton," Dwelling #415

[52] U. S. Federal Census, Chowan County, NC, 1860, M653, #893, p. 44, "Dist. above Edenton,: Dwelling #435

[53] Hinshaw, William W., *Encyclopedia of American Quaker Genealogy, Vol. I, North Carolina*, c. 1936, p. 66

[54] Ibid., p. 66

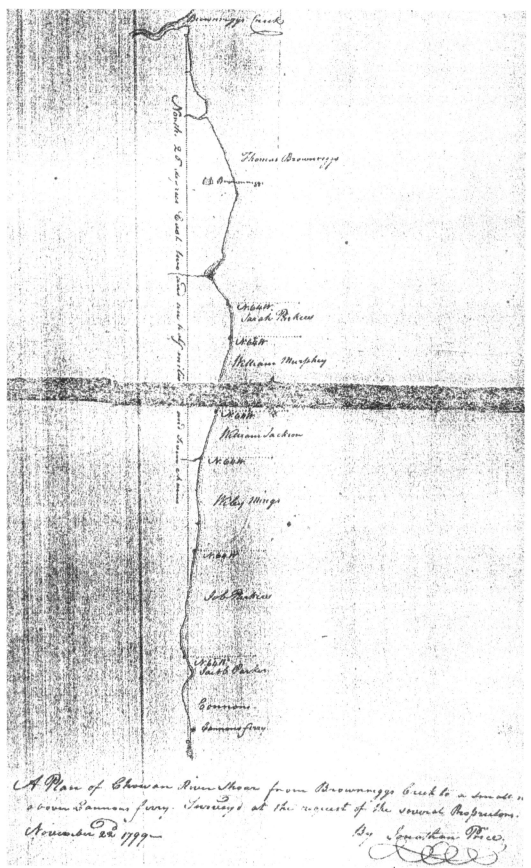

Map depicting survey of 22 November 1799, by the 18th Century cartographer, Jonathan **PRICE**. "A Plan of Chowan River Shoar from **BROWNRIGG**s Creek to a small m[arsh] above **CANNON**s ferry. Surveyed at the request of the several Proprietors." [NCSA, MC.024/1799 CL]

## Thomas[3] PARKER *(Thomas[2] William[1])*

Thomas[3] **PARKER** *(Thomas[2] William[1])* is the son of Thomas[2] **PARKER** of Nansemond County, VA, and was called "Thomas **PARKER**, Jr.," when he was granted land near Kingsale in 1690. He was touched upon briefly at the beginning of Chapter 7. His brother, Peter[3] **PARKER** was discussed in Chapter 10.

Thomas[3] **PARKER** had an assignment of "all our Right Title & Interest of ye within mentioned Sale" from George **WHITE**, and Francis his wife, on 7 October 1707.[1] Further research on this property eventually reveals its description and location in Chowan County, NC.

Working backwards in the chain of title, the following deed begins the search: It is a deed of sale of land from Edward **WILLIAMS** and wife Mary, to George **WHITE** on 7 October 1707. It is described as "all that our plantation & 100 acres on ye Indian Town Creek at the head of our line where we live lying directly opposite to ye plantation of James **HARLO** [sic]..." Witnesses were Tho. **SNODEN** and Daniell **HALLSEY**.[2]

The second document in this search is an assignment of a patent from Thomas **POLLOCK**, Merchant, to Edward **WILLIAMS**, Cooper, on 14 June 1701.[3] The third is that patent to Thomas **POLLOCK**, which provides the description and location of this land: "To all ye Know ye &c Doe hereby give and grant unto Colo. Tho: **POLLOCK** a Tract of land qt. [sic] Six hundred and forty Acres lying in Chowan prct. &c Beginning at a Gum, Standing at ye. mouth of old Town Creek, then up the River by Various Courses to a pine, then East 14[d]. South 320 po. to a pine, S. 396 pole to a Gum, Standing in the Long branch, then down the s[d]. branch by various Courses to a white Oak, Standing by the old Town Creek, then down ye. s[d]. Creek by Various Courses to the first Station. To Hold &c. Given &c. the 20th. of April 1697..."[4]

These four documents provide the facts that Thomas[3] **PARKER** owned 100 acres in Chowan County, near Old Town Creek/Indian Town Creek, Long Branch and Chowan River, on 7 October 1707.

The name "**HARLO**" is actually one of the several spelling variations of "**FARLEE**." James "**FFARLO**" patented 216 acres "on ye West side of ye. head of old Town Creek Swamp," next to Richard **SEWILL**, on 9 January 1702/03.[5] The double "ff" can be easily misread as an "H." The current name of "Indian Creek" has been variously "Old Town Creek," "Old Indian Town Creek," "Indian Town Creek," "**DILLARD** Creek" and "**BALLARD**'s Creek."

On 30 August 1714, Thomas[3] **PARKER** patented "a Tract of Land Containing 387 Acres lying in Chowan precinct, Beginning at a pine in Petr. **PARKER**s line, then So. 186 pole to a Red Oak then Et. 42 pole to a pine, then No. 70 Et. 120 pole to a pine, then No. 5 Et. 156 pole to a red Oak, then No. 20 Et. 100 pole to a pine, then No. 20 Wt. 30 pole to a pine by the Meadow, then No. 60 Wt. 96 pole to a pine, then No. 20 Wt. 76 pole to a pine Thos. **PARKER**s Corner tree, then along his line So. 25 Wt. 158 pole to a pine, then No. 45 Wt. 144 pole to a pine Petr. **PARKER**s Corner tree, then along his line to the first Station..." This patent lapsed to Peter[4] **PARKER** 11 November 1719.[6]

On 7 January 1716/17, Thomas[3] **PARKER** gave a deed of gift of 180 acres of land to Benjamin **EVANS**, for the "love, good will and affection I have & do bear towards my Loving Son in Law." It is described as part of a patent and part of a sale, "Begining at the mouth of Poplar Run so up the said Run to the Mouth of a branch Call'd Meadow branch to a mark'd Pine yn up the sd. Branch to a mark'd Gum thence by a Line of marked trees to Thos. **PARKER**'s Line yn along his line to Stumpy Creek Swamp so down ye sd. Swamp to the first station..." He signed this deed with the letter "P" and

---

[1] Chowan County, NC, Deed Book W#1:76
[2] Ibid., W#1:77, abstract courtesy of Weynette Parks Haun, Durham, NC
[3] Ibid., W#1:166, abstract courtesy of Weynette Parks Haun
[4] NCLG, 1:68, File #19
[5] Ibid., 1:115, File #57
[6] Ibid., 1:240, File #177

the witnesses were Jno. **PARKER** and Henry (O) **LAM**.[7]

The use of the term "son-in-law" sometimes denoted a relationship now known as "step-son." Some researchers have misinterpreted the term in this instance, taking it for granted that Benjamin **EVANS** was the son of Jane **PARKER**, Thomas[3] **PARKER**'s wife. She has been claimed by others as the "widow of Peter **EVANS**," and variously, the daughter of William **BUSH** and John **EARLY**. This writer has never seen any form of documentation to substantiate any of these claims. Further research readily refutes them.

Peter **EVANS** was still living in October of 1718, when he proved the will of Charles **MERRITT** in Chowan County Court.[8]

Benjamin **EVANS** was the son of John and Jane **EVANS**, as evidenced by John's Chowan County will, made 24 August 1739. In that will, he names his wife, Jane, sons John, Thomas and Benjamin **EVANS**, as well as daughters Jane, Mary and Rachel **EVANS**. His eldest son, John **EVANS**, and Charles **JORDAN** witnessed that will and it was probated 15 January 1739/40.[9]

William **BUSH** made his will in the precinct of Chowan, Albemarle County, 5 April 1716. He names his wife as Martha, eldest son William, Jr., youngest son John **BUSH**, daughters Mary **EARLY**, Marth **WILLIAMS**, Rose **WINNS**, Elinore **MACKLENDON**, and youngest daughter Elizabeth **BUSH**.[10]

John **EARLY**, Sr., made his will in Bertie County 6 August 1740. He names his wife as Ann, son John, daughters Margaret **MACKHENRY**, Martha **THOMS**, Mary **BLAKE**, Sarah **KEEF**, Elisabeth **ALBERSON**, Bethshaba **MORRIS** and Rebekah **MORRIS**.[11] Jane **PARKER** fails to appear in any of these documents.

There may be a clue as to her identity in the following deeds. On 26 September 1722, Paul **PHILIPS** of Chowan, Schoolmaster, gave 30 acres to "Jane **PARKER**, Widow." He used the phrase, "for the Love, Good Will and affection I bear towards my loving friend." This land lies on the south side of Poplar Run and was part of a patent to Paul for 130 acres.[12] "My loving friend" is most often used for a family member. It was used again, by Jean/Jane **PARKER** on 26 7ber 1723 [sic,] when she so termed Paul **PHILIPS** in a deed of gift of 100 acres on the north side of Poplar Run, "formerly belonging to Benjamin **EVANS** and was part of a patent containing 370 acres belonging to me." Both these deeds were witnessed by John **CHAMPION** and Mary **FOXWORTH**, and each was acknowledged by the grantor on 30 March 1723.[13] Was Jane **PARKER** a sister to Paul **PHILIPS**?

Thomas[3] **PARKER** meant what he said and Benjamin **EVANS** actually was his son-in-law. It becomes obvious that Benjamin **EVANS** was married to a predeceased daughter of Thomas[3] **PARKER**, whose name is suspected, but not confirmed by this writer. His daughter Sarah was termed "Sarah **PARKER**," not "Sarah **EVANS**," in his will.

Thomas[3] **PARKER** made his will 23 January 1717, in Chowan Precinct. It is transcribed here in full:

"In The name of God Amen the twenty third day of January in the year of our Lord God one thousand seven hundred and seventeen [sic] I Thomas **PARKER** of y[e] precinct of Chowan in the County of Abermarl [sic] in y[e] province of north Carolina being very sick and weak in body but of perfect mind and memory thanks be given unto God therefore Calling to mind the mortality of my body and knowing that it is Appointed for all men once to dye do make and ordain this my last will and testament that is to say principaly and first of all I give and recommend my soul into the hands of God that gave it and my body I recommend to the earth to be buryed in a desent and Christian /manner/ at the descretion of my executrix nothing doubting but at the generall Resurrecttion I shall receive the same again by the Almighty Power of God and as for touching such worldly estate where

---

[7] Chowan County, NC, Deed Book B#1:516

[8] Hofmann, Margaret M., *Chowan Precinct North Carolina Genealogical Abstracts of Deed Books 1696 to 1723*, c. 1976, p. 240, #1734, Court Records in Chowan County, NC, Deed Book B#1:43-44

[9] NCSA, Chowan County, SS Wills John Evans

[10] Ibid., Chowan County, SS Wills William Bush

[11] Ibid., Bertie County, SS Wills John Early

[12] Hofmann, Margaret M., *Chowan Precinct North Carolina Genealogical Abstracts of Deed Books 1696 to 1723*, c. 1976, 196:#1577, Chowan Deed Book C#1:386

[13] Ibid., 196:#1575, Chowan Deed Book C#1:385

with it hath pleased God to bless me with in this life I give demise and dispose of the same in the following manner and form

Imprimis  I give and bequeath unto my son Thomas **PARKER** one Cow an Calf to be paid
unto him out of my stock at his freedom ~~sh~~ they an their increes for ever

Imprimis  I give and bequeath unto my son Joseph **PARKER** one Cow an Calf to be paid unto
him out of my stock at his freedom they and their increes for ever

Imprimis  I give and bequeath all my moveable estate goods and Chatels to be equaly devided
amongst my Children Thomas **PARKER** an Joseph **PARKER** Sarah **PARKER** John **PARKER**
William **PARKER** and ffrances **PARKER**

Item  I do desier my dearly beloved wife Jeane **PARKER** whome I like wise Constitu/te/
make and ordain my soul executrix of this my last will and testament to have the /use/ of my moveable
estate tell my Children Shall be of age or so long as She remains a widow and if she doth mery for her
to have a Childs portion and I do desier my Sons shall be of age to [?] posse [sic] what they have at y^e
age of eighteen years and my daughter at y^e age of sixteen years and i do hereby utterly disallow Revoke and disannul all and every other former testament wills legaces and ~~beque—~~ Requests and exe-
cuters by me in any ways before named willed and Bequeathed Ratifiing and Confirming this and no
other to be my last will and testament in witness where of I have hereunto set my hand and seal the
day and year first above == writen          Thomas his T [?] mark **PARKER**
signed sealed published pronounced and declared by the said Thomas **PARKER** to be his last will and
testament in the presents of us the subscribes [sic]

John **PARKER** Jurat

Henry his O mark **LAM**

Benjamin **EVANS**

Chowan ss October Court 1717 [sic]

Provd in Open Court by y^e

Oath of Jn^o: **PARKER**

___ **HICKS** Clk"[14]

Not all of Thomas[3] **PARKER**'s children are mentioned in his will.  It appears that he was
most probably married at least twice.  He had a predeceased daughter who married Benjamin **EVANS**,
as shown above.  In a Perquimans Precinct Court held 9 January 1704/05, there was a petition "of
Thomas **PARKER** praying to be admitted to prove Rights to A Hundred acres of Land by the Importation of Elizabeth **PARKER** & Lucy **PARKER** & is admitted & assigned them to Henry
**SPRING**."[15]  Were they his first wife and daughter?  All his sons were considered to have been in
Perquimans County at a much later date.

His eldest son's name was Peter[4] **PARKER**, as evidenced by the following petition to the
General Council: "Upon Petition of Peter **PARKER** therein Setting forth that his Father Thomas
**PARKER** four years agoe Surveyd and patented a Tract of Land lying in Chowan Precinct adjoyning
to his Own line and his Brother Peter **PARKER**s Containing about Three hundred and fifty Acres
which land is now Elapsed for want of being Seated in due time pursuant to the Tenore of the said Pat-
ent and there fore prayes the Same may be Granted him  Ordered that the Same be Granted as pray'd
for"[16]  This document is not dated, but the petition of Peter[4] **PARKER** was made after the death of
Thomas[3] **PARKER** in late 1717, and prior to 11 November 1719, when that patent lapsed to Peter[4]
**PARKER**.[17]  Peter[4] made an assignment of the above patent, specified as 377 acres, to "Jean
**PARKER** Widow," on 15 December 1719.  He signed his name with the letter "P," and Jno.
**PARKER** and Robt. **HICKS** witnessed that deed.[18]  Peter[4] **PARKER** will be remembered from the
will of Peter[3] **PARKER**, wherein he was keeping a mare for his cousin, Joseph[4] **PARKER**.

Peter[4] **PARKER** *(Thomas[3], Thomas[2], William[1])* made a deed of gift to Benjamin **EVANS**,
probably in 1717, proved by John **PARKER** in October Court of that year.  The deed has not been

---

[14]  NCSA, C.R.024.801 Chowan County Wills 1694-1938

[15]  Haun, *Old Albemarle County North Carolina Perquimans Precinct Court Minutes 1688 thru 1738*, c. 1980,
69:#177

[16]  NCSA, G.O. 111 Council Journal., 1712-1728, p. 152

[17]  NCLG, 1:240, File #177

[18]  Chowan County, NC, Deed Book C#1:104

preserved in the records, thus nothing more is known of it.[19]

On 10 December 1715, Richard and Jane **CHURCH** sold Peter[4] **PARKER** 90 acres of land described as "beginning at a white oak the corner tree of the main survey then along ye sd. head line 90 po. to a small hickory then by a line of marked trees 160 po. to a white oak thence by a line of marked trees 90 po. to a red oak standing near the upper side line then along the sd. line 160 po. to the first station..." This deed was signed Richd (RC) **CHURCH** and Jane (RC) **CHURCH**, and was witnessed by Wm. **CRAWFORD** and Jno. **JORDAN**.[20] This deed does not specify on which side of the Chowan River the land lies, but other deeds concerning Richard **CHURCH** are for lands on the west side, in present-day Bertie County. This Peter **PARKER** is Peter[4] **PARKER**, Jr., as evidenced by a 1717 Tax List for Chowan County, wherein he owned 90 acres of land and was charged for one tithable person. He was listed as living near Charles **GAVIN**, John **EARLY** and Wm. "**GRANFIELD**," which may well be "**CRANFORD**."[21] Aberrant spellings are very common in these old records.

Peter[4] **PARKER** married Grace **COPELAND**, daughter of William and Christian **COPELAND**, of Chowan Precinct, prior to 17 July 1714. That was the date of a deed of gift from them to their "well beloved Son in Law Peter **PARKER**," and "his heirs begotten of the Body of my Daughter Grace ye wife of sd **PARKER**." The land was 200 acres "on ye So. side of Sandy Run Swamp beginning at the mouth of a branch of sd Sandy Run Swamp commonly called ye Spring Branch & so running wt. ye sd branch to a Pine being one of the line trees of sd Wm. **COPELAND**s land & so running with ye sd line to a markd Poplar standing in ye head of a branch known as meadow Branch & so running down ye sd branch & with sd branch to ye sd Sandy Run Swamp to ye first station...sd **PARKER** is not to Let Lease for Mortgage sd land without consent of sd Wm. **COPELAND** & if Grace wife of sd **PARKER** should die without Issue then ye sd land to return to Wm. **COPELAND**..." Witnesses were Jno. **JORDAN** and Robt. **HOLBROOK**, and this deed was registered 14 February 1714/15.[22] Peter[4] and Grace **PARKER** returned that gift 14 April 1716.[23]

William **COPELAND** became ill and made his will 23 October 1720. He survived that illness and his will was not probated until 21 July 1724. The land whereon he lived was bequeathed to his son, William, along with all the land he owned on the south side of Sandy Run. His lands between Sandy Run and Bear Swamp went to his youngest sons, John, James and Charles. His two younger daughters, Christian and Sarah **COPELAND**, were each given 50 Shillings, to be paid to them at age 16, or the day of marriage. The remainder of his estate was bequeathed to his wife, Christian, whom he also appointed his executrix. John **JORDAN**, George **TURNEDGE** and Elizabeth her E mark **TURNEDGE** witnessed this will.[24] As his daughter Grace **PARKER** was already married, she was not provided for in his will. Other children may also have been omitted.

Peter[4] **PARKER** appears in a 1721 Chowan County Tax List as living near Will **CURLEE**, James **PAGE**, Aaron **OLIVER**, Thomas **DAVIS** and the Widow **GAVEN**, with 300 acres of land.[25] Bertie County was formed in 1722, thus he and Grace may be traced somewhat further in that county.

By 1758, Peter[4] **PARKER**'s situation had deteriorated dramatically, as he appears to have come to Chowan County to live with his brother, Joseph[4] **PARKER**. This is evidenced by the following record: "At a Vestry met at **CONSTANT**s Chapel on Satterday The seventh Day of January 1758," it was "Ordered That Joseph **PARKER** son of Thomas **PARKER** ___ Allowed at The Rate of Six pounds Proclamation Money a year for The Mentainance of his Brother Peter **PARKER** a Poor

---

[19] Hofmann, Margaret M., *Chowan Precinct North Carolina Genealogical Abstracts of Deed Books 1696 to 1723*, c. 1976, 232:#1680, Deed Book B#1:32

[20] Chowan County, NC, Deed Book B#1:291

[21] Haun, *Old Albemarle County North Carolina Miscellaneous Records 1678 to ca 1737*, c. 1982, 97:#274

[22] Chowan County, NC, Deed Book W#1:178, courtesy of Weynette Parks Haun

[23] Hofmann, Margaret M., *Chowan Precinct North Carolina Genealogical Abstracts of Deed Books 1696-1723*, c. 1976, 104:#830, Deed Book B-1:279

[24] NCSA, Manuscript and Archives Reference System, hereafter (MARS) Id: 12.96.1.471 (Folder) No county is given in this will, but the Chowan County deed of gift to Peter and Grace Parker clearly provides that information.

[25] Haun, *Old Albemarle County North Carolina Miscellaneous Records 1678 to ca 1737*, c. 1982, 123:#328

helpless man in This Parish."[26] By 9 September 1758, Peter[4] **PARKER** was dead. In a Vestry meeting of that date, it was "Ordered That Joseph **PARKER** be Allowed forty six Shillings proc for his charge in keeping his brother Peter, a poor man in this parish, three months and Burying him."[27]

Thomas[4] **PARKER** *(Thomas[3], Thomas[2] William[1])* first appears in Perquimans County deeds as a witness to a deed from Jacob **PERRY** to Philip **PERRY**, dated 7 July 1732. That land is located on "Perquimans River Swamp." Perquimans River is within about a mile of the Chowan/Perquimans County line today. That line was "flexible" for a very long time before it was settled, thus people who lived near it were in two different counties at different times, without moving. Thomas[4] **PARKER** used the letter "T" as his mark.[28] Jacob **PERRY** will be remembered from a mention of a deed from him to John **WHITE**, in Chapter 10.

Just over a week later, on 15 July 1732, Caleb **ELLIOTT** of Perquimans Precinct, and Mary his wife, sold Thomas[4] **PARKER** 50 acres for £60. It is described as "begining at the mouth of the gum branch then runing up the sd. branch to the line formerly Thomas **ELLIOTT**s then along Thomas **ELLIOTT**s line to a branch Known by the name of Ephraim **LISLES** branch then down the said branch to the run of the Cypress Swamp then along the said run to the first station..." Joshua and Ann her A mark **ELLIOTT** witnessed this deed.[29] Thomas[4] **PARKER** appears on a 1740 list of taxables for Perquimans County, with one poll.[30]

On 2 February 1742/43, Thomas[4] **PARKER** of Perquimans, Planter, sold that 50 acres to John **BOYCE**. He still used his mark of the letter "T" as his signature. The witnesses to this deed were Nicholas **STALLINGS**, Isaac **BOYCE** and Sarah her S mark **PARKER**. Thomas[4] acknowledged the sale in open court in April 1743.[31] Sarah's relationship to Thomas[4], if any, is unknown.

Just nine days later, on 11 February 1742/43, it becomes obvious that Thomas[4] **PARKER** was preparing to leave the area. On that date, he sold Caleb **ELLIOTT** 20 head of cattle, 30 head of hogs, a white cow, gray mare, bay horse and household and kitchen utensils, including beds and furniture, pots, pans and other items. The witnesses to this transaction were John and Peter **PARKER**. Thomas also acknowledged that deed in April Court 1743.[32] Was he the Thomas **PARKER** for whom widow Elizabeth **PARKER** submitted an inventory to Pasquotank County Court 18 July 1752?[33] No further information.

On 12 July 1718, John[4] **PARKER** *(Thomas[3], Thomas[2] William[1])* purchased of John **JORDAN** 110 acres "beginning at a marked maple on ye mouth of a branch adjoining to the Old Town Creek Swamp on ye North Side said Swamp and up said branch and with the said branch to a poplar in the line of ye said land, various courses to a white oak by the Old Town Creek Swamp so down the swamp to first station..." The only witness to this deed was Jno. C. **EVANS**.[34]

On 3 June 1734, John[4] and Solome **PARKER** sold the 110 acres purchased of John **JORDAN**, to Thomas **HERENDON**. All three persons were termed "of Albemarle County in Chowan Precinct." The land is described as "the Plantation whereon the said John **PARKER** formerly lived and is now in the Possession of him the Sd. Thomas **HERENDEN** lying and being in the precinct of Chowan...Beginning at a marked maple Standing in the Mouth of a Branch Joyning to the Old Town Creek Swamp on the North Side of the Swamp then up the Said Branch and with the Said Branch to a Marked Popler Standing in the line of the Sd. Land then with the line of the Sd. Land by it Various [sic] to Marked White Oak Standing by the Old town Creek Swamp thence down the said Swamp and with the Sd. Swamp to the first station..." Joseph[4] and James[5] **PARKER** witnessed this deed.[35] On 9

---

[26] Fouts, *Vestry Minutes of St. Paul's Parish Chowan County, North Carolina 1701-1776, 2d Edition*, c. 1998, 87:#195

[27] Ibid., 90:#200

[28] NCSA, C.077.40002, Perquimans County Record of Deeds 1729-1744, Vol: C,D, C:#55.

[29] Ibid., C:75

[30] Haun, *Perquimans County North Carolina County Court Minutes 1738 thru 1754 Book II (with Deeds 1735 thru 1738)* c. 1987, 70:#144-57

[31] Ibid., D:229-231, Deed #106

[32] Ibid., D:159-160, Deed #78

[33] NCSA, C.C.R.185, MARS Id: 401.3.372 (Folder) Courtesy of NCSA

[34] Chowan County, NC, Deed Book B#1:583

[35] Ibid., A#1:341

March 1744/45, Thomas **HERENDEN** sold to Charles **JORDAN** the 110 acres that he had purchased of John[4] **PARKER**.  Both James[5] and Joseph[4] **PARKER** also witnessed that deed.[36]

The given name "John" is extremely popular in most of the **PARKER** families, which contributes to the difficulty of distinguishing them, one from the other.  The name "Solome" is unique, thus very helpful to that end.  The late Eleanor Davis **MC SWAIN**, of Macon, GA, fortunately located this couple in Craven County, NC, in the course of her research.[37]

Although John[4] and Solome were termed "of Albemarle County in Chowan Precinct" in 1734, they may have already removed to Craven at that time.  John[4] **PARKER** was dead by 1737, as evidenced by a September Court order showing that Solome **PARKER** was granted administration on the estate of John[4] **PARKER**, deceased.  The order reads as follows:  "Upon the petition of Sollome **PARKER** praying letters of administration on the Estate of John **PARKER** Decd. the same granted She giving Security according to law Jacob **SHEETS** Esqr. and Martin **FFRANCKS** Came into Court & acknowledged themselves Securities to be bound in a bond of one hundred pounds order the Secretary have notice thereof.  Ordr the Clrk Take the Bonds."[38]

The following is a verbatim transcription of the original document:  "North Carolina Craven precinct} ss  At a Court held at the Court house in <u>n</u>ewbern Town the 20th of Sep[r] 1737  Present his Majesties Justices Esqrs &c  Upon the petition of Sollome **PARKER** widdow of John **PARKER** late of this prec[t] Dece[d]: praying an order for Letters of Adm[en] on all y[e] goods & Chattles of the s[d] John **PARKER** Dece[d]: the same is granted & these are to Certifie She the s[d] Sollome **PARKER** has Complied as the Law Directs Jacob **SHEETTS** & Martin **FFRANCKS** Esqrs became her Securities Sep[r] y[e] 30th 1737 James **COOR** Clk Cur"[39]  No further information.

On 14 January 1716/17, Thomas[3] **PARKER** gave a deed of gift of an unspecified number of acres of land to his two sons, William[4] and Francis[4] **PARKER**.  It specifically states "love good will & affection which I have & do bear to my Loving Sons," and is described as "one part the Plantation whereon I now Live & all the Land thereto belonging Except ye part which I have before given to my Son in Law Benjn. **EVANS** ye other part a Pattent of three hundred & Eighty Seven Acres...with all the other parcell before mentioned between my two sons William **PARKER** & Francis **PARKER** the one part to one of ym. ye other part to the other..."  Wm. **CRAWFORD** and Jno. **PARKER** witnessed this deed.[40]

On 28 June 1735, Jeane **PARKER** sold Benjamin **EVANS** 100 acres of land for £20 "in the County of Albemarle."  It is described as "Beginning at a pine Standing in the old Line which was formerly George **WHITE**s in the head of a Branch Known by the Name of the Lightwood Knott Branch then along a Line of Markd. Trees to Jno. **OVERTON**s Line then along ye. said **OVERTON**s Line to a pine a Corner Tree Standing in John **PARKER**s line yn. along ye. sd. **PARKER**s Line to Jno. **WELSH**'s Line then along his Line to a Pine a Corner tree Standing in the Meadow then ___ ye. said **WELSH**'s Line to a poplar Run at ye. mouth of the Lightwood Knot Branch, then along the afsd. **WHITE**s old ____ to the first Station..."  Jane used the mark of "♉" as her signature.  This deed was witnessed by Joseph his P. mark **PARKER**, John **PARKER** and John **CHAMPEN**.[41]

When Thomas[3] **PARKER** died in 1717, he had not seated the land that he was granted 30 August 1714, within the required three years.  Jean **PARKER** became the owner of that land with the assignment of the patent made to her by Peter[4] **PARKER** 15 December 1719.  Neither Francis[4] nor William[4] were of age to claim that land as of 1720.  It was listed under Jean's name that year as 370 acres "near Stumpy Creek," in Chowan Precinct and held by patent.[42]  This sequence of events necessitated Jean's signature on the subsequent deeds to John **PARKER** from her and her sons, William[4]

---

[36]  Haun, *Chowan County, North Carolina Deed Books: A-1, E-1, F-1, F-2, G-1 (Deeds dated 1701-1755) Vol. II*, c. 1999, 58:#259

[37]  McSwain, Eleanor Davis, *Some Ancestors and Some Descendants of Richard Parker, Chirurgeon 1629-1680*, c. 1980, p. 152

[38]  Haun, *Craven County, North Carolina, Court Minutes, 1730-1751, Book II*, c. 1981, 50:#93

[39]  NCSA, SS 1-20, Parker, John  Craven 28

[40]  Chowan County, NC, Deed Book B#1:515

[41]  Ibid., W#1:261

[42]  NCSA, C.024.99011, Chowan County Miscellaneous Papers, Vol. XIX-no dates, p. 70.  Date is provided by NCSA, C.C.R. 187, Lists of Acreage 1697-1720, MARS Id: 401.7.3, courtesy of NCSA

and Francis⁴.

Jean **PARKER**'s name has been spelled both as "Jeane" and "Jane." Her lands were mentioned as being on Old Town Creek Swamp, adjoining John **PARKER** and John **OVERTON**, in a deed from Philip **MAGUIRE** of Bertie Precinct, to Jno. **OVERTON** dated 26 January 1725/26. This deed was witnessed by Jno. and Sarah her X mark **BYRUM**.[43]

The following is all that remains of the land descriptions in the two **PARKER** deeds mentioned above: The first was made 8 June 1738, "Jane **PARKER** widow of Thos. **PARKER** late of Chowan deceased and Will **PARKER**, her son both of afsd. Province to John **PARKER**, 38 pds., on South side of Poplar Run...beginning "at the Mouth of a Branch formerly ye line __ Frank **PAR___** the abovesaid Jno. **PARKER** __ up that Bra___ a line of Mark'd trees to the ___ halfway place ___ his ___ns Line then ___ poplar run _____ ___tion." No signatures remain. Witnesses were Jas. **WILLIA**[MS], Jas. **PARKER**, Martin his M mark **NOWEL**.[44] The second was made 29 December 1738, from "Jane **PARKER** widow of Thos. **PARKER** late of Chowan deceased & Frans. **PARKER** her son both of the prect. aforesaid of the one part & Jno. **PARKER** of the Province afsaid of the other part...in Consideration of the Sum of Eighteen pounds...Sell all that piece or parcel of Land lying & being in the prct of Chowan, Beginning at ____ Branch at Will **PARKER**s Line ___ Branch which ___ Line of ___ & then along ye. ___ **PARKER** ___ ___ ___ Courses to Charles _____ Line to Mat. **GUMBS** Line ___ **EVINS**es Line then along his ___ ___ ___ Pond & then by a Line of Markt ___ ___ ___ of the Little Branch whereon it ___ down the Branch to ye. first Station ___ ___ fifty Acres of Land more or less..." ___ **PARKER** & Frak. [sic] **PARKER**. Witnesses were Jos. **COCKRIL**, Jos. **PARKER** and Jas. **FARLER**.[45] Chowan County Deed Book W#1 is a copy of an earlier book that had deteriorated. It was fortunate that even this much of these deeds survived.

Jane **PARKER** made one final deed to John **PARKER** on 3 March 1739/40, both of Chowan County. It was for 15 acres, sold to him for £18:0:0, and described as "Beginning on Stumpy Creek Swamp at the mouth of poplar run then up the said poplar run to the mouth of a branch on the south side of the said run then up the said branch to a pine a corner tree of the sd. Jno. **PARKER**, then along his line to Stumpy Creek Swamp then up the said swamp to the first station..." It was signed by Jane her ᵻ mark **PARKER**, with James and Peter **PARKER** as witnesses.[46] This land appears to be the same that was given to her in the deed of gift from Paul **PHILIPS**.

As early as 1751, Jane [Jean] **PARKER** was in need of financial assistance from St. Paul's Parish. In a delayed account of William **HORSKINS** [sic,] recorded in 1756, dated 28 March 1751, he paid Jane **PARKER** £13:04:0 "in her distress." She was also paid £1:0:0 in 1752, in that same account.[47] Yet another delayed account of Mr. **HORSKINS**' expenditures shows that on 10 December 1753, there was £1:11:0 paid to Jane **PARKER** "before she was on ye Parish." On 5 November 1754, he paid Robert **MC CLALAND** £1:16:0 "for bording Jane **PARKER**."[48] At a Vestry met 1 May 1754, there was a motion made by "Robert **MC CLELAND** praying that Jean **PARKER** may have a Maintainence [sic] from this Parish." It was then "Ordered that the said Robert **MC CLELAND** be Allowed the sum of Six [?] Shillings Proclamation per Mounth for keeping the said Jean **PARKER**."[49]

Jane **PARKER** was dead before 15 October 1754. John **HALSEY** submitted his account to the Vestry 9 August 1755. It began on that October date and shows that he paid cash "for Burying Jean **PARKER**, £0:15:0."[50] There is no known reason for her family not taking care of her and making her dependent on the Parish. She was apparently a second and much younger wife to Thomas³ **PARKER** and her only known children were William⁴ and Francis⁴ **PARKER**.

Francis⁴ **PARKER** *(Thomas³,Thomas²,William¹)* appears on a list of jurymen in Perquimans

---

[43] Chowan Co., NC, Deed Book C#1:512

[44] Ibid., W#1:387

[45] Ibid., W#1:386

[46] Ibid., C#2:82

[47] Fouts, *Vestry Minutes of St. Paul's Parish Chowan County, North Carolina 1701-1776, Second Edition*, c. 1998, 82:#185

[48] Ibid., 83:#186

[49] Ibid., 70:#159

[50] Ibid., 76:#172

County in 1740.[51] He also appears on a list of tythables there for that same year.[52] No further information.

William[4] **PARKER** *(Thomas[3], Thomas[2] William[1])* appears in the same records as his brother, Francis[4], and no further information has been found on him. It can be speculated that they were both dead prior to 1751, leaving their mother in destitute circumstances. No proof whatsoever has been found to substantiate that speculation.

Sarah[4] **PARKER** *(Thomas[3], Thomas[2] William[1])* has left no identifiable records pertaining to her life.

Joseph[4] **PARKER** *(Thomas[3], Thomas[2] William[1])* appears on a 1740 list of jurymen in Perquimans County, along with his brother, Francis[4] **PARKER**.[53] He also appears in a list of tythables in Perquimans for 1740, under the name Joseph "**PARCARE**." His brothers, Francis[4], Thomas[4] and William[4] **PARKER**, all appear in that same list.[54]

Joseph[4] **PARKER**'s next appearance is on a 1751 Chowan County Tax List taken by Thomas **LUTEN**. He is listed with one tithable person next to William **HILL** and Gabriel **LASETOR** [**LASSITER**.][55] Both of those men lived near Watery Swamp in present-day Gates County, just southeast of Merchant's Millpond and in **HUNTER**'s Mill Township.

Joseph[4] served in the Chowan County Militia, under Captain James **FARLEE**. He appears as "Joseph **PARKER**, Sr." on a list of **FARLEE**'s men taken 25 November 1754, along with Joseph **BROWN**, James and Joseph **HAYS**, Maxemilon **MINCHEAD**, Gabriel **LASITOR** and Abel **MARTIN**, all known to live in the Watery Swamp area.[56] Joseph[4] **PARKER** witnessed the Chowan County will of John **ALSTON** 20 February 1755, which he and another witness proved in court on 2 December 1758.[57] He has already been mentioned as caring for and burying his brother, Peter[4] **PARKER**, in 1758.

In a Chowan County Court begun 15 October 1760, it was "Ordered that the following Persons work on the Road leading from the watery Swamp to **BENNET**s Creek Road by James **HINTON**s Plantation Vizt. James **HINTON**, William **HAYS**, Maximilian **MINCHEW** John **BROWN** John **LASSITER** Joseph **ALPHIN** Solo. **ALPHIN**, John **SLAVENS**, Ahrom [sic] **LASSITER** Joseph **PARKER**, Sarah **MIANED** [sic] and that Maximilian **MINSHEW** Act as overseer over said Road. Order iss[d]."[58]

Joseph[4] **PARKER** left no record of purchases or sales of land, thus the date of his initial residence in the Watery Swamp area is unknown.

Joseph[5] **PARKER** *(Joseph[4], Thomas[3], Thomas[2] William[1])* appears on a tax list in Richard **WALTON**'s district in 1765. Joseph[5], James **PARKER** and John **FALEE** [**FARLEE**] appear together as white polls, with no slaves. Gabriel **LASSITOR** and Sarah **MINARD** also appear on this list, both of whom appear in the previous documents.[59] The James **PARKER** on this list may be James[5] **PARKER**, *(Joseph[4], Thomas[3], Thomas[2] William[1])* a brother of Joseph[5] **PARKER**, but no other documentation of such an individual has been found. The only other known James[5] **PARKER** *(John[4], Peter[3], Thomas[2], William[1])*, in the same area, was Joseph[5]'s cousin who died in 1766. Both these men had close associations with the **FARLEE** family. The significance of the John **FARLEE** on that same tax list is unknown.

Joseph[5] **PARKER**, Planter, made his first recorded purchase of land from Amos **FREEMAN**,

[51] Saunders, *Colonial Records of North Carolina*, Vol. IV, pp. 517-518, scanned by Harold Colson in April 2000, http://perqtax.homestead.com/files/perqjury1740.html

[52] Haun, *Perquimans County North Carolina County Court Minutes 1738 thru 1754 Book II (with Deeds 1735 thru 1738)* c. 1987, 70:#144-57

[53] Saunders, *Colonial Records of North Carolina*, Vol. IV, pp. 517-518, scanned by Harold Colson in April 2000, http://perqtax.homestead.com/files/perqjury1740.html

[54] Haun, *Perquimans County North Carolina County Court Minutes 1738 thru 1754 Book II (with Deeds 1735 thru 1738)* c. 1987, 70:#144-57

[55] NCSA, C.R.024.701.2 Chowan County Taxables 1717-1769

[56] NCSA, MIL TR.1-19

[57] NCSA, SS 882/128 Chowan County Wills

[58] NCSA, C.024.30002, Chowan County Court Minutes 1755-1772, [1755-1761] p. 78

[59] NCSA, C.R.024.701.2 Chowan County Taxables 1717-1769

Planter, on 14 February 1765. It was 50 acres, for £20, and is described as "part of a grant to the Chowan Indians...beginning at the mouth of a small branch that issueth out of the West side of Katherine Creek & from thence up the said branch, its several courses to a pine being a corner tree & from thence a line of Marked trees to head of another branch that issueth out of aforesaid Katherines Creek & from thence down this said branch its several courses to the aforesaid creek & from thence up the Creek its several courses to the first station..." The witnesses were Garrett his X mark **DAVIS**, Robert **WALTON** and Timy. **WALTON**. It was proved in April Court 1765.[60] He sold this parcel to George **OUTLAW** 6 August 1771.[61]

The term "Planter" indicates that Joseph[5] **PARKER** owned at least 100 acres of land, and quite probably more.[62] There is no record of any earlier purchases of land by this man, thus whatever acreage he owned at that time was most probably inherited from his father, Joseph[4] **PARKER**.

On 10 February 1770, Josiah **BLANSHARD**, of South Carolina, sold 250 acres of land to Joseph[5] **PARKER**, for £84 Proclamation Money. It was in Chowan County and described as "on the West side of the Indian Swamp, Begining at the Mouth of a Small Branch, that maketh out of the said Swamp, upon the North side of the said Swamp, begining at a White oak standing in Richard **MINCHEY**'s Line, so runing up the Branch to a Marked Pine that stands in Aaron **BLANSHARD**'s line, and runing along the said Line to the Main Road, and along the said road, to the aforesaid Swamp, and up the said Swamp to the first Station..." The witnesses were Seasbrook **WILSON**, Demsey **HINTON**, Jurat, and Sabrill **SOLLERS**. It was proved in September Court and registered 24 September 1770.[63] This land is now known as "Elmwood" and is located south of Merchant's Millpond, near Watery Swamp. It is still in the possession of Joseph[5] **PARKER**'s descendants.

There is a family cemetery on the property, in a field south of the residence, but there is no marker for Joseph[5] **PARKER**, if he is buried there. In Thomas R. **BUTCHKO**'s book, *Forgotten Gates The Historical Architecture of a Rural North Carolina County*, there is a description of an interesting little building on this property. It is: "Behind the house is a small, one-and-a-half story gambrel-roof structure that is dominated by a large double-shoulder chimney on the north; extending from the chimney is a small rectangular brick potato house. Used as the main kitchen from 1822 until the late nineteenth century, the distinctive little building was most likely built during the late eighteenth century as the farm's primary dwelling. It is covered with beaded weather boards and has a facade of wide flush sheathing. ... The room is dominated by a large fireplace, opposite of which is a partially enclosed corner stairs. Recently renovated, the building is one of the unique architectural treasures of the Albemarle region."[64] This description certainly implies that the building was built by, or for, Joseph[5] **PARKER**.

Joseph[5] **PARKER**'s name appears on "A List of person [sic] that hath taken the Oath of Allegiance & Or Affirmation to the State of North Carolina before Tho[s] **HUNTER** at [?] Chowan County 1778." Garrett **DAVIS**, as well as many others, also appears on this list. It was submitted to June Court 1778.[65] This is the last Chowan County record for Joseph[5] **PARKER** as he lived in the part that was cut off to Gates County in 1779. He was first called for jury service in Gates County in August Court 1780.[66]

On 29 April 1780, Garrett and Hester **DAVIS** made the following unrecorded deed to Joseph[5] **PARKER**, transcribed here in full: "A Deed of Sale To all People to Whom these Presents Shall Come greeting &c Know ye that We garrett **DAVIS** and Hester **DAVIS** of gates Countey in the Province of North Carolina for and in Consideration of the Sum of one thousand Pounds Lawful money of this State Do Sell all hour goods and Chattels hogs and Catt[le] horses for one thousand

---

[60] Chowan County Deed Book M#1:216

[61] Ibid., O#1:339

[62] *North Carolina Research Genealogy and Local History*, Edited by Helen F. M. Leary and Maurice R. Stirewalt, c. North Carolina Genealogical Society, 1980, p. 583

[63] Chowan County Deed Book O#1:243

[64] Butchko, Thomas R., *Forgotten Gates The Historical Architecture of a Rural North Carolina County*, c. 1991, Gates County Historical Society, p. 187

[65] NCSA, C.024.99009, Chowan County Miscellaneous Papers 1772-1782, Vols. 15, 16, Vol. XVI:33

[66] Fouts, *Minutes of County Court of Pleas and Quarter Sessions Gates County, North Carolina 1779-1786*, c. 1994, 23:#42

Pounds Current money of this State unto the Said Joseph **PARKER** him and his hears forever We garrett **DAVIS** & Hester **DAVIS** Do warrent and Deffend the above mensied [sic] good and Chattels Cattels hogs and horses unto the Sd Joseph **PARKER** him and his hears for Ever the Said Joseph **PARKER** further a grees to maintain Safissiently the Sᵈ garrett **DAVIS** & Hester **DAVIS** his Wife as Long as it Shall Pleas god they Shall Liv Either in good helth or Ele [Ill?] for the a bove mensied one thousand Pound[s] We the Said garrett **DAVIS** & Hester **DAVIS** do give up unto the Sᵈ Joseph **PARKER** him and his hears administrators from hence forth as his and there Proper goods and Chattles Cattels hogs and horses absolutly With out any manner of Condit___ in Witness Where of We have here unto Set hour hands and Seals this Twenty Ninth Day of April by the grace of god and State of North Carolina and Countey of gates in the year of our Lord one thousand Seven hundred and Eightey Ackᵈ garrett his + mark **DAVIS** {Seale} Hester her H mark **DAVIS** {Seale}
Signed Sealed and Delivered in the Presents of Test Jonas **FALLAR** James **FREEMAN** Gates County sst. August Inferior Court of Pleas &c 1780 the Above Deed of Sale was duly Acknowledged in open Court by the above said Garrott **DAVIS** and on Motion was ordered to be Registered. Test Law **BAKER** Clerk"⁶⁷

A second deed concerning these same parties is also transcribed here in full: "A Deed of Gift This Indenters maid [sic] this Twenty Seventh Day of June in the year of our Lord one Thousand Seven hundred and Eightey one By and betwen Joseph **PARKER** & garrett **DAVIS** & Hester **DAVIS** his Wife all of gaites Countey in the Province of North Carolina Witnes that I the Saᵈ Joseph **PARKER** Do give up all that was /given/ me by a Deade of gift by the Sᵈ **DAVIS** & his Wife unto the Saᵈ garrtt **DAVIS** & hester his Wife to them and thers Earse or orders for Ever Exepting one Cow & Calf & one Dry Cow and two year old heffer & one Lardge Puter Dish Which the Said **PARKER** Keeps by bargin and Like Wise I the Sᵈ Joseph **PARKER** Do Compell my Ears and assines to give up unto the Sᵈ garrett **DAVIS** ~~DAVIS~~ & hester his Wife /all the hole Estate/ to Dsspose With as they See fit to them and ther Ears forever Exceptin What Was a bove mensied Which is one Cow & Calfe one Cow Dry & a two year old heffer and one Lardge Puter Dish and that I the Said Joseph **PARKER** hath a good right and Lawful authorrity to Sel or give up unto the Sᵈ garrett **DAVIS** & hester his Wife & thers Ears for Ever and the a bove to Remain in full forse and Virtue Sealed With my Seal Daited in Gaites Countey the Day and year first a bove Written Joseph his ⅄ mark **PARKER** {SealeSined Sealed and Delivered in the Presents of James **FREEMAN** William **FREEMAN** Junr."⁶⁸ This deed was proved by the oath of James **FREEMAN** in May Court 1782.⁶⁹

The 29 April 1780 deed appears to be that of a father-in-law to his son-in-law, assuring himself and his wife of a decent level of care in their declining years. There are no extant marriage records for Joseph⁵ **PARKER** and a **DAVIS** woman, but this deed is the best evidence available for that marriage. The 27 June 1781 deed of gift from Joseph **PARKER** to Garrett and Hester **DAVIS**, just over a year later, makes it appear that Joseph's wife had died within that time span.

On 6 July 1781, Garrett **DAVIS** made his will. He was "sick and weak" and left his estate to his wife, Hester, then to his son-in-law, Thomas **MANSFIELD**. He named **MANSFIELD** as his executor and the will was witnessed by James **OUTLAW**, George **OUTLAW** and James **FREEMAN**. It was proved in May Court 1782.⁷⁰ As Joseph⁵ **PARKER**'s wife was apparently dead, it seems that **DAVIS** no longer considered him as a "son-in-law."

Joseph⁵ **PARKER**'s second wife was named Catherine, of uncertain parentage. She may have been a **HINTON** by birth. That possibility is made evident by the fact that Kedar **HINTON**, eldest son of Jonas **HINTON**, was named as one of Joseph⁵ **PARKER**'s executors. He was also a bondsman on a marriage bond for Catherine **PARKER**, at a later date. Jonas **HINTON**'s wife was named Christian and their children were Cader, James, Noah, Jonas, Seasbrook, Christian, Judith and Priscilla **HINTON**. Several of these names also appear in Joseph⁵ **PARKER**'s family. Demsey **HINTON**, a

---

⁶⁷ NCSA, C.R.041.401.3 Gates County Miscellaneous Deeds 1776-1908
⁶⁸ Ibid. These two deeds were never recorded in the Gates County Deed Books and were found in the North Carolina State Archives by my husband, Robert J. Fouts.
⁶⁹ Fouts, *Minutes of County Court of Pleas and Quarter Sessions Gates County, North Carolina 1779-1786*, c. 1994, 44:88
⁷⁰ Almasy, *Gates County, North Carolina Wills 1779-1807*, c. 1984, p. 23-24, Will Book 1:24-25

brother to that Jonas, was a witness to the 1770 deed from Josiah **BLANSHARD** to Joseph **PARKER**. The long and close association between the two families, and the use of the same names, lends weight to that possibility. It appears that Catherine married Joseph[5] **PARKER** circa 1781.

In 1784, the first extant tax list for Gates County shows Joseph[5] **PARKER** with 250 acres of land and one poll. He lived in Joseph **RIDDICK**'s captaincy that year, and in 1785.[71] He still owned the 250 acres in 1786, then in Isaac **HUNTER**'s captaincy and continued to be listed with one poll.[72] The taxing district [captaincy] changed every few years. No record of sale has been found, but Joseph[5] appears in the tax list for 1787 with only 175 acres and no longer paying a poll tax.

In the 1786 State Census, Joseph[5] **PARKER** is listed as follows:
"White Males 21-60  White Males under 21 & above 60  White females every age
--                                    5                                    3"[73] This record, in conjunction with the above tax lists, proves that Joseph[5] **PARKER** was born circa 1726.

Joseph[5] **PARKER** made his will in Gates County 21 July 1789. It is transcribed here in full:
"I Josepth [sic] **PARKER** of gates county North Carolina do make my last will and Testament in maner follering
I Give to my /wife/ Catren fifty Akers of land whareon my Housses stands with one third of the Orchard as long as She lives my weddow
also one Bay Horse two Cows and Calfs and 1 Beef Stere fore Sheep two Beds and furnerture with the Rest of my House hold goods of Evary kind Except two Beds also one Negro woman Named **PRISS** untill my yongest dafter coms of age to work to mentane my children and after that to be Sold and hur in Crese if En/e/y and the money after Sold to be devided betwent Josept [sic] **PARKER** my son and and [sic] John **PARKER** and Cader **PARKER** and James **PARKER** and polly **PARKER** and alizabeth **PARKER** And Nance **PARKER** And pressa **PARKER** I give allso to my /wife/ two Sows /w [?]/ pigs and one Thousand wate of pork fowls of Evry kind that I have allso I give to my /wife/ when the Crop coms of Twenty Barrils of corn ten Bushells of peese all so the potators that is made
I give the Other part of my plantation to my Son Josspth [sic] **PARKER** and my Still /and 2 thirds of the orchard/ and the Other part of my plantation when my wife marres or dise also one mare  I give to Sary **JONES** on Sow and pigs all my other Estate to be Sold and the money a Rising To be devided /with all my Depts due to me/ be twene Josepth **PARKER** and John **PARKER** and Cader **PARKER** and James **PARKER** and polly **PARKER** and Elezabeth **PARKER** and Nance **PARKER** prisse **PARKER** allso I give polly a Bed and tw [sic] Blankitts  also I do give to Elisabith **PARKER** 1 Bed}
July the Twenty first one thousand Seven hundred and Eighty Nine
last will and testamen [sic] of Josepth **PARKER**              Joseph his ꝟ mark **PARKER**
Wits[d] in the presents of
John **ROBBINS** Sener
John **ROBBINS** Juner
I leve John **ROBBINS** /Juner/ and Cader **HINTON** my Excerters
State of N° Carolina}
    Gates County    } ss: Aug[st] Inferior Court of Pleas &c 1789
The within and above Will was exhibited into Court by John **ROBBINS** junior Executors therein appointed & was proved by the oath of John **ROBBINS** Senior one of the Subscribing Witnesses thereto and then the said Will was Ordered to be Recorded at the same time the said Executor came into Court and quallified himself for that Office and prayed an Order for Letters Testamentary thereon, which was accordingly granted  Teste Law **BAKER** cc  Recorded in Book A folio 82. & 83. Teste Law **BAKER** cc"[74] This will appears to have been penned by John **ROBBINS**, Sr.

An inventory of Joseph[5] **PARKER**'s estate was taken 13 October 1789 by John **ROBBINS** Junr., Executor, and exhibited by him in November Court of that year. It is transcribed here in full:
"A True Inventery of the Goods and Chattles of the Estate of Joseph **PARKER** Deceased Taken octo-

[71] NCSA, C.041.70001, Gates County Tax List 1784-1831 [1784-1806], p. 9;22
[72] Ibid., p. 43
[73] NCSA, G.O. 130 [1786 State Census]
[74] NCSA, C.R.041.801.9, Gates County Wills 1762-1904. The name "PARKER" is written in all lower case in the original will.

ber the 13th Day 1789. one Negro woman one mans Sadle Two Sider Trof[s]. Two plou/ghs/ Two pair of Traces one Cleve Iron Two axes one pair of weges one Hand Saw one drawing knife Eleven Emty Barrels five Hogsheads one Cart & whels Twenty one head of Cattle Three Horses Eight Sheep fourteen Stocks of bees Two Bushels of flax seed fifteen hundred hand fulls of flax on Broak [unbroken] one Gun one Gun Barrel Two Rasors one press Basket and flatform Two chesels Two pair of Stillards one file one Still and Still Tub fifteen Gees Twelve fouls Three Beeds and Bed Steds four Blankets four Chests one Desk one Stand of Drors one Trunk one Sugar Box one Box iron Two heters one Table Twelve Earthen plates Eight puter Dishes Two Basons Six puter plate one Tea pot one Earthen pan Two Quart Bottles one Looking Glass Two womons Sadles one hackle and a half one Barrel of fish one hundred pounds of pork five Gallons of honey one Linnen whel one wolling whel Six Chears one frying pan four Iorn pots one Skillet Three weeding hoes one Gobing [Grubbing] hoe one Loomb & harness Two pot hangers Two Bells one Grind Stone one Set net Thre Bushels of oats four Baskets Two water pales one Tra Thirty one head of hogs Seventy four pounds in Notes Bonds an accounts a crop of corn unmeasure/e/d a crop of Pease Unmeasureed 20 Bushel of Pertators   John **ROBBINS** State of N° Carolina}

    Gates County} ss November Inferior Court of Pleas &c 1789 The above Inventory was exhibited into Court by John **ROBBINS** Junr. Executor on oath and on Motion was Ordered to be Recorded Teste Law **BAKER** CC  Recorded in Libra A Folio 340 & 341  Teste Law **BAKER** CC"[75]

    John **ROBBINS**, Jr., sold Joseph[5] **PARKER**'s goods and chattels 2 December 1789, for a total of £155:19. The purchasers were "Catron" **PARKER**, John **ROBINS**, Kedar **HINTON**, John **STEPTO**, Demsey **JONES**, Jr., Isaac **ESON** [**EASON**,] Thomas **TRAVIS**, Searsbroc [sic] **HINTON**, Mary **PARKER**, Henery **HILL**, Jethro **MELTEAR**, John **ROBINS**, Sr., Jonathan **ROBERTS**, James **FREEMAN**, Thomas **MARSHAL**, William **BOND**, Bashford **ROBINS** and Daniel **POWEL**.[76] The account of this sale was exhibited into court in February, 1790, by John **ROBBINS**.[77]

    Jonathan **ROBERTS** was appointed guardian to the orphans of Joseph[5] **PARKER** as evidenced by the following, and later, guardian returns. The detailed return for Joseph[6] **PARKER** is transcribed here in full:

"Dr Joseph **PARKER** Orphan of Joseph **PARKER** Decd. in account Currant with Jonathan **ROBERTS** Guardian

| | £ S C | | | £ S C |
|---|---|---|---|---|
| 1790 To 1 Hatt @ 15/ | 15 | 1790 | by Cash for a Mare | 20 1 .. |
| July 12th To 3¼ y[ds] of Check @ 4/6 | 14 7½ | May 20 | by Cash for the rents of Land & Still | 7 12 .. |
| To 1½ y[ds] of Striped Linnen @ 5/ | 7 6 | | by Interrest for Two years | 18 9 |
| 17  To 1 quir or paper @ 3/ | 3 .. | 1791 | by Cash his Equal part of his fathers Estate | 14 3 8¾ |
| August 26 To 5½ y[ds] Sheeting @ 4½ | 1 2 .. | | by Interest for one year | 16 11¾ |
| December To 2½ y[ds] of Corderoy @ 11/ | 1 7 6 | | by Cash for rents of Land & Still | 6 10 .. |
| To Buttons & Twist | 5 6 | | by Interrest for one year | 7 9½ |
| To 1½ y[ds] of Cloth @ 20/2 | 1 10 3 | | | 50 10 3 |
| To 3 y[ds] of Linnen @ 5/6 | 16 6 | | | 20 14 2½ |
| To 1 Pair of Buckles @ 2/9 | 2 9 | | Ballance Due the Orphans | £29 16 ½ |
| To 1 Pair of Hose @ 8/3 | 8 3 | | | |
| To 3 hanks of Silk | 3 8 | | Jonathan **ROBERTS** Guardian | |
| To Making one Shirt | 4 [?] | | | |
| To money paid the Taylor for making his Cloths | 1 2 .. | | | |
| To 2½ Dozen Buttons for Do | .. 3 8 | | | |
| To 7 months & 20 Days Schooling | 2 6 .. | | | |
| To 7 months & 20 Days Board | 7 12 .. | | | |
| To Clerks fees | .. 7 .. | | | |
| To my own Trouble | 1 .. .. | | | |
| To 1 quir of paper @ 3/ | .. 3 .. | | | |

---

[75]  NCSA, C.R.041.508.86 Gates County Estates Records, 1765-1920, Folder: Parker, Joseph 1789

[76]  Ibid.

[77]  Fouts, *Minutes of County Court of Pleas and Quarter Sessions Gates County, North Carolina 1787-1793*, c. 1995, 56:#99

**Chapter 13**: Thomas[3] **PARKER** *(Thomas[2] William[1])*

£20 14 2½"[78]

In February Court 1791, it was "Ordered that Jonathan **ROBERTS**, William **LEWIS** & Thomas **MARSHAL** & John B **WALTON** auduit state and settle the accounts of John **ROBBINS** Executor of Joseph **PARKER** dec."[79] That account still exists, undated, but transcribed here in full:

"D[r] The Estate of Joseph **PARKER** Decs[d]. in Account with John **ROBBINS** his Executor — C[r]

| | | | | |
|---|---|---|---|---|
| To paid William **HINTON** prov[d]. Acc[t]. | 1 .. .. | By Amount of Account Sail | 155 19 |
| To paid W[m]. **BOOTH** prov[d]. Acc[t]. | 2 .. .. | By Cash p[r]. Bond & Intrest | 32 12 3½ |
| To paid Samuel **HARRIL** for Commissions Sail | 3 .. .. | By Cash p[r]. Bond & Intrest | 16 4 9½ |
| To paid Demsy **JONES** prov[d]. Acc[t]. | 4 8 .. | By Cash p[r]. Bond & Intrest | 22 4 4½ |
| To paid Samuel **BROWN** prov[d]. Acc[t]. | 3 .. | | 227 .. 5½ |
| To Scrasbrook [sic] **HINTON** prov[d]. Acc[t]. | 1 3 .. | | 76 .. 1 |
| To paid W[m]. **BRISTER** prov[d]. Acc[t]. | 1 2 4 | Ballance Due | 151 .. 4½ |
| To paid Thomas **MARSHALL** prov[d]. Acc[t]. | 0 8 0 | | |
| To paid Isral **MINNARD** prov[d]. Acc[t]. | .. 16 .. | | |
| To paid Jn[o] **ROBBINS** prov[d]. acc[t]. | 4 15 9 | | |
| To paid Willis **BROWN** p[r]. Note | 5 5 .. | | |
| To paid Mary **PARKER** part of her Legatee [sic] | 13 6 6 | | |
| To paid Wm. **TIVATHEN** prov[d]. acc[t]. | .. 18 .. | | |
| To paid W[m]. **BAKER** p[r]. Recept.. | .. 6 .. | | |
| To paid Isaac **EASON** p[r]. Bond | 10 18 .. | In Obediance to the annxe[d]. Ordr of Cort | |
| To paid Orderters [Auditors] | 1 4 .. | we have Settled the accounts of John | |
| Alow[d]. Executor for Servises | 10 .. .. | **ROBBINS** Executor of Joseph | |
| To paid Kader **HINTON** for working in the Crop | 3 4 | **PARKER** Decs[d] and find a | |
| To paid William **HINTON** for work Dun in Crop | 6 1 6 | Ballance Due the Orphans | |
| ~~To work dun by Jn[e] **ROBINS** in Crop~~ | [blank] | Tho[s] **MARSHALL** | |
| To paid for Cort Charges | 2 9 .. | Jonathen **ROBERTS** | |
| To paid Isaac **EASON** prov[d]. Acc[t]. | 3 12 .. | W[m]. **LEWIS**"[80] | |
| | 76 .. 1 | | |

In May Court 1791, it was "Ordered that Jonathan **ROBERTS** Thomas **MARSHALL** William **LEWIS** & John Bunbery **WALTON** or any three of them make a Division of the Estate of Joseph **PARKER** dec/d/ agreeable to the Will."[81] That division was then made and is transcribed here in full:

"D[r]. The Estate of Joseph **PARKER** Decs[d]. in Acc[t]. C__rent __n **ROBINS** his Execu___ — C[r].

| | £ S C | | |
|---|---|---|---|
| | | 1791 | |
| To paid W[m]. **BAKER** p[r] Bond | 10 5 5¾ | By amount of Money due y[e] Orphan from | £ S C |
| To paid Humphey **HUDGINS** for Feas | 13 .. | a Return maid by Orderters to Cort (may Turm) | 151..4½ |
| To paid P.. **HEGETHY** for Feas | 12 | | 37 10 5¾ |
| To paid Readick **HUNTER** prov[d] Acc[t] | 1 16 | Ballance due y[e] Orphan to Devide | £113 9 10¾ |
| To Cash Allow[d]. Jn[o] **ROBINS** Executor | 10 .. .. | | |
| To paid Dividers of y[e] Estate | 1 4 .. | | |
| To paid Orphan in Sted of a Bed | 13 .. .. | | £ S C |
| | £37 10 5¾ | Polly **PARKER**s part | 14 3 8¾ |
| | | Joseph **PARKER**. part | 14 3 8¾ |
| | | Betsy **PARKER**. part | 14 3 8¾ |
| | | John **PARKER**s part | 14 3 8¾ |
| | | Kadear **PARKER**. part | 14 3 8¾ |
| | | James **PARKER**s part | 14 3 8¾ |
| | | Nansy **PARKER**. part | 14 3 8¾ |
| | | Pressy **PARKER**. part | 14 3 8¾ |

In Obediance to y[e] anex[d] Order of Cort. we have
Devided y[e] estate of Joseph **PARKER** Decs[d].

---

[78] NCSA, C.R.041.508.86 Gates County Estates Records, 1765-1920, Folder: Parker, Joseph 1789

[79] Fouts, *Minutes of County Court of Pleas and Quarter Sessions Gates County, North Carolina 1787-1793*, c. 1995, 78-79:#144

[80] NCSA, C.R.041.508.86 Gates County Estates Records, 1765-1920, Folder: Parker, Joseph 1789

[81] Fouts, *Minutes of County Court of Pleas and Quarter Sessions Gates County, North Carolina 1787-1793*, c. 1995, 88:#163

Jonathan **ROBERTS** John B **WALTON** Thomas **MARSHALL**"[82]

Sarah[6] **PARKER** does not appear in this list of heirs, though she does in a later division. A bill of sale from Cathren **PARKER** to Jonathan **ROBERTS** is transcribed here in full: "Know all men by these presents that I Cathren **PARKER** of the County of Gates & State of North Carolina have Bargained and Sold and Delivered unto Jonathan **ROBERTS** of the County and State aforsaid Two Beds & Furniture Eight Puter dishes one Mair and Colt and one young Mare Two Cows & calvs one Cow and yearling and one Cow Nine Sows and Twenty five Pigs three Iron potts six head of Sheap one desk & Chest of Draws Two Chests for and in Consideration of the Sum of Sixty pounds Current Money of the State aforsaid to me in hand paid before the Insealing and Delivering of these presents in Satisfaction of the Same I do Warrent and for Ever defend the S[d].. Mentioned articles from the Claim or Claims of any person or persons What ever Unto the Said Jonathan **ROBERTS** his Heirs & assigns for Ever as witness my hand & Seal this 16th Day of May 1791

Test David **HARRELL**                                    Cathren + **PARKER**

State of N[o]. Carolina }

Gates County}ss  May Term 1791

The above Bill of Sale was in Open Court duly Proved by the Oath of David **HARRELL** the Subscribing Witness thereto and on Motion was Ordered to be Registered. Test Law **BAKER** CC Christ[r]. **RIDDICK** P.R."[83]

On 16 August 1791, Jonathan **ROBERTS**, Timothy **LASSITER** and William **HARRISS**, all of Gates County, entered into bond in the sum of £400 for Jonathan **ROBERTS** to be guardian to "~~Mary **PARKER**~~, Elizabeth **PARKER** John **PARKER**, Kadah **PARKER**, James **PARKER**, Nancy **PARKER** & Christian **PARKER**, Orphans of Joseph **PARKER** dec[d]."[84] "Christian" **PARKER** in this record is undoubtedly "Priscilla Christian" **PARKER**. Mary **PARKER** may have come of age by that date, thus was excluded from the guardian bond.

This guardian bond appears to be a renewal of a former bond as Jonathan **ROBERTS** made a guardian return from May, 1791, for John, Kedar, James, Nancy and "Pressy" **PARKER**.. Cash for each child's part of their father's estate was £14:3:8¾, plus £3:17:8¼, "by four years and Nine months Interest," less £1:7:0 for court charges and his "trouble," left the sum of £16:14:6 due to each orphan.[85]

This record is puzzling on its face, with the "four years and Nine months Interest," less than two years after Joseph[5] **PARKER**'s death. The puzzle is solved when it is realized that this guardian account was not exhibited into court until February 1796.[86] The cause of the long delay is unknown to this writer, but submission of this account was probably precipitated by the death of two of the children.

Among the numerous spellings of her name, Catherine **PARKER** appears as "Katherine"on a marriage bond with Micajah **BLANSHARD**, dated 20 November 1791. Kedar (X) **HINTON** was his bondsman and Richard **BARNES** was the witness.[87] Four years later, Micajah **BLANSHARD**, of Chowan County, appears on another marriage bond dated 2 November 1795, with one Milley **CARTER**. William **WILLIAMS** was his bondsman then.[88]

Apparently, Catherine died some time in those intervening years. The most likely time for that event was near 20 May 1793, when Micajah **BLANSHARD** entered into a guardian bond with Amariah **BLANSHARD** and William **WILLIAMS**, in the sum of £250. The minors named in that bond were Jno.[6], Kedar[6], Jas.[6] & Nancy[6] **PARKER**, orphans of Joseph[5] **PARKER**. Priscilla Christian "Pressy"[6] **PARKER** was not included on that bond, thus was probably dead at that time. In August Court of that year, Micajah **BLANSHARD** "came into Court and mooved for Administration on the Estate of Priscilla **PARKER** orphan of Joseph **PARKER** dec[d] Ordered that he give Bond and Secu-

[82] NCSA, C.R.041.508.86 Gates County Estates Records, 1765-1920, Folder: Parker, Joseph 1789

[83] NCSA, C.041.40002 Gates County Real Estate Conveyances 1786-1795 Vol: 2,3, 2:227

[84] NCSA, C.R.041.508.86 Gates County Estates Records, 1765-1920, Folder: Parker, Joseph 1789

[85] NCSA, G.041.2194761 Gates County Estates, Record of 1765-1920, Folder: Parker, Joseph 1789, Doc. #1600

[86] Fouts, *Minutes of County Court of Pleas and Quarter Sessions Gates County, North Carolina 1794-1799, Vol. I*, c. 1984, 50:#104

[87] Almasy, *Gates County, North Carolina Marriage Bonds 1778-1868*, c. 1987, p. 9.

[88] Ibid.

rity in the sum of One hundred pounds at same time John B **WALTON** & William **WILLIAMS** came into Court and offered themselves as Securitys &c" That bond was entered into 22 August 1793.[89] In that same court, it was also ordered that Simon **STALLINGS**, James **FREEMAN**, John B. **WALTON** and Timothy **WALTON**, or any three of them were to audit, state and settle his accounts with her estate and make a division thereof. [90]

The division did not survive, but that account is still extant and is transcribed here in full:
"D[r] The Estate of Prissilla **PARKER** decs[d] Orphan of Joseph **PARKER** decs[d] In Accnt Current with Micajah **BLANSHARD** Adm[r]                                                                          C[r]

May 1793 To Cash p[d] Clk Court, Administration

| | | | | |
|---|---|---|---|---|
| /orders/&c | 0 12 0 | May 1791 By Cash as p[r] division | 14 3 8¾ |
| To Cash p[d] Jonathan **ROBERTS** p[r] Accnt | 1 7 0 | By Interest on the above Sum 3 yrs. | 2 11 1¾ |
| To tending On the Child in her Sickness} | | | |
| and other Services as adm[r]. &c } | 6 0 0 | | 16 14 9½ |
| To Cash to Auditors, dividers &c | 1 0 0 | Ballance due the Estate £6.9.9½ | |
| To attending Court With these returns} | | | |
| Clks fees &c } | 1 6 0 | | |
| | 10 5 0 | | |
| Ballance brought p[r] Contra | 6 9 9½ | | |
| | 16 14 9½ | | |

_ay 1794 In Obedience to Order of Court hereunto annexed we the Subscribers have Audited Stated and Settled the Accnts of Micajah **BLANSHARD** Adm[r] of Prissilla **PARKER** decs[d] (Minor) Orphan of Joseph **PARKER** decs[d], as above   Simon **STALLINGS** James **FREEMAN** Timothy **WALTON**"[91] This account and the division of estate were returned to May Court 1794.[92]

On 22 November 1797, Joseph[6] **PARKER** entered into an administration in the sum of £100 on the estate of "Kadar"[6] **PARKER**, deceased, with Elisha **CROSS** and Demsey his O mark **ODAM** as bondsmen.[93] There is also an identical bond of the same date for James[6] **PARKER**'s estate.[94] They were both minors and appear to have died about the same time. There is no way to determine the cause of their deaths, be it by accident, or disease.

Undated, but identical, inventories were taken for Kedar[6] and James[6] **PARKER** by Joseph[6] **PARKER**. They each consist of "Cash in the hands of his Guardian as appears by his Settlement with Court Feby Term 1796, at that time there was a ballance in his hands of £16.14.6."[95]

The account current and division on these two estates is extant and is transcribed here in full:
"D[r] The Estates of James **PARKER** & Kedah **PARKER** decs[d] in Account with Joseph **PARKER** administrator   C[r]

| | | | |
|---|---|---|---|
| 1797 To burying the decs[d] funeral Expenses &c | 5 3 9 | Feby 1797 By Cash as pr Settlement with} | 16 14 6 |
| To Cash p[d] Clerk, Court, at Sundry times | 0 15 0 | Court which appeared to be due Kedah **PARKER**} | |
| To Cash p[d] Jonathan **ROBERTS** p[r] Accnt | 1 0 0 | By Cash as p[r] Settlement with Court} | |
| | £6 18 9 | which appeared to be due James **PARKER**} | |
| Brought from Contra | 26 10 3 | | 16 14 6 |
| | 33 9 0 | | 33 9 0 |

Interest on £26.10.3 three years
is                4.15.5¼
Ballance due the Estates  £31. 5.8¼
Feby 1800 We the Subscribers have proceeded to devide the above Sum of 31.5.8.¼ amongest the heirs
of the deced.'s in the following Manner-     To Sarah **JONES**       5.4.3¼

[89]  NCSA, G.041.2194762 Gates County Estates, Record of 1765-1920, Folder:  Parker, Prissilla 1794, Doc. #228

[90]  Fouts, *Minutes of County Court of Pleas and Quarter Sessions Gates County, North Carolina 1787-1793*, c. 1995, 137:#255;138:#256

[91]  NCSA, C.R.041.508.86 Gates County Estates Records, 1765-1920, Folder:  Parker, Joseph 1789

[92]  Fouts, *Minutes of County Court of Pleas and Quarter Sessions Gates County, North Carolina 1794-1799, Vol. I*, c. 1984, 9:#17

[93]  NCSA, G.041.2194761 Gates County Estates, Record of 1765-1920, Folder:  Parker, Joseph 1789, Doc. #1602

[94]  Ibid., Folder:  Parker, James and Kedar 1797, Doc. #714

[95]  NCSA, C.R.041.508.86 Gates County Estates Records, 1765-1920, Folder:  Parker, Joseph 1789

|                          |          |
|--------------------------|----------|
| To Mary **FAIRLESS**     | 5.4.3¼   |
| To Joseph **PARKER**     | 5.4.3¼   |
| To Elizebeth **PARKER**  | 5.4.3¼   |
| To John **PARKER**       | 5.4.3¼   |
| To Ann **PARKER**        | 5.4.3¼   |

In Obedience to Order of Court hereunto Anexed we the Subscribers have proceeded to Audite the Accounts of Joseph **PARKER** Admʳ of Kedah **PARKER** James **PARKER**, Minors, decsᵈ, as above Stated, And also have proceeded to divide the Estates of the two decds, and Each Share appear as above in Witness Whereof we have hereunto Subscribed Our names

Kedar his + mark **HINTON**

David **HARRELL**

Jethro **MELTEAR** Senʳ...”[96]

The order of court for the audit of accounts and division of these estates was made in November 1799.[97] It was exhibited into the next court, held in February 1800.[98]

In February Court 1804, Nancy⁶ **PARKER**, orphan of Joseph⁵ **PARKER**, came into court and chose Joseph **RIDDICK** Esquire as her guardian.[99] On 21 February 1804, Joseph **RIDDICK**, Joseph⁶ **PARKER** and Elisha **TROTMAN** entered into a guardian bond in the sum of £500 for Joseph **RIDDICK** to be guardian to Nancy⁶ **PARKER**.[100] In February Court 1804, the following order was issued: “Agreeable to the Petition of Joseph **RIDDICK** Esquire Guardian to Ann **PARKER** orphan of Joseph **PARKER** deceased, it was then and there Ordered that the Sheriff of this County sell certain Negroes belonging to the Estate of Joseph **PARKER** deceased, which Negroes was left in the last Will and Testament of the Decedent to be sold when one of his children arrived to age, which child is now Dead And that he make report of his proceedings to this Court at next sitting and hereunto annexed Copy Test L. **BAKER** C.C.” That sale was made in April of that year and is transcribed here in full:

“Pursuant to the Order of Court hereunto annexed I have sold the negroes above mentioned in said Order, as follows,

| | | | | | |
|---|---|---|---|---|---|
| 1 Negro Woman, Named **PRISSY** | | | To Joseph **PARKER** | £145..0..0 |
| 1 Dᵒ. | Boy | dᵒ | **JACK** | To Joseph **PARKER** | 70..0..0 |
| 1 Dᵒ | Boy | dᵒ | **PAUL** | To Elizabeth **PARKER** | 68. 0. 0 |
| 1 Dᵒ | Girl | dᵒ. | **HANNAH** | To Joseph **PARKER** | <u>116. 0. 0</u> |
| | | | | | £399. 0. 0 |

The purchaser's have given their Bonds with security, payable to Joseph **RIDDICK** Guardian to one of the Orphans, and in trust for the other Heirs of the said Joseph **PARKER** deceased.

April 26ᵗʰ. 1804                    J. **SUMNER** Shff.”[101]

In the February 1805 term of Gates County Court, orders were issued that John B. **WALTON**, Esquire, Timothy **WALTON**, Richard **BOND**, Sr., and John **ROBERTS**, or any three of them, were to make a division of the estate of Joseph **PARKER**, deceased. They reported their proceedings to May Court of that year.[102] In the August 1805 term of Gates County Court, orders were issued that Richard **BOND**, John **ROBERTS**, Thomas **MARSHALL** and Joseph **RIDDICK**, or any three of them, were to audit and state the accounts of Joseph⁶ **PARKER**, Administrator of Kedar⁶ and James⁶ **PARKER**, orphans of Joseph⁵ **PARKER**. At the same time, they were also ordered to make a division of the personal estates of Kedar⁶, James⁶ and Priscilla⁶ **PARKER**.[103] As a division of James⁶ and

---

[96] NCSA, G.041.2194761 Gates County Estates, Record of 1765-1920, Folder: Parker, James and Kedar 1797, Doc. #716

[97] Fouts, *Minutes of County Court of Pleas and Quarter Sessions Gates County, North Carolina 1794-1799, Vol. I*, c. 1984, 132:#255

[98] Fouts, *Minutes of County Court of Pleas and Quarter Sessions Gates County, North Carolina 1800-1805, Vol. II*, c. 1985, 5-6:#266

[99] Ibid., 93:421

[100] NCSA, G.041.2194761 Gates County Estates, Record of 1765-1920, Folder: Parker, Joseph 1804, Doc. #1608

[101] Ibid., Doc. #1606

[102] Fouts, *Minutes of County Court of Pleas and Quarter Sessions Gates County, North Carolina 1800-1805, Vol. II*, c. 1985, 119:#460; 124:468

[103] Ibid., 127:#473

Kedar[6]'s estates had been made in 1800 and there is no record of such for Priscilla[6], it may be that Nancy[6] "Ann" **PARKER** came of age in 1805, permitting a final settlement to all the orphans. No other record of the above divisions has been found.

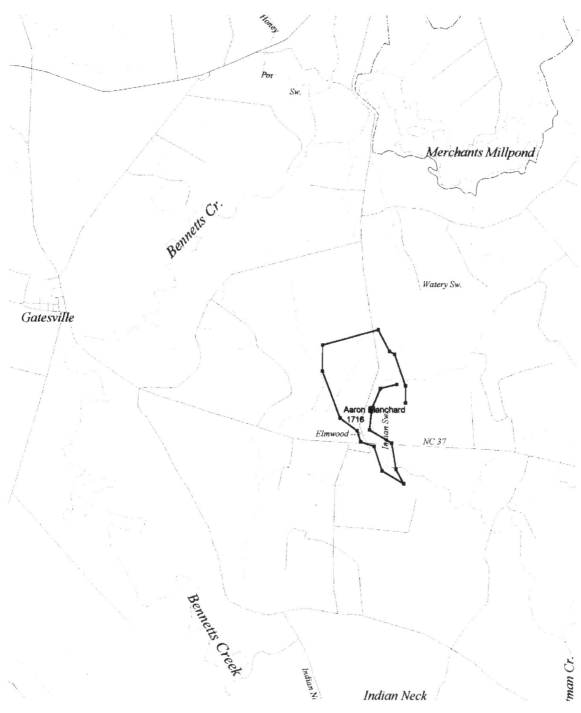

Scale: 0.76 mi/in

Map depicting location of the land Josiah **BLANSHARD** sold to Joseph⁵ **PARKER** 10 February 1770. It was part of a patent to Aaron **BLANSHARD** 29 March 1716, "on Indian Swamp in Meherrin Neck."[104]

---

[104] NCLG, 8:285, File #979

## Children of Joseph[5] PARKER (*Joseph[4],Thomas[3],Thomas[2],William[1]*)

Sarah[6] **PARKER** (*Joseph[5],Joseph[4],Thomas[3],Thomas[2],William[1]*) is estimated here to have been born circa 1763, to Joseph[5] **PARKER** and his first wife, Miss **DAVIS**. That would place her age at circa 20 years when she appeared on a marriage bond with Joseph **NESBITT**, dated 11 May 1783. John **ROBBINS** was his bondsman.[1] He will be remembered as the executor of Joseph[5] **PARKER**'s will.

Joseph **NESBITT** was "sick and weak in body," when he made his will 6 November 1784, and the first bequest he made was of his wearing apparel to his "father in law **PARKER**." He left the re-mainder of his estate to his beloved wife Sarah, also naming her as his executrix. The witnesses to this will were Thomas **BRICKELL** and Spenko his X mark **MENCHEY**.[2] It was proved by Thomas **BRICKELL** in November Court 1784, and Sarah[6] qualified herself as his executrix.[3] She would have been of age by that year, thus could legally assume the responsibility of that office.

Sarah[6] (**PARKER**) **NESBETT** next appeared on a marriage bond with Demsey **JONES**, dated 29 July 1785. Richard (x) **FREEMAN** was his bondsman.[4] Dempsey **JONES** made his will 10 Septem-ber 1823. He left his "Loving wife Sarey **JONES**" the use of his plantation whereon he lived and all his Negroes with the exception of one named **RUBEN**, whom he left to his daughter Elizabeth[7] **JONES**. All his lands were to be Sarah's for her life, then to be divided between his sons John[7], Sam[7] and William[7] **JONES**. He also mentioned daughters named Nancy[7] and Mary[7] **JONES** and left his "worthy friend" John **ROBERTS**, and son John[7] **JONES**, as his executors. Witnesses to this will were R. **PARKER** and William his x mark **TVATHAN** [sic]. It was proved in February Court 1825, by the oath of Robert **PARKER**.[5]

Sarah[6] (**PARKER**) **NESBETT JONES** was also dead by February, 1825, as evidenced by the order for Nathaniel **JONES** to be granted letters of administration on her estate with a bond of $500.00.[6] An inventory of her estate was exhibited into May Court of that year and James W. **RIDDICK**, John **WALTON**, Robert **PARKER** and David **PARKER** were ordered to settle and divide her estate. Their report was made in that November Court.[7]

An interesting petition for division of Negroes was made to February Court 1836, by John **JONES**, William **JONES**, Jethro **HARRELL** and wife Nancy, Riddick **SMITH** and wife Mary, and Elizabeth **BRIGGS**. It mentions that "Elizabeth intermarried with ___ **BRIGGS** who departed this life before the said Sarah."[8] Charles **BRIGGS** appeared on a marriage bond with Elizabeth[7] **JONES** dated 23 January 1828. John **WALTON** was his bondsman.[9] No further information.

Mary[6] "Polly" **PARKER** (*Joseph[5],Joseph[4],Thomas[3],Thomas[2],William[1]*) was born circa 1768, to Joseph[5] **PARKER** and his first wife, Miss **DAVIS**. She made purchases at her father's estate sale in 1789 and her name was crossed off of the guardian bond for her brothers and sisters in 1791. She married a **FAIRLESS**, of unknown given name, probably between 1791 and 1800, when she was termed "Mary **FAIRLESS**" in the division of the estates of her younger half-brothers. Their descendants may have mi-grated to Hertford County. No further information.

Joseph[6] **PARKER** (*Joseph[5],Joseph[4],Thomas[3],Thomas[2],William[1]*) was born circa 1770, to Joseph[5] **PARKER** and his first wife, Miss **DAVIS**, as evidenced by his appearance on the Gates County Tax List of 1793, paying for one poll.[10] He was a minor up until May of 1791, as evidenced by the previous

---

[1] Almasy, *Gates County, North Carolina Marriage Bonds 1778-1868*, c. 1987, p. 64

[2] Almasy, *Gates County, North Carolina Wills 1779-1807, Vol. I*, c. 1984, p. 40-41, Will Book 1:43-44

[3] Fouts, *Minutes of County Court of Pleas and Quarter Sessions Gates County, North Carolina 1779-1786*, c. 1994, 82:#163

[4] Almasy, *Gates County, North Carolina Marriage Bonds 1778-1868*, c. 1987, p. 51

[5] Almasy, *Gates County, North Carolina Wills 1807-1838, Vol. II*, c. 1985, p. 105, Will Book 2:232-233

[6] Fouts, *Minutes of County Court of Pleas and Quarter Sessions Gates County, North Carolina 1824-1827, Vol. VI*, c. 1988, 46:#1362

[7] Ibid., 58:#1379;75:#1402

[8] NCSA, C.R.041.508.62, Gates County Estates Records, 1765-1920, Folder: Jones, Demsey 1836

[9] Almasy, *Gates County, North Carolina Marriage Bonds 1778-1868*, c. 1987, p. 11

[10] NCSA, C.041.70001, Gates County Tax Lists 1784-1831 [1784-1806] Isaac Hunter's Captaincy, p. 149

**Chapter 14:** Children of Joseph⁵ **PARKER** (*Joseph⁴,Thomas³,Thomas²,William¹*)

guardian account with Jonathan **ROBERTS**. He did not appear on the August 1791 guardian bond with the other children of Joseph⁵ **PARKER**. That account shows that Joseph⁶ **PARKER** received an education to some unknown level. Only the more affluent families could afford to provide any of their children with an education during that era. This was quite often only for the eldest son in the family and was very rarely provided for daughters. His administration on the estates of his brothers, Kedar⁶ and James⁶, was explained in the previous chapter.

The first record found within the Gates County Deed Books for Joseph⁶ **PARKER** was a bill of sale to him from Holoday **WALTON**, of Chowan County, for a Negro girl named **PENNY**, for £62:10. It was dated 7 January 1799, with Kedar his X mark **HINTON** and Jeremiah **JORDAN** as witnesses.[11]

On 2 October 1800, Joseph⁶ **PARKER** purchased a Negro man named **SAM** from Seth **TROTMAN**. The purchase price was £125, "if found on the other Side of Rown Oake River" and "if found on this Side of Rown Oake," the price was to be £150. John **HOFFLER** and Jacob **SPIVEY** witnessed this deed.[12] Runaway slaves were often sold while they were still at large.

Joseph⁶ **PARKER** appears on a marriage bond with Rodey **HARRELL**, dated 16 March 1801. John **MARSHALL** was his bondsman.[13] Rodey [Rhoda] **HARRELL** was the daughter of Isaac, Sr., and Judith **HARRELL**, as evidenced by the will of Isaac, Sr., made 20 March 1805, probated in November, 1805. He left "to my daughter Rhoday **PARKER** five shillings Virginia currency as her full part of my estate to her & her heirs & assigns forever."[14]

On 10 November 1806, Joseph⁶ witnessed a deed from Barnaby **BLANCHARD** to his brother, John⁶ **PARKER**.[15]

On 17 August 1807, Nathaniel his + mark **JONES** sold Joseph⁶ **PARKER** a "Negro Boy about 9 years of age Named **PAWL**," for the sum of £51 "<u>v</u>irginia money." P. **HEGERTY** was the sole witness.[16] This child is the same that Elizabeth **PARKER** purchased in April, 1804, in the sale of her father's slaves, prior to her marriage to Nathaniel **JONES**. It appears that Joseph⁶ **PARKER** desired to reunite this child's family.

On 13 March 1810, John his X mark **JONES** sold Joseph⁶ **PARKER** 34½ acres of land for $75.00. This parcel joined on Jeremiah **JORDAN**, David **HARRELL** dec^d., Charles **SMITH** and Nathaniel **JONES**. It was "One half of the land that Demsey **JONES** Sen^r. gave to be divided Between his Two Sons Joseph & Nathaniel **JONES**'s [sic] this being the part that was Josephs part..." James his X mark **HINTON** and Nathaniel his .N. mark **JONES** witnessed this deed.[17] John **JONES** is the sole signatory to this deed, yet when it was proved in May Court 1810, it was stated as "Deed of sale of land John **JONES** & Rachel **JONES** to Joseph **PARKER** was proved by the Oath of James **HINTON** &c."[18]

On 7 January 1812, Joseph⁶ **PARKER** sold Nathaniel **JONES** 60 acres of land for $150 silver dollars. It is described as "beginning at Jeremiah **JORDAN**s Corner tree from thence along Charles **FELTON**s line from thence to Noah **HINTON**s line thence up the flat Branch to James **TREVATHAN**s line thence along **TREVATHAN**s line to Charles **SMITH**s line then Runing a West Course or thereabout to A Corner Tree a Black Gum Standing in the Cypress Branch then by a line of Marked trees to a Sweet Gum A Corner tree Standing in the deep branch thence up the said branch to the first Station..." It was signed by Joseph **PARKER** and Rachal her X mark **JONES**. William A. **JORDAN** and John **HARE** witnessed this deed.[19] Rachal **JONES** appears to be the widow of one Demsey **JONES**.[20] Her signature on this deed likely makes up for that deficit in the former deed from John **JONES** to Joseph⁶ **PARKER**. This 60-acre tract appears to encompass the 34½ acres purchased from John **JONES** in 1810.

---

[11] NCSA, C.041.40003, Gates County Real Estate Conveyances 1794-1803, Vol. 5, 5:202

[12] Ibid., 5:244

[13] Almasy, *Gates County, North Carolina Marriage Bonds 1778-1868*, c. 1987, p. 68

[14] Almasy, *Gates County, North Carolina Wills 1779-1807, Vol. I*, c. 1984, p. 185-186, Will Bk. 1:221-222

[15] Gates Co. Deed Book 6:336

[16] NCSA, C.041.40004, Gates County Real Estate Conveyances 1803-1810, Vol: 6,7,8, 7:191

[17] Ibid., 8:140

[18] Fouts, *Minutes of County Court of Pleas and Quarter Sessions Gates County, North Carolina 1806-1811, Vol. III*, c. 1985, 114:#660

[19] NCSA, C.041.40005, Gates County Real Estate Conveyances 1811-1812, 1815-1819, Vol: 9,10, 9:113

[20] Almasy, *Gates County, North Carolina Marriage Bonds 1778-1868*, c. 1987, p. 50, shows Demsey Jones of Nansemond Co., VA, and Rachel Bond, on a bond dated 2 March 1789.

**Chapter 14:** Children of Joseph[5] **PARKER** (*Joseph[4],Thomas[3],Thomas[2],William[1]*)

In February Court 1812, Joseph[6] **PARKER** was appointed overseer of the road in the room of Reuben **HINTON**, who had resigned that post. In May Court 1813, it was ordered that his hands were to work on the road under William A. **JORDON**.[21]

On 16 March 1814, Noah **HINTON** sold Joseph[6] **PARKER** 20 acres of land for $100 silver dollars. It is described as "Begining and runing as follows begining at a pine stump standing on the East side of the main lane that Leads from the said Noah **HINTON** to John **HAIR** Land thense Runing South Corse Binding on the said Joseph **PARKER** [s] Line to a white Oake a Corner tree then Runing wess [sic] Corse Binding on John **HEIR**s line to the End of the aforesaid main lane thense up the said main lane a North corse as the ditch Runs on the East side of the said lane to the first station." Thos. **BOND** witnessed this deed.[22]

Joseph[6] **PARKER** made his will 25 February 1820, probated in November Court of that same year. It is transcribed here in full: "In the Name of God Amen. I Joseph **PARKER** Being of sound and Perfect Mind and memory Blessed Be God Do this the Twenty Fifth Day of February in the year of our Lord One thousand Eight Hundred and Twenty make and Publish this my Last will and Testament in manner following. First it is my wish and will that my Beloved son David **PARKER** Should have a surtain negro fellow By the name of **PALADORE** also a negro woman By the name of **PENNEY** also a negro Boy By the name of **ADDER** also a negro Boy By the name of **DAVE** an also a negro Girl By the name of **HANNAH** it is my will and wish that my son David **PARKER** shall have fifteen Hundred Dollars In Cash which is in notes and Bonds for him two Beds and furniture and further it is my wish and will that my Son David **PARKER** should have my young Horse its my wish and will that my son David **PARKER** should have the gun that I Bought for him at Chs. **TOWNSEN**s [sic] all of this to him his heirs and assigns forever.

It is my wish and will that my Beloved wife Rodah **PARKER** should have a surtain negro fellow By the name of **JACOB** and a negro woman by the name of **PRISE** and a woman by the name of **SEALEY** one riding Gigg & Harness and my oald Horse and one Bed and furniture to her and hur heirs and assigns forever and it is also my will and wish that my Beloved wife Rodah **PARKER** should have the use of all of my Lands and Plantation utensils House Hould and Kitchen furniture Besides what I have already given to David **PARKER** hur natural life, and it is my wish and will that my beloved wife Rodah **PARKER** should have the use of all of my stock consisting of cattle Hoggs and sheep untill my son David **PARKER** arrives to Twenty one years of age then and in that case it is my wish and will that my stock Be Equally divided Between my Beloved wife Rodah **PARKER** and my two sons David **PARKER** and James **PARKER**, and it my [sic] wish and will that my Beloved son James **PARKER** should have all of my lands and Plantation and Plantation utensils House Hold and kitchen furniture after the Death of my beloved wife Rodah **PARKER** it is also my Wish and will that my son James **PARKER** should have a surtain negro Fellow by the name of **JACK** and a negro woman by the name of **PATIENCE** and a negro Boy by the name of **WILLIS** and a negro girl By the name of **LUISER** and two Feather beds and furniture and one gun to him his heirs and assigns forever.

It is my wish and will that my Beloved wife Rodah **PARKER** should keep the three small negroes that I gave to my son David **PARKER** by the name of **ADDER, DAVE** and **HANNAH** untill David **PARKER** should arrive to the age of Twenty one years, and also my wish that she should Keep the Horse that I gave him until he becomes of age, and it is also my wish and will that my beloved wife Rodah **PARKER** should Keep all the Property of Every description that I gave to my Beloved son James **PARKER** until he should arrive to the age of Twenty one years. And I hereby make and Ordain my beloved wife Rodah **PARKER** and my son David **PARKER** Executrix and Executor of this my Last will and Testament. in witness whereof I the said Joseph **PARKER** have to this my Last will and Testament set my hand and Seal the day and year above written. sign[d]. sealed Published and declared

By the said Joseph **PARKER** the testator

as his last will and Testament in

the presence of us who were Present at the time of

Signing & sealing thereof                                  Joseph **PARKER** {Seal}

---

[21] Fouts, *Minutes of County Court of Pleas and Quarter Sessions Gates County, North Carolina 1812-1817, Vol. IV*, c. 1986, 1:#736; 34:#797

[22] NCSA, C.041.40005, Gates County Real Estate Conveyances 1811-1812, 1815-1819, Vol: 9,10, 10:28-29

R. **PARKER** (Jurat)
Salley **LEWIS** (Jurat)
State of North Carolina} November County Court of Pleas
   Gates County } ~~May~~ &c 1820
The above will was exhibited into Court by Rhoda **PARKER** the executrix therein appointed, and was proved by the oath of Robert **PARKER** & Sally **LEWIS**."[23]

   David[7] **PARKER** (*Joseph[6],Joseph[5],Joseph[4],Thomas[3],Thomas[2],William[1]*) was called upon to accept legal responsibilities before the age of 21. He was born 1 June 1803, on the land in Gates County now known as "Elmwood Plantation."[24] On 25 October 1823, he entered into a Special Administration bond with Reuben **HINTON** in the sum of $1,000.00, to serve as administrator on the estate of Rhoda **PARKER**, deceased, until the next court.[25] David[7] conducted the sale of her perishable property 6 November 1823, and bought Negroes **JACOB**, **SEALEY** and **PRISE** for $240.00 on 22 December 1823.[26] In February Court 1825, Henry **GILLIAM**, James W. **RIDDICK** and B. **WALTON** made report of their proceedings of auditing and stating the accounts of David[7] **PARKER** on the estate of Rhoda **PARKER**, deceased, and making a division of her personal estate.[27] No record of that division has been found.

   On 31 January 1822, David[7] **PARKER** purchased 200 acres from Frederick **HINTON** for $1,625.00. It is described as "a certain tract of land or Plantation, whereon I now live, Beginning at a Post Oak standing in the main path from Noah **HINTON**s to Tho[s] **PEARCE**'s James **HINTON**s corner in Robt. **PARKER**s line thence binding said Robt. **PARKER**s line by various courses to John **WALTON**s line thence on his line to the run of the Flatt branch thence down the run to a water Oak thence by a line of marked trees along the old path to a red Oak on the edge of Noah **HINTON**s plantation thence crossing the same to a persemon at the corner of Noah **HINTON**s Orchard thence by a line of trees S[o].70.E. or thereabout to the aforesaid public path thence binding said path to the first station..." Witnesses to this deed were R. **PARKER** and Reuben **LASSITER**. It was proved in February Court 1822, by the oath of Robt. **PARKER**.[28] It will be recalled that Joseph[6] **PARKER** left his land to his wife, Rhoda, then to James[7] after her death.

   In a Gates County Court held 17 November 1823, it was "Ordered that David **PARKER** be appointed Guardian to Jame_ **PARKER** orphan of Joseph **PARKER** decd. & that he give bond & Security in the sum of Three thousand dollars."[29] No record of that bond has been found. David[7] **PARKER** made a sale of "the moveable property belongin to James **PARKER** Olphin [sic] of Joseph **PARKER** Deseast Sold on a credit of Six months December the 22[st] day 1823." That sale netted $259.19.[30] The reverse of that document shows "Account of Sales of the perishable Estate of James Parker *decd*." That clerical error is most misleading as James[7] **PARKER** lived until 1882. That account of sales was also submitted to February Court 1825. David[7] and William **HINTON** were appointed administrators on the estate of his uncle, John[6] **PARKER**, in that same court. [31]

   There is no extant marriage record for David[7] **PARKER**, but it appears that he married Sarah G. **HINTON** circa 1828. She was the daughter of Reuben and Penelope **HINTON**, as evidenced by the will of Reuben **HINTON** of 28 March 1837, probated August 1837. He bequeathed his daughter, Sarah **PARKER**, $200.00.[32] Sarah G. (**HINTON**) **PARKER** was born 7 January 1805, and died 20 December

---

[23] Gates County Will Book 2:173-175

[24] On-site transcription of gravestone in Elmwood Cemetery, Gates County, NC, by Raymond Parker Fouts, March 1975, hereafter, Elmwood Cemetery.

[25] NCSA, G.041.2194762, Gates County Estates, Record of 1765-1920, Folder: Parker, Rodah 1823, Doc. #454

[26] Ibid., Doc. #459-462; #466

[27] Fouts, *Minutes of County Court of Pleas and Quarter Sessions Gates County, North Carolina 1824-1827, Vol. VI*, c. 1988, 49:#1366; 50:#1367

[28] Gates County Deed Book 11:193

[29] Fouts, *Minutes of County Court of Pleas and Quarter Sessions Gates County, North Carolina 1818-1823, Vol. V*, c. 1987, 168:#1293

[30] NCSA, G.041.2194761, Gates County Estates, Record of 1765-1920, Folder: Parker, Joseph 1821, Doc. #1620

[31] Fouts, *Minutes of County Court of Pleas and Quarter Sessions Gates County, North Carolina 1824-1827, Vol. VI*, c. 1988, 43:#1358, 44:#1360

[32] Almasy, *Gates County, North Carolina Wills 1807-1838, Vol. II*, c. 1985, pp.171-172, Will Book 2:391-394. Sarah's maiden name was contributed by the late Mildred (Cross) Woodside.

1861. She is buried in Elmwood Cemetery.[33] They have been reputed to have been married in 1821, but their first child was not born until 1829, and it would have been most unusual for them to have remained childless for the first eight years of their marriage.

David[7] **PARKER** was appointed Constable in **HUNTER**s Mill district in November Court 1828. William **HINTON** and Reuben **HINTON** were his securities.[34] In May Court 1829, he was appointed overseer of the road "from **NORFLEET**'s Mill to John **WALTON**s, and that he have the following hands to work on said road viz. his own, Noah **HINTON**s, James **PARKER**s, Ann **BOND**s, Mary **HINTON**s & Reuben **HINTON**s &c."[35] In November Court 1831, David[7] **PARKER** was allowed $5.56 in payment for serving as a Patrolman.[36]

On 18 November 1834, an "Indenture of agreement" was made between Bryant B. **BEST** and wife Mary **BEST** that for $100.00 they sold to David[7] **PARKER** "one Certain tract of Land in Gates County bounded by David & James **PARKER**s Ann **BOND** Federbrick [sic] **JONES** & Noah **HINTON** & others & is the /same/ tract of Land assigned to /the/ above named Mary **BEST** as her Dower in the Estate of Reuben **HINTON** Junior. To have and to hold to the said David **PARKER** his heirs & assigns for & during the natural life of the Said Mary **BEST**..." C. R. **KINNEY** witnessed this document.[37] The number of acres in this tract is not specified.

On 19 November 1834, Benbury **WALTON** sold David[7] **PARKER** 35 acres for $75.00. It is described as "a Certain piece of Land in said County and by refference to the report made in the division of Land belonging to the heirs of James **HINTON** dec[d]. find that the no...drawn by his son Reuben **HINTON** dec[d]. to run as follows, viz. Beginning at a large White Oak a Corner of Noah **HINTON** Jun[r]. in Fred[d]. [sic] **JONES**'s line, thence S. 8½° E. 153 poles to /a/ small pine a corner of N. **HINTON**s in James **PARKER**'s line thence S. 85° E 32½ poles to a pine Stump a corner of James **PARKER** in Nancy **BOND**s line thence N. **BOND**s line 144 poles to a Persimmon tree a corner in said James line thence N. 80° W. 27 poles N. 71° W. 18 poles to the first Station..." **WALTON** had purchased this land from Jephtha **FOWLKES**, guardian to the heirs of Reuben **HINTON**, Jr., 18 November 1834. Willis J. **RIDDICK** witnessed this deed.[38]

On 23 March 1841, James **SMITH** sold David[7] **PARKER** 75 acres of land for $300.00. It is described as "Beginning at a hollow bridge across the main Road leading from Sunsbury to Gatesville at the mouth of a ditch in Hance **HOFLER** & wife Elizabeth **HOFLER**'s, being cut down the run of the Holly-tree branch, and running up said ditch or branch along said **HOFLER**'s road field on the West side of the big ditch, thence along said **HOFLER**'s line a straight course to a red oak at the corner of my low ground fence, thence running on the West side of the fence to a post Oak a corner in said **HOFLER**'s line, thence running across the field on the South side of the line fence something of an Easterly course to an ash over the fence in the edge of the woods, on the East side of said **HOFLER**s fence, thence running along said fence to a white oak a corner, thence running down said fence something of a Westerly course to the run of the holly-tree branch, thence up said branch to David **PARKER**'s line, thence to a post oak a corner of James **HINTON**'s heirs, & Nathan **PEARCE**, thence to the heirs of Abram **GREEN**'s line, thence along said **GREEN**'s line to the aforesaid road, thence up said road to the first station, it being a part of the tract of Land formerly owned by Richard **CROSS**, and given to him by his Grand-Father Bond **MINCHEW**, and lying on the South side of the road beforementioned [sic] and is the land that I purchased of James R **RIDDICK** & Elizabeth **HAYS**, now **HOFLER**..." Hance **HOFLER** and Willis J. **RIDDICK** witnessed this deed and it was acknowledged in August Court 1841.[39].

His next purchase was from his brother, James H.[7] **PARKER**, on 20 October 1842, for the sum of $3,000.00. This parcel contained 295 acres, "it being the same tract of land devised to the said James H. **PARKER** by his father Joseph **PARKER**, with a tract of land purchased by the said James H.

---

[33] Elmwood Cemetery
[34] Fouts, *Minutes of County Court of Pleas and Quarter Sessions Gates County, North Carolina 1828-1831, "Rough Minutes" May 1827-May 1833, Vol. VII*, c. 1990, 29:#42
[35] Ibid., 50:#67
[36] Ibid., 125:#174
[37] Ibid., 15:149-150
[38] Ibid., 15:165-166
[39] NCSA, C.041.40009, Gates Co. Real Estate Conveyances 1841-1847, Vol: 18,19, 18:37-38

**PARKER** of Jas. **HARE** by deed bearing date the 2ⁿᵈ.. day of February 1837, and is the same lands upon which the said James H. **PARKER** now lives...” It is described as “lying & being in the County of Gates & State aforesaid, on the West side of the Indian swamp, Beginning at the mouth of a small branch that maketh out of said swamp upon the North side of said swamp so running up the branch to David **PARKER**’s line formerly James **HINTON**’s, thence along said **PARKER**’s line to Noah **HINTON**’s orphan of James **HINTON** deceased, thence to James **HINTON**’s line & running said line to Noah **HINTON**’s Sr. line, & binding on said **HINTON**’s line to John **WALTON**’s line, thence along said **WALTON**’s line to the Edenton road near said **WALTON**’s gate, and along the aforesaid road to the aforesaid Indian swamp, & up the said swamp to the first station...” For that same consideration, James H.⁷ sold David⁷ “one brandy still, all the hogsheads, apple mill, & implements for making cider & brandy which are now on the aforesaid land.” This deed was witnessed by W. G. **DAUGHTRY** and Will: J. **BAKER**.⁴⁰ This land adjoined his purchase of 200 acres from Frederick **HINTON** in 1822, and is the same purchased by his grandfather, Joseph⁵ **PARKER**, on 10 February 1770.

David⁷ **PARKER** continued to add to his plantation on 18 September 1844, when he purchased 33 acres for $94.00 from Noah **HINTON**. It is described as “Beginning at a stake in the path leading from Ann **BOND**’s to the road that leads from the Edenton road to **NORFLEET**’s mill, it being where a pine stood a corner of Willis J. **RIDDICK** in James H. **PARKER**’s line formerly, but the said David **PARKER**’s at present thence N 15° W. 176 poles along the said **RIDDICK**’s line to a pine in the said David **PARKER**’s line on the West side of the old path called the Amos **LASSITER** path, thence N 50° E 28 poles to a post oak standing in said path, a corner formerly of Frederick **JONES** & others thence S. 1½° W. 15 poles, thence S 5½° W. 21 poles, thence S 5° E. 14½ poles to a white oak a corner of said **JONES**, thence N 64° E. 30 poles to a large white oak a corner of the said David **PARKER** in a tract of land formerly owned by Reuben **HINTON** dec’d thence S 8½° E 153 poles to a stake where a small pine stood a corner of the said David **PARKER** standing in the lands formerly owned by James H. **PARKER**, now the said David **PARKER**, thence N 85° W. 24½ poles to the first station, containing thirty-three acres be the same more or less, it being the lands that was devised to the said Noah **HINTON** by the death of his father and the same land the said Noah **HINTON** drew in the division of the lands belonging to James **HINTON** dec’d...” Joseph **PARKER** and Henry his X mark **TREVATHAN** witnessed this deed.⁴¹

David⁷ **PARKER** continued to buy and sell land and took many deeds in trust which were subsequently sold. He made application for a fire insurance policy 18 February 1851. It is an interesting document and is transcribed here in full: “Application of David **PARKER** Esqr of the County of Gates for insurance against Fire by the “North Carolina Mutual Insurance Company for the sum of Forty Three hundred & Fifty dollars to wit on his dwelling house fifteen hundred dollars at Ten per cent on his house hold furnitur [sic] therein five hundred dollars at Ten per cent on his provisions in Smo hous [sic] five hundred dollars at Ten per cent office one hundred dollars at Ten per cent Kitchen one hundred dollars at Ten per cent 2 Smo house at fifty dollars at Ten per Cent, Barn Two hundred dollars at Ten pr cent Grain in Said Barn one thousand dollars at Ten per cent Carriage house ~~House~~ one hundred dollars at Ten per cent Stables fifty dollars at Ten per cent 7 Mules & Horses at the Sum of Three hundred dollars, amount of premium net Four hundred and forty dollars. This property is situated 4 Miles South east from Gatesville on road leading from Edenton to **NORFLEET** Mill bounded North by land of Ro [?] **HINTON** E by J **WALTON** South Jno **WALTON** & Edenton road west is R **HINTON** of wood & in good repair no Scuttle to roof, 32 ± 32-2 Stories high and addition of 14 + 18 all 2 Stories high 2 chimneys 6 fire places no Stoves at present Kitchen is 60 feet s. west from house smoke hous [sic] are the same distance J. **HUSMAN** agent David **PARKER** applicant” Before Henry M **DAUGHTRY**, Justice of the Peace for the County of Gates, the execution of this memorandum was proved and ordered to be registered with the certificate 18 February 1851.⁴² This document describes the home on Elmwood Plantation.

This beautiful home is reputed to have been built by David⁷ **PARKER** in 1822. That date is unlikely as he was only 19 years of age at that time and his mother, Rhoda **PARKER**, had possession of that land until her death in 1823. It then fell to his brother, James H.⁷ **PARKER**, from whom he pur-

---

⁴⁰ NCSA, C.041.40009, Gates Co. Real Estate Conveyances 1841-1847, Vol: 18,19, 18:37-38, 18:326-327
⁴¹ Ibid., 19:80-81
⁴² NCSA, C.041.40010, Gates Co. Real Estate Conveyances 1847-1857, Vol: 20,21, 20:436-437

chased it 20 October 1842. If Elmwood actually was built in the 1820's, it was built for James H.[7] **PARKER**, not David[7] **PARKER**. If David[7] had it built, it was more likely to have been in 1843, instead of 1822.

David[7] **PARKER** lived a long and prosperous life and made his will 17 December 1874, transcribed here in full: "I David **PARKER**, of the County of Gates and State of North Carolina being of sound mind and memory do make publish and declare the following to be my last Will and Testament hereby revoking and declaring null and void all other wills and testaments heretofore made by me.

Item 1st I direct my Executors hereinafter named to provide for my body suitable burial and to pay all my just debts.

Item 2nd I give and devise to my three sons Dr. Joseph **PARKER**, James **PARKER** and John D. **PARKER** and their heirs all of my land and real estate of every kind and description where ever situated and being, to have and to hold to them and their heirs as tenants in common.

Item 3rd I give and bequeathe to my daughter Diana E. **BURGESS** to her sole and separate use the sum of Twenty five thousand dollars to be paid to her by my executors herein named: and I request my said daughter and her husband William B. **BURGESS** to Keep the said sum or a portion of it invested in her own name.

Item 4th I give and bequeathe to my son-in-law William B. **BURGESS** all of his indebtedness to me whether due by bond, note or account, and I direct my executors herein named, at my death, to cancel and deliver same to him.

Item 5th I give and bequeathe to my daughter Margaret J. **BUFFKIN** to her sole and separate use the sum of Ten thousand dollars to be paid to her by my executors hereinafter named.

Item 6th I give and bequeathe to my son-in-law Malachi W. **BUFFKIN** a certain bond or promissory note which I hold against him for the sum of one thousand dollars bearing date October 24th in the year one thousand eight hundred and sixty six: and I direct my executors hereinafter named at my death, to cancel and deliver the same to him.

Item 7th I give and bequeathe to my daughter Amazon **ASKEW** the sum of five dollars to be paid to her by my executors hereinafter named.

Item 8th I give and bequeathe to Ann **DELK** in consideration of her Kind and faithful service to me, the sum of Sixty dollars annually so long as she continues to live with Dr. Joseph **PARKER** and James **PARKER** or with either of them and I hereby direct my executors hereinafter named to pay the said sum of sixty dollars to her each and every year so long as she continues to live as aforesaid and no longer.

Item 9th It is my will and desire that Napoleon B. **DELKE** receive a good English Education and that Cleopatria **DELKE** be taught to read and write and I give and bequeathe to my executors hereinafter named a sum of money out of my estate sufficient to educate them as aforesaid and direct my said executors to hold the same in trust and expend it for the said purpose.

Item 10th I direct my executors hereinafter named to enclose my family grave yard with an iron railing, and to place suitable marble Slabs or tomb Stones over the graves of my deceased wife, my son Augustus and John P. C. **DELK** and over my own grave and pay for the same out of my estate.

Item 11th I give, devise and bequeathe all the rest and residue of my property and estate of every Kind and description, not herein before devised and bequeathed to my three sons Dr. Joseph **PARKER**, James **PARKER** and John D. **PARKER** to them, their heirs, executors and administrators.

Item 12th I hereby name, constitute and appoint my two sons Dr. Joseph **PARKER** and James **PARKER** executors to this my last will and Testament in manner and form above written and charge them with the faithful execution of the trusts herein imposed.

In testimony whereof I David **PARKER** have hereunto set my hand and seal this the 17th day of December A. D. 1874.                              (Signed) D. **PARKER** {seal}

Signed, sealed, published and declared by the said David **PARKER** to be his last will and testament in the presence of us who at his request and in his presence and in the presence of each other do subscribe our names as witnesses thereto. M. L. **EURE**, John **BRADY**, A. F. **HARRELL**

In Probate Court 23 April 1875, the personal and real property in this estate was declared to be $150,000.00. The heirs were named as Mrs. Diana E. **BURGESS** and William B. **BURGESS** of Portsmouth, Virginia, Mrs. Margaret J. **BUFFKIN** and Malachi W. **BUFFKIN** of Pasquotank County, North Carolina, Amazon **ASKEW** of Bertie County, North Carolina, John D. **PARKER** of Perquimans County, North Carolina, Joseph **PARKER** and James **PARKER** of Gates County, Ann **DELKE**, and N. B. and

**Chapter 14:** Children of Joseph[5] **PARKER** (*Joseph[4],Thomas[3],Thomas[2],William[1]*)

Cleo **DELKE**, minors without guardian, of Gates County, North Carolina.[43]

The terms of this will were disagreeable to two of his daughters. A caveat was brought into Superior Court in Gates County on 19 October 1875, with Thomas R. **ASKEW** and wife Amazon[8], and M. W. **BUFFKIN** and wife Margaret[8], versus Joseph[8] **PARKER**, James[8] **PARKER** and J. D.[8] **PARKER**.[44] The complaint in the petition was that none of them were given notice of the probate and that they lived 50 or 60 miles from Gatesville at that time. William B. and Diana E.[8] **BURGESS** were residents of Virginia. Thomas R. and Amazon[8] **ASKEW** resided in Bertie County, and M. W. and Margaret[8] **BUFFKIN** were residents of Camden County. They alleged undue influence of David[7]'s sons, "men of strong intellect and great force of character." They wanted a trial by jury on the validity of the will as they believed themselves "entitled to $40,000.00 each."[45]

An affidavit for removal of the cause to another county was entered and Judge Allmand A. **MC KOY** ordered the trial moved to Camden County on 20 June 1876. The trial was held in a Special Term of Superior Court in Camden County on 13 December 1876. The jury declared it to be the will of David[7] **PARKER**.[46] He died 17 April 1875, and is buried in Elmwood Cemetery.[47]

On 17 December 1877, Joseph[8] **PARKER** and wife, Annie M. **PARKER**, and John D.[8] **PARKER** sold James[8] **PARKER** 1,100 acres for $5,000.00. It is described as "land whereon the late David **PARKER** dec'd. lived and died situated in County of Gates and state of N. C. in **HUNTER**s Mill and Mintonsville Townships, bounded on the west by the lands of Thomas **SMITH**, W. P. **ROBERTS** and Mary **BOND**, Peter **NIXON** and others, on the south by the lands of Mary **HARE**, Henry **WILLIAMS** and others...excepting and assuring from the operation of this deed one third of the Family Grave Yard to said Joseph **PARKER** and one third of the said Grave Yard to the said John D. **PARKER** and the right of ingress and egress through said land to said Grave Yard..." John **BRADY** witnessed this deed.[48]

Margaret J.[8] **PARKER** (*David[7],Joseph[6],Joseph[5],Joseph[4],Thomas[3],Thomas[2],William[1]*) was born 18 May 1829, and died 22 June 1901. She is buried in Pasquotank County, NC. She married William **MESSENGER** in 1855, then secondly, married Malachi W. **BUFFKIN**, son of John **BUFFKIN**, who was born circa 1836, Perquimans County. He died 9 June 1909, and is also buried in Pasquotank County.[49] No further information.

Joseph[8] **PARKER** (*David[7],Joseph[6],Joseph[5],Joseph[4],Thomas[3],Thomas[2],William[1]*) was born circa 1830. He had completed his education as a physician by 1860, as he appears in that U. S. Census, in **HUNTER**'s Mill Township, as 30 years of age and his occupation was "Dr."[50] He continued to live with his father and brother James[8], until at least 1870.[51]

Dr. Joseph[8] **PARKER** and his wife, Annie M. **PARKER**, were residents of Wake County, NC, in 1886.[52] They were married between 1870 and 1877, as evidenced by the foregoing deed. James[8] and Lavinia L. **PARKER** and John D.[8] and Mary R. **PARKER**, of Gates and Perquimans respectively, sold to Joseph[8] **PARKER**, of Wake County, 140 acres for $300.00 on 20 February 1886. It was devised to them by David[7] **PARKER** and was known as the Jno. C. **WOLFLEY** tract, lying near Merchants Mills. It adjoined the Mill tract and the lands of Frank **SPEIGHT**s heirs, the Blake **JONES** tract, White Pot Swamp and **BENNETT**s Creek.[53]

He was dead before September 1889. In the Superior Court of Chowan County, NC, Annie M.

---

[43] Gates County, NC, Will Book 4:61-63

[44] Gates County, NC, Special Proceeding in the Superior Court, 1:21

[45] NCSA, G.042.2194760, Gates Co. Estates, Record of 1765-1920, Vol. Odom-Parker, Folder: Parker, David 1875 Doc. #1667-1677

[46] Ibid., Doc. #1678-1679; Doc. #1773-1779

[47] Elmwood Cemetery

[48] Gates County, NC, Deed Book 28:241

[49] Spence, Wilma Cartwright, *Tombstones & Epitaphs of Northeastern N. C., Consisting of Beaufort, Camden, Chowan, Currituck, Gates, Hyde, Pasquotank, Perquimans and Washington Counties*, Gateway Press, Inc., c. 1973, p. 207

[50] U. S. Census, 1860, Gates Co., NC, M653 Roll #898, p. 79, #782

[51] Ibid., 1870, M593 Roll #1139, p. 34, #254

[52] Gates County, NC, Deed Book 37:442

[53] Ibid., 37:442

**PARKER**, Administratrix of Joseph[8] **PARKER**, entered a suit against her son, Moore[9] **PARKER**, and his guardian ad litem, W. M. **BOND**, and was appointed Commissioner to "make sale of the lands of Joseph **PARKER**, deceased," 12 September 1889. The petition states that the personal estate of the decedent **PARKER** is insufficient to pay his debts and charges of administration. Her dower was to be allotted to her out of cash, "the funds arising from the said land according to the annuity tables, it being found a fact and adjudged that the said Widow is 38 years old and that the funds other than that allotted as dower constitute assets in the hands of the administratrix to pay such debts." These lands were located in Chowan, Gates and Perquimans Counties and totaled 2,507 acres.[54] She sold one of those parcels of 700 acres to L. L. **SMITH** 6 March 1891, for $1,900.00. It was the tract known as the Dr. **PARKER-JORDAN** place, in Mintonsville Township, Gates County, and is described as "beginning at Catharine Creek or Mill Creek bridge on the river road, thence down the said Creek to the other branch of Catharine Creek, thence up said Creek towards Old Town Landing to Leander **HOWARD**s line, his line back to the creek, up the Creek to the Little Mill run, thence up the run of Little Mill Swamp across the river road and adjoining the lands of Martin **STALLINGS**, Joseph **RIDDICK** and Wm. **WHITE** to the **WELCH** Mill Pond, thence run of the said Millpond & race to the first station... Annie M. **PARKER**, Commissioner."[55] **WELCH** Millpond lies on the border of Gates and Chowan Counties on Catherine Creek.

Little is known of Moore[9] **PARKER** (*Joseph[8],David[7],Joseph[6],Joseph[5],Joseph[4],Thomas[3],Thomas[2], William[1]*) of Raleigh, Wake County, NC, the only known issue of Joseph[8] and Annie **MOORE**. It is estimated here that he was born circa 1878 and died between 1917 and 1919, in Raleigh. He appears to have married a young woman of unknown name who was born circa 1886. She is listed in the 1920 Census as "Mrs. Moore **PARKER**." They had daughter Annie M.[10] **PARKER**, born circa 1906; daughter Bettie[10] **PARKER**, born circa 1908; son R. Moore[10] **PARKER**, born circa 1910 and son James M.[10] **PARKER**, born circa 1918. They lived on E. Edenton Street in Raleigh in 1920.[56] No further information.

🙢🙠🙢🙠🙢🙠🙢🙠🙢🙠🙢🙠🙢🙠🙢🙠🙢🙠🙢🙠🙢🙠🙢🙠🙢🙠🙢🙠🙢🙠🙢🙠🙢🙠🙢🙠🙢🙠🙢🙠🙢🙠🙢🙠

Diana E.[8] **PARKER** (*David[7],Joseph[6],Joseph[5],Joseph[4],Thomas[3],Thomas[2],William[1]*) was born circa 1833.[57] She appears on a Gates County marriage bond dated 17 December 1851, with William B. **BURGESS**.[58] When her father died in 1875, she and William were residents of Portsmouth, VA. No further information.

Sarah L.[8] **PARKER** (*David[7],Joseph[6],Joseph[5],Joseph[4],Thomas[3],Thomas[2],William[1]*) was born circa 1835 and was 15 years of age in 1850.[59] As she does not appear in the 1860 U. S. Census, she may have died in the interim. No further information.

James[8] **PARKER** (*David[7],Joseph[6],Joseph[5],Joseph[4],Thomas[3],Thomas[2],William[1]*) was born 29 January 1836, and died 4 February 1908. He is buried in Elmwood Cemetery.[60] He married Lavinia Louise **WHEDBEE** 5 October 1876, at J. S. **WHEDBEE**'s residence.[61]

The most significant purchase made by James[8] **PARKER** was the one made in 1877, from his brothers. He made several other purchases, among which are the following deeds. The first was from his cousin, Joseph W.[8] **PARKER**, of Hertford County, of 300 acres for $1,200.00, on 11 January 1883. It was known as the John R. **HOFLER** place on the road from Gatesville to Somerton, two miles north of Gatesville, on Lassiter **RIDDICK** to the Winton Road, east on that road to the John **ROBERTS** tract, south to James R. **BROWN**, to the road leading from Honey Pot Swamp to Gatesville, along that road toward Gatesville to a corner on the **BENBURY** tract, then northwest on **BENBURY** to the Gatesville and Somerton Road to the beginning.[62]

On 10 April 1883, James[8] purchased 160 acres for $350.00 from L. L. **SMITH**. It was known as the "Nancy **BOND** tract between the Edenton Road and the road leading from Gatesville to Sunbury back

---

[54] NCSA, C.R.024.508.79, Chowan County Estates Records 1728-1951, Folder: Parker, Joseph 1789

[55] Gates County, NC, Deed Book 45:509

[56] U. S. Census 1920, Wake Co., NC, T625, Roll: 1326, p. 58B Enumerated 14 January 1920.

[57] U. S. Census 1850, Gates Co., NC, M432, Roll: 631, p. 101, Fam. # 810

[58] Almasy, *Gates County, North Carolina Marriage Bonds 1778-1868*, c. 1987, p. 15

[59] U. S. Census 1850, Gates Co., NC, M432, Roll: 631, p. 101, Fam. # 810

[60] Elmwood Cemetery

[61] Gates County Historical Society, *Bible Records of Gates County, N. C.*, c. unknown, p. 146.

[62] Gates County, NC, Deed Book 34:165

of James **HINTON**s and the Peter **NIXON** tract." It adjoined Walter **HINTON**, Jacob R. **HATHA-WAY**, Rufus **BLANCHARD** and James[8] **PARKER**.[63]

On 29 April 1892, James[8] and Lavinia L. **PARKER** sold all the juniper timber seven inches and over in diameter to the John L. **ROPER** Lumber Company for $300.00. The land containing that timber is near **BOND**'s Landing on **BENNETT**'s Creek and was formerly known as the John W. **HINTON** Swamp, then as the **PARKER** Swamp. It contained 50 acres and was bounded on the north by the swamp land belonging to the heirs of Henry B. **LASSITER**, on the east by the **BAKER** Swamp, now owned by the lumber company, and on the south and west by **BENNETT**'s Creek.[64]

On the following day, 30 April 1892, "Annie M. **PARKER**, Administratrix, against Moore **PARKER**," in the Superior Court of Chowan County, sold the above 50 acres to James[8] **PARKER**, called "the Juniper Swamp tract," for $275.00. The other parcel in that same deed was the Peter **NIXON** place of 36 acres, adjoining James **PARKER** and James **HOLLAND**.[65]

James[8] **PARKER** made his will 20 January 1808, in Gates County, transcribed here in full: "I James **PARKER** of the County and State aforesaid, being of sound mind and understanding, but Considering the uncertainty of my earthly existence, do make and declare this my last Will and Testament. First. It is my will and desire, and I so order and direct, that the premises and plantation on which I now live, Known as the "Home Place" situated in said County adjoining the lands of E. F. **TURNER**, J. B. **HOLLAND**, the heirs of Jno. R. **WALTON**, J. E. **HARRELL**, Edwin **JONES** and others and Containing One thousand three hundred acres more or less, be and remain as a home for my wife Lavinia L. **PARKER** and my Children Viz: Sallie Parker **CROSS**, Hulda Parker **HAYES**, J. Louise **PARKER** and Ethel **PARKER** during their natural lives, and that said premises and plantation then go to the heirs of my said Children as the law directs.

Second. All the rest and residue of my Estate of every nature and Kind I give devise and bequeath to my heirs at law, to be divided equally among them, according to law and in such way and manner as if I had died intestate. In the final distribution of my Estate, I direct that those of my children to whom I have made advances be required to account for the same.

Lastly: I hereby Constitute & appoint all my Children, Viz: Sallie Parker **CROSS**, Hulda Parker **HAYES**, J. Louise **PARKER** and Ethel **PARKER** my lawful executrixes to all intents and purposes to execute this my last will and testament according to the true intent and meaning of the same and every part and Clause thereof. In witness whereof I the said James **PARKER** do hereunto set my hand and seal this 20th day of January 1908. James **PARKER** {Seal}" John G. **CROSS** and Charles G. **ELLIS** witnessed this will.[66]

On 22 February 1908, an application was made for letters testamentary on the estate of James[8] **PARKER**, considered to be worth about $75,000.00, by Lavinia L. **PARKER**, widow, Sallie Parker[9] **CROSS**, Hulda Parker[9] **HAYES**, J. Louise[9] **PARKER**, "all of full age of Gates Co. N. C. and Ethel[9] **PARKER** a minor without Guardian of Gates Co. N. C."[67] They took an inventory of his estate 3 March 1908.[68]

In her petition for a year's support on 30 April 1908, "Lavinia L. **PARKER** widow of James **PARKER** vs. Sallie Parker **CROSS**, Hulda Parker **HAYES** and J. Louise **PARKER** Executrixes of said James **PARKER** Dec'd.," she stated that "her late husband died in Gates county on the 4th day of February 1908, leaving a last will and Testament, from which she has dissented." No allowance had been made for her and she requested that "an order issue to the Sheriff Comanding him to sumon a Justice of the Peace and two indifferent persons qualified to act as Jurors of the County, to assign to her, from the Crop, stock and provisions of the deceased a sufficiency for the Support of herself and her family for one year from the death of her husband." That order was carried out and she had an allotment of $750.00, filed 28

---

[63] Gates County, NC, Deed Book 34:438

[64] Ibid., 44:210

[65] Ibid., 44:313

[66] Gates County, NC, Will Book 5:86

[67] NCSA, G.042.2194761, Gates Co. Estates, Record of 1765-1920, Vol. Parker, E.-Parker, M., Folder: Parker, James 1908, Doc. #866-867

[68] Ibid., Doc. #902-917

**Chapter 14:** Children of Joseph⁵ **PARKER** (*Joseph⁴,Thomas³,Thomas²,William¹*)

May 1908.[69]

On 27 May 1908, Lavinia's dower of one-third of James⁸'s lands was laid off to her under a writ of dower issued 15 May 1908, for the term of her natural life. The land is described as "1. The Home place, situated in both **HUNTER**s Mill and Mintonsville Townships Gates County, adjoining the lands of Edwin **JONES**, the heirs of Thos. E. **SMITH**, E. F. **TURNER**, James B. **HOLLAND** the heirs of Jno. R. **WALTON**, James E. **HARRELL** and others, Containing 1300 acres more or less and being the place at which said James **PARKER** resided at the time of his death.

2. The tract of land situated in Gatesville Township said County near the town of Gatesville Known as the **HOFLER** place and bounded as follows: On the North by the lands of Elijah **PHELPS**, the Lassiter **RIDDICK** lands and others; On the East by the lands of O. C. **TURNER**, L. L. **SMITH**, and others; On the South by the lands of G. K. **RIDDICK** the **BENBURY** lands and others, And On the West by the Main road leading from Gatesville to Gates Station, Containing 250 acres more or less.

3ʳᵈ. The Hotel lot and land belonging thereto situated in the town of Gatesville and bounded as follows: On the North by Court Street and the lands belonging to Gates County, On the East by Main Street; On the South by **BENNETT**s Creek and the lands of A. O. **HILL**, On the West by said **HILL** and the Gates Ferry road, Containing 10 acres, more or less and including the Post Office building, the place now occupied by Q. H. **TROTMAN**, the Ware house and land lying on **BENNETT**s Creek.

4ᵗʰ The Stable lot situated on Church Street in the town of Gatesville Known as the Hotel Stables and bounded as follows: On the North by the lane or Street recently opened, which runs from Main Street at the North East Corner of the S. P. **CROSS** Brick store to Court Street; On the East by the S. P. **CROSS** Brick store lot and the H. C. **ROUNTREE** Stable lot, On the South by Court Street, the land of R. M. **RIDDICK** and the lands belonging to Gates County And On the West by Church Street, Containing ¼ of an acre more or less.

5ᵗʰ. The Store lot in the town of Gatesville now occupied by W. R. **HAYES** and bounded as follows: On the North by the H. C. **ROUNTREE** Stable lot; On the East by Main Street; On the South by the Joe **DUNN** Corner Store lot And On the west by the lane which runs from Court Street to the Stable lot mentioned above, Containing ⅛ of an acre more or less.

6ᵗʰ One half undivided interest in a Certain tract of land situated in Mt. Herman Township Pasquotank County North Carolina adjoining the lands of D. C. **PERRY**, Exum **CHAPPELL** Foreman **BLADES** Lumber Company, the heirs of T. G. **SKINNER** & others Containing (2000) Two thousand acres more or less and Known as the **SANDERLIN** farm."[70] This document describes all of James⁸ **PARKER**'s known real estate holdings at the time of his death.

On 28 May 1908, a more detailed description of Lavinia's dower in the "Home Place" appears in the report of the jury allotting dower. It is described as "Beginning in the public road, leading from Gatesville to Zion M. E. Church, in the run of the "Indian Swamp," a corner on the lands of James N. **CARTER**, W. R. **HATHAWAY** and the lands belonging to the estate of John R. **WALTON**, dec'd. formerly the Thomas B. **WALTON** land; thence along said road, nearly a West Course, to the road leading from the Gatesville-Zion road to Merchant Mills; thence along the Merchant Mills road so far as the J. R. **WALTON** land extends; thence along the line of the said **WALTON** land (that part lying on the North side of the Gatesville-Zion road.) its various courses back to the Gatesville-Zion road; thence along the last named road in a westerly direction to the land now owned by Edwin **JONES**; thence, leaving the road along the line of the Edwin **JONES** land, the George **RIDDICK** land, the James I. **SMITH** land, the F. E. **BAINES** land and the lands of E. F. **TURNER** to the aforesaid Merchant Mills road; thence along this last named road, its various courses, to that corner of the James **HINTON** land nearest the late residence of the aforesaid James **PARKER**, dec'd;; thence along the line of the James **HINTON** land, (now owned by Penina **HOFLER**, wife of Johnson **HOFLER**,) to a path leading to James B. **HOLLAND**s; thence along said path to the land of said **HOLLAND**; thence along said **HOLLAND**'s line to the "Indian Swamp"; thence down said swamp binding on the lands of J. E. **CARTER**, Alex **CARTER** and J. N. **CARTER** to the Gatesville-Zion road the first station, including the dwelling house, offices, outhouses, buildings and improvements thereon. This 28 day of may 1908.{H. C. **WILLIAMS** E. R. **ROBERTS**

---

[69] NCSA, G.042.2194761, Gates Co. Estates, Record of 1765-1920, Vol. Parker, E.-Parker, M., Folder: Parker, James 1908, Doc. #931-933; #934-937

[70] Ibid., Doc. #951-954

**Chapter 14:** Children of Joseph[5] **PARKER** (*Joseph[4],Thomas[3],Thomas[2],William[1]*)

Lycurgus **HOFLER.**[71]

Sallie[9] **PARKER** (*James[8],David[7],Joseph[6],Joseph[5],Joseph[4],Thomas[3],Thomas[2],William[1]*) was born 5 July 1877, at Elmwood. She was the eldest of the four daughters of James[8] and Lavinia Louise **(WHEDBEE) PARKER.** On 20 April 1898, she married Simon Peter **CROSS**, at Elmwood. He was born in Alabama, 1 May 1873, and died 9 February 1964.[72] They lived in Gatesville and he was the proprietor of the S. P. **CROSS** "Brick Store," as noted above. Sallie[9] **(PARKER) CROSS** died 21 July 1955 and is buried at Elmwood. Simon Peter **CROSS** died 7 February 1964, and is also buried there

James Parker[10] **CROSS** (*Sallie[9],James[8],David[7],Joseph[6],Joseph[5],Joseph[4],Thomas[3],Thomas[2],William[1]*) was born 9 April 1899, and died 17 December 1968. He married Mary Emily **GATLING** 25 August 1925. Their only known issue was James Parker[11] **CROSS**, Jr. Mary Emily **(GATLING) CROSS** died 1 April 1973.[73] No further information included here.

Catherine[10] **CROSS** (*Sallie[9],James[8],David[7],Joseph[6],Joseph[5],Joseph[4],Thomas[3],Thomas[2],William[1]*) was born 13 November 1900. She married Thomas Jefferson **GREY**, Jr., 2 December 1931, in St. Mary's Episcopal Church, Gatesville. She died 21 September 1978, Bridgeville, Sussex County, Delaware, and is buried in the Bridgeville Cemetery. Dr. Catherine **(CROSS) GREY** was a general practitioner, specializing in obstetrics in Bridgeville for 38 years, until her retirement in 1969.[74] No further information.

Mildred[10] **CROSS** (*Sallie[9],James[8],David[7],Joseph[6],Joseph[5],Joseph[4],Thomas[3],Thomas[2],William[1]*) was born 9 August 1903 and married Joseph Owen **WOODSIDE** 16 September 1924, in St. Mary's Episcopal Church, Gatesville. Their daughter, Nancy Cross[11] **WOODSIDE**, was born 30 August 1926, and married Chester Sears **JENKINS** 1 January 1943. Their daughter was Sallie Ann[12] **JENKINS.**[75] No further information.

Dorothy[10] **CROSS** (*Sallie[9],James[8],David[7],Joseph[6],Joseph[5],Joseph[4],Thomas[3],Thomas[2],William[1]*) was born 16 January 1907. She married Neely Jenkins **CROMER** in May 1933.[76] No further information.

Hulda[9] **PARKER** (*James[8],David[7],Joseph[6],Joseph[5],Joseph[4],Thomas[3],Thomas[2],William[1]*) was born 9 March 1879, at Elmwood. She married Thomas Gatling **HAYES** 7 November 1905, at St. Paul's Church, Norfolk, Norfolk County, Virginia. Thomas was born 20 November 1865, and died 28 December 1944. Hulda[9] died 3 December 1940, and both are buried in Elmwood Cemetery.[77] No further information.

Jimmie Louise[9] **PARKER** (*James[8],David[7],Joseph[6],Joseph[5],Joseph[4],Thomas[3],Thomas[2],William[1]*) was born 11 March 1884, at Elmwood. She married William John **HAYES** 16 January 1932, in Virginia Beach, Princess Anne County, Virginia.[78] William was born 9 October 1870, the son of Lemuel P. and Ella Virginia **(PARKER) HAYES**. He died 23 January 1938, in Gates County.[79] Jimmie Louise died 30 September 1958, and both are buried in Elmwood cemetery. No further information.

Ethel[9] **PARKER** (*James[8],David[7],Joseph[6],Joseph[5],Joseph[4],Thomas[3],Thomas[2],William[1]*) was born 23 September 1888, at Elmwood. She never married and died without issue 22 January 1972, and is buried at Elmwood.[80] No further information.

〰〰〰〰〰〰〰〰〰〰〰〰〰〰〰〰〰〰〰〰〰〰〰〰〰〰〰〰〰〰〰〰〰〰〰

John David[8] **PARKER** (*David[7],Joseph[6],Joseph[5],Joseph[4],Thomas[3],Thomas[2],William[1]*) was born 22 August 1838, at Elmwood. He died 29 December 1902, and is also buried there.[81] He married Mary

---

[71] NCSA, G.042.2194761, Gates Co. Estates, Record of 1765-1920, Vol. Parker, E.-Parker, M., Folder: Parker, James 1908, Doc. #965-968

[72] Gates County Historical Society, *Bible Records of Gates County, N. C.*, c. unknown, p. 146-147; U. S. Census 1900, Gates Co., NC, T623, Roll: #1196, Gatesville Twp., p. 1, Sheet 1B, Fam. #18

[73] Gates County Historical Society, *Bible Records of Gates County, N. C.*, c. unknown, p. 146-147

[74] Ibid.; Obituary, *Gates County Index*, 4 October 1978, p. 12

[75] Gates County Historical Society, *Bible Records of Gates County, N. C.*, c. unknown, p. 146-147; courtesy of Mildred Cross Woodside

[76] Ibid.

[77] Ibid.;Elmwood Cemetery

[78] Gates County Historical Society, *Bible Records of Gates County, N. C.*, c. unknown, p. 146-147

[79] Gates County Death Records, Book 10:60

[80] Elmwood Cemetery

[81] Elmwood Cemetery

Rebecca **WHEDBEE**, daughter of Joshua Skinner and Diana (**HINTON) WHEDBEE**, on 14 December 1878.[82] She was born in 1858 and died in 1926. She is also buried in Elmwood Cemetery. Their only known issue was one daughter, Nina⁹ **PARKER**, born in January 1881.[83]

Augustus M.⁸ **PARKER** (*David⁷,Joseph⁶,Joseph⁵,Joseph⁴,Thomas³,Thomas²,William¹*) was born 9 May 1841, and died 5 December 1863. He is buried in Elmwood Cemetery.[84]

Amazon⁸ **PARKER** (*David⁷,Joseph⁶,Joseph⁵,Joseph⁴,Thomas³,Thomas²,William¹*) was born circa 1847. She was one of the plaintiffs, with her husband, Thomas R. **ASKEW**, in the contest of the will of David⁷ **PARKER**, on 19 October 1875.

Thomas R. **ASKEW** appears in the Bertie County, NC, U. S. Census for 1870, as 40 years of age, with wife Mary O. **ASKEW**, and seven children. The youngest was Robert Lee **ASKEW**, age one month.[85] Amazon⁸ **PARKER** is known as Thomas' wife by 19 October 1875. The U. S. Census for 1880, in Bertie County, shows Thomas R. **ASKEW**, age 50, Amizon, age 32, five of his children, including Robert Lee , age 9, and Annie S., age 7, Willie H., age 4, and Margaret M., age 2.[86] At least the last two, Willie H.⁹ and Margaret M.⁹ **ASKEW**, were Amazon⁸'s children. No further information.

〰〰〰〰〰〰〰〰〰〰〰〰〰〰〰〰〰〰〰〰〰〰〰〰〰〰〰〰〰〰〰〰〰〰〰〰〰

James H.⁷ **PARKER** (*Joseph⁶,Joseph⁵,Joseph⁴,Thomas³,Thomas²,William¹*) was born 27 March 1809, and was the younger brother of David⁷ **PARKER**. The abstract of the following deed describes part of the land sold to David⁷ **PARKER** 20 October 1842: 2 February 1837 James **HARE** to James H. **PARKER** 25 acres $75.00, "beginning at a pine in James H. **PARKER**s line near his fence and John **WALTON**s corner then binding said **WALTON**s line to a Water oak a corner between Said James **HARE** and John **WALTON** and standing in John **HARE** Decst line then binding said John **HARE** Decst. line to Noah **HINTON**s ~~line~~ /lane/ from his House to the Edenton road and then runing up said lane to James **PARKER**s line thence runing said **PARKER** line to the first Station...the land devised to the Said **HARE** by the death of his father..." Witnesses: James **SMITH** D. **PARKER**[87]

One week later, James H.⁷ **PARKER** received a deed of gift from his father-in-law, William **LASSITER**, in Hertford County, NC. That deed of 640 acres was made 27 October 1842, for $5.00 and "love and affection...for the son in law of Sd. William **LASSITER**...and for the purpose of advancing him in life..." The land adjoined the lands of John B. **SHARP** on the west, heirs of John **BACON** and the lands of Sipha **SMITH** on the south, the lands of Jacob **SHARP** on the east "and his on the North side of Wicacon Creek...being the same tract purchased by sd. William **LASSITER** of George **GORDON** by deed 8 December 1819 and is the same upon which the sd. William **LASSITER** now lives..." He also included "the following negroes all of which have heretofore since the intermarriage of him the sd. James H. **PARKER** with the daughter of him the sd. Wm. **LASSITER** been put in possession of sd. **PARKER** by sd. **LASSITER** as an advancement, to wit, negroes **LEWIS, WASHINGTON, MILLY** and her child **DENNISON** and girl **CHARLOTTE**, with all their future increase and boy **MASON**..."[88]

The 1850 U. S. Census for Hertford County shows James H.⁷ **PARKER**, age 40, Martha, age 26, William⁸, age 7 and David⁸ **PARKER**, age 5.[89] In 1860, Joseph⁸, age 8, and Florence⁸, age 5, also appear.[90] In 1870, they were living in Harrellsville Township and the names of the children in this family were listed as William L.⁸, age 26, David⁸, age 24, Annie⁸, age 22, Joseph⁸, age 18 and Florrence⁸, age 14. The latter two were attending school that year.[91] "Annie **PARKER**" is a new name in this family and her whereabouts in the earlier enumeration is unknown. In the 1880 Census, only James H.⁷ and Joseph W.⁸ **PARKER** are listed.[92]

On 1 December 1873, James H.⁷ **PARKER** made an application in Hertford County for an ad-

---

[82] Gates County Marriage Register 1878

[83] U. S. Census, 1850, Perquimans Co., NC, T623, Roll: #1211, p. 161, Sheet 8A, Fam. #142

[84] Elmwood Cemetery

[85] U. S. Census, 1870, Bertie Co., NC, M593, Roll: #1123, p. 59

[86] U. S. Census, 1880, Bertie Co., NC, T9, Roll: #953, p. 302C

[87] NCSA, C.041.40008 Gates County Real Estate Conveyances 1836-1842 Vol: 16, 17, 16:103-104

[88] Hertford County, NC, Deed Book K:461

[89] U. S. Census, 1850, Hertford Co., NC, M432, Roll: #634, p. 334, Fam.#340

[90] U. S. Census, 1860, Hertford Co., NC, M653, Roll: #902, p. 104, Fam. #804

[91] U. S. Census, 1870, Hertford Co., NC, M593, Roll: #1143, p. 30, Fam. #231

[92] U. S. Census, 1880, Hertford Co., NC, T9, Roll: #968, p. 205, Fam. #23

ministration bond on the estate of David[8] **PARKER**. Amason **PARKER** and James H.[8] were named as heirs. She may have been the "Annie" mentioned above.[93] No further information.

On 7 December 1874, James H.[7] **PARKER** relinquished his right of administration on a second son's estate, transcribed here in full: "I James H.[7] **PARKER** hereby renounce my right and claim to administer on the estate of my son William L. **PARKER** and respectfully recommend that Letters be granted to Jno. F. **NEWSON** Public Administrator of Hertford County. J. H. **PARKER**." W. J. **GATLING** witnessed this document. The estate was valued at $100. A sale of his property was made 1 February 1875, where a violin was sold to J. B. **HARE** for $5.65 and a banjo to Jesse H. **MITCHELL** for $5.00.[94]

James H.[7] **PARKER** died 27 May 1882, and is buried in Elmwood Cemetery.[95] About two weeks after his death, Joseph W.[8] **PARKER** signed the following receipt in Gates County on 15 June 1882: "Received of James **PARKER** Twenty Thousand Nine Hundred and Five 73/100 Dollars in full of all notes, bonds, accounts, money or other matters in his hands or due by him to the estate of James H. **PARKER** deceased late of Hertford County North Carolina: and in consideration of the said sum, I Joseph W. **PARKER** personal representative and sole heir of the said James H. **PARKER**, deceased, do hereby release the said James **PARKER** from all claim demand and cause of action whatsoever on account of the said James H. **PARKER** and his Estate from the beginning of the World down to this present time. Witness my hand and seal this 15th day of June 1882. Joseph W. **PARKER** Administrator of James H. **PARKER** dec'd and as his sole heir at law."[96]

As James H.[7] **PARKER** died intestate and Joseph W.[8] **PARKER** stated that he was the "sole heir at law," it would appear that the other four children were deceased by 1882. No identifiable record of any of the children was found in the 1900 U. S. Census for Hertford County.

The deed from Joseph W.[8] **PARKER** (*James H.[7],Joseph[6],Joseph[5],Joseph[4],Thomas[3],Thomas[2],William[1]*) to his cousin, James[8] **PARKER**, on 11 January 1883, has already been mentioned. He made at least three more deeds in Hertford County. The first was made 27 May 1886, by J. W.[8] **PARKER** and wife Minnie H. **PARKER**, to Nannie E. **WILLIAMS**, all of Hertford County, in consideration of the said Nannie E. **WILLIAMS** "paying off and fully cancelling all the judgments together with all cost as record of said County doth more fully show...over $5,000, and one dollar to them paid...sell 800 acres known as a part of the James H. **PARKER** tract of land...beginning at the lane ditch on Mt. Pleasant road and up said road to C. L. **SHARP**'s line, thence along said old line to the creek, thence down the creek to John **SHARP**'s line, thence up John **SHARP**'s line to a post at the corner of J. W. **PARKER**'s new line, thence said new line to first station at the said road..." They both signed the deed and D. L. **JERNIGAN** witnessed it.[97]

The other two deeds were to his wife, Minnie H. **PARKER**. The first was a deed of gift for a 100-acre tract known as part of the J. H. **PARKER** tract, made 27 May 1886. It adjoined H. **HAYS**, Jno. **SHARP** and others. It was made to her "during her natural life and then to her heirs the children of the said J. W. **PARKER** her husband..." W. J. **LASSITER** witnessed this deed.[98] The second was another deed of gift, made 1 July 1886, of "one gray mare named Mollie, one top buggy, one open buggy, and all of my household and kitchen furniture of every kind and description and carpet..." W. R. **MILLER** witnessed this deed and Joseph W.[8] **PARKER** acknowledged it 4 October 1886.[99] No further information

The Logan H. **PARKER** family occupied the home known as "the old man Jim **PARKER** place" in Harrellsville, in the early 1900's. It seems to have been quite "haunted" at times. There are stories of the sound of several horses galloping across the roof on bright, moonlit nights. They were heard by a number of people, none of whom could see any visible cause for the sound. Another story concerned a man sitting at the base of a tree, wearing a Confederate soldier's uniform and whom, when spoken to, instantly disappeared. This home was said to have been owned by one John D. **ASKEW** in the 1920's. It was torn down within the last 10 years.

---

[93] NCSA, C.R.051.508.32, Hertford County Estates Records, Parham-Parker, Oris, Folder: Parker, David 1873
[94] Ibid., Folder: Parker, William L. 1874
[95] Elmwood Cemetery
[96] Gates Co., NC, Deed Book 32:455
[97] Hertford Co., NC, Deed Book O:379
[98] Ibid., O:381
[99] Ibid., O:463

**Chapter 14:** Children of Joseph[5] **PARKER** (*Joseph[4],Thomas[3],Thomas[2],William[1]*)

〰〰〰〰〰〰〰〰〰〰〰〰〰〰〰〰〰〰〰〰〰〰〰〰〰〰〰〰〰〰〰〰〰〰〰〰〰〰〰

Elizabeth[6] "Betsy" **PARKER** *(Joseph[5],Joseph[4],Thomas[3],Thomas[2],William[1])* is estimated here to have been born circa 1771, to Joseph[5] **PARKER** and his first wife, Miss **DAVIS**. She was a minor as of 16 August 1791, as she was under the guardianship of Jonathan **ROBERTS** on a bond of that date. She does not appear on the guardian bond entered into by Micajah **BLANSHARD** on 20 May 1793.

Elizabeth[6] **PARKER** appears on a marriage bond with Nathaniel (X) **JONES** dated 6 January 1807. William **HAYS** was his bondsman.[100] Nathaniel **JONES** was deceased by 15 March 1838, when David **PARKER** conveyed 50 acres of land to Mills **ROBERTS** for $75.00. It was a deed in trust from Nathaniel **JONES**, and the land was where he lived. On that same date, Elizabeth **JONES** relinquished her dower in the above land to Mills **ROBERTS**, stating that "Whereas my late Husband Nathaniel **JONES** of the County and State aforesaid conveyed a certain tract or parcel of land whereon he lived (being all that he possessed) to David **PARKER** by a deed of Trust bearing date the 11th day /of / August 1837..." Elizabeth her X mark **JONES** Witnesses D. **PARKER**, James H **PARKER**.[101] No further information.

James[6] and Kedar[6] **PARKER** *(Joseph[5],Joseph[4],Thomas[3],Thomas[2],William[1])* are most likely to have been born between 1780 and 1783, children of Joseph[5] **PARKER** and his second wife, Catherine. Both were deceased by November 1797, as outlined in the previous chapter.

Nancy[6] "Ann" **PARKER** *(Joseph[5],Joseph[4],Thomas[3],Thomas[2],William[1])* is estimated here to have been born circa 1784, daughter of Joseph[5] **PARKER** and his second wife, Catherine. She was still a minor when Joseph **RIDDICK** became her guardian in February 1804, as mentioned in the previous chapter. Nancy[6] **PARKER** appears on a marriage bond with John **HARE**, dated 11 October 1813. Frederick (X) **HINTON** was his bondsman. Many women died in childbirth and she may have died within that first year as John **HARE** appears on another marriage bond with Christian **HAYSE**, dated 27 June 1814. John **HARE**, Sr., was his bondsman.[102] No further information.

John[6] **PARKER** *(Joseph[5],Joseph[4],Thomas[3],Thomas[2],William[1])* is estimated here to have been born circa 1785, to Joseph[5] **PARKER** and his second wife, Catherine. More of him in the following chapter.

Priscilla Christian[6] **PARKER** *(Joseph[5],Joseph[4],Thomas[3],Thomas[2],William[1])* was the youngest daughter of Joseph[5] **PARKER** and his second wife, Catherine. She is estimated here to have been born circa 1786 and was deceased by 1793, as outlined in the previous chapter. No further information.

---

[100]  Almasy, *Gates County, North Carolina Marriage Bonds 1778-1868*, c. 1987, p. 52

[101]  NCSA, C.041.40008 Gates County Real Estate Conveyances 1836-1842 Vol: 16, 17 16:330-331

[102]  Almasy, *Gates County, North Carolina Marriage Bonds 1778-1868*, c. 1987, p. 36

**Chapter 14:** Children of Joseph[5] **PARKER** (*Joseph[4],Thomas[3],Thomas[2],William[1]*)

**Chapter 15:** John[6] **PARKER** *(Joseph[5],Joseph[4],Thomas[3],Thomas[2],William[1])*

John[6] **PARKER** *(Joseph[5],Joseph[4],Thomas[3],Thomas[2],William[1])*

John[6] **PARKER** *(Joseph[5],Joseph[4],Thomas[3],Thomas[2],William[1])* is estimated here to have been born circa 1785, to Joseph[5] **PARKER** and his second wife, Catherine. He appears on the last extant guardian bond for Joseph[5] **PARKER**'s orphans on 20 May 1793, as previously mentioned. He was 21 years of age by 1806, as he appears on the Gates County Tax List for that year as paying for one poll, but no land.[1]

That status changed when John[6] **PARKER** purchased 111 acres 10 November 1806, from Barneby **BLANCHARD** for $500. It is very briefly described as "bounded as follows, on the East by Mr. Samuel **BROWN** and on the West by Mr. Benjamin **BLANCHARD**..." Benjamin **BLANCHARD** and John[6]'s brother, Joseph[6] **PARKER**, witnessed this deed.[2]

On 24 November 1808, John[6] **PARKER** and Levina **CLEVES** appeared on a Gates County marriage bond, with Bray **BAKER** as his bondsman.[3] Levina, also called "Lavinia," was the widow of Solomon **CLEVES**. They appeared on a marriage bond dated 19 May 1803, with Benjamin **BEEMAN** as his bondsman.[4] She was called "Livina" **BROWN** and was the daughter of Samuel **BROWN** and his first wife, of unknown name.[5] Solomon **CLEVES** was deceased by November 1807, as evidenced by an order of court to lay off and allot a year's provision to Levenia **CLEVES**, widow of Solomon **CLEVES**.[6] Solomon and Lavinia (**BROWN**) **CLEVES** had one son, John **CLEVES**, who was born circa 1805. He appears on a Gates County marriage bond with Ann **EURE** dated 5 January 1826, with "Sipran" **EURE** as his bondsman.[7] In 1850, he was 45 years of age, living in Nansemond County, VA, with his wife Nancy, age 44, Leah **STRINGER**, age 19 and Harriet **CLEVES**, age 11.[8]

On 16 November 1818, John[6] **PARKER** purchased 50 acres from William **DANIEL** for $175.00. It is described as "Beginning at a sweet gum on George **BROOKS** line Standing in the watery Swamp thence running along s[d]. **BROOKS** line to a pine a corner tree Standing in a valley thence running a west course to a Post Oak standing on the old ditch, thence up said ditch to a persimmon tree, a corner tree, thence a west course a forward line to a maple on the line of Aaron **BLANCHARD** decs[d]. thence along Said line to a Sweet gum a corner tree Standing in the s[d] Watery Swamp, thence up s[d] Swamp to the first Station..." William and Sarah her X mark **DANIEL** signed this deed and the witnesses were J. **WALTON** and Jno. B. **WALTON**.[9]

The following deed is the last known purchase of land made by John[6] **PARKER** and is the parcel on which his home stood. It was later known as the "Nathan **PARKER** place," and the "Tom **HURDLE** place." Janice **OWINGS**, (Mrs. Walton A.) was the last owner known to this writer. On 2 November 1819, Elisha H. **BOND** sold John[6] **PARKER** 300 acres, for $2,000.00. It was the land whereon **BOND** lived at the time. It is described as "comprising within the said tract the farm, Several tracts or messuages respectively purchased of Timothy **FREEMAN** Robert **TAYLOR** & Henry [sic] **TAYLOR** Embracing the Fishery &c adjoining the Lands of Demsy **BOND** Noah **ROUNTREE** John **DAVIS** Clement **HILL** & Elisha **ROBERTSON**..." It was witnessed by B. **BLANCHARD** and Robt. **RIDDICK**.[10]

On 2 March 1820 a covenant was made between Elisha H. **BOND** and John[6] **PARKER**. It states that "whereas the Garbage which may arise from the mouth of the Creek Fishery is not specially

[1]  NCSA, C.041.70001, Gates County Tax Lists 1784-1831 [1784-1806,] 1806, Isaac Costen's Captaincy, p. 363
[2]  NCSA, C.041.40004, Gates County Real Estate Conveyances 1803-1810, Vol. 6,7,8, 6:336
[3]  Almasy, *Gates County, North Carolina Marriage Bonds 1778-1868*, c. 1987, p. 68
[4]  Ibid., p. 16
[5]  NCSA, C.R.041.508.1, Gates County Estates Record, Brown, Samuel 1849
[6]  Fouts, *Minutes of County Court of Pleas and Quarter Sessions Gates County, North Carolina 1806-1811, Vol. III*, c. 1985, 46:#558
[7]  Almasy, *Gates County, North Carolina Marriage Bonds 1778-1868*, c. 1987, p. 17
[8]  U. S. Census, 1850, Nansemond Co., VA, M432 Roll: #962, p. 156, #467
[9]  NCSA, C.041.40005, Gates County Real Estate Conveyances 1811-1812, 1815-1819, Vol. 9,10, 10:492
[10]  Ibid., 10:539

named in my deed of sale of land to John **PARKER** of the s[d] County to be an appertenant [sic] article in the right to s[d] **PARKER**, and to his own proper & legitimate use & benefit, This is to confirm unto him the s[d] John **PARKER** a firm & indesbitable [sic] right to the s[d]. Garbage free & clear of all persons whatever..." It was witnessed by Rob[t]. **RIDDICK** and Jonas **HINTON**.[11] Herring fisheries on the Chowan River and its tributaries were a profitable enterprise and the "garbage" from the operation was used to fertilize crops.

The following two deeds more fully describe parts of the land included in the above deed. The first is a deed dated 8 February 1798, from "Robert **TALOR** & his Brother Hilry **TALOR** of the State of north Carolina & County of Hardford [sic] of the one part & Elisha H **BOND** of the County of Gates," for 160 acres for £225. It is described as being "on **BENET**s Creek in Indian Neck Beginning at A Maple Standing on the Edge of **BENET**s Creek Swamp from thence to A pine from thence Runing A Straite Course to A pine A Corner Tree of Timothy **FREEMAN** so Runing along a [?] line to Jacob **OUTLAW** line & from thence a place Called the head of the Pond from thence along a line of Marked trees to the Head of the Musey Branch so Runing down the said branch to **BENET**s Creek Swamp so runing down s[d] Swamp to the first Station..." Robert his X mark **TALOR** and Hillry **TAYLOR** both signed this deed and it was witnessed by Richard **BOND** and Timothy **FREEMAN**.[12]

The second deed was made 2 June 1803, from Timothy **FREEMAN** to Elisha H **BOND** for 10 acres for £200. It is described as "Beginning at the South East Side of the Causway from then Runing along the side of s[d] Swamp [sic] to a Juniper a Corner tree from thence along Riddick **TROTMAN**s line to the lane down the s[d] lane to the Swamp with the Causway and Fishery all thereunto Belonging...lying and being on **BENETT**s Creek..." Richd. **BOND** and William **FREEMAN** witnessed this deed.[13]

On 15 November 1820, John[6] sold 20 acres, of the 300 purchased from Elisha H. **BOND**, to Moses **LASSITER**. It is described as being "on the East side of **BENNET**s Creek. Beginning at a post Oak a corner of Clement **HILL**s & runing a westardly course by a line of marked trees 87 Rods to a pine a corner of said **PARKER**s thence S. 8[d]. E 63 rods by a line of marked trees to a pine a corner on s[d]. **PARKER**s thence along the path N. 55°. E. 96 Rods to the first station..." Clement **HILL** was the sole witness to this deed and it was acknowledged in May County Court 1822.[14]

On 19 November 1820, John[6] **PARKER** sold the 50 acres he purchased from William **DANIEL** to James **BLANCHARD**. Benjamin **BLANCHARD** was the sole witness to this deed.[15] On 27 February 1821, he sold the 111 acres purchased from Barnaby **BLANCHARD** to John B. **WALTON**. J. W. **RIDDICK** and L. **ELLIOTT** witnessed this deed.[16]

John[6] **PARKER** made his will 4 January 1825. It is transcribed here in full: "In the name of God amen I, John **PARKER** of the county of gates in State of north Carolina being weak in body, but of Sound ~~mind~~ and perfect mind and memory Blesed be Almighty God for the same do make and publish this my last will and testament – first I give and bequeth unto my beloved wife Levina **PARKER** all my Cleard land tenaments building[s] and as much as she may think proper to clear of the wood land untill the children becomes of age, all the above mentioned land She is to hold untill her death or in case of her marriage again the abve [sic] mentioned property is to be returned to my sons She has full power to sell Light wood &c to assist her in suporting of my children and her self the children to be schooled if can be done with convenience, my black man **ISACK** to remain with my wife untill her death or marriage if the Said black man is then alive then to belong to my youngest daughter Martha of all my movable property when sold to be divided equaly betwen my daghters Nancy & Martha Nancy receiving fifty dollars more as an equvalant [sic] for the Black Man I bequeth unto my oldest Son Isack **PARKER** all that piece or parcel of land commencing at the old mill branch Joining Elisha **ROBINSON**s line in a direct course to **MANING**s ridge keeping the ridge unto the back line with all the high land on the North side of the Boare swamp

---

[11] NCSA, C.041.40005, Gates County Real Estate Conveyances 1811-1812, 1815-1819, Vol. 9,10, 10:539-540

[12] NCSA, C.041.40003, Gates County Real Estate Conveyances 1794-1803, Vol: 4,5, 4:196-197

[13] NCSA, C.041.40004, Gates County Real Estate Conveyances 1803-1810, Vol: 6,7,8, 6:34-36

[14] NCSA, C.041.40006, Gates County Real Estate Conveyances 1819-1829, Vol: 11-13, 11:326-327

[15] Ibid., 11:139-140

[16] Ibid., 11:169

To my youngest Son Nathanial **PARKER** I bequeth the Land South of the Boare Swamp the swamp included the Landing and Juniper Pecoson with all the Buildings thare on I[n] case of one of thair deaths /without an heir/ the other takes the whole if both of them, then it is to be divided betwen the girls

I Bequeath unto my Sone [sic] in law my /John **CLEAVES**/ land pattent in western Country if he will go to it if not to be given to Isack & Nathaniel my sons has not power to sell any of the above mentioned Land untill thay are thirty years of age

here by revoking all other wills by me made In witness whereof I have hereunto set my hand & Seal the 4th day of January Eighteen hundred & twenty five

Signed sealed published and declaired by the above John **PARKER** to be his last will and testament in the presence of us who have here unto subscribed our names as as [sic] witnesses in the presence of the testator

My Still I Give to my wife during her life and arfter her death unto my Son Nathanied [sic]

My Mill & piece of Swamp Land to be sold

Clement **HILL** {Seal}

Henry **JOCELIN** {Seal}

G. **HOFLER** Jurat {Seal}

State of North Carolina}

Gates County } February County Court of Pleas &c 1824 [sic]

The last will and Testament of John **PARKER** dec[d]. was exhibited into Court by William **HINTON** & David **PARKER** and was proved by the oath of Garrett **HOFFLER** and Ordered to be recorded and on Motion Ordered that the Said William **HINTON** & David **PARKER** administer on the said estate of the dec[d]. with the will annexed, and that they give bond and Security in the Sum of five thousand pounds the Said administrators were duly qualified for that Office &c Teste J **SUMNER** Clk"[17]

This verbatim transcription of a copy of the original will differs slightly from the copy found in Gates County Will Book 2, pp. 227-229. The Will Book shows the black man's name as "**JACK**," which is in error. The clerk also "corrected" the spelling and punctuation of the original document, which was a very common practice. As John[6] **PARKER** did not name an executor, a Special Administration, with the will annexed, was required. In this instance, son-in-law means step-son.

The application for and issuance of the Special Administration Bond for William **HINTON** and David[7] **PARKER** on the estate of John[6] **PARKER**, deceased, is dated 26 January 1825. An order to sell the perishable estate was included. Their bond in the sum of $2,000.00 was given on that same date.[18]

The inventory of John[6] **PARKER**s estate was taken 20 January 1825, though the document is dated "1824," a very human error at the beginning of a new year. It is transcribed here in full: "A True and purfect Invontary [sic] of all and Singler The goods and Chattes of the Estate of John **PARKER**s Decase Jinuary the 20 Day 1824.

| | | | |
|---|---|---|---|
| 2 | Beds and furneture | 1 | Tub |
| 4 | Chears | a | Parsel of Sider Caske |
| 2 | pine tables | 15 | Gees |
| a | parsel of wooden ware | 1 | Barrll of herrings |
| 2 | Trays | 2 | axes |
| 2 | Pots | 4 | Barrels of Sider wine |
| 1 | Duchoven | 1 | Canoe |
| 1 | Set of Earthen ware | 1 | horse |
| 1 | Pare of Side Irons | 1 | Bare of Iron |
| 1 | Looking glass | 1 | Parsel of Salt pork |
| 2 | Safe | 2 | Sauderirons |
| 1 | Chist | 1 | Pare of Iron wedges |
| a | Parsel of Pees | 23 | Head of Sheep |

[17] NCSA, C.R.041.801.9 Gates County, NC, Wills 1762-1904

[18] NCSA, G.041.2194761, Gates County Estates, Record of 1765-1920, Folder: Parker, John 1821 [sic] Doc. #1208-1209; #1207

| | |
|---|---|
| a Parsel of Cotton | 1 Basket of old Iron |
| a Parsel of rice | a Parsel of Corn |
| 1 Gun | 3 weding hose |
| a Parsel of flax | 2 grubing D° |
| 1 Pare of traces | 1 Set of Black Smith Tools |
| 4 Plows | 1 Stock of bees |
| 1 Sider astablishment | 1 Top Stack |
| 1 Chart and whels [Cart and wheels] | 5 gots [goats] |
| 20 Head of Cattle | |
| 43 Head of hogs | a parsel of lard |
| 1 ox yoke | a /parsel?/ Shucks |
| 1 Pan | 1 grin Stone |
| 1 Skillet | 6 Raw hids |
| 2 Basons | a Parsel of plank |
| 1 Dish | a Parsel of Skanling [Scantling] |
| 1 Dresing table | 2080 lb of frish [or Irish] pork |
| 1 Trunk | a parsel of Bacon |
| 1 pare of Stillards | 1 Bushel of Salt |
| a Parsel of Blade fodder | Sundry account untried |
| 5 Ducks | William **HINTON** } |
| 1 pare of Saddle bags | David **PARKER**   }  Admrs."[19] |
| a parsel of youpon | |
| 1 frow | |

The date on this inventory predates the granting of the administration on this estate by six days. John[6] **PARKER** most probably died very near that 20 January 1825 date. There is an extensive cemetery on what was his property, with many unmarked graves. He, and other members of his immediate family, are most likely buried there. He appears to have been a blacksmith, as well as owning a mill and fishery. His lack of a formal education did not prevent him from being prosperous. The above inventory was exhibited into May Court 1825, by David[7] **PARKER**, Administrator.[20]

On 22 February 1825, David **PARKER** and William **HINTON** sold the land and mill as directed in John[6] **PARKER**'s will. The deed is abstracted and transcribed here: "Whereas John **PARKER** late of Gates County in the State of north Carolina departed this life being possessed of a certain messuage or Tenement or parcel of Land on which is situated a Saw & Grist mill formerly known by the name of **WALTON**s mill lying in the County aforesaid on the main road leading from Suffolk to Edenton and the said John **PARKER** by his last will & Testament give the aforesaid Saw & Grist mill with its privelidges [sic] and appurtenances to be Sold for the purpose of discharging the debts of the Said John **PARKER** dec[d]... after advertiseing to same agreeable to law did on the 22 day of February 1825, expose to public Sale at Gates C. House...when Timothy **FREEMAN** of the County aforesaid being present, bid therefore the Sum of Four Hundred dollars and he being the highest & best bider the said Saw & grist mill with all the privelidges &c was struck off to him at the price aforesaid..." There were no witnesses to this deed and it was acknowledged in November Court 1825, and ordered to be registered.[21]

In an account of sales made 3 February and 15 March 1825, the personal property of John[6] **PARKER** was sold on a credit of six months. The piece of swamp land was sold to James **PHELPS** for $40.00 on a credit of 12 months. The sale of **ISAAC** was made to the widow for $225.00, on 12 July 1826. No deed, nor bill of sale, was registered for either of these transactions. The total amount of sales was $1,151.63.[22]

---

[19] NCSA, G.041.2194761, Gates County Estates, Record of 1765-1920, Folder: Parker, John 1821 [sic] Doc. #1215

[20] Fouts, *Minutes of County Court of Pleas and Quarter Sessions Gates County, North Carolina 1824-1827, Vol. VI*, c. 1988, 57:#1378

[21] NCSA, C.041.40006, Gates County Real Estate Conveyances 1819-1829, Vol: 11-13, 12:71-72

[22] NCSA, C.R.041.508.86, Gates County Estates Record, Folder: Parker, John 1821

**Chapter 15:** John[6] **PARKER** *(Joseph[5],Joseph[4],Thomas[3],Thomas[2],William[1])*

In November Court 1826, an order issued for Henry **GILLIAM**, James W. **RIDDICK**, Henry **BOND** and Charles **FELTON** or any three of them to audit and state the accounts of David **PARKER** and William **HINTON** administrators of John **PARKER** deceased. The audit of the estate was done 23 January 1827, by the last three auditors named. After the payment of numerous small debts, deduction of commissions and additions of income from sales and notes paid, the amount due to the estate was $64.09.[23]

No previous guardian accounts have been found, but in February Court 1827, it was "Ordered that Lavinia **PARKER**, be appointed Guardian to Isaac, Ann, Nathan G. and Martha **PARKER** orphans of John **PARKER** decd. and that she give bond and security in the sum of $1000 each, James W. **RIDDICK** and William **HINTON** securities."[24]

An account of Lovina **PARKER**, guardian of the orphans of John[6] **PARKER**, was exhibited into February Court 1828.[25] She stated that as of 1 January 1828, "The accounts are ballanced there remains nothing due said orphans. Lovina **PARKER** Guard" She listed one item as "amt Charged for Board & schooling for the years 1826 and 1827 said orphans viz Isaac, Nathan, Nancy & Margaret **PARKER**s at $15.99 each} $63.96"[26] In all other extant records, "Margaret" is called "Martha."

Lavinia **PARKER** appears in the Gates County Tax Lists, with 350-355 acres of land from 1825-1833. Isaac[7] **PARKER**, her eldest son, has that number of acres listed under his name for 1834-1835. Lavinia last appears with that 355 acres in 1837.[27]

On 13 February 1840, Lavinia **PARKER**, Miles **BROWN** and David **PARKER**, mutually chosen trustee, entered into a deed in trust wherein she secured a debt to Miles **BROWN** by selling property to David **PARKER** for $1.00. It is described as "a certain tract or parcel of land, that is to say, during my natural life, situate lying & being in the County of Gates, adjoining the lands of James T. **FREEMAN**, Henry B. **LASSITER** & Elisha **BOND**, it being the land whereon the said Lovenia **PARKER** now lives, and was the land devised to her by her husband John **PARKER**, one Negro man by the name of **ISAAC**, three feather beds & furniture, one sorrel mare, three head of Cattle, 15 head of hogs, one cart & wheels, with all my Household & Kitchen furniture, and my farming Utensils, my corn & fodder, and all the ballance of my estate of every kind whatever." It was further agreed that Lavinia was to "retain possession of the lands &c, before conveyed until demanded for the purpose of carrying this Trust into execution. If she paid the debt, the deed would be null and void. It was witnessed by Isaac his x mark **PARKER** and James his x mark **EURE**.[28]

On 20 May 1841, James **EURE** and Lavinia **PARKER** sold Nathan[7] **PARKER** seven acres of land that had been conveyed to them in a deed in trust from Isaac[7] **PARKER**. It was "knocked off" to Nathan **PARKER** for $19.25, as the highest bidder, and is described as "all said Isaac **PARKER**'s land on the west side of the main road called the orchard piece." It was signed by James his x mark **EURE** and Lavinia her x mark **PARKER**, and witnessed by Mills **ROBERTS** and John W. **HINTON**. This deed was not registered until August Court 1844, three years after its execution.[29] Lavinia **PARKER** does not appear in the 1850 U. S. Census, nor did she leave any estate records. It is most likely that she died in 1844 and the registration of this deed secured a valid title to Nathan[7] **PARKER** shortly thereafter.

Lavinia was still living as of 18 May 1842, as she is mentioned as an adjoining landowner in a deed from the Sheriff of Gates County to James T. **FREEMAN**, for land that had belonged to Enoch **PEARCE**.[30]

Nancy[7] "Ann" **PARKER** *(John[6],Joseph[5],Joseph[4],Thomas[3],Thomas[2],William[1])* is estimated here to have been born circa 1810. No identifiable records have been found for her. No further infor-

---

[23] NCSA, C.R.041.508.86, Gates County Estates Record, Folder: Parker, John 1821, Doc. #1194-1199

[24] Fouts, *Minutes of County Court of Pleas and Quarter Sessions Gates County, North Carolina 1824-1827, Vol. VI*, c. 1988, 136:#1475

[25] Ibid., *1828-1831, Vol. VII*, 5:#7

[26] NCSA, G.041.2194761, Gates County Estates, Record of 1765-1920, Folder: Parker, John 1821 Doc. #1224

[27] NCSA, C.041.70001, Gates County Tax Lists 1784-1831 [1807-1831] pp. 323;341;357;377;395; 416;437. C.041.70002, 1832-1851 [1832-1841] 17;41;160

[28] NCSA, C.041.40008, Gates County Real Estate Conveyances 1836-1842, Vol: 16,17, 17:116-118

[29] NCSA, C.041.40009, Gates County Real Estate Conveyances 1841-1847, Vol: 18,19, 19:30

[30] Ibid., 18:376-377

mation.

Isaac[7] **PARKER** *(John[6],Joseph[5],Joseph[4],Thomas[3],Thomas[2],William[1])* is estimated here to have been born circa 1812. He first appears on the Gates County Tax List in 1833 as one taxable poll, with no land, in Bushrod **RIDDICK**'s Captaincy. Isaac[7] appears on the Tax Lists in 1834 and 1835, with the 355 acres previously listed for his mother in 1833. In the lists for 1836-1837, he appears with only 20 acres and Lavinia lists the 355 acres again, for the latter year.[31] He appears to have died some time after 1842, as will be shown.

On 5 February 1836, Isaac[7] **PARKER** purchased 20 acres from Starky **EURE**, for $25.00. It was witnessed by J. T. **BENTON** and John **MORRIS**. It was acknowledged and ordered registered in May Court 1840.[32] It is the identical parcel that John[6] **PARKER** had sold to Moses **LASSITER** 15 November 1820.[33] Isaac[7] sold that same 20 acres to Reuben **LASSITER** 19 March 1838. It was witnessed by Jas. T. **FREEMAN** and Henry **BOND**, who proved it in May Court 1840, where it was ordered to be registered.[34]

In November Court 1836, it was "Ordered that Isaac **PARKER** be appointed Overseer of the Road leading from **BOND**s Landing to the fork near Mills **ROBERTS**'s and the following hands work on same to wit: James **EURE** /Jr./ John **MORRISS** Jr. Robert **PARKER**, Nathan **PARKER** Cannon [?] **HALL**, Elisha **BOND** Isaac **PARKER** & Henry B **LASSITER**."[35]

On 12 February 1840, Isaac[7] **PARKER** made a deed in trust to Lovenia **PARKER** and James **EURE**, securities on notes to John **ROBERTS** and James T. **FREEMAN** and a judgment due to James T. **FREEMAN** and stayed by Nathan[7] **PARKER**. For the liabilities of $112.00, and $1.00, Isaac sold to Lovinia **PARKER** and James **EURE**, "all my right, title & interest to & in a certain tract or parcel of land...it being part of the tract of land on which my Father John **PARKER** died Seized & possessed of̲f̲, and which he devised to me in his last will & Testament, adjoining the lands of James T **FREEMAN** Dempsey **BOND** & others, containing by estimation Two hundred acres..." Isaac his X mark **PARKER**, James his X mark **EURE** and Lovinia her X mark **PARKER** all signed this deed. It was witnessed by Mills **ROBERTS** and Nathan[7] **PARKER**. This deed was delivered to John **WALTON**, Public Register, and was registered 13 February 1840. It was again returned to him for registration 25 October 1843, which seems to indicate that Isaac[7] **PARKER** was most probably deceased by then.[36]

Isaac[7] **PARKER** last appeared in the Gates County Tax Lists in 1842, listed as one poll and without land.[37] Family tradition has been that Isaac[7] "died in his 30's," possibly in a logging accident. He never married and died without issue. No further information.

Nathaniel Gabriel[7] **PARKER** *(John[6],Joseph5,Joseph[4],Thomas[3],Thomas[2],William[1])* was born 20 April 1819, and died 3 August 1890.[38] More of him later.

Martha[7] **PARKER** *(John[6],Joseph5,Joseph[4],Thomas[3],Thomas[2],William[1])* was born circa 1820. She appears on a Gates County marriage bond with Levi **CRANK**, dated 18 June 1838. Isaac[7] (X) **PARKER** was his bondsman.[39] Levi **CRANK** appears only once in the Gates County Tax Lists, with four acres of land and no polls listed in 1848.[40]

They appear in the Gates County 1850 Census as "Levi **CRANK**, 34 M, Sailor; Martha **CRANK**, 30 F; Lavinia **CRANK**, 1 F; Levi B. **CRANK**, 5 [?] M, and Jane **BROWN**, 23, F."[41] They

---

[31] NCSA, C.041.70002, Gates County, NC, Tax Lists 1832-1851 [1832-1841] Bushrod Riddick's Captaincy, p. 41; 1834, p. 79; 1835, p. 101; 1836, p. 134; 1837, p. 160

[32] NCSA, C.041.40008 Gates County Real Estate Conveyances 1836-1842 Vol: 16, 17, 17:234-235

[33] See footnote #14.

[34] NCSA, C.041.40008 Gates County Real Estate Conveyances 1836-1842 Vol: 16, 17, 17:247-248

[35] NCSA, C.041.30003, Gates County Court Minutes 1827-1850, November Court 1836. Pages are unnumbered in this volume.

[36] NCSA, C.041.40008 Gates County Real Estate Conveyances 1836-1842 Vol: 16, 17, 17:114-115

[37] NCSA, C.041.70002, Gates County, NC, Tax Lists 1832-1851 [1832-1841] Mintonsville Dist., p. 34

[38] Nathan G. Parker Cemetery. Transcription of gravestone inscriptions made 20 September 1977, by Raymond P. Fouts. Hereafter, Nathan G. Parker Cemetery.

[39] Almasy, *Gates County, North Carolina Marriage Bonds 1778-1868*, c. 1987, p. 19

[40] NCSA, C.041.70002, Gates County, NC, Tax Lists 1832-1851 [1842-1851] Mintonsville Dist., p. 220

[41] Almasy, *Gates County, North Carolina Census 1850 & 1860*, c. 1987, p. 80

removed to Currituck County, NC, between 1850 and 1860, as evidenced by their appearance in that county on the 1860 U. S. Census. This family is listed as "Levi **CRANK**, 46, M, none [Occupation;] Martha **CRANK**, 40 F; Bembrey[8] **CRANK**, 12, F [sic;] Levina[8] **CRANK**, 11, F; John[8] **CRANK**, 10 M; Thomas[8] **CRANK**, 6, M; Caroline[8] **CRANK**, 2 F, and Caleb[8] **CRANK**, 1, M."[42] Martha[7] **(PARKER) CRANK** appears to have died between 1863 and 1870 as she does not appear in the 1870 U. S. Census and one other child, named William[8] **CRANK**, age 6, does appear in that Census.[43]

Nathaniel Gabriel[7] **PARKER** *(John[6],Joseph5,Joseph[4],Thomas[3],Thomas[2],William[1])* was born 20 April 1819, and died 3 August 1890, as previously noted. He is buried in the Nathan G. **PARKER** Cemetery, near NCSR #1103, known as Indian Neck Road. His gravestone reveals that he was 71 years, 3 months and 13 days old. There are numerous graves in this cemetery, only three of which bear markers. John[6], Lavinia, Isaac[7] **PARKER** and several other family members are most likely also buried in this cemetery.[44]

Nathaniel Gabriel[7] **PARKER** is always referred to as "Nathan," or "Nathan G." in all extant legal records. The name "Gabriel" has been preserved by the memory of his granddaughter, the late Mary Agnes[9] **(PARKER) TAYLOR**.

On the "Marriages" page of the Nathaniel Gabriel[7] **PARKER** Family Bible, the initial entry is "Gates Co NC March 12th 1837 On this Day & date I Nathan G. **PARKER** and Mary A. **POWELL** was married."[45] "Mary A." was Mary Ann **POWELL**, daughter of Thomas and Mary **POWELL**, of **POWELL**'s Crossroads, Gates County.

On 21 November 1837, Peter B. **MINTON** sold a tract of land to Mary **POWELL** and Nathan **PARKER**, for $75.00. The number of acres was not specified and it was described as "bounded on the North by lands of Charles **POWELL** on the West by land of the heirs of John **OUTLAW** on the South by lands of John **WHITE** and on the East by lands of Jacob N. **PARKER** and is the same tract of land now occupied by the said Mary **POWELL** To have and to hold to the said Mary **POWELL** for and during the time of her natural life and from and after her death To have and to hold to the said Nathan **PARKER** his heirs and assigns forever..." This deed was witnessed by C. R. **KINNEY**.[46] This parcel had been purchased by Peter B. **MINTON** for $20.50 at a public auction of the lands and tenements of Thomas **POWELL** 7 August 1831. It was not proved until August Court 1832.[47]

On 18 February 1840, Nathan[7] **PARKER** entered into an "Indenture of agreement" with John **MORRIS** and Robert **SIMONS** to sell them 52½ acres of land for $150.00. It is described as "Beginning at a small oak on the edge of the Pocoson corner on Nathan **PARKER** thence along the Pocoson S. 40° E. 53 poles to the road leading to **BOND**'s landing thence up the road N. 40° E. 40 poles to the fork of the road thence along the road /nearly/ an East course to a small oak corner on Thomas **COLLINS** and Elisha **BOND** thence N. 15° E. a straight line to a pine corner on Nathan **PARKER** thence said **PARKER**'s line to the first station..." This deed was witnessed by Allen **SMITH** and H. **WILLEY**. After Nathan[7] **PARKER**'s signature to this deed, the relinquishment of rights to this land is specified as follows: "The Land in this deed conveyed to **SIMONS & MORRESS** I Lovenia **PARKER** do relinquish to the said **SIMONS & MORESS** all my right title & interest in said land thus conveyed by my son Nathan **PARKER** against myself & all claimants Given under my hand & seal the 20th day of February 1840. Lovenia her x mark **PARKER**." This deed of relinquishment was witnessed by Mills **ROBERTS** and proved in May Court 1840.[48] This parcel is part of the "land South of the Boare Swamp the swamp included the Landing and Juniper Pecoson," left to him in his father's will. He was barely under the age of 21, which would necessitate his mother's relinquishment of rights to the land.

---

[42] U. S. Census, 1860, Currituck Co., NC, M653, Roll: 895, p. 639, Dw. #385, Fam. #834

[43] U. S. Census, 1870, Currituck Co., NC, M593, Roll: 1133, p. 325, Dw. #213, Fam. #213

[44] Nathan G. Parker Cemetery

[45] The Nathaniel Gabriel Parker Family Bible was in poor condition and missing the cover and first 130 pages. It was published by John E. Potter and Co., 614 & 617 Sansom Street, Philadelphia, PA. The family information pages have been preserved. It was owned by the late Hazel (Taylor) Bunting, of Chesapeake, VA, and its present provenance is unknown to this writer. Hereafter, Nathan G. Parker Bible.

[46] NCSA, C.041.40008 Gates County Real Estate Conveyances 1836-1842 Vol: 16, 17, 16:302-303

[47] NCSA, C.041.40007 Gates County Real Estate Conveyances 1829-1836 Vol: 14, 15, 14:414-415

[48] NCSA, C.041.40008 Gates County Real Estate Conveyances 1836-1842 Vol: 16, 17, 17:242-244

**Chapter 15:** John[6] **PARKER** *(Joseph[5],Joseph[4],Thomas[3],Thomas[2],William[1])*

On 14 April 1840, Mary **POWELL** sold Nathan[7] **PARKER** 27 acres for $50.00. It is described as "Beginning in Catharine creek a corner tree in the land of Jacob **OUTLAW** thence running **OUTLAW**'s line an East course to Noah **ROUNTREE**'s line a corner thence **ROUNTREE**'s line a North course to the main road thence down the road to the creek thence down the creek to the first station..." It was signed by Mary her x mark **POWELL** and witnessed by Nathan **NIXON** and Zechariah **NIXON**.[49]

In August Court 1845, it was "Ordered that Nathan **PARKER** be appointed overseer of the road leading from the fork near Mills **ROBERTS** to **PARKER**'s landing." On 19 February 1849, he was once again appointed overseer of the same road and the landing was referred to as "**BOND**'s Landing, a name it still retains.[50]

On 24 June 1856, Nathan[7] **PARKER** sold 50 acres of land to John W. **HINTON** for $250.00. It adjoined Jno. **MORRIS**, Jr., Wiley **PILAND**, James **GREEN** and others, "it being the land whereon the Steam Mill stands together with all the appurtenances thereunto affixed." It was "one half only of the above described tract of land..." This deed was witnessed by E. T. [F?] **HURDLE**, Thos. A. **JORDAN** and Joseph G. **COBBITT** [sic.] It was not proved in court until 31 December 1885.[51]

On 14 January 1857, Nathan[7] sold John W. **HINTON** 40 more acres for $1,700.00. It is described as "The land where the steam mill stands, one half of that tract of land, one half of all the buildings and improvements, one half of the steam mill and contents of every description and timber sawed at said mill, Bounded by John **MORRIS**, James **EURE** and others. It was witnessed by E. T. **HURDLE** and James G. **COBBETT**. This deed was also proved 31 December 1885.[52]

On 7 July 1857, Nathan[7] **PARKER** sold Gisbourne J. **CHERRY**, of Washington Co., NC, and Thomas P. **CHERRY**, of Gates, the timber on 50 acres for $135.00. It is described as "all the Juniper trees for full term of three years...Commencing at the Mill Branch on high land running thence nearly a Southerly course to **BENNETT**'s Creek thence down the Creek to **BOND**'s Landing Causeway, thence the Causeway to the edge of the high land thence along the high land to the first Station...the said Juniper Swamp & Juniper trees and Juniper Timber..." John B. **JONES** was the sole witness to this deed, which was registered 7 October 1857.[53] Juniper Swamp runs directly behind the site of the Nathan[7] **PARKER** home on Indian Neck Road.

On 26 July 1859, Nathan[7] **PARKER** sold 35 acres to Calvin **EURE** for $400.00. It is described as "commencing at a gate corner of land of E. **LASSITER** running a South course to a pine corner tree on James H. **FREEMAN** land, his line to corner on the **HILL** tract, that line North to a post oak stump thence down a path to the first station..." The sole witness was Job **FREEMAN**.[54]

On 8 February 1869, Leah **STRINGER**, the daughter of John **CLEAVES** and Ann "Nancy" **EURE**, gave a Power of Attorney to Nathan[7] **PARKER**. It was for the purpose of enabling him to sell her "distributive share of the estate of James **EURE**, late of Gates County now in the hands of James R. **HOFLER** administrator of the said James **EURE**, and also to manage, farm rent out and exercise general control over my interest in the real Estate of the late James **EURE**, which said distributive share and real estate belong to me by reason of my being one of the next of kin, and one of the heirs-at-law of the said James **EURE**."[55]

On 3 January 1876, Nathan[7] and Mary A. **PARKER**, and Leah **STRINGER** of Nansemond County, VA, sold 91½ acres to Simon **NOWELL**. This tract lies on the road near **BOND**'s Landing, "beginning at a small hickory on the south side of the road corner on Isaac **PARKER**, thence along road 66 po. to a corner on Mrs. **ROUNTREE**'s dower, a corner on the river pocoson, to run of a Branch, up the run and various courses of branch to corner on Isaac **PARKER**..." Jacob M.[8]

---

[49] NCSA, C.041.40008 Gates County Real Estate Conveyances 1836-1842 Vol: 16, 17, 17:248-249

[50] NCSA, C.041.30003, Gates County Court Minutes 1827-1850. Pages are unnumbered in this volume.

[51] Gates County, NC, Deed Book 37:69-70

[52] Ibid., 60:70

[53] Ibid., 22:63

[54] Ibid., 23:271

[55] Ibid., 24:445

**PARKER** and Charles A.[8] **PARKER** witnessed this deed and it was proved in court 3 January 1877.[56] Isaac[8], Jacob M.[8] and Charles A.[8] **PARKER** are all sons of Nathan[7] and Mary Ann (**POWELL**) **PARKER**, as will be shown.

Nathan[7] **PARKER** served on both Grand and Petit juries in Gates County on several different occasions.[57] He was on both sides of the bar, at different times. During the Fall Term of 1870, Nathan[7], sons Millard[8], Jacob M.[8] and one John **STALLINGS** were named on a Warrant taken out by Rufus **LASSITER**. The reason for the warrant is not stated and it was "dismissed at the cost of the defendants." There were controversies between Nathan and his cousins, James H. and David **PARKER** and one with Mary C. **LASSITER** and others, all with Nathan[7] named as defendant.[58]

Nathan[7] **PARKER** and Mary A., his wife, made a deed in trust to L. L. **SMITH** 30 November 1888, on 200 acres lying on both sides of Indian Neck Road. It was bounded by Henry B. **LASSITER**'s heirs on the north, James H. **FREEMAN** and Calvin **EURE** on the east, Wiley **PILAND** and John **MORRIS** on the south and swamp lands on the border of **BENNETT**'s Creek on the west.[59]

The final deed found for Nathan[7] G. **PARKER** was a mortgage of $300.00 to **EASON** and **RIDDICK**, dated 7 March 1889. It was for 50 acres of pine-timbered land in Water Swamp, bounded on the north by Henry **HOFLER**, Sr., Jos. N. **BROWN** on the east, James **HINTON** on the west and Jethro **EURE** on the south. This land was "descended to N. G. **PARKER** from his mother." This mortgage also included stock and other items, including "one large sized clock," which remains in the family. It was paid in full 16 March 1892.[60]

The Nathan[7] **PARKER** home place has been known by his name and was later called "the Tom **HURDLE** place." Janice **OWINGS**, (Mrs. Walton A.,) Thomas **HURDLE**'s niece, kindly contributed the following anecdotes concerning this home and its residents. They were recounted to her by her mother, Monterey M. (Mrs. C. C.) **PARKER**, of Northampton County, NC. "Nathan was a great outdoorsman; raised the most bountiful crops, kept the premises up best and had the prettiest flower garden of any other person around. He had an Irishman who stayed 20 years as a gardener. There was a white picket fence all the way across the front of the house and extending 10 to 20 feet beyond on the sides. There were beautiful flower beds, laid out in the style of an English garden, with many boxwoods. A huge white, wild rose bush covered the left side (south) fence and a large oak tree on the right was covered with beautiful ivy. Beyond the picket fence, on each side, stretched the large vineyards; Scuppernong on the left and Nish, a blue grape, on the right. All were supported by frameworks about 12 to 15 feet square. The winepress was in the back yard, made into two huge sycamore trees. There were about 100 acres under cultivation, in front of the house and on each side, back to the **PARKER** graveyard. Part of the house was built prior to the American Revolution.

The second-floor porch had a railing all around, about three to four feet high. This porch was about 12 by 15 feet. The columns in the front porch were white, square and large. The front columns, four of them, ran to the ceiling of the second floor porch. The others, on each side, were half-high columns and ran to the tin roof of the first-floor porch. This was a long, inviting porch for children to play on all day long. Beyond the picket fence in front were two long rows of huge Cedars, parallel with Beeches. On the right, in the yard, was a long carriage house for four or five buggies, sulkies, and the carriage. There was a ramp all the way across the front. There were three or four barns, including one log barn in back.

Inside the house there were beautiful mantels, wainscoting three feet high, paneled, wide plank floors, some long windows to the porch floor, some short, old iron door latches and a huge chimney in the kitchen that, if you bent over, you could walk into [the fireplace.] As you entered the front door, with glass panels on each side of the door, you walked into a 10 or 12 feet wide front hall,

---

[56] Gates County, NC, Deed Book, 27:412

[57] Superior Court, Gates County, NC, Record Book Minute Docket 1859 to 1887, p. 1, 1859; p. 26, 1861; p. 49, 1866; p. 68, 1868; p.125, 1872

[58] Gates County Criminal Docket 1861-1919, p. 16, #10; Judgements in Civil Actions in Superior Court, Book E:20,35; Book F:3

[59] Gates County, NC, Deed Book 40:338

[60] Ibid., 41:277

cut off midway with portieres. The staircase, which was entered from the back hall, had the prettiest little newel and high risers, pretty side railing and wainscoting running beside the wall side of the steps up to the second floor. The upstairs hall was large enough for a single bed at the front. The upstairs hall windows went all the way to the floor, paneled in glass and leading to the second floor porch.

As to the Nathan **PARKER** family, they were delightful and here at this home was much gaiety and entertaining, with warm friendliness abounding for everyone. At 70, Nathan sat his horse like a young man, erect and tall. Mrs. **PARKER** was an unusually calm, sensible and well-poised woman, whom neither time nor change could disturb. Some of the children of Nathan's children were very beautiful. It was a handsome family, both old and young members.

Mother told me about this Christmas party when she was quite young. [Mrs. C. C. **PARKER** was born about 1864.] All the young people in the neighborhood were invited to a 4:30 A.M. Christmas eggnog party at Nathan **PARKER**'s. The night before, it snowed until time to go and Mother and her brother walked, being hardly one-quarter mile away. Everyone came, either on horseback or walking, with boots on. She wore her father's. When they arrived, such warmth and glee with open fires all over the house for everyone to dry out by, then down to the big parlor, a very large room, where they had a wonderful time with all the neighborhood young people. At six, Mrs. **PARKER** served a delicious Christmas morning breakfast with all the trimmings. After much Christmas happiness, all the visitors left about 9:30 A. M. and she and her brother got home just as their parents were ready for breakfast. It was the largest snow of the season, to their knees."

When this writer found the remains of the Nathan[7] **PARKER** home in 1975, it still retained the shake-shingle roofing and the large chimney on the southwest side of the front part of the house. The chimney on the northeast side was already tumbled down. There were fireplaces in both chimneys for the first and second floors. They were made of hand-molded bricks, a few of which retained finger-impressions. The base of that remaining chimney measured five feet, nine and one-half inches across. The kitchen, shed-room and ell at the back of the house had been destroyed, with only remnants of their chimneys remaining. The interior of the house had been stripped of all vestiges of paneling or other wood trim, including the mantels and stairs. The width of the front of the house is about 44 feet and the front part that remained at that time measured 14 feet in depth. The walls were plastered and finely finished.

The huge oak in the front yard is a Swamp Chestnut Oak and had attained a diameter of just under five feet, at its base. The Sycamore trees that once supported the winepress were dead, but still standing. The brick outlines of the flower beds in the English garden were still in place, covered by several inches of pine needles and leaf-litter. An ornamental plant, with a burgundy blossom and strong scent of ripe apples, still bloomed in the front yard in May. It is variously known as "Sweet Betsy" and "Sweet Bush." Four of the enormous Beech trees still remained on the north side of the driveway. On counting the rings in a fallen limb, those trees were found to be at least 140 years old in 1977. The Cedar trees had been cut long before. The house and the remaining chimney are now completely down.

Nathan G.[7] **PARKER** died intestate 3 August 1890. Family tradition relates that the cause of death was "cholera morbus." He is buried on his own land, next to his wife, Mary Ann.[61]

Letters of Administration on his estate were granted to Mary A. **PARKER** 25 August 1890, by her entrance into a bond for $1,200.00. Alexander **CARTER** and B. F. **WILLEY** were her sureties.[62] The application for administration is transcribed here in full: "In the matter of the administration of the estate of Nathan G. **PARKER**, Dec'd. Before W. T. **CROSS** C. S. C. Mary A. **PARKER** being sworn, doth say: That Nathan G. **PARKER** late of said County, is dead, without leaving any Will and Testament and that she, Mary A. **PARKER** is the proper person entitled to Letters of Administration on the Estate of the said Nathan G. **PARKER**, Further, that the value of the said Estate, so far as can be ascertained at the date of this application, is about $600.00 and that Isaac W. **PARKER**, M. F. **PARKER**, Addie F. **CROSS**, Margaret **ELLIS**, & T. W. **PARKER**, all of full age of Gates Co., N. C. & Martha **GRIFFIN**, Norfleet **WARD**, Kate **WARD**, Eva **WARD**, Nathan **WARD**, Noah **WARD** & Eliza **WARD** all of Chowan Co. & of full age except the last four who are

---

[61] Nathan G. Parker Cemetery
[62] Gates County Book of Bonds, p. 127

minors with Guardian, and Job H. **PARKER** of Walker Co., Texas, and L. H. **PARKER** & Sallie **PARKER** of Kitsof Co., [Kitsap Co.] Washington, and Jacob **PARKER** & Harriet **PARKER** of Portsmouth, Va., and C. A. **PARKER** of Hertford Co., N. C. all of full age are entitled as heirs and distributees thereof. Sworn and subscribed before me, this 25 day of Aug. 1890. W. T. **CROSS**, Clerk Superior Court     Mary A. **PARKER**"[63]

Mary Ann (**POWELL**) **PARKER** died 18 February 1901, intestate, reputedly from complications of asthma. She is buried next to her husband in the Nathan G. **PARKER** Cemetery. Her gravestone reveals that she was 78 years, eight months and 30 days old.[64]

In June, 1901, L. L. **SMITH** had written letters to several of the heirs, requesting their agreement to the sale of the lands of Nathan **PARKER**, and received responses from some of them.[65] On 30 October 1901, there was a petition entered into court to sell land to pay off the mortgage, and for distribution of the balance of the estate among the petitioners. The petitioners were named as "Logan H. **PARKER**, Isaac W. **PARKER**, Harriet A. **TURNER**, Margaret J. **ELLIS**, Wife of Alexander **ELLIS**, Job H. **PARKER**, Sallie A. **PERRY**, wife of Ivey D. **PERRY**, Millard F. **PARKER**, Jacob M. **PARKER**, C. A. **PARKER**, Jno. N. **PARKER**, Martha L. **GRIFFIN**, Addie F. **CROSS**, wife of R. L. **CROSS**, T. W. **PARKER**, Children & heirs of Mary E. **WARD**, to wit: (1) Kate **WARD**, (2) John N. **WARD**, (3) Eva D. **EASON**, wife of John **EASON**, (4) Nathan **WARD**, (5) Noah **WARD**, (6) Mary E. **MITCHELL**, wife of George L. **MITCHELL**."[66]

On 15 January 1908, L. L. **SMITH**, "Commissioner for sale of the Nathan **PARKER** lands," gave three deeds to grantees who had purchased those lands 1 December 1902. The first was to T. W. **HURDLE** and C. C. **PARKER** for $600.00. It is described as the "Nathan **PARKER** Home Place bounded by Isaac **BELL**'s line, thence up the branch to County road, thence up the road north to H. B. **LASSITER** line, along **LASSITER** line to another corner thereof Easterly, then south on **LASSITER** line up the lane east to Calvin **EURE** tract, then south to a corner on sd. tract, then east on sd. tract to R. M. **REDDICK** land along line to that tract to James H **FREEMAN**'s, then **FREEMAN**'s line on the north side of Boar Swamp to the line of the A. W. **HENRY** tract at the County road thence the County road to the Indian Neck Road, then up the Indian Neck a west course to the corner on John **MORRIS** tract, north on **MORRIS**'s line then a west a strait line to the Juniper Swamp known as Henry B. **LASSITER** Swamp, up the Swamp to the first station 200 acres and including one acre known as the **BOND** landing and fishery bounded on north by "landing Causeway" on east by James **PARKER** Swamp, on south by a cove and the James **PARKER** Swamp and on west by **BENNETT**'s Creek..."

The second was to T. W. **HURDLE** and Monterey M. **PARKER**, for $40.00, "known as the Jimmie **EURE** land...beginning at a cypress in **BAKER** Swamp then E. F. **HURDLE** land line north to a corner on Wiley **PILAND**, along that line to the **KLEGG** tract, that line to Simon **NOWELL**, along a branch on his line to **BAKER** Swamp, bounds of **BAKER** Swamp to the first station..."

The third in this series was to N. L. **ROUNTREE** for 35 acres at $58.00. It was known as the Isaac **PARKER** tract and is described as "Beginning in the Indian Neck road at a pine stump, thence the County road to Simon **NOWELL**'s line to the Mary **KLEGG** tract, thence the line of the **KLEGG** tract to the Jimmie **EURE** tract, thence along the line of the Jimmie **EURE** land to a pine in the line of the Wiley **PILAND** tract, thence the line of the **PILAND** tract to the first station..."[67]

The Nathan G.[7] **PARKER** home place, along with other lands of Mrs. **OWINGS**', is now almost an island, in a vast expanse of cultivated fields.

---

[63] NCSA, G.041.2194762, Gates County Estates, Record of 1765-1920, Vol. Parker-Pierce, Folder: Parker, Nathan G. 1890, Doc. #100

[64] Nathan G. Parker Cemetery

[65] NCSA, C.R.71.508.86, Gates County Estates Records, 1765-1920, Folder: Parker, Nathan 1890

[66] Gates County, Special Proceedings in the Superior Court, Book 1:161

[67] Gates County, NC, Deed Book 61:239, 243, 245

Gravestones of Mary Ann (**POWELL**) **PARKER** and Nathaniel G.[7] **PARKER**.

Placement of gravestones above in the Nathan G. **PARKER** Cemetery, near Indian Neck Road in Gates County, NC.  Photo taken by the author June 2000.

## Descendants of Nathan G.[7] PARKER *(John[6],Joseph[5],Joseph[4],Thomas[3],Thomas[2],William[1])*

Jobe Henry[8] **PARKER** *(Nathan G.[7],John[6],Joseph[5],Joseph[4],Thomas[3],Thomas[2],William[1])* was the eldest child of Nathan G.[7] and Mary Ann **(POWELL) PARKER**, born 25 February 1838, in Gates County, NC.[1] No record of land ownership has been found for Jobe Henry[8] **PARKER**.

He enlisted in the Army of the Confederacy in Gatesville 8 July 1861, as a private in Company C, 19th Regiment NC State Troops, (2d Regiment, NC Cavalry.) His Compiled Military Service Record shows that he was absent without leave 20 June 1863 and was listed as "deserted 17 June 1863."[2] According to one family member, troops came to Nathan[7]'s home, searching for Jobe Henry[8]. The one who discovered him in the bed of a wagon, concealed by a load of hay, was a friend who carefully replaced the hay and continued "searching" the premises.[3] Hunger, fatigue and the horrors of having fought in the battle of Brandy Station, Culpeper County, VA, on 9 June 1863, may well have precipitated his desertion.

Jobe Henry[8] **PARKER** appears on a Gates County marriage bond with Margaret **SIMONS**, dated 27 December 1865. Isaac W. (x) **PARKER** was his bondsman. They were married the following day.[4] He and his family were living in Sleepy Hole Township, near Suffolk in Nansemond County, VA, as of 18 August 1870. They were listed as Job H. **PARKER**, age 30, "Works on farm;" Margaret age 27, "Keeping house;" Patrick H., age three and William E., age one, all born in North Carolina.[5] He was not in either Gates or Nansemond Counties in the 1880 U. S. Census, but was believed to be residing in Walker County, TX, in 1890, at the death of his father.[6]

According to family tradition, he did not stay in touch with his family in North Carolina, other than to occasionally send them a newspaper from wherever he was living at the time. It was also said that he, and all his family, "died in the 1900 Galveston Hurricane." The latter statement has proved to be completely baseless.

On the Widow's Application for a Pension to the State of Texas, dated 7 May 1917, Margaret Ann **PARKER** stated that she was born in Gates County, NC, and was 75 years of age. She had resided in Texas for 34 years and in Smithville, Bastrop County, for 25 years. That statement places this family as coming to Texas in 1883 and to Smithville in 1892. That same application and associated papers gives the date of Jobe Henry[8] **PARKER**'s death as 26 November 1916. Her answer to the question "How long did your husband serve?" was "From 1861 to 1865. See affidavit attached hereto made by W. P. **ROBERTS**." The first of two copies of that affidavit is transcribed here in full: "Gatesville, N. C. Sept. 27 1904. To whom it may concern! Job H. **PARKER**, formerly of Gates County North Carolina, was a member of Co. "C". 2nd. North Cavalry [sic] (19th Regt. No. Car. State Troops,) and served continuously from 1861 to 1865. He was a good soldier and deserves well of the people among whom he is now living. W. P. **ROBERTS** Late Sergt. Co. "C" 2nd No. Car. /Cav/ and Capt of said Co. Colonel of the same Reg't., and Brigadier Geneneral [sic] P. A. C. S. Sworn to before me this 27. of Sept. 1904. W. T. **CROSS** Clerk Superior Court of Gates Co. N. C. (L. S.)"

The second copy of this affidavit differs little from the first, except for the date. "North Carolina Gates County} I hereby Certify that Job H. **PARKER** originally of Gates County, North Carolina was a Member of Company C, 2nd. N. C. Cav. (19th N. Ca. State Troops) And served during war as a gallant Soldier. W. P. **ROBERTS**. (Capt & Brig. General C S A) Subscribed and sworn to before me Dec. 19. 1904. W. T. **CROSS** Clerk Superior Court of Gates Co. N.C."[7] William P. **ROBERTS** was a neighbor

---

[1] Nathan G. Parker Family Bible

[2] National Archives, Washington, DC, File M4877; Compiled Military Service Record courtesy of Jason Walker, Historian, Texas State Cemetery, Austin, TX, personal correspondence of 17 November 2003.

[3] Contributed by his nephew, the late Vernon Bryant Parker.

[4] Almasy, *Gates County, North Carolina Marriage Bonds 1778-1868*, c. 1987, p. 68; Nathan G. Parker Family Bible

[5] U. S. Federal Census, 1870, M593, Roll: #1664, Nansemond Co., VA, pp.33-34, Fam. #234

[6] NCSA, G.041.2194762, Gates County Estates, Record of 1765-1920, Vol. Parker-Pierce, Folder: Parker, Nathan G. 1890, Doc. #100

[7] Copies of Records reproduced from the holdings of the Texas State Archives, P-18. Hereafter, Texas State Archives

and probably a boyhood friend.

The Application for Admission to the Texas Confederate Home from Job H. **PARKER** was received by them 13 February 1905, and approved by Val C. **GILES** 31 March 1905. He was admitted 30 May 1905, as "disabled and indigent...and not receiving a pension from any source." The disability is not described in these papers. The attached letter from S. L. **STAPLES**, Attorney at Law in Smithville, is transcribed here in part: "Supt. Confederate Home Austin Tx Dear Sir: Enclosed please find application of Mr. J. H. **PARKER** who desires to enter your Institution. He is a most estimable gentleman; you will find him courteous and will at all times observe the rules & regulations prescribed by you. I trust you will be able to make room for him." The final document in this series is a letter from J. C. **JONES**, Commissioner [of Pensions,] dated 21 May 1917, to Mrs. Margaret Ann **PARKER**, Smithville, Texas. It states that "Your application for a confederate pension has been rejected, as your deceased husband's war record at Washington, D. C. is not good."[8]

Jobe Henry[8] **PARKER** is buried in the Texas State Cemetery, Confederate Field, Section 3, Row H, #16. He died 26 November 1916 and was buried 27 November 1916. His gravestone reads "Joel H. **PARKER**," which has been corrected on his website, accessible through the address in this footnote.[9]

Patrick Henry[9] **PARKER** *(Jobe H.[8],Nathan G.[7],John[6],Joseph[5],Joseph[4],Thomas[3],Thomas[2],William[1])* was the eldest son of Jobe Henry[8] and Margaret Ann **(SIMONS) PARKER**. He was born in November, 1866, in North Carolina.[10] Patrick Henry[9] went to Texas with his parents and married "Lizzie" **KELLY** on 5 July 1894, in Bastrop County.[11] His name appears in that record as "Henry **PARKER**."

In the 1900 U. S. Census enumeration, he is listed as Patric H.[9] **PARKER**, W M Nov. 1866, 33, married five years and he and both parents born in North Carolina. His wife, Elizabeth A., W F Feb 1877 23, married five years, mother of three children and three living. She was born in Texas, her father in Georgia and her mother in Alabama. Their children are listed as Ida M.[10], daughter, W F Mar [May?] 1896, age four; Nathan G.[10], Son, W M Dec 1897, age two, and Mary M.[10], daughter, W F Jan [?] 1900, age 4/12 [?][12]

Patrick Henry[9] **PARKER**'s wife, Elizabeth A. **(KELLY) PARKER**, apparently died between 1900 and 1904. He appears once again as "Henry" **PARKER**, on a marriage record with Mrs. Mary **OGLA** [?] 3 July 1904.[13] They appear in the U. S. Census, 1910, Bastrop Co., TX, as P. H. **PARKER**, with wife Mary, her sons Frank and Robert **WEST** [?], his daughters, Ida May[10], Mary[10] and son Nathan[10].[14] They were both still living in 1920 and none of their children appear with them in that U. S. Census.[15] No further information.

Nathan G.[10] *(Patrick Henry[9],Jobe H.[8],Nathan G.[7],John[6],Joseph[5],Joseph[4],Thomas[3],Thomas[2],William[1])* **PARKER**, the only known son of Patrick Henry[9] and Elizabeth A. **(KELLY) PARKER**, was born in December 1897, as shown above. He appears on a marriage record of Bastrop County, TX, with Miss Nettie **COX** on 14 October 1915. Nathan G.[10] **PARKER** does not appear in any available census records after 1910. He does appear on a marriage license issued in Bastrop County, TX, 28 November 1945, with Mrs. Ima **BROWN**. They were married on that same date, but by A. B. **MC FALL**, a Justice of the Peace for Prec. #6, Bee County, TX.[16]

Nathan G.[10] **PARKER** died 8 May 1976, in Victoria, Victoria County, TX.[17] No further information.

William E.[9] **PARKER** *(Jobe H.[8],Nathan G.[7],John[6],Joseph[5],Joseph[4],Thomas[3],Thomas[2],William[1])* was the only other known child of Jobe Henry[8] and Margaret Ann **(SIMONS) PARKER**. He was born circa 1869, in North Carolina, and was living with his parents in Nansemond County, VA, in 1870. He appears

---

[8] Texas State Archives, P-18

[9] Texas State Cemetery-Section Map, http://www.cemetery.state.tx.us/pub/sect_map.asp?sect=E&sub=B

[10] U. S. Census, 1900, T623, Roll: 1609, p. 89B, Dw. #74, Fam. #77

[11] Bastrop County, TX Marriages, Book F:404, scanned images, courtesy of Tammy Owen, Rootsweb website coordinator @ http://www.rootsweb.com/~txbastro/bastrop.htm Hereafter, Bastrop County, TX Rootsweb

[12] See Footnote #10. This record is partially illegible.

[13] Bastrop County, TX Rootsweb, Book H:526

[14] U. S. Census, 1910, T624, Roll: 62, p. 16, Dw. #29, Fam. #29

[15] Ibid., 1920, T625, Roll: 1774, p. 96A, Dw. 300, Fam. #329, on Rose Street, Smithville, TX

[16] Bastrop County, TX Rootsweb, Book L:126; Book S:389

[17] Social Security Death Index, http://ssdi.genealogy.rootsweb.com/

to have died at an early age, as he never appears in any other records of this family. No further information.

Harriet Ann[8] **PARKER** *(Nathan G.[7],John[6],Joseph[5],Joseph[4],Thomas[3],Thomas[2],William[1])* was the eldest daughter of Nathan G.[7] and Mary Ann **(POWELL) PARKER**, born 8 March 1840, in Gates County, NC.[18] She was a resident of Portsmouth, VA, at the time of her father's death in 1890. She was married to ___?___ **TURNER** by 2 September 1897, when she was received as a member of **FLETCHER**'s [Methodist] Chapel under the name "Harriet A. **TURNER**."[19] In the U. S. Census, 1900, Gates County, she is shown as a widow and as the mother of two, one living.[20] In the U. S. Census, 1880, Nathan[7] **PARKER** is listed with two grandsons. The first is Thomas C.[9] **PARKER**, age 10, and the second is Dunn[9] **PARKER**, age 6.[21] Those two names do not appear in any of the families of the other children of Nathan G.[7] and Mary Ann **(POWELL) PARKER** and family tradition gives one of Harriet[8]'s children the name "Duanie." One of them was said to have died "at age nine." Which of the two survived until 1900 is unknown, but the more likely one would be Thomas C.[9] **PARKER**. No further information.

John Thomas[8] **PARKER** *(Nathan G.[7],John[6],Joseph[5],Joseph[4],Thomas[3],Thomas[2],William[1])* was the third child and second son of Nathan G.[7] and Mary Ann **(POWELL) PARKER**, born 29 March 1842, in Gates County, NC.[22] This child died young as he does not appear in the 1850 U. S. Census for Gates County, nor any subsequent records. No further information.

Isaac William[8] **PARKER** *(Nathan G.[7],John[6],Joseph[5],Joseph[4],Thomas[3],Thomas[2],William[1])* was the fourth child and third son of Nathan G.[7] and Mary Ann **(POWELL) PARKER**, born 22 January 1844, in Gates County, NC.[23] He married Elizabeth "Bettie" J. **MORRIS**, daughter of John and Harriet **MORRIS**, in Gates County on 15 February 1870, by G. W. **PHELPS**, Minister.[24] She was born in November, 1846, as shown in the 1900 Census for Chowan County.[25] His date of death is unknown to this writer.

On 20 February 1882, Isaac W.[8] **PARKER** and wife, Elizabeth, entered into a deed in trust on 40 acres of land with Dr. Richard E. **PARKER** of Nansemond County, VA. The land was on the road leading from **BOND**'s Landing to Mintonsville and was bounded by Willis **PILAND**, Mrs. Martha **ROUNTREE** and others.[26] No record of any land ownership has been found for this man in the extant tax lists, but he made another deed in trust 12 November 1901. It was to Lycurgus **HOFLER** for a total of 223 acres. It was stated to be the estate of Nathan **PARKER**, deceased, and consisted of the following tracts: 1. Home tract on Indian Neck Road, bounded on north by Rufus **LASSITER** and Isaac **EURE**, on the east by R. M. **RIDDICK** and James **FREEMAN**, on the south by Sam **PERKINS** and on the west by **LASSITER** heirs and contained 96 acres. 2. The Water Swamp tract adjoining Owen **SPIVEY** and contained 50 acres. 3. The "Isaac" tract, adjoining N. L. **ROUNTREE** and S. D. **NOWELL** and contained 37 acres. 4. The Jimmie **EURE** tract, adjoining E. F. **HURDLE** and N. L. **ROUNTREE** and contained 40 acres.[27] This deed was made just under two weeks after the date of the petition to sell the lands to pay off the mortgage. Isaac William[8] **PARKER**'s authority to make such a deed has never been determined.

Their children were Carl Cavana[9] **PARKER**, born in February, 1871; John W.[9] **PARKER**, born circa 1873; Mary F.[9] **PARKER**, born in November 1876; Nathan[9] **PARKER**, born in March, 1880; Jacob A.[9] **PARKER**, born in December 1882, and Luther[9] **PARKER**, born in September 1884.[28]

---

[18] Nathan G. Parker Family Bible. Her name is written as "Harriet An. Parker."

[19] LDS film #434943, Fletcher's Chapel Register of Members, p. 121, hereafter Fletcher's Chapel Register of Members

[20] U. S. Census, 1900, Gates Co., NC, T623, Roll: 1196, p. 80B, Dw. #26, Fam. #38

[21] U. S. Census, 1880, Gates Co., NC, T9, Roll: #964, Mintonsville Twp., p. 27, Fam. #238

[22] Nathan G. Parker Family Bible. His name is written as "John Thos. Parker."

[23] Ibid.

[24] Gates County Marriage Register, 1870

[25] U. S. Census, 1900, Chowan Co., NC, T623, Roll: 1188, p. 217B, Dw. #192, Fam. #192

[26] Gates County Deed Book 33:142

[27] Ibid., Book 51:93

[28] U. S. Census, 1880, Gates County, NC, T9, Roll: 964, Mintonsville Twp., p. 25, Fam. #226; U. S. Census, 1900, Chowan County, NC, T623, Roll:1188, Upper Twp., p. 217B, Dw. #192, Fam. #192

**Chapter 16:** Descendants of Nathan G.[7] **PARKER** *(John[6],Joseph[5],Joseph[4],Thomas[3],Thomas[2],William[1])*

Carl Cavana[9] **PARKER** *(IsaacW[8], Nathan G.[7],John[6],Joseph[5],Joseph[4],Thomas[3],Thomas[2],William[1])* was born 21 February, 1871, and died 27 November 1952, in Gates County. He is buried in the **BYRUM** Family Cemetery, Ryland, Chowan County, NC.[29] He married Martha Jane **BYRUM**, daughter of Isaac and Elizabeth **(TAYLOR) BYRUM**, 7 February 1894, in Chowan County, NC.[30] Martha Jane **(BYRUM) PARKER** was born 8 January 1871, in Chowan County, NC, and died 20 October 1946, in Gates County, NC. She is also buried in the **BYRUM** Family Cemetery in Ryland, NC.[31]

Their children were John Thomas[10] **PARKER**, born October 1894, died 5 October 1918; James Watson[10] **PARKER**, born 30 April 1897, died 22 June 1898; Ora Penelope[10] **PARKER**, born 31 May 1899; Linsy Lycurgus[10] **PARKER**, born 2 October 1902, died 13 October 1909; William Walter[10] **PARKER**, born 21 January 1905, died 27 March 1964; Martha Cavana[10] **PARKER**, and her twin, Mary Elizabeth[10] **PARKER**, born 11 October 1909, died 16 February 1911, and Gertrude M.[10] **PARKER**, born 8 October 1912.[32]

Carl C.[9] **PARKER** made his will 27 February 1939, naming one son, three daughters and one grandson. He mentioned the farm known as "the John Lee **ALPHIN** Place," adjoining the lands of Richmond Cedar Works, John T. **BARNES**, Mamie **ALPHIN**, Mable **JONES** and W. W. **PARKER**. It consisted of 100 acres on the Sandy Ridge public road at Acorn Hill, in **HUNTER**'s Mill Township, Gates County. All the land was bequeathed to W. W. **PARKER**, provided that he paid each of his sisters $833.33 within six months of Carl's death.[33] As he failed to name an executor, W. O. **CRUMP** was appointed administrator to his estate.[34]

William Walter[10] *(Carl C.[9],Isaac W[8], Nathan G.[7],John[6],Joseph[5],Joseph[4],Thomas[3],Thomas[2],William[1])* **PARKER** was born 21 January 1905, and died 27 March 1964. He is buried in Damascus Congregational Christian Church Cemetery, Sunbury, Gates County, NC.[35] He made his will 5 February 1964 and it was proved in Gates County Superior Court 14 April 1964. He devised all personal property and land to his wife, Louise S. **PARKER**, for life and then to be equally divided between his two sons, not named in the will.[36] The only known children in this family are William Walter[11] **PARKER**, Jr. and "Jay[11]" **PARKER**.[37] No further information.

Margaret Jane[8] **PARKER** *(Nathan G.[7],John[6],Joseph[5],Joseph[4],Thomas[3],Thomas[2],William[1])* was the fifth child and the second daughter of Nathan G.[7] and Mary Ann **(POWELL) PARKER**, born 23 August 1845, in Gates County, NC.[38] Family tradition states that she died circa 1918, in Norfolk, Norfolk County, VA. She married Alexander Elbert **ELLIS**, son of Alfred and Lavinia **ELLIS**, of Nansemond County, VA, 15 January 1890, at the Nathan **PARKER** home. Alexander Elbert **ELLIS** was born in July, 1836, and predeceased Margaret Jane[8] by an unknown span of time. He is said to have "died in his sleep," of unknown causes.[39]

Margaret Jane[8] had no children of her own and was fondly known to her nieces and nephews as "Aunt Puss." Alexander **ELLIS** enlisted in the Confederate States Army 22 June 1861, in the 19th Regiment, Co. "C" (2nd Regiment N. C. Cavalry,) as a private. He enlisted in Hertford County, NC, and was "Present or accounted for through September 1864."[40] No further information.

---

[29] Gates County, NC, Death Records, Book 18:89

[30] Chowan County Marriage Register, 1894

[31] Gates County Death Records, Book 15:138

[32] Bible Records of Carl C. Parker family, courtesy of Harvey B. Harrison, III, in personal correspondence of 29 August 2000; U. S. Census, 1910, Gates County, NC, T624, Roll: 1101, Mintonsville Twp., p. 258, Dw. #68?, Fam. #67. Carl C. Parker is erroneously listed as "Carroll C." Parker.

[33] Gates County Will Book 7:357

[34] Gates County Superior Court, Administrators, Executors & Guardians Book 6:238

[35] Fouts, Raymond Parker, personal transcription of gravestone.

[36] Gates County Will Book 7:593

[37] Gates County Will Book 7:357. William Walter Parker, Jr., named as grandson of Carl C. Parker. The name "Jay" was courtesy of the late W. T. Cross, Gatesville, NC

[38] Nathan G. Parker Family Bible

[39] Gates County Marriage Register, 1890; U. S. Census, 1850, Nansemond County, VA, M432, Roll: 962, Dw. #143, Fam. #256; U. S. Census, 1900, Gates County, NC, T623, Roll: 1196, Mintonsville Twp., p. 80B, Dw. 26, Fam. #38

[40] Jordan, Weymouth T. and Louis H. Manarin, compilers, *North Carolina Troops 1861-1865, A Roster,* c. 1989,

**Chapter 16:** Descendants of Nathan G.[7] **PARKER** *(John[6],Joseph[5],Joseph[4],Thomas[3],Thomas[2],William[1])*

Sallie Ann[8] **PARKER** *(Nathan G.[7],John[6],Joseph[5],Joseph[4],Thomas[3],Thomas[2],William[1])* was the sixth child and the third daughter of Nathan G.[7] and Mary Ann (**POWELL**) **PARKER**, born 15 June 1847, in Gates County, NC.[41] She died at age 77, 8 March 1924, of "broncho-pneumonia," in the State Hospital, Raleigh, NC. She is buried in Ocean View Cemetery, Beaufort, NC.[42]

Sallie Ann[8] **PARKER** married Ivey Dowdy **PERRY**, son of Josiah D. **PERRY** and Nancy **SAWYER**, on 11 September 1879, in Gates County. Ivey D. **PERRY** was born 19 September 1854, and died at age 82 years, five months and 24 days, on 13 March 1937, in Springfield, Greene County, MO.[43]

Ivey D. **PERRY** is known to have been a steamboat captain on the Chowan River, in North Carolina, and the James in Virginia. Logan Hurst[8] **PARKER**, Sallie's brother, went with him and his family to the Seattle, WA, area and they settled in Pearson, Bainbridge Island, Kitsap County, WA, circa 1890. They traveled to Chicago, IL, then took a covered wagon the rest of the way there. They were there when Mary Ann (**POWELL**) **PARKER** filed the application for administration on the estate of her husband, Nathan G. **PARKER** on 25 August 1890.[44] Ivey farmed land and also went into the real estate business.[45] There is a tradition that he participated in the Yukon Gold Rush, though unconfirmed.

Their children were a little girl, Birtie D.[9] **PERRY**, born 24 August 1880, died 20 September 1881[46]; Willie I.[9] **PERRY**, born 12 September 1883, lost in wilderness around Seattle, WA; Merritt Sawyer[9] **PERRY**, born 21 August 1884, Berkley City, VA, died 22 November 1965, Kansas City, MO, and Logan H.[9] **PERRY**, born 19 November 1887, died 9 July 1888.[47]

Willie[9] and Merritt[9] were enlisted in the U. S. Navy at an early age. In the U. S. Census, 1900, Sallie Ann[8] (**PARKER**) **PERRY** was listed as "Mother of 0, 0 living," and her birth month and year as "June 1846," all of which are incorrect.[48] These errors may have been by the census enumerator. Others are researching this family. No further information included here.

Mary Eliza[8] **PARKER** *(Nathan G.[7],John[6],Joseph[5],Joseph[4],Thomas[3],Thomas[2],William[1])* was the fourth daughter and seventh child of Nathan G.[7] and Mary Ann (**POWELL**) **PARKER**, born 19 March 1849, in Gates County, NC.[49] She died in Chowan County, NC, circa 1878 as her husband appears in the 1880 Census as "widowed."[50] She appears on a Gates County marriage bond with "Umphrey" **WARD**, dated 12 January 1866. Elisha F. **HURDLE** was his bondsman. They were married 18 January 1866.[51] Humphrey N. **WARD** was the son of Noah and Elizabeth **WARD**, born in September 1847.[52]

Their children were Kate[9] **WARD**, born circa 1867; John Norfleet[9] **WARD**, born circa 1869; Eva D.[9] **WARD**, born in November 1872 [twin,] and Nathan Q.[9] **WARD**, born in November 1872 [twin;] Noah C.[9] **WARD**, born circa 1875, and Mary Eliza[9] **WARD**, born 24 August 1877.[53]

Eva D.[9] **WARD** *(Mary Eliza[8],Nathan G.[7],John[6],Joseph[5],Joseph[4],Thomas[3],Thomas[2],William[1])* was the third child of Humphrey N. and Mary Eliza[8] (**PARKER**) **WARD**, born in November 1872. On 29 January 1891, she married John R. **EASON**, son of Timothy and Sarah **EASON**, born in May 1866.[54]

---

Vol. 2, p. 124

[41] Nathan G. Parker Family Bible. Her name was written as Sallie "An" Parker.

[42] NC State Board of Health, Death Certificate, Volume 845:160. Courtesy of Rex Perry, Stillwater, MN.

[43] Nathan G. Parker Family Bible; Missouri State Board of Health, File #11913. Courtesy of Rex Perry, Stillwater, MN.

[44] Gates County Book of Bonds, p. 127

[45] Family tradition courtesy of the late Mary Agnes (Parker) Taylor; courtesy of Rex Perry

[46] Nathan G. Parker Cemetery

[47] Courtesy of Rex Perry

[48] U. S. Census, 1900, T623, Roll: 1746, p. 43B, Dog Fish Bay Pct., Kitsap County, WA, Dw. #274, Fam. #274

[49] Nathan G. Parker Family Bible

[50] U. S. Census, 1880, T9, Roll: 958,Chowan County, NC, Upper Twp., p. 12, Fam. #103

[51] Almasy, *Gates County, North Carolina Marriage Bonds 1778-1868*, c. 1987, p. 95; Nathan G. Parker Family Bible

[52] U. S. Census, 1860, M653, Roll: 893, Chowan County, "District above Edenton," p. 35, Fam. #283; Ibid., 1900, T623, Roll: 1188, Chowan County, NC, p. 215B, Upper Twp., Dw. #157, Fam. #157

[53] U. S. Census, 1870, M593, Roll: 1130,Chowan County, NC, p. 24, Fam. #202; Ibid., 1880, T9, Roll: 958, p. 12, Fam. #103

[54] Chowan County Marriage Register, 1891; U. S. Census, 1900, Chowan County, NC, T623, Roll: 1188, p. 209, Fam. #40

**Chapter 16:** Descendants of Nathan G.[7] **PARKER** *(John[6],Joseph[5],Joseph[4],Thomas[3],Thomas[2],William[1])*

Their children were Evvis [?] C.[10] **EASON**, born July 1891; Leroy F.[10] **EASON**, born December 1892; Minnie E.[10] **EASON**, born September 1894; Orther [Arthur] R.[10] **EASON**, born September 1896, and Linzy[10] [Lindsay ?] **EASON**, born February 1898.[55] No further information.

Nathan Q.[9] **WARD** *(Mary Eliza[8],Nathan G.[7],John[6],Joseph[5],Joseph[4],Thomas[3],Thomas[2],William[1])* was the fourth child of Humphrey N. and Mary Eliza[8] **(PARKER) WARD**, born in November 1872, fraternal twin to Eva D.[9] **WARD**.

He married Cora J. **COPELAND** circa 1897, probably in Chowan County, NC.[56] Their children were Viola[10] **WARD**, born August 1898; Jamima, also called "Leona" M.[10] **WARD**, born May 1900; Lycurgus C.[10] **WARD**, born circa 1903; Eugene N.[10] **WARD**, born circa 1907; Lester E.[10] **WARD**, born circa 1911, and Ruth Y.[10] **WARD**, born circa 1915. They moved from Chowan County to Perquimans County between 1910 and 1920.[57] No further information.

Mary Eliza[9] **WARD** *(Mary Eliza[8],Nathan G.[7],John[6],Joseph[5],Joseph[4],Thomas[3],Thomas[2],William[1])* was the sixth child of Humphrey N. and Mary Eliza[8] **(PARKER) WARD**, born 24 August 1877. She died 15 October 1952, in Hertford County, NC.[58] She married George Locke **MITCHELL**, son of Bryant and Mary Elizabeth **(TAYLOR) MITCHELL**, circa 1900-1901.[59]

Their children were George Locke[10] **MITCHELL**, Jr., born 20 May 1902, and married Gladys Warrick **JERNIGAN**; Ernest Linwood[10] **MITCHELL**, born 19 June 1905, died 24 February 1935; Elizabeth[10] **MITCHELL**, born in March, 1906, married 25 November 1931, Hertford County, NC, Thomas R. **ROGERS**, Mary E.[10] **MITCHELL**, born 1909, married an **EVERETT**; Robert Lewis[10] **MITCHELL**, died before 1914; Lucille[10] **MITCHELL**, married George E. **WETHERINGTON**, all born in Hertford County.[60] No further information.

Martha Luvina[8] **PARKER** *(Nathan G.[7],John[6],Joseph[5],Joseph[4],Thomas[3],Thomas[2],William[1])* was the eighth child and fifth daughter of Nathan G.[7] and Mary Ann **(POWELL) PARKER**, born 15 August 1850, in Gates County, NC.[61] She married Franklin **GRIFFIN**, son of Simeon and Penina **(HOBBS) GRIFFIN**, 20 December 1866. They were married by John **BRADY**, J. P., in Gates County. Her brother, Isaac W.[8] (x) **PARKER**, was his bondsman.[62]

Their children were Emily[9] **GRIFFIN**, born circa 1868; Millard[9] **GRIFFIN**, born February 1870; Penina[9] "Penny" **GRIFFIN**, Roxy[9] **GRIFFIN**, Charles[9] **GRIFFIN**, and Eliza[9] **GRIFFIN**.[63] No further information.

Millard Filmore[8] **PARKER** *(Nathan G.[7],John[6],Joseph[5],Joseph[4],Thomas[3],Thomas[2],William[1])* was the ninth child and fourth son of Nathan G.[7] and Mary Ann **(POWELL) PARKER**, born 19 March 1852, in Gates County, NC.[64] On 11 February 1875, he married Amanda E. "Mandy" **WILLIFORD**, daughter of Richard F. and Elizabeth **WILLIFORD**, of Hertford County. They were married in Harrellsville by Wm. P. **WRIGHT**, Methodist Minister.[65] She was born in Hertford County in January 1850 and died 11

---

[55] U. S. Census, 1900, T623, Roll: 1188, Chowan County, NC, p. 209, Dw. #40, Fam. #40

[56] U. S. Census, 1910, T624, Roll: 1098, p. 254B, Chowan County, Upper Twp., Dw. #128, Fam. #129, shows that they were married 12 years by the date of the enumeration, 26 April 1910. Nathan's 15-year old sister-in-law, Annie Copeland, reveals Cora's maiden name.

[57] U. S. Census, 1900, T623, Roll: 1188, Chowan County, NC, p. 214B, Dw. 128, Fam. #128; U. S. Census, 1910, T624, Roll: 1098, p. 254B, Chowan County, NC, Upper Twp., Dw. #128, Fam. #129; U. S. Census, 1920, T625, Roll: 1317, Perquimans County, NC, Belvidere Pct., p. 1, Fam. #6

[58] Hertford County, NC, Death Records, Book 21:69

[59] U. S. Census, 1900, T623, Roll: 1196, Gates Co., NC, p. 81, Mintonsville, Twp., Dw. #33, Fam. #53, shows Mary E. Ward as single. Gates County, Special Proceedings in the Superior Court, Book 1:161, the petition concerning the estate of Nathan G. Parker states that she is "wife of George L. Mitchell," and is dated 30 October 1901.

[60] All undocumented information in this paragraph was courtesy of the late George L. Mitchell, Jr.

[61] Nathan G. Parker Family Bible

[62] U. S. Census, 1850, M432, Roll: 625, Chowan County, NC, p. 86, Fam. #105; Chowan County, NC, Will Book C:167, will of Emily Hobbs; Ibid., p. 275, will of Simeon Griffin; Gates County, NC, Almasy, *Gates County, North Carolina Marriage Bonds 1778-1868*, c. 1987, p. 35

[63] U. S. Census, 1870, M593, Roll: 1130, Chowan County, NC, Third Twp., p. 440, Dw. #226, Fam. #226; last four names courtesy of the late Mary Agnes (Parker) Taylor.

[64] Nathan G. Parker Family Bible

[65] U. S. Census, 1860, M653, Roll: #902, Hertford County, NC, p. 107, Fam. #844; Hertford County Marriage

January 1904. Millard died 14 November 1930.[66]

Millard Filmore[8] **PARKER** owned the M. F. **PARKER** and Company sawmill operation in Gates County. The sawmill was in Indian Neck and was probably the one later known as "**HURDLE**'s Mill." He and his brother, Logan Hurst[8] **PARKER**, along with their nephew, John Norfleet[9] **WARD**, traded as M. F. **PARKER** and Company and entered into a deed in trust 5 September 1889, with J. A. **EASON** and D. E. **RIDDICK**, trading as **EASON** and **RIDDICK**. The purpose of that deed was to pay off the debts of their company. It included "all the sawed pine lumber, logs, etc., four trams road trucks, two dwelling houses occupied by M. F. and T. W. **PARKER**, situated on the land of John B. **LASSITER**, and near said mill, also on **LASSITER**'s land."[67]

He resided in Gates County as late as 1890 and removed to Hertford County, Harrellsville Twp., NC, prior to 1900. He moved to Bertie County, NC, in Colerain Township, prior to 1910.[68] Their children were Lella [or "Lelia,"] Maud[9] **PARKER**, born 5 December 1875, died 25 August 1881; Theodore[9] **PARKER**, born 19 February 1877, died August 1957; John Nathan[9] **PARKER**, born July 1878, died 1937; Della Elizabeth[9] **PARKER**, born 20 August 1880, died 13 February 1942; Millard Fillmore[9] **PARKER**, born 17 April 1882, died 1921; Walter Leroy[9] **PARKER**, born 12 October 1885, died 17 November 1937.[69]

Millard Filmore[8] **PARKER** married secondly Hilda Beamon **STOKES**, 2 October 1907. She was born 8 June 1886, and died 3 November 1910. Their only child was Susie Clair[9] **PARKER**, born 20 June 1909. His third and final marriage was to Ida Margaret **HUTCHINS**, 1 January 1917.[70] No further information.

Adlina Felton[8] **PARKER** *(Nathan G.[7],John[6],Joseph[5],Joseph[4],Thomas[3],Thomas[2],William[1])* was the 10th child and sixth daughter of Nathan G.[7] and Mary Ann (**POWELL**) PARKER, born 6 November 1853, in Gates County, NC.[71] She married Richard L. **CROSS**, son of Richard **CROSS**, 12 May 1870.[72] Richard **CROSS** was a dry goods merchant in Gates County, NC, in 1870, in **HUNTER**'s Mill Township.[73]

Their children were Correa[9] [Corrie A.?] **CROSS**, born circa 1871; John R.[9] **CROSS**, born December 1872; Mary[9] "Mollie" **CROSS**, born circa 1877; Lonnie Raleigh[9] **CROSS**, born May 1879; Essie V.[9] **CROSS**, born December 1881; Addie S.[9] **CROSS**, born April 1884, and Rosa B.[9] **CROSS**, born August 1889. The 1900 Census for Holy Neck District, Suffolk, Nansemond County, VA, shows that "Addie" was the mother of 11 children, with five surviving, in the 30 years of their marriage.[74] The names, birth and death dates of the other children are unknown to this writer.

John R.[9] **CROSS** *(Adlina F.[8],Nathan G.[7],John[6],Joseph[5],Joseph[4],Thomas[3],Thomas[2],William[1])* was the son of Richard L. and Adlina Felton[8] (**PARKER**) **CROSS**, born December 1872, in North Carolina. He was living in Nansemond County, VA, in 1900, and was employed as a laborer in a "butter dish factory." His wife, Margaret P. **CROSS**, was born in 1876, and they had been married three years as of 2 June 1900. Their children were George W.[10] **CROSS**, born June 1898, and John W.[10] **CROSS**, born February 1900.[75] No further information.

Jacob Mask[8] **PARKER** *(Nathan G.[7],John[6],Joseph[5],Joseph[4],Thomas[3],Thomas[2],William[1])* was the 11th child and fifth son of Nathan G.[7] and Mary Ann (**POWELL**) PARKER, born 6 April 1855, in Gates

---

Register, 1875

[66] Courtesy of Betty Parker Nash, personal correspondence 11 July 1994. Information was transmitted to her from the late Susie (Parker) Hawk, from a reputed Millard Filmore Parker Family Bible. Hereafter, M. F. Parker Family Bible.

[67] Gates County, NC, Deed Book 42:63

[68] U. S. Census, 1880, T9, Roll: 964, Gates County, NC, p. 27, Fam. #239; Ibid., 1900, T623, Roll: 1200, Hertford County, NC, p. 165, Dw. #293, Fam. #298; Ibid., 1910, T624, Roll: 1098, Bertie County, NC, p. 30, Fam. #17

[69] M. F. Parker Family Bible

[70] Ibid.

[71] Nathan G. Parker Family Bible

[72] Gates County, NC, Marriage Register, 1870

[73] U. S. Census, 1870, M593, Roll: 1139, Gates County, NC, p. 21, Fam. #152

[74] U. S. Census, 1900, T623, Roll: 1719, Nansemond County, VA, p. 169, Dw. #61,Fam. #62

[75] Ibid., Fam. #61

**Chapter 16:** Descendants of Nathan G.[7] **PARKER** *(John[6],Joseph[5],Joseph[4],Thomas[3],Thomas[2],William[1])*

County, NC.[76] He died 1 December 1936, Norfolk, Norfolk County, VA.

He is reputed to have married Amanda **DUCK**, who died in childbirth, dates unknown. His second marriage was to Louise **MARKHAM**, in Pasquotank County, NC, date unknown. His third marriage was to Annie Wood **MITCHELL**, daughter of Bryant and Mary Elizabeth (**TAYLOR**) **MITCHELL**, on 4 October 1899, in Powellsville, Bertie County, NC.[77] Annie was born 16 May 1877, in Hertford County, NC, and died 8 January 1940, in Norfolk, Norfolk County, VA.

Their children were Jacob Mask[9] **PARKER**, Jr., born 23 August 1900; Mildred Irene[9] **PARKER**, born 5 October 1902; Leon Ashburn[9] **PARKER**, born 10 September 1906, and Paul Bryant[9] **PARKER**, born 10 January 1909. Jacob Mask[9], Jr., was born in North Carolina and the other three were born in Virginia. They resided at 131 Seaboard Avenue, Washington District of Norfolk, Virginia, where Jacob, Sr., was employed as a ship carpenter.[78]

Jacob Mask[9] **PARKER**, Jr., *(Jacob M.[8],Nathan G.[7],John[6],Joseph[5],Joseph[4],Thomas[3],Thomas[2],William[1])* was the son of Jacob Mask[8] and Annie Wood (**MITCHELL**) PARKER, born 23 August 1900, in Bertie County, NC. He died 10 May 1970, in Suitland, Prince George County, Maryland. He married Freida **SCHMIDT**, date unknown. Their children were "Jackie"[10] **PARKER**; Andrew Lee[10] **PARKER**, born 14 August 1938, died 31 January 1999, gravestone in Nathan G. **PARKER** Cemetery, and Robert W. **PARKER**. No further information.

Mildred Irene[9] **PARKER** *(Jacob M.[8],Nathan G.[7],John[6],Joseph[5],Joseph[4],Thomas[3],Thomas[2],William[1])* was the daughter of Jacob Mask[8] and Annie Wood (**MITCHELL**) PARKER, born 5 October 1902, Suffolk, Nansemond County, VA. She married Albert Curby **FRIZZELL** 31 July 1922, in Elizabeth City, Pasquotank County, NC. Their children were Shirley Mae[10] **FRIZZELL**, born circa 1924, and Roy Wheeler[10] **FRIZZELL**, born circa 1928. Annie and Jacob[8] were living with them on Corprew Avenue, Norfolk, VA, in 1930.[79] No further information.

Leon Ashburn[9] **PARKER** *(Jacob M.[8],Nathan G.[7],John[6],Joseph[5],Joseph[4],Thomas[3],Thomas[2],William[1])* was the son of Jacob Mask[8] and Annie Wood (**MITCHELL**) PARKER, born 10 September 1906, in Berkley, VA. He married Josephine **PALIDENO** in Brooklyn, Kings County, NY, on 16 August 1936.

Their children were Judith Ann[10] **PARKER** and Virginia Dorothy[10] **PARKER**. No further information.

Paul Bryant[9] **PARKER** *(Jacob M.[8],Nathan G.[7],John[6],Joseph[5],Joseph[4],Thomas[3],Thomas[2],William[1])* was the son of Jacob Mask[8] and Annie Wood (**MITCHELL**) PARKER, born 10 January 1909, in South Norfolk, Norfolk County, VA. He married Margaret **WALSH** in Brooklyn, Kings County, NY, on 30 June 1935.

Their children were Paul Bryant[10] **PARKER**, Jr., and Donald Francis[10] **PARKER**. No further information.[80]

John Nathan[8] **PARKER** *(Nathan G.[7],John[6],Joseph[5],Joseph[4],Thomas[3],Thomas[2],William[1])* was the 12th child and sixth son of Nathan G.[7] and Mary Ann (**POWELL**) PARKER, born 23 November 1856, in Gates County, NC.[81] He married Annie F. **SADLER**, daughter of J. M. **SADLER**, circa 1878, probably in Virginia. She was born there in September 1858.[82]

Their children were John W.[9] **PARKER**, born in May 1879; Annie C.[9] **PARKER**, born in January 1885; Bessie P.[9] **PARKER**, born in September 1886, and Arthur F.[9] **PARKER**, born in October 1894. They had two other children who did not survive to 1900. They resided on Virginia Avenue, in Crewe Town, VA.[83]

John Nathan[8] **PARKER** owned his own business as evidenced by the letterhead he used to answer L. L. **SMITH** concerning the sale of his father's lands in 1901. It reads "John N. **PARKER** & Co.,

---

[76] Nathan G. Parker Family Bible

[77] Bertie County, NC, Marriage Register, 1899

[78] U. S. Census, 1910, T624, Roll: 1638, Norfolk County, VA, Washington Dist., , p. 165, Dw. #403, Fam. #125

[79] U. S. Census, 1930, T626, Roll: 2469, Norfolk County, VA, 4th Precinct, p. 254, Dw. 182, Fam. #204

[80] All information, other than the marriage and Census references, on the family of Jacob Mask[8] Parker is courtesy of the late Leon Ashburn Parker and Mildred Irene (Parker) Frizzell.

[81] Nathan G. Parker Family Bible

[82] U. S. Census, 1900, T623, Roll: 1721, Nottaway County, VA, Crewe Town, p. 221B, Fam. #195

[83] Ibid.

Merchant Tailors, Our Motto: Fine Goods, Good Workmanship, Low Prices and Latest Styles." John W.[9] **PARKER** was also a tailor and appears to have been his partner. [84] No further information.

Charles Arthur[8] **PARKER** *(Nathan G.[7],John[6],Joseph[5],Joseph[4],Thomas[3],Thomas[2],William[1])* was the 13th child and seventh son of Nathan G.[7] and Mary Ann **(POWELL) PARKER**, born 12 May 1858, in Gates County, NC.[85] He died 25 May 1929, at 1:30 PM, in the community of Drum Hill, Gates County, NC.[86] He is buried on Mooretown Road, Bertie County, NC.[87] He married Lula Sophie **MITCHELL**, daughter of Bryant and Mary Elizabeth **(TAYLOR) MITCHELL**, 20 December 1887, in Harrellsville, Hertford County, NC.[88] She was born 22 July 1866, in Harrellsville, and died 27 September 1945, in South Norfolk, Norfolk County, VA. She is buried next to her husband, in Bertie County, NC, north and east of Powellsville.

Their children were Mary Ruth[9] **PARKER**, born 4 October 1888; Lula Wood[9] **PARKER**, born 10 October 1890; Charles Arthur[9] **PARKER**, Jr., born 17 June 1892; Bessie May[9] **PARKER**, born 22 May 1894, Powellsville, Bertie County, NC; Pauline[9] **PARKER**, born 28 May 1896; Walter Stallings[9] **PARKER**, born 30 January 1899; Minnie Smith[9] **PARKER**, born 27 October 1901; Alton Bryant[9] **PARKER**, born 21 September 1904, and John Mitchell[9] **PARKER**, born 2 May 1910.[89]

Mary Ruth[9] **PARKER** *(Charles A.[8],Nathan G.[7],John[6],Joseph[5],Joseph[4],Thomas[3],Thomas[2],William[1])* was the daughter of Charles Arthur[8] and Lula Sophie **(MITCHELL) PARKER**, born 4 October 1888, in Harrellsville, Hertford County, NC. She died 30 December 1908, in Powellsville, Bertie County, NC. She married Herman Jerry **HOLLOMAN**, son of Magruder and Temperance **HOLLOMAN**, 15 January 1908, in Bertie County, NC. He was born circa 1885.[90] Their only child was Herman Parker[10] **HOLLOMAN**, born 23 October 1908, in Powellsville, Bertie County, NC. He died 6 August 1993, in Norfolk, VA.[91] He married Lucille **WORRELL**, date unknown. No further information.

Lula Wood[9] **PARKER** *(Charles A.[8],Nathan G.[7],John[6],Joseph[5],Joseph[4],Thomas[3],Thomas[2],William[1])* was the daughter of Charles Arthur[8] and Lula Sophie **(MITCHELL) PARKER**, born 10 October 1890, Harrellsville, Hertford County, NC, died 8 June 1961, Suffolk, Nansemond County, VA. She married Joe Mark **HARRELL**, date unknown.

Their children were Ruth[10] **HARRELL**, Josie[10] **HARRELL** and George Arthur[10] **HARRELL**. No further information.

Charles Arthur[9] **PARKER**, Jr., *(Charles A.[8],Nathan G.[7],John[6],Joseph[5],Joseph[4],Thomas[3],Thomas[2],William[1])* was the son of Charles Arthur[8] and Lula Sophie **(MITCHELL) PARKER**, born 17 June 1892, Harrellsville, Hertford County, NC, died 7 December 1952, Norfolk, Norfolk County, VA. He married Mary Louise **HARRELL**, daughter of Lazarus **HARRELL**

Their children were Arthur[10] **PARKER**, Hubert[10] **PARKER** and Judith Harrell[10] **PARKER**. No further information.

Pauline[9] **PARKER** *(Charles A.[8],Nathan G.[7],John[6],Joseph[5],Joseph[4],Thomas[3],Thomas[2],William[1])* was the daughter of Charles Arthur[8] and Lula Sophie **(MITCHELL) PARKER**, born 28 May 1896, Powellsville, Bertie County, NC. She married Ernest Granville **STEINMETZ** 20 June 1916, in Powellsville. He was born circa 1887, in Virginia. His father was born in Germany and his mother in Virginia.[92]

Their children were Granville H.[10] **STEINMETZ**, born circa July 1917,[93] and Ernest Parker[10] **STEINMETZ**. No further information.[94]

Walter Stallings[9] *(Charles A.[8],Nathan G.[7],John[6],Joseph[5],Joseph[4],Thomas[3],Thomas[2],William[1])* **PARKER** was the son of Charles Arthur[8] and Lula Sophie **(MITCHELL) PARKER**, born 30 January

[84] Gates County Estates Records, 1765-1920, C.R.71.508.87, Folder: Parker, Nathan 1890

[85] Nathan G. Parker Family Bible

[86] Gates County, NC, Death Records, Book 4:55

[87] Courtesy of Sally Koestler, transcribed by her 24 April 2000, and transmitted to the writer 19 July 2003.

[88] Hertford County, NC, Marriage Register, 1887

[89] Charles Arthur Parker Bible, birth page, courtesy of USAF Major John W. Parker, Jr., 14 July 1977

[90] U. S. Census, 1910, T624, Roll: 1098, Bertie County, NC, Roxobel Twp., p. 101B, Dw. 35, Fam. #35

[91] Obituary, courtesy of Mrs. Wayne H. Holloman in correspondence of 13 January 1994.

[92] U. S. Census, 1920, T625, Roll: 1909, Henrico County, Richmond City, VA, p. 260, Dw. #182, Fam. #213

[93] Ibid.

[94] All information on the Charles Arthur Parker family, prior to this footnote, was courtesy of the late Miss Bessie May Parker and USAF Major John M. Parker, Jr.

1899, Powellsville, Bertie County, NC.  He married Mary Sally **WILLOUGHBY**, daughter of Thomas Ely and Betty **(DOUGHTIE) WILLOUGHBY**, 29 December 1924, in Winton, Hertford County, NC.  She was born 1 October 1899, and died in February, 1994.[95]  He died 19 December 1977, in Ahoskie, Hertford County, NC, and is buried in the **WILLOUGHBY** Family Cemetery.[96]

Their children were Elizabeth[10] **PARKER**, and Ruth[10] **PARKER**, born in Gates County, NC.

Elizabeth[10] *(Walter Stallings[9],Charles A.[8],Nathan G.[7],John[6],Joseph[5],Joseph[4],Thomas[3],Thomas[2], William[1])* **PARKER** married James Dale **CAVENDER**, son of Elijah W. and Nora Bell **(WALDEN) CAVENDER**, in South Mills, Camden County, NC.  He was born 14 September 1922, in Rock River, Wyoming, and died in January, 1996.[97]

Their children are James Dale[11] **CAVENDER**, Jr., born 20 March 1947, in Colerain, Bertie County, NC, and died 23 August 1947, in Alma, Ware County, GA; Brenda[11] **CAVENDER** married Sherrill Anthony **BALDREE**, son of Sherrill Hammond and Helen **(EUBANKS) BALDREE**, and Walter **CAVENDER**.  No further information included here.[98]

Ruth[10] *(Walter Stallings[9],Charles A.[8],Nathan G.[7],John[6],Joseph[5],Joseph[4],Thomas[3],Thomas[2],William[1])* **PARKER** married ___ **OVERTON**.  No further information.

Minnie Smith[9] **PARKER** *(Charles A.[8],Nathan G.[7],John[6],Joseph[5],Joseph[4],Thomas[3],Thomas[2],William[1])* was the daughter of Charles Arthur[8] and Lula Sophie **(MITCHELL) PARKER**, born 27 October 1901, Powellsville, Bertie County, NC.  She married Thomas Starling **HARRELL** son of Lazarus **HARRELL**, 21 February 1925, in Gates County, NC.[99]

Their children were Thomas Starling[10] **HARRELL**, Jr., and Phillip Allen[10] **HARRELL**.  No further information.

Alton Bryant[9] **PARKER** *(Charles A.[8],Nathan G.[7],John[6],Joseph[5],Joseph[4],Thomas[3],Thomas[2],William[1])* was the son of Charles Arthur[8] and Lula Sophie **(MITCHELL) PARKER**, born 21 September 1904, Powellsville, Bertie County, NC.  He married Blanch **LAMB**, daughter of Hettie **LAMB**.

Their only known child was Thomas Arthur[10] **PARKER**.  No further information.

John Mitchell[9] **PARKER** *(Charles A.[8],Nathan G.[7],John[6],Joseph[5],Joseph[4],Thomas[3],Thomas[2],William[1])* was the son of Charles Arthur[8] and Lula Sophie **(MITCHELL) PARKER**, born 2 May 1910, Powellsville, Bertie County, NC.  He married Thelma Isabel **BATTLEY**, who died 20 January 1954.

Their children were John Mitchell[10] **PARKER**, Jr., and Barbara Jean[10] **PARKER**.  He married secondly Geraldine Annie **CLARK**, daughter of John **CLARK**.[100]  No further information included here.

Thomas Walter[8] **PARKER** *(Nathan G.[7],John[6],Joseph[5],Joseph[4],Thomas[3],Thomas[2],William[1])* was the 14th child and eighth son of Nathan G.[7] and Mary Ann **(POWELL) PARKER**, born 24 June 1860.[101]  Family tradition states that he was an accomplished violinist and lived in Norfolk, VA, where he was employed as a "motorman" on street cars there.  He is reputed to have been held in high esteem by his employers and to have died in 1920.[102]  He was still living as of 13 January 1920, the date of the census enumeration mentioned later.  He married Dora F. **OUTLAND**, daughter of John M. **OUTLAND**, 23 December 1887.  She was 17 years of age.[103]

This family appears in both Gates and Camden Counties in the 1900 U. S. Census, within a few days.  The Gates County Census was enumerated 6 June 1900, in Mintonsville Township, and shows Doro [sic] **PARKER** as Head, W[hite] F[emale], [born] Jan 1870, [age] 30, M[arried] 13 [years,] [mother of] 4, 4 [living.]  Listed with her was her daughter, Gracy V. **PARKER**, born September, 1888, age 11; son, John U. **PARKER**, born July 1892 and daughter, Doro F., born September 1896, age 3.[104]

---

[95] Courtesy of Elizabeth (Parker) Cavender, personal correspondence 15 May 1999.

[96] Courtesy of the late Edna C. (Parker) Breland, from an unidentified newspaper obituary.

[97] Courtesy of Elizabeth (Parker) Cavender, personal correspondence 15 May 1999.

[98] Courtesy of Elizabeth (Parker) Cavender, personal correspondence of 1981.

[99] Gates County, NC, Marriage Register, 1925

[100] All information on the Charles Arthur Parker family, not otherwise referenced, was courtesy of the late Miss Bessie May Parker and USAF Major John M. Parker, Jr.

[101] Nathan G. Parker Family Bible

[102] Courtesy of the late Vernon B. Parker, Sr., and Edna C. (Parker) Breland

[103] Gates County, NC, Marriage Register, 1887; Fletcher's [Methodist] Chapel Marriage Records, LDS Microfilm Reel #434943.

[104] U. S. Census, 1900, T623, Roll: 1196, Gates County, NC, Mintonsville Twp., pp. 81A-81B, Dw. #45, Fam. #57

**Chapter 16:** Descendants of Nathan G.[7] **PARKER** *(John[6],Joseph[5],Joseph[4],Thomas[3],Thomas[2],William[1])*

The Camden County 1900 enumeration was made 29 June 1900, and shows Thomas **PARKER**, Head, W M, Jan 1860, 40, married 12 years; Dora **PARKER**, Wife, W F <u>May 1882</u>, <u>38</u>, married 12 years, mother of 4, 4 living; Grace[9] **PARKER**, daughter, W F, Apr 18<u>90</u>, <u>10</u>, <u>S</u>ingle; Ethel[9] **PARKER**, daughter, W F, May 1892, 8, S; John[9] **PARKER**, son, W M, Apr 189<u>4</u>, <u>6</u>, S; Dora[9] **PARKER**, daughter, W F, May 1897, 3, S, and **OUTLA<u>W</u>**, Godwin, Bro in law, W M, Mar 1870, 30, S.[105]  The Gates County Census appears to be the more accurate record for birthdates and ages.

In 1910, this family appears in Norfolk, VA, where Thomas Walter[8] **PARKER** was employed as a street car conductor, living at 219 Highland Avenue.  He is listed as 49 years of age, Dora was 39, John N.[9] **PARKER** was 16, Dora F.[9] **PARKER** was 13, and son Walter T.[9] [sic] **PARKER** was age seven.  John H. **OUTLAND** was listed as his brother-in-law, aged 23.[106]

On 13 January 1920, they were living at 317 East 25th Street, in the 18th precinct of Norfolk, VA.  He was listed as Thomas W. **PARKER**, age 58, Dora O. **PARKER**, was age 49, Thomas W.[9] **PARKER**, Jr., was age 12, and daughter Mary[9] was age 8.  In this same household, Herman L. **BARNETT** was listed as Thomas' son-in-law, age 29, along with Thomas' daughter, Ethel P.[9] **BARNETT**, age 29, and their son, Herman L.[10] **BARNETT**, Jr., age one year, two months.  Herman L. **BARNETT**, Sr., was employed as an electrician at the Norfolk Navy Yard.[107]  No further information.

Kate[8] **PARKER** *(Nathan G.[7],John[6],Joseph[5],Joseph[4],Thomas[3],Thomas[2],William[1])* was the 15th child and seventh daughter of Nathan G.[7] and Mary Ann (**POWELL**) **PARKER**, born 6 October 1863, in Gates County, NC.  She is reputed to have lived only one year.[108]  No further information

Logan Hurst[8] **PARKER** *(Nathan G.[7],John[6],Joseph[5],Joseph[4],Thomas[3],Thomas[2],William[1])* was the 16th child and eighth son of Nathan G.[7] and Mary Ann (**POWELL**) **PARKER**, born 15 March 1865.[109]  He died 16 March 1941, Norfolk, Norfolk County, VA, and is buried there, in Forest Lawn Cemetery.[110]

Logan Hurst[8] **PARKER** married Mary Agnes **MITCHELL**, daughter of Bryant and Mary Elizabeth (**TAYLOR**) **MITCHELL**, 9 January 1895, in Hertford County, NC, by the Rev. Braxton **CRAIG**, at Elizabeth **MITCHELL**'s home.[111]  Mary Agnes was born 3 June 1870[112], near Cofield, Hertford County, NC.  She died 4 December 1929, Camden, Camden County, New Jersey, and is buried in the **HOGGARD-MITCHELL** Cemetery on land known as the "**BASNIGHT** Estate."[113]  She was much admired and loved by all her children.

Logan was a partner in the M. F. **PARKER** and Company, sawmill operation in Gates County, as of 5 September 1889, as mentioned earlier.  He went to Seattle, Washington, in 1890, with his sister, Sallie Ann[8] (**PARKER**) **PERRY** and her husband Ivey Dowdy **PERRY**.  He remained there until circa 1892, then returned to Gates County.  He and Mary Agnes (**MITCHELL**) **PARKER** were received as members of **FLETCHER**'s Chapel 2 September 1897, on profession of F. B. **MC CALL**.[114]  They resided at the Nathan G.[7] **PARKER** home with Mary Ann **PARKER** until her death in 1901.

Logan cultivated grapes and corn at the old home place, as his father before him, and made and sold wine.  It was transported to Gatesville by horse and wagon.  The family moved frequently as evidenced by the various birthplaces of their children.

Mary Agnes[9] *(Logan H.[8],Nathan G.[7],John[6],Joseph[5],Joseph[4],Thomas[3],Thomas[2],William[1])* **PARKER** was the first child and first daughter of Logan Hurst[8] and Mary Agnes (**MITCHELL**) **PARKER**, born Monday, 21 October 1895, in Gates County, NC.[115]  She married Jesse Eugene **TAYLOR**, son of Isaac Madison and Martha Ann (**HOLLOMAN**) **TAYLOR**, 9 January 1916, near Har-

---

[105] U. S. Census, 1900, T623, Roll: 1186, Camden County, NC, Shiloh Twp., p. 199, Dw. #395, Fam. #404

[106] U. S. Census, 1910, T624, Roll: 1637, Norfolk, VA, pp. 225B, 226, Dw. # 148, Fam. #158

[107] U. S. Census, 1920, T625, Roll: 1902, Norfolk, VA, p. 218, Dw. #190, Fam. #257

[108] Nathan G. Parker Family Bible; Courtesy of Betty Parker Nash, personal correspondence 11 July 1994.

[109] Nathan G. Parker Family Bible

[110] Certificate of Death, Commonwealth of VA, State File #7960

[111] Hertford County Marriage Register, 1895

[112] Logan H. Parker Family Bible births page, courtesy of the late Della F. M. Parker, hereafter Logan H. Parker Family Bible.  This record shows her date of birth as "June 8, 1870, on Sat."

[113] Camden Health Dept., Camden, Camden County, NJ, Death Certificate Reg. #1521

[114] Fletcher's Chapel Register of Members, p. 121

[115] Logan H. Parker Family Bible

Harrellsville, Hertford County, NC. He was born 14 October 1892, near Harrellsville, and died 2 March 1965, Williamsburg, James City County, VA.

Their children are Jesse Gray[10] **TAYLOR**, Mary Agnes[10] **TAYLOR**, Margaret Ruth[10] **TAYLOR**, the late Hazel Parker[10] **TAYLOR**, Jean Marie[10] **TAYLOR**, and Gordon Gale[10] **TAYLOR**.[116] No further information included here.

Maude Valeria[9] *(Logan H.[8],Nathan G.[7],John[6],Joseph[5],Joseph[4],Thomas[3],Thomas[2],William[1])* **PARKER** was the second child and second daughter of Logan Hurst[8] and Mary Agnes (**MITCHELL**) **PARKER**, born Thursday, 18 May 1897.[117] She died 20 January 1974, in Norfolk, VA. She married Richard Willis **CROSS**, son of Tobe **CROSS**, 27 December 1919. He was born 29 February 1896, Portsmouth, Norfolk County, VA, and died in May 1964.

Their children were Richard Willis[10] **CROSS**, Jr., and Helen Anne[10] **CROSS**.[118] No further information included here.

Logan Hurs*e*[9] *(Logan H.[8],Nathan G.[7],John[6],Joseph[5],Joseph[4],Thomas[3],Thomas[2],William[1])* **PARKER**, Jr., was the third child and first son of Logan Hurst[8] and Mary Agnes (**MITCHELL**) **PARKER**, born Friday, 17 February 1899.[119] He died 8 October 1933, in Norfolk, Norfolk County, VA, and is buried in Forest Lawn Cemetery, in Norfolk. He married Abbie Lucretia **HARRELL** on 1 March 1922, in Norfolk. She was the daughter of William Mills and Lucretia (**WILLIAMS**) **HARRELL**, born 17 October 1905, in Gates County, NC, died 13 April 1988.

Logan Hurse[9] **PARKER**, Jr., served on the Norfolk Police Force for six months and was appointed to the Fire Department in 1923. He held the rank of Private, First Class. He was a member of the Norfolk Fire Department, attached to the Berkley station. He resided at 1748 Gowrie Avenue, Gowrie Park, with his wife and two children. He held a transport pilot's license and was flying a Gee Bee biplane when it crashed into a ditch at the end of the Tidewater Airport, beside the Virginian Railway track. He had cut the switches on the plane before the crash, which action averted a fire. He and his passenger, James Robert **BENNETT**, were tragically killed almost instantly.[120]

Their children are Allen Leon[10] **PARKER** and Jeane Barbara[10] **PARKER**. No further information included here.

Vernon Bryant[9] *(Logan H.[8],Nathan G.[7],John[6],Joseph[5],Joseph[4],Thomas[3],Thomas[2],William[1])* **PARKER** was the fourth child and second son of Logan Hurst[8] and Mary Agnes (**MITCHELL**) **PARKER**, born on Tuesday, 25 June 1901.[121] He died 7 November 1981, in the Veterans' Administration Hospital, Salisbury, Rowan County, NC. He married Anna Belle **CLARK**, daughter of David Columbus and Annie Hopper (**BURROUGHS**) **CLARK**, date unknown. She was born 17 January 1908, Mobile County, Alabama and died 18 May 1973, Levittown, Bucks County, Pennsylvania. They were divorced at some unknown date.

Vernon Bryant[9] **PARKER** served in the United States Army, Air Service Balloon Company #13. He enlisted 28 July 1919 and was awarded an honorable discharge 23 July 1921, with the rank of Private, First Class. He was variously employed as a streetcar motorman in Norfolk, VA, punch-press operator and service station owner and operator. He also worked for Merchants and Miners Transportation Company, as an oiler, on the steamships Grecian and the well-known Dorchester, out of Baltimore, Maryland. He retired 25 June 1966, from Mid-Florida Gas Company, Orlando, Florida, and removed to Charlotte, NC.

The children of Vernon Bryant[9] and Anna Belle (**CLARK**) **PARKER** are Vernon Bryant[10] **PARKER**, Jr., and Anna Belle[10] "Ann" **PARKER**.

Vernon Bryant[9] **PARKER** married secondly Jessie Raymond **HILL**, daughter of Rowland and Elizabeth Raymond (**GEROW**) **HILL**, 24 April 1933, Baltimore, Baltimore County, Maryland. She was born 4 October 1892, Norfolk, VA, and died 24 May 1955, Orlando, Orange County, Florida.

---

[116] Information on this family courtesy of the late Mary Agnes (Parker) Taylor

[117] Logan H. Parker Family Bible

[118] Information on this family was courtesy of the late Mary Agnes (Parker) Taylor and Della F. M. Parker.

[119] Logan H. Parker Family Bible

[120] Newspaper articles from *Virginian Pilot & The Norfolk Landmark,* 9 October 1933 edition; *The Norfolk Ledger-Dispatch,* 9 October 1933 edition.

[121] Logan H. Parker Family Bible

Their only child is Raymond Aileen **PARKER**, who began research on the **PARKER** families in North Carolina and Virginia in 1973 and is the author of this book.

Vernon Bryant[9] **PARKER**, Sr., married thirdly Elva Ray **HUMPHRIES**, daughter of Marion F. and Fannie **(FORTNER) HOWARD**, born 2 February 1901, Iredell County, NC, reputed to have died in 1984. No further information included here.[122]

Margaret Jane[9] *(Logan H.[8],Nathan G.[7],John[6],Joseph[5],Joseph[4],Thomas[3],Thomas[2],William[1])* **PARKER** was the fifth child and third daughter of Logan Hurst[8] and Mary Agnes **(MITCHELL) PARKER**, born on Saturday 8 May 1904.[123] She died, unmarried, 16 September 1998.[124] No further information.

Thomas Walter[9] *(Logan H.[8],Nathan G.[7],John[6],Joseph[5],Joseph[4],Thomas[3],Thomas[2],William[1])* **PARKER** was the sixth child and third son of Logan Hurst[8] and Mary Agnes **(MITCHELL) PARKER**, born on Tuesday, 31 July 1906, in Cofield, Hertford County, NC.[125] He died 12 March 1995, in Pennsylvania. He was a retired marine engineer with the Army Corps of Engineers. His last assignment was the dredging of the Delaware River as a chief marine engineer working out of Fort Mifflin, in Philadelphia.[126]

He married Bessie Lee **CLARK**, daughter of David Columbus and Annie Hopper **(BURROUGHS) CLARK**, 21 August 1931, in Philadelphia, Philadelphia County, Pennsylvania. She was born 9 August 1910 in Creola, Mobile County, Alabama, and died 19 April 1990.

Their children are Thomas Walter[10] **PARKER**, Jr., Ronald Allen[10] **PARKER** and Elizabeth Lee[10] **PARKER**. No further information included here.[127]

Edna Cooper[9] **PARKER** *(Logan H.[8],Nathan G.[7],John[6],Joseph[5],Joseph[4],Thomas[3],Thomas[2],William[1])* was the seventh child and fourth daughter of Logan Hurst[8] and Mary Agnes **(MITCHELL) PARKER**, born on Saturday, 14 May 1910, in South Norfolk, Norfolk County, VA [twin.][128] She died in Concord, Cabarrus County, NC, 20 April 2004. She married Earl Dewey **WILKINSON** 11 May 1928, in Norfolk County, VA.

Their children are Margaret Jane[10] **WILKINSON** and Earl Dewey[10] **WILKINSON**, Jr., both later **BRELAND**, by adoption.

Edna Cooper[9] **(PARKER) WILKINSON** was divorced 2 January 1942, and married secondly Marion Harbrook **BRELAND**, son of Wyman Franklin and Barbara Catherine **BRELAND**, 17 May 1943, in Norfolk, Norfolk County, VA. He was born 25 May 1913, Cottageville, Colleton County, South Carolina, and died 2 March 1969, Fort Lauderdale, Broward County, Florida.

Their child is Dolores Dee[10] **BRELAND**.[129] No further information included here.

Harry Hilborn[9] *(Logan H.[8],Nathan G.[7],John[6],Joseph[5],Joseph[4],Thomas[3],Thomas[2],William[1])* **PARKER** was the eighth child and fourth son of Logan Hurst[8] and Mary Agnes **(MITCHELL) PARKER**, born on Saturday, 14 May 1910 [twin.][130] He was born in South Norfolk, Norfolk County, VA, and died 12 May 1982, in Winton, Hertford County, NC. He was a past Master of the Harrelsville and Winton Masonic Lodges and was an Army veteran of World War II.[131] He married Eva Nita **MATTHEWS**, daughter of Almond J. and Eva Ann **(CREEKMORE) MATTHEWS**, 21 March 1932, in South Mills, Camden County, NC. Eva Nita was born 31 December 1909, in Norfolk, Norfolk County, VA.

Their children are Grace Joyce[10] **PARKER**, Eva Nita[10] **PARKER**, Harry Hilborn[10] **PARKER**, Jr., and Joan Annette[10] **PARKER**.[132] No further information included here.

Ivey D.[9] **PARKER** *(Logan H.[8],Nathan G.[7],John[6],Joseph[5],Joseph[4],Thomas[3],Thomas[2],William[1])* was the

---

[122]  Information on the family of Vernon Bryant Parker is from personal knowledge of the writer and courtesy of both the late Vernon Bryant Parker, Sr., and Junior.

[123]  Logan H. Parker Family Bible

[124]  Courtesy of the late Edna C. (Parker) Breland.

[125]  Logan H. Parker Family Bible

[126]  Obituary, Wednesday, 15 March 1995, *The Philadelphia Inquirer*, courtesy of his daughter, Betsi Parker.

[127]  Information on this family was courtesy of the late Thomas Walter Parker, Sr., and his daughter, Betsi Parker.

[128]  Logan H. Parker Family Bible

[129]  Information on this family was courtesy of the late Edna C. Breland and personal interview with family members. She made many contributions of names and addresses of family members and numerous updates of information, as they occurred.

[130]  Logan H. Parker Family Bible

[131]  Obituary, Thursday, 13 May 1982, *The Virginian-Pilot*, Norfolk, VA, courtesy of the late Edna C. Breland.

[132]  Information on this family was courtesy of the late Eva Nita (Matthews) Parker.

**Chapter 16:** Descendants of Nathan G.[7] **PARKER** *(John[6],Joseph[5],Joseph[4],Thomas[3],Thomas[2],William[1])*

ninth child and fifth son of Logan Hurst[8] and Mary Agnes (**MITCHELL**) **PARKER**, born 2 September 1912, in Cremo, Bertie County, NC.[133] He died 12 January 1988, in New Jersey. He married Grace **WEAVER** in 1933. They were divorced in 1942.

Their children are Donald Ivey[10] **PARKER** and Robert Edward[10] **PARKER**.

Ivey D.[9] **PARKER** married secondly Della Frances **MASKELL**, daughter of John Wood and Caroline (**DARE**) **MASKELL**, 11 December 1943. She was born 15 February 1905, in Camden County, New Jersey, and died 21 October 1986.[134] She made many valuable contributions to the research that has been done on the family of Nathan G.[7] and Mary Ann (**POWELL**) **PARKER** and their many descendants. No further information included here.

Robert Mitchell[9] **PARKER** *(Logan H.[8],Nathan G.[7],John[6],Joseph[5],Joseph[4],Thomas[3],Thomas[2],William[1])* was the 10th child and the sixth son of Logan Hurst[8] and Mary Agnes (**MITCHELL**) **PARKER**, born Sunday, 14 February 1915, in Cremo, Bertie County, NC, and died 26 July 2002, in Voorhees, Camden County, New Jersey.[135] He married Jane Harriet **WALLINGTON**, daughter of Charles Edwin and Alice May (**SHEPHERD**) **WALLINGTON**, 12 September 1938, in Camden County, NJ. She was born 11 April 1919, Lucas County, Ohio, and died 9 August 2001, in Voorhees, Camden County, New Jersey.[136]

Their children are Wendy Jane[10] **PARKER** and Wayne Robert[10] **PARKER**.[137] No further information included here.

*END*

---

[133] Logan H. Parker Family Bible

[134] Information on this family was courtesy of the late Della F. (Maskell) Parker and the late Ivey D. Parker.

[135] Logan H. Parker Family Bible; courtesy of Wayne Parker and Beth Covan.

[136] Courtesy of Wayne Parker and Beth Covan.

[137] Information on this family was courtesy of Wendy Jane (Parker) Johnson.

Mary Ann (POWELL) and Nathan G.[7] PARKER, taken at Rockwell's Gallery, Petersburg, VA. Date is unknown, but possibly 1864. Courtesy of the late Mildred Frizzell and Hazel P. Bunting.

Remains of Nathan G. Parker home in Indian Neck, taken by the late Hazel P. Bunting-1981.

Margaret Jane "Aunt Puss" Parker Courtesy of Rex Perry.

Ivey D. and Sallie A. (Parker) Perry-1898, Seattle, WA.  Courtesy of Rex Perry.

Charles Arthur and Lula S. (Mitchell) Parker-1925. Courtesy Hazel Bunting.

Charles A. and Thomas W. Parker
Courtesy of Hazel P. Bunting.

Isaac William Parker. Courtesy of Harvey B. Harrison, III

APPENDIX
*Family Photos*

Pvt. Bryant MITCHELL, Blacksmith, 17th Regiment, Co. D, North Carolina Troops. Gen. WHITING assigned him as blacksmith to the citizens of Hertford County, NC, from 1 March 1864 to 1 October 1864. Courtesy of Hazel P. Bunting.

# FEMALE NAME INDEX

**Abbie Lucretia**
HARRELL 226
(HARRELL) PARKER 226
**Abigail**
ELLIOTT 163
MORGAN 40,44
PARKER 25,39,
40,155,156
(PARKER) JUDKINS 155
PARKER MORGAN 39
**Abigal**
CHITREL 24
PARKER 38
(PARKER) CHITREL 24
**Abtgall**
PARKER 38
**Adaline**
PARKER 163
**Addie**
CROSS 221
**Addie F.**
(PARKER) CROSS 212,
213
**Addie S.**
CROSS 221
**Adlina Felton**
PARKER 221
(PARKER)CROSS 221
**Alba**
PARKER 65
**Alesey**
PARKER 65,67
(PARKER) BALLARD 67
**Alice**
BROWN 120,121
PARKER 37
**Alice E.**
PARKER 36,37
**Alice May**
(SHEPHERD)
WALLINGTON 228
**Alice O**.
BABB 101
**Alizabeth**
PARKER 179
**Allice Olivia**
BABB 101
**Almedia Lucrecy** BAKER
101
**Almeta**
BAKER 120,121
**Alse**
DAUGHTREY 20
(PARKER) DAUGHTREY
20

**Alsey Ailery**
BABB 101
**Amanda**
DUCK 222
(DUCK) PARKER 222
**Amanda E. "Mandy"**
WILLIFORD 220
(WILLIFORD) PARKER
220
**Amason**
PARKER 200
**Amazon**
PARKER 199
(PARKER) ASKEW
193,194,199
**Amizon**
ASKEW 199
**Ann**
BALLARD 65
BOND 191,192
(BRADY) PARKER 78
CROOM 25
DELK 193
DELKE 193
EARL 137
EARLY 170
ELLIOTT 173
EURE 203
(EURE) CLEAVES 203
FARMER 150
HINES 16
JONES 49,50
KING 47
NICHOLLS 87
PARKER 7,10,48,49,66,
107,126, 139,184,207
(PARKER) BALLARD
57,64
(PARKER) FRENCH 48
(PARKER) SPIVEY 20
SPIVEY 20
WILLIAMS 109,136
**Ann E.**
PARKER 75
**Ann F.**
PARKER 140
**Ann Mariah**
PARKER 166,167
**Ann "Nancy"**
(EURE) CLEAVES 210
**Ann Robinson**
PARKER 162,163
(PARKER) ELLIOTT 163
**Anna Belle**
CLARK 226

**Anna Belle** (Cont.)
(CLARK) PARKER 226
**Anna Belle "Ann"**
PARKER 226
**Annette**
PARKER 165,167
**Annie**
MOORE 195
(MOORE) PARKER 195
PARKER 199,222
**Annie C.**
PARKER 222
**Annie E.**
HOFLER 79
(HOFLER) PARKER 79
**Annie F.**
SADLER 222
(SADLER) PARKER 222
**Annie Hopper**
(BURROUGHS) CLARK
226,227
**Annie M.**
PARKER 194-196
**Annie S.**
ASKEW 199
**Annie Wood**
MITCHELL 222
(MITCHELL) PARKER
222
**Armesia**
EURE 112

**Barbara Catherine**
BRELAND 227
**Barbara Jean**
PARKER 224
**Bathsheba**
ARNOLD 55
**Bessie Lee**
CLARK 227
**Bessie May**
PARKER 223
**Bessie P.**
PARKER 222
**Bethany**
PARKER 25
**Bethshaba**
(EARLY) MORRIS 170
**Betsey**
BROWN 77
(BROWN) PARKER 42,77
PARKER 42
(PARKER) SOUTHALL 66
SMALL 141
(SMALL) PARKER 141

**Betsy**
  PARKER 36,181
  (PARKER) ROGERS 36
**Bettie**
  PARKER 195
**Betty**
  (DOUGHTIE)
  WILLOUGHBY 224
**Birtie D.**
  PERRY 219
**Blanch**
  LAMB 224
  (LAMB) PARKER 224
**Brenda**
  CAVENDER 224
  (CAVENDER) BALDREE
  224

**Caroline**
  CRANK 209
  (DARE) MASKELL 228
  HOFLER 79
  PARKER 100,102
**Caroline Virginia**
  PARKER 101
**Carrie**
  HOLLAND 79
**Catharine**
  PARKER 154,155
**Catherine**
  CROSS 198
  (CROSS) GREY 198
  HINTON 178
  (HINTON?) PARKER 178
  KING 25
  LANGSTONE 87
  PARKER
  178,179,182,201,
  203
**Cathren**
  PARKER 182
**Catren**
  PARKER 179
**Catron**
  PARKER 180
**Charity**
  (BENTON) PARKER 29
  (COPELAND) WINSLOW
  152
  PARKER 29,35,41-43,
  105
**Cherry**
  CROSS 34
  (CROSS) PARKER 34
  PARKER 33,35,41,45
**Chetta**
  PARKER 117,118,120,

**Chetta** (Cont.) 121
  SPIVEY 120
**Chetty**
  PARKER 118-120
**Chittey**
  PARKER 118
**Chitty**
  JONES 117
  JONES PARKER 117
  PARKER 109,117,118
**Christian**
  BROWN 43,45
  COPELAND 172
  FARLEE 24,135,151
  HAYSE 201
  (HAYSE) HARE 201
  HINTON 178
  OUTLAW 165
  PARKER 33,40,182
  (PARKER) BROWN 40,77
**Christiana**
  PARKER 42
**Cinthia**
  PARKER 107
**Clamilia**
  PARKER 111
**Clarkey**
  (EURE) PARKER 89
  PARKER 89,90,93,111
**Claudia**
  BRADY 121
**Clementine**
  PARKER 111
**Cleo**
  DELKE 194
**Cleopatria**
  DELKE 193
**Cora J.**
  COPELAND 220
  (COPELAND) WARD 220
**Correa**
  CROSS 221
**Corrie A.?**
  CROSS 221
**Cynthia**
  PARKER 108,115,116,
  118
  (PARKER) SAUNDERS
  108

**Deborah Ann**
  PEELE 163
  (PEELE) PARKER 163
**Della Elizabeth**
  PARKER 221
**Della Frances**
  MASKELL 228

**Diana**
  (HINTON) WHEDBEE
  199
**Diana E.**
  PARKER 195
  (PARKER) BURGESS
  193-195
**Dolores Dee**
  BRELAND 227
**Dora**
  PARKER 225
**Dora F.** OUTLAND 224
  (OUTLAND) PARKER
  224
  PARKER 225
**Dora O.**
  PARKER 225
**Doro**
  PARKER 224
**Doro F.**
  PARKER 224
**Dorothy**
  BEHETHLAND 4
  (CROSS) CROMER 198
  PARKER 6
  (WELLS) IRONS 69
**Dorothy Beresford**
  MC CULLOCH 157
  (MC CULLOCH) WHITE
  157

**Easter**
  PARKER 33
**Ede**
  PARKER 21,22
**Edith**
  PARKER 25
  (PARKER) VANN 24
  VANN 24
**Edna Cooper**
  PARKER 227
  (PARKER) WILKINSON
  227
  (PARKER) WILKINSON
  BRELAND 227
**Eleanor**
  (DAVIS) MC SWAIN 174
**Elezabeth**
  PARKER 179
**Elezebth**
  (PARKER) HARRELL 134
**Elinore**
  (BUSH) MACKLENDON
  170

**Elisabeth**
(EARLY) ALBERSON 170
JONES 48
PARKER 50,156,162
PERISHO 134
(PERISHO) PARKER 134
**Elisabith**
PARKER 179
**Eliz.**
BULLOCK 41
CRANFORD 126
PARKER 99,126
**Eliz. J.**
PARKER 100
**Eliza**
BULLOCK 42
GRIFFIN 220
PARKER 41,42,80,124,
130
(PARKER) BULLOCK 42
(PARKER) CROSS 77,78
(PARKER) PARKER 41
WARD 212
**Elizabeth**
ARNOLD 56
(ARNOLD) NORFLEET
55
BAILEY 9
BRISCOE 116,118,120
BROWN 40
(BROWN) PARKER 115
BULLOCK 43,45
BUSH 1,170
CARTER 99
CRAWFORD 79
(GRIFFIN) PARKER 50
HAYS 191
(HAYS) HOFLER 191
HOFLER 191
HUNTER 20
JONES 52,93,187
(JONES) BRIGGS 187
MINOR 65
MITCHELL 220,225
(MITCHELL) ROGERS
220
MORRIS 162
(MORRIS) PARKER 162
NORFLEET 56
PARKER
6,7,9,29,36,40,41,44,45,
51,65,66,76,81,89, 91,95-
97,102,104,105,108,124,
126,127,133,134,138-142,
147,148,151,155,156,167,
171,173,182,184,188,217,
224

**Elizabeth** (Cont.)
(PARKER) BRISCO 93,94
(PARKER) BRISCOE
105,106,115
(PARKER) CAVENDER
224
(PARKER) EASON 33
(PARKER) HUNTER 20
(PARKER) JONES 201
(PARKER) MINOR 57
(PARKER) PARKER 95
(PARKER) PEELE 156
(PARKER) SOUTHALL 66
(PARKER) SOUTHALL
MINOR 66
PARKS 133
PRICE 141
(PRICE) PARKER 141
ROGERS 35
SKINNER 139
(SKINNER) PARKER
139
(TAYLOR) BYRUM 218
THOMAS 148
TOPPING 140
(TOPPING) PARKER 140
TURNEDGE 172
WALLES 132
(WALLES) PARKER 131,
132,136
WALLIS 129
(WALLIS) PARKER 129
WARD 219
WELCH 142,143,151
WILLIAMS 65
(WILLIAMS) PARKER 65
(WILLIAMS) ROGERS
104
**Elizabeth A.**
(KELLY) PARKER 216
PARKER 79,80,216
(PARKER) CRAWFORD
79
**Elizabeth Ann**
HOFLER 80
(HOFLER) PARKER 80
**Elizabeth "Betsy"**
PARKER 201
**Elizabeth "Bettie" J.**
MORRIS 217
(MORRIS) PARKER 217
**Elizabeth J.**
(CARTER) PARKER 99
PARKER 100
**Elizabeth Lee**
PARKER 227

**Elizabeth Margaret**
MC CULLOCH 157
(MC CULLOCH)
MEREDITH 157
**Elizabeth P.**
PARKER 34
**Elizabeth Pipkin**
PARKER 34,36
**Elizabeth Raymond**
(GEROW) HILL 226
**Elizabeth**
WILLIFORD 220
**Elizebeth**
PARKER 147,184
**Elizth.**
PARKER 147
**Ella**
EURE 80
**Ella Virginia**
(PARKER) HAYES 198
**Elmira**
PARKER 111
**Elmirah**
PARKER 111
**Elva Ray**
(HOWARD) HUMPHRIES
227
(HOWARD) HUMPHRIES
PARKER 227
**Emeline**
LANGSTON 108
**Emiline**
EURE 108
**Emily**
CROSS 28
GRIFFIN 220
PARKER 27,28,79
(PARKER) CROSS 28
ROUNTREE 79
**Emily Hortense**
ROUNTREE 79
(ROUNTREE) PARKER
79
**Emily O.**
BROWN 79
(BROWN) PARKER 79
**Emma**
PARKER 80
**Emma Jane**
PARKER 80
**Emmy**
EURE 112
PARKER 79
**Essie V.**
CROSS 221
**Esther**
ARNOLD 55

Esther (Cont.)
BLADES 112
HARE 57
PARKER 33,51
**Ethel**
PARKER 196,198,225
**Ethel P.**
(PARKER) BARNETT 225
**Eva**
WARD 212
**Eva Ann**
(CREEKMORE)
MATTHEWS 227
**Eva D.**
WARD 219,220
(WARD) EASON 213
**Eva Nita**
MATTHEWS 227
(MATTHEWS) PARKER
227
PARKER 227

**Faith**
JUDKINS 155
(JUDKINS) PARKER 155
PARKER 156
**Fannie**
(FORTNER) HOWARD
227
**Febury**
PARKER 25
**Fereby**
PARKER 25,26
**Florence**
PARKER 199
**Florrence**
PARKER 199
**Frances**
LANGSTON 84
MONTAGUE 6
MONTAGUE PARKER 6
PARKER 7,171
**Freida**
SCHMIDT 222
(SCHMIDT) PARKER 222

**Gaberiellar**
BABB 101
**Gabrella**
BABB 101
**Geraldine Annie**
CLARK 224
(CLARK) PARKER 224
**Gertrude M.**
PARKER 218
**Gladys Warrick**
JERNIGAN 220

**Gladys Warrick** (Cont.)
(JERNIGAN) MITCHELL
220
**Grace**
COPELAND 172
(COPELAND) PARKER
172
PARKER 225
WEAVER 228
(WEAVER) PARKER 228
**Grace Joyce**
PARKER 227
**Gracy V.**
PARKER 224

**Hannah**
PARKER 22,23,47,147
**Harriet**
CLEAVES 203
MORRIS 217
OUTLAW 165
(OUTLAW) PARKER 165
PARKER 167,213
**Harriet A.**
(PARKER) TURNER 213
TURNER 213,217
**Harriet Ann**
PARKER 217
(PARKER) TURNER 217
**Harriet E.**
(OUTLAW) PARKER 167
PARKER 165-167
**Harriet E. G.**
PARKER 165
**Harriett Ann**
PARKER 81
**Hazel Parker**
TAYLOR 226
**Helen**
(EUBANKS) BALDREE
224
**Helen Anne**
CROSS 226
**Henrietta May**
MC CULLOCH 157
(MC CULLOCH)
BROWNRIG 157
**Hester**
DAVIS 177,178
**Hettie**
LAMB 224
**Hilda Beamon**
STOKES 221
(STOKES) PARKER 221
**Hulda**
PARKER 198
(PARKER) HAYES 198

**Hulda Parker**
(PARKER) HAYES 196
**Huldah**
WHITE 131

**Ida**
MULLEN 101
(MULLEN) PARKER 101
**Ida M.**
PARKER 216
**Ida Margaret**
HUTCHINS 221
(HUTCHINS) PARKER
221
**Ida May**
PARKER 216
**Ima**
BROWN 216
BROWN PARKER 216
**Indiana Riddick**
PARKER 81
(PARKER) BROWN 81
**Isabel**
PARKER 159,160,
167
(PARKER) TOWNSEND
167
PEELE 158
(PEELE) PARKER 158
**Isabella**
PARKER 162,164
(PARKER) ELLIOTT 162
(PARKER) TOWNSEND
164
TOWNSEND 164
**Isabellah**
TOWNSEND 164
**Issabella**
PARKER 65
(PARKER) WHITE 65

**J. Louise**
PARKER 196
**Jael**
PARKER 134
**Jail**
PARKER 135
**Jamima**
WARD 220
**Jane**
(BABB) COLLINS 101
BROWN 41-43,208
CHURCH 172
COLLINS 120,121
EVANS 170
JONES 52
(JONES) CHAMPION 52

**Jane** (Cont.)
  PARKER 91,105,111,
128,156,162,170,174,
175
**Jane Harriet**
  WALLINGTON 228
  (WALLINGTON) PARKER
228
**Jane R.**
  ARLINE 37
  (ARLINE) PARKER 37
**Jane Rebecca**
  ARLINE 37
  (ARLINE) PARKER 37
**Jane T.**
  BAKER 120,121
**Janice**
  (PARKER) OWINGS
203,211
**Jean**
  GREGORY 40
  PARKER 126,170,171,
**Jean**
  PARKER 174,175
**Jean Marie**
  TAYLOR 226
**Jeane**
  PARKER 171,174,
175
**Jean Barbara**
  PARKER 226
**Jemima**
  PARKER 154,155
**Jessie Raymond**
  HILL 226
  (HILL) PARKER 226
**Jimmie Louise**
  PARKER 198
  (PARKER) HAYES 198
**Joan Annette**
  PARKER 227
**Joane**
  PARKER 6
**Josephine**
  PALIDENO 222
  (PALIDENO) PARKER
222
**Josie**
  HARRELL 223
**Judah**
  GRIFFIN 24
  PARKER 75
  (PARKER) GRIFFIN 24
**Judeth**
  (PARKER) DUKE 48
**Judith**
  (BEEMAN) PARKER 102

**Judith** (Cont.)
  (BENTON) RABEY 29
  EURE 78,106
  (EURE) BEEMAN 106
  (EURE) BEEMAN
PARKER 106
  HARRELL 188
  HINTON 178
  PARKER 53,75-77,107,
108,154,155
  (PARKER) COPELAND
155
  PARKER EURE 76
  SAVAGE 106,110,119
  (SAVAGE) BRISCOE 106
**Judith Ann**
  PARKER 222
**Judith** Harrell
  PARKER 223
**Julia**
  PEELE 156
  (PEELE) PARKER 156
**Julia Etta**
  PARKER 81

**Kate**
  PARKER 225
  WARD 212,213,219
**Kath.**
  CRAWFORD 125
**Katherine**
  (HINTON?) PARKER
BLANSHARD 182
**Katherine**
  LANGSTONE 87
  PARKER 182
  PILAND 89
**Keran**
  NEWBY 154
**Keren**
  PARKER 155
**Keron**
  NEWBY 154
  (NEWBY) PARKER 154
**Kiziah**
  PARKER 134

**Lavenia**
  HARRELL 106,120
**Lavinia**
  BRISCOE 106
  (BRISCOE) HARRELL
106
  (BROWN) CLEAVES 203
  CLEVES 203
  CRANK 208
  ELLIS 218

**Lavinia** (Cont.)
  PARKER 197,207,209
  SMITH 118
**Lavinia L.**
  PARKER 194,
196
**Lavinia Louise**
  WHEDBEE 195
  (WHEDBEE) PARKER
195,198
**Leah**
  PARKER 152
  STRINGER 203,210
**Lelia Maud**
  PARKER 221
**Lella Maud**
  PARKER 221
**Leona M.**
  WARD 220
**Levenia**
  CLEAVES 203
**Levina**
  CLEVES 203
  CLEVES PARKER 203
  CRANK 209
  LANDEN 88
  PARKER 204
**Lidia**
  PARKER 42
**Livina**
  BROWN 203
  (BROWN) CLEAVES 203
**Lizzie**
  KELLY 216
  (KELLY) PARKER 216
**Louisa**
  (BROWN) PARKER 42
  EURE 112
  JONES 117
  PARKER 41,42,45
  SPIVEY 120
**Louise**
  MARKHAM 222
  (MARKHAM) PARKER
222
**Louise S.**
  PARKER 218
**Lovenia**
  PARKER 207-209
**Lovina**
  PARKER 207
**Lovinia**
  PARKER 208
**Lucille**
  MITCHELL 220
  (MITCHELL)
WETHERINGTON 220

**Lucille** (Cont.)
WORRELL 223
(WORRELL) HOLLOMAN
223
**Lucrecia**
BEEMAN 107
**Lucretia**
(WILLIAMS) HARRELL
226
**Lucy**
PARKER 79,171
**Lucy L.**
TURNER 120
**Luisa**
PARKER 41
**Luiza**
BROWN 40
**Lula Sophie**
MITCHELL 223
(MITCHELL) PARKER
223,224
**Lula Wood**
PARKER 223
**Lyda**
PARKER 134
**Lydia**
ELLIOTT 153
PARKER 131,132,134,
153
(PARKER) ELLIOTT 152,
153
(PARKER) ELLIOTT
MURPHY 153

**Mable**
JONES 218
**Magaret**
PARKER 42
**Magt**.
PARKER 41,42
**Mamie**
ALPHIN 218
**Margaret**
(EARLY) MACKHENRY
170
JUDKINS 155
(JUDKINS) PARKER 155
MARCH 120,121
PARKER 28,34,53,57,
58,65,67,162,207,215
(PARKER) BALLARD 64,
67
(PARKER) BUFFKIN 194
(PARKER) ELLIS 212
(PARKER) WHITE 162
PARKER WILLIAMS 36

**Margaret** (Cont.)
SIMONS 215
(SIMONS) PARKER 215
TEAKLE 9
TOWNSEND 164
(TOWNSEND) PARKER
164
WALSH 222
(WALSH) PARKER 222
WILLIAMS 35
**Margaret A.**
BALLARD 64
PARKER 28,163
**Margaret Ann**
BALLARD 57,58,64,65,
67
(NEWBY) PARKER 163
PARKER 28,163,215,
216
(SIMONS) PARKER 216
**Margaret E.**
(BABB) MARCH 101
PARKER 28
**Margaret J.**
PARKER 194
(PARKER) BUFFKIN
193
(PARKER) ELLIS 213
(PARKER) MESSENGER
194
(PARKER) MESSENGER
BUFFKIN 194
**Margaret Jane**
BRELAND [nee
WILKINSON] 227
PARKER 218,227
(PARKER) ELLIS 218
WILKINSON 227
**Margaret M.**
ASKEW 199
**Margaret Morris**
PARKER 163
**Margaret P.**
CROSS 221
**Margaret Ruth**
TAYLOR 226
**Margaret W.**
PARKER 164
**Margarett**
MARCH 120,121
**Margarett A.**
PARKER 65
**Margret**
ROBERTSON 88
**Maria**
HARRELL 120,121
TOWNSEND 164,167

**Mariah**
HARRELL 108
TOWNSEND 164
**Mariam**
(PARKER) WOODWARD
138
**Marth**
(BUSH) WILLIAMS 170
**Martha**
BUSH 170
BUTTLER 92
CRANK 209
(EARLY) THOMS 170
FOXWORTH 128
PARKER 26,28,107,108,
115,116,136,155,156,159,
160,163,167,199,204,207,
208
(PARKER) CRANK 208,
209
(PARKER) EURE 108
(PARKER) GRIFFIN 212,
213
(PARKER) WHITE 163,
164,167
PEELE 155
(PEELE) PARKER 155
PIPKIN 83
ROUNTREE 217
SAUNDERS 26
SAUNDERS PARKER 26
SOUTHALL 63
TAYLOR 115,119
WHITE 162
(WHITE) PARKER 162
**Martha A.**
RODGERS 96
**Martha Ann**
(HOLLOMAN) TAYLOR
225
PARKER 26,27
RODGERS 96
ROGERS 95,102
SOUTHALL 66
**Martha B.**
SUMNER 66
**Martha Cavana**
PARKER 218
**Martha E.**
GOODMAN 29
(LASSITER) PARKER
199
PARKER 27,28
(PARKER) GOODMAN 28
**Martha Jane**
BYRUM 218
(BYRUM) PARKER 218

238

**Martha Luvina**
PARKER 220
(PARKER) GRIFFIN 220
**Mary**
ARLINE 37
ARNOLD 55
(ARNOLD) PARKER 55
(BENTON) PARKER 29
BOND 42,194
BRADY 121
BROTHERS 45
BROWN 38,39
(BROWN) EVANS 41
BUSH 1
(BUSH) EARLY 170
CANNON 149
CARTER 97
CHITREL 24
COPELAND 25
CRAPER 41,42,45
CROOM 25
CROSS 41
CULLENS 115
DAULDING 6
EARLY 123,125
(EARLY) BLAKE 170
ELLIOTT 173
EURE 80,94,104,112
(EURE) CROSS 112
(EURE) LANGSTON 89
EVANS 41,42,170
FARLEE 24,135
(FARLEE) PARKER 24,
135,151
FARMER 150
FOXWORTH 170
GOODWIN 116
HARE 194
HICKS 155
(HICKS) PARKER 155
HINTON 191
HINTON BEST 191
HOWELL 96
JONES 187
(JONES) SMITH 187
JORDAN 158
KING 47
KLEGG 213
LANGSTON 91,108
(LANGSTON) PARKER
91,99,101,102
LONG 131
MC CULLOCH 157
MINOR 57
NICHOLLS 87
ODOM 59-62,64,65
OGLA 216

**Mary** (Cont.)
OGLA PARKER 216
PARKER 7,24,27,32,
34,36,38,39,42,51,65,66,
80,89,90-92,102,103,110,
113,114,126,133,135,136,
141,147,149,150,154-156,
162,163,167,180-182,216,
225
(PARKER) BROWN 136
(PARKER) CANNON 130,
148,150
(PARKER) CHITREL 24
(PARKER) CRAPER 39,
42
(PARKER) CRAPER
BROTHERS 45
(PARKER) EURE 80
(PARKER) FAIRLESS
184, 187
(PARKER) FRYER 48
(PARKER) GOODIN 110
(PARKER) GOODWIN
110, 115
(PARKER) GRIFFIN 33
(PARKER) HENDRIN 76
(PARKER) HOFLER 99
(PARKER) HOWELL 95,
102
(PARKER) HOWELL LEE
97
(PARKER) JONES 141
(PARKER) MING 134
(PARKER) ODOM 57,66
(PARKER) ROGERS 36
(PARKER) SMALL 142
(PARKER) WILSON 162
PARKS 133
PERKINS 9
POWELL 209,210
ROADS 145
ROGERS 35
SAUNDERS 26
TAYLOR 104
THOMAS 148
(WALLES) PARKER 131,
132,136
WILLIAMS 73,123,169
**Mary A.**
BRADY 120
LEE 97
PARKER 210-213
(PARKER) HOFLER 100
(PARKER) HOWELL LEE
(PARKER) HOWELL LEE
103
POWELL 209

**Mary Agnes**
(MITCHELL) PARKER
225-228
PARKER 225
(PARKER) TAYLOR 209,
225
TAYLOR 226
**Mary Ann**
PARKER 27,101,114,
212,225
(PARKER) HOFFLER 101
(POWELL) PARKER 209,
211,213-215,217-225,
228,229
**Mary C.**
LASSITER 211
**Mary E.**
(EURE) CROSS PARKER
112
MITCHELL 220
(MITCHELL) EVERETT
220
PARKER 36,37,80
(PARKER) COBB 37
(PARKER) WARD 213
RODGERS 96
SAVAGE 106
(SAVAGE) BRISCOE 106
(WARD) MITCHELL 213
**Mary Eliza**
PARKER 219
(PARKER) WARD 219,
220
WARD 219,220
(WARD) EASON 219
**Mary Elizabeth**
PARKER 36,163,218
SOUTHALL 66
(TAYLOR) MITCHELL
220,222,223,225
**Mary Emily**
GATLING 198
(GATLING) PARKER 198
**Mary F.**
PARKER 217
**Mary Jane**
PARKER 26,27
**Mary Jane R.**
PARKER 37
**Mary, "Jr."**
(PARKER) BROWN 136
**Mary**
PARKER, Jr. 136
**Mary L.**
PARKER 36
HARRELL 223
(HARRELL) PARKER 223

**Mary M.**
  PARKER 216
**Mary "Mollie"**
  CROSS 221
**Mary O.**
  ASKEW 199
  (EURE) CROSS PARKER
BALLARD 114
**Mary "Polly"**
  PARKER 187
**Mary R.**
  PARKER 194
**Mary Rebecca**
  WHEDBEE 199
  (WHEDBEE) PARKER
199
**Mary Ruth**
  PARKER 223
**Mary Sally**
  WILLOUGHBY 224
  (WILLOUGHBY) PARKER
224
**Mary Susan**
  (BABB) BAKER 101
  PARKER 80
**Mary W.**
  PARKER 114
**Maude Valeria**
  PARKER 226
  (PARKER) CROSS 226
**May**
  (JONES) LOVEL 52
**Mildred**
  CROSS 198
  (CROSS) WOODSIDE
198
HARRELL 27
  LEE 104
  PARKER 105,
155
  (PARKER) PILAND 76
  WILLIAMS 104
**Mildred A.**
  PARKER 36
  (PARKER) WIGGINS 37
  SPEIRS 37
  (SPEIRS) PARKER 37
**Mildred Ann**
  PARKER 36, 37
**Mildred Irene**
  PARKER 222
  (PARKER) FRIZZELL 222
**Milley**
  ARLINE 104
  CARTER 182
  (CARTER) BLANSHARD
182

**Milley** (Cont.)
  PARKER 75
**Milly**
  PARKER 75,76
  (WILLIAMS) ARLINE 104
**Minnie E.**
  EASON 220
**Minnie H.**
  PARKER 200
**Minnie Smith**
  PARKER 223,224
  (PARKER) HARRELL 224
**Miriam**
  MORRIS 162
  PARKER 152
  THOMPSON 137
**Monterey M.**
  PARKER 211,213
**Morning**
  JORDAN 161

**Nance**
  PARKER 179
**Nancey**
  PARKER 42,75, 134
  BOND 41
  (PARKER) BOND 42
**Nancy**
  BOND 38,41,42,
45,191,195
  BROWN 40
  (BROWN) LASSITER 42
  COLLINS 41
  EURE 115,203
  JONES 187
  (JONES) HARRELL 187
  LASSITER 41,42,115
  LAWRENCE 96
  NEWBY 163
  PARKER 33,38-40,
42-44,65,66,75,102,
107-109,115,116,118,182,
184,204,207
  (PARKER) BENTON 66
  (PARKER) BENTON
BALLARD 66
  (PARKER) BOND 39
  (PARKER) HARE 201
  (PARKER) LANGSTON
108
  (PARKER) LAWRENCE
95,102
  SAWYER 219
  (SAWYER) PERRY 219
  WILLIAMS 104
  (WILLIAMS) PARKER
104,105

**Nancy "Ann"**
  PARKER 185,201,207
**Nancy Cross**
  WOODSIDE 198
  (WOODSIDE) JENKINS
198
**Nannah**
  HUMPHFLET 104
**Nannie E.**
  WILLIAMS 200
**Nansey**
  BENTON 66
  PARKER 109
**Nansy**
  PARKER 181
**Naomi**
  WILLIAMS 73
  (WILLIAMS) PARKER 74
***NEGRO WOMEN***
ABA 93
AGGY 41
AMA 89
AMEY 89,90
AMY 117
ANN 28
BRIDGET 137
CATE 89,90
CELEA 138
CELIA 138
CHARLOTTE 199
DINAH 57
DOLL 20
EDITH 89
EDNEY 138
FRANKEY 138
HAGAR 21
HAGOR 24
HANNAH 29,184,189
KIDDY 28
KITTY 28
LAURA 28
LUCINDY 101
LUCY 28
LUISER 189
MARY 89,90,138
MILLEY 41
MILLY 199
PATIENCE 189
PEG 137
PEGG 89
PEGGY 90
PENEY 93
PENNEY 189
PENNY 188
PLEASANT 117
PLESANT 136
PRESILLER 90

**NEGRO WOMEN** (Cont.)
PRISE 189,190
PRISS 179
PRISSY 184
RHODA 24
SEALEY 189,190
SILLA 89
SILLAH 138
**Nell Marion**
  NUGENT 9
**Nettie**
  COX 216
  (COX) PARKER 216
**Nina**
  PARKER 199
**Nora Belle**
  (WALDEN) CAVENDER
224

**Oma** [Naomi]
  PARKER 74
**Ora Penelope**
  PARKER 218

**Patience**
  FRYER 23
  PARKER 20,22
  (PARKER) FRYER 23
**Pauline**
  PARKER 223
  (PARKER) STEINMETZ
223
**Peggy**
  PARKER 33,34,65,
67
**Peminah**
  FULLENTON 134
**Penanah**
  (PARKER) MOORE
160,167
**Penelope**
  BRISCOE 106
  (EURE) HARRELL 89
  HINTON 190
  LAWRENCE 120
  MC CULLOCH 157
  (MC CULLOCH) PARKER
157,158
  PARKER 101,104,
105
  (PARKER) ROGERS 95,
101,102
  RODGERS 102
  ROGERS 102
  WALTON 65
  (WALTON) PARKER 65
**Penina**

**Penina** (Cont.)
  (HOBBS) GRIFFIN 220
  HOFLER 197
  PARKER 134,149,151
  (PARKER) MOORE 167
  (PARKER) NICHOLSON
134
**Penina "Penny"**
  GRIFFIN 220
**Peninah**
  FULLINGTON 134
  MOORE 164
  PARKER 155,164,167
  (PARKER) BLANCHARD
155
**Pennina**
  ROGERS 101
**Penninah**
  AVERY 152
  PARKER 45
**Penny**
  CARTER 117-119
  PARKER 41,42
**Penonne**
  (PARKER) NEWSOM 136
**Persilia**
  PARKER 29
**Pharaba**
  (PARKER) GRANBERY
160
**Phebe May**
  PARKER 155
**Pheraby**
  PARKER 167
  (PARKER) GRANBERY
167
**Phereba**
  GRANBERY 164
**Pherebe**
  (PARKER) GRANBERY
164
**Pheriby**
  PARKER 25
**Pleasant**
  (ARNOLD) KNIGHT 55
**Polley**
  BROWN 40
  MULLEN 101
  PARKER 75
**Polly**
  PARKER 25,26,39,
50,75,76,179,181
  WILLIAMS 104
**Polly L.**
  PARKER 34
**Polly Lee**
  PARKER 34,36

**Pressa**
  PARKER 179
**Pressy**
  PARKER 181,182
**Pricilla**
  PARKER 53
**Priscilla**
  HAYES 79
  (HAYES) PARKER 79
  HAYS 41,42,44
  HINTON 178
  HUMPHLET 107
  PARKER 40,54,96,97,
101,103,182,184,185
  (PARKER) HAYS 42
  WILLIAMS 104
  (WILLIAMS) PARKER 95,
97,102,103
**Priscilla Christian**
  PARKER 182,201
**Priscilla Christian
"Pressy"**
  PARKER 182
**Prisillar**
  (WILLIAMS) PARKER 91
**Priss**
  LANGSTON 108
**Prisse**
  PARKER 179
**Prissila** HAYS 41
  PARKER 91
**Prissilla** HAYS 43
  PARKER 183
**Prissillar**
  WILLIAMS 91
**Prissillia**
  PARKER 97

**Rachael**
  (PARKER) WOOTTEN
152
**Rachal**
  JONES 188
**Rachel**
  EVANS 170
  FAR.EE 24,135,151
  JONES 188
  PARKER 29,153
  (PARKER) WOOTEN 153
  SMITH CANNON 150
  WOODWARD 158
**Raymond Aileen**
  PARKER 227
**Rebecca**
  PARKER 155
  WARREN 129

**Rebecka** (Cont.)
(WARREN) PARKER 129
**Rebekah**
(EARLY) MORRIS 170
**Rhoda**
DRAPER 155
(DRAPER) PARKER 155
(HARRELL) PARKER 188,190
JORDAN 154
PARKER 156,190,192
**Rhoday**
PARKER 188
**Roadeth**
PARKER 137
**Rodah**
PARKER 137,189
**Rodath**
PARKER 137
**Rodey**
HARRELL 188
(HARRELL) PARKER 188
**Rodith**
PARKER 136
**Rosa B.**
CROSS 221
**Rosa E.**
CROSS 28
**Rose**
(BUSH) WINNS 170
**Rosella**
PARKER 105
**Rosetta**
PARKER 105
**Roxanna**
PARKER 79
(PARKER) HOLLAND 79
**Roxy**
GRIFFIN 220
**Ruth**
BRINKLEY 65
FARMER 151
HARRELL 223
LILLY 131,151
PARKER 53,65,67,108,134,149,150,153,224
(PARKER) BRINKLEY 57,64,67
(PARKER) BUNDY 134
PARKER FARMER 150
(PARKER) OVERTON 224
(PARKER) RIDDICK 24
PEELE 163
RIDDICK 24
**Ruth Y.**
WARD 220

**Ruthy**
BRINKLEY 66

**Salley**
LEWIS 190
**Sallie**
PARKER 25,99,100,101,198,213
**Sallie**
(PARKER) CROSS 198
**Sallie A.**
(PARKER) PERRY 213
**Sallie Ann**
JENKINS 198
PARKER 219
(PARKER) PERRY 219,225
**Sallie Parker**
(PARKER) CROSS 196
**Sally**
LEWIS 190
PARKER 40,42
(PARKER) JACKSON 136
**Sally E.**
PARKER 76
**Sally Mary**
PARKER 81
**Sarah**
BABB 96,101
BRINKLEY 65
BROTHERS 51
(BROTHERS) PARKER 51
(BROTHERS) PARKER BRINKLEY 51
BYRUM 175
CANNON 150
(CANNON) ARNOLD 150
COPELAND 172
DANIEL 203
(EARLY) KEEF 170
EASON 219
ELLIOTT 153
FARLEE 24,135,151
(FARLEE) PARKER 151
FARLER 151
HORTON 24
JONES 52,183
(JONES) PARKER 52
MASON 6
MIANED 176
MINARD 176
NICHOLLS 87
PARKER 6,40,45,51,53,65,66,79,80,101,134,135,138,141,142,152-156,160,164,167,170,171,173,176,

**Sarah** (Cont.)
PARKER 182,187
(PARKER) ALBERTSON 164,167
(PARKER) BABB 95,101
(PARKER) BRINKLEY 57,64,66
(PARKER) ELLIOTT 152
(PARKER) EVANS 170
(PARKER) HORTON 24
(PARKER) JONES 183
(PARKER) NESBETT 187
(PARKER) NESBETT JONES 187
(PARKER) NESBITT 187
PEELE 155
(PEELE) PARKER 155
RUSSELL 120,121
SUMNER 23
WARREN 129
WELCH 142,143
(WELCH) PARKER 142
WHITE 123
**Sarah A.**
PARKER 79
**Sarah Ann**
(BABB) RUSSELL 101
PARKER 140
**Sarah E.**
PARKER 78,98
**Sarah Eliza**
PARKER 80, 97
(PARKER) CROSS 78
**Sarah Elizabeth**
PARKER 140
**Sarah G.**
HINTON 190
(HINTON) PARKER 190
**Sarah Isabella**
PARKER 163
**Sarah L.**
PARKER 195
**Sarey**
JONES 187
**Sary**
(PARKER) JONES 179
**Scynitha**
PARKER 108
**Scyntha**
PARKER 108
**Scynthy**
PARKER 107
**Sele**
PARKER 137
**Selea** EURE 106
**Seley**
PARKER 137

**Shirley Mae**
FRIZZELL 222
**Siddy**
DUNFORD 78
(PARKER) PARKER 77
of Sophie, (PARKER)
DUNFORD 77
**Sidey**
PARKER 42
**Sidney**
PARKER 42
(PARKER) PARKER 78
**Sidny**
PARKER 41
**Silva**
PARKER 133,134
**Silvia**
PARKER 134
**Sollome**
PARKER 174
**Solome**
PARKER 173,174
**Sophia**
HARRELL 108
PARKER 41,42,45,107,
115,116
(PARKER) HARRELL 107
**Sophia Ann**
PARKER 78
**Sophie**
PARKER 77
**Sousan**
BAKER 120,121
**Sue**
PARKER 99,100
**Sue M.**
GOODMAN 29
**Susan**
PARKER 79,80, 101
**Susannah**
WILLIAMS 123,124,154
**Susie**
PARKER 100
**Susie Clair**
PARKER 221
**Syntha**
PARKER 107

**Tamur**
PARKER 136
(PARKER) BURGES 136
**Telpah**
PARKER 53
**Telpha**
(PARKER) ROGERS 54
**Temperance**
HOLLOMAN 223

**Terese**
KING 110
**Tersecia**
PARKER 111
**Tex E.**
CROSS 28
**Texana**
PARKER 28
**Texana T.**
PARKER 27
**Texanna**
PARKER 28
(PARKER) CROSS 28
**Texas T.**
PARKER 28
**Thelma Isabel**
BATTLEY 224
(BATTLEY) PARKER 224
**Theresa**
PARKER 90,106, 111
(PARKER) KING 111
(PARKER) WIGGINS 51
**Theressa**
PARKER 111
**Thirsa**
PARKER 41,42
**Thursa**
PARKER 42
**Treacy**
KING 107
PARKER 50
**Treasey**
(PARKER) KING 93,109
**Treasy**
(EURE) SPARKMAN 89
**Trecey**
JAMISON 159
**Trecy**
PARKER 89
**Treecy**
PARKER 91,94
(PARKER) KING 94

**Ursula**
BAYLY 9

**Viola**
WARD 220
**Virginia**
BABB 120,121
**Virginia Dorothy**
PARKER 222
**Waunita**
POWELL 9
**Wendy Jane**
PARKER 228

# NAME INDEX

## A

**ABRAMS**
Robert 16
**ADDISON**
John 9
**ALBERSON**
Elisabeth (EARLY) 170
**ALBERTSON**
Benjamin 164,167
Sarah (PARKER) 164, 167
**ALFIN**
Humphry 139
**ALLEN**
George 92
**ALPHIN**
Humphry 140
John Lee 218
Joseph 176
Mamie 218
Solo. 176
**ALSTON**
--- 23
John 21,22,37,176
Wm. 37
**ARLINE**
James 55
Jane R. 37
Jane Rebecca 37
Jesse 37
John 129
Mary 37
Milley 104
Milly (WILLIAMS) 104
*ARMY*
Confederate States 103
Corp of Engineers 227
United States 226,227
................................................
**ARNALL**
Edward 53
**ARNELL**
Edward 49,51,55
**ARNOLD**
Bathsheba 55
Benjamin 150
Edward 50,55,56,60-62
Elizabeth 56
Esther 55
James B. 58
John 55
Mary 55
Richard 55
Sarah (CANNON) 150
William 50,55,56,66

**ARNOLD** (Cont.)
Wm. 56
**ASKEW**
Amazon (PARKER) 193, 194,199
Amizon 199
Annie S. 199
John D. 201
Margaret M. 199
Mary O. 199
Robert Lee 199
Thomas R. 194,199
Willie H. 199
**AVERITT** (See also EVERET, EVERETT)
James 145
**AVERY**
John 152
Penninah 152

## B

**B.**
W. L. 110
**BABB**
Alice O. 101
Allice Olivia 101
Alsey Ailery 101
Gaberiellar 101
Gabrella 101
James B. 101
John C. 101
John E. 120,121
Lewis 120,121
Lewis H. 101
Lewis Henry 101
Sarah 96,101
Sarah (PARKER) 95,101
Thomas W. 101,120,121
Thos. W. 101,103,120
Virginia 120,121
William 35,101,109,110, 120,121
William K. 101,120,121
Wm. K. 101
**BACKUS**
John 24,151
**BACON**
John 199
**BAGLEY**
Jacob 38
**BAGNOLL**
James 6
**BAILEY** (See also BAILY, BAYLEY,BAYLY)
Elizabeth 9

**BAILEY** (Cont.)
Richard 9
**BAILY**
Jno. L. 42
**BAINES**
F. E. 197
William 160
William, Jr. 160
**BAKER**
--- 31,36,76,91,196,213
Almedia Lucrecy 101
Almeta 120,121
Bennet 146
Blake 120,121
Blake, Jr. 101
Bray 203
Henry 84,88
James 74
James Thomas 101
Jane T. 120,121
L. 184
Law 86,178-180,182
Lawrence 37
Mary Susan (BABB) 101
Richard 31,32
Richard B. 118
Sousan 120,121
Sylvester 10
W. J. 96,102,119
Will J. 109,116,118,119, 192
William 86
Wm. 29,181
Wm. J. 78,110
**BALDREE**
Brenda (CAVENDER) 224
Helen (EUBANKS) 224
Sherrill Anthony 224
Sherrill Hammond 224
**BALLARD**
--- 24,26,60,112,115, 125,129,135-137,148, 159,169
A. 63
Afred 62
Alesey (PARKER) 67
Alfred 58-64,67
Ann 65
Ann (PARKER) 57,64
Ben 62,63
Benj. 59,62,63
Benjamin 64,67
Jethro 56
Joseph 25,27
Kedar 51,57,59-62, 64-66
Margaret A. 64

BALLARD (Cont.)
Margaret Ann 57,58,64, 65,67
Margaret (PARKER) 64,67
Mary (EURE) CROSS PARKER 114
Nancy (PARKER) BENTON 66
R. H. 59,62
Richard A. 67
Richard H. 57
Richd. H. 60
Robert 114,119
Robert H. 114,119
Robert M. 96
Robt. H. 110,119
Thomas 51

**BARBER**
--- 136,160
Isaac 159

**BAREFIELD**
Richard 70,71
Richd. 70,71

**BARFIELD**
John 72
Richard 72

**BARKER**
John 70
Joseph 136

**BARNES**
--- 108
Benjamin 25
John 67
John T. 218
Richard 89,182
Thomas 75,87,91

**BARNETT**
Ethel P. (PARKER) 225
Herman L. 225
Herman L., Jr. 225
Herman L., Sr. 225

**BARR**
Isaac 60

**BARROW**
Sherrard 25

**BASNIGHT**
--- 225

**BASS**
Lemuel 127

**BATTAILE**
John 127

**BATTLE**
John 127

**BATTLEY**
Thelma Isabel 224

**BAYLEY** (See also BAILEY)
Richard 9

**BAYLY**
Richard 9
Ursula 9

**BEAGLIN** (See also BENGLIN)
Thos. 16

**BEAMAN** (See also BEEMAN, BEMAN)
David 106

**BEASLEY**
William 27

**BEEMAN**
--- 107
Abraham 44,90,92,106
Benjamin 203
David 106
Israel 23,88
Isreal 21
Jno. 92
John 105,106,112,114, 116
Joseph 92
Judith (EURE) 106
Lucrecia 107

**BEHETHLAND**
Dorothy 4

**BELL**
Isaac 213

**BEMAN**
John 114

**BENBURY**
--- 195,197

**BENET**
--- 19,38,204

**BENETT**
--- 4,204

**BENGLIN** (See also BEAGLIN)
Thos. 16

**BENNET**
--- 37-39,43,44,74,115, 176
Wm. F. 113

**BENNETT**
--- 13,15,16,21,24,38, 42,47-49,74,165,194,196, 197,204,210,211,213
James Robert 226

**BENNITT**
-- 13,44

**BENTON**
--- 47,49
David 58,60-62,64
Elijah 29,49
Epaphro__tus 29
Epaphroditus 47,49
J. T. 208
Jacob 66

**BENTON** (Cont.)
James 47,49,57
Jethro 29,32,49,51,53, 54
John 16,21,22,29,31,47, 49,52,60-62
John, Jr. 16,31
Jonhn 19
Josiah 32
Miles 51,66
Moses 56
Nancy (PARKER) 66
Nansey 66

**BERRYMAN**
Richard 31

**BEST**
Bryant B. 191
David Rice 120
Mary HINTON 191

**BIRD** (See also BYRD)
Jesse 21,22
John 21,22

**BIRUM** (See also BYRUM)
William 142

**BLADES**
--- 94,104
Esther 112
Foreman 197

**BLAKE**
Mary (EARLY) 170

**BLANCHARD**
Aaron 203
B. 203
Barnaby 188,204
Barneby 203
Benjamin 203,204
Ephrim 129
James 204
Jonathan 155
Peninah (PARKER) 155
Rufus 196

**BLANSHARD**
Aaron 177,186
Amariah 182
Josiah 177,179,186
Katherine (HINTON?) PARKER 182
Micajah 182,183,201
Milley (CARTER) 182

**BLOUNT**
Charles 129

**BOAZMAN** (See also BOUZMAN, BOZEMAN)
Saml. 127

**BOND**
--- 196,208,209,210, 213,217
Ann 191,192

**BOND** (Cont.)
Dempsey 208
Demsy 203
Elisha 207-209
Elisha H. 203,204
H. 157
Henry 157,207,208
Mary 42,194
N. 191
Nancey 41
Nancey (PARKER) 42
Nancy 38,41,42,45,191,
195
Nancy (PARKER) 39
Rd. 53
Richard 15,25,184,204
Richard H. L. 120
Richard, Sr. 184
Richd. 204
Thomas 39
Thos. 189
W. M. 195
William 135,180
**BONNER**
Henry 52
John 139
**BOOTH**
Harry 113
James 38,39,117
W. L. 116
Wm. 181
Wm. L. 107
**BOOTHE**
W. L. 120
William L. 95,107
William S. 108
Wm. L. 104,106,107,
110,112
**BOREMAN** (See also
BOAZMAN, BOUZMAN,
BOZEMAN)
Samll 127
**BOSTICK**
Francis W. 111
**BOUZMAN**
Saml. 127
**BOYCE**
-----136,166
Epaphroditus 31
Isaac 173
John 173
Moses 16,31
William 39
**BOYD**
William 24,136
William, Jr. 151
Wm. 131,136
**BOYET**

**BOYET** (Cont.)
David 26
**BOYT**
Thomas 15
**BOZEMAN**
**BOZEMAN** (See also
BOAZMAN,BOREMAN,
BOUZMAN)
Samll. 127
**BOZEMAN** (Cont.)
Samuel 127
**BRADDEY**
James 14,15
**BRADDY**
James 23,75
John 113
Jos. 71
**BRADEY**
James 84
Jeames 84
**BRADLEY**
Jos. 71
**BRADY**
--- 96
Andrew 121
Blake 77
Claudia 121
James 95
John 93,95,96,120,193,
194,220
Mary 121
Mary A. 120
Quinton 80,120
**BRASHER**
--- 94
**BRATTLE**
W. 124
**BRELAND**
Barbara Catherine 227
Dolores Dee 227
Earl Dewey 227
Edna Cooper (PARKER)
WILKINSON 227
Margaret Jane 227
Marion Harbrook 227
Wyman Franklin 227
**BRICKELL**
John 23
Thomas 187
**BRIGGS**
Charles 187
Elizabeth (JONES) 187
**BRINCKLEY**
Josiah 50
**BRINKLEY**
Jethro 58-64,66,67
Ruth 65
Ruth (PARKER) 57,64,67

**BRINKLEY** (Cont.)
Ruthy 66
Sarah 65
Sarah (BROTHERS)
PARKER 51
Sarah (PARKER) 57,64,
66
William 51,64,65,67
**BRINN**
James 153
**BRISCO**
--- 94
Ebron 89,105
**BRISCO**
Elizabeth (PARKER) 93,
94
Timy 105
**BRISCOE**
Elizabeth 116,118,120
Elizabeth (PARKER) 105,
106,115
John 106
John W. 106
Judith (SAVAGE) 106
Lavinia 106
Mary E. (SAVAGE) 106
Penelope 106
R. D. 106
Richard 106
Richard D. 106,120
Richd. 106
**BRISTER**
Wm. 181
**BROOKS**
George 203
William 39
Wm. 38,44
Wm. C. 43
**BROTHERS**
Bryant 45
Mary 45
Mary (PARKER) CRAPER
45
Sarah 51
**BROWN**
A. 63
Albridgeton 62
Alice 120,121
Betsey 77
Christian 43,45
Christian (PARKER) 40,
77
Elizabeth 40
Emily O. 79
Harrison L. 81
Ima 216
Indiana Riddick
(PARKER) 81

**BROWN** (Cont.)
Ja. 42
James 37,40-43,45,77, 114-116,119
James, of Willis 41
James R. 195
Jane 41-43,208
Jas. 41
Jesse 37-39,41
John 119-121,176
Jos. N. 211
Joseph 176
Josiah 136
Livina 203
Luiza 40
Mary 38,39
Mary, "Jr." (PARKER) 136
Mary (PARKER) 136
Miles 207
Nancy 40
Polley 40
Richard 146
Robert 40
Samuel 181,203
Willis 38-42,44,45,181
Willis, Jr. 40
**BROWNE**
Willis 40
**BROWNRIG**
Henrietta May (MC CULLOCH) 157
Mark 157
**BROWNRIGG**
--- 168
John 152,158
Thomas 134,159,167
Thos. 159
**BRYAN**
John 145
**BRYANT**
Edward 146
John 70
**BUFFER** (See also BUTLER)
Wm. 124
**BUFFKIN**
John 194
M. W. 194
Malachi W. 193,194
Margaret J. (PARKER) 193
Margaret J. (PARKER) MESSENGER 194
Margaret (PARKER) 194
**BUFKIN**
Ralph 150
**BULLOCK**

**BULLOCK** (Cont.)
David 42
Eliz. 41
Eliza 42
Eliza (PARKER) 42
Elizabeth 43,45
**BUNCH**
--- 145
James L. 139
**BUNDY**
Nathan 134,135
Ruth (PARKER) 134
Samuel 134,135
**BUNTING**
Hazel P. 229
**BURBAGE**
James R. 164
**BURGES**
Tamur (PARKER) 136
**BURGESS**
--- 95
Diana E. (PARKER) 193-195
Edward W. 102
Penelope (PARKER) ROGERS 95,102
William B. 193-195
**BURNSTIE**
Lott 157
**BUSH**
Elizabeth 1,170
John 1,5,139,166,170
Martha 170
Mary 1
Thomas 3
William 69,164,170
William, Jr. 170
**BUTCHKO**
Thomas R. 177
**BUTLER** (See also BUFFER)
Wm. 124
**BUTTLER**
James 92
Martha 92
**BYRAM** (See also BIRUM)
Bryant 150
James 161
**BYRD** (See also BIRD)
William 36,92
**BYRUM**
--- 218
Bryant 132
Elizabeth (TAYLOR) 218
Isaac 218
Jno. 175
John 166
Martha Jane 218

**BYRUM** (Cont.)
Sarah 175

# C

C___
William 164
**CALDWELL**
Spiner 25
**CAMPBELL**
John 3,24,151
**CANNON**
--- 133,150,152,158, 159,160,164,167,168
Henry 164,165
J. 166
Jacob 150
James 167
James J. 166
Jeremiah 130,133,143, 149-151,155
Jereremiah 149
Joseph 131,150,164
Mary 149
Mary (PARKER) 130, 148,150
Rachel SMITH 150
Sarah 150
**CARR**
--- 60
T. W. 58,59,61,62,64
**CARTER**
Alex 197
Alex. 83
Alexander 91,92,212
Elizabeth 99
Henry 108,112
J. E. 197
J. N. 197
James 110,116
James N. 197
John 2,9,10
Mary 97
Milley 182
Moor 38,73
Penny 117-119
Wiley 115
**CASPEY**
Thomas 55
William 55
**CAVENDER**
Brenda 224
Elijah W. 224
Elizabeth (PARKER) 224
James Dale 224
James Dale, Jr. 224
Nora Bell (WALDEN) 224
Walter 224

**CHAMPEN**
John 129,148,174
**CHAMPION**
Jane (JONES) 52
John 170
Percivall 2,3
**CHAPPELL**
Exum 197
James 159
John T. 149
**CHERRY**
Gisbourne J. 210
Thomas P. 210
**CHITREL** (See also
KITTERELL, KITTRELL)
Abigal 24
Abigal (PARKER) 24
Benjamin 24
Mary 24
Mary (PARKER) 24
Willis 24
**CHURCH**
Jane 172
Richard 172
Richd. 172
**CLARK**
Anna Belle 226
Annie Hopper
(BURROUGHS) 226,227
Bessie Lee 227
David Columbus 226,
227
Geraldine Annie 224
John 224
Thomas 164
**CLEAVES** (See also
CLEVES)
Ann (EURE) 203
Ann "Nancy" (EURE) 210
Harriet 203
John 203,205,210
Lavinia (BROWN) 203
Levenia 203
Livina (BROWN) 203
Solomon 203
William 39
***CLERK OF COURT***
BAKER
L. 184
Law 86,178-180,182
Will J. 116
BOSTICK
Francis W. 111
BURNSTIE
Lott 157
BUSH
John 139
COOR

***CLERK OF COURT*** (Cont.)
James 174
CRAVEN
J. H. 49
Jas. 20
CROSS
W. T. 212,213,215
DAUGHTRY
W. G. 107,113
EURE
Henry L. 105
GILLIAM
H. 113
HATHAWAY
H. T. 166
T. V., Deputy 139
HICKS
___ 171
HOSKINS
Edmd. 138
MEARNS
Will 149
NORFLEET
James 133,134,160
Jas. 137,153
RIDDICK
N. J. 95
Nathaniel J. 95
SUMNER
J. 41,58,90,205
WILLS
Henry 142

**CLEVES** (See also
CLEAVES)
Lavinia 203
Levina 203
**COAKE**
Edward 4
**COBB**
F. W. 37
Fred 37
Mary E. (PARKER) 37
**COBBETT**
James G. 210
**COBBITT**
Joseph G. 210
**COCKRIL**
Jos. 129,175
**COFFIELD**
John 143
**COLE**
--- 32,112,115
**COLES**
John, Jr. 22
**COLLINS**
--- 36
James 69,70

**COLLINS** (Cont.)
James, Jr. 69
Jane 120,121
Jane (BABB) 101
John 71
Miles 101,120,121
Nancy 41
Thomas 209
Thos. 41
***COMPANIES***
Chowan & Southern
Railroad 100
EASON & RIDDICK 221
Foreman BLADES Lum-
ber 197
John L. ROPER Lumber
196
John N. PARKER, & 222
M. F. PARKER 221,225
Merchants and Miners
Transportation 226
Mid-Florida Gas 226
Norfolk & Carolina Rail
Road 100
North Carolina Mutual
Insurance 192
Richmond Cedar Works
218

**CONELL**
Edmond 148
***CONSTABLES***
CRANFORD
William 124
PARKER
David 191

**CONSTANT** (See also
COSTEN)
--- 151,172
**COOGAN**
Daniell 2
**COOK** (See also COAKE)
Edward 2
**COOR**
James 174
**COPELAND** (See also
COPLAND, COUPLAND)
--- 26
Charles 132,133,172
Christian 172
Cora J. 220
Grace 172
Henry 35,75,108
James 25,129,172
Jesse 25,150,152
John 25,172
Joseph 132

**COPELAND** (Cont.)
Josiah 154
Judith (PARKER) 155
Mary 25
Sarah 172
Silas 25
William 125,132,133, 155,172
Wm. 124,125,127,154, 172
Wm., Jr. 133
Wm., Sr. 133
**COPLAND**
Elisha, Sr. 87
Henry 87
Jesse 130
**COSTEN** (See also CONSTANT)
James 14,15
**COUNSIL**
Charles 152
*COUNTY SURVEYOR*
HEGERTY
Pa. 76,91
Patrick 39
SMITH
Allen 107,119
WALTON
Benbury 42
WYNNS
John, [Deputy] 145,146

**COUPLAND** (See also COPELAND)
William 151
**COWPER**
R. B. G. 37,100
W. W. 118
William 89,107,114
Wm. W. 78,116
**COX**
Nettie 216
**CRAFFORD**
James 88
**CRAIG**
Braxton 225
**CRAIN**
--- 11
**CRANFORD** (See also CRAWFORD)
Eliz. 126
Will. 125
William 124
Wm. 126,172
**CRANK**
Bembrey 209
Caleb 209
Caroline 209

**CRANK** (Cont.)
John 209
Lavinia 208
Levi 208,209
Levi B. 208
Levina 209
Martha 209
Martha (PARKER) 208, 209
Thomas 209
William 209
**CRAPER**
Mary 41,42,45
Mary (PARKER) 39,42
Warren 39
**CRAVEN**
J. H. 49
Jas. 20
**CRAWFORD** (See also CRAFFORD,CRANFORD, GRANFIELD)
Abram 79
Elizabeth 79
Elizabeth A. (PARKER) 79
Isaac W. 79
Joseph 83
Kath. 125
William 124,125
Wm. 124,172,174
**CREECE**
Levi 109
**CREECEY**
Levy 109
**CREW**
Randall 3,4,5,11
Randolphe 10,11
**CREWE**
Randall 11,12
**CROMER**
Dorothy (CROSS) 198
Neely Jenkins 198
**CROOM**
Ann 25
Isaac 25
Mary 25
Richard 25
**CROSS**
Addie 221
Addie F. (PARKER) 212, 213
Addie S. 221
Adlina Felton (PARKER) 221
Catherine 198
Cherry 34
Correa 221
Corrie A. ? 221

**CROSS** (Cont.)
David 112
David C. 115
Dorothy 198
E. 28
Edwin 28
Elisha 28,33,34,183
Eliza (PARKER) 77,78
Emily 28
Emily PARKER 28
Essie V. 221
Etheldred 113
George W. 221
Hardy 34,35,94,102
Helen Anne 226
Henry P. 29
James Parker 198
James Parker, Jr. 198
John 34,35
John G. 196
John, Jr. 34
John R. 221
John W. 221
Lemuel E. 28
Lonnie Raleigh 221
Margaret P. 221
Mary 41
Mary (EURE) 112
Mary "Mollie" 221
Maude Valeria (PARKER) 226
Mildred 198
R. L. 213
Richard 77,78,191
Richard L. 221
Richard [Riddick] 77
Richard Willis 226
Richard Willis, Jr. 226
Riddick 78,95
Rosa B. 221
Rosa E. 28
S. P. 197,198
Sallie (PARKER) 198
Sallie Parker (PARKER) 196
Sarah Eliza (PARKER) 78
Simon Peter 198
Taylor 91
Tex E. 28
Texanna (PARKER) 28
Tobe 226
W. T. 212,213,215
William 94
William H. 118
Willis 118
Wm. 94
**CRUMP**

250

**CRUMP** (Cont.)
W. O. 218
**CULLENS**
Amos 100
Jacob 134
Mary 115
**CULLIN**
Nathan 165
**CULLINS**
Jacob 158
**CUMMING**
William 150
**CUMMINGS**
E. 133
**CURL**
Richd. 94
**CURLEE**
Will 172

# D

**DANIEL**
Sarah 203
William 203,204
**DARDEN**
John 49
**DAUGHTIE** (See also
DOUGHTIE,DOUGHTRIE)
Wm. 17
**DAUGHTREY**
Alse 20
Alse (PARKER) 20
**DAUGHTRY**
Henry M. 94,192
Mills 114
W. G. 78,107,113,192
William G. 94,104,115,
119
Wm. 94
**DAULDING**
Mary 6
**DAVIS**
--- 187,201
Garrett 177,178
Garrott 178
Garrtt 178
Hester 177,178
John 21,60,146,203
Moses 43,44
Thomas 172
**DAVY**
--- 13
**DELK**
Ann 193
John P. C. 193
**DELKE**
Ann 193
Cleo. 194

**DELKE** (Cont.)
Cleopatria 193
N. B. 194
Napoleon B. 193
**DESHAN**
Ganston 136
**DEW**
Thomas 3-5,9-12
**DEWE**
Thomas 2,12
**DILLARD**
--- 128,169
**DOE**
Samuel 9
**DONEN**
John 130,151
**DOUGHTIE**
William 20,22
Wm. 20
**DOUGHTRIE** (See also
DAUGHTIE,DAUGHTRIE)
Wm. 16,31
**DOUGHTY**
Edward 29
**DRAKE**
Thomas 58
Thos. 60-62,64
**DRAPER**
Rhoda 155
**DUCK**
Amanda 222
**DUKE**
John 13,50,51,55,57
Judeth (PARKER) 48
Thomas 12,13,48
Thomas, Jr. 13
Thos. 12
**DUNFORD**
Jesse 77,78
Siddy 78
Siddy (PARKER) of
Sophie 77
Siddy (PARKER) PARKER
77
**DUNN**
Joe 197

# E

**EALBANKS**
Henry 159
**EARL**
Ann 137
**EARLY**
Ann 170
John 123,125,126,148,
170,172
John, Sr. 170

**EARLY** (Cont.)
Mary 123,125
Mary (BUSH) 170
**EASON** (See also ESON)
--- 211,221
Andrew 119
Arthur R. 220
Elizabeth (PARKER) 33
Eva D. (WARD) 213
Evvis 220
Isaac 180,181
J. A. 221
Jesse 113
John 213
John R. 219
Leroy F. 220
Lindsay 220
Linzy 220
Mary Eliza (WARD) 219
Minnie E. 220
Orther R. 220
Sarah 219
Timothy 219
**EDWARDS**
--- 5,97
**ELEY**
Eli 26
**ELLICE** (See also ELLIS)
--- 103
**ELLINOR**
Francis 74
**ELLIOT**
Caleb 150
**ELLIOTT**
Aaron 163
Abigail 163
Ann 173
Ann Robinson (PARKER)
163
Caleb 150,151,173
Ephraim 134,164
Ephriam 164
Exum 153
Francis 139
Henry 142
Humphry 139,140
Isabella (PARKER) 162
James 52
Joseph 162,163
Joseph Parker 163
Joshua 173
L. 204
Lydia 153
Lydia (PARKER) 152,153
Mary 173
Sarah 153
Sarah (PARKER) 152
Thomas 163,173

**ELLIOTT** (Cont.)
William Lancaster Bailey
163
**ELLIS** (See also ELLICE)
Alexander 213,218
Alexander Elbert 218
Alfred 218
Charles G. 196
Daniel 84
Jacob 84
James 20,83,84
James, Jr. 83,84
Joseph 84
Lavinia 218
Margaret J. (PARKER)
213
Margaret Jane (PARKER)
218
Margaret (PARKER) 212
Mills 56
Solomon 63
William 56,84
**ESON** (See also EASON)
Isaac 180
**EUER**
Saml. 83
**EUR**
Charles 88
Sephen 88
Stephen 88
**EURE**
--- 97
Ann 203
Armesia 112
Benjeman 88
Blake 91
Boon 94,104,115
Calvin 210,211,213
Charles 91,104,106
Charly 80
D. 111
Daniel 165
Dempsey 96,103,110,
111,114,119
Demsey 112
Elisha 109
Ella 80
Emiline 108
Emmy 112
Henry 108,112
Henry L. 80,104,105
Hy. H. 93,109
Isaac 217
James 207,208,210
James, Jr. 208
James O. 80,99
Jas. O. 80
Jethro 115,211

**EURE** (Cont.)
Jimmie 213,217
Joseph 108,118
Judith 78,106
Judith PARKER 76
L. 94
Lenward 80
Leonard 80
Levey 91
Levi 94,106,116
Levy 91,92,104
Lewis 26,112,117,119
Louisa 112
M. 107,110
M. H. 97,98
M. L. 97,121,193
Martha (PARKER) 108
Mary 80,94,104,112
Mary (PARKER) 80
Mills 93,107,110-112,
114
Mills H. 27,97,103
Nancy 115,203
Nathanil 112
Nathl. 113
Nolley 80
Nollie E. 80
Parker 108
Peter 114
Riddick 99
Samuel 87,112,114
Selea 106
Sipran 203
Starky 208
Stephen 86,89,90,91
Tenson 94
Thos. R. 100
Tinson Y. 104
Uriah 112
Whitmel 75,106
Whitmill 92,106
**EVANS** (See also EVINS)
Beniamin 171
Benjamin 142,148,169,
170,171,174
Benjn. 174
Jane 170
Jno. C. 173
John 41,170
Mary 41,42,170
Mary (BROWN) 41
Peter 170
Rachel 170
Sarah (PARKER) 170
Thomas 170
**EVERET** (See also
AVERITT)
William 19

**EVERETT**
--- 220
James E. 97,99
Mary E. (MITCHELL)
220
**EVINS** (See also EVANS)
--- 175
**EYRES**
William 6

**F**

**FAIREFAX**
James 9
**FAIRLESS** (See also
FEARLESS,FERRELL,
FERRILL)
--- 187
Mary (PARKER) 184,187
Nichollas 148
**FALEE** (See also FARLEE)
John 176
**FALLAR**
Jonas 178
**FARLEE**
**FARLEE** (See also
FALEE,FARLER,FFARLO)
--- 169
Christian 24,135,151
James 24,135,151,176
John 176
Mary 24,135
Rachel 24,135,151
Saml. 135
Samuel 24,135,151
Sarah 24,135,151
**FARLER**
Jas. 129,175
Sarah 151
**FARMER**
Ann 150
John 150
Jos. 150
Joseph 150
Mary 150
Ruth 151
Ruth PARKER 150
Thomas 130,150,151
William 150
**FEARLESS** (See also
FAIRLESS, FERRELL,
FERRILL)
Joseph 165
**FELTER**
Boon 100
**FELTON**
Boon 100
Charles 188,207

**FELTON** (Cont.)
  Richard 24,31,52
  Richd. 52
**FELWELL** (See also
  THELWELL)
  Edward 70
**FERRELL** (See also
  FAIRLESS,FEARLESS)
  Nicholas 125
  Nichollas 148
**FERRILL**
  Nic. 126
  Nichollas 148
**FFARLO** (See also
  FALEE,FARLER,FFARLO)
  James 169
**FFOXWORTH** (See also
  FOXWORTH)
  Moses 124
**FIELD**
  Lemuel K. 94
  Mills R. 40
**FLEMING**
  James 125
  Jams 125
**FLETCHER**
  --- 217,225
**FLOURNY**
  George H. 111
**FLOYD** (See also LOYD)
  David 69
**FORD**
  Rogr. 152
**FORREST**
  Henry 39
**FOWLER**
  James H. 92
**FOWLKES** (See also
  FULKS)
  Jeptha 191
**FOXWORTH** (See also
  FFOXWORTH)
  Martha 128
  Mary 170
  Moses 128,142
**FRANCKS**
  Martin 174
**FRAZER**
  Thomas 52
**FRAZIER**
  Thomas 17
**FREEMAN**
  Amos 176
  James 39,145,147,178,
  180,183,217
  James H. 210,211,213
  James T. 207,208
  Jas. T. 208

**FREEMAN** (Cont.)
  Job 210
  John 145-148
  Richard 187
  Thomas 40
  Timothy 74,203,204,206
  William 204
  William, Jr. 178
**FRENCH**
  Ann (PARKER) 48
**FRIER** (See also FRYER)
  William 83
**FRIOR**
  --- 16
**FRIZZELL**
  Albert Curby 222
  Mildred 229
  Mildred Irene (PARKER)
  222
  Roy Wheeler 222
  Shirley Mae 222
**FRYER** (See also FRIER)
  Mary (PARKER) 48
  Patience 23
  Patience (PARKER) 23
  Tho. 84
  Thomas 23,24,72
**FULKS** (See also
  FOWLKES)
  John 53
**FULLENTEN**
  John 158
**FULLENTON**
  John 159
  Peminah 134
**FULLINGTON**
  John 134
  Peninah 134

## G

**GAFFIN** (See also
  GAVEN,GAVIN)
  Charles 124
**GAINES**
  --- 103
**GARRET**
  John 4
  Lazarus 146
**GARRETT**
  --- 6,38
  Richard 135
  Richd. 135
  Thomas, Sr. 125
  Thos. 125
  Thos., Jr. 38
**GARROT**
  Thomas 129

**GARWOOD**
  John 10
**GATLIN**
  Joseph 114
**GATLING**
  James 51,75,76,91
  Jno. J. 99,100
  John 104
  John J. 100
  Mary Emily 198
  Miles 39
  Riddick 26-28,93,110,
  114,119
  Riddick, Jr. 79
  Riddick, Sr. 28
  W. J. 200
  William, Sr. 24
**GAVEN** (See also GAFFIN)
  --- 172
**GAVIN**
  Charles 172
  Chas. 125
**GAY** (See also GRAY)
  Henry 70
**GEORGE**
  --- 3,4
**GILES**
  Val C. 216
**GILLIAM**
  --- 113
  H. 41,45,113
  Henry 41,113,117,190,
  207
**GILMER**
  J. F. 3
**GLAUGHANGN** (See also
  MAGLOHAN)
  Richard 136
**GLOVER**
  --- 145
**GOFF**
  Thomas 14,19,29
**GOLSON** (See also
  POLSON)
  Geo. 17
**GOODIN** (See also
  GOODWIN)
  James 110
  Mary (PARKER) 110
  Will 110
**GOODMAN**
  --- 21
  Barnes 36
  Harry H. 29
  Henry 75,83,113
  James I. 29
  Jethro D. 112
  Joel 75

**GOODMAN** (Cont.)
Martha E. 29
Martha E. (PARKER) 28
Sue M. 29
William 25,26,73,75
William M. P. 29
William, of Joel 75
William T. 29
Wm. 83
Wm. H. 93,113
Wm. Mac. 28
**GOODWIN** (See also
GOODIN)
James 110
Jas. 110
Job 140
John 140
Mary 116
Mary (PARKER) 110,115
**GORDAN**
John C. 58
John, Jr. 150
Robert A. 164
**GORDON**
George 199
John C. 57,58,61,63,64
Joseph 64,65
**GOURDON**
George 2,4
**GOWIN** (See also
GUINNS,GWIN)
Christopher 16
**GRANBERRY**
Josiah T. 166
**GRANBERY**
Jos. T. 165,166
Josiah T. 166
Pharaba (PARKER) 160
Pheraby (PARKER) 167
Phereba 164
Pherebe (PARKER) 164
Thomas 160,167
Thos. 160,162
**GRANFIELD** (See also
CRAFFORD,CRANFORD,
CRAWFORD)
William 124
Wm. 172
**GRANVILLE**
--- 131
**GRAY** (See also
GAY,GREY)
Henry 70
John 145,148
**GREEN**
--- 103,146
Abram 191
Exum 97

**GREEN** (Cont.)
James 210
Samuel 88
**GREGORY**
James 40
Jean 40
**GREY** (See also GRAY)
Catherine (CROSS) 198
Thomas Jefferson 198
**GRIFFEN**
Henry 48,49
**GRIFFIN**
Charles 220
Elial 131
Eliza 220
Emily 220
Franklin 220
Hugh 50
Humphrey 50
James, Jr. 53
John 33,47,154
Judah 24
Judah (PARKER) 24
Martha Luvina (PARKER)
220
Martha (PARKER) 212,
213
Mary (PARKER) 33
Matthew 154
Millard 220
Penina (HOBBS) 220
Penina "Penny" 220
Roxy 220
Simeon 220
William 24
Willis 158
**GRIFFITH**
John 150
**GUINS** (See also
GOWIN,GWIN)
Leonard 2,69
**GUMBRE**
Abraham 132
**GUMBS**
Mat. 129,175
**GWIN**
John 57

# H

**HAGERTY** (See also
HEGARTY,HEGERTY,
HEGETHY,HERGERTY)
Pa. 34
**HAIR** (See also HARE)
John 189
Moses 52,83
**HALL**

**HALL** (Cont.)
A. E. 97
Cannon 208
Edward 129
Moses 19,49,52
Nathl. 55
**HALLSEY**
Daniell 169
**HALSEY**
John 175
**HAMPTON**
Thomas 9
**HANIFORD**
Joseph 60
**HARE** (See also
HAIR,HEIR)
Christian (HAYSE) 201
E. 118
Edward 83
Edwd. 83
Elijah 117,118,120
Elisha 51
Esther 57
Harrison 117,118
Henry 26
J. B. 200
James 199
Jas. 192
Jesse L. 57-60,62
John 61,188,199,201
John, Sr. 201
Mary 194
Moses 56,71,83
Nancy (PARKER) 201
Thomas 25
**HARLO** (See also FARLEE)
James 169
**HARPER**
William 24,135
**HARRALL**
Jesse 86
**HARREL**
Thomas 90,92
**HARRELL**
A. F. 193
Abbie Lucretia 226
David 182,184,188
E. R. 52
Elezebth (PARKER) 134
Elisha 90,92,102,
106-108,114,118,120
Elisha B. 119
Ervin 94
George Arthur 223
Isaac, Sr. 188
J. E. 196
James 110,118,119
James E. 197

254

**HARRELL** (Cont.)
 Jesse 86
 Jethro 106,187
 Joe Mark 223
 John 159
 John, Jr. 31
 Josie 223
 Judith 188
 Lavenia 106,120
 Lavinia (BRISCOE) 106
 Lazarus 223,224
 Lucretia (WILLIAMS) 226
 Maria 120,121
 Mariah 108
 Mary Louise 223
 Mildred 27
 Mills 106
 Minnie Smith (PARKER) 224
 Nancy (JONES) 187
 P. 118
 Penelope (EURE) 89
 Phillip Allen 224
 Reuben 76,110
 Rodey 188
 Rufus 120,121
 Ruth 223
 Samuel 31,32,37,113
 Sophia 108
 Sophia (PARKER) 107
 Theops. 58
 Thomas 10,12,88
 Thomas Starling 224
 Thomas Starling, Jr. 224
 Washington 108
 William 108
 William Mills 226
 Wm., of Mills 106
**HARRIL**
 Samuel 181
**HARRILL**
 John 152
**HARRIS**
 James 53
**HARRISS**
 William 23,56,182
**HARROW**
 Thomas 10
**HARVEY**
 Wm. M. 92
**HARWOOD**
 Thomas 10
**HASKET**
 Silas 135
 William 135
**HASLET**
 Jethro S. 113

**HASLIT**
 John 19
**HATFEILD**
 William 3,4,5,11
**HATHAWAY**
 Burton W. 140
 H. T. 166
 Jacob R. 196
 T. V. 139
 W. R. 197
**HAYES**
 Benjamin 44
 Ella Virginia (PARKER) 198
 Hulda (PARKER) 198
 Hulda Parker (PARKER) 196
 Jimmie Louise (PARKER) 198
 Lemuel P. 198
 Priscilla 79
 Thomas Gatling 198
 W. R. 197
 William John 198
**HAYS**
 Benja. 41
 Benjamin 43,44
 Benjn. 43
 Elizabeth 191
 H. 89,200
 James 176
 John 154
 Joseph 176
 Priscilla 41,42,44
 Priscilla (PARKER) 42
 Prissilla 43
 Robert 119
 Thos. 154
 William 176,201
 Willis R. 119
**HAYSE**
 Benjamin 40
 Christian 201
 James 37
 Timothy 74
 William 74
 Zacheriah 74
**HEARENDEN** (See also HERENDEN)
 Thomas 145
**HEGARTY** (See also HAGERTY)
 Patrick 33
**HEGERTY**
 P. 188
 Pa. 39,76,91
 Patrick 39
**HEGETHY**

**HEGETHY** (Cont.)
 P. 181
**HEIR** (See also HAIR,HARE)
 John 189
**HENDRIN**
 Mary (PARKER) 76
**HENNEFORD**
 James 147
**HENRY**
 A. W. 213
**HENTON** (See also HINTON)
 James 83
**HERENDEN** (See also HEARENDEN)
 Thomas 173,174
**HERENDON**
 Thomas 173
**HERGERTY** (See also HAGERTY)
 Pa. 33
**HERRON**
 Wm. 131
**HICKS**
 --- 171
 Mary 155
 Robert 124
 Robt. 171
**HILL**
 --- 210
 A. O. 197
 Asa 79,95
 Clement 45,203-205
 Elizabeth Raymond (GEROW) 226
 Henery 180
 Jessie Raymond 226
 Rowland 226
 William 3,176
**HINES** (See also HYNDS)
 Ann 16
 Moses 32
 Richard 16
**HINSHAW**
 William Wade 136
**HINTON** (See also HENTON)
 Cader 178,179
 Catherine 178
 Christian 178
 Demsey 177,178
 Frederick 190,192,201
 Gordon 119
 James 176,178,188, 190-192,196,197,211
 John W. 196,207,210
 Jonas 178,179,204

**HINTON** (Cont.)
Judith 178
Kader 181
Kedar 178,180,182,184,
188
Mary 191
N. 191
Noah 178,188,189,
190-192,199
Noah, Jr. 191
Noah, Sr. 192
Penelope 190
Priscilla 178
R. 192
Reuben 189-192
Reuben, Jr. 191
Ro. 192
Sarah G. 190
Scrasbrook 181
Searsbroc 180
Seasbrook 178
Walter 196
William 38,181,190,191,
205-207
**HIRBY**
William 158
**HOBBS**
Miles 159
Moses 158
**HOFFLER**
Garrett 205
Henry 113
John 58-60,188
Mary Ann (PARKER) 101
Willis 99,101
**HOFLER**
--- 99,197
Annie E. 79
Caroline 79
Elizabeth 191
Elizabeth Ann 80
Elizabeth (HAYS) 191
G. 205
Hance 79,191
Henry, Sr. 211
J. H. 100
James R. 210
John R. 195
Johnson 197
Lycurgus 198,217
Mary A. (PARKER) 100
Mary (PARKER) 99
Penina 197
Willis 100
Willis J. 99
**HOGGARD**
--- 225
**HOLBROOK**

**HOLBROOK** (Cont.)
Robt. 172
**HOLLADAY**
Thomas 148
**HOLLAND**
Carrie 79
J. B. 196
J. J. 79
James 196
James B. 197
Roxanna (PARKER) 79
Thomas 79
**HOLLBROOK**
Robert 126
**HOLLIDAY**
Thos. 136
**HOLLOMAN**
Herman Jerry 223
Herman Parker 223
Lucille (WORRELL) 223
Magruder 223
Temperance 223
**HOOD**
--- 11-13
**HOOKS**
William, Jr. 25
**HORN**
William 92
**HORSKINS** (See also
HOSKINS)
William 175
**HORTON**
Charles 37
Joseph 14,19,20
Sarah 24
Sarah (PARKER) 24
**HOSKINS**
Edmd. 138
Thomas 153,154
Thos. 155
**HOUSE**
Robert 150
Thos. 16
**HOWARD**
Fannie (FORTNER) 227
Leander 195
Marion F. 227
**HOWELL**
David 118
Dixon 95-97,102
Jas. E. 120
Mary 96
Mary (PARKER) 95,102
Miles 26,27,117,118
**HUBARD**
John 51
Mathew 51
**HUBBARD**

**HUBBARD** (Cont.)
James 47,48,52
John 49,52,55
Mathew 52,55
Matthew 50
**HUDGINS**
Humphey 181
**HUGHS**
William, Jr. 22
**HUMFLEET** (See also
UMFLEET)
William 90
**HUMPHFLET**
Nannah 104
**HUMPHLET**
Priscilla 107
**HUMPHRIES**
Elva Ray (HOWARD) 227
**HUNTER**
--- 176,191,194,197,
218,221
Elizabeth 20
Elizabeth (PARKER) 20
Hardy 146
Isaac 179
Isaac R. 65
Isaac, Sr. 57
Jacob 44,66
Job 146
John O. 59,60
R. 33,34
Readick 181
Riddick 33
Thos. 177
**HUNTOR**
Isaac 14
**HURDLE**
--- 221
E.F. 210,213,217
E. T. 210
Elisha F. 219
Hardy 132
James R. 210
T. W. 213
Thomas 211
Tom 203,211
***HURRICANE***
Galveston 215
ooooooooooooooooooooooooooooooooooooo
**HUSMAN**
J. 192
**HUTCHINS**
Ida Margaret 221
**HUTSON**
--- 165
Uriah 132
**HYATT**
Isaac 165
**HYNDS** (See also HINES)

**HYNDS** (Cont.)
Jno. 83

# I

*INDIANS*
Chowan 74,177

**IRONS**
Dorothy (WELLS) 69
Symon 69

# J

**JACKSON**
John 125
Richard 5
Salley (PARKER) 136
William 167
**JAMERSON** (See also
JIMERSON)
--- 96
**JAMESON**
William P. 92
**JAMISON**
Bond 159
Trecey 159
**JEAMESON**
William P. 93
**JENKINS** (See also
JINKINS)
Chester Sears 198
Nancy Cross
(WOODSIDE) 198
Sallie Ann 198
**JERNIGAN** (See also
JOURNIGAN)
D. L. 200
Gladys Warrick 220
James 120
Wm. 120
**JIMERSON**
--- 95
**JINKINS** (See also
JENKINS)
Isaac H. 35
Wiley W. 35
**JOCELIN**
Henry 205
**JOHNSON**
Andrew 112
Charles E. 138,139
William 112,115
Wm. 112
**JOHNSTON**
Charles E. 140
Jno. 53

**JONES**
--- 109,120
Allen 135
Ann 49,50
Benj. 62
Benjamin 64
Blake 194
Charles 50
Chitty 117
David 49
Demcy 50
Dempsey 187
Demsey 187,188
Demsey, Jr. 180
Demsey, Sr. 188
Demsy 181
Edwin 196,197
Elisabeth 48
Elizabeth 52,93,187
Elizabeth (PARKER) 201
Epaphrods. 83
Federbrick 191
Fredd. 191
Frederick 192
Hardy 117,118
Hardy C. 109,118
Henry 26,52,117,118,
120
Henry, Jr. 109,117
Henry, Sr. 109,117
J. C. 216
Jacob P. 64,65
James 21,48,51,76
Jams 76
John 27,48,49,109,117,
118,187,188
John B. 210
John M. 139
Joseph 49,52,53,188
Louisa 117
Mable 218
Mary 187
Mary (PARKER) 141
Mikel 19
Nancy 187
Nathaniel 187,188,201
Rachal 188
Rachel 188
Sam 187
Sarah 52,183
Sarah (PARKER) 183
Sarah (PARKER)
NESBETT 187
Sarey 187
Sary (PARKER) 179
Tho. 143
Washington 64
William 49,50,52,56,87,

**JONES** (Cont.)
William 93,187
Wm. 49,50,83,113
Wm., Sr. 49
**JORDAN**
--- 159,166,195
Charles 129,148,150,
170,174
Ed. 148
Jacob 132,137,150,154,
158,159
Jacob, Jr. 133,152,158
Jeremiah 188
Jno. 124,127,172
John 128,148,172,173
John, Sr. 150
Jonathan 133,158,159
Joseph 158
Mary 158
Morning 161
Nathan 159,161
Rhoda 154
Thos. A. 210
William A. 188
**JORDON**
William A. 189
**JOURNIGAN** (See also
JERNIGAN)
Henry 48
*JUDGE*
COWPER
R. B. G. 37
FLOURNY
George H. 111
MC KOY
Allmand A. 194
SHIFF
Wm. M. 81

**JUDKINS**
Abigail (PARKER) 155
Faith 155
James 155
Margaret 155
*JUSTICE OF THE PEACE*
BRADY
John 220
DAUGHTRY
Henry M. 192
PARKER
Richard 14
SAVAGE
O. B. 103

# K

**KEEF**

257

**KEEF** (Cont.)
Sarah (EARLY) 170
**KEEFE**
Treddell 124
**KELLY**
Elizabeth A. "Lizzie" 216
**KING**
--- 83
Ann 47
Catherine 25
Henry 21,23,25,27,47,
83
Jno. 110
John 23,29,47,111
Mary 47
Solomon 25
Terese 110
Theresa (PARKER) 111
Treacy 107
Treasey (PARKER)
93,109
Treecy (PARKER) 94
**KINNEY**
C. R. 191,209
**KITTERELL** (See also
CHITREL)
--- 16
Johnan 16
Johnn 15
Jonathan 15
**KITTRELL**
George 65,66
H. 19
John 33
**KITTRLIN**
H. 19
**KLEGG**
--- 213
Mary 213
**KNIGHT**
Dempsey 58,59,61,63,
113
Demsey 64
J. A. 65
James 51,55,66
John 14
John A. 65
Pleasant (ARNOLD) 55

**L**

**L**.
M. E. 98
**LAM**
Henry 170,171
**LAMB**
Blanch 224
Hettie 224

**LANDEN**
Elisha 88
Levina 88
**LANDING**
--- 92
James 87
Mills 91
**LANG**
--- 26
**LANGSTON**
--- 98
Demsey 87,88
Emeline 108
Frances 84
Francis 108
Isac 88,108
Jno. B. 26
John 83,88
Lenord 83
Mary 91,108
Mary (EURE) 89
Nancy (PARKER) 108
Priss 108
Thomas 83
Thos. 83
Timothy 92,104
Timothy E. 28
William 83
William, Jr. 83
Wm. 83
Wm., Jr. 83
Wm., Sr. 83
**LANGSTONE**
Catherine 87
John 87
Katherine 87
**LASETOR**
Gabriel 176
**LASITER**
Jacob 147
**LASITOR**
Gabriel 176
**LASSITER**
--- 31,217
Ahrom 176
Amos 192
E. 210
Ezekiel 41,115
Ezikiel 41
Gabriel 176
H. B. 213
Henry B. 196,207,208,
211,213
Jacob 147
John 53,176
John B. 221
Mary C. 211
Moses 204,208

**LASSITER** (Cont.)
Nancy 41,42,115
Nancy (BROWN) 42
Reuben 190,208
Riddick 113
Rufus 211,217
Timothy 182
W. J. 200
William 199
Wm. 199
**LASSITOR**
--- 52
Gabriel 176
**LAUGHLY**
Pat. 125
**LAVEY**
John 158
**LAW** (See also LEE)
Jesse 113
**LAWRENCE**
--- 33
George 117
James 95,96,102
Kendrid 102
Kindred 102
M. K. 97,121
Michael 39
Mills K. 106,120
Nancy 96
Nancy (PARKER) 95,102
Penelope 120
**LEARY**
Jno. 158
Job 134
**LEE** (See also LAW)
B. B. 99
J. M. H. 28
Jack 100
Jesse 108,113
John 94,105,110,119
Levi 91
Levy 91
Mary A. 97
Mary A. (PARKER)
HOWELL 103
Mary (PARKER) HOWELL
97
Mildred 104
Titus J. 97,103,108
William 35,117
William Henry 28
Wm. H. 28,98
**LEMMON**
John 154
**LEWIS**
--- 112
David 91,112,116,119
John 38,75,83,92,129

**LEWIS** (Cont.)
   Mills 75,76,92
   Patrick 124
   Philip 25,87
   Salley 190
   Sally 190
   William 56,181
   Wm. 181
**LILLY**
   Ruth 131,151
**LISLES**
   Ephraim 173
**LIVETT**
   Jos. 153
**LONG**
   Mary 131
**LOVEL**
   May (JONES) 52
**LOYD** (See also FLOYD)
   David 69
**LUTEN**
   John 52
   Samuel 52
   Thomas 176

## M

**MACE**
   Frances 13
**MACKHENRY**
   Margaret (EARLY) 170
**MACKLENDON** (See also MC CLENDON)
   Elinore (BUSH) 170
**MAGLOHAN** (See also GLAUGHANGN)
   James 142
**MAGLOHON**
   James 148
**MAGUIRE**
   Philip 175
**MANDEW**
   Thomas 124
**MANDUE**
   Thomas 69
**MANING**
   --- 204
**MANNEY**
   --- 28,92
**MANOR**
   Robert 83
**MANSFIELD**
   Thomas 178
**MARCH**
   John A. 26
   John Anthony 26
   John B. 101,120,121
   Margaret E. (BABB) 101

**MARCH** (Cont.)
   Margarett 120,121
**MARKHAM**
   Louise 222
**MARSHAL**
   Thomas 180,181
**MARSHALL**
   Humphrey 124
   John 188
   Thomas 39,181,182, 184
   Thos. 181
**MARTIN**
   Abel 176
**MASKELL**
   Caroline (DARE) 228
   Della Frances 228
   John Wood 228
**MASON**
   John 6
   Sarah 6
   Thomas 70
**MATHEWES**
   Wm. 103
**MATHEWS**
   James 72
   John 116
**MATHIAS**
   Jesse 59,61
**MATTHEWS**
   Almond J. 227
   Anthony 113
   Etheldred 59
   Eva Ann (CREEKMORE) 227
   Eva Nita 227
   Isaiah 45,112
   John 45
   John W. 116
**MC CALL**
   F. B. 225
**MC CLALAND**
   Robert 175
**MC CLELAND**
   Robert 175
**MC CLENDON** (See also MACKLENDON)
   Thomas 146
**MC CULLOCH**
   Dorothy Beresford 157
   Elizabeth Margaret 157
   Henrietta May 157
   Henry 157
   James 157
   Mary 157
   Penelope 157
   William 157,158
**MC FALL**

**MC FALL** (Cont.)
   A. B. 216
**MC KOY**
   Allmand A. 194
**MC SWAIN**
   Eleanor Davis 174
**MEARNS**
   Will 149
**MEASELLS**
   John 147
***MEETING, MONTHLY***
   Dartmouth 163
   Jack Swamp 155
   Milford 163
   Pasquotank 134,162,163
   Perquimans 134,150,152, 153,154,157,158,163-165, 167
   Piney Woods 134,162,163
   Rich Square 136,152,154, 155,158,163
   Short Creek 155,156
   SUTTONs Creek 134
   Welles 154
   Western Branch 154
   White Water 155
   ▭▭▭▭▭▭▭▭▭▭▭▭▭▭▭▭▭▭▭▭▭▭▭▭▭▭▭▭
**MELTEAR**
   Jethro 180
   Jethro, Jr. 44
   Jethro, Sr. 184
**MENCHEY** (See also MINCHEAD,MINCHEY, MINSHEW)
   Spenko 187
**MEREDET**
   --- 137
**MEREDITH**
   Elizabeth Margaret (MC CULLOCH) 157
   Joseph 157,158
**MERRELL**
   Samuel 71
**MERRIOTT**
   Samuel 71
**MERRITT**
   Charles 170
   Samuel 71
**MESSENGER**
   Margaret J. (PARKER) 194
   William 194
**MIANED** (See also MINARD)
   Sarah 176
**MIERS**
   Nathan 142
**MIL__**

**MIL__** (Cont.)
--- 73
**MILES**
--- 71
**MILLER**
Isaac 23,32,39
W. R. 200
**MILLES**
--- 73
**MILLS**
71-76,82
Henry 71
**MILNER**
Thomas 51,53,55
**MINARD** (See also
MIANED,MINNARD)
Sarah 176
**MINCHEAD** (See also
MINSHEW)
Maxemilon 176
**MINCHEW**
Bond 191
Maximilian 176
**MINCHEY**
Richard 177
**MINER** (See also MINOR)
Will 63
William 58-61,63,66
Wm. 59,61-63
**MING**
--- 158
Francis 134
Mary (PARKER) 134
Thomas 158
Wiley 167
Wyley 159
**MINNARD** (See also
MINARD)
Isral 181
**MINOR**
Elizabeth 65
Elizabeth (PARKER) 57
Elizabeth (PARKER)
SOUTHALL 66
Mary 57
William 55
**MINSHEW** (See also
MENCHEY,MINCHEAD,
MINCHEY)
Maximilian 176
**MINTON**
Peter B. 209
**MITCHELL**
--- 225
Annie Wood 222
Bryant 220,222,223,
225
Elizabeth 220,225

**MITCHELL** (Cont.)
Ernest Linwood 220
George L. 213
George Locke 220
George Locke, Jr. 220
Gladys Warrick
(JERNIGAN) 220
Jesse H. 200
Lucille 220
Lula Sophie 223
Mary E. 220
Mary E. (WARD) 213
Mary Elizabeth (TAYLOR)
220,222,223,225
Robert Lewis 220
**MONTAGUE** (See also
MOUNTAGUE)
Frances 6
Peter 6
**MOOR**
Jno. 83
**MOORE**
Annie 195
Aug. 116,165
John 17,20-22
Joseph 160,162,167
Penanah (PARKER) 160,
167
Penina (PARKER) 167
Peninah 164
**MORE**
John 19,21
**MORESS** (See also
MORRIS)
--- 209
**MORGAN**
Abigail 40,44
Abigail PARKER 39
Abraham 56
Abrm. C. 61
Abrm., Sr. 61
James 58-60,64,65,67
John T. 66
Lewis 39
Matthias 62,63
Saml. 60
Samuel 59
Seth R. 59
**MORGIN**
Hardy 52
Henry 29
**MORRESS**
--- 209
**MORREY** (See also
MURREY)
Thomas 5
**MORRIS**
Aaron 162

**MORRIS** (Cont.)
Bethshaba (EARLY) 170
Elizabeth 162
Elizabeth "Bettie" J. 217
Harriet 217
Jno., Jr. 210
John 208-211,213,217
Miriam 162
Rebekah (EARLY) 170
**MORRISS**
John, Jr. 208
**MOSELEY**
Edwd. 125
James D. 75
**MOUNTAGUE** (See also
MONTAGUE)
Peter 6
*MULATTOES*
HALL
Nathl. 55
ooooooooooooooooooooooooooooooooooooooo
**MULLEN**
George M. 104
Ida 101
James 100,101
Polley 101
**MURFREE**
William 84
**MURPHERY**
Evans 38
**MURPHEY**
William 167
**MURPHRY**
Lydia (PARKER) ELLIOTT
153
William 153
**MURPHY**
Lydia (PARKER) ELLIOTT
153
William 153
**MURREY** (See also
MORREY)
Thomas 5

# N

**NAIRNE**
John 125
*NAVY*
U. S. 219
ooooooooooooooooooooooooooooooooooooooo
*NEGROES*
ABA 93
ABRAM 117
ADDER 189
AGGY 41
AMA 89
AMEY 89,90

**NEGROES** (Cont.)

AMY 117
ANN 28
ASHLY 28
BEN 166
BRIDGET 137
CATE 89,90
CELEA 138
CELIA 138
CHARLOTTE 199
DAVE 28,141,189
DAVID 28,117
DAVY 117
DENNISON 199
DINAH 57
DOLL 20
EDITH 89
EDNEY 138
FRANKEY 138
GERRY 138
GILES 41
HAGAR 21
HAGOR 24
HANNAH 29,184,189
HENRY 28
ISAAC 28,138,206,207
ISACK 204
JACK 28,184,189,205
JACOB 89,90,138,189,
190
JAMES 89,90
JANE 28
JERRY 138,166
JILES 33
JIM 28
KIDDY 28
KITTY 28
LAURA 28
LEWIS 28,35,199
LUCINDY 101
LUCY 28
LUISER 189
LUTAN 89
MARY 89,90,138
MASON 199
MAYOR 141
MILLEY 41
MILLS 28
MILLY 199
MOSES 141
NED 28
PALADORE 189
PATIENCE 189
PAUL 184
PAWL 188
PEG 137
PEGG 89
PEGGY 90

**NEGROES** (Cont.)

PENEY 93
PENNEY 189
PENNY 188
PLEASANT 117
PLESANT 136
PRESILLER 90
PRISE 189,190
PRISS 179
PRISSY 184
RHODA 24
RUBEN 187
SAM 57,141,188
SEALEY 189,190
SILAS 28,166
SILLA 89
SILLAH 138
TOM 101
WASHINGTON 199
WILLIS 189

□□□□□□□□□□□□□□□□□□□□□□□□□□□□□□□□□□□□□□□□□□

**NESBETT**
  Sarah (PARKER) 187
**NESBITT**
  Joseph 187
  Sarah (PARKER) 187
**NEWBY**
  Keran 154
  Keron 154
  Nancy 163
  Thomas 163
**NEWSOM**
  Charles 44
  E. H. 45
  M. E. 45
  Penonne (PARKER) 136
**NEWSON**
  Jno. F. 200
***NEWSPAPERS***
  *Old North State, The* 95

□□□□□□□□□□□□□□□□□□□□□□□□□□□□□□□□□□□□□□□□□□

**NICHOLLS**
  --- 98
  Ann 87
  John 87
  Mary 87
  Sarah 87
**NICHOLS**
  John 87
**NICHOLSON**
  John 134
  Nathan 134
  Penina (PARKER) 134
**NIXON**
  N. 167
  Nathan 210
  Peter 194,196
  Zechariah 210

**NORFLEET**
  --- 56,191,192
  Abraham 56,140
  E. 157
  Elizabeth 56
  Elizabeth (ARNOLD) 55
  Jacob 49,53,56
  James 133,134,160
  Jas. 137,153
  John 22
  Kinchen 40,42,56,66,
109
  Wm. 153
**NORFLET**
  John 52
**NORFLETT**
  Kinchan 109
**NORSWORTHY**
  --- 6
  Tristram 6
**NOWEL**
  Martin 128,175
**NOWELL**
  S. D. 217
  Simon 210,213
**NUGENT**
  Nell Marion 9
**NURNEY**
  John 154
***OATH***
  Allegiance, of 177
***OCCUPATIONS***
  Blacksmith 103,146,206
  Carpenter 145
  Chirurgeon [Surgeon] 9
  Cooper 50,55,70,76,92,
93,106,169
  Cordwainer 132
  Electrician 225
  Farmer 103,163
  Fireman 226
  House Carpenter 56,76
  Joiner 56
  Laborer, in a butter dish
factory 221
  Merchant 114,169
  Oiler 226
  Policeman 226
  Punch-press operator 226
  Schoolmaster 170
  Service station owner 226
  Ship carpenter 222
  Street car conductor 225
  Street car motorman 226
  Surveyor 145,146
  Tailor 50
  Teacher 167
  Turner 145

Weaver 130
Wheelwright 47,146
**OFFICE**
Virginia Land 16
□□□□□□□□□□□□□□□□□□□□□□□□□□□□□□□□□□□□□□□□□□□□□□□□□
**ODAM**
Aaron 21
Demsey 183
John 83
Moses 83
Tho. 21
Thomas 21
William 25
**ODOM**
--- 108
Aaron 84
Abraham 72
Asa 94,104
Benjamin 66
Dempsey 35
Demsey 40,66
Jacob 84
Jno. 91
John 72,83,84,88,91,92
Mary 59-62,64,65
Mary (PARKER) 57,66
Richard 83,84,98,104
Rodon 104
Thomas 21
William 25
**ODOMOM**
Richard 88
**ODUM**
Thomas 14
**OGLA**
Mary 216
**OHDOM**
Richard 88
**OLIVER**
--- 13
Aaron 126,172
Alexander 83
**O'NEAL**
Charles 142
**OQUIN**
Bryant 16
**OSBORNE**
--- 69
**OSTEEN**
Samuel 146
**OUTLAND**
Dora F. 224
John H. 225
John M. 224
**OUTLAW** (See also
OUTLAND)
Christian 165
David 114

**OUTLAW** (Cont.)
George 74,165,177,178
Godwin 225
Harriet 165
Jacob 204,210
James 178
John 209
**OVERTON**
--- 224
Jno. 174,175
John 128,142,175
Ruth (PARKER) 224
**OWINGS**
--- 213
Janice 203,211
Walton A. 203,211

## P

**P.**
H. 51
R. 94
S. 94
**PADGET**
Samuel 126
**PADGETT**
William 124
**PAGE**
James 172
**PAGETT**
Wm. 125
**PALIDENO**
Josephine 222
**PAR___**
Frank 175
**PARCARE**
Joseph 176
**PARKE**
Reuben 118
**PARKER**
--- 10-12,18,56,57,65,
67,99,112,143,164-166,
174,195,196,210,211, 227
A. 41
A. W. 94,112,113,115,
117
Aaron 162
Abbie Lucretia
(HARRELL) 226
Abigail 25,39,40,155,
156
Abigal 38
Abm. 42,53
Abm. W. 112,113
Abr. 42
Abraham 21,22,40,41,
43-45,58,90,91,106,110,
112,146,147

**PARKER** (Cont.)
Abraham W. 94,112-114
Abram 22,41-43,59,104,
105,111
Abram W. 89,93,94,
106-109,112-116
Absolam 53
Abtgall 38
Adaline 163
Adlina Felton 221
Alba 65
Alesey 65,67
Alexander 154,155
Alfred 57,58,64,65
Alice 37
Alice E. 36,37
Alizabeth 179
Allen Leon 226
Alton Bryant 223,224
Amanda (DUCK) 222
Amanda E. "Mandy"
(WILLIFORD) 220
Amason 200
Amazon 199
Amos 24,50,51,132,135,
136,150,151
Andrew Lee 222
Ann 7,10,48,49,66,107,
126,139,184,207
Ann (BRADY) 78
Ann E. 75
Ann F. 140
Ann Mariah 166,167
Ann Robinson 162,163
Anna Belle "Ann" 226
Anna Belle (CLARK) 226
Annette 165,167
Annie 199,222
Annie C. 222
Annie E. (HOFLER) 79
Annie F. (SADLER) 222
Annie M. 194-196
Annie (MOORE) 195
Annie Wood (MITCHELL)
222
Arthur 223
Arthur F. 222
Asa 75,76
Asa H. 76
Asy 75,76
Augustus 193
Augustus M. 199
B. F. 79
Barbara Jean 224
Benjamin 49,52,87,155
Benjamine 48
Bessie May 223
Bessie P. 222

**PARKER** (Cont.)

Bethany 25
Betsey 42
Betsey (BROWN) 42,77
Betsey (SMALL) 141
Betsy 36,181
Bettie 195
Blanch (LAMB) 224
Bray 88-94,103-105,
108,113,115,116,118,120
C. A. 213
C. C. 211-213
C. V. 99
Cader 179
Carl C. 218
Carl Cavana 217,218
Caroline 100,102
Caroline Virginia 101
Catharine 154,155
Catherine 178,179,182,
201,203
Catherine (HINTON?)
178
Cathren 182
Catren 179
Catron 180
Charity 29,35,41-43,105
Charity (BENTON) 29
Charles A. 211
Charles Arthur 223,224
Charles Arthur, Jr. 223
Charles Thomas 81
Cherry 33,35,41,45
Cherry (CROSS) 34
Chetta 117,118,120,121
Chetty 118-120
Chittey 118
Chitty 109,117,118
Chitty JONES 117
Christian 33,40,182
Christiana 42
Cinthia 107
Clamilia 111
Clarkey 89,90,93,111
Clarkey (EURE) 89
Clementine 111
Cornelius 80
Cynthia (See also Cin-
thia,Syntha,Scynitha,
Scyntha) 108,115,116,
118
D. 110,117-119,193,
199,201
Daniel 13,16,17,19-21,
23,24,29,31-35,133,136
Danl. 33,34
David 21,22,57,187,
189-194,199-201,

**PARKER** (Cont.)

David 205-207,211
David W. 65
Dawson 78
Deborah Ann (PEELE)
163
Della Elizabeth 221
Dempsey 89,93,94,96,
104,105,107,109,110,
115-117,119,120
Dempsey, of John 117,
118
Dempsy 114,118,119
Demsey 24,31,90,106,
113,114,116-118
Diana E. 195
Dilday 25
Donald Francis 222
Donald Ivey 228
Dora 225
Dora F. 225
Dora F. (OUTLAND) 224
Dora O. 225
Doro 224
Doro F. 224
Dorothy 6
Dossey 77
Duanie 217
Dunn 217
E. J. 37,100
Easter 33
Ede 21,22
Edith 25
Edmon J. 36,37
Edmond J. 36,37
Edmund J. 37
Edna Cooper 227
Edward 55,57,65,79
Edward J. 65
Edward Peele 163
Edwin 77,80
Elezabeth 179
Elias 160,164
Elias T. 160,163,164
Elisabeth 50,156,162
Elisabeth (PERISHO)
134
Elisabith 179
Elisha 21,24,32-36,104,
105,115,116,118,129,
132,136-139
Elisha, Jr. 34
Eliz. 99,126
Eliz. J. 100
Eliza 41,42,80,124,130
Eliza (PARKER) 41
Elizabeth 6,7,9,29,36,
40,41,44,45,51,65,66,

**PARKER** (Cont.)

Elizabeth76,81,89,91,
95-97,102,104,105,
108,124,126,127,133,134,
138-142,147,148,151,155,
156,167,171,173,182,184,
188,217,224
Elizabeth J. (CARTER)
99
Elizabeth A. 79,80,216
Elizabeth A. (KELLY)
216
Elizabeth Ann (HOFLER)
80
Elizabeth "Betsy" 201
Elizabeth "Bettie" J.
(MORRIS) 217
Elizabeth (BROWN) 115
Elizabeth (GRIFFIN) 50
Elizabeth J. 100
Elizabeth Lee 227
Elizabeth (MORRIS) 162
Elizabeth P. 34
Elizabeth (PARKER) 95
Elizabeth Pipkin 34,36
Elizabeth (PRICE) 141
Elizabeth (SKINNER)
139
Elizabeth (TOPPING) 140
Elizabeth (WALLES) 131,
132,136
Elizabeth (WALLIS) 129
Elizabeth (WILLIAMS) 65
Elizebeth 147,184
Elizth. 147
Elmira 111
Elmirah 111
Elva Ray (HOWARD)
HUMPHRIES 227
Emily 27,28,79
Emily Hortense
(ROUNTREE) 79
Emily O. (BROWN) 79
Emma 80
Emma Jane 80
Emmy 79
Enoch 132,134,135
Enock 131,132
Esther 33,51
Ethel 196,198,225
Eva Nita 227
Eva Nita (MATTHEWS)
227
Faith 156
Faith (JUDKINS) 155
Febury 25
Fereby 25,26
Florence 199

**PARKER** (Cont.)

Florrence 199
Frak 175
Frances 7,171
Frances MONTAGUE 6
Francis 6,7,11,12,19,20,
22,25,80,128,174-176
Francis, Jr. 12
Frank 80,128
Frans. 175
Freida (SCHMIDT) 222
G. W. 167
Geo. 37
George 7,105,155,156,
166
George E. 36,37
George T. 37,65
George Thomas 36
George W. 165,167
Geraldine Annie (CLARK)
224
Gertrude M. 218
Grace 225
Grace (COPELAND) 172
Grace Joyce 227
Grace (WEAVER) 228
Gracy V. 224
Hannah 22,23,47,147
Hardy 34-36,96,99,102
Hardy D. 34-37
Hardy W. 95,96,100,
103,106,120
Harriet 167,213
Harriet Ann 217
Harriet E. 165-167
Harriet E. G. 165
Harriet E. (OUTLAW)
167
Harriet (OUTLAW) 165
Harriett Ann 81
Harrison 28
Harry Hilborn 227
Harry Hilborn, Jr. 227
Henderson 135,136
Henry 41-43,45,216
Hilda Beamon (STOKES)
221
Hubert 223
Hugh Griffin 50,51
Hulda 198
Humphey 59,63
Humphrey 33,34,50,51,
57-60,63,65
Humphry 50,51,64
Ida M. 216
Ida Margaret
(HUTCHINS) 221
Ida May 216

**PARKER** (Cont.)

Ida (MULLEN) 101
Ima BROWN 216
Indiana Riddick 81
Isaac 24,95,96,101,105,
137,141,147,154-156,
207-211,213
Isaac W. 212,213,215,
217,220
Isaac William 217
Isaack 137
Isabel 159,160,167
Isabel (PEELE) 158
Isabella 162,164
Isack 204,205
Issabella 65
Ivey D. 227,228
J. D. 194
J. H. 200,216
J. Louise 196
J. R. 80,81
J. W. 200
Jackie 222
Jacob 20,22,29,130,
135,138-140,146,147,
149,151,154,155,160,
164,167,213,222
Jacob A. 217
Jacob, Jr. 156
Jacob M. 211,213
Jacob Mask 221
Jacob Mask, Jr. 222
Jacob Mask, Sr. 222
Jacob N. 160,163-167,
209
Jacob, Sr. 156
Jacub 149
Jael 134
Jail 135
James_ 190
James 24,37,41,48-53,
55,73-79,87,111,129-133,
135,136,142,145,148,150,
151,153,155,157,173-176,
179,181-184,188-191,
193-198,200,201,213
James B. 78,79
James Edward 81
James H. 113,191-193,
199-201,211
James M. 195
James Peele 163
James R. 65
James, Sr. 49,129,132
James Watson 218
Jane 91,105,111,128,
156,162,170,174,175
Jane Harriet

**PARKER** (Cont.)

(WALLINGTON) 228
Jane R. (ARLINE) 37
Jane Rebecca (ARLINE)
37
Jas. 29,75,128,130,175,
182
Jas. R. 80
Jay 218
Jean 126,170,171,174,
175
Jeane 171,174,175
Jeane Barbara 226
Jemima 154,155
Jeremiah 154,155
Jes 29
Jess 29
Jesse 29,33-35,40,42,
45,63,75,76,78,141,142,
155
Jesse A. 37
Jesse Benton 29
Jesse E. 36
Jessee 42
Jessie Raymond (HILL)
226
Jethro 36
Jethro W. 36,37
Jethrow W. 36
Jim 200
Jimmie Louise 198
Jno. 88,124,126,170,
171,174,175,182
Jno. F. 99,113
Jno. N. 213
Joan Annette 227
Joane 6
Job 130,138,149,151,
153-155,157-160,
162-164,167
Job H. 212,213,215,
216
Jobe 149,151,157
Jobe Henry 215,216
Joel H. 216
John 6,7,14,15,32,33,
40,43,44,48,50,51,53,70,
75-77,81,83-90,92,98,
105,117,123,126-129,
131-135,141-145,148,
151,152,154-156,158,
171,173-175,179,181,
182,184,188,190,201,
203-209,225
John Baptist 88
John D. 193,194
John David 198
John F. 95,96,99,100,

**PARKER** (Cont.)

John F. 101,102,105, 119-121,166
John Frank 99
John Franklin 163,164, 167
John H. 79
John, Jr. 87
John Mitchell 223,224
John Mitchell, Jr. 224
John N. 222,225
John Nathan 221,222
John Newby 163
John Peele 162
John, Sr. 85
John Thomas 217,218
John U. 224
John W. 79,217,222,223
Jonas 20,29
Jonathan 13,15-17,20, 23,24,29,31,109,135,152, 153
Jordan 57,58,64,65
Jordan Williams 65
Jos. 126,129,152,153, 159,175
Joseph 35,126,128-131, 135,142,143,145,148-151, 153-155,157-160,162, 163,164,171-174, 176-184,186-195,199, 201,203
Joseph A. 36,37
Joseph R. 165
Joseph Robinson 162, 163
Joseph, Sr. 148,176
Joseph W. 195,200
Joseph Wilson 163
Josephine (PALIDENO) 222
Josept 179
Josepth 179
Josiah 53,72-74,136, 154,155
Josiah, Jr. 73,74
Josiah, Sr. 73,74
Josspth 179
Judah 75
Judith 53,75-77,107, 108,154,155
Judith (EURE) BEEMAN 106
Judith Ann 222
Judith (BEEMAN) 102
Judith Harrell 223
Julia Etta 81
Julia (PEELE) 156

**PARKER** (Cont.)

Junius H. 37
Junius Hardy 36
K. 93
Kadah 51,182
Kadar 183
Kadear 181
Kate 225
Katherine 182
Kedah 51,183,184
Kedar 50,51,182-185, 188,201
Keren 155
Keron (NEWBY) 154
Kindred 88-97,99, 100-103,106,108-111, 113,115,116,118,120
Kiziah 134
L. E. 28
L. H. 212
L. W. 81,111
Langston 102
Lavinia 197,207,209
Lavinia L. 194,196
Lavinia Louise (WHEDBEE) 195,198
Lazarus J. 36,37
Leah 152
Lelia Maud 221
Lella Maud 221
Lem. 28
Leml. 27
Lemuel 26,27
Lemuel E. 27,28
Leon Ashburn 222
Levi 105,110,115,116, 118,120
Levi W. 110,111
Levina 204
Levina CLEVES 203
Levy 91
Lidia 42
Linsy Lycurgus 218
Lizzie (KELLY) 216
Logan H. 200,213
Logan Hurse, Jr. 226
Logan Hurst 219,221, 225-228
Louis Claiborne 81
Louisa 41,42,45
Louisa (BROWN) 42
Louise (MARKIIAM) 222
Louise S. 218
Lovenia 207-209
Lovina 207
Lovinia 208
Lucy 79,171
Luisa 41

**PARKER** (Cont.)

Luke 24,53
Lula Sophie (MITCHELL) 223,224
Lula Wood 223
Luther 217
Lyda 134
Lydia 131,132,134,153
M. E. 36
M. F. 212,221,225
Magaret 42
Magt. 41,42
Margaret 28,34,53,57, 58,65,67,162,207,215
Margaret A. 28,163
Margaret Ann 28,163, 215,216
Margaret Ann (NEWBY) 163
Margaret Ann (SIMONS) 216
Margaret E. 28
Margaret J. 194
Margaret Jane 218,227
Margaret (JUDKINS) 155
Margaret Morris 163
Margaret (SIMONS) 215
Margaret (TOWNSEND) 164
Margaret W. 164
Margaret (WALSH) 222
Margarett A. 65
Martha 26,28,107,108, 115,116,136,155,156, 159,160,163,167,199, 204,207,208
Martha Ann 26,27
Martha Cavana 218
Martha E. 27,28
Martha Jane (BYRUM) 218
Martha (LASSITER) 199
Martha Luvina 220
Martha (PEELE) 155
Martha SAUNDERS 26
Martha (WHITE) 162
Mary 7,24,27,32,34,36, 38,39,42,51,65,66,80,89, 90-92,102,103,110,113, 114,126,133,135,136, 141,147,149,150,154-156, 162,163,167,180-182, 216,225
Mary A. 210-213
Mary Agnes 225
Mary Agnes (MITCHELL) 225-228
Mary Ann 27,101,114,

**PARKER** (Cont.)

Mary Ann 212,225
Mary Ann (POWELL)
209,211,213-215,217,
218-225,228,229
Mary (ARNOLD) 55
Mary (BENTON) 29
Mary E. 36,37,80
Mary Eliza 219
Mary Elizabeth 36,
163,218
Mary Emily (GATLING)
198
Mary (EURE) CROSS
112
Mary F. 217
Mary (FARLEE) 24,135,
151
Mary (HICKS) 155
Mary Jane 26,27
Mary Jane R. 37
Mary, Jr. 136
Mary L 36
Mary (LANGSTON) 91,
99,101,102
Mary Louise (HARRELL)
223
Mary M. 216
Mary OGLA 216
Mary "Polly" 187
Mary R. 194
Mary Rebecca
(WHEDBEE) 199
Mary Ruth 223
Mary Sally
(WILLOUGHBY) 224
Mary Susan 80
Mary W. 114
Mary (WALLES) 131,
132,136
Maude Valeria 226
Micajah 155,156
Mildred 105,155
Mildred A. 36
Mildred A. (SPEIRS) 37
Mildred Ann 36,37
Mildred Irene 222
Miles 24-27,75,117
Miles H. 27,28
Miles Harrison 28
Millard 211,221
Millard F. 213
Millard Fillmore 221
Millard Filmore 220,221
Milley 75
Mills 80
Mills H. 28
Milly 75,76

**PARKER** (Cont.)

Minnie H. 200
Minnie Smith 223,224
Miriam 152
Monterey M. 211,213
Moore 195,196
Moses 31,32,53
Myles 26,27
N. G. 211
Nance 179
Nancey 42,75,134
Nancy 33,38-40,42-44,
65,66,75,102,107-109,
115,116,118,182,184,204,
207
Nancy "Ann" 185,201,
207
Nancy (WILLIAMS) 104,
105
Nansey 109
Nansy 181
Naomi (WILLIAMS) 74
Nathan 130-135,
149-155,158,203,
207-213,216-218
Nathan G. 207,209,
211-225,228,229
Nathanial 205
Nathanied 205
Nathaniel 141,142,151,
205
Nathaniel G. 214
Nathaniel Gabriel 208,
209
Nettie (COX) 216
Nina 199
Noah 135
Offa (See Theophilus) 78
Oma (See Naomi) 74
Ora Penelope 218
Orpha (See Theophilus)
78
P. 97
P. H. 216
Patience 20,22
Patric H. 216
Patrick H. 215
Patrick Henry 216
Paul Bryant 222
Paul Bryant, Jr. 222
Pauline 223
Peggy 33,34,65,67
Penelope 101,104,105
Penelope (MC CULLOCH)
157,158
Penelope (WALTON) 65
Penina 134,149,151
Peninah 155,164,167

**PARKER** (Cont.)

Penninah 45
Penny 41,42
Persilia 29
Peter 16,17,19-24,31,32,
33,37,41,42,46,70,75-78,
80,81,123-127,129,131,
132,136-140,144-148,
154,169,171-176
Peter, Jr. 124,127,172
Peter, Sr. 124,125
Petr. 126,169
Petr., Sr. 125
Petter 137
Phebe May 155
Pheraby 167
Pheriby 25
Philip 136
Phillip 9
Polley 75
Polly 25,26,39,50,75,76,
179,181
Polly L. 34
Polly Lee 34,36
Pressa 179
Pressy 181,182
Pricilla 53
Priscilla 40,54,96,97,
101,103,182,184,185
Priscilla Christian 182,
201
Priscilla Christian
"Pressy" 182
Priscilla (HAYES) 79
Priscilla (WILLIAMS) 95,
97,102,103
Prisillar (WILLIAMS) 91
Prisse 179
Prissila 91
Prissilla 183
Prissillia 97
R. 187,190
R. Moore 195
Rachel 29,153
Randel 111
Rasco 105
Raymond Aileen 227
Rd. 16
Rebecca 155
Rebecka (WARREN) 129
Redden 111
Reuben 88,90,92-94,
102,106-108,110-112,
115-118,122
Rhoda 156,190,192
Rhoda (DRAPER) 155
Rhoda (HARRELL) 188
Rhoday 188

**PARKER** (Cont.)

Richard 9-17,19-25,
29-32,40-42,44-47,69,
149,154,155
Richard E. 217
Richard H. 65
Richard, Sr. 11,12,15,83
Richard, the Elder 21
Richd. 12,13,17,21,42
Richd., Sr. 13
Roadeth 137
Robart 19,20,38
Robert 15,24,31,37-45,
72-78,154,155,187,190,
208
Robert Edward 228
Robert, Jr. 38,40
Robert Mitchell 228
Robert, Sr., 37-39
Robert W. 222
Robt. 42,190
Rodah 137,189
Rodath 137
Rodey (HARRELL) 188
Rodith 136
Ronald Allen 227
Rosella 105
Rosetta 105
Roxanna 79
Ruben 89
Rubin 90,118
Ruth 53,65,67,108,134,
149,150,153,224
S. E. 28
Salley 25
Sallie 99-101,198,213
Sallie Ann 219
Sally 40,42
Sally E. 76
Sally Mary 81
Saml. 14,29
Samuel 13,14,131-136,
152,155,158,159
Samuell 132
Sarah 6,40,45,51,53,65,
66,79,80,101,134,135,
138,141,142,152-156,
160,164,167,170,171,
173,176,182,187
Sarah A. 79
Sarah Ann 140
Sarah (BROTHERS) 51
Sarah E. 78,98
Sarah Eliza 80,97
Sarah Elizabeth 140
Sarah (FARLEE) 152
Sarah G. (HINTON) 190
Sarah Isabella 163

**PARKER** (Cont.)

Sarah (JONES) 52
Sarah L. 195
Sarah (PEELE) 155
Sarah (WELCH) 142
Saul 135
Scynitha 108
Scyntha 108
Scynthy 107
Sele 137
Seley 137
Seth 89,90,92-97,102,
107-110,115,116,118,
134-137,141,142
Seth, Jr. 142
Seth, Sr. 118,141
Seth (the elder) 115
Siddy (PARKER) 77
Sidey 42
Sidney 42
Sidney (PARKER) 78
Sidny 41
Silva 133,134
Silvia 134
Sollome 174
Solome 173,174
Sophia 41,42,45,107,
115,116
Sophia Ann 78
Sophie 77
Stephen 19,20,22,25,29
Stephen Arnold Douglas
81
Sue 99,100
Susan 79,80,101
Susie 100
Susie Clair 221
Syntha 107
T. J. 99
T. W. 212,213,221
Telpah 53
Tersecia 111
Texana 28
Texana T. 27
Texanna 28
Texas T. 28
Thelma Isabel (BATTLEY)
224
Theodore 221
Theophilus 76-78
Theresa 90,106,111
Theressa 111
Thirsa 41,42
Tho. 11,124
Thomas 2,5,6,7,11-13,
36,47-58,64-70,81,126,
127,128,130,144-148,
163,167,169-176,225

**PARKER** (Cont.)

Thomas Arthur 224
Thomas C. 217
Thomas J. 99,101
Thomas Jefferson 101
Thomas, Jr. 69,70,169
Thomas, son of Thomas
55
Thomas, Sr. 69,70
Thomas W. 225
Thomas W., Jr. 225
Thomas Walter 224,225,
227
Thomas Walter, Jr. 227
Thos. 47,52,53,58,99,
127,130,169,175
Thursa 42
Timothy 79
Timothy Edward 79
Tom 97
Treacy 50
Trecy 89
Treecy 91,94
Umphry 50
Vernon Bryant 226
Vernon Bryant, Jr. 226
Vernon Bryant, Sr. 227
Virginia Dorothy 222
W. 47,52
W. W. 218
Walter Leroy 221
Walter Stallings 223
Walter T. 225
Warren 111
Wayne Robert 228
Wendy Jane 228
Westley 77
Westly 77
Wilday 25,26
Wiley 76,77,79,80
Will 128,175
Will. 42
William 1,2,4,5,7,9,10,
20,21,29,40-45,47-53,
55,68,70-72,79,82,105,
111,155,163,171,174,
175,176,199
William Ambrose 81
William E. 215,216
William J. 105
William, Jr. 51
William L. 37,199,200
William Lafayette 36
William, Sr. 49-51
William Thomas 163
William Walter 218
William Walter, Jr. 218
Willis 23,38,40,42,50,

PARKER (Cont.)
Willis 51,137,140-142
Wm. 4,37,42,55,70,71
Wm. J. 105
Wm., Jr. 51
Wm., Sr. 51
PARKS
Daniel 133
Elizabeth 133
John 133
Mary 133
Samuel 133
PATTERES
--- 71
PEARCE
Enoch 207
Nathan 191
Thos. 190
PEELE
Deborah Ann 163
Elizabeth (PARKER) 156
Isabel 158
James 163
John 156
Julia 156
Martha 155
Ruth 163
Sarah 155
PELTREE
Abraham 4
PERCE
George 69
PERISHO
Elisabeth 134
John 160
PERKINS
Mary 9
Nicholas 9
Sam 217
PERREY
Jacob, Jr. 130,151
PERROT
Nicholas 69
PERRY
Birtie D. 219
D. C. 197
Ivey D. 213,219
Ivey Dowdy 219,225
Jacob 130,131,151,173
Josiah D. 219
Logan H. 219
Merritt Sawyer 219
Nancy (SAWYER) 219
Philip 173
Sallie A. (PARKER) 213
Sallie Ann (PARKER)
219,225
Willie I. 219

PETERS
--- 72,82,93
Lawrence 10
PETERSON
--- 93
PETTERS
--- 71,72
PETTEVER
John 128
PHEBUS
Peter 70,72
PHELPS
Elijah 197
G. W. 217
James 206
PHILIPS
Paul 170,175
PILAND
Edward 112
George 37,38
Jesse 110
Katherine 89
Mildred (PARKER) 76
Peter 76,107,114
Reuben 115,119
Thoma_ 73
Thomas 71-73,88
Thos. 83
Wiley 210,211,213
Willis 217
PILANT
Stephen 88
Thomas 88
PILINT
Thomas 83
Thos. 83
PIPKIN
--- 42,43
Isaac 75,87,93
Isaac, Jr. 25
Jno. D. 77,113
Jno., Jr. 71
John 87
John D. 42,45,78
John, Jr. 71
Martha 83
POLLOCK
Tho. 169
Thomas 169
POLSON (See also
GOLSON)
--- 39
Geo. 17
John 38
POOL
John 135
POWEL
Daniel 180

POWELL
--- 2,47,209
Charles 209
Jacob 33
John 57
John, of Jacob 33
Mary 209,210
Mary A. 209
Thomas 2-4,9,209
Waunita 9
PRATT
--- 36
PRICE
Elizabeth 141
Jonathan 168
PRISHARD
Abselom 142
PRITCHARD
Absm. H. 142
PRIVETT
Saml. 138
Samuel 138
Wm. 138
PRUDEN
James 32
*PUBLIC ADMINISTRATOR*
GATLING
Jno. J. 99,100
John J. 100
NEWSON
Jno. F. 200
*PUBLIC REGISTER*
RIDDICK
Christr 182
RIGHTON
Wm. 158
WALTON
Jno. R. 105
John 208
PUGH
--- 19,33
Daniel 16,25
Fra. 21
Francis 23,29
Henry 60,111
Wm. E. 112

## R

RABEY
Adam 31
Jacob 21,23
Judith (BENTON) 29
RABIE
--- 31
RABY
Adam 31,113

268

**RALLS**
--- 117
**RANER**
Richard 146
**RAWLS**
--- 117
Richard 76
Rizup 113
**RAYNOR**
Amos 89
**REDDICK**
R. M. 213
Robert 71
***REVOLUTIONARY WAR***
139,211

**RICE**
John 148
Nathaniel 49,149
William 146
**RICKS**
Robert 124
**RIDDICK** (See also REDDICK)
--- 211,221
Abm. 38
Alfred M. 102
Bushrod 208
Christopher 40
Christr. 182
D. E. 100,221
Edward 113
Etheldred 116
G. K. 197
George 197
I. H. 113
J. 165
J. R. 119
J. W. 204
James 74
James M. 58
James R. 94,102,104, 109,110,117,118,191
James W. 187,190,207
Jas. 106
Jesse 31
John 77,78,104,110, 112,119
Joseph 179,184,195,201
Lassiter 45,195,197
M. 44
Mills 43
N. J. 95
Nathaniel J. 95
R. M. 197,217
Robt. 203,204
Ruth 24
Ruth (PARKER) 24

**RIDDICK** (Cont.)
Saml. 165
Seth 86
Thomas 42,113,114, 118,119
W. T. 103
William W. 38,39,42,89
Willis J. 191,192
Wm. W. 39,42
**RIGHT** (See also WRIGHT)
William 159
**RIGHTON**
Wm. 158
**ROADS** (See also RODES)
Henry 145,146
Mary 145
**ROBBINS** (See also ROBINS)
Jno. 181
John 180,181,187
John, Jr. 179,180
John, Sr. 179
**ROBENSON** (See also ROBINSON)
John 132
**ROBERTS**
E. R. 197
Edward 14
Jas. W. 103
John 70,124,184,187, 195,208
John S. 119
Jonathan 180-183,188, 201
Jonathen 181
Mills 26,201,207-210
Thomas 124
W. P. 194,215
William P. 215
**ROBERTSON**
--- 91,111
Elisha 203
Margret 88
Thomas 88
**ROBINS**
___n 181
Bashford 180
Jno. 181
John 180
John, Sr. 180
**ROBINSON**
Elisha 204
**RODES** (See also ROADS)
Henry 145
**RODGERS**
Jacob 72
James 102
John F. 96

**RODGERS** (Cont.)
Martha A. 96
Martha Ann 96
Mary E. 96
Penelope 102
Thos. 125
**ROGERS**
--- 73,88,90,91,94,95
Betsy (PARKER) 36
Elisha 35,36
Elizabeth 35
Elizabeth (MITCHELL) 220
Elizabeth (WILLIAMS) 104
Enos 35,36,54
Frank 36
James 101,102
John F. 95,101
John Francis 95
Jonathan 34
Levi 104
Martha Ann 95,102
Mary 35
Mary (PARKER) 36
Penelope 102
Penelope (PARKER) 101
Pennina 101
Philip 104
Robert 83,88,94,101
Stephen 88
Telpha (PARKER) 54
Thomas R. 220
William 15
**ROGERSON**
Abel 167
**ROGGERS**
--- 84
**ROOKS**
Elisha 79
James 79
Joseph 72
Thomas 72
**ROPER**
John L. 196
**ROSS**
Andrew 84
Callum 83
Calum 83
**ROUNTREE**
--- 210
Emily 79
Emily Hortense 79
H. C. 197
James 165
John A. 79
Martha 217
N. L. 213,217

269

**ROUNTREE** (Cont.)
Noah 165,167,203,210
Seth W. 165,167
Solomon 113,119
**RUSSEL**
Charls 19
**RUSSELL**
--- 120
Charles 83
Dempsey 101,120
Demsey 101
Sarah 120,121
Sarah Ann (BABB) 101
Thomas 120,121

## S

**SADLER**
Annie F. 222
J. M. 222
**SANDERLIN**
--- 197
**SANDERS**
Abraham 25
Charles 25
Henry 70
William 2
**SATTERFIELD**
Thomas 139
Thos. 141
**SAUNDERS**
Abraham 25
Benjamin 25
Bray 26
Brian 26
Charles 25
Cynthia (PARKER) 108
D. M. 118
Francis 25,27
James 26
Jason 26
Jesse 25,26
John 93
Lawrance 26,28
Lawrence 26,27
Martha 26
Mary 26
Richard 108
Robert 26
Robert H. 120
Thomas 26
**SAVAGE**
--- 36
Cordy Y. 119
Jesse 34,35
Judith 106,110,119
Mary E. 106
O. B. 96,97,103,105

**SAVAGE** (Cont.)
Oliver H. 113
Pryer 42
Pryor 42
R___ 99
William H. 119
**SAWYER**
Nancy 219
**SCHMIDT**
Freida 222
**SCOTT**
Charles 71
Jos. 131
Jos., Jr. 153
Joseph 159
Robert 124
Robt. 124
William, Jr. 124
**SEARS**
Belver 96
Henry 92
Henry Ebron 39
J. 81
William 93,108
**SEAWARD**
--- 5
John 5
**SEWARD**
--- 5
**SEWILL** (See also
SHOWLES,SOWELL)
Richard 169
**SHARP**
C. L. 200
Jacob 199
Jno. 200
John 200
John B. 199
**SHEETS**
Jacob 174
**SHEETTS**
Jacob 174
**SHEPARD** (See also
SHIPPARD)
Stephen 71-73
**SHEPHARD**
--- 74
Stephen 72,73
**SHEPHERD**
--- 74
John 75,76
Stephen 73
**SHERARD** (See also
SHERROD)
Randol 111
***SHERIFF***
GATLING
James 51

***SHERIFF*** (Cont.)
HILL
Asa 95
PIPKIN
Isaac 87
RIDDICK
D. E. 100
James R. 104,109,118
Thomas 119
SUMNER
J. 184
ɑɑɑɑɑɑɑɑɑɑɑɑɑɑɑɑɑɑɑɑɑɑɑɑɑɑɑɑɑɑɑɑɑ
**SHERROD** (See also
SHERARD)
Randal 110,111
**SHIFF**
Wm. M. 81
**SHIPPARD** (See also
SHEPARD)
Stephen 72
***SHIPS***
Charles 1,4,5
Dorchester 226
Grecian 226
Guift 1
Neptune 1
ɑɑɑɑɑɑɑɑɑɑɑɑɑɑɑɑɑɑɑɑɑɑɑɑɑɑɑɑɑɑɑɑɑ
**SHOWLES** (See also
SEWILL,SOWELL)
Richard 127
**SIMONS**
--- 209
Margaret 215
Robert 209
**SIMPSON**
James 109
**SIMSON**
John 131
**SKINNER**
Elizabeth 139
Evan 135
James C. 140
John 83
T. G. 197
William R. 140
Willm. 83
Wm. R. 140
**SLAVENS**
John 176
**SMALL**
Allen 142
Betsey 141
Jno. 52
John 11,16,19,25
John, Jr. 47,48
John, Sr. 48
Joshua 57
Mary (PARKER) 142

SMALL (Cont.)
Moses H. 33,50
SMITH
--- 36,90,110,119
Allen 107,119,209
Charles 74,188
Cyprian 113
Edwin 101
Geo. W. 105
George 36
Henning T. 96
James 191,199
James I. 197
John 150
Jonathan 40
Joseph 92,118
L. L. 80,81,99,195,197,
211,213,222
Lavinia 118
Lewis L. 80
Mary (JONES) 187
Na. 108
Nathan 117
Nicholas 7
Riddick 187
Robt. 83
S. E. 97
Samuel 140
Samuel E. 96
Sipha 113,199
Thomas 194
Thos. E. 197
Toby 2
Wm. 6
SMYTH
Toby 2
SNODEN
Tho. 169
SOLLERS
Sabrill 177
SOUTHALL
--- 38,39
Betsey (PARKER) 66
Daniel 38,40,43-45,66
Danl. 42
Davis 45
Elizabeth (PARKER) 66
James 66
Jesse 40,44,66
John W. 43
Martha 63
Martha Ann 66
Mary Elizabeth 66
Thomas James 66
SOWELL (See also
SEWILL,SHOWLES)
John 145,146
Richd. 124,125

SPARKMAN
D. 107
Dempsey 107,114-116,
118,119
Dempsy 114,119
John 109,111,116
Lewis 88,91,92,106,116
Mills 107,110,118,119
Treasy (EURE) 89
SPARLING
--- 33
SPEED
Rufus K. 78
SPEIGHT (See also
SPIKES,SPIGHT,SPITES)
Francis 25,83
Frank 194
Henry 25
Isaac 136
John, Jr. 112
Joseph 25
Moses 57
Thomas T. 79
SPEIRS
Mildred A. 37
SPIGHT (See also
SPEIGHT)
Thomas 25
Thos. 16
SPIKES
William 23
SPITES
William 14
SPIVEY
--- 115
Ann 20
Ann (PARKER) 20
Chetta 120
Geo. 16
Georg 12
Jacob 188
James T. 120
Jas. 16
John 52
Littleton 52
Louisa 120
Moses 115
Nathan 120
Owen 217
Seth 165
SPRING
Henry 171
STALLINGS
--- 104
Jno. 15,16
John 211
Joseph 3
Martin 195

STALLINGS (Cont.)
Miles 161
Nicholas 159,173
Simon 183
Whitl. 113
STALLINS
Elias 146
Whitmil 113
STAPLES
S. L. 216
STEINMETZ
Ernest Granville 223
Ernest Parker 223
Granville H. 223
Pauline (PARKER) 223
STEPHENS
Richard 2
Samuel 2
STEPTO
John 180
STEVENSON
George 167
STOKES
Hilda Beamon 221
STORY
William 10
STRICKLAND
Matthew 69
STRINGER
Leah 203,210
SUMNER
--- 23,24,26,47-49,150
Abraham 32
Benjamin 64
David E. 109
Dempsey 21,22
Demsey 15,17,21,22,25,
31,32,48,49,52,72
Demsey, Sr. 72
Edwin 24
J. 41,58,90,184,205
Ja. 124
Jacob 20,23,24,32
James 27,117,118,132,
147
Jethro 41,55,58,60,66
Jno. 53,124
John 14,25,26
Joseph John 66
Luke 23,66
Martha B. 66
Sarah 23
William 16,47
SUTTON
-- --134
SWEETE
John 5

271

# T

**TABER**
William 60
Wm. 62
**TALOE**
Wm. 83
**TALOR** (See also TAYLOR)
Hilry 204
Robert 204
Wm. 83
**TAPSCER**
--- 5
**TAPSTER**
--- 6
**TAPTSTER**
--- 6
**TAYLOE**
John 83
William 83
**TAYLOR**
Gordon Gale 226
Hazel Parker 226
Henry 203
Hillery 109
Hillry 204
Isaac Madison 225
Jean Marie 226
Jesse 88,91,92
Jesse Eugene 225
Jesse Gray 226
Jno. 59
Kedar 62
Margaret Ruth 226
Martha 115,119
Martha Ann
(HOLLOMAN) 225
Mary 104
Mary Agnes 226
Mary Agnes (PARKER)
209,225
Richard 31
Robert 74,203
Wm. 83
**TEAKLE**
Margaret 9
Thomas 9
**THELWELL** (See also
FELWELL)
Edward 69,70
**THOMAS**
Elizabeth 148
Frances 148
Jno. 83
John 148
Joseph 126,127
Mary 148
Stephen 148

**THOMAS** (Cont.)
Thomas 148
William 148
**THOMPSON**
Miriam 137
**THOMAS**
Martha (EARLY) 170
**TIVATHEN** (See also
TREVATHAN,TVATHAN)
Wm. 181
**TOPPING**
Elizabeth 140
John 133,152,158
**TOWNSEN**
Chs. 189
**TOWNSEND**
Isabel (PARKER) 167
Isabella 164
Isabella (PARKER) 164
Isabellah 164
Josiah 164
Margaret 164
Maria 164,167
Mariah 164
**TRADER**
Jonathan 37,39
**TRAVIS**
Thomas 180
**TREVATHAN** (See also
TIVATHEN,TVATHAN)
Henry 192
James 188
William 32
**TROTMAN**
--- 164,165
Elisha 184
Q. H. 197
Riddick 74,204
Seth 188
**TUCKER**
William 9
**TURNEDGE**
Elizabeth 172
George 172
**TURNER**
--- 217
E. F. 196,197
Harriet A. 213,217
Harriet A. (PARKER) 213
Harriet Ann (PARKER)
217
Lucy L. 120
O. C. 197
**TVATHAN** (See also
TIVATHEN,TREVATHAN)
William 187

# U

**UMFLEET** (See also
HUMFLEET)
Job 87
**UMFLET**
William 83
Wm. 83
**UMPHFLEET**
William 92
**UMPHFLET**
Elisha 117
**UMPHLET**
Charney 119
David 88
Thomas 102
William 88,90,92
**UMPHLETT**
William 92
**UMPPHLET**
William 92
**UNFLEET**
--- 81
**UNPHET**
William 90

# V

**VAHANE** (See also
VAUGHN)
Edmund 10
**VALENTINE**
--- 117
**VANN**
Charles 87
Dempsey 60
Demsey 109
Edith 24
Edith (PARKER) 24
Edwd., Jr. 83
Jesse 87
John 38
Jos. 83
Thomas 73
**VANPELT**
Simon 147
Simon, Sr. 147
**VAUGHN** (See VAHANE)
Edward 10
**VINCENT**
Abraham 50
**VOLENTINE**
--- 117

# W

**WALLACE**

WALLACE (Cont.)
John 136
Wm. 83
WALLES
Elizabeth 132
John 131,132,136
WALLINGTON
Alice May (SHEPHERD) 228
Charles Edwin 228
Jane Harriet 228
WALLIS
--- 136
Elizabeth 129
John 131
WALSH (See also WELCH)
John 143
Margaret 222
WALTERS (See also WALTORS,WATERS)
--- 36
Isaa 32
Isaac 32-35,55
William 31,32
Willm. 32
WALTON
--- 39,206
B. 190
Benbury 42,191
Henry 59
Holoday 188
J. 192,203
J. R. 197
Jno. 192
Jno. B. 203
Jno. R. 105,196,197
John 39,40,187, 190-192,199,208
John B. 181-184,204
John Bunbery 181
John R. 100,197
Penelope 65
Richard 176
Robert 177
Thomas 14,15
Thomas B. 197
Timothy 74,112,183,184
Timothy, Jr. 44
Timy. 143,177
WALTORS
William 49
WARD (See also WORD)
Cora J. (COPELAND) 220
Eliza 212
Elizabeth 219
Eugene N. 220
Eva 212

WARD (Cont.)
Eva D. 219,220
Humphrey 153
Humphrey N. 219,220
Isaac 161
Jamima 220
John L. 167
John N. 213
John Norfleet 219,221
Kate 212,213,219
Leona M. 220
Lester E. 220
Lycurgus C. 220
Mary E. (PARKER) 213
Mary Eliza 219,220
Mary Eliza (PARKER) 219,220
Nathan 212,213
Nathan Q. 219,220
Noah 212,213,219
Noah C. 219
Norfleet 212
Ruth Y. 220
Thomas 129,133
Thomas, Jr. 148
Umphrey 219
Viola 220
William 153
Wm. 153
WARREN (See also WOREN)
Abraham 129
Edwd. 83
James 129
John 75,76
Joseph 84
Rebecka 129
Robert 146
Sarah 129
WATERS (See also WALTERS)
--- 31
William 48
WATSON
Saml. 70
Samuell 69
WEAVER
Grace 228
John 29
WEEKES
Thomas 129
WELCH (See also WALSH,WELSH,WOLCH)
--- 150,165,195
David 132,135,150,159
Edward 129,133,142, 143,152,158
Elizabeth 142,143,151

WELCH (Cont.)
James 142
Jno. 124,126
John 127,129,142,143
Michael 130,135,150
Miles 134
Sarah 142,143
WELLS
Fran 69
Francis 69
John 146
WELSH
David 24,135
Jno. 174
WEST
Frank 216
Robert 216
WETHERINGTON
George E. 220
Lucille (MITCHELL) 220
WHEDBEE
Diana (HINTON) 199
J. S. 195
Joshua Skinner 199
Lavinia Louise 195
Mary Rebecca 199
WHITE
--- 133,136,163,167
Arnold 131
Dorothy Beresford (MC CULLOCH) 157
Elias 162
Exum 65
Francis 169
Gabriel 163-165,167
George 124,169,174
Huldah 131
Issabella (PARKER) 65
James 136
Jeptha 140
Jno., Jr. 124,125
Jno., Sr. 124
John 128,131,133,145, 165,173,209
John, Jr. 126,148
John, Sr. 124,126
Jon. 123
Jonathan 140
Jordan 157,160
Luke 131
Margaret (PARKER) 162
Martha 162
Martha (PARKER) 163, 164,167
Sarah 123
Wm. 195
WIGGINS
--- 47

**WIGGINS** (Cont.)
Jesse 26,36
Mildred A. (PARKER) 37
Theresa (PARKER) 51
Thomas 48
Wilie 37
**WILKINSON**
Earl Dewey 227
Earl Dewey, Jr., 227
Edna Cooper (PARKER) 227
Margaret Jane 227
**WILLEROTS**
--- 36
**WILLES**
William 154
**WILLEY**
B. F. 212
H. 209
H. C. 106
Henry C. 79,102
Hillery 34,109
Hillory 25,29,35
J. 114
John 78,94-96,102,113, 115
John, Sr. 79
**WILLIAMS**
Ann 109,136
Arthur 43,44
D. 109
Demsey 32
Edward 169
Elisha 35
Elizabeth 65
George 36,38,40,43,44, 86,92,104
H. 104
H. C. 197
H. G. 81
Halan 39
Henry 109,194
Henry G. 81,109
Isaac 71,83,136
James 42,148
James G. 94
Jas. 128,175
Jethro 40
John 14,19
Jonathan 34-36,57,89, 104,109
Lewis 123,124,154
Margaret 35
Margaret PARKER 36
Marth (BUSH) 170
Mary 73,123,169
Mildred 104
Nancy 104

**WILLIAMS** (Cont.)
Nannie E. 200
Naomi 73
Nath. 84
Polly 104
Priscilla 104
Prissillar 91
Richard 72
Samuel 73
Susannah 123,124,154
William 123,124,154, 182,183
**WILLIAMSON**
John 20,22,48,49
Richard 125
**WILLIFORD**
Amanda E. "Mandy" 220
Elizabeth 220
Richard F. 220
**WILLOUGHBY**
--- 224
Betty (DOUGHTIE) 224
Mary Sally 224
Thomas Ely 224
**WILLS**
Henry 142
**WILLY**
H. C. 98
John 77
**WILSON**
John 145
Mary (PARKER) 162
Robert 35,128
Robt. 128
Seasbrook 37,38,177
William 162
**WINNS** (See also WYNNS)
Rose (BUSH) 170
**WINSLOW**
Charity (COPELAND) 152
John 152
Nathan 140
**WOLCH** (See also WELCH)
John 127
**WOLFLEY**
A. 96
Augustus 97,101,120
Conrad 93
Jno. C. 194
**WOLFREY**
Aug. 103
**WOOD**
John 139
Moses 131
Patrick 127
Seth 161
**WOODS**

**WOODS** (Cont.)
--- 52
**WOODSIDE**
Joseph Owen 198
Mildred (CROSS) 198
Nancy Cross 198
**WOODWARD**
James 158
Mariam (PARKER) 138
Nathaniel 165
Rachel 158
Saml. 131
Samuel 136
**WOOTEN**
Arthur 153
Rachel (PARKER) 153
**WOOTTEN**
Arthur 152
Jonathan 152
Nathan 152
Rachael (PARKER) 152
**WOOTTON**
Jonathan 152
**WORD** (See also WARD)
John L. 167
**WOREN** (See also WARREN)
--- 97
**WORRELL**
Lucille 223
S. W. 110
**WRAYFORD**
Phillip 69
**WRIGHT** (See also RIGHT)
John 2,3,5
William 10-12
Wm. P. 220
**WYNNS** (See also WINNS)
Benjamin 111,114
Benjn. 146
John 145,146

# X

None

# Y

None

# Z

**ZEHENDER**
Isaac 125

# LOCATION INDEX

**AIRPORT**
  Suffolk Municipal  3
  Tidewater  226
**ARCHIVES**
  North Carolina State
167

**BANK**
  Oyster  6
  Sand  26,84
**BAY**
  New Town haven river  6
  South  5
**BRANCH**
  Bay  19,32
  Bay Tree  16,31
  Bear  16
  Beargarden  72
  Beaver Dam  71
  Boregarden  71,72
  Buckland Mill  15
  Bulls Skull  31
  Cock Fighting  142
  Crooked  74
  Cypress  27,188
    Little  88,117
  Cypruss  87
  DAVYes mare  13
  Deep  44,130,133,137,
148,151,152,188
  Deep Run  126,131
  Duck Pond Pond  159
  Ephraim LISLES  173
  Fago  148
  Femur  145
  Flat  48,49,188
  Flatt  47,190
  Forked  16
  Fox  148
  Fugo  123
  Fugoa  125
  Fumur  145
  Galbush  26
  Gaul Bush  26
  Goodwater  123
  Gum  31,32,173
  Gumbling  145
  Half Way Run  37
  Haw Tree  37,38,88,117,
118
  Hog Yard  159
  Hogg Yard  128
  Holly-tree  191
  HOODs Mare (See also
Mare Branch)  13
  Indian Pond  124
  Jimmies  36,37

**BRANCH** (Cont.)
  Lickaroot  110
  Lickel root  92
  Licking  84
  Licking root  84
  Lickingroot  84,88,90,91,
93,112
  Lightwood Knott  174
  Liking Root  88
  Liking Rute  88
  Likingroot  84
  Little house neck  154
  Long  71,125,145,153,
154,158,159,169
  Maer, Great  17
  Mare  14,29,48
    fork of  19,21
    Little  16,19,31,32
      fork of  21
  Meadow  169,172,
174
  Meeting House Spring
158
  Middle  130
  Miery  91
  Mill  210
  Mill Dam  16,31,32
  Mirey  91
  Miry  88
  Musey  204
  Norwest  31
  Old Mill  204
  Pine, Great  142
  PIPKIN's  42
  Ready  92
  Reedy  25,26
  Robert PARKERs  39
  Robert ROGERS  83,88
  ROGERS  88,90,91,94
  ROGGERS  84
  Rooty  137
  Spring  24,135,172
  Tumbling  145,146
  Walnut  148
  White Oak  155
**BRIDGE**
  BALLARD's  24,125,129,
135,137,148
  BENNETT's Creek  15
  Catherine Creek  195
  Cow  74
  James River  6
  JORDANs  159
  Long Branch  125
  Mill Creek  195
  Poly  131
  Timothy WALTON's  74

**CAUSEWAY**
  BOND's Landing  210
  Landing 213
**CAVE**
  Indian  165
**CEMETERY**
  BALLARD  112,115
  Bridgeville, DE  198
  BYRUM Family  218
  Damascus Congrega-
tional Christian  218
  Elmwood  191,194,195,
198-200
  family burying ground
166
  Forest Lawn, Norfolk, VA
225,226
  HOGGARD-MITCHELL
225
  Nathan G. PARKER  209,
213,214,222
  Ocean View, Beaufort,
NC  219
  Texas State Confederate
Field  216
  WILLOUGHBY Family
224
**CHAPEL**
  CONSTANT's  151,172
  FLETCHER's  217,225
  Indian Town  14
  James BRADDEY's, at
15
  James COSTEN's, at  15
  Knotty Pine  29
  Meherin, at  15
  Piney Wood  14
**CHURCH**
  Episcopal  14
  Methodist Episcopal  57
  PARKER's Methodist  57,
67
  St. Mary's Episcopal  198
  St. Paul's, Norfolk, VA
198
  Zion M. E.  197
**CITIES**
  Austin, TX  216
  Baltimore, MD  226
  Beaufort, NC  219
  Berkley, VA  226
  Berkley City, VA  219
  Bridgeville, DE  198
  Brooklyn, NY  222
  Camden, NJ  225
  Charlotte, NC  226
  Chicago, IL  219

**CITIES** (Cont.)
Concord, NC 227
Dartmouth, MA 163
Doublin, Ireland 157
Dublin, Ireland 158
Elizabeth City, NC 222
Fort Lauderdale, FL 227
Galveston, TX 215
Kansas City, MO 219
London, England 1
Macon, GA 174
Norfolk, VA 198,218,
222-227
  South, VA 222,
223,227
Orlando, FL 226
Philadelphia, PA 227
Portsmouth, VA 3,193,
195,213,217,226
Raleigh, NC 167,195,
219
Richmond, VA 103
Salisbury, NC 226
Seattle, WA 219,225
Springfield, MO 219
Suffolk, VA 3,5,13,42,
65,206,215,221-223
Suffolk City, VA 1,13
Suitland, MD 222
Virginia Beach, VA 198
Voorhees, NJ 228
Washington, DC 216
Williamsburg, VA 226

**COMMUNITIES** (See also
CITIES,TOWNS)
Acorn Hill 218
Cofield 225,227
Colerain 145,221,224
Corapeake 52,65
Cremo 228
Drum Hill 17,223
Eure 84,87
Gates Station 197
Harrellsville 221,226
HUTSON Corner 165
PARKER's Fork 57,67
Powellsville 222-224
Ryland 218
Sarem 71,72,74,101
Sarum 83
Scratch Hall 83
Sunbury 15,218
Sunsbury 191
WELCH 150,165

**CORPORATION**
Charles City, VA 4

**COUNTRIES**
China 149

**COUNTRIES** (Cont.)
England 1,5,9,10,71
Germany 223
Gr. Brit. 136
Great Britain 157
Ireland 157
Western 205

**COUNTIES**
Accomack, VA 9
Albemarle 124,126,142,
148,170,173,174
Amelia, VA 66
Baltimore, MD 226
Bastrop, TX 215,216
Bee, TX 216
Bertie 24,25,29,50,71,
103,123,145-148,151,
170,172,193,194,199,
221-224,228
Broward, FL 227
Bucks, PA 226
Cabarrus 227
Camden 194,224,225,
227
Camden, NJ 225,228
Charles City 4,9
Chowan 14-17,19,21,22,
24,25,29-32,37,47-50,
52-55,70-72,83,123,124,
126-137,139-145,148-
150, 152-155,157-159,
162-165,167,169-173,
175-177,182,188,
194-196,212,217-220
Colleton, SC 227
Craven 174
Culpeper, VA 215
Currituck 209
Dobbs 25
Duplin 146
Edgecomb 110,111
Edgecombe 111
Fairfax, VA 103
Gaites 178
Gates 13-15,17,20,21,
23-27,29,30,32,33,35,
37-41,43,44,47-52,55,
57,58,64,66-68,70,71,73,
74,77-80,82,84,86,87,89,
90,93-96,98-100,102-107,
109,115,117-121,128,
165,167,176-180,182,184,
187,188,190-198,200,
203-212,214,215,217-226
Greene, MO 219
Hardford (See also Hert-
ford) 204
Hartford 20,21

**COUNTIES** (Cont.)
Henderson, TN 44
Henrico 9
Hertford 20-24,26,29,
30,32,37,38,44,49,71,
73,84,87,91,120,123,
145,187,195,199,200,204,
213,218,220-227
Iredell 227
Isle of White, VA 124
Isle of Wight, VA 1,3,
5-7,13,22,69,70,81,123,
124,126,154
James City, VA 226
Jefferson, OH 155,156
Kings, NY 222
Kitsap, WA 219
Kitsof, WA 213
Lucas, OH 228
Mobile, AL 226,227
Nansemond, VA [All
spellings] 1-10,12-16,18,
20-23,25,26,29,30,32,35,
47,48,53,55,69,70,72,81,
83,87,117,123,124,127,
128,169,203,210,215-218,
221-223
New Norfolk, VA 9
  Upper 2,3,6
New Norfolke, VA 3
  Upper 2-4
  Upper County of 4
Norfolk, VA 218,222,
223,225-227
  Upper 2,5,6,9
North Hampton 130
Northampton 123,131,
133,135,136,150-152,
154-156,211
Orange 37
Orange, FL 226
Pasquotank 134,162,
163,173,193,194,197,
222
Pequimons 129
Perquimans 37,129-135,
139,140,148,150-153,157,
158,162-165,167,171,173,
175,176,193-195,220
Philadelphia, PA 227
Pickens, AL 110,111
Pitt 25
Prince George, MD 222
Princess Anne, VA 198
Rowan 226
Rutherford, TN 29
Sussex, DE 198
Victoria, TX 216

**COUNTIES** (Cont.)
Wake 194,195
Walker, TX 212,215
Ware, GA 224
Warrisquoake 1,2
Washington 210
Wayne, IN 155,163
**COURT HOUSE**
the 44,45
Bertie County 147
door in Gatesville 78,81
Edenton 22,149
Gates (See also TOWNS) 40,42-44,116,206
Gatesville, in 113
**CREEK**
Back 6
Ballard 6
BALLARDs 136,159,169
BALLARDs Bridge 137
Ballasting Marsh 6
Beaver Dam 167
Beaverdam 3
BENNETT's 13,15,16, 19,21,24,37-39,42-44, 47-49,74,115,165,176, 194,196,197,204,210, 211,213
head of 47
BROWNRIGGs 168
Catherine (See also Katherine) 74,124,165, 167,195,210
Chinkapen 145
Chuckatuck 5
COLE, commonly called new Bay 115
COLE's 112
Contenteney, Little 25
Crainy 12
Craney 3,5,11
Craneyed 5
Crany 4,12
DILLARD 128,169
Dumpling Island 1-3,8, 69
EDWARDS 5
Herring 115
Indian 4,10,128,138, 169
Indian Town 124,128, 129,148,151,169
Katherine 125,177
Kathren 125
Long Pond 6
Long Ponds 6
Marracoones 10,12
Middle 133,158

**CREEK** (Cont.)
Mill 195
Newbegun 162
Newbiggin 162
Old Indian Town 169
Old Town 128,169,173, 175
Oyster House Creek 1
PARKER's 10,11
POWELLs 2
Rugged Island 6
S_____ 149
Salmon 125
Sarem 99
Sarum 87,110,115,118, 119
SEAWARDs 5
Somerton 120
South Bay 5
Stopping 125
Stumpey 158
Stumpty 145
Stumpy 128,130,151, 152,169,174,175
SUTTON's 134
TAPSCERs 5
TAPSTERs 6
TAPTSTERs 6
TROTMAN 165
Wicacoane, commonly called Bear Swamp 123
Wicacon 199
Wiccacon 123,148
Wickacon 125
Wickacone 125,126,148
Wickacorn 128
**CROSSROADS**
BALLARDs 112
GLOVER's 145
PARKER's 112,164,165
POWELL's 209
WIGGINS 47
**DISTRICT**
Ballahack 140
Christopher RIDDICK's 40
Columbia, of 216
Hall 105
Haslett 36
Holy Neck, VA 221
HUNTER's Mill 191
James ARLINE 55
James ROUNTREE's 165
Jethro SUMNER 55
John COFFIELD's 143
Richard WALTON's 176
Salmon Creek/Wickacon 125

**DISTRICT** (Cont.)
Washington, of Norfolk 222
**ESTATE**
BASNIGHT 225
**FARM**
SANDERLIN 197
**FERRY**
CANNON's 143,168
Gates 197
Jeremiah CANNON's 150
MANNEYs 28,92
PUGHs 19
**FIELD**
BRADY's 93
GEORGEs 3,4
Indian old 125
Long neck 159,160
old Indian 9
**FISHERY**
Bell Grade 166
BOND Landing and 213
Creek 203
PARKER 166
**FORT**
Mifflin, PA 227
**GLADE**
Pine 134
**HILL**
Clay 44
High 26
**HOLE**
Cat 167
**HOME**
Texas Confederate 216
**HOSPITAL**
State 219
Veteran's Administration, Salisbury, NC 226
**HUNDRED**
West & Sherley 4
**ISLAND**
Bainbridge, WA 219
COLE's 32
Craney 3,11
Dumpling 69
Dumplinge 1
Fort 116,119
Holiday 143,148,150
HOODs Neck 11
Long Ponds 6
New haven 3
a point of land called the 5
Rackoone 12
Ragged 1,6
Rugged 6
SUMNER's 150

**LAKE**
Kilby 3
**LANDING**
BOND and fishery 213
BOND's 196,208-210,
217
Indian 130
Ingen 148,149
old 43
Old Town 195
PARKER's 210
Stoney 26
Thompson 4
**LINE**
Chowan/Perquimans
135,173
Country 14,16,19,31,
32,49
County 21,49,69
Perquimans 15,83
State 36,37
Virginia 15,21,83
**MARSH**
Great 26
Reedy 94
Stopping Creek 125
White Oak Spring 66
**MEETING** HOUSE
Newbegun Creek 162
PARKER's 65
Piney Woods 162
Rich Square 153,155,
156,158
**MILL**
BRADY's 93
Buckland 15
Elisha PARKER's 21
GAINES' 103
HUNTER's 191,197,218
HURDLE's 221
Merchant 197
Merchant's 194
NORFLEET's 191,192
Peter PARKERs 16,21
Steam 210
WALTON's 206
WELCH 195
**MILLPOND**
Elisha PARKER's 21,32
Merchant's 45,176,177
old 165
Peter PARKER's 31
Robert BALLARDs 119
**NECK**
HOODs 11-13,18
Indian 74,165,167,204,
209,221
Little 127

**NECK** (Cont.)
Little house 154
Long 159,160
Meherrin 186
St. John's 145
**PARISH**
Kiccoughton, Corpora-
tion of Elizabeth City 1
Lower, of Isle of Wight
County 6,70
St. Paul's 14,143,151,
175
**PATCH**
Turnup 55
**PATENT**
Cross Swamp 11-13,18,
47,69
HOOD Neck 11
John SMALL 48
SPIVEY 115
**PATH**
cart, that leads towards
POLSON's 39
old, called the Amos
LASSITER 192
PRATT 36
**PLACE**
Bear Garden 100
Bray PARKER 105
called head of the Pond
204
crossing 159
going over 158
Half Way 128,175
HOFLER 197
John Lee ALPHIN 218
Nathan G. PARKER home
213
Nathan PARKER 203
home 211,213
PARKER, old man Jim
200
SMITH 110
St. George's, New 87
Tom HURDLE 203,211
**PLANTATION**
Ballyhack 140
Edward WELCHes old
158
Elmwood 177,190,192,
193,198,199
forck of the Duckinstool
148
Harmony Hall 159,160
Henry JONES 117,120
James HARLO, of 169
Jerrico 12
JONES 109

**PLANTATION** (Cont.)
old 135
River 162
SOUTHALL's 39
**POCOSON**
BALLARDs 26
BENNETT's Creek 74
Bound 16
FRIORs 16
Galberry 21
gaulberry 19
great reedy 3
Horse 71
Juniper 205,209
maine 3,4
Maple 16,25
Mehearon 19
Merry Hill 24,31-33
Middle 118
River 84,115,125,210
Roap [ROASS?] 71
Stopping Creek 125
Thicket 56
Timber 19
Toe? 73
White Pott 15
woody, great 11
**POINT**
Brock 4
GARRETTs 6
**POND**
--- 129
Duck 159
head of the 204
near the Country line 19
old 93
Perseman 154
Peter PARKERs mill 16
WELCH Mill 195
**PRECINCT** (See also
COUNTY)
18th, of Norfolk, VA 225
Bertie 145,148,175
Chowan 14,15,21,71,83,
123-128,142,147,148,
169-175
Craven 174
Onsloe 145
Perquimans 128,171,
173
**PROVINCE** (See also
COUNTY, STATE)
Chowan 24,135,175
North Carolina 48,49,
72,126,130,136,148,154,
170,177,178
**REGION**
Albemarle 177

**RIDGE**
MANINGs 204
Pitch old point 138
**RIVER**
Beaverdam 3
Beverdam 12
Blackwater 70
branches of 69
Chowan 26,47,115,
123-128,130,145,148,
150-153,155,160,
167-169,172,204,219
Chowan, No. Et. Shore of
125
Chuckatuck 5
Delaware 227
Elizabeth 3
James 6,219
Little 134
Maine 4,6
Matrevers 4
Namsamund, Southerne
branch of 3,4
Nancemond, Southern
branch of 4
Western branch of 4
Nansamond 3,4
Nansamund 2
Southward Branch of 3
Nansemond 3-5
North west branch of
10
Southern branch of 2,
8-13,69
Southward branch of 9
Western branch of 2,5,
8-10,70
Nansimond 2
Nansimum, Western
branch of 4
Nansmund 2
Nanzemund 1
New Town Haven 5,6
Perquimans 173
Rown Oake 188
Warresquicke 5
**ROAD**
BENNETT's 37
BENNETT's Creek 38,
176
old, that leads to the
Court House 44
CANNON Ferry 150
County 213
County #1217 101
Edenton 39,88,92,150,
192,195,199
Ferry 112,164,165

**ROAD** (Cont.)
fork just above Gates
Court House 40
Fort Island 116,119
Gates Ferry 197
from Gatesville to Somer-
ton 195
Gatesville-Zion 197
Honey pot 38,40,44
Indian neck 209-211,
213,214,217
leading from BOND's
Landing to Mintonsville
217
from BOND's Landing
to the fork near Mills
ROBERTS 208
from Gates Court House
to Suffolk 42
from Gates Court House
to the Honey Pots 43
from Gatesville to Sun-
bury 195
from Gatesville to Win-
ton 94,119
from George ALLEN's
Shop to MANNEY's Ferry
92
from Honey Pot Swamp
to Gatesville 195
from the fork near Mills
ROBERTS to PARKER's
landing 210
from the Gatesville-Zion
road to Merchant Mills
197
leads from Gates Court
House to Winton 116
from the Edenton road
to NORFLEET's mill 192
Main 40,49,90,140,164,
177
from Somerton to
MANNEYs Ferrey 28
leading from Gatesville
to Gates Station 197
leading from Suffolk to
Edenton 206
leading from Sunsbury
to Gatesville 191
leads from Gates Court
House 44
Merchant Mills 197
Mooretown 223
Mt. Pleasant 200
New 40,44
fork of the 39
old, that leads from the

**ROAD** (Cont.)
Court House 44
Perquimans 15
Pinewoods 159,160
Public 36,135
leading from Gatesville
to Zion M. E. Church 197
Publick 56
Pynewoods 158
Rich Thicket 56
Ridge Thicket 55
River 195
Ryland 165
Sandy Ridge Public 218
Sarum Creek 115
Suffolk 65
Thicket 55,56
Virginia 150,159,160,
164
Winton 92,195
**RUN**
Chinkapen Swamp 145
Deep 126,145
Half Way 37,38
Little Mill 195
Marsh Cyprus 83
OLIVERs 13
Poplar 24,128,158,169,
170,174,175
Popler 135
Poppler 142
Sandy 125,128,132,
151,172
**SCHOOL**
Central Junior High 45
County High 45
Friends 163
**SCHOOL HOUSE**
--- 66
Common 119
**SHOP**
George ALLEN's 92
**SPRING**
John BRADY 95
Meeting House 158
White Oak 66
**STATES**
Alabama 110,111,120,
198,216,226,227
Confederate, of America
103
Delaware 198
Florida 226,227
Georgia 174,216,224
Illinois 219
Indiana 155,163
Maryland 222,226
Massachusetts 163

**STATES** (Cont.)

Missouri 219

New Jersey, 225,228

New York 222

North Carolina 13-16, 19-23,25,29-32,37,40, 41,46,49,57,58,65,67,68, 70,71,77,78,82,83,86-88, 93,95,96,103,107,110, 111,114,115,117,118,120, 121,123,124,127,130,133, 137,139,144,145,147,149, 152,155,157,159,165, 167,169,174,177,179,180, 182,190,193-197,199, 200,204-206,209-211, 214-228

Ohio 155,156

Pennsylvania 226,227

Rhode Island 163

South Carolina 177,227

Tennessee 29,44,109

Texas 212,215,216

United, of America 57

Virginia 1-6,8,9,14-16, 18,20-23,25,26,30-32, 35,36,47,55,66,68,69,70, 72,81,83,84,87,102,103, 117,123,124,126-128, 150,154,169,193-195, 198,203,210,213,215-219, 221-227

Washington 213,219, 225

Wyoming 224

**STATION**

Berkley (Fire) 226

Brandy, VA 215

**STREET**

Edenton, E. 195

**SWAMP**

Arrow reed, great 2

Ashen 5

Back 37-39

BAKER 196,213

BALLARDs Crek 159

Barbaque 146

Barbique 146

Bare 165

Bear 123,125,149,150, 172

Beaver Dam 125

Beaverdam 3

Beech 14,21,71

Beechy 125

BENNETT's Creek 15, 204

big, in the fort Island

**SWAMP** (Cont.)

Road 116

Blackwater, Maine 124

Boar 165,167,213

Boare 204,205,209

BRADY's Mill 93

Chincopin 146

Chinkapen 145

Coropeak 127

Creek 42,43

Cross 11-13,18,47,69

Cypress 25-27,88,91, 117,118,146,173

Deep 25,27

Flat 25,27

little 118,119

Cyprus 84,87,146

Cypruss 145

Dismal 48

Great 66

Elm 16,126,127

Elme 127

Elmn 52

Flat 71

Folly 15,48

Fork 134

GOODMAN 21

Haw Tree, Great 39

Henry B. LASSITER 213

Honey Pot 43,45

Horse 123

Horsepen 74

Hunting Quarter 150

Indian 177,186,192,197

Indian Town Creek 128

James PARKER 213

John W. HINTON 196

Juniper 167,196,210, 213

Kingsale 70,169

Knotty Pine 15,81,83,92

Little Mill 195

Loosing 15,19,47,83

Lossing 48

Meherrin 15

Middle Creek 133,158

MIL_ 73

MILES 71

Mill 14,19,71,95

MILLS 73,82

MILLS's 71,72,74-76

North West 32

Nottaway 69

Nottoway 124

Notty Pine 29

Oarepeak 49

Old Town Creek 169, 173,175

**SWAMP** (Cont.)

Oropeak 127

PARKER 196

PATTERES 71

Perquimans River 173

Peter PARKERs mill 21

PETER's 72,82,93

PETERSON's 93

PETTERS 71,72

Poly Bridge 131

reedy 4

Rich Thicket 49,50,53, 55

Sand Bank 84

Sandy Run 133,172

bend of 133

fork of 133

Saram, main 70

Sarum 71

Somerton 14,15,19

Stumpey Creek 158

Stumpty Creek 145

Stumpy Creek 169,175

Sypress 87,88

Main 87

Thicket 56

Warrick 125,147

Warwick 129,148

Water 211,217

Watery 176,177,203

White Oak 36,125,148

White Pot 194

Wht. Oake 126

Wiccacon Creek 148

Wilroy 1

**TOWNS**

Ahoskie 224

Alma, GA 224

Bartlett, VA 5

Camrly, Ireland 157

Cornwall, England 9

Cottageville, SC 227

Creola, Al 227

Crewe Town, VA 222

Crittenden, VA 5

Edenton 14,15,22,39, 83,92,150,166,192,199, 206

Gatesville 74,78,81,94, 95,113,119,191,192,194, 195,197,198,215,225

Gowrie Park, VA 226

Hampton, VA 157

Harrellsville 199,200, 220,223,227

Holland, VA 69,70,81

Indian 124

old 3

**TOWNS** (Cont.)

Kingsale  69,169
Levittown, PA  226
Newbern  174
Pearson, WA  219
Providence, RI  163
Rich Square  136,
152-156,158,163
Rock River, WY  224
Smithville, TX  215,216
Somerton, VA  195
South Mills  224,227
Sunbury  195
Sunsbury  191
Victoria, TX  216
Windsor  147
Winton  92,94,116,119,
195,224227

**TOWNSHIP**

Colerain  221
Gatesville  197
Harrellsville  199,221
Hunter's Mill  176,194,
197,218,221
Mintonsville  194,195,
197,224
Mt. Herman, Pasquotank
Co.  197
Sleepy Hole, VA  215

**TRACT**

A. W. HENRY  213
Bear Garden  96,99
BENBURY  195
BLADES  94,104
Boon EURE  94,104
BOYCE  166
BRADY  96
Bray PARKER  104
Calvin EURE  213
Chetta PARKER  121
Dempsey EURE  96,103,
110,119
Dempsey PARKER  96
PARKER-JORDAN  195
ELLICE  103
George LAWRENCE  117
GREEN  103
HILL  210
Home  65,217
Isaac  217
Isaac PARKER  213
J. H. PARKER  200
JAMERSON  96
James H. PARKER  200
James HARRELL  110,
119
Jimmie EURE  213,217
John ROBERTS  195

**TRACT** (Cont.)

JONES Plantation  109
JORDAN  166
Joseph SMITH old place
118
Juniper Swamp  196
Mary KLEGG  213
Nancy BOND  195
Peter NIXON  196
RALLS  117
RAWLS  117
ROBERTSON  91,111
Ruthy BRINKLEY  66
SMITH  119
STALLINGS  104
Tenson EURE  94
Tinson Y. EURE  104
VALENTINE  117
VOLENTINE  117
Water Swamp  217
Wiley PILAND  213
WOREN  97

**WOODS**

Piney  134

**YARD**

Norfolk Navy  225

# NOTES

Made in the USA
Coppell, TX
15 September 2022